A Survey of English Spelling

A Survey of English Spelling

Edward Carney

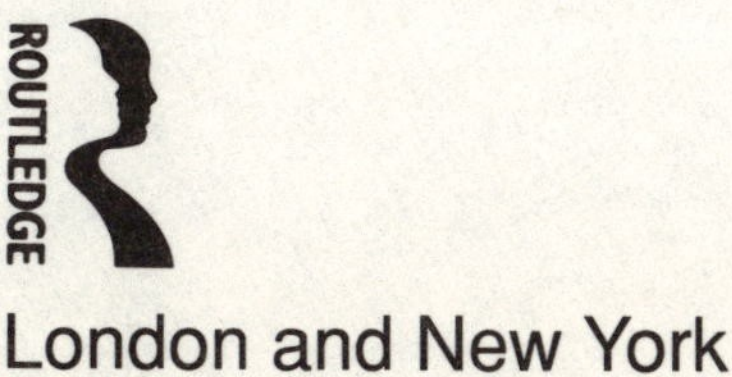

London and New York

First published 1994
by Routledge
11 New Fetter Lane, London, EC4P 4EE

Simultaneously published in the USA and Canada
by Routledge Inc.
29 West 35th Street, New York, NY 10001

Typeset in 10/12pt Times Linotronic 300 by
Florencetype Ltd, Kewstoke, Avon
Printed in Great Britain
by Clays Ltd, St Ives plc

British Library Cataloguing-in-Publication Data
A catalogue record for this book is available from the British Library

Library of Congress Cataloging-in-Publication Data
A catalog record for this book is available from the Library of Congress
0-415-09270-1

Contents

Acknowledgements

Here at Manchester, I am surrounded by colleagues who know more about the English writing system than I do. William Haas, founder of the Department of Linguistics at the University of Manchester, first interested me in writing systems. Of the many other colleagues who have helped me very generously with their time and patience, I wish to single out Martin and Sue Barry, Dennis Bradley, Neville Collinge, Katharine Perera and the present Mont Follick professor, Nigel Vincent. If they and other long suffering colleagues have failed to save me from error, the fault can only be mine. I am also indebted to Eunice Baker and Irene Pickford for data preparation and secretarial help in the book's early stages.

I had the privilege of presenting some of the theoretical sections of the book in three of the annual Mont Follick Lectures at the University of Manchester. I am grateful to the Mont Follick Trust for defraying some of the data preparation costs of the research.

Preface

Page for page, most of what has been written about English spelling has had a particular and often practical aim in view – to show how the writing system has evolved over the centuries as an integral part of the history of the English language, to advocate some reform of the writing system, to lay down a framework for the teaching of literacy or to provide the foreign learner with a guide to pronunciation. Few people have set out to describe the English writing system in its present state as a working system. Yet there does seem to be a need for more insight into how our writing system actually manages to function. Unhappily, the spelling literature is beset with disagreements based on ignorance and with controversies fuelled by prejudice.

If we take a radical reformist standpoint, the present English writing system is simply not worth describing:

> Our present spelling is just a chaotic concoction of oddities without order and cohesion.
>
> (Follick 1965: 1)

Present-day reformers are equally insistent:

> proper analysis of the synchronic and diachronic evidence shows rather that [English spelling] is unplanned, phonographically highly inconsistent, and historically, pragmatically and geographically fluid. Its lack of coherent system and its unpredictable deviations from the spelling of other languages are detrimental to its role as a medium of international communication, while to native speakers of English it has proved a serious obstacle to the acquisition of literacy.
>
> (Upward 1988: 3)

Such a view has been frequently stated. Ever since English spelling settled down in the seventeenth and eighteenth centuries, the consensus seems to have been that the conventions we have inherited are ill-suited:

> Such indeed is the state of our written language, that the darkest hierogliphics, or most difficult cyphers which the art of man has hitherto

> invented, were not better calculated to conceal the sentiments of those who used them from all who had not the key, than the state of our spelling is to conceal the true pronunciation of our words, from all except a few well educated natives.
>
> (Sheridan 1780: 13)

Happily, rather more than a few well-educated natives seem to cope with the present system, though after a heavy investment of time and effort. Linguists today are even prepared to concede that, in spite of its imperfections, the English writing system has some virtue:

> our orthography is possibly not the least valuable of the institutions our ancestors have bequeathed to us.
>
> (Sampson 1985: 213)

The extreme statement of this point of view is the provocative declaration by Noam Chomsky and Morris Halle that:

> English orthography turns out to be rather close to an optimal system for spelling English.
>
> (1968: 184)

Nor does a linguistic analysis of the writing system necessarily end in a pessimistic outlook for the educational task of teaching literacy:

> most English speakers learn our writing system, to one degree or other, without much explicit analysis of it to guide them. They do not do this by learning each item separately, but by making some sort of analysis themselves. If they can do so well without much explicit description, the system need not be beyond anyone when understood and presented systematically.
>
> (Albrow 1972: 51)

It is part of the recently established national curriculum for British schools that 'the rules of spelling' in traditional orthography should, and presumably can, be learnt. What these rules might be and how they should be taught is another matter.

Public concern about falling standards of literacy is reinforced by the national press. In the educational debate, spelling mistakes provide powerful ammunition:

> She had spent 'houres' over her essay but she had no 'apptitude' and no 'flare' for spelling. Even after a 'brake' for lunch, it was still 'suprisingly' bad, though you could see what she 'ment'. An 'independant' girl, she did not find it 'forefilling'. Despite 'baring' a good 'refrence' and a respectable 'adress', her hopes of college 'enterance' were dashed because she was not 'apreciated'.

(All those spelling mistakes were taken from an essay written by an

18-year-old student of English literature and reassembled in this concentrated form by Peter Wilby as copy for an article in the *Sunday Times* 3 February 1985.)

Faced with frequent statements that there are no rules for traditional English spelling and with curricula which require that the rules should be learnt, we may conclude that there must still be scope for neutral explorative studies of the English writing system. We still do not seem to know enough about it. This present study tries to deal equally with the problems of the writer and the reader, which are rather different.

Computer analysis has provided some statistical insights, especially on the interrelationship of text frequency and lexical frequency. The present account is also different in that it covers in some detail the spelling of names. I have not made excursions into the general theory of writing systems, but I have made some comparisons with the Swedish writing system to show the workings of spelling reform in a more 'managed' system and a different approach to the spelling of loan-words. I have drawn attention to differences between British and American spelling. I have taken Southern British Standard pronunciation as the basis for analysing spelling correspondences with selective cross-reference to American English and other accents

I am shy of calling this study 'a survey', since some aspects of the English writing system deserve a far more detailed treatment than I have been able to give them. It is, however, something of a survey in the sense that I have trawled through a fairly large database to find what regularities I could in the English writing system and to see how they might best be described. This is a strictly functional approach. My main object has been to see how traditional orthography works, or fails to work. I have not been concerned with tracing the development of the present system over the centuries. Only occasionally have I referred to the past to explain the present.

To make the book more accessible as a work of reference, I have provided a detailed list of contents and five different indexes. I have also tended to repeat brief glosses of technical terms in the text to save the reader from interruptions. There is also some repetition of data, where variant pronunciations are logged under different phonemes and spellings. In quotation, I have preserved the writer's idiosyncratic spellings, such as Shaw's spelling of <Shakespear>. This does not, of course, imply any recommendation.

Occasionally, I have strayed from my descriptive brief to make prescriptive comments on features of traditional orthography that seem inconsistent or undesirable. Spelling reform as it has been implemented in the United States and as it has been variously planned in Britain has been dealt with selectively in §7.3. Detailed proposals for spelling reform in Britain have been discussed for many years through the publications of the Simplified Spelling Society and it is to them, or to their American and

Canadian counterparts, that anyone interested in that aspect of literacy should turn.

The current addresses of some active associations, to which any enquiries should be made, are as follows:

1 The Simplified Spelling Society, 39 Chepstow Rise, Croydon CR0 5LX, England
2 American Literacy Council, 106 Morningside Drive, New York City 10027, USA
3 BEtSS, 24034 Bingham Pointe Drive, Birmingham, Michigan 48010, USA (BEtSS = 'Better Education thru Simplified Spelling')
4 The Internasional Union For The Kanadian Langwaje, 94 Glenholm Avenue, Toronto ONT M6H 3B1, Canada

I have tried to leave a few warning signs on entrenched heresies that still thrive in works on reading, writing and spelling. In §2 particularly, I have sought out some examples of how not to describe English spelling. My excuse for this missionary zeal is that all too often the literature of literacy is taken up by non-arguments about non-problems.

Conventions, symbols and technical terms

SBS stands for **'Southern British Standard'** and refers to the speech of educated English speakers from London and the surrounding counties and across southern Britain generally (Wells 1982: 117). This is the accent of standard British English used here as the basis of the description of spelling correspondences. Other accents are referred to when there are differences that affect spelling.

I have used the term 'Southern British Standard' in preference to '**RP**' (or '**Received Pronunciation**') for several good reasons. It is not merely that the term 'Received Pronunciation' has a Victorian stuffiness. SBS is a much wider concept. I wish to prevent an assumption that all the phonetic detail of the pronunciation of RP, or of any other accent, is relevant in tracing the correspondences between spellings and phonemes. What is important for literacy is the number of contrasting phonemes in the accent and their distribution, not the minutiae of how they are pronounced (their phonetic realization).

However, RP is simply a socially defined subsystem within SBS. Readers used to the term 'RP' may, for our purposes, regard them as equivalent. The two terms refer to speakers who have the same number of phonemes with essentially the same distribution. To refer restrictively to RP in describing English spelling, rather than the wider notion of SBS, would be to accept a narrow social irrelevance:

> Socially, [RP] is characteristic of the upper and upper middle class . . . Occupations perhaps most typically associated with RP are barrister, stockbroker, and diplomat. . . . Typically [RP speakers] belong to families whose menfolk were or are pupils at one of the 'public schools' (exclusive private schools standing outside the state education system)
>
> (Wells 1982: 117)

AmE stands somewhat naively for '**American English**'. I have used this as a loose cover term for general features which distinguish the speech of most Americans from Southern British Standard in phoneme contrasts and in the distribution of phonemes in words. These are the main factors that affect the description of spelling correspondences. It would have been unwise to use the term 'General American', claiming it to be a standard American accent, since its definition, and indeed existence, is a matter of some controversy. What is here taken to be 'American' may well not be valid for Eastern or Southern accents of American English. For instance, AmE is here taken to be 'rhotic' speech which has not lost //r// before a consonant in words such as *farm*. So, AmE does not here refer to any strictly definable accent of American English, but to features of pronunciation shared by many Americans.

The bearing of accent and dialect on spelling is discussed in §2.7.

IPA stands for **The International Phonetic Association**, particularly with reference to their system of phonetic symbols.

Phoneme symbols

The phoneme symbols here used for representing Southern British Standard are the IPA symbols used in Gimson's *Pronunciation of English* (Cruttenden 1994). They are shown in table 1 below. Alongside I have given the spelling-based letter symbols of Cummings *American English Spelling* (1988), which are derived from the symbols used in the Webster dictionaries (W3NID).

Table 1 Vowel phoneme symbols

	Keyword	*IPA*	*Cummings symbol*	
Short vowels				
1	bit	ɪ	i	('short *i*')
2	bet	e	e	('short *e*')
3	bat	æ	a	('short *a*')
4	full	ʊ	u̇	('high short *u*')
5	dull	ʌ	u	('low short *u*')
6	bomb	ɒ	ä	('low short *o*')
Long counterparts of the short vowels				
7	bite	aɪ	ī	('long *i*')
8	beet	iː	ē	('long *e*')
9	bait	eɪ	ā	('long *a*')
10	bout	aʊ	au̇	
11	boat	əʊ	ō	('long *o*')
Long vowels and diphthongs wholly or partly associated with //r//				
12	bard	ɑː		(see note 2 below)
13	board	ɔː	ôr	(see note 3 below)
14	bird	ɜː	ur	
15	beard	ɪə	êr	
16	bear	ɛə	âr	
17	boor	ʊə	u̇r	
18	fire	aɪə	īr	

	Keyword	*IPA*	*Cummings symbol*	
19	flour	aʊə	au̇r	
Other long vowels and diphthongs				
20	booty	uː	ū	('simple long *u*')
21	beauty	juː	yū	('complex long *u*')
22	boy	ɔɪ	ȯi	
Reduced vowel				
23	about	ə	ə	('schwa')

Notes on the vowel phonemes and their symbols

1 The group of short vowels, (1) to (6) in Table 1, are sometimes called 'checked' vowels, because of their distribution. They do not occur in final open syllables, so /kæt/ *cat* is a possible English word, but there can be no English word */kæ/. Long vowels and diphthongs have no such restriction and are in consequence 'free' (/kaʊl/ *cowl*, /kaʊ/ *cow)*. Since the length difference between 'short' and 'long' is less marked in some accents of English, the terms 'lax' and 'tense' may also be used. The short vowels vary with their long counterparts in some morphemes:

/aɪ/ – /ɪ/ *sign – signal mime – mimic line – linear*
/iː/ – /e/ *redeem – redemption plenary – replenish serene – serenity*
/eɪ/ – /æ/ *vain – vanity mania – manic inflame – inflammatory*
/aʊ/ – /ʌ/ *renounce – renunciation South – Southern*
abound – abundance
/əʊ/ – /ɒ/ *tone – tonic omen – ominous know – knowledge.*

2 In SBS the vowel /ɑː/ occurs not only before //r//, but also in words such as *after, bath, cast, dance,* where many other speakers, including AmE, would have /æ/. (See §3.3.3.1 pp. 177ff.) In AmE the vowel /ɑː/ also takes in the vowel of *bomb* (= *balm*), *box, dodge, stop, watch*, which in SBS is 6 above, the short low back rounded /ɒ/.

3 In SBS, the vowel /ɔː/ occurs in both *caught* and *court* as /kɔːt/, since //r// has been lost before a consonant. In rhotic accents, as in most AmE, they will differ as /kɔːt/ and /kɔrt/. A halfway stage may keep *caught* and *court* distinct as /kɔːt/ and /kɔət/.

4 In SBS and some other British accents unstressed /ɪ/ can end a word such as *city*, *happy*, where other accents including AmE have /iː/.

5 Some writers on AmE merge the stressed vowel [ʌ] of *dull* together with the unstressed schwa [ə] of *about* in a single phoneme, using /ə/ as the symbol for both, since they are phonetically very similar.

6 Cummings (1988), uses W3NID symbols, slightly modified. This system tries to help the reader by choosing phoneme symbols which mirror the most common spelling. In the vowel symbols, there may be some

advantage in using terms and symbols such as 'long *i*' /ī/ and 'short *i*' /i/ for the /aɪ/ and /ɪ/ of *mime* and *mimic*. It draws attention to the phonological relationship. It cannot, however, entirely free the reader from the task of remembering different phoneme symbols. (See pp. 8f.)

7 There are minor differences of phonetic detail between SBS and other accents which are reflected in the SBS phoneme symbols, but which have little bearing on spelling. For instance, the /əʊ/ vowel (11 above) starts without lip rounding in SBS: *coat* is [kəʊt], but before a dark [ɫ] SBS does have rounding as in *coal* [kɒʊɫ]. In other accents lip rounding remains as [oʊ], or as a pure vowel [oː]. Similarly the vowel length marker [ː] for /iː/, /ɑː/, /ɔː/, /ɜː/ and /(j)uː/ may be inappropriate for accents in which the difference between 'short' and 'long' vowels is more a matter of vowel quality than length. The quality differences are indicated by the vowel symbol itself /u/ – /ʊ/, /i/ – /ɪ/, etc. However, I have kept Gimson's redundant and sometimes misleading length marks for a practical reason: simply to make the symbols appear different to the rapid reader.

More detailed comments will be found under each vowel phoneme in §3.3.

Table 2 Consonant phoneme symbols

Stops	p pan	t ten	k cap	ʧ choke
	b ban	d den	g gap	ʤ joke
Fricatives	f ferry	θ thin	s sat	ʃ ship
	v very	ð then	z zeal	ʒ measure
Nasals	m met	n net	ŋ long	
Liquids	l late	r rate		
Glides	h hat	w wet	j yet	

Notes on the consonant phonemes and their symbols

Unlike the vowels, the system of consonant phonemes shows little difference across accents. SBS and AmE, for instance, are here identical. Usually the symbol reflects a common spelling, as in the case of /p b t d k g f v s z h m n l r w/.

The symbol /ŋ/ does not include a following /g/: in SBS *finger* and *singer* differ as /ˈfɪŋgə/ and /ˈsɪŋə/; in Northern British English they may both have /-ŋgə/.

The glide /h/ is traditionally classed as as ninth member of the set of fricatives (as in §3.3.7), though unlike them it does not enter into a voicing contrast (/f/ – /v/, /s/ - /z/, etc.). The glides /w/ and /j/ are traditionally referred to as 'semivowels' (as in §3.3.10).

Some alternative symbols in common use for English consonants are shown below in Table 3. The standard IPA use of /j/ for the semivowel in *yet* (not the affricate in *jet*) needs noting.

Table 3 Alternatives to the IPA consonant symbols

	IPA	*Non-IPA*	*Cummings*
thin – then	θ ð		th th
choke – joke	ʧ ʤ	č ǰ	ch j
ship – measure	ʃ ʒ	š ž	sh zh
yet	j	y	y

Other phonetic symbols used

[-] is sometimes used to show a syllable boundary, as /uː-ɪ/ in *fruition.*
[ʔ] is the symbol for a glottal stop sound.
[ˈ] placed before a symbol indicates that the following syllable is stressed, as in /təˈmɒrəʊ/.
[ˌ] placed underneath a symbol indicates that a consonant is syllabic, as in [litl̩].

Other phonetic symbols found occasionally in the text are briefly explained where they occur.

Types of bracketing

[ ] – square brackets with phonetic symbols enclose **sounds** or strings of sounds without necessarily assigning them to any particular English phoneme (thus, [ʔ] represents a glottal stop sound and [l̥] represents the voiceless variant of the /l/ phoneme found after voiceless /p/ in /plɒt/). For 'phoneme' see p. xxvii.

/ / – single diagonal slashes with phonetic symbols enclose **phonemes** or strings of phonemes (thus, *box* ends in /ks/ and *seraph* ends in /f/). These are traditional 'surface' phonemes, which are directly represented by a sound.

// // – double slashes enclose a more abstract 'underlying' phoneme. Thus //r// does not necessarily refer to present-day SBS /r/, but effectively to the /r/ of early Modern English, which in SBS and many other dialects does not now survive finally (*far*), or before a consonant (*farm*). In SBS the word *far* has an 'underlying' final //r// but no actual 'surface' /r/ unless a vowel follows immediately (*far away*). In AmE and other 'rhotic' accents //r// has not been lost in these contexts, so, as captured in the spellings, *far* is /fɑr/ and *farm* is /fɑrm/.

< > – angled brackets enclose **letters** or strings of letters (thus, *box* ends in <x> and *seraph* ends in <ph>).

/ /≡< > – indicates a spelling **correspondence** between a string of one or more phonemes and a string of one or more letters: at the end of *box* we have /ks/≡<x> and at the end of *seraph* we have /f/≡<ph>. The order of the two sides depends on the topic: speech-to-text /ks/≡<x> or text-to-speech <x>≡/ks/. Often the order is not critical. These are often referred to as 'phoneme-grapheme correspondences'.

{ } – curly brackets enclose **morphemes** (minimal units of word structure) cited in ordinary spelling. Thus the word *photograph* contains the morphemes {photo} and {graph}, *unreliably* contains the morphemes {un-}, {rely}, {able} and {-ly}. {photo} and {graph} are **free morphemes**: they can form a word on their own. {un-} and {-ly} are **bound morphemes**: they do not appear on their own, but are always attached to other morphemes. The phonetic form of a morpheme often varies from context to context: {photo} varies as /fəʊtəʊ/, /fətɒ/, /fəʊtə/ in *telephoto*, *photographer*, *photographic*. The English writing system contains spelling correspondences with whole morphemes such as {-ed}≡<ed>, where {-ed} varies phonetically as /ɪd/ (*wanted*), /d/ (*begged*), or /t/ (*washed*).

Notational symbols

≠ 'is not equal to', 'contrasts with'.

* – an asterisk attached to a written form, may denote either a wrong, unconventional, reformed, hypothetical or dialect spelling, such as *<stoopid>, *<sed>, *<woz>. An asterisk is also used in formulae to indicate some specific restriction which is indicated in the following text (e.g. '<C>*' may exclude some letters specified in a note).

∅ – **zero**, as in <h>≡∅ for the initial spelling in *hour*, where <h> has no phonetic counterpart.

– a word boundary, possibly followed by suffixes that can attach to free forms (see pp. 269ff). So the context ' –<e> #' would apply not only to *care*, but also to *carer*, *caring*, *careful*, *careless*, *carelessly*, *carelessness*. The text-to-speech rules of §4 include a 'compound-guesser', which tries to find a boundary in compounds such as *carefree*, *careworn*, by using possible letter sequences.

The following capital letters will be found in rule formulae with particular uses:

/V/ any vowel phoneme.
<V> any vowel letter, any letter from the set: < a, e, i, o, u, y >.
/C/ any consonant phoneme (including glides /h, j, w/ and liquids /l, r/).
<C> any consonant letter, any letter from the set: < b, c, d, f, g, h, j, k, l, m, n, p, q, r, s, t, v, w, x, y, z >.

The letter <y> belongs to both the <C> and <V> sets.

<C_0> zero or more consonant letters.
<C_1> one or more consonant letters.

<C>* the asterisk indicates some specific restriction which is indicated in the explanation that follows.

<C>-doubling refers to the doubling of a consonant letter as in *matting* compared with *mat*.

TF, LF refer to the text frequency and lexical frequency of words in the database described in §3.1.1. The percentage figures quoted for word frequency in §3 exclude grammatical words such as pronouns, auxiliaries, articles, and only refer to the frequency of lexical words.

F+, F- are used in the description of speech-to-text correspondences in §3 to draw attention to a difference between the text frequency and lexical frequency of a particular spelling. 'F-' indicates a tendency to occur in low frequency words, where the per cent share of lexical frequency for a particular spelling is notably higher than the per cent share of text frequency. 'F+' shows a tendency to occur in high frequency words, where the per cent share of text frequency for a particular spelling is notably higher than the per cent share of lexical frequency.

Some technical terms

affix, prefix, suffix – these terms are normally applied to bound morphemes added to other morphemes in the process of word-formation: the added units have a distinct function or meaning. For example, the suffix <-ness> does not occur on its own, but only when bound to a stem, as in *goodness*, where it turns the adjective into a noun. In describing English spelling, it is sometimes convenient to refer to initial and final strings of letters that do not have an add-on meaning or a clear marking function. So, <-tion> in *suggestion* is often referred to as a unit, even though the division is then <sugges>+<tion>, with the <t> arbitrarily separated from <suggest>. The string <-ant> may be dealt with as a unit not only in *accountant*, but also in *covenant*, *elephant*. I have used the general terms '**beginning**' and '**ending**' when the letter strings referred to are not strictly affixes.

auxiliary, inert, empty letters refer to different functional types of letter. See §2.6.5 pp. 40ff.

bias, workload refer to the performance of text-to-speech rules in §4 and are explained in §4.2.2 pp. 270ff.

consonant, vowel refer only to sounds, not letters. A statement such as: 'the stressed vowel is followed by a single consonant' would apply to both *lemon* and *common*. There is a double consonant letter in *common*, but not a double consonant. See §2.2 pp. 9ff.

diphthong, digraph –'diphthong' is a purely phonetic term and refers to a vowel glide, as distinct from a relatively 'pure' vowel, within a single syllable. The words *cycle*, *omen*, *mouse*, *mice*, all contain diphthongs. The words *react*, *poet*, (with two vowels) and *head*, *brawn*, (with a single 'pure' vowel) do not contain diphthongs. 'Digraph' refers to a string of two letters: in *head* the digraph <ea> represents the vowel /e/; in *react* it represents the vowels /iːæ/.

divergence – a lack of one-to-one correspondence between phonemes and spellings shows divergence from the alphabetic principle of one symbol per phoneme and one phoneme per symbol (Haas 1970: 51). There may be divergence on the phonetic side of a correspondence: <th>≡/θ/ and <th>≡/ð/; or on the graphic side: /f/≡<f>, /f/≡<ff> and /f/≡<ph>. More often than not we find divergence on both sides: /iː/≡<ea>, /iː/≡<ee>, and <ea>≡/iː/, <ea>≡/e/, etc.

grapheme – this term has a number of different meanings in the study of writing systems. It is not used here as an abstraction of 'letter' (the set of different written shapes of 'the same' letter), but for any minimal letter string used in correspondences. So, <ea> in *head* may be referred to as a single (but complex) grapheme.

phoneme – this term is used in the traditional sense for contrasting units of sound. The words *exit* and *seraph* are each pronounced with three consonant phonemes and two vowel phonemes. Readers unused to phonetics will probably find that their notion of 'speech sound' is effectively the same as 'phoneme'. A phoneme may be realized by a range of slightly different sounds with different speakers and in different contexts.

lexeme – a word defined semantically. *Gaol* and *jail* represent the same lexeme.

long, short – vowels are referred to as 'long' and 'short', rather than 'tense' and 'lax'. The shortening of the vowel in words such as *sanity* (from *sane*), is here referred to as '**third-syllable shortening**'. It is otherwise known as 'trisyllabic laxing'.

rhotic, non-rhotic – a rhotic accent is one, such as AmE, Scottish or Irish English, in which underlying //r// survives in all contexts, so *a firm offer* is pronounced with two instances of /r/. A non-rhotic accent is one, such as SBS, in which //r// is lost before a consonant and in final position, so *a firm offer* has no instances of /r/ in SBS.

§Basic, §Greek, §Latinate, etc. refer to subsystems of spelling conventions in the English writing system, but not directly or by definition to the historical origin of words. The symbol '§' attached to such a label indicates 'subsystem'. The word *deacon* (of Greek origin) has the characteristics of a §Basic word as does *beacon* (of Germanic origin). See §2.9.

Chapter 1

Alternative approaches to describing English spelling

1.1 A PHILOLOGICAL APPROACH

How did the present system come about?

English spelling, like most of our institutions, has a history. So, in matters of spelling, the past can help us to explain the present. We can see that loan-words acquired from particular languages at particular times have brought with them their own spelling conventions. The words *village* and *entourage* are both borrowed into English from French. *Village* was borrowed in the Middle Ages, but *entourage* seems to have been first used in written English in the 1830s. The final French stress has shifted to the front in the early borrowings, making them more like other English words and the <-age> of *village* has become an unstressed /-ɪʤ/. In a late borrowing such as *entourage* the <-age> is usually unchanged as /-ˈɑːʒ/. Studying the changing relationships between written and spoken English through time is the business of **philology**.

Philology studies language as part of cultural history. Its viewpoint is **diachronic**, looking at language evolution, showing how the present-day state of the language has developed over the centuries. A study of English spelling that is primarily philological, such as Cummings (1988), will consequently focus on the writing system as a transmission of culture. This will include material which, though interesting in itself, need have no relevance at all to the purely **synchronic** problems of achieving literacy in the language as it is today.

The philological approach can dig out an interesting antiquarian diversity often unsuspected by the common reader. Cummings (1988: 332), for instance, points out that the double <bb> spellings of *chubby* and *shabby* come before a word boundary: 'apparently the adjective came from *chub*, a fattish fish'; '*shab* reflects an obsolete word used to refer to a skin disease of sheep and to a low fellow'. But for all practical spelling purposes, *chubby* and *shabby* are to be treated as simple forms on a par with the nouns *hobby*, *lobby*, *tabby* or the adjectives *silly*, *merry*, *happy*. Similarly, it has no bearing on the problems of literacy to know that : 'The only known Romance instance of /ů/ = *oo* is the monosyllabic *rook* "chess piece"'. The word did indeed come into English via French. Before that, along with the game of chess itself, it came into French by way of Arabic and beyond that from Persian. Yet, in spite of this chequered history, it is spelt by §Basic spelling conventions and is identical to *rook* 'type of crow', a purely Germanic word.

On the other hand, it would be useful to keep apart (unlike Cummings 1988: 356) instances of <cc>≡/k/ with §Latinate prefixes in words such as *accumulate*, *occasion*, *occupy*, from the <cc> of §Italianate words such as *peccadillo*, *staccato*, *toccata*. The <cc> of *accumulate* has to be linked to the double letters found with other prefixes, as in *affiliate*, *alleviate*, *annihilate*, *appreciate*. The *staccato*-type words have the common feature of penultimate stress and a final vowel. These two groups of words with the spelling <cc>≡/k/ belong to different subsystems for practical spelling.

In a philological approach, the concept of 'rule' may be rather different from the kind of rules (or generalizations) that might underlie competence in spelling (see §2.8.1). For instance, Cummings has a 'Stress Frontshift Rule' (ibid.: 127), which simply reflects the fact that the final stress of French loan-words, as we saw in *village*, tended to shift to the first syllable. This has happened in *cover*, *honest*, *gravel*, *lemon*, *model*, *refuge*, *river*, *scholar*. The importance for present-day spellers in this group of words is that a short vowel followed by a single consonant then became stressed in a spelling context where you would expect a long vowel – cf. *over, navel, demon, modal, polar*. This stress shift was a 'rule' in that the historical process affected most of the early French loan-words. It is not a rule in any synchronic sense, since there are no criteria for identifying these early loan-words by their present-day pronunciation or any other marker of 'Frenchness'. They are simply a group of exceptions. The consequences, too, are different for reader and writer: the writer must avoid putting a <CC> spelling after the short vowel (*<lemmon>); the reader must avoid 'saying' a long vowel */ˈliːmən/.

Framing such rules as active processes may be slightly misleading in a philological framework. This is so of the rules which account for the short vowel before the suffix <-ity> (ibid.: 112) and before the suffix <-ic> (ibid.: 115). The underlying form is taken to be the vowel of the base form. So the long vowels of *sane* and *mime* are 'shortened' in the derived forms *sanity* and *mimic*. The rule is explicitly framed as a process: 'instances of /i/ = *i* in VCV strings whose head vowels have been shortened (*sic*) by the Suffix *-ic* Rule', 'head vowels have been shortened by the Suffix *-ity* Rule' (ibid.: 224). Many of the words given as examples of the 'shortening' process did not have a long vowel to shorten, either in their etymology or in related forms in English: *critic, monolithic, prolific*; *acidity, humidify, ability*; *logic, symbolic, topic*. The process of 'shortening' means, of course, that the vowel 'ends up as' short. So, here the historical difference between the stressed vowels of *mimic* and *topic* is lost sight of by the descriptive device.

1.2 A FUNCTIONAL APPROACH

How does the present system work?

A philological approach is very much concerned with asking: How did these spellings come about? The present study is primarily concerned with the question: How does our spelling system work? The two approaches are not at odds; they are complementary.

The difference between the two approaches can be shown by comparing what they would say about one particular spelling problem: the difference between final <-o> in words such as *bingo*, *fresco*, *limbo*, and words with final <-ow> such as *billow*, *farrow*, *follow*. The philological approach would tell you that *halo* is one of some old adoptions from French and Latin, that *photo* is one of a number of back-formations or 'clippings', that *motto* is one of several similar loans from Italian, that *mango* is from Portuguese, and that there are several words, such as *jumbo*, of obscure origin. The <-ow> words, such as *follow*, got their <-ow> spelling in Middle English as a regularization of a number of Old English word endings: <we>, <rg>, <lg>, <rh> and <u>.

On the other hand, the present study is concerned with how spellers can distinguish between the two groups of words as they are today, so that they do not make errors such as *<sallo>, *<mangow> for *sallow* and *mango*. If we look at the structure of the two groups of words, we find a pattern which could be exploited to provide teaching material. None of the disyllabic <-ow> words has stress on the second syllable as does *hello*, or a long vowel in the first syllable as does *photo*, or medial consonants outside the range /d, n(d), l, r/, as does *mango* (see §3.3.2.5, pp.173f.). This approach to the description of spelling conventions is best described as functional.

Since exceptions do invite comment, it may be of occasional interest to mention the historical reason for an exception even in a strictly functional approach. For instance, *pickerel* has an exceptional 'doubled' <ck> in the third syllable from the end (see #D6 p.123). The word means 'a young pike', so there is a hidden boundary after the first syllable, which makes the word rather like *shrubbery* in structure, where the <CC> is regular. *Frippery*, *gallery* and *scullery* are similar exceptions to the doubling rules, compared with *celery, misery*, but to add that *frippery* comes from Old French *fripe*, meaning 'rag', would not help. The <frip(p)> has no claim to be an English morpheme. The reverse is the case in *shabby* and *chubby* (see p. 1), where there is a hidden boundary that need not be known to explain the doubling.

If we are to focus on the problems of literacy in English, we are not primarily concerned with how the writing system came to be in its present state. We shall try to look at the system as it functions today for a normal literate adult and uncover those regularities that appear to be exploitable by a competent speller. These will not usually be in the form of recallable and explicit 'spelling rules' to be chanted in moments of insecurity. They will often be letter patterns which correlate well with speech patterns, with types of word-formation or with the various subsystems of foreign loan-words. In trying to describe the system by exploring the awareness of an average literate adult, we shall not assume knowledge outside the adult's competence as a speaker and reader of English.

Chapter 2

Literacy and English spelling: methods and problems

2.1 WRITING WITHOUT SPEECH

Can the written forms of English be described systematically without linking them to spoken forms?

It would be quite feasible, though far from easy, to describe the English writing system without referring to speech. Egyptian hieroglyphs and Chinese characters are examples of writing systems that were originally designed to encode meanings directly, without indicating what the spoken forms were. Even when a writing system is based on an alphabet, as is English, the written form of the language can be studied as an independent system of purely graphic signs. This is obviously true of those signs in the English writing system which are not made up of letters: written signs such as <$>, <%>, <+>. The ampersand <&> was originally a manuscript ligature of Latin <et> 'and', but for present English users, it is just a single squiggle. For ordinary silent reading, we do not need to know a way of saying these signs as /ˈdɒlə/, /pəˈsent/, /plʌs/ or /ænd/. Indeed, in the case of <@> we probably do not know a way of 'saying' it. These signs, like numbers and scientific symbols, are international and independent of speech.

The writing system also includes punctuation signs such as <. , : ; - ! ?> and indeed the space between words. These relate to speech, but only indirectly. Their main function is to show grammatical structure and its boundaries, and to some extent the attitude of the writer. We know that 'Doesn't she enjoy a game of bridge!' is not expressing doubt, as it would if <?> were used. We know that '. . . bridge!' will probably have a falling tone as an expression of certainty. But <!> can associate directly with the certainty; there is no need to imagine the speech.

Usually, of course, the signs of the English writing system are made up of letters strung together and we can make more or less regular connections between the letters of the spelling and the phonemes of the pronunciation. But we do not have to make this connection. Quite early in their schooling, competent readers acquire the skill of skimming over the written text without referring to the corresponding spoken forms. Indeed it comes as a surprise to learn later on, if they ever take a course in phonetics, that the single written form of a morpheme such as {-ed} or {photo} has several different contextual pronunciations in their speech.

In describing such complex written signs we are quite free to ignore speech altogether and simply say which letters go with which and, conversely, which fail to go with which. The letter <q> is always followed by <u>, except in foreign names such as <Iraq>. That a similar-sounding <w> never follows <q> is, however, no more interesting in such a description than the fact that <t> or <p> never follows <q>. We can relate a final <-ed> to {past tense} without being bothered by its different phonetic correlates: /ɪd/ (*waited*), /d/ (*begged*) and /t/ (*watched*). We would note that <h> occurs as the second member of some common clusters which seem to have the status of units: <ch>, <gh>, <ph>, <rh>, <sh>, <th>, <wh> as in *church*, *ghost*, *physics*, *rhetoric*, *show*, *thin*, *when*. Other clusters with <h> might only be found at morpheme boundaries: <nh> in *inhuman*, <yh> in *boyhood*, <lh> in *girlhood*, etc. It would not be part of such a description to say that in some accents of English the graphic contrast <wh> – <w>, as in *whine – wine*, correlates with a phonemic contrast /hw/ – /w/, but not in all accents. Nor would it be necessary to point out that <th> has the phonetic correlate /ð/ initially in demonstratives (*this*, *there*, *then*, *those*, . . .) and a different phonetic correlate, /θ/, initially in lexical words (*thin*, *theorem*, *thesis*, . . .). These would be just a few of the consequences of describing the English writing system as if it were simply a system of graphic signs. There are indeed several practical reasons why one might profitably study the way letters and strings of letters are distributed: for instance, in studying the purely visual aspect of reading, or in the technology of text processing.

2.2 LINKING SPEECH TO WRITING: SOUNDS AND LETTERS

Points of view

The more common alternative, however, is to describe English spelling by exploring the relationship between spoken and written forms. We then show how spelling relates to sound: how letters and strings of letters map on to phonemes. This approach serves a wide range of practical needs and interests: in the pursuit of spelling reform; in the technology of man-machine communication; in theories of perception and in the teaching of literacy, both to native English speakers and where English is a foreign language. For foreign learners the spelling of an unfamiliar word is, for better or worse, a reference from which to attempt its pronunciation. But this wide range of practical applications brings problems. It is scarcely surprising that when people with a particular interest set out to describe

English spelling from their particular angle, the picture that emerges may not be a fully objective record. Perspective may so easily shade off into distortion. Since the aim of this present survey is to bring out whatever regularities we can find in the English writing system, we ought to begin by noting that the search for regularities and the business of describing them is far from straightforward.

Classroom units

Many descriptions of English spelling conventions are bound up very intimately with the teaching of reading to young children. The question usually asked is: how is this string of letters pronounced and how is it associated with a meaning? It is a very different question to look from the other direction and ask: how is this string of phonemes (and the chunk of meaning it associates with) represented in writing? The emphasis on reading is natural enough. Literacy teaching is more often concerned with the receiving of written messages than with sending them. Systematic teaching of spelling can only be undertaken when pupils are well-launched into reading. So, the educational process is naturally rather more concerned with reading than with writing since reading is the basic means of acquiring information. Consequently, if we want to take a fresh look at the regularities of English orthography we need only approach it from the less usual point of view: from speech to spelling. Parts of this study will explore this less familiar approach.

The close ties between published descriptions of the English writing system and the teaching of reading have had some unhappy consequences. It might be expected that the units and rules which one would set up to describe a system of correspondences between sounds and spellings would naturally form a basis for the structural units to use in teaching – subject to a grading for difficulty, productivity and other educational considerations. The converse is certainly not true. It does not follow that units and rules used by teachers and set up for classroom convenience will serve as an adequate description. We can take a few examples from a classroom primer intended for foreigners.

Old-fashioned spelling primers often use units of correspondence in their spelling drills which are incompatible with any consistent and economical linguistic description. Morpheme boundaries may be ignored, even when a complex spelling is clearly made up of two simple spellings split by a morpheme boundary. There is no need to consider the <ayi> of *playing*, *saying*, as a unit of spelling (as Hill and Ure 1962) because it comes about by the straightforward addition of <ing> to <play> and <say>. Nonetheless they have <ayi> and similar complex strings as single units of description: <eei> in *agreeing*, *seeing*; <eea> in *agreeable*; and even <ewa> in *chewable*, *sewable*, *beware*, *homewards*, *reward*, *prewar*. Unlike the previous strings, which were at least unambiguous, <ewa> has a whole range of different phonetic counterparts. But the apparent variety of these counterparts is illusory. Once the morpheme boundaries in these words are recognized, the variability is accounted for. The intention in such drills is probably to warn the reader to look out for morpheme boundaries.

It is clear that units such as <ewa> would never figure in a properly systematic description of how English spelling relates to speech. They are mentioned here simply to show that there are no generally accepted and explicit criteria for establishing the units of description. We are unlikely to find such criteria by hunting through the spelling books. If <ewa> is a unit, why not <opi> or <ene>? Units such as these could only crop up in spelling books destined for use by pupils who are already readers. Classroom-oriented accounts of English spelling tend to highlight pitfalls for the unwary reader, rather than to present a systematic description of the regularities of English spelling.

Finding symbols for phonemes

Perhaps the greatest practical problem in dealing with spelling is that people do not have a familiar and generally accepted way of tackling the phonetic side of correspondences. There is plenty of evidence that native speakers are passively aware of the phonemes of their particular language: English speakers are aware that the commutation list *pat*, *bat*, *mat*, *cat*, *hat*, *rat*, *sat,* etc. involves minimal distinctive changes. They know that what is substituted here is a minimal distinctive unit of sound. Equally well they know that what is substituted in *flat*, *brat*, *slat*, etc., is more complex and involves a cluster of two such units. Yet there is no easy way for them to refer to these units phonetically: no way of dealing with phonemes rather than letters. There are, of course, phonetic symbols readily available which can be used with a minimal knowledge of speech production, but few people have access to them. Phonetics does not seem to play a significant role in the training of primary-school teachers and many writers on spelling deliberately avoid all reference to phonetic symbols and categories. It is commonly held that to use IPA phonetic symbols for English phonemes when writing about spelling is to add unnecessary technical complexity. Cummings decided that since he was writing for:

> teachers and others who are deeply engaged with English spelling without necessarily being trained linguists, it seemed better to use a system of pronunciation symbols that was less technical and perhaps less intimidating.
>
> (Cummings 1988: xxxi)

Taking this view, Cummings borrows the letter symbols used in W3NID, slightly modified. This simply shows a preference for phoneme symbols more or less isographic with the spelling. There may well be some minimal advantage in using ‘a’, ‘ā’;‘ä’ rather than /æ/, /eɪ/, /ɑː/ to woo the reader. But surely anyone ‘deeply engaged with English spelling’ would be well-advised to learn a little phonetics. Krapp (1925: 333) thought that Webster-type symbols were a handicap in distinguishing between speech and writing. He comments: ‘This was the characteristic contribution of the Webster dictionaries to the popular understanding of phonetics in America and remains today the chief obstacle in the way of securing a treatment of the subject in elementary books which is based on scientific principles’. Certainly, it can be shown that this use of spellings as phoneme symbols caused problems for the Hanna (1966) study of phoneme-grapheme correspondences (see §2.8.5).

Since speech is often referred to by using common regular spellings as a substitute for standard phoneme symbols, it follows that correspondences are not usually stated in the direction /p/≡<p>, but only in the direction <p>≡/p/. Writers usually refer the reader to a *phoneme* by quoting a *letter* in a given keyword:

> ‘*th* as in *then*’, ‘*th* as in *think*’, ‘*o* as in *hop*’, ‘*o* as in *hope*’.

Such a formula takes the roundabout route: the phoneme represented by the spelling <th> in the word *then*. The lack of a simpler technique for dealing with phonemes helps to ensure that the usual direction of description is from writing to speech.

Sounds and letters: the misuse of ‘vowel’ and ‘consonant’

(Note: in this section some of the references are drawn on simply to illustrate misleading use of terminology and inadequate methods. Literacy studies are a minefield of misunderstandings.)

The published literature on spelling is bedevilled by failure to distinguish between speech and writing, between sounds and phonemes on the one hand and letters on the other. ‘Vowel’ and ‘consonant’ are generally used to refer to letters rather than sounds. This is bad practice because it is bound to lead to misunderstanding. In many contexts the writer gets away with it because the statement is ambiguous and could apply equally to sound or spelling, but sooner or later the practice ends in confusion. Not every statement that is true of vowel and consonant letters in English will also be true of vowel and consonant sounds:

> Monosyllables ending in *b* double it before suffixes beginning with vowels if the sound (*sic*) preceding it is a single vowel (a, e, i, o, u, or y), but not if it is a diphthong or a vowel plus r: *cabby*, *webbed*, *glibbest*, *bobbed*, *shrubbery*; but *daubed*, *barbed*.
>
> (Fowler 1926: 44)

In the 2nd edition, Gowers quite rightly revised this to 'if the sound preceding it is a short vowel, but not if it is a long vowel or a vowel and *r*'. (Fowler 1965: 52).

But if we are indeed talking about **sounds** and not specifically about **letters**, the vowel /ɔː/ of *daubed* is just as much a single vowel as /æ/ or /ɪ/ and in phonetic terms it is not a diphthong. So, the <u> in *quick* is a vowel letter representing a consonant /w/; the <w> in *jaw* is a consonant letter used as part of a vowel spelling.

In adult literacy primers, which are naturally very careful to distinguish statements involving sounds and those involving letters, we can find oddities like: '*q* is always followed by *u* and at least one other vowel, e.g. quit' – [why 'one other vowel', when <u> here represents a consonant /w/?]; 'the (f, l, s, z) sounds are usually doubled when spelled at the end of one-syllable words' – [the 'sounds' are not doubled]. It is admittedly more cumbersome to be explicit. Where Fowler, in the first edition of his *Modern English Usage*, writes about 'double and single consonants' (Fowler 1926: 554), Gowers alters the text to 'double and single letters for consonantal sounds' (1965: 575), showing a willingness to pay the price of accuracy. Similarly, Fowler calls those vowels after which <l> is not doubled before a suffix, such as the /eɪ/≡<ai> in *failed* (cf. *equalled*) 'a compound vowel sound, as *ai*, *ea*, *ee*, *oi*, *ow*, *ur*'. One might expect a 'compound vowel sound' to be a diphthong, but what 'compound' refers to here is evidently not the sounds but the spellings. Gowers in the 2nd edition alters this to 'a long vowel sound made up either of two vowels or a vowel and a consonant', specifically mentioning 'sound', but he is still using 'vowel' and 'consonant' to refer to letters (ibid.: 340). Gowers clearly felt that something was wrong in the original text, but did not quite make a clear distinction between letters and sounds.

Recognized authorities may use 'vowel' and 'consonant' to mean both letters and sounds in the belief that this makes life easier for their readers, but it does make for some awkward statements. Cummings (1988: 212), for instance, refers to 'the letter *w*, a consonant in *wed* but a vowel in *dew*' and 'the letter *h* . . . is a vowel only when it is the second letter in a vowel digraph, as in *ah*, *oh*, *uh*, *John*, *ohm*, *dahlia*'. This is not perhaps so serious, but taken at face value it means that there are two 'vowels' (as letters) in *wed* but only one 'vowel' (as phoneme). This may well confuse some readers. The problem surfaces again when Cummings classifies the vowel of *bite* along with those of *beat*, *bait*, *boat*, *boot*, *beaut-*, as a 'long vowel sound' and the vowels of *oil* and *owl* as diphthongs (ibid.: 203). Admittedly, he is using the word 'sound' here 'for stylistic ease' to cover a more abstract unit, which he calls a 'morphophone', but the vowel phoneme in *bite* is as much a diphthong phonetically as those in *oil* and *owl*. The difference is one of letters not of sounds. The 'long vowels' have single-letter spellings and alternate with short vowels in the pronunciation of morphemes. So we have the pairs /aɪ/ – /ɪ/ (*define*, *definitive*), /iː/ – /e/ (*serene*, *serenity*), /eɪ/ – /æ/ (*mania*, *manic*), /əʊ/ – /ɒ/ (*sole*, *solitude*). The 'diphthongs' /aʊ/ and /ɔɪ/ cannot be spelt with single letters. If 'vowel' has to bridge both sound and spelling, a solution might be to call the alternating vowels 'basic vowels' with long and short values.

In this study 'consonant' and 'vowel' are used only to refer to sounds or phonemes. When talking about letters, I have used 'consonant letter' or '<C>' to refer to letters in the set <b, c, d, f, g, h, j, k, l, m, n, p, q, r, s, t, v, w, x, y, z> and 'vowel letter' or '<V>' to refer to letters in the set <a, e, i, o, u, y>. The letter <y> is a member of both sets: it is a consonant letter in *youth* and a vowel letter in *myth*. Some consonant letters may be used as auxiliary letters (see §2.6.5) in making up complex vowel spellings such as <igh> *sigh*, <ow> *now*.

In the rest of this section we can profitably examine some of the dangers inherent in the traditional misuse of 'vowel' and 'consonant'. The references used are not necessarily important in the field of literacy studies. They are chosen to highlight a problem that is endemic.

Making spelling an authority for pronunciation

Failure to realize that the relationship between letters and sounds is purely conventional may have quite bizarre consequences. Because of the 'authority' of written language, people are tempted to use spelling conventions as evidence of what goes on in speech production. Consider the following speculation as to why the consonant letter is doubled after a short vowel in *latter* but not after a long vowel in *later*.

> Vowel sounds are of two species, long and short, i.e. those which, like the *a* in 'father', can be prolonged, and those which, like the *e* in 'let', cannot. The reason of this seems to be that in forming the short vowels the throat is in such a position as to emit a large quantity of air, so that the lungs are immediately emptied of wind; hence it is necessary to close or partly close the mouth in order to lessen the expense of wind, if speech is to continue; in other words, such vowels must always be followed instantly by a consonant; from this cause is derived the rule that short vowels are followed by double consonants, e.g. 'letter', and long vowels by single consonants, e.g. 'later'. After a short vowel, as in 'letter', the shutting of the mouth is done with some force and quickness, and is clearly audible and distinguishable from the noise of the subsequent opening. After a long vowel, however, as in 'later', the closing of the mouth is clearly heard; the two sounds of shutting and opening after the short vowel are represented by the double consonant. Hence the double consonant has come to indicate the shortness of the vowel preceding it.
>
> We have seen that after a short vowel the consonant follows instantly,

> and is made audible by means of this vowel preceding, e.g. 'nod'; but that after a long vowel the consonant is not so made audible, therefore it needs a vowel to follow it, e.g. 'no-de'. Hence it has come about that the *e* following a consonant indicates that the preceding vowel is long.
>
> These facts are important, because the practice of indicating the short and long vowels in English in this way has been called irrational.
>
> (Willis 1919: 34)

This piece of evident nonsense will serve as a lead towards recognizing less obvious misunderstandings. The 'immediate emptying of the lungs', or the existence of a final vowel in *node* are not of course real observations of natural speech. Yet, at the time Willis wrote, classical phonetics was in its heyday and the real nature of speech production was well understood. Even today people have problems in keeping apart the written and the spoken medium. The heresy of thinking that mere spelling conventions are a reliable encapsulation of phonetic facts still thrives.

This is the main reason why phonetics is wrapped in mystery for ordinary people. Anyone who has an accent that does not fit the provisions of the writing system will risk being told that their speech is 'wrong' or even that their hearing is defective. Someone who does not contrast /hw/ and /w/ in *which* and *witch*, may be told that they have 'lost' a consonant 'h', or more confusingly that they are 'not hearing' a consonant 'h'.

Those who practise phonetic methods in the teaching of reading might even find it useful to be aware of phonetic detail below the level of phonemic contrasts. Some of their operations used in taking words apart and putting them back together may have unforeseen phonetic consequences. The idea of 'blends' and 'blending', where clusters are assembled from their independently taught members, must take the subtleties of phonetic context into account. If you associate a voiceless [p] with <pay> and a voiced [l] with <lay>, it does not follow that the co-articulation of /p/ and /l/ in <play> is phonetically straightforward, since the whole /pl/ cluster in <play> is voiceless.

The failure to distinguish between sounds and letters may produce non-problems and non-arguments which are ultimately used as evidence of the complexity or irregularity of the English writing system. The following example is all the more interesting in that it occurs in a book which tries to include some explanation of what phonemes and allophones are, and which has a section devoted to 'the surface structure of language' (Smith 1971: 30). In discussing 'phonics' as a method of teaching reading Smith says:

> Here is a phonic rule that would appear to have impeccable antecedents: final *e* following a single consonant [*sic* = letter] indicates that the preceding vowel [*sic* = phoneme] should be tense, as in *hat* and *hate*, or *hop* and *hope*. And here is an instant exception: *axe* has a single consonant but a lax (short) /a/ (while *ache*, which has a double consonant, takes a

> tense /a/). We have the choice of admitting that our traditional rule is not impervious to exceptions, or else we have to make a rule for the exceptions. One explanation that might be offered is that *x* is really a double consonant, *ks* (and that *ch* is really a single consonant, *k*). But then we are in the rather peculiar position of changing the notion of what constitutes a single letter simply because we have a rule that does not fit all cases. If we start to say that the definition of what constitutes a letter depends on the pronunciation of a word, how can we say that the pronunciation of a word can be predicted from its letters?
>
> (ibid.: 166)

This has all the outward appearance of a rational argument, but it depends purely on confusion between 'sound' and 'letter'. The message is that one cannot rely on 'phonic rules' because the one discussed is apparently flawed. The flaw is only in Smith's use of 'consonant' to refer to a consonant letter. There is no problem with either *axe* or *ache* if 'consonant' is used phonetically in the rule. The only exception in §Basic vocabulary is the use of <-e> as a marker after <v> as in *love, have.* (See p. 121; see also p. 220 for *ache* and, in the context of the 'short word rule', p. 133 for *axe.*)

There may be some advantage to be gained by this exploitation of the confusion between sounds and letters. Smith finds it necessary to challenge all phonographic regularities in the interests of his own theory of lexical access in reading, which is based on sampling the text for visual features. A 'regularity' is what you find; an 'irregularity' may be a regularity that would be inconvenient for your purposes to find. This could be the reason why Smith (1971) and Venezky (1967), writing about the very same data, can come to quite different conclusions:

> (a): Some aspects of spelling are simply unpredictable, certainly to a reader with a limited knowledge of word derivations, no matter how one tries to define a spelling unit. An example of a completely unpredictable spelling to sound correspondence is *th*, which is pronounced in one way at the beginning of words like *this*, *than*, *that*, *those*, *them*, *then*, *these* but in another way at the beginning of *think*, *thank*, *thatch*, *thong*, *theme*, and so on. There is only one way to tell whether *th* should be pronounced as in *this* or as in *think*, and that is to remember every instance.
>
> (Smith 1971: 167)

> (b): A final example of where form class identity is necessary for correct pronunciation is in initial *th*. Functors beginning with this cluster have the voiced inter-dental spirant /ð/: *the*, *then*, *this*, *those*, while contentives have the voiceless spirant /θ/: *thesis*, *thin*, *thumb*.
>
> (Venezky 1967: 92)

If we take Venezky's point to be valid, as indeed we must, Smith is clearly quite wrong to refer to the <th> spellings as 'completely unpredictable'. There is nothing very esoteric about their distribution. Primary-school teachers certainly need not brandish terminology such as 'functor' or 'contentive' at children to make them aware of the difference.

'Learning the alphabet'

Much of the confusion between sounds and letters derives from the business of 'learning the alphabet' as a preliminary to reading. Alphabet books for small children need careful design and material to do what they are intended for: to bring out an awareness of letter-sound correspondences. However good the pictures, no child will get very far with 'O is for owl', 'O is for orange', 'S is for sugar', 'S is for ship'. The whole long business of formal education should not begin with the rote learning of manifest inconsistencies. This important first step in literacy does not seem to attract much attention from educationalists. (A notable exception is the critical survey of alphabet books written by Suria Perera for Knowsley Council Remedial Services.) 'Knowing the alphabet' involves learning a letter's shape(s), its usual phonetic counterpart(s) and its 'name'. A great deal of mystique attaches to the name of the letter, because in some vowel correspondences 'the letter says its name'. The letter <a> 'says its name' in *mate* but not in *mat*. Problems arise if the names of letters are taken to be a basis for describing the writing system in relation to speech. For instance, Follick (1965: 98), a leading spelling reformer, in a scheme designed to teach English spelling and pronunciation to foreigners, groups vowels into:

'pure vowels': as in *mate*, *mete*, *mite*, *mope*, *tube*;
'impure vowels': as in *mat*, *met*, *bit*, *mop*, *tub*;
'diphthongs': as in *brawn*, *brown*, *rood*, *stood*;
'continental a': as in *father*.

This use of the term 'pure' obviously derives from the correspondence of the '*name* ' of the letter with its '*value*'. By comparison the short vowels are 'impure' since name and value are out of step. There is an irony here because, in Mont Follick's reformed spelling scheme, the simple vowel letters have their short value and the long vowels require digraphs. The fact that they 'say their name' is not exploited. What is wrong with these categories is not so much that they are in drastic conflict with the phonetic use of the terms 'pure' and 'diphthong'. It is simply that they would form a very confusing basis for teaching English pronunciation to foreigners.

Apart from how the letter 'says its name', the other criterion used in this classification is whether the spelling consists of one letter or two. The term diphthong properly refers to vowel sounds, not vowel spellings. A diphthong is a vowel glide within a single syllable, that is, a vowel in which there is a perceptible change of quality during its production. What is common to *brawn*, *brown*, *rood*, *stood* is that the vowels are represented by digraphs: strings of two letters. The only one of the four to contain a diphthong is *brown*. In later stages of Follick's scheme for reformed spelling the 'pure'/'impure' categories are dropped but the confusion of sounds and letters persists to some extent:

> Diphthongs : ei ii ai ou iu aa au aw.
> Digraphs : ch sh th dh kh zh.
>
> (Follick 1965: 201)

Some of these 'diphthongs' do not, of course, represent diphthongs at all but, in the phonetic sense, pure vowels. The spelling <aa> represents /ɑː/, <au> usually represents /ɔː/. What Mont Follick really has here are a set of vowel digraphs and a set of consonant digraphs. The ingrained idea that a diphthong is a vowel spelt with two letters persists throughout the literature on reading and spelling and is a prime source of confusion (cf. the example quoted from Fowler at the beginning of this section). Most people would be aware that the element <graph> has to do with writing, but unfortunately the element <phthong> is so infrequent in English words that it carries no association with 'sound'.

2.3 DIVERGENCE

Departures from one-to-one correspondence

The alphabetic principle, in theory at least, requires not only that a given phoneme is represented by a constant symbol but also that the symbol involved does not represent other phonemes. This requirement is referred to in phonological theory as 'biuniqueness'. As we have already seen, the English writing system is by no means entirely based on the alphabetic principle: to a very large extent it seeks to secure a constant spelling for a given morpheme. Partly because of this, partly because of large-scale borrowing from other languages, and partly because of the effect of sound-changes, the phoneme–grapheme correspondences of English usually fall far short of biuniqueness. But individual phonemes and individual graphemes vary considerably in the extent of their divergence from biuniqueness. This is fairly obvious to any speller: the spelling of /p/ is more straightforward than the spelling of /k/, for instance.

We shall use the term 'divergence' (Haas 1970: 51) to cover this aspect of spelling. We may find divergence on the phonic side of a correspondence: <th>≡/θ/ and <th>≡/ð/; or on the graphic side: /f/≡<f>, /f/≡<ff> and /f/≡<ph>. More often than not we find divergence on both sides: /iː/≡<ea>, /iː/≡<ee>, and <ea>≡/iː/, <ea>≡/e/, etc.

The terms '**conditioned variant**' and '**competing variant**' would seem to be useful in differentiating between real and apparent divergence. Consider the different spellings of /p/ and the different spellings of /ɜː/. The <pp> spelling is largely predictable either as consonant-letter doubling to mark a previous short vowel in §Basic words (*apple*, *copper*, *supper*) or as prefix assimilation in §Latinate words (*approve*, *apprehend*, *appreciate*). If we can state general rules for the distribution of two alternative spellings, then they can be regarded as conditioned variants in complementary distribution. If we look, however, at the spellings of /ɜː/ in SBS, we do not find that the distribution of the spellings can be described by rule to any marked extent. The choice between, say, <ir> and <ur> as spellings of /ɜː/ cannot be explained by context. We might tentatively call them competing variants. Any divergence requires more effort by the reader/writer, but competing variants are clearly much more troublesome than conditioned variants. They make the task of differentiating word-shapes more difficult, especially for the writer. For the reader, the cost might well be justified if it gives a different shape to homophones such as *seen* – *scene* (see §5.3).

The temptation to overstate irregularities

The divergence found in English spelling is often overstated. This is largely because people fail to realize that some spellings are conditioned variants which do not in effect compete with each other. Henderson and Chard (1980: 111) in an article devoted, ironically, to the reader's implicit knowledge of orthographic structure, provide a listing of what they consider to be the 'mapping options' for the spellings and sounds of the word *fake* (<fake>≡/feɪk/) reproduced below as Table 4. This is supposed to represent the choices open to the reader. The correspondences they use derive from Hanna (1966).

Commenting on this table they note that the reader has 19 options in putting together the string of phonemes and the writer has 27 options in putting together the string of letters. They conclude that correspondences are more ambiguous in the phoneme to grapheme direction. This may well be true, but the assumption is falsely made. The mapping of letters on to phonemes and vice versa is seen as a series of 'pathways'. They find that there is also asymmetry in the relative frequency of a given pathway: /k/ is the regular sounding of <k>, while <c> is the regular spelling of /k/. They go on to admit that 'some of these asymmetries of choice can be reduced by applying other constraints, ranging from position within the syllable up to more complex linguistic considerations'. That is so very obviously the case that it is difficult to imagine any valid use to which such a table might be put.

Table 4 'Mapping options' for *fake* <fake>≡/feɪk/ (as in Henderson and Chard)

Grapheme–phoneme correspondences			*Phoneme–grapheme correspondences*		
Grapheme	*Phonemic options*	*Example*	*Phoneme*	*Graphemic options*	*Example*
<f>	/f/	fake	/f/	<f>	fake
				<ph>	phone
<a>	/eɪ/	fake		<ff>	buff
	/ɑː/	arm		<gh>	rough
	/iː/	eat			
	/e/	many	/eɪ/	<a–e>	fake
	/aɪ/	aisle		<a>	angel
	/əʊ/	coat		<ai>	aid
	/ɔː/	all		<ai–e>	aide
	/ə/	canal		<aigh>	straight
	/uː/	beauty		<au–e>	gauge
				<ay>	way
<k>	/k/	fake		<e>	cafe
	silent	knee		<ea>	break
				<ei>	vein
<e>	silent	fake		<eigh>	weigh
	/ɛə/	there		<et>	beret
	/iː/	feel		<ey>	they
	/e/	end			
	/aɪ/	eye	/k/	<k>	fake
	/uː/	sleuth		<c>	orc
	/ə/	angel		<cc>	occupy
				<cch>	saccharine
				<ch>	echo
				<ck>	back
				<cq>	acquire
				<kh>	khaki
				<qu>	bouquet
				<sc>	viscount

What is wrong here is the curious disregard for context. This takes two forms. A 'grapheme' is taken to be a single letter, as if reading and spelling were done with units of one letter at a time. This seems to entail that a single letter <a> in the slot <f–ke> is somehow able to be confused with <ea>≡/iː/ in *eat*, <ai>≡/aɪ/ in *aisle*, <oa>≡/əʊ/ in *coat*, and <eau>≡/juː/ in *beauty* and so denies these letter complexes the status of units. It also assumes that the <e>-marker is not read as part of the correspondence <a–e>, though they allow this in the other direction, speech-to-text. This brings us to the other way in which context is here disregarded. The authors ignore the fact that correspondences may be conditioned variants. The final single <e> of <fake> cannot in any way form a correspondence with the vowels of *there, feel, end, eye, sleuth* or *angel*. The 'silent' <k> is limited to the initial cluster <kn>. The same point can be made for most of the correspondences cited for the speech-to-text direction. For instance, the <ff> and <ck> options would only occur after a short vowel. The <gh> option for /f/ does not occur initially. Here we are on the familiar ground of Shaw's comic suggestion that *fish* may equally well be spelt *<ghoti> (see p. 21). In fact, in English the spelling <fake> can only be a spelling of /feɪk/. On the other hand, there are a few marginal ways in which the utterance /feɪk/ might otherwise be spelt:

1 as *<phache> (cf. *phase*, and the discussion of *ache*, p. 472;
2 as *<feak> which is only feasible on the remote analogy of *break*);
3 as *<faik> (though<ai> does not seem to occur before <k>, except in a few names such as *Aiken, Blaikley, Craik, Raikes*).

All in all, a better example of the difference between apparent and real divergence could hardly have been given.

Disregard for context is a recurring problem in literacy studies. It lies at the heart of Smith's treatment of *axe* (p. 12), <th-> (p. 13), {-ed} (p. 20) and <ho-> (p. 33).

2.4 LEXICAL SPELLING

Keeping the spelling of a morpheme constant

The English writing system is not simply concerned with mapping phonemes on to letters. To a large extent it tries to offer the reader a constant spelling for a morpheme in spite of the varying pronunciation of the morpheme in different contexts. Children are taught both a long and a short phonemic value for the simple vowel letters. In spite of the very considerable present-day phonetic differences in pronunciation, the pairs /eɪ/ – /æ/ (*sane*, *sanity*), /aɪ/ – /ɪ/ (*mime*, *mimic*), /əʊ/ – /ɒ/ (*cone*, *conical*), /iː/ – /e/ (*diabetes*, *diabetic*) have a constant vowel letter. Only in the pair /aʊ/ – /ʌ/ (*pronounce*, *pronunciation*) do the vowel letters used in the spelling (<ou> – <u>) sometimes vary to reflect the surface difference. But even here there are long–short differences such as *South*, *Southern* where the morpheme keeps its spelling identity. Similarly the different correspondences /s/≡<c>, /k/≡<c>, and /ʃ/≡<ci> allow a constant morphemic spelling in words such as *electricity*, *electrical*, *electrician*. The past tense and participle morpheme {-ed} in regular verbs (ignoring forms such as *spelt*, *spent*, *dreamt*) has a constant <-ed> spelling in spite of the phonemic variation /ɪd/ (*waited*), /d/ (*warned*) and /t/ (*watched*).

There is very similar allomorphic variation in the noun plural and 3rd person singular present tense of the verb with its variants /ɪz/ (*watches*), /z/ (*warns*) and /s/ (*waits*). The two sets of phonetic variants are often cited together as equivalent examples of morphemic spelling. If we look closely at the details, however we find in fact that they are dealt with rather differently in the writing system (table 5).

Table 5 English plural and past tense inflections

	{-ed} ending	*{-(e)s} ending*
1	/-ɪd/ *matted*	/-ɪz/ *masses*
2	/-ɪd/ *mated*	/-ɪz/ *maces*
3	/-t/ *hopped*	/-s/ (No **hoppes*)
4	/-t/ *hoped*	/-s/ *hops, hopes*
5	/-d/ *planned*	/-z/ (No **plannes*)
6	/-d/ *planed*	/-z/ *plans, planes*
7	/-d/ *hurried*	/-z/ *hurries*
8	/-d/ *radioed*	/-z/ *radios*
9	/-d/ *vetoed*	/-z/ *vetoes* or *vetos*

Table 5 gives examples of each suffix in its three phonemic variants. The words provided as contexts include a preceding long vowel followed by a single consonant, a preceding short vowel followed by a single consonant, and the spelling variation found after <o>. The past tense has a constant <ed> spelling across all these contexts which is only varied by merging with a final <-e> in the long vowel words (e.g. *hope – hoped*). The marking of the long vowels is also done indirectly by using <C>-doubling to mark a previous short vowel – absence of doubling marks the long vowel. This is not done in the noun plural suffix, so there are no equivalents in rows 3 and 5 to <hopped> and <planned>, that is *<hoppes> and *<plannes>. Nor is there a variant spelling *<vetod> to spoil the uniformity of <-ed>. The <e> of <-oes> and <-ies> is best treated as a marker of the long vowel. Grammarians refer to the two inflections as the *-s* form and the *-ed* form and this is in accordance with the traditional spelling rule that one adds <-s> and <-ed> respectively to the base form.

If we try to use a consistent <-ed> morphemic spelling in chopping up words into correspondences without any overlap, this lack of symmetry becomes apparent. In *scribbles* we have /əl/≡<le> and in *scribbled* we have /əl/≡<l>; in *hopes* we have <e>-marking of the vowel as /əʊ/≡<o..e>, /p/≡<p>, /s/≡<s>, but in *hoped* we have /əʊ/≡<o>, /p/≡<p>, /t/≡<ed>, while the long vowel is marked by absence of <C>-doubling. In a process description, and indeed for any human speller, this is catered for by 'dovetailing' so that <hope>+<ed> becomes <hoped>, <eight>+<ty> becomes <eighty>, etc.

Not all past tense and participle forms have the <ed> spelling. The group *burn*, *dwell*, *learn*, *smell*, *spill*, *spoil* have two alternative forms (*burned* /d/≡<ed>, *burnt* /t/≡<t> etc.). Some irregular verbs have two such forms but with a different vowel in the /t/ form as well (*dream*, *dreamed* and *dreamt* /dremt/, *lean*, *leaned* and *leant* /lent/), or just one form with a different vowel and /t/≡<t> (*deal*, *dealt*; *creep*, *crept*; *buy*, *bought*). The group *bend*, *build*, *lend*, *rend*, *send*, *spend*, have a single form with /t/≡<t> replacing the /d/≡<d> of the base form. The group *sell*, *tell*, *say*, *hear* have a single /d/≡<d> with a stem vowel change. These do not present a problem in spelling since the <t> or <d> spellings only occur where the stem vowel changes or where the /t/ suffix irregularly follows a vowel or voiced consonant or both. There should be no temptation to write *<creped> (for *crept*) or *<bened> for *bent*.

The system also maintains a constant morphemic spelling in instances where an underlying phoneme does not surface and the letter in question has a zero phonetic counterpart – cf. *sign* with /Ø/≡<g> and *signature* with /g/≡<g>. The <g> in *sign* is an example of what is here called an 'inert letter' (see §2.6.5 p. 41).

In arguments about the English writing system, a good head of steam can easily be generated simply by regarding morphemic spellings as failed phonemic spellings. For instance: 'it is often impossible to know for certain which phonic rules apply. The rule that specifies how to pronounce *ph* in *telephone* falls down in the face of *haphazard*, or *shepherd*, or *cuphook*' (Smith 1971: 168). These alarming lapses can easily be cured by recognizing a morpheme boundary. Smith considers that there are three important aspects of spoken language that 'our writing system does not even pretend to represent'. They are, in his view, intonation, syntax (e.g. whether *permit* is a noun or a verb), and 'finally, and perhaps surprisingly, spelling does not really attempt to represent sounds at all, but rather phonemes'. Reluctantly accepting that the English writing system does seem to represent phonemes, he goes on to illustrate its failure to do so consistently:

> Sometimes a single letter that we may think has only one sound is pronounced as three different *phonemes* [*sic*]; the *s* at the end of a plural noun or present tense verb may be pronounced /s/ as in 'walks', /z/ as in 'runs', or /ez/ [*sic*] as in 'judges'. Similarly the past tense *ed* may be pronounced /t/ as in 'walked', /d/ as in 'charged', or /ed/ [*sic*] as in 'landed'. None of these distinctions is indicated by the spelling, and they are generally disregarded in 'phonic rules '.
>
> (Smith 1971: 168)

Here again, one can only note that regularity is in the eye of the beholder. Smith assumes that the only function of spelling is to represent phonemes. Then he criticizes the writing system when it chooses to represent morphemes instead of phonemes.

Processes and underlying forms

Keeping the spelling of a morpheme constant entails some graphic units having several different phonetic counterparts. Usually this variation is catered for by regular correspondences between letters and phonemes already provided in the system. So the /s/ and /k/ values of <c> in *electrical*, *electricity* are not only used to give morphemes such as *electric* a constant spelling, they are in use throughout the system (*cat*, *city*). However, derivation processes do produce correspondences only found in allomorphic variation and not elsewhere. Sound changes, such as palatalization, which operate in word-formation, highlight the difficulty of working with surface phonemes in setting up simple correspondences. Palatalization, in English word-formation, is where an alveolar consonant has become palato–alveolar by merger with a following /i/ or /j/ or with a palato-alveolar consonant (/ʃ/, /ʒ/, /ʧ/, /ʤ/) and where special correspondences have to be set up to capture the result. The word *picture* was probably pronounced as /pɪktjuːr/ in Early Modern English; now it is pronounced /pɪkʧə(r)/. The spelling reflects the earlier pronunciation, which would give the straightforward correspondences /t/≡<t>, /juː/≡<u>, /r/≡<r>. But how are we to cope with the present-day /ʧ/? Setting up /ʧ/≡<t> is inevitably going to add to the complexity of the description.

We could of course avoid the problem and say that the spelling system does not pretend to represent the present-day pronunciation: that as a system it represents more or less the pronunciation of Early Modern English. The modern pronunciation can be derived from the earlier 'underlying' form by a number of fairly simple rules. This type of description requires phoneme-encoding (if and when phoneme-encoding takes place in any stage or type of reading activity) to be a two-stage process. We would interpret <picture> as //pɪktjuːr// and then apply some rough-and-ready sound changes by which //t//+//j// became /ʧ/ and the /r/ before the boundary was lost. At first sight this looks like an absurdly complex way of going about it. However, the sound changes involved in this process are not really long-dead and fossilized, they are still an active and normal part of the speaker's control of allegro forms. In quick speech, palatalization occurs across word-boundaries to produce *might you* as /maɪʧʊ/ from /maɪt/+/juː/ and speakers of SBS and similar accents are aware of a word-final latent //r// which will surface only before a vowel in a close-knit phrase (*picture it*).

We can note in passing Bernard Shaw's comic suggestion that *fish* might equally well be spelt *<ghoti> (by analogy with *tou*__gh__, *w*__o__*men*, and *na*__ti__*on*). It is not just that these correspondences never occur in the phonetic contexts in which he has put them (Haas 1970: 57, Stubbs 1980: 51). The correspondence /ʃ/≡<ti> only occurs as palatalization in §Latinate words and *fish* is clearly §Basic.

An optimal orthography? The views of Venezky and Chomsky and Halle

It is possible, then, to describe the English writing system as a system of greater inherent simplicity by going beyond the surface correspondences in some cases and using underlying phonological forms. These often reflect an earlier pronunciation which became fixed in the orthography. Readers are then left to use a battery of familiar sound-changes to help them identify the morpheme. Of course, readers do not necessarily have to work their way through all of them to trace every underlying phoneme to its present surface pronunciation. All they need is to collect enough clues to allow them to jump to a hypothesis of recognition. The underlying form usually has the great advantage of being adequate for a wide range of surface variation across dialects.

Venezky (1967: 94) gives the following examples of how spelling-to-sound rules organized in this way would predict the pronunciation of *social* and *signing* (I omit technical details of the various levels):

> *social* would be mapped into //sosɪæl// by the . . . rules for the separate units *s*, *o*, *c*, *i*, *a*, *l*. . . . The main word stress would be placed on the first syllable, resulting in //sósɪæl//. Then, through vowel reduction, //ɪæl// would become //jəl// and the resulting //sj// would be palatalized to //ʃ// . . . giving /sóʃəl/.
>
> *signing* would first be broken into *sign* and *ing* and then each . . . would be mapped onto . . . //sɪgn// and //ɪng//. Upon combination of the two forms and the application of stress and certain phonotactical rules, the form //sɪ́gnɪŋg// would result. By the rules for leveling consonant clusters, final //ŋg// would become //ŋ// and //gn// would become //n// with compensatory alternation of //ɪ// to //aɪ// . . . /sáɪnɪŋ/.
>
> (Venezky 1967: 94)

There is no doubt that a spelling-to-sound description of the English writing system using such abstract underlying forms is quite feasible. Chomsky and Halle (1968: 49) firmly state that 'an optimal orthography would have one representation for each lexical entry'. They find that in many cases 'English orthography turns out to be rather close to an optimal system for spelling English' (ibid.: 184n).

Their main evidence is the vowel alternations found in derived forms such as *mania – manic*, *serene – serenity*, *divine – divinity*, *cone – conic*, *manager – managerial*, *Canada – Canadian*, and similar consonant variation in *electric – electricity*, *sign – signature*. But their complex analysis of English phonology provides other, less obvious evidence that English orthography is largely a system of 'lexical spelling' – a term added by Carol Chomsky (1970). So, the spelling often mirrors the underlying form which is required for the stress assignment rules. It is difficult to summarize the evidence cited, which often involves special pleading for intractable spellings, but they regard the following examples as phonologically well-founded. The final <-y> of *economy*, *industry*, is conveniently ambiguous as a vowel letter or a consonant letter. On the surface, of course, it represents a final vowel, but for assigning stress Chomsky and Halle's Main Stress Rule (Chomsky and Halle 1968: 40) requires that it should be counted here as a consonant. If the <-y> were counted as a vowel spelling, then *industry* would be stressed wrongly on the second syllable from the end. The final 'cluster' <-ustry> is skipped because it ends a noun and contains a lax (short) vowel, so the stress comes forward to <in->. On the other hand, the final <-e> of *Neptune* (ibid.: 46) and of *burlesque*, *eclipse*, (ibid.: 147–8) has somehow to be treated as a vowel to get the stress right: the <-e> is skipped as a lax (short) vowel and the stress is placed on <-esqu->. Ideally, *cement* ought to have such an <-e>, too, to keep the stress on <-ment>. However, what is good for *Neptune* does not seem to fit *Canute*. The endings of words such as *ferocious*, *audacious*, have to be analysed for stress assignment into an <i> and an <ou> for two separate vowels; so a surface analysis into <ci>≡/ʃ/ and <ou>≡/ə/ would be misleading.

Similarly, the <C>-doubling of *Kentucky*, *confetti*, *abscissa*, *Philippa*, marks a 'strong cluster', which attracts the stress (ibid.: 148–9). In *budget*, *butcher*, *bushel*, the letter clusters <dg>, <tch>, <sh> mark the vowel as short, even though phonetically they represent a single consonant (ibid.: 204). The same is true of the double letters in *Maxwellian*, *perennial*, which prevent the lengthening of the vowel as in *manager – managerial* (ibid.: 182n). More subtle is the effect of rule ordering as it affects the voicing of //s// to /z/ in *resume*, *deserve*, *preserve*, *resist*, *resign*, *design*, compared with *consume*, *conserve*, *consist*, *insist*, *persist*, *consign*. The phonetic context for the /z/ is obvious enough: the voicing is found where the §Latinate prefix ends in a vowel. But words spelt with <c>≡/s/, such as *recite*, *recede*, do not become voiced in this way. This is accounted for in their generative model by the ordering of two phonological rules: the velar softening rule which gives *medical – medicine*, *rigour – rigid*, *allegation – allege*, is made to operate after the voicing rule. The underlying velar of *recite* is not then affected by the voicing rule, since it has not yet become /s/ (ibid.: 221).

These examples of how the spelling reflects the underlying phonology vary in importance. The general vowel and consonant alternations of §Latinate words are an essential part of full literacy. The contortions necessary to get the stress right on *Neptune* or to prevent *industry* from being an exception to the Main Stress Rule may be over-ingenious. It could be cheaper to admit exceptions. They are certainly too subtle for the classroom.

How much this approach to the description of English spelling will have relevance to the teaching of reading is a matter for the educational psychologist. It does have some general disadvantages as a method of description which lie beyond arguments about its classroom feasibility. Such a view of the relationship between speech and writing will undoubtedly reinforce the normative, prescriptive view of language so cherished by the general public and even by some educationalists. The underlying form will be seen as the 'real' pronunciation and the actual pronunciation will be misinterpreted as slovenliness. Vowel reduction becomes evidence of a decline in standards. People nowadays will simply not pronounce words properly. These attitudes do affect our appreciation, understanding and effective use of language.

However, there is a more immediate disadvantage in a description which makes extended use of underlying forms that only match up with their pronunciation by further processing. It offers no help to the writer. The surface pronunciation is the undeniable minimum of relevant information that writers start with. Whether, as part of their competence, or from their accumulated experience as readers, they have underlying phonological forms available to them is open to question. Working from print to sound in the other direction, one can make quite economical hypotheses about what the printed morpheme is. It is probably easier to get from a written form <picture> to an abstract phonological form //pɪktju:r// and then to /pɪkʧə(r)/ than to arrive at a written form <picture> by first turning /pɪkʧə(r)/ into //pɪktju:r//. The present study does not make use of abstract underlying forms as a descriptive device. It is largely concerned with the problem of how far the surface phonetic forms can be exploited by writer and reader. Assumed phonetic awareness is restricted to surface pronunciations such as /pɪkʧə(r)/. There is no obvious way in which underlying forms could be generated from this raw data in order to keep the description of the system of correspondences simple. That could only be done by feeding back information from the desired spelling, which would defeat the object of the exercise. Something perilously close to this was in fact done in Hanna's algorithm for English spelling (see §2.8.5). In practice, these restrictions are loosened considerably if one treats each spelling correspondence along with its immediate context as a complex data item. So, for instance, the results of palatalization are separable, by context, from 'original' palatals: the /ʧ/ of *picture* can be analysed in context as /ʧ≡<t> with /ə/≡<u> and the /ʧ/ of *watch* can be analysed as /ʧ/≡<tch> with #.

An untidy alphabetic system?

Though there is a fairly wide spectrum of differing opinions about the relative abstractness and regularity of the present English writing system, there is general agreement about how it fits into the overall typology of writing systems. It is an untidy alphabetic (phonemic) system – in which single letters or strings of letters make up symbols to represent phonemes, but it has been allowed and encouraged to preserve as far as possible a constant orthographic shape for morphemes in spite of their varying pronunciation. So, in spite of variation in their vowels and consonants, the visual shapes of morphemes recur unchanged, for instance, {cynic} in *cynic*, *cynicism;* {hilar} in *hilarious*, *hilarity;* {-s} in *kits*, *kids;* {-ed} in *wanted*, *washed*, *wagged*. Hence the system is in part morphophonemic rather than purely phonemic. This insight has in fact to be unlearnt by language students attempting a purely phonemic transcription, who are tempted, for instance, to transcribe *scratched* as */skræʧd/ instead of /skræʧt/. The close bond between, say, phonetically different pairs of long and short vowels: /aɪ/ – /ɪ/, /iː/ – /e/, /eɪ/ – /æ/, /aʊ/ – /ʌ/, /əʊ/ – /ɒ/, and the way in which these vowel pairs alternate in allomorphs of the same morpheme, can be described fairly informally. Primary-school teachers have successfully taught morphophonemics for generations without knowing it. Successful graduates of the primary school have a very abstract //A//, //E//, //I//, //O//, //U// with their long and short values firmly built into their literacy skills even after a 'phonic' training. Robert Bridges (1919: 41ff) even suggested that children should be taught a formal style of speech, not unlike the public oratory of the day, with unreduced vowels in unstressed syllables. Elocution would become part of the process of acquiring literacy:

> In the natural order of things, children would be taught a careful 'high standard' articulation as a part of their elemental training, when in their pliant age they are mastering the co-ordinations which are so difficult to acquire later. Then when they have been educated to speak correctly, their variation from that full pronunciation is a natural carelessness and has the grace of all natural behaviour, and it naturally obeys whatever laws have been correctly propounded by phoneticians.
>
> (Bridges 1919: 41)

Phoneticians, chiefly in the person of Daniel Jones, came in for strong criticism from Bridges. 'Mr. Jones' had misleadingly transcribed the stressed vowel of *bit* and the unstressed vowel of *Margate* with the same phoneme symbol. Bridges maintains, in effect, that children who say /ˈmɑːgɪt/ should be told that they ought to be saying /ˈmɑːgeɪt/. Perhaps they would in a better ordered society. In his tract, he roundly blames phoneticians for contributing to 'the impoverishment of the language':

> 7 Attention is called to the low standard of pronunciation adopted by our professional phoneticians, and to the falsity of their orthodox teaching.
> 8 The damage to the language which is threatened by their activity is exposed.
>
> (ibid.: 47)

Underlying Bridge's reaction is the realization that the English writing system cannot be described as 'phonemic', but rather 'morphophonemic', since it tries to provide a consistent spelling for morphemes. It has been suggested, however, (Stubbs 1986: 5) that 'morpholexical' might be a better typological label for the English writing system than 'morphophonemic'. This term has been used to describe allomorphic variation which required reference to indexed classes of lexemes. The rules describing the phonemic variation in allomorphs in English cannot work simply by processing the morphophonemes into surface phonemes, so that //e// becomes /iː/ in the base-form of *serene* and /e/ before {ity} in *serenity*. There are exceptions. This variation does not occur in *obese*, *obesity*, both with /iː/. So it is essential to know that *serene* is in one class of lexemes and *obese* in another, otherwise the unwary reader would wrongly read */əʊˈbesətɪ/. Similarly we would presumably have *mime*, *cone*, *mania*, *diabetes* in one lexical class and *scene*, *base*, in another because of their variant treatment before {-ic}. The label 'morpholexical' does cover this variation more precisely than 'morphophonemic'. The consequences of such variation are, of course, more significant to the reader than to the writer – both /e/ and /iː/ have the default spelling <e> in §Latinate words and both *serenity* and *obesity* are spelt as a straightforward string of correspondences.

2.5 READING

What does a reader read?

Reading a text, silently or aloud, is successful if the strings of letters in the text are eventually associated with the meanings of intended morphemes and words. This is usually termed 'lexical access' in psychological studies of reading. A wide range of recent psycholinguistic testing has sought to establish how lexical access is achieved. In the present state of the art, however, only a small proportion of this work has any direct bearing on the task of describing the writing system as a mapping of spoken language on to written language.

A basic problem for the psycholinguist is whether the reader analyses the letter strings at any stage of the reading process (or the process of learning to read) into their corresponding phonemes to recognize a word, or whether the operation by-passes speech altogether. One argument against phonemic-encoding as part of the reading process is that the rate at which letters are read is too rapid for the phoneme associations to be made. This, however, ignores the considerable redundancy in a continuous printed text. On the other hand there is ample evidence from reaction-time measurements that real words or 'pronounceable' word-shapes are processed more quickly than non-words. Gibson *et al.* (1962) in a relatively early study, put this down to the reader's use of grapheme-phoneme correspondences in the processing. However, a repetition of the test with a group of profoundly deaf subjects (Gibson *et al.* 1970: 71) showed that this did not necessarily involve internalized speech. It was presumably orthographic regularities *reflecting* the phoneme-grapheme correspondences which were available to the deaf readers.

> Orthographic rules are rules in their own right and apparently can be learned as such, quite aside from the fact that any word they produce maps predictably to speech sounds. Sound would seem thus to be not necessarily a part of the individual's processing in forming higher units of reading, although historically it formed them in the spelling patterns of the written language.
>
> (Gibson *et al.* 1970: 71)

Roger Brown, in a discussion of this article (in Levin & Williams, 1970: 165ff) suggests as an alternative explanation that simple frequency of letter combinations may well account for the quicker reaction time to regular word-shapes. That is to say, there is no apparent need for the string to relate to vowels, or consonants, or the onset, peak and coda of a syllable. His argument leaves one with the impression that psycholinguists are anxious to avoid such linguistic categories. This caution seems to be the complete obverse of the earlier reluctance by American structuralists to accept any linguistic categorizations or arguments based on psychological criteria. The Gibson study had already rejected simple bigram (two-letter strings) and trigram (three-letter strings) letter counts (which of course have no linguistic basis as units) as predictors of their results with the deaf children, because, hardly surprisingly to a linguist, they did not correlate very well with the results. Brown suggests an equally arbitrary unit:

> One might hypothesize that the perceptual device incorporated a model of the structure of English in which letter strings have the bigram frequencies of English but no other constraints and further hypothesize that the perceivability of a letter string would be proportional to the logarithm of the probability of the string in the model. To find the frequency of a string in the model, . . . one would take the product of the bigram frequencies of all the bigrams and divide it by the product of the frequencies of all the letters in the string except the end letters.
>
> (ibid.: 165)

Now let us suppose these more subtly processed but still arbitrary frequency units did give a better correlation with the Gibson test results. What have we explained? Nothing at all. We have merely established that some bigrams are more frequent than others. But no-one is suggesting that readers process letter strings in chunks of two letters at a time. We surely need something more explanatory than operational mathematical convenience. What units were the readers in these tests actually exposed to?

The regular pseudo-words used in the original Gibson tests were items such as: DINK, VUNS, GLOX, KLERFT; the irregular word shapes were transforms of these: NKID, NSUV, XOGL, FTERKL, etc. In structuralist terms, these monosyllables, consisting of onset-peak-coda, had their (written) onsets and codas exchanged. It was not simply a matter of taking letters off the end and putting them on the beginning, where they would be equally valid: the experimenters did not create *NKDI, *NSVU or *XGLO from DINK, VUNS and GLOX. In effect, the units involved were letter strings corresponding to syllable onsets and syllable codas (some simple, some complex) and the frame within which the changes were rung was essentially the syllable. The irregular word shapes were still shaped like monosyllables around a peak vowel. They were made up of constituents, not of arbitrary strings of letters. What was odd about them was that the increasing/decreasing sonority of the clusters was reversed by the switching. Looked at from a linguistic point of view the test material was not therefore a full coverage of the problem. The non-words should have included words made up with irregular onsets which were not (in another context) regular codas, and irregular codas which were not (in another context) regular onsets. The fact that the Gibson tests were not juggling with arbitrary bigrams but were switching immediate constituents of (written) syllables was overlooked even more in the general debate which followed. Aderman and Smith (1971), for instance, who use the same kind of material, call the switched clusters 'unrelated letters (UL)' as distinct from the regular 'spelling patterns (SP)'. It should be obvious that <ng> is not a string of unrelated letters in the sense that, for instance <jt> or <wg> would be.

Later cognitive studies of reading also use 'non-words' as experimental material to test for awareness of sound and letter correspondences. These sometimes stray outside the regularities of the system. Young children may be asked to read, as the names of imaginary creatures, <ka>, <ko>, <ja>, <ji>, with the expectation that they will say a final short vowel: /kɒ/, /ʤæ/, etc., and taking /kəʊ/ to be an unsatisfactory response. Short vowels do not occur in such a context in English. I have also seen in reading research projects <CVC> non-words such as <poc>, <rif>, <nol> in a list alongside more normal strings <lep>, <rom>, <mab>. These are only marginally odd, given the messy ways in which <C>-doubling is used to mark a short vowel, but, to be really safe, non-words should be constructed within the regularities of the writing system.

Should spelling be taught deliberately or should it seep in?

Before modern linguistics deepened our insight into the structure of language, written English was innocently thought to be a direct representation of speech. Hence children were taught to read by hit-and-miss 'phonic' methods: <plot> spells [pə-lə-ɒ-tə], /plɒt/. With the growing interest in linguistics, from the 1950s more informed methods were used to draw attention to the system of written and spoken contrasts within the shape of whole words. This was based essentially on the structuralist notion of **commutation**: showing that the substitution of one phoneme for another in a particular context may produce a new word-shape – *pat*, *pet*, *pit*, *pot*, *put*.

The material offered to the child, however, was often mind-numbing: 'The cat can bat the pan. Dan can pat the cat. The man ran the van.'

Wardhaugh (1971: 346) sums up this approach: 'in essence, the method entails little more than the presentation of regular phoneme–grapheme, or sound–spelling relationships in beginning reading texts, in many ways a kind of neo-phonics'. Chomsky and Halle, together with Venezky at the end of the 1960s, required much more linguistic competence in their models of the reading process: boundaries and stress patterns need to be recognized and the orthographic symbols relate to actual sounds by way of phonological rules.

Phonological awareness and taught spelling

Meanwhile, the aridity of the 'Dan can pat the cat' material had caused a reaction against methods which tried to draw attention to spelling-to-sound correspondences. This led to a 'look and say' approach, which encouraged the child to remember the graphic shape of a word without analysing it into spelling-to-sound correspondences. It was assumed that children would work out such correspondences for themselves, if they needed them, without intervention from the teacher. Developing out of this is the theory proposed by Frank Smith, which has many followers (see Perera 1980). Smith maintains that reading is a process of continuous prediction of the meaning of a written text. The prediction is controlled by intermittent sampling of its visual features. The role of the teacher is simply to provide feedback, but no detailed scheme is proposed for how this should be done. The difference between this approach and the original 'look and say' proposals is that, for Smith, the reading process is not tied to the individual words. Smith's theory seems to require that sound-to-spelling correspondences ought not to be actively used in the teaching of literacy at any stage. Certainly, in the examples quoted in this and the next section, he decries any suggestion of usefulness in what he takes to be 'phonic' methods.

For Smith, spelling skills and phonological awareness can only be relevant to writing. They have no part to play in reading:

> I am not saying that knowledge of spelling is not important, only that it does not have a role in reading, and that undue concern with the way in which words are spelled can only interfere with a child's learning to read.
> (Smith 1973: 143)

Dogmatic assertions are not always easy to disprove. Here, the onus of disproof has been on cognitive psychologists. Recent 'longitudinal' or diachronic studies of the early stages of reading do seem to have proved that Smith's view is wrong. Ellis and Cataldo (1990), summarizing the results of one such developmental study, claim that: 'the teaching of spelling and phonological awareness is an integral and important part of early reading instruction' (ibid.: 1).

The children studied were tested individually on four separate occasions over a three-year period in reading and spelling and by several different tests of phonological awareness. A 'pathway' analysis of the developmental interaction between the various skills identified spelling as an important contributor to early reading, but the influence was clearly not reciprocal. Good spelling at one stage predicted good reading at a later stage, but good reading did not predict good spelling: 'the early flow of information between reading and spelling appears to be unidirectional' (ibid.: 10).

In the early stages of learning to read, children seem to develop a complex strategy in which alphabetic decoding may play an important and productive part:

> Children are able to shift from one level of reading strategy to another, depending on the demands of the task. Beginners attempt to read unknown words via a strategy of combining context, visual and phonetic cues, and only when this fails, switch to deciphering. Initially, deciphering is used exclusively for reading unknown words when other strategies fail, but with practice children integrate this alphabetic approach into their repertoire set of strategies and eventually the beginner comes to appreciate the general usefulness of this deciphering strategy, perhaps temporarily reneguing other approaches to word recognition for the sake of practising this skill and gaining automaticity.
>
> (ibid.: 11)

The Ellis and Cataldo results and similar cognitive work may still not convince those who are locked in to a 'look and say' approach to reading, but they are certainly sufficient to shift the onus of proof. The English writing system, for all its blemishes, is an alphabetic system and the natural assumption to make is that a growing awareness of sound and letter correspondences should play an active, significant and constructive role in the development of reading skills. There is no reason to doubt this. Anyone who wishes to say otherwise has the task of providing proof. Dogma will not do.

What if you look, but cannot say?

Amid all the arguments about how literacy should be acquired, there are two quite separate questions to be addressed:

1 How should children, or illiterate adults for that matter, be taught to read? To what extent should spelling-to-sound correspondences be exploited in teaching them?
2 What goes on in the mind of a literate person reading a text? Do

remembered spelling-to-sound correspondences play a part, either in confident, free-flowing reading, or when the reader stumbles across an unfamiliar word which cannot be read effortlessly?

We can make a few assumptions about skilled reading without getting involved too deeply in controversy. We shall assume that the skilled reader makes an informed guess at the identity of the written words. Rapid readers will not necessarily focus on each word in the line, but hop along in little jumps, with the accumulated context helping their guesses. The reading is successful if the string of words perceived matches the writer's intention. For fluent readers, recognition may well be direct and purely visual, without the mediation of the spoken form. That seems to be a consensus view of what the skilled reader does.

Anyone who believes in a thoroughgoing 'look and say' approach to reading as the direct recognition of whole chunks of text, would hardly disagree with the notion that the reader is making informed guesses. They would, of course, deny any significant role for spelling-to-sound correspondences. However, let us assume that we are dealing with a more-or-less literate person who, while reading, comes across a word which is not immediately recognizable in a context where no reasonable guess springs to mind. Whatever holistic processes may be involved in relating letter strings to known words, they will presumably have failed. The 'visual features' lying there in the printed text evoke no recognition. The only strategy open to the reader at this point is to convert the letters into a string of sounds by rule to trigger an association with a known word, or provide a pronunciation for a new word. 'Look and say' methods have little to offer when the reader has looked but cannot say. Spelling-to-sound correspondences may at least be part of a back-up system for the reader, keeping open the possibility that correspondence rules might also be used effectively in the initial teaching of reading skills.

Literacy for foreign learners of English is a special case. In the absence of a live informant, the orthography is the main indication available of the pronunciation of an unfamiliar word, short of looking it up in a pronouncing dictionary. They need, from the very beginning, some awareness of spelling–phoneme correspondences as a key to the phonetics of English and to prevent them from being misled by the writing system of their first language, in which they will usually be literate.

The information we need for making an informed guess at the identity of a written word may come from a range of different sources. These may comprise the overall syntactic and semantic context in which the word occurs. What we clearly do not do in reading continuous English text is to focus all our faculties on a left to right scan, matching letters to phonemes until we reach the end of the word, and then looking for its meaning in our internal lexicon. Fluent reading cannot effectively be such a tedious one-channel linear process; it must involve some form of parallel processing and some awareness of probabilities and redundancy. If the spoken form does mediate in the reading process, the reader will also need to monitor the accumulating grammatical context. If we are expecting a verb, after having read '*he always* . . .', the form <analyses> will be /'ænəlaɪzɪz/, but when we expect a noun after '*the most thorough* . . .', it will be /ə'næləsiːz/. We may also need to recognize structural boundaries within the word to distinguish *react* from *reach*, or *an axis* from *three taxis*, or to note that <e> does not represent /e/ in *bumblebee*, *thistledown*. Since stress is not independently marked by the orthography – cf. <invalid> as /'ɪnvəlɪd/ (n.), /ɪn'vælɪd/ (adj.) – we need to be aware of potential stress patterns for appropriate vowel reduction; this clearly requires lexical and grammatical information. The view we are taking is that the identification of a word in reading is an informed guess and that several channels more-or-less simultaneously bring relevant information to bear, one of which channels may be spelling-to-sound correspondences. A detailed review of these correspondences is given in §4. A similar review of sound-to-spelling correspondences which might have relevance for the writer is given in §3.

2.6 FINDING CORRESPONDENCES

Splitting the string of letters into units to match up with phonemes

(Note: the criteria used, consciously or not, to segment the string of letters into units of correspondence, are numbered #S1 to #S7 for reference purposes. They represent well-motivated practice. The '#S" stands for 'segmentation guideline'.)

2.6.1 Segmentation

Where to chop. The size of units

In a great many English spellings one phoneme maps on to one letter: *cat* is <c>≡/k/,<a>≡/æ/,<t>≡/t/. The extent of this simple mapping is often overlooked, since discussion is usually centred on peculiar and more complex correspondences for purely argumentative reasons. When we do have to depart from the correspondence of single phonemes to single letters we may have an apparent choice of where to make the cut. Do we split up the word <sign> in the matching process as <s-i-gn> or <s-ig-n>, or as <s-i-g-n> with some kind of dummy <g>? What guidelines can be drawn up to ensure that in such cases we make the cuts consistently and sensibly using criteria similar to those used in linguistic analysis generally? This is not a question that writers on English spelling seem to ask themselves. One has only to glance through any half dozen manuals on English spelling to see that practice varies widely and that the variation is not explained. Few writers have bothered to make explicit their reasons for chopping up the string of letters into graphic units in their own particular way. It has always been a matter of personal choice. The usual ground rules of linguistic analysis: explicitness, consistency, exhaustiveness and simplicity, are not easy to apply in the study of the English writing system. Indeed, the wide range of varying practice among those who try to describe it is yet more fuel for those who deny that the English writing system has any worthwhile regularities. Where there does seem to be agreement on what the units of spelling are, it is not always easy to pin down the principle which underlies this agreement.

Why, for instance, does R.A. Hall (1961) give <e..e>≡/iː/ in *mete*, but <i>≡/iː/ (not <i..e>≡/iː/) in *machine*? He also has <gu>≡/g/ in *guard*, <cu>≡/k/ in *biscuit*, but not <bu>≡/b/ in *build*. He treats <gh> as 'silent letters' in *high*, but <w> is not 'silent' in *two* (<wo>≡/uː/). There may be good reasons for doing this, and many other people may well do exactly the same, but, as is usual, Hall gives no reasons. Yet if Hall, as a linguist, were to carry out some phonological or morphological analysis, he and his readers would expect the methodology to be fully explicit. The methods used in such an exercise might even overshadow the object of analysis in academic interest.

Wilfully juggling the units of correspondence provides the basis for yet another spurious argument for those with a vested interest in denying the validity of phonic methods in the teaching of reading. Consider yet another example of Smith's highly individual views:

> I think it would be difficult to exaggerate the complexity and unreliability of phonics. To take just one very simple example, how are the letters *ho* pronounced? Not in a trick situation, as in the middle of a word like *shop*, but when *ho* are the first two letters of a word? Here are eleven common words in each of which the initial *ho* has a different pronunciation – *hot*, *hope*, *hook*, *hoot*, *house*, *hoist*, *horse*, *horizon*, *honey*, *hour*, *honest.* Can anyone really believe that a child could learn to identify any of these words by sounding out the letters?
>
> (Smith 1978: 56)

Despite the disclaimer that there is no trickery in this argument – which should, of course, alert the reader – this is really quite spurious. There are one or two irregularities in the sample. But *hot*, *hope*, *hook*, *hoot*, *house*, *hoist* and *horse* are straightforward enough when taught by analogy. The point is that Smith's *ho* is not a unit by which one would teach the sound-spelling correspondences for reading purposes. The units <o..e>, <oo>, <ou>, <oi> and <or> are regular enough and so is <oo> before the following <k>. One cannot deny the complexity, but Smith greatly and deliberately exaggerates it. A further example of needlessly overstating irregularity may be found in the section on divergence §2.3, pp. 16–8.

One likely reason for the lack of interest in the methodology of writing systems is that the object of study is usually a set of contrived conventions gradually adopted over a long period of time. How we now write is the result of a long tradition of changing scribal practice stretching back in time and frequently borrowing from the traditions of other writing systems. It does not, however, follow that the result is a mere hotch-potch which does not merit consistent and explicit analysis. Certainly if we are attempting to present a detailed picture of the deployment of English spelling conventions in the lexicon, we should have some explicit and sensible guidelines on how to set up the units of spelling correspondence. But since there is undoubtedly some fuzziness, some anomaly in the writing system itself, we may not be able to demand more than a measure of general tidiness. The guidelines which follow do go some way to ensuring a consistent analysis and seem to codify common sense. Yet they cannot be entirely self-evident, since each has been ignored by some or other writer on English spelling.

There is one obvious basic assumption which underlies the whole business of relating phonemes to letters: simply that it can be done. We do not expect to find that words have to be treated as whole units of correspondence and cannot be broken down into smaller correspondences. Some archaic proper names come perilously close to this, however. *Featherstonehaugh* may be pronounced /'fænʃɔː/. All that one can pick out as correspondences here are perhaps the initial <f>≡/f/ and the final <augh>≡/ɔː/. What to do with the remainder is quite a problem. In ordinary words such extreme cases do not occur; intractable spellings are rare. The old spelling *gaol* is perhaps the extreme case. *OED* comments: ‘though both forms *gaol*, *jail* are still written, only the latter is spoken’ (*OED* under *jail*). The contrived spelling *choir*, which gradually replaced *quire*, is dealt with similarly: ‘the spoken word is still *quire*, though since the close of the seventeenth century this has been fictitiously spelt *choir*’ (*OED* under *choir*). As it stands, the statement: ‘the spoken word is still *quire*’, is nonsense. How can the phonetic form of a word be a string of letters? But what is meant is quite clear: the spelling <quire> is more appropriate than <choir> because it can be broken up into regular correspondences. Any attempt to break up <choir> or <gaol> would give some nonce correspondences. Though there are such nonce spellings in current use, we have to proceed on the assumption that analysis into recurrent phoneme-letter correspondences is normally possible: that the system is more or less alphabetic.

2.6.2 Simplicity

How many units of correspondence?

As in all linguistic analysis, we then need a ‘**simplicity**’ (or ‘**economy**’ or ‘**minimization**’) criterion. That is essential to the rigorous description of any system. One of several possible formulations is:

#S1 The number of different correspondences set up to describe the system should be as small as possible.

It then follows that we cannot base our correspondences on, say, syllables or parts of syllables (e.g. *sat* as /s/≡<s>, /æt/≡<at>), but must base them as far as possible on single phonemes, since these are the minimal contrasting units in the spoken medium. In effect, #S1 in this wording simply states the alphabetic principle; it implies that the English writing system is fundamentally an alphabetic system. It is, however, a system that has been modified in many ways. Complex graphic units have been introduced to eke out the Roman letters and plurality of correspondence has been encouraged, especially in the representation of vowels. But although we frequently have to deal with a string of several letters as a unit, or, more rarely, a string of more than one phoneme as a unit (e.g. /ks/≡<x> in *tax*), this does not mean that we are free to set up units of any length. Strings such as <eei>, <ayi>, <ewa>, which clearly span more than one unit (see pp. 7–8), are not viable. The simplicity criterion allows us to make such a distinction.

The simplicity criterion alone will often determine where to cut the graphic string into units. Some writers (e.g. Albrow 1972: 38) would set up <aig>≡/eɪ/, <eig>≡/eɪ/, <ag>≡/eɪ/ as vowel correspondences in *campaign*, *deign*, and *champagne*, but these correspondences would then be restricted to the context of a following /n/. It would clearly be uneconomic to make such an analysis if the correspondence <gn>≡/n/ and the correspondences <aɪ>≡/eɪ/, <ei>≡/eɪ/ and <a>≡/eɪ/ are elsewhere required and available. Looking at the system as a whole, however, it might in the end be most economical to set up the <g> as an empty letter: <g>≡∅ <n>≡/n/. Cummings (1988: 102, 247, 345) similarly has <i>≡/aɪ/ in both *nigh* and *night*, leaving as a remainder <gh>≡/∅/ and <ght>≡/t/. This not only violates the simplicity criterion (#S1) by not recognising <igh>≡/aɪ/, but also the phonetic transparency criterion (see #S4 p. 38) in setting up <ght>≡/t/. Even more troublesome is his <a>≡/ɔː/ before <lk>≡/k/ to account for *talk*, *walk*. Why not have a more generally useful <al>≡/ɔː/?

Complex phonemes

The simplicity criterion must make us look very hard at phonetically complex phonemes such as the affricate consonants /ʧ/ and /ʤ/ and the diphthongs, to see whether there would be any economy of description by chopping them up. As phonological units, the English diphthongs are often analysed as a simple vowel plus a glide, especially in the American linguistic tradition (Cruttenden 1994: 5.3.1). *Pie* is taken to be a sequence of three units, as is *yap*. Since diphthongs frequently correspond with more than one letter: /eɪ/≡<ay> in *day*, /aʊ/≡<ow> in *how*, /ɔɪ/≡<oi> in *boil*, there might well be some economy in treating a diphthong as two separate parts corresponding to different letters. On reflection though, this will not be found to be the case. There is certainly nothing to be gained by splitting the SBS diphthongs /eɪ/, /aɪ/, /əʊ/ and /aʊ/. To chop /eɪ/≡<ay> into /e/≡<a> and /ɪ/≡<y>, would give a marginal correspondence for /e/. We should presumably have to group the beginning of /aʊ/ in *how* with /æ/ in *hat* giving an equally peculiar correspondence in /æ/≡<o>. A further consideration is that /eɪ/, /aɪ/ and /əʊ/, as in *paper*, *trident*, *bonus*, often have single letter correspondences. These three and /aʊ/ also serve as single units alternating with short vowels in allomorphs: *state – static*, *bile – bilious*, *tone – tonic*, *profound – profundity*. A fifth 'closing' diphthong /ɔɪ/ , however, is different: it does not pair up with a short vowel alternant. Its correspondences, <oi> as in *boil* and <oy> as in *boy*, could easily be split, but for consistency it is treated as a unit like the others. The 'centring' diphthongs of SBS, /ɪə/, /ɛə/ and /ʊə/, largely owe their origin to loss of post-vocalic /r/ and the writing system reflects this original /r/. Higginbottom (1962: 101) points out that as a consequence there is no contrast between /iː/ – /ɪə/ and between /eɪ/ – /ɛə/ in final position in a word or morpheme. So, effectively, SBS may be considered to have <eer>≡/iːr/ *peer*, <air>≡/eɪr/ *pair*, <oar>≡/əʊr/ *roar* and <oor>≡/uːr/ *poor*, with phonetic realization rules to give [pɪə] before a consonant or boundary and [pɪəɹ] before a vowel.

2.6.3 Exhaustiveness and discreteness

Remainders, overlaps and morpheme boundaries

In addition to the simplicity criterion, we also need an '**exhaustiveness**' criterion and a '**discreteness**' criterion. We can group them together as:

#S2 On both the phonetic and graphic planes of correspondence, the strings of phonemes and letters should normally be analysed:

(a) without remainder
(b) without overlapping, and, as far as possible
(c) without crossing morpheme boundaries

Hence we cannot simply ignore awkward data such as the <b> in *debt*. The <b> has to appear somewhere in one of the correspondences; it cannot be an unaccounted-for remainder. But we may under certain circumstances wish to set up empty letters which have a zero phonetic correspondence (/∅/≡<b>). If our description is based on letter strings and their distribution, we ought not to winkle out some letters as special markers which are not really part of a string. Cummings (1988: 350) analyses *guest*, *guide*, *guy*, as having simple /g/≡<g> with an added 'diacritic' <u>. In *guard*, *guarantee*, however, he treats the <u> as part of a correspondence /g/≡<gu>. There is undoubtedly a difference, but it is best seen as a difference of context, not a difference of correspondence. If we find /g/≡<gu> in both, we can still say that the <u> has a marking function in *guest*, since *<gest> would be read as /ʤest/. The <u> in *guard* would have a redundant marking function, since *<gard> could only spell /gɑːd/.

The discreteness condition (#S2b) means that in cutting up the string of letters into units, we should as far as possible make clean cuts without overlapping. A particular letter would then belong to only one unit in the string of letters. The consequences of not doing this may be seen in Cordts (1965), where overlapping is, for reasons not explained, a deliberate and constant feature of the analysis. Thus the <e> of *cake* appears in two correspondences: /k/≡<ke> and also /eɪ/≡<a..e>; in *guess* we have both /g/≡<gu> and /e/≡<ue>; in *choir* we have both /kw/≡<cho> and /aɪ/≡<oi>. The overlapping even ignores morpheme boundaries: we have /uː/≡<oo> in *mood* and /uː/≡<ooe> in *mooed*. This clearly flouts the basic simplicity criterion by multiplying the number of units required. Moreover, it would be extremely difficult to justify as classroom practice in a phonic approach to reading. Occasionally we do come across cases where we might be tempted to relax the discreteness criterion as an analysis of last resort. Albrow (1972: 41) suggests that, in *picture*, the <u> belongs partly to the correspondence /ʧ/≡<tu> and partly to the following vowel correspondence. The problem is that if you allow overlapping in this instance, how do you disallow the widespread overlapping practised by Cordts?

To disallow, or at least discourage, overlapping does of course not mean that letter strings must always be continuous. It is perfectly in order to analyse the vowel correspondence in *take* as <a..e>≡/eɪ/, since the final <e> has everything to do with the vowel and in most cases nothing to do with the consonant after the vowel. But in *rage* the <e> is also serving another function: to mark the correspondence of <g> to /ʤ/ rather than to /g/. That the <e> serves two functions is clear if we compare the spelling of *rag*, where both the vowel and the final consonant differ from those of *rage*. Indeed, when the long vowel /eɪ/ is followed by /g/, as in *vague*, we have to bring in the <u> to mark the consonant.

Allowing morpheme boundaries to be a criterion in deciding graphic units helps to assure that morphemes keep a constant spelling. This applies particularly to affixes. In cutting <righteous> into units, the morpheme boundary criterion is one of the reasons for preferring /ʧ/≡<te> and /ə/≡<ou> to /ʧ/≡<t> and /ə/≡<eou>. The former helps to give the suffix a constant <ous> spelling.

In deciding what constitutes a minimal graphic unit and where the string of letters is to be cut, we are relying on our awareness of the possibilities of substitution in English spellings. A similar kind of awareness underlies a native speaker's passive knowledge of what the phonemes of his language are. If we have two phonemes in each of *see*, *saw*, *sigh*, and if /s/≡<s> is a default correspondence, then whatever remains will normally be the graphic unit corresponding to the vowel in each case. Hence, /iː/≡<ee>,

/ɔː/≡<aw>, /aɪ/≡<igh>. Consistency then encourages us to use these units elsewhere. It is not really necessary to state this as a separate principle since it so clearly follows from the simplicity criterion.

But what is to prevent us from setting up /e/≡<ue> in *guest* or /aɪ/≡<uy> in *buy*, since /g/≡<g> and /b/≡<b> are default correspondences? The simplicity criterion #S1 would clearly prevent this, since to set up /e/≡<ue>, /ɑː/≡<ua>, /ɪ/≡<ui> in *guest*, *guard*, *guinea* etc, would increase the overall number of correspondences more than if we set up /g/≡<gu>. This is reason enough. The same is true of *buy* and *buoy*. A further factor is that the two spellings <bu> and <gu> support each other by sharing a common orthographic device. It is common practice, for instance, in phonology to justify a particular analysis because it involves units or conventions already employed elsewhere, rather than make an analysis peculiar to that one case.

2.6.4 Distinctiveness and appropriateness

Take it to the left, or take it to the right?

There are however two other considerations which probably play a part in deciding to chop up *guest* as <gu/e/s/t> rather than <g/ue/s/t>. They are respectively a **distinctiveness** criterion and an **appropriateness** criterion (for want of better labels).

In *guest* the problem is what to do with the <u>. In effect we assign it to the graphic unit where it is really needed. Commonly before the vowel letters <i> and <e>, a <g> represents /ʤ/ and, as all spelling books point out, the <u> is used to mark the correspondence with /g/ instead. That is what makes the spelling distinctive. The <u> disambiguates the <g>. Hence a distinctiveness criterion:

#S3 Letters are allocated to adjacent strings for greater distinctiveness.

This distinctiveness criterion (#S3) merely takes into account the difference between graphic units, but we also need to take into account their phonetic transparency. The relative appropriateness of spelling units varies quite widely and cannot be considered a major criterion for deciding what constitutes a graphic unit. Moreover, the simplicity criterion (#S1) usually covers the same cases. But since appropriateness is so important as a factor in reading, it is worth noting separately:

#S4 Complex graphic units will normally have a degree of phonetic transparency, especially in their first element.

Letters used in complex graphic units are reasonably consistent in the phonetic values assigned to them. Take the obvious cases of English vowels as spelt by the Roman alphabet in the present writing system. There is considerable under-differentiation, since we only have five single vowel letters available (or six with <y>) to represent 20 vowel phonemes.

Consequently complex graphic units are needed to cope with the range of vowel contrasts. In addition there is frequent plurality of correspondence (*talk*, *taught*, *taut*, *tawny*, etc) – which may have value for the reader, if not for the writer. Even so, the various complex units used to cover the vowels usually maintain a modicum of phonetic transparency. The first letter of the unit usually has a phonetic association with an appropriate sub-range of the vowel system and the second letter often acts as a correcting or restricting influence. Thus the spellings cited above for /ɔː/ start with <a>, which indicates a low vowel, and the following <u> or <w> indicates lip-rounding; even the <l> of *talk* is not entirely inappropriate. An /l/ in this position, if there was one, would be the 'dark' variety with a secondary raising of the back of the tongue (velarization). We cannot make very positive claims for phonetic appropriateness as a guideline in finding the units of correspondence, but looking at things negatively, we can often **exclude** some ways of dividing the letter string simply because of the restrictions on our phonetic expectations. One reason why we cannot decide to have /g/≡<g>, /e/≡<ue> in *guest* is that it is difficult to associate <u . . .> with a mid front unrounded vowel such as /e/.

The phonetic transparency involved is not necessarily based on the conventions of the usual phonetic alphabets. Some of the conventions used are peculiar to the English writing system, but within that system they are used with consistency. Since the English phoneme /h/ has a highly restricted distribution, the letter <h> is available to make up extra consonant symbols (<ch>, <sh>, <th>) which would not evoke a phonetic interpretation as consonant clusters, though the reader needs to notice a morpheme boundary in *carthorse*, *mishap* etc. The <h> in <ch>, <sh> and <ph> is an appropriate marker of the voiceless and fricative features of /ʧ/, /ʃ/ and /f/. Less naturally, <gh> can occur as auxiliary letters in vowel spellings such as <igh>. The symbol <h> without the <g> is quite appropriate phonetically as a marker of vowel length, since /h/ shapes the vocal tract ready for a following vowel, with no inherent place of articulation above the glottis. It is quite often used to mark long vowels in other writing systems, as in German *Fahne*, *Ehre*, *ihr*, *Sohn*, *Kuh*. These considerations are not to be misinterpreted as a defence of /aɪ/≡<igh> as an efficient spelling. They are simply meant to show that, although it is not entirely unreasonable to set up <igh> as a single graphic unit, there is good reason not to set up <ue> (in *guest*) as a graphic unit.

Phonetic transparency is often a secondary consideration in the organization of writing systems: it is usually bypassed in the interests of preserving the constant shape of a morpheme. In German, for instance, the absence of contrast between /t/ and /d/ in final position is not evident from the spelling. The inflected forms /bʊntəs/≡<buntes> 'coloured' and /bʊndəs/≡<Bundes> 'union' have the contrast, but the base forms /bʊnt/≡<bunt> and /bʊnt/≡<Bund> do not. Keeping a constant morpheme spelling is probably an advantage for the native speaker and, in the long run, for the foreign learner. In the short term, however, such conventions may prompt inappropriate spelling pronunciations, as when English learners of German pronounce a word-final [d]. Similarly English learners of French may wrongly attempt a final consonant in words such as *loup*, *droit*, *frein*, where the consonant 'is silent'.

2.6.5 Auxiliary, inert and empty letters

All letters are 'silent', but some are more silent than others

Opinions are sharply divided on whether to allow the use of 'silent letters' in a description of English orthography so as to cater for spellings such as the <b> in *debt*, *doubt*. If we are to find our way in this controversy, we clearly need to clarify our terminology. The term 'silent letters' is an extension of a metaphor commonly used in the teaching of reading, where letters are often supposed to 'speak' to the reader. When a simple vowel letter, as the <a> in *latent* has its long value /eɪ/, 'the vowel says its name'. A commonly-used classroom rule for reading vowel digraphs, such as <oa>, <ea>, is: 'when two vowels go walking, it's the first that does the talking' – a comment on the greater phonetic transparency of the first element in a complex graphic unit. But, as Albrow (1972: 11) points out, all letters are silent: 'the sounds are not written and the symbols are not sounded; the two media are presented as parallel to each other'. He suggests the term 'dummy letters' for letters with no direct phonetic counterpart but, as far as possible, tries to do without them in his analysis.

Auxiliary letters: making do with the Roman alphabet

If we take a closer look at the problem, it appears that there are three distinct types of letters that we need to take note of, which I have called 'auxiliary', 'inert' and 'empty' letters.

Auxiliary letters, as we have seen in #S3, are extra letters which help to make up complex graphic units. Thus, the <h> in /θ/≡<th> and the <g> in /ŋ/≡<ng> are necessary to keep these graphic units distinct from others. Auxiliary letters are clearly needed to compensate for the underdifferentiation of the Roman alphabet in coping with English phonemes. Rather different are auxiliary letters added before or after a basic letter which is already in itself an adequate spelling (cf. the <ea> in *bread*, *leather* with the <e> of *bred*, *tether*, or the <wr> and <r> of *wrest*, *rest*, or the <wh> and <w> of *whine* (SBS), *wine*). Katharine Perera (personal communication) has suggested that complex spellings of the type <th>≡/θ/ and <sh>≡/ʃ/ are conveniently classified as '**exocentric**' since they are not used to represent the same phoneme as either letter would on its own. Other complex spellings are '**endocentric**', since a unit such as <ea> represents the same phoneme (in *bread*, *leather*) as one of the letters, <e>, can do on its own. In *ghost* the <gh> is endocentric; in *tough* it is exocentric. The two terms are not always easy to apply: whether a spelling is endocentric or exocentric may depend on the context: <ch>≡/k/ is endocentric in *choral*, but exocentric in *chemist*, since <c>≡/k/ can occur before <o> but not before <e>. Those phonemes which do not have a 'normal' single letter spelling provided by the Roman letter set, as for instance /θ/, /ð/, /ʃ/, /ʒ/, /ŋ/, and many of the vowels, will inevitably have only exocentric spelling. With endocentric spellings, such as the <kn> of *knob* or the <mb> of *lamb*, we seem to have the choice of regarding the whole string as a unit or treating the <k> of *knock*, or the <b> of *lamb*, as some kind of 'dummy' letter. This term 'dummy' letter, if we are to use it at all, will require some delimitation. While auxiliary letters usually have some distinctive function, there are letters which clearly do not. It is these that are often referred to as 'dummy' letters, but there are in fact two distinct kinds.

Inert letters: now you hear them, now you don't

Inert letters are letters which occur in all the spellings of a morpheme (thus helping to give it a constant shape), but in some forms of the morpheme they do not have a phonetic counterpart. In those allomorphs they are 'inert'. Thus the <g> is constant in all spellings of {sign} and forms the correspondence /g/≡<g> in *signature*, *signatory*, *signal*, but in *sign*, *signed, signer, signing*, there is no phonetic counterpart. Rather than put these inert letters with either of the adjacent correspondences, it would seem to make better sense to give them a zero phonetic counterpart: /∅/≡<g>. In this case the <g> can be said to be 'inert', meaning not active. For SBS and other accents of English where postvocalic /r/ has disappeared in pre-consonant and pre-pause position (as in *farm*, *spar*), the <r> which remains in the spelling is an inert letter (cf. *spa*, *spar*, *sparring*). But it is only by taking into account accents which have not lost this /r/ that we could really regard the pre-consonantal <r> of *farm* as inert. We have in fact opted out of the distinctiveness criterion to cater for this by using /ɑː/≡<ar> in *farm*, *far* and both /ɑː/≡<ar> and /r/≡<r> in *sparring*. The reason is that for most cases with /ɪə/ and /ʊə/ and for all cases with /ɛə/ the latent //r// is necessary to the occurrence of that phoneme.

<e> before /r/ becomes inert when /ə/ is lost by a common reduction process in allegro pronunciations of *dysentery*, *etcetera*, *interested*, *mackerel*, *temperature* and perhaps even in *conqueror*. The <a> may similarly be inert in allegro forms of *dictionary*, *ordinary*, *secretary* (in SBS but not in AmE) and in the suffix <-ally>, where **economicly* and *economically* are identical. Presumably the /CC/ cluster is less effortful than having to make the

unstressed syllabic. The <e>-marking in *vineyard* is superfluous due to the shortening of the original long vowel of *vine*, but the lexical spelling is kept. The <d> is inert due to cluster simplification in *grandma*, *handsome*, *handkerchief*, *sandwich*, *landscape*, etc.

Empty letters and special markers

Empty letters are a second kind of dummy letter. They have no real distinctive function (as do auxiliary letters) and not even a latent distinctive function (as do inert letters). The classic example of an empty letter is the <b> in *debt*, *doubt*. The <b> recurs in *debit, dubious*, *dubiety* as <b>≡/b/, however, so if we make that connection, then the <b> in *doubt* is inert. But once we look beyond a handful of similar cases, the notion of 'empty' letter becomes very difficult to handle. Yet, statistically, the simplicity criterion (#S1) is an obligation to find as many empty letters as possible, in order to cut down the number of correspondences used in the description. It is surely simpler to use the notion of empty letter in cases where there has been historical elision, rather than proliferate correspondences – as in Cummings (1988: 352), where we find /g/≡<ckgu> in *blackguard* and /g/≡<tg> in *mortgage*. Not only are these nonce correspondences, but they violate the requirement for phonetic transparency of the initial letter(s) of the string. On the other hand, the exhaustiveness criterion #S2 requires that, on both the phonetic and graphic planes of correspondence, the strings of phonemes and letters should normally be analysed without remainder. Clearly there are empty letters in the present orthography. Some of these are simply redundant, but others can be seen as having some kind of function outside the range of correspondences.

Empty letters are naturally a target for the spelling reformers, but one should not rush in with the scissors too hastily. A favourite target is final <-e>. The instances of <-e> at the end of *copse, bottle, file, giraffe,* are often referred to as 'silent' letters, but they are very different. The <-e> of *copse* marks the word as different from the plural *cops*. The word *bottle* cannot sensibly be spelt as *<bottl>, since syllabic consonants are always spelt with a vowel letter and a consonant letter, except for <sm> in *sarcasm, prism*. Similarly it might be thought that *file* could be spelt *<fil>. It would still be different from *fill*, as it is in *filing, filling*. However, some degree of redundancy is essential to human language and that justifies taking the unit of correspondence to be <i..e>≡/aɪ/. Even the <-e> at the end of *giraffe* has something to be said in its favour. It can be said to mark the unusual final stress of the noun as in the <-CCe> of *brunette, cassette, corvette, largesse, bagatelle, gazelle*.

For empty letters which can be considered to have a marking function of some kind, Venezky sets up a special category of 'markers'. He caters for marking functions by using two different types of unit. Where we have been dealing solely with correspondences he employs *relational units* and *markers*:

> A *relational unit* is a string of one or more graphemes which has a morphophonemic correspondent which cannot be predicted from the behaviour of the unit's smaller graphemic components.
>
> A *marker* is a string of one or more graphemes whose primary function is to indicate the correspondences of relational units or to preserve a graphotactical or morphological pattern. It has no sound correspondence.
>
> (Venezky 1967: 85ff)

This means that some letters are regarded as outside the stripped-down phoneme–grapheme correspondences. Instead they are responsible for resolving ambiguities between, for instance, the divergent pronunciations of <g> and <c>. Their function is 'to indicate the pronunciation of a preceding grapheme' (1970b: 50). So the <u> in *guest* is not part of a correspondence /g/≡<gu> but a separate entity /Ø/≡<u> which serves to distinguish /g/≡<g> from /ʤ/≡<g>. At first sight this seems very neat. The most persuasive example is that of <e>-marking of a preceding <c> or <g> in *notice* or *manage* as representing /s/ and /ʤ/ rather than /k/ and /g/. The <e> marker is dropped from the spelling in *noticing* and *managing* because the following <i> takes over the marking function and does away with the need for a separate marker segment. The marker is not dropped in *noticeable* and *manageable* because a following <a> would indicate a previous <c>≡/k/ and <g>≡/ʤ/. In addition to its normal distinctive function any correspondence such as the /ɪ/≡<i> in *noticing*, *city*, *electricity* can have a marking function. These marking functions are referred to as 'influences' in Venezky (1970b: 113), though the term is not discussed in detail. Before <ld>, the letter <o> can only refer to a long vowel /əʊ/ because the sequence */ɒld/ is not found. This is a marking function.

The simplicity criterion #S1 would seem to favour setting up separate markers where possible because the overall number of units deployed in the description would thereby be reduced. However, if we try to do this consistently, we end up with an analysis very different from Venezky's or any other.

The words *cote*, *coat* and *cot* would all have correspondences with the 'primary' unit <o>, but *cote* and *coat* would have the vowel marked as long by the markers /Ø/≡<e> (after the consonant) and /Ø/≡<a> (before the consonant). A similar analysis could be made for *bait*, *bate* and *bat* and, with some ingenuity, most of the other vowel digraphs. Similarly we could do away with the need for consonant digraphs such as <gh> and <sh> on the lines of Venezky's analysis of /g/≡<gu>. We would have /Ø/≡<h>

serving as a marker to distinguish the phonetic value of <s> in *seen* and *sheen*.

It would seem, then, that the idea of separate marker units with a zero phonetic counterpart, if applied consistently, would produce an oddly fragmented analysis. Venezky himself only seems to have used these 'markers' in occasional instances and it is difficult to see what economy has been achieved. If the beginning of *guest* is differentiated from the beginning of *gesture* by the <u> marker following the <g>, this appears to offer no economy over a simple analysis into /g/≡<gu> and /ʤ/≡<g>, given the context of a following /e/≡<e>. Moreover, in Venezky's scheme, these special markers do not account for all marking. Any correspondence, such as the /e/≡<e> of *gesture* can have a marking function.

There are, of course, problems in using empty letters without restraint. How are we to decide between an auxiliary letter in an endocentric setting and an empty letter? No-one wants to set up /aɪ/≡<ig> in *tight*, *fright* and treat the <h> as an empty letter (as it is in *hour*, *honest* – a very different context). We must bear this in mind in defining an **empty** letter:

#S5 Empty letters have no distinctive function. They may not follow auxiliary letters in endocentric strings.

This simply says that if we are adding trailing letters to make up an endocentric graphic unit, a string such as <igh> must be regarded as a single unit. This would not prevent the <b> of *doubt* from being an empty letter since the <ou> string which it follows is not endocentric. A further condition is necessary to distinguish the **inert** letters:

#S6 Inert letters have a latent distinctive function. They have a zero phonetic counterpart in some allomorphs of a morpheme and a full phonetic counterpart in other allomorphs.

At first sight it would seem that the use of empty letters is adequately regulated by a simple redundancy criterion. We could argue that the <b> in *debt*, *doubt* is redundant because we should still have perfectly adequate spellings if we simply omitted it. Compare *let*, *lout; bet*, *bout; get*, *gout.* But could we omit the <l> of *salmon* as redundant? Is *<samon> an acceptable spelling? This is difficult to judge: it has no <C>-doubling (as in *gammon*) and might otherwise well contain /eɪ/≡<a> (as in the name *Damon*). On the other hand, such a redundancy criterion would suggest, against our better judgment, that the <a> in *bread*, *leather* is an empty letter, since we also have *bred*, *tether*. Certainly most spelling reformers would simply drop it. Similarly, we could treat the <u> of *gauge* as empty, since we also have *gage*. Amongst consonants, we should also find the <h> of *whine* (in SBS and many other accents) to be an empty letter and the <w> of *wring* and *sword*, disallowing <wh>, <wr> and, in this case, <sw> as graphic units. But to treat all endocentric strings in this way would only seem to complicate the business of description.

Phonetic transparency and functional load

We clearly need other criteria to support the basic notion of redundancy. Two supportive criteria are **phonetic transparency** and **functional load**. Both are, of course, relative notions, so we must hope that there will be a fairly clear split between the more frequent and less frequent and between the more transparent and the less transparent. We can lump these three criteria into a single rough-and-ready guideline:

#S7 Empty letters, with a zero phonetic counterpart, may be used when they are best excluded from the previous or following correspondence for any of the following reasons:

(a) lack of phonetic transparency,
(b) low functional load,
(c) qualitative redundancy,
(d) transferability.

Let us try this out on the <l> in *salmon*. As for #S7(a) neither /æ/≡<al> nor /m/≡<lm> can be considered phonetically transparent. In assessing phonetic transparency the first letter of the string is of principal importance: <lm> is worse as a potential counterpart of /m/ than <al> as a counterpart of /æ/. As for #S7(b) there are no other instances of either /æ/≡<al> or /m/≡<lm>. As for #S7(c) the <l> may be considered redundant (i.e. an empty letter) in that the phoneme string is competently spelt by normal correspondences without involving any '<l>-ness'. That is why the term 'qualitative redundancy', rather than sheer redundancy is used. We are not trying to judge whether *<samon> is an inadequate spelling. The <l> may be an empty letter, but it still counts as a consonant letter. Consequently we should be wrong to compare *<samon> with <gammon>, since <C>-doubling as a marker of a short vowel only occurs if there is no intervening consonant letter. 'Empty' does not always mean ignorable. The rules which involve *numbers* of consonant letters will still count empty letters.

A rather different type of problem is whether to take the <a> in *head* or the <w> in *wrung* to be an empty letter and to treat other endocentric strings similarly. Phonetic transparency is difficult to interpret. The criterion is partly satisfied if the auxiliary letter is not phonetically misleading. In the case of <wr> in *wrung* we can point to the lip-protrusion associated with both /r/ and /w/; /w/ is a frequent substitute for /r/ in child speech. Acoustically /w/ and /r/ are very similar. The <h> of <wh> is justified as a marker of the voicelessness found in those accents of English where /hw/ and /w/ contrast. In all three cases there is nothing positively misleading about the auxiliary letters used, given the choice available. We can also find further support for not analysing them as empty letters in these cases from the functional load criterion. This does not necessarily require a high frequency of use, but it does require the complex spelling to be used contrastively with the basic spelling. We require <ea>-<e>, <wr>-<r> and <wh>-<w> contrasts, minimal if possible. Such contrasts need to be and are found in more than one isolated example:

lead–led; bread–bred; leaven–seven; etc.,
wring–ring; wrest–rest; write–rite; etc.,
whine–wine; which–witch; where–wear; etc.

These contrasts override the redundancy criterion, which is satisfied by default in all endocentric units. By virtue of their being in endocentric units we could treat all those auxiliary letters as empty letters were it not for the argument from functional load. A factor which strengthens the functional load argument is a restricted or concentrated distribution. The spelling <ea> is particularly frequent before voiced apical (coronal) consonants, such as /d ð ʒ/ (*head*, *leather*, *treasure*). The spelling <wh> is typical of interrogative and relative function words (*what*, *which*, etc).

Phonetic transparency and functional load are considerations which apply to reading rather than writing. If the phonetic associations do not mislead the reader and if the spelling has some currency, it is obviously desirable to distinguish the graphic shapes of different morphemes and words. In that sense there is a distinctive function. But, however transparent to the reader a pair of spellings such as <r-> and <wr-> may be, such overdifferentation is still a problem for the writer.

Transferability: using what you've got

There is one further guideline (#S7d) which we tend to use in splitting strings. One might call it '**transferability**'. If a graphic string is used and acceptable in correspondences with other phonemes, it is likely to find acceptance even in a correspondence where it is clearly anomalous. If the <l> in the string <al> is taken to be an auxiliary letter in *talk* (/ɔː/≡<al>) or *palm* (/ɑː/≡<al>), then it is more likely to be accepted as one in *salmon*, even though /æ/≡<al> is a nonce form. Similarly, if <gu>≡/g/ fulfils a need to distinguish /g/ and /ʤ/ before /e/ (*guest – gesture*), then the phonetically improbable spelling <bu>≡/b/ in *buy*, *buoy* stands a better chance of acceptance.

Using the category of empty letters in the description of correspondences seems natural enough if one considers extreme cases such as *debt*, *doubt*, where there is absolute redundancy, but it is very difficult to constrain their use by predefined guidelines in less clear cases. Empty letters are by definition only found in anomalous spellings and, even in English spelling, anomalies are by definition infrequent.

On the phonetic side of correspondences, there is clearly no such thing as a zero unit. Since alphabetic writing is intended to encode speech, an alphabetic system requires every phoneme in the string to have some graphic expression. There can be no empty phonemes.

Some hard cases

The criteria #S1 to #S7 given above seem well founded but need testing against a range of suitably troublesome examples. We can begin with some problem spellings cited by Albrow (1972:50) . He is reluctant to allow the use of dummy letters except in cases such as the <b> in *debt*, *doubt* and the <t> in *castle*, *fasten*, where the dummy letters could be seen as 'merely characterizing the usual shape of the words in which they occur and playing no part in symbolization'. This seems to be an argument based on phonetic transparency. However, the <b> of *debt* fits our #S7c as an empty letter, since the spellings *<det>, *<dout> would be quite normal (cf. *pet*, *pout; get*, *gout; let*, *lout* etc.). The <t> of *castle*, *fasten* can be treated as an inert letter under #S6, since we have other allomorphs (*castellar*, *fast*) in which the <t> does have a phonetic counterpart: /t/≡<t>. This interpretation is supported by instances of /Ø/≡<t> as a result of regular cluster simplification in *Christmas*, *postman*, etc. Albrow is reluctant to use dummy letters in other cases. He suggests that <ig> in *sign*, <ic> in *indict*, <is> in *isle*, <ais> in *aisle*, <ug> in *impugn*, <os> in *Grosvenor* and similar strings can be treated as units.

Our criteria would not agree in all of these other cases. The <g> of *sign* is, in our terms, an inert letter. Since <ile> is a perfectly valid spelling for *isle*, the <s> must be regarded as an empty letter (#S7). There are problems with *aisle*, however. The correspondence /aɪ/≡<ai> only occurs otherwise in *naiad* and *shanghai*; <ai> normally corresponds to /eɪ/. Whatever we do in analysing the spelling of *aisle* is bound to be exceptional. This may be thought an argument for treating the <ais> as a single unit.

Whether we have /əʊ/≡<os> in *Grosvenor* or treat the <s> as an empty letter depends partly on whether we regard *<Grovenor> as a realistic spelling. Presumably it is, since in three-syllable words we often find no indication of the distinction between long and short vowels. Compare long: *copious*, *topiary*; short: *popular*, *ominous*. Indeed, *<Grovenor> may be better than the actual spelling <Grosvenor>, since /əʊ/≡<o> is much less common before consonant clusters than /ɒ/≡<o>. The <c> and <g> of *indict* and *impugn* are empty letters by #S7. In judging them to be redundant we are not claiming *<indit> and *<impun> to be adequate spellings. The strings of two consonant letters <-ct> and <-gn> obviate <e>- marking of the vowel. So in classifying the <c> and <g> as empty, we are comparing the spellings with *indite*, the normal spelling before 1600, and **impune*. These words are analogous to *salmon*, discussed above.

It might seem that such a close consideration of the less common spellings in the system is purely academic and uneconomic and that they should simply be labelled irregular and left to the scalpel of the spelling reformers. It is, however, quite important to be aware of the criteria which we may be using, wittingly or unwittingly, to establish spelling correspondences.

2.6.6 The punctuation of words

Spaces and hyphens

'Spelling' may involve more than stringing letters together into word-shapes. There is an overlap with punctuation. The space at the beginning and end of the word defines what is a 'word' for the writing system. We are so accustomed to this use of spaces that it is difficult to imagine that spacing and other punctuation devices were a late improvement to alphabetic writing systems. We can soon see how important spacing is by trying to read a passage without spaces, or capitals, or word-internal hyphens and without the convention of beginning a new line of text with a new word (or ending the previous line with a hyphen). Try reading:

themainproblemwithasimpleswitchisthatitisanallornoneoronoroffdevice

The first couple of words can be read off easily enough, but as we proceed, alternative places for possible word boundaries start to compete. The written shape of a word may also contain marks which are not letters. The most important of these marks are the apostrophe and hyphen. The special letter shapes called 'capitals' may be also be used to mark different kinds of words.

Written words are delimited by spaces. A hyphen brings together two or more units into a single space-delimited 'word' and records the novelty of their union. The suffix <-like> is found in frequently-used terms without a hyphen: *businesslike, godlike, ladylike, suchlike*. If I were to make up a new collocation 'a pagoda-like building', the use of the hyphen makes it easier for the reader to see the structure. It might be confusing to come across <pagodalike> written without the hyphen. The reader might have to flick through possible units such as *<pagodal>, *<god>,*<alike>, before seeing the structure.

Prefixes ending in a vowel often have a hyphen when attached to a free form with an initial vowel, as in *re-enact*, *co-exist*, *de-escalate*. Unhyphenated examples are more common: as in *react*, *reinstate*, *coaxial*. Unusual uses of a suffix can also be hyphenated: <a Shaw-ism>.

The main use of hyphens is to help to distinguish **compounds** from **phrases**. This can be done without a hyphen, using simple spaces. The phrases *green house* and *black board* are distinguished by spacing from the compounds *greenhouse* and *blackboard*. Compounds have a specialized meaning, often described as 'close connection' between the elements. Phrases are open to expansion by inserting other words: *a green and yellow house*, *a green private house*, *a very green house*. Since spacing can evidently cope with this kind of distinction, the hyphen is very much an optional extra tool for drawing attention to internal boundaries. Its use is very variable, especially in noun+noun collocations. Common collocations are usually written as one word, as in: *lamplight, lamplighter, lamppost, lampshade*, or with a hyphen as in *lamp-light, lamp-lighter, lamp-post, lamp-shade*. Less common collocations would be more likely to have a hyphen, as *lamp-base, lamp-fitting, lamp-standard*. The use of a hyphen is to some extent influenced by the stress pattern. Though compounds tend to have stress on the first element, there are many similarly specialized collocations which do not. Those which, like phrases, have stress on the second element may be written as two words or hyphenated: *head master, kitchen sink, town centre, district nurse*, etc. This can point up differences such as *sleeping partner* ('inactive business associate') and *sleeping-partner* ('that you sleep with'), *hard core* ('nucleus') and *hardcore* or *hard-core* ('aggregate'). American writing conventions make much less use of hyphenation than British.

A hyphen has to be used in compounds such as *fighter-bomber, fridge-freezer, hunter-gatherer, washer-drier*. In these examples the two elements cannot be written separately and cannot be fused into a single orthographic word. They resemble noun+noun collocations where the referent is both a {noun1} and a {noun2} such as *baby boy, city state, clock radio, prince regent, queen mother*. The difference seems to be that in the *hunter-gatherer* group the relationship is 'either. . . or' rather than 'both . . . and'. This use of the hyphen is like the use of the oblique stroke '/' to mean 'or' in <and/or>

The hyphen comes into its own as a second layer of boundary marking in various kinds of complex adjective or adverb, as in: *a blue-grey tinge, forty-five degrees, large-scale efforts, parish-pump politics, I'll talk to him man-to-man*. Part of the complex word may be missed out in repetition: '*such type-setting or -casting machines*', '*the fox- and deer-hunting fraternity*'. In the same way, a hyphen is used to represent the absent stem when citing bound morphemes: '*the comparative ending* -er *and superlative ending* -est'. When a suffix is added to a two-element name the two elements are not hyphenated: 'Elvis Presley-like', 'Welcome to Gracelands, Elvis Presley-dom'. A hyphenated personal name is usually a surname showing two branches of a family. Compare 'the Elvis Presley home', 'the Cabot-Lodge home'.

The use of a hyphen to split words up at the end of a line of text is discussed in §2.8.3.

The flight from the apostrophe

A common mistake in spelling is to write <it's>, as in (*on *it's own*), for the possessive pronoun <its>. Writing <its> as the truncated form of <it is> is less likely. This wrong use of <it's> is a very natural mistake to make, since here the two main uses of the apostrophe are in conflict with each other. The most common use of the apostrophe is to show that the possessive (*Mark's*) is different from the noun plural (*marks*). A reply /ðə ˈbɜːdz ˈtwɪtə/ to the question *What wakes you up so early?* can have three different structures, since *twitter* can be either a verb or a noun. The different structures are: 'the birds are in the habit of twittering' or 'the twitter of a bird' or 'the twitter of several birds'. The three are distinguished in writing as <birds>, <bird's> and <birds'>. There is a complication, though. Pronouns differ from nouns in having possessive forms without the apostrophe: his *her* and *hers, our* and *ours, their* and *theirs, your* and *yours*. This is one of several differences between the spelling of grammatical words and lexical words. So, as a possessive pronoun, the spelling <its> is regular. But the misuse of *<it's> is much more extensive than misspellings such as *<their's>, *<your's>. That is because of confusion with the other main use of the apostrophe.

The apostrophe also serves to indicate a pronunciation in which sounds (and letters) are missing. So <it's> represents *it is* in <it's going> or *it has* in <it's gone>. This use of the apostrophe is particularly common with *not* and auxiliary verbs, such as *can't, don't, shouldn't, I'll, we'll, they've, you've, I'd, she'd*. Since these reduced forms represent colloquial speech, they are rather frowned upon in formal prose. But even in academic writing they can show the voice of the author coming through in asides and comments outside the flow of the argument. More colloquial forms, however, can only reflect a spoken register: <the Cap'n>, <'Fraid so>, <'E's gone>, <'cos I like it> (*because*). This is obviously so in the spelling of vocal gestures such as <H'm>.

Such an apostrophe is dropped when the shortened noun form overtakes the full form in common use. So *bus, cello, flu* and *phone*, which are shortenings of *omnibus, violoncello, influenza,* and *telephone* do not now have an apostrophe as <'phone>, etc. 'Common use' comes gradually. Fowler (1926: 62) writes: '*bus* is sufficiently established to require no apostrophe', but he is slightly more diffident about *cello* as <'cello>. 'Being now much commoner than *violoncello*, it might well do without its apostrophe' (ibid.: 72). The case of *flu* is rather special because something is missed from the beginning and from the end, so the spelling should have been marked as <'flu'>, not <'flu>. This double apostrophe was clearly doomed from the outset, since it looked like single quotation marks.

A further use of the apostrophe is to make plurals for numbers and letter symbols, as in <three 7's in a row>, <mind your P's and Q's>,

<the regiment has three V.C.'s>. The plural of common acronyms is often printed without an apostrophe as in <M.P.s>, rather than <M.P.'s> and increasingly without full stops as in <MPs>. Year numbers can be truncated with an initial apostrophe if the century is obvious: *the '14 – '18 war*.

The complex of information coded by the apostrophe: whether a letter is missing, or whether a noun is possessive or just plural, or whether it is both possessive and plural, has made spellers feel insecure about its use. The apostrophe always required a certain amount of formal teaching and that is less available in schools nowadays. This has encouraged some welcome simplifications in apostrophe use. In collocations such as *the students union*, current practice manages without an apostrophe. Paraphrase with *of* is possible and it is clear that you cannot have a union of only one student. Yet it would seem pedantic to write <students' union>. Doing without an apostrophe in premodifiers can spread to irregular plurals, where there is no doubt about where an apostrophe would go, as in <the mens room>. Names are allowed a great deal of freedom in spelling, so it is not surprising to find the flight from the apostrophe here too: *Butchers Lane, Earls Court, Gerrards Cross*. There is no need to think of these <-s> names as possessives.

Apostrophes are so revered as a token of educational prowess that they have become a favourite device in creative spelling: 'Leave your *trolley's here'; '*Property's in your area' (discussed further on p. 80).

In print the apostrophe keeps the shape of the letter '9' even when it comes at the beginning of a word. In this respect it differs from single quotation marks, which are paired as '6'-shaped initially and '9'-shaped finally in most fonts of type.

Capital letters

A capital (upper-case) letter differs in size and usually in shape from a small (lower-case) letter. As a punctuation device, it is used to mark the beginning of a sentence. Initial capitals also redundantly mark the beginning of a line in regular verse forms, even those beginning with a function word:

> Among thy mountains did I feel
>   The joy of my desire;
> And she I cherished turned her wheel
>   Beside an English fire.
>
> (W. Wordsworth 1807 poems)

Capitals also have several uses, which we need not consider in detail, in marking word-types. The main use is to mark the names of places, institutions and persons, or words which have a specific reference or a technical meaning:

> . . . on the terms of the letter to Shareholders and the Memorandum and Articles of Association of the Company and subject to the proposed dividend being declared by the Directors and approved by the Shareholders and the admission of the New Shares to the Official List by the London Stock Exchange. We are not electing on behalf of any person who is a North American Person (as defined in Appendix II to this letter).

Similarly, as a formal literary device capitals were used when ordinary nouns were personified or became the focus of attention:

> A Rock there is whose homely front
>   The passing traveller slights
> And one coy Primrose to that Rock
>   The vernal breeze invites.
>
> (W. Wordsworth *The Primrose of the Rock* in 1835 poems)

This highlighting may seem odd to the modern reader, but it was a reflection of Wordsworth's belief in the active forces of nature.

The use of a capital 'I' in English for the first person pronoun is highly unusual. It seems to have developed as a printing device because of the lack of bulk in a single small 'i'. On the other hand in many languages the second person pronouns are given a capital letter as a polite mark of deference to the other person(s). This is so in Swedish: <jag> ('I') does not have a capital but both forms of 'you' in formal writing (<Du>, <Ni>) do have a capital. Inevitably, the contrariwise English use of pronoun capitals is taken to be clear evidence of the self-centredness of native English speakers. English speakers themselves are wary of this to some extent. In learning to write letters as school, pupils may be advised not to use 'I' too frequently because it sticks out so much on the written page. In contrast to this self-effacement, a capital letter is a natural device for referring to God with the pronoun set 'Thou', 'Thee', 'Thine', 'Thy'.

Capitals are also used extensively in trade-names (see §6.2).

2.7 ACCENT AND DIALECT: LITERACY IS HARDER FOR SOME

2.7.1 Differences between accents

Four types of difference between accents (Wells 1982)

The English writing system is better suited for some speakers of English than for others, depending upon the type of English they speak, their particular accent. If we assume that a child's accent does affect its approach to literacy, a working-class child in East Lancashire should find it easier to acquire literacy than a London child of whatever class, simply because the writing-system is a better fit for the Northern child's accent. 'It is probably the Southerner and the person with an RP accent for whom the writing system is most obscure. Other speakers seem in many cases to have the 'foresight' to keep their pronunciation more overtly in step with the way they are expected to write' (Albrow 1972: 4). The poet laureate Robert Bridges expressed horror at an early version of Daniel Jones's EPD: 'it represents a pronunciation so bad that its slovenliness is likely to be thought overdone' (Bridges 1919: 31), but he grudgingly admitted that it did represent what educated Southerners actually said. In effect he was bewailing the difficulty of relating these spoken forms to the spelling.

Foreigners learning English in Britain and through British institutions are usually taught a Southern accent (SBS). No doubt for social reasons this is the right choice. Yet it would be far easier for the foreign learner to acquire literacy in English by learning a 'rhotic' accent, such as East Lancashire or Devonshire English, which has kept /r/ intact in all positions and still distinguishes *paw–pour–poor*, *caught–court*. The spelling would then be a more reliable guide to the pronunciation. The fact that SBS is a standard accent for 'establishment' purposes does not mean that it is the easiest accent for acquiring literacy.

To assess how a phonetic difference between speakers will affect the relationship of speech to writing, we need to distinguish several types of difference. Wells (1982: §1.3) discusses the phonetic and phonological differences between any two speakers of English under four major categories:

1 differences of phonetic realization,
2 differences of phonotactic distribution,
3 differences of phonological system,
4 differences of lexical distribution.

These categories are sometimes difficult to apply to particular data and they often interact, but they do bring some order to the description of accent differences. We can borrow them to explore the range of problems which differences of accent and dialect present in acquiring literacy. These are, however, only potential problems. It does not follow that speakers of a dialect for which the writing system is a poor fit will turn out to be worse spellers than their luckier counterparts. Their awareness of the difference may stimulate them to take greater care with spelling. Recent research projects in Denmark and West Germany found that speakers of a dialect for which the standard orthography was a less good fit did not necessarily make more spelling errors (reported in Cheshire *et al.* (1989)), though dialect-based spelling errors will inevitably surface in the writing of the less literate or the less well taught.

Differences of phonetic realization

Differences of phonetic realization, the first of Wells's four categories, is perhaps the least important for spelling. The phonetic differences involved are minor in that they are non-distinctive: they are not able to distinguish different word-forms. A Yorkshire speaker with a relatively unaspirated [p$^{=}$] [t$^{=}$] [k$^{=}$], a Merseyside speaker with a relatively affricated [pɸ] [ts] [kx] and an SBS speaker with an aspirated [p^{h}] [t^{h}] [k^{h}] have different realizations of their /p/, /t/ and /k/ phonemes in *pan*, *tan*, and *can*. There should be no spelling problem arising from these phonetic differences. The only consequence of any importance for such differences of realization is the relative phonetic appropriateness of the spelling. For an AmE speaker with an unrounded vowel in words like *bomb*, instead of a rounded /ɒ/, the correspondence is less close to general orthographic conventions for the use of vowel letters. This in itself is hardly a problem for individual spellers, who take the conventional spellings and map them on to their own phonemes. There will be a problem for people who do not contrast the vowels in *bother* and *rather*, but have the same unrounded [ɑː] in both. That, however, is the very different problem of distribution.

Writers who want to represent traditional dialect in phonetic detail do try to account for differences of realization by manipulating the spelling with varying consistency and varying success. In representations of Lancashire dialect the spelling <eaw> is used in **teawn*, **seawnd*, **eawr*, **meawth*, etc. for *town*, *sound*, *our*, *mouth* (see Pomfret (1969), from whose anthology of dialect verse further Lancashire examples will be taken). This leading <e> is evidently meant to indicate a fronted starting point for a glide [æʊ] rather than a more open and back SBS [ɑʊ]. Similarly an offglide to [ə] can be indicated by a following <o> or <a> in **leeod* or **leod*, **meeon*, **clooas* for (*to*) *lead*, *mean*, *clothes*.

This ambition to record phonetic detail by varying the conventional spelling even leads to changes in spelling where the dialect pronunciation is not markedly different from that of most English speakers. This kind of re-spelling tends to regularize the more irregular spellings or give a different spelling of unstressed syllables: **sed*, **woz*, **Omerika*, **tooathry* or **toothrie*, **ov*, **surelee* ([-iː]), **agen*, **sur*, for *said*, *was*, *America*, *two or three*, *of*, *surely*, *again*, *sir*. These examples are picked at random from Pomfret. Even George Bernard Shaw, who, more than any other dramatist, specifies the accents of his characters in detail as part of their personae uses the same graphic trick: **sallery* (*salary*), **nacher* (*nature*), or *sure me* **fut* **slipt* (*my foot slipped*), for the Irish English in *John Bull's Other Island*. This kind of re-spelling is simply a cosmetic means of persuading the readers that they are reading dialectal speech. A rather snide consequence of this is to convey the impression that the speaker in the text is illiterate, simply because the speech is not spelt properly. (See the journalistic example on p. 80). It is a favourite device of Dickens and other nineteenth-century novelists for representing low-life characters. In the text of stage plays it counts for nothing in actual performance.

The possibilities of varying the spelling to show differences of phonetic realization are fairly limited and rather crude. In many parts of Lancashire the definite article is represented by a glottal stop, so [tə tæʊn] and [təʔ tæʊn] represent *to town* and *to the town* respectively. Texts usually represent the latter as *to th' *teawn*, a spelling which is phonetically not very transparent. Side by side with attempts at phonetic precision, an author may have to be content with the conventional spelling even when there are noteworthy dialectal pronunciations which would be worth recording. For instance, in Lancashire texts the pure vowel pronunciations of the mid long vowels [eː] and [oː] (equivalent to SBS /eɪ/ and /əʊ/) may be spelt with their standard spellings, as in *veil*, *faces*, alongside phonetic respellings of other phonemes in the following verse:

> Flashy clooas an' bits o' foinery
> Help to mend sich loike as me:
> Veils improve some women's faces
> But, owd friend, they'll noan mend thee.
>
> (Samuel Laycock d.1893)

It follows that literary dialect texts require of the reader some direct familiarity with the spoken dialect if they are to be interpreted with any degree of phonetic accuracy. The dialect spellings can only be suggestive. The phonetic realization of a phoneme in particular accents is unlikely, of itself, to disadvantage one speller more than another.

Differences of phonotactic distribution

Phonotactic distribution involves the privilege of occurrence of (equivalent) phonemes in particular contexts. This can have extremely important consequences for spelling, since the writing system reflects only one particular pattern of distribution. Some accents of English may have very different patterns. The outstanding example here is whether or not the original //r// survives before a consonant in words such as *farm* and finally, as it does in AmE and in Scottish and Irish English. The writing system reflects an English which has not lost 'post-vocalic' (or rather, pre-consonantal and final) /r/. Those who have lost it, such as SBS speakers, have the problem of differentiating the various spellings of /ɜː/ such as <er>, <ir>, <or>, <ur> (*term*, *thirst*, *worst*, *burst*), and of deciding whether /ɔː/ and /ɑː/ and /ɪə/ are spelt with an <r> or not (*caught–court*, *spa–spar*, *idea–dear*. So, although every English speaker has an /r/ phoneme, its possible distribution is crucial. Those who only have /r/ before vowels have problems. A recent article in the *Guardian* newspaper explained that, to produce a new queen bee in a beehive, royal jelly was fed to 'a *lava'. On the very next page one could read '. . . at the top of the *peninsular.' Not all distributional differences, however, have important consequences for spelling. For instance, the variation found across speakers between /iː/ and /ɪ/ in final open unstressed syllables (as in *lady*, *story*) does not seem to complicate the spelling task for either group of speakers. One can, however, only guess at what may be the case. It is difficult to put a costing on such differences and envisage their consequences.

It is sometimes difficult to decide whether a difference of distribution is phonotactic (and so subject to a general rule) or lexical (and so found simply in a given list of words). There is a difference of distribution between the vowels of Northern speakers of British English who retain a short vowel before /f, θ, s/ in words such as *after*, *path*, *glass*, and those of Southern speakers who have their long /ɑː/ instead. The same difference holds between AmE and SBS. But since there are words such as *gas*, *aster*, which escaped the lengthening, it should perhaps be considered a difference simply of lexical distribution.

Differences of phonological system

The most important of the four categories in its relevance to spelling is systemic difference. This is when the two speakers differ in the number of contrasting phonemes. If a speaker has fewer contrasts than the kind of English on which the present writing system was based, there will be under-differentiation. In foreign language learning this is a constant problem. A Greek who has five vowel phonemes in his own language, has to contrast as many as 20 in learning to speak English. Predictably he conflates /iː/ – /ɪ/, /uː/ – /ʊ/, /eɪ/ – /e/, /ɑː/ – /æ/, etc. This means that he cannot rely on his own pronunciation as a guide to the spelling of, say, *steal* – *still*, when he has to write English rather than read it.

English has millions of speakers as an official language of India. Naturally enough, Indian English is heavily influenced by the native language of the area in which it is spoken. Even though Indian English is institutionalized with its own norms of pronunciation, lexis and grammar, the literacy problems due to interference are essentially those facing any foreign learners. Lack of contrast is bound to affect literacy. For instance, in the consonant system, depending on the area, there may be a lack of contrast between plosives and fricatives /p/ – /f/ *paint –faint,* /t/ – /θ/ *tank–thank*, /d/ – /ð/ *dare–there*, or between /s/ – /ʃ/ *same–shame,* or /v/ – /w/ *viper–wiper*. Here, too, this is bound to be a source of spelling problems if the pronunciation does not maintain the contrasts. A Scottish speaker who does not have a contrast between /uː/ and /ʊ/ will have a more complex task in learning which words to spell with <oo> and which with <u> as in *pool*, *pull*.

SBS itself is underdifferentiated with respect to other accents in several ways. For instance, the vowel /eɪ/ occurs in both *wait* and *weight*, but North Lancashire and Yorkshire speakers may have a contrast here between a pure mid vowel /eː/ in *wait* and a diphthong with a more open starting point /ɛɪ/ in *weight* (and in other pairs involving the <eigh> spelling). The difference stems from an original velar consonant, reflected in the <gh>, which once occurred in the /ɛɪ/ words. Speakers who still maintain this contrast will find it easier to differentiate the <ai> and <eigh> spellings since they have two different vowel pegs on which to hang them. For SBS speakers there is no such support. An SBS speaker has a similar disadvantage in dealing with *wail–whale*, *witch–which*, *wear–where*, etc., compared with a Scottish, Irish or AmE speaker who has a contrast between [w] and its voiceless fricative counterpart [ʍ] (phonemically analysed as a cluster /hw/). In this case there is an added advantage for these others, since the spellings are phonetically transparent: the <h> marks voicelessness and friction.

Cheshire *et al.* (1989: 238) cite some German examples. There is no contrast in the Swabian dialect between rounded and unrounded front vowels: the rounded /yː/ of standard German, for instance, is merged with /iː/. So, one finds Swabian speakers making errors, such as *<zwelf> with <e> and *<Phisik> with <i>, using unrounded vowel spellings, instead of *zwölf* and *Physik*, where <ö> and <y> are rounded vowel spellings. Hypercorrections also occur, where the spelling for the standard rounded vowel is used for a standard unrounded vowel: *<vermüssen> for *vermissen* or *<mölken> for *melken*. These clearly stem from underdifferentiation.

There are a few complications, however. Systemic differences are not just a case of more or fewer phonemes in the system. What is important in spelling is how the contrasts are maintained. Consider a Northern speaker who has not lost the final //g// in *sing*, *bang*, etc., but who says [sɪŋg], [bæŋg] rather than [sɪŋ], [bæŋ] and for whom *singer* rhymes with *finger*. Such speakers do not have a separate /ŋ/ phoneme: the [ŋ] is simply a velar allophone of Northern /n/, conditioned by the following velar /g/ or /k/. So, with no phonemic /ŋ/, they have one phoneme less compared with SBS. On the surface this is a systemic difference. However, there is no loss of contrast between *sing* and *sin* in either accent. In *sing*, this Northern accent has <ng>≡[ŋg] (=/ng/); SBS has <ng>≡[ŋ] (=/ŋ/). Similarly, it does not matter for the spelling that a Welsh speaker has [ŋ] rather than [ŋg] in *language*, *stronger*. Here, the theory might conceal the practical effect. The only slight consequence for spelling is that the <ng> has greater phonetic transparency for the Northern speaker, who has two segments. The SBS speaker has a clumsy but adequate digraph: <ng>≡/ŋ/ in *singer*, and within a morpheme <ng>≡/ŋg/ as in *finger*. The simplest phonological account would be a process description. Both speakers have an underlying //ng// which they process differently: the Northern speaker does not delete the

//g//. This would then seem to be a distributional difference like that due to the loss of //r//, but the consequences are different: //r// does cause spelling problems for some vowels, such as *<sorcer> for *saucer*.

A further complication in assessing the effect of differences of accent is that each individual speaker need not have just a single phonological system. Everyone uses a number of different styles and registers. This variability makes it difficult to decide in some cases whether a speaker is sufficiently in command of a contrast to use confidently the different spellings associated with it. A case in point is whether a Cockney speaker lacks the contrast between /f/ and /θ/ in *fought*, *thought*. This would appear to be a straightforward systemic difference between Cockney and other accents due to 'TH fronting' (as Wells (1982: 328ff) calls it), whereby the /θ/ of other accents is merged with /f/, and /ð/ with /v/. Wells is adamant, however, that this is not a systemic difference:

> Even the broadest-speaking Cockneys clearly have /θ/ and /ð/ as items in their (underlying) phonemic inventory. But for the broader speakers, underlying /θ, ð/ are subject to the variable rule of TH fronting leading to their frequent realization as [f, v].
>
> (ibid.: 328)

The main evidence for this is an apparently complete absence of hypercorrections such as *[θaɪv] for *five*. A similar problem is whether Cockney speakers have an /h/ phoneme or not. Left to themselves, Cockneys would no doubt quite happily do without /θ/, /ð/ and /h/ in their consonant system. But the whole community has been exposed to literacy. They have had to learn a writing system that caters for a distinctively spelt /θ/, /ð/ and /h/. Cockneys can only become literate by realising that *fought* is not *thought* and *art* is not *heart*, etc. Radio, films and television have made it increasingly likely that people will have a passive awareness of other accents. For the teaching of literacy this can only be to the good. SBS-speaking children must surely derive benefit from being aware of 'rhotic' American accents in coping with /ɔː/ and /ɑː/, phonemes which can have spellings both with and without <r>.

Differences of lexical distribution

Difference of lexical distribution refers to the incidence of phonemes in words. It does not always present spelling problems. It is often the case that the variant phonemes are phonologically very close and the spelling is the same. Take, for instance, *economics* (/ekə'nɒmɪks/ – /iːkə'nɒmɪks/). The vowels /e/ and /iː/ regularly alternate in allomorphs for which the system provides a constant spelling (as in *serene* – *serenity*). The <a> spelling is common to /'plæstɪk/ and /'plɑːstɪk/. However, spelling problems may stem from lexical distribution. This would be clearly so for any AmE speaker who says /və'nelə/ for *vanilla*, especially when there are words such as *novella*, *patella*, *umbrella*. It might seem reasonable to allow dialect speakers to have variant spellings as **vanella* in such cases, but that would begin a free-for-all of spelling variance which would be difficult to regulate.

Differences of lexical distribution will inevitably occur if there is a difference in the number of phonemes in the system. The set of words in which Northern British speakers have /ʊ/ will be different in size from the set of words with SBS /ʊ/, where the original //ʊ// has split into SBS /ʊ/ and /ʌ/ (see pp. 144ff.). So the Northern /ʊ/ set includes not only *bush*, *butcher*, *could*, *courier*, *cushion*, *pudding*, *put*, *wolf*, etc., but also *mud*, *putt*, *rush*, *thudding, touch, wonder,* etc. There is further complication. The SBS /ʊ/ set will also include *book*, *cook*, *hook*, *look*, *rook*, *shook*, *took*, which for the Northerner would have /uː/.

We find an even more complex pattern in the low back vowels of SBS and AmE. For AmE speakers outside the Eastern and Southern states, the parallels are usually as shown below in table 6. They have no low back rounded short vowel that is phonetically equivalent to SBS /ɒ/. The vowel has lost its rounding in many words and fallen in with the /ɑː/ of *balm*, *bra*, *bravado*, *calm*, *mirage*, *palm*, *psalm*, *sonata*, *suave* and, for some speakers, *father*, *rather*. *Bomb* and *balm* are usually homophones in AmE. The rounding may be kept before /θ/, /f/, /s/, /g/, /ŋ/ and the vowel will merge with the /ɔː/ of *caught*. There is a further complication in the scope of /æ/. In SBS before /f/, /θ/, /s/ or a nasal and consonant cluster /æ/ has lengthened to /ɑː/, but not in AmE.

Table 6 Low vowels of SBS (top row) and AmE (bottom row)

æ	ɑː	ɑː(r)*	ɑː	ɒ	ɒ
cat	after	card	balm	bomb	across
man	path	farm	calm	drop	coffee
lamp	past	far	father	wad	moral
traffic	dance	spar	spa	holly	dog
æ	æ	ɑːr	ɑː	ɑː	ɔː

* The /r/ only follows before a vowel in a word or close-knit phrase as 'linking /r/'.

The four categories of difference between speakers inevitably interact in other ways. The most salient difference between the long vowels and diphthongs of SBS and AmE is an effect of the different distribution of /r/. The difference in phonotactic distribution between AmE as a 'rhotic' accent in which the original //r// remains in all positions, and SBS, where the original //r// has been lost before a consonant, has a consequent effect on the two vowel systems. Several new diphthong phonemes gliding to [ə] have developed in SBS resulting from the loss of //r//. In AmE these correspond to one of the other vowel phonemes plus /r/.

2.7.2 Recognizing problems due to phonological interference

Difference of accent evidently has an important bearing on literacy, but, strangely enough, its implications for speakers of a particular dialect are rarely drawn out. The *Studies in Spelling* volume (Robbie 1961), published by the Scottish Council for Research in Education, addressed itself to the problems of English spelling for Scottish children. As a source of specific Scottish problems, however, the book is curiously uninformative. The phonological aspects of the subject are not addressed. The nearest one gets to peculiarly Scottish spelling problems is the chapter called 'The Scottish Pupil's Spelling Book' by R.R. Rusk. This is concerned simply with selecting a basic word list for reading and writing in Scottish schools. The editor of the Scottish National Dictionary was consulted on whether certain terms were peculiar to Scottish English and he came up with the following advice:

> I have now gone through the list and I should say that the following words are purely Scottish: *wee*, *tig*, *burn*, *jag*, *peevers*, *dresser*, *bools*, *peat*, *loch*, *neeps*, *tatties*, *bure*, *Hallowe'en*, *guise/r/ing*, *dook*, *champers*, *bee-baw-babbity*, *brae*, *bramble*, *janitor*, *higher grade*, *currant bun*, *first footing*, *dyke* (in the sense of wall). . . . I am glad to see that an attempt is now being made to permit the inclusion of Scotticisms in the compositions of Scottish children.
>
> (op. cit.: 109f)

The aim of all this is to warn Scottish children about the use of dialect words in formal written English. South of the Border they have *lakes*, not *lochs*. But what has this to do with 'spelling'? What is remarkable in this list is that from the reading/writing point of view only a small proportion of these words presents a peculiarly Scottish spelling problem. Scottish children need to know that *neeps* and *brae* are not **neaps* and **bray*, but *higher grade* and *currant bun* (whatever specialized meanings they may have in Scotland) are common English forms and are, in any case, not simple words. Why they should be included as separate entries in a word list meant to define the words a Scottish pupil should be able to read and spell is something of a mystery. The greater mystery, however, is that the phonetic and phonological differences between Scottish English and SBS (or any other English accents) are not mentioned either as a source of advantage or disadvantage to the Scottish speller. This raises again (see §2.2) the lack of phonetic awareness in works on literacy and spelling.

There have been few attempts to pinpoint the phonological problems of dialect speakers in tackling standard orthography. Bojarsky (1969) examined the spelling errors made by children at a rural high school in the Appalachian mountains of West Virginia. The front vowels of this dialect differ from those of 'Standard English', which in this case was represented by her own speech, the speech of Philadelphia. This caused literacy problems, since, as Bojarsky one-sidedly puts it, 'the mountain man often has difficulty understanding those outside his community'. A group of Appalachian and a group of Philadelphia pupils were asked to write down some test words spoken by the author. Needless to say the Appalachian pupils produced more errors than the control group of Philadelphia pupils. Strangely enough the words were not read as a second test to both groups by an Appalachian speaker; the reciprocity was not explored. We can briefly consider the spelling errors made for the /iː/ – /ɪ/ contrast in *steal*, *still*. The Appalachian children seem to have had lower variants, so that the vowel of Appalachian *steal* approached that of Philadelphian *still*, while Appalachian *still* had a more open vowel than [ɪ]. In 26% of cases the Appalachian children took Philadelphian *still* to be *steal*, but they interpreted Philadelphian *steal* as *still* in only 4% of cases. This is what one would expect from the phonetic discrepancy.

Despite appearances, however, this does not appear to be a study of how the speakers of a particular dialect are disadvantaged by the writing system as a system. It is a study of how the relationship between speech and writing may be thrown into confusion when the speech patterns are those of a different dialect. It says nothing at all about purely Appalachian spelling problems in relation to traditional orthography.

2.7.3 Phonological interference in Black American English

Recent work on Black American English has explored dialect and literacy in some detail in the general context of educational and social problems. Black English in inner-city New York has several systemic and phonotactic differences from those dialects of English that fit traditional orthography better. O'Neal and Trabasso (1976) examined spelling errors made by Black children in the third and fifth grades to see if they were attributable to surface phoneme differences. They found that the younger children especially relied on the phonemic level in their spelling strategy. The errors made were clearly due to phonological difference rather than mere letter confusion. The errors increased if the word was tested outside a sentence context and errors were more frequent in longer and less common words.

The absence of /θ/ and /ð/, a systemic difference, appeared to have some bearing on spelling errors such as *<ver> *there*, *<brave> *brother*, *<too> *tooth*, *<mout> *mouth*, *<toh> *throw*, *<someing> *something*, *<souf> *south*, *<trought> *throat*. Absence of pre-consonantal /r/, a distributional difference, appeared to underlie *<amy> *army*, *<famer> *farmer*, *<flooh> *floor*. There may then be some insecurity about <r>, giving *<potes> *protest*. The contrast between /ɪ/ – /e/ is neutralized before /n/, another distributional difference, which appears to have prompted *<wenter> *winter*, *<intear> *enter*, *<sin> *send*, *<when> *win*, *<wend> *wind*, *<pliny> *plenty*. The most striking distributional difference, however, is the simplification of consonant clusters by dropping a final stop. Loss of the stop means that there is no difference between /t, d/ forms of {-ed} and the base form: *wash – washed*, *beg – begged*. Spelling errors from the tests included: *<coldes> *coldest*, *<wilds> *wildest*, *<rise> *rest*, *<tese> *test*, *<guess> *guest*, *<caes> *cashed*, *<finsh> *finished*, *<cole> *cold*, *<hole> *hold*, *<minn> *mind*, *<sin> *send*, *<win> *wind*.

The literacy problem for such speakers may not be intractable. Though the /d/ is lost in speech word-finally in *cold*, it is not lost before a vowel in *colder*. The spelling of the base form can be got at and remembered by looking at derived forms: *mist* from *misty*, *wind* from *windy*, etc. (Desberg, Elliott and Marsh 1980: 73).

There is some evidence, however, that the omission of the suffixes /-t/, /-d/ and /-s/, /-z/ in the writing of Black American children may not be a simple matter of phonetic cluster reduction. Whiteman (1981: 158) has some evidence for this view, part of which is shown in table 7.

Table 7 Percentage of <-s> suffix absence in speech and writing of South Maryland Blacks and Whites

	Verbal <-s>		Plural <-s>	
	Black	White	Black	White
Speech	83.3%	14.5%	29.6%	3.9%
Writing	50.0%	30.8%	26.9%	13.1%

In Table 7 both Blacks and Whites in South Maryland are shown to have a tendency to omit both verbal <-s> and noun plural <-s> in speech and in writing. The figures for Whites show a much larger percentage of omissions in writing than in speech, so some factor other than phonological must be reponsible. Another relevant fact is that, in writing, the clusters formed by adding a suffix, as in *pulled*, were affected significantly more than the same cluster in a single morpheme, as in *cold*. The reason why suffixes are dropped so frequently in writing may be part of a 'simplification' process applied to the new task of writing. A simplification like those made in the early stages of language development in young children, or like those made in naively 'simplifying' the language when talking to foreigners.

2.7.4 An orthography to cope with dialect variation

Wells's four categories have been used by Allerton (1982) in exploring how different regional pronunciations can be accommodated in a single orthography. 'It should be possible to represent in the orthography the maximal number of distinctions, even though no one dialect has all of them' (op. cit.: 63). This is the principle of 'maximal differentiation'. *Saw*, *law* would have to be distinguished from *sore*, *lore*, as <oh>, <or>. Allerton sees no reason why dialect speakers, within this overall system, should not write their own phonemes: a Northerner writing *last* as <last> and a Southerner as <lahst>, or even individuals writing their own pronunciation of *economics* with the first vowel as <e> or <iy>. 'This practice would surely be the simplest for the writer; and the reader, once used to it, would find it no more difficult than regarding *honour* and *honor* or *shown* and *shewn* as variant spellings of the same words' (ibid.: 64f). Presumably schools would then have regional initial reading schemes.

2.7.5 Stage dialect: spelling out the intentions of the playwright

George Bernard Shaw has a good claim to having been the most ambitious user of accent differences in the theatre. He often tried to exploit different registers for the same character in different situations. In *John Bull's Other Island*, the character Keegan sometimes uses 'a brogue which is the jocular assumption of a gentleman and not the natural speech of a peasant', but with educated listeners 'dropping the broad Irish vernacular of his speech to Patsy'. Hannigan puts on 'a rollicking stage brogue', but when exposed, 'his brogue decays into a common would-be genteel accent with an unexpected strain of Glasgow in it'. Hodson, the valet, normally is 'well-spoken' in the course of his duties but breaks out into Shaw's favourite Cockney under stress:

> 'You talk of your rotten little fawm cause you mide it by chackin a few stowns dahn a ill! Well, wot prawce maw grenfawther, Oi should lawk to knaow, that fitted ap a fust clawss shop . . . and then was chacked aht of it on is ed at the end of is lease withaht a penny for his goodwill. . . . They took the door off its inges and the winder aht of its seshes on me, an gev maw wawf pnoomownia'.
>
> (*John Bull's Other Island* London: Constable 1914: 75)

Irishness in the play is conveyed partly by vocabulary and grammar, with well-known phrases such as 'at all at all', 'I'll do it, so I will'. The phonetic indicators are fairly restricted. The commonest is to indicate a dental before /r/ in **afthernoon*, **aither* (*eater*), **counthry*, **dhrain*, **dhrinker*, **flatthery*, **matther*, **Misther*, **murdher*, **sthring*, **wather* (*water*). The ending <-ing> is /-ən/ not /-ɪŋ/: **admyerin*, **goin*, **mornin*, **shillin*. Final /-əʊ/ becomes /-ə/ spelt as <-a> in **barra*, **shadda*. Words with the SBS correspondence <ea>≡/iː/ have an <a..e> spelling to indicate [eː], so *weak* is spelt <wake>: the Middle English vowels of *week* and *weak* not having merged as they have in SBS. Compare also **mane*, **lave*, **spakin*. Words with /ɪ/ rather than /e/ are **expinses*, **hwin*, **innimy*, **respict*, **riverence*, **sind*. That seems to be lexical distribution rather than a general lack of contrast. The <wh> spelling is often written as <hw> in **hwat*, **hwin*, etc. to show a voiceless fricative. Merger of /ɪ/ and /ə/ is reflected in **sammin* (*salmon*), **sympithy*. Affrication is indicated by **schoopid*, **widja* (*with you*). Since the number of these respellings varies directly with the 'lowness' of the character, there may be a tendency for the writer, unconsciously or not, to select words that will carry them, so that the speech is adequately seeded with dialect markers.

At the least Irish end of the scale is Doyle, a professional man, who has lived in England for many years. His Irishness is marked only occasionally, as in the stage direction: 'He pronounces *post offices* with the stress on *offices* instead of on *post*' – which simple respelling could not indicate.

In *Captain Brassbound's Conversion*, Shaw sketched in Captain Kearney, commander of the USS 'Saratoga', as a 'Western American'. This was done quite economically. The short <o> spelling is respelt <aw> presumably to indicate an unrounded [ɑ] in **clawck*, **cawnsulted*, **cawnsidered*, **fawlly*, **respawnsible*, and similarly **wawnt* for *want*. The <a> spelling is respelt <ah> in **ahct*, **Ahdmiralty*, **ahsked*, **bahck*, **chahplain*, **fahstnesses*, **glahd*, **hahnd*, **hospitahlity*, **lahst*, **pahssion*, **Rahnkin*. The <ah> spelling is presumably meant to represent a front [æː]. The choice of these two respellings is not very appropriate, but they were similarly used in Shaw's representation of Cockney. As used in traditional orthography, <ah> would be associated with a back vowel quality and <aw> with a rounded vowel (cf. *saw*). Nor are these spellings used consistently: *understand, Brassbound, man, conduct, fashion, knots, passed*, all occur in Kearney's speeches with normal spelling. But **chahm* with no <r> is clearly a mistake. The absence of [j] before [uː] is indicated in **cawndooce*, **doo* (for *due*), **dooty*. Stress differences with vowel changes are indicated in **customairily*, **innquery* (['ɪŋkwəri]). The respelling of <c> as <s> in **sertnly*, **sertn* is redundant. The intervocalic <-rr-> of **Amerrican*, **verry*, may be intended to indicate a fully retroflex approximant, but surely not a trill. As a simple respelling it is inexplicit. For such a devoted spelling reformer as Shaw, there is an odd inconsistency in the American Kearney "saying" in the printed text: 'We will wait on the governor of the gaol (*sic*) on our way to the harbor (*sic*)' with a mixture of British and American spelling (*Three Plays for Puritans* London: Constable 1906: 290).

Intonation differences can play a part in indicating accent, but they are beyond the resources of punctuation or respelling and would require special markers. Such systems have been used in textbooks on rhetoric, but no dramatist seems to have employed detailed intonation marking in the text of a play, other than punctuation, either to realize an accent, or in discourse structure to indicate contrast or 'givenness' or attitude. Nucleus shift for emphasis or a difference of stress in a word can be shown in the text by italics or capitals. Punctuation indicates intonation to some extent:

Doesn't she enjoy a game of bridge! Doesn't she enjoy a game of bridge?

with respectively a falling and a rising nucleus. The first demands agreement, the second is unsure.

Direct comparison of different pronunciations is the theme of the song 'Let's call the whole thing off!' from the musical *Shall we dance?* (George and Ira Gershwin 1937). The text is based on lexical distribution differences, indicated rather inconsistently by respelling.

You say ee-ther and I say eye-ther, You say nee-ther and I say ny-ther;
Ee-ther, eye-ther, nee-ther, ny-ther, Let's call the whole thing off!
You like po-ta-to and I like po-tah-to, You like to-ma-to and I like to-mah-to;
Po-ta-to, po-tah-to, to-ma-to, to-mah-to! Let's call the whole thing off! . . . . .
So, if you like pa-ja-mas And I like pa-jah-mas,
I'll wear pa-ja-mas and give up pa-jah-mas. . . . . .
You say laugh-ter And I say lawfter. You say af-ter And I say awfter;
Laugh-ter, lawf-ter, af-ter, awf-ter, Let's call the whole thing off!
You like va-nil-la and I like va-nel-la, You sa's'-pa-ril-la and I sa's'-pa-rel-la;
Va-nil-la, va-nel-la, Choc'-late, straw-b'ry!! Let's call the whole thing off! . . . . .
So, if you go for oysters And I go for erst-ers,
I'll or-der oysters and can-cel the ersters.

(lyrics: Ira Gershwin)

Some of these differences look more fanciful than real and some of the spellings are not explicit. In reality, differences of system and differences of phonotactic distribution would have been more likely to make life difficult for the two people, but that would have certainly demanded more from the already overtaxed librettist.

Literary characters, we find, are not merely walking shadows, they are also talking shadows. Writers are not bound by absolute consistency or real phonetics. Nor, in the end, can they exercise much control on the actors who have to interpret their intentions. For all his care in spelling out the kinds of accent that he wanted his various characters to speak, Shaw did not always get cooperation. In a letter printed in *The Author* (Summer 1944), he admits:

> My own experience as a playwright in efforts to write modern cockney dialect phonetically with 26 letters has convinced me of its impossibility. Actors who specialize in cockney have had to transcribe my text into conventional spelling before they could study their parts.

That, if anything, is evidence of the flexibility of conventional spelling.

2.8 RULES AND ERRORS

2.8.1 Types of rule

Correspondence, adaptation, graphotactic and reference rules

The spelling of English words is now relatively fixed in a traditional orthography, even though there is no official 'Academy' in any English-speaking country vested with authority to decide what the 'correct' spelling of a word should be. We turn to the dictionaries printed by respected publishers to find how a particular word 'should be' spelt. The *OED*, with its derivative smaller dictionaries, is a standard work in Britain. Equally respected are the dictionaries of well-known publishers, such as Collins or Longman. In the United States the usual standard is *Webster's New International Dictionary*. This is specified as a standard in the style manual of the Government Printing Office.

The clear consequence of having a standard orthography is that you can make spelling errors. If *scoff* were spelt *<skoff>, most people would accept that a spelling rule had been broken because <sc> normally occurs before <o> and <sk> doesn't. Similarly we expect final /f/ to be spelt <ff> in lexical words after a stressed short vowel, so *<scof> would also break a spelling rule. But there might be some reluctance to say that to spell *cough* wrongly as *<coff> breaks any actual rule, since <ough>≡/ɒf/ is virtually a nonce correspondence. That is one point of view. A different, generative view of spelling would see every aspect of successful spelling as rule-governed. So the correspondence <ough>≡/ɒf/ in *cough*, *trough*, would be dictated by a very marginal word-specific rule, but a rule nevertheless. This is what you would be forced to do in programming a computer to spell English words by rule from speech input, mimicking the competence of a human speller. Even if the computer has a preliminary look-up list of 'irregular' spellings to consult first, before applying more general rules, the list simply represents rules of minimal generality. In practice we shall here use the term 'rule' rather loosely for varying degrees of generality.

Three main types of spelling rule occur in descriptions of English spelling conventions (Stubbs 1986: 6):

1 **correspondence rules**: these may apply in either the speech-to-text direction: '/h/≡<h>', or in the text-to-speech direction '<h>≡/h/'. In a strictly alphabetic system, correspondences would be consistently true in both directions. This is certainly not so for correspondence rules in English.

  The examples just given are context-free correspondence rules: the rule is not stated as applying only to specified contexts. But there are also rules which are restricted to particular contexts: '/ɒ/≡<ɑ> after /w/' (*watch*, *quarrel*).

There is some reluctance to think of such correspondences as being 'rules', whatever their generality: 'Rather than talk of correspondence rules, it is better to say that the analyst can establish correspondences between some letters, or letter groups, and some phonological segments' (Stubbs 1986: 7).

2 **adaptation rules** – rules which adapt the spelling of a morpheme to the structure of complex words: '{full} is spelt <ful> as a suffix (*spoonful*)'; or, as a fairly general rule: 'one letter of a complex spelling is elided when the same letter follows or precedes across a morpheme boundary' *threshold* (not <-shh->), *eighth* (not <-tth>)'. In so far as these rules restrict the possible sequences of letters in a word, they have a graphotactic bearing.

3 **graphotactic rules** (or **letter-distribution rules**): These are rules which restrict possible letter sequences. For instance: 'words do not usually end in <j>, <q>, <u>, <v>, or a single <z>, unless they are distinctly foreign (*raj, Iraq, guru, fez*), or slang (*spiv, baz*)'.

There are relatively few generalizations like this, which simply say where letters as such can or cannot occur. More often we say where a correspondence rather than a letter can or cannot occur:

'<c>≡/s/ does not occur before a consonant or word-boundary'.

Any correspondence rule restricted to a particular context has a graphotactic bearing.

Both adaptation rules and graphotactic rules can usually be recast as correspondence rules. Certainly, in putting together a computer algorithm for spelling, it would be convenient to do so. The nature of a graphotactic rule depends on what is meant by a grapheme. Phonotactic rules define the possible sequences of phonemes in a language, so we might reasonably expect graphotactic rules to define possible sequences of graphemes in a writing system. If we take 'grapheme' to be a hypostasis of 'letter', so that 'G' and 'g' are different realizations ('allographs') of the same grapheme, then graphotactic rules would presumably define what letter sequences are possible in English.

The letter string <o>+<u>+<g>+<h> is possible, but not *<o>+<u>+<h>+<g>; phonotactic rules for English allow /str/ as a possible initial cluster, but not */srt/. One important difference between phonotactics and graphotactics is that the former can use the distinctive features of phonemes to set up natural classes of phonemes and frame the phonotactic rules in terms of those classes. Initially in English syllables, plosives must be followed by an oral sonorant, that is a vowel or /l, r, w, j/, but not a nasal /m, n, ŋ/. Useful general statements about letter sequences are not easily made.

In practice it is rules like the '<i> before <e> except after <c>' rule, which would tend to be called graphotactic. The more closely one looks at that supreme, and for many people solitary, spelling rule, the more peculiar it seems. Its practical use for the most part is restricted to deciding between /iː/≡<ie> in *believe*, etc. and /iː/≡<ei> in *deceive*, etc., that is in simply deciding between two correspondences for /iː/ that are a visual metathesis of each other. It is not a general graphotactic rule applicable to other phonemes. So, although *seize* and *heinous* (if you pronounce it with /iː/ rather than /eɪ/) are exceptions, *heifer*, *leisure* with /e/≡<ei> or *rein*, *vein* with /eɪ/≡<ei> are not exceptions; <ie> is not a usual spelling of /e/ or /eɪ/. An adequate wording of the rule would be: 'in spelling /iː/ with an <i> and an <e>, the <i> goes before the <e> except after <c>'.

Haas (1970: 59) uses 'graphotactic rule' in tandem with 'phonotactic rule' to describe reading and writing as processes of phono-graphic translation:

> if we say (with certain qualifications) "Grapheme <c> sounds /k/ if it occurs before <a, o, u>, but /s/ before <e, i, y>", we are referring to purely graphemic conditions of the occurrence of <c>; we are stating a *graphotactic* rule for the *reader*. Similarly, when we say (in the other direction) "phoneme /k/, initially in a stressed syllable, is generally written <k> before /i, ɪ, e/, but <c> before other phonemes", we are stating a *phonotactic* rule for the *writer*.
>
> (ibid.: 59)

Some linguists do not use the term grapheme to mean the set of possible shapes of a single letter, but to refer to a string of one or more letters on the graphic side of a correspondence. In this usage, <ough> may be considered a grapheme in *fought*, where /ɔː/≡<ough>. With this use of the term grapheme, it is difficult to see what a graphotactic rule would be other than a context-sensitive correspondence rule. The term graphotactic rule might then conceivably be used for rules which are statements about what *cannot* occur in sequence, that is as a kind of negative correspondence rule. One may wish to point out that /s/≡<c> does not occur before a consonant or word boundary, or that /k/≡<c> does not occur finally in native words, as part of a general indication of where <c> does and does not occur in spellings. But clearly the same information can be conveyed by a series of adequate correspondence rules for /k/ and /s/.

Although a set of correspondence rules (with lists of exceptions) would serve to describe the English writing system, graphotactic rules may have explanatory value in laying bare some of the general design principles. There is the so-called 'short word rule' or '3-letter rule', which provides a minimum bulk for lexical words as opposed to function words (see §3.2.5). The rules for <e>-marking of long vowels and <C>-doubling as a marking of short vowels depend on whether the vowel in question is spelt by one or more letters: we have <bedding> but not *<headding>, <grate> but not *<greate> (see #D11 in §3.2.2 p. 124). The <o> spellings brought in as early as the Middle English period to replace <u> are a graphotactic device. Sequences of downstrokes of the pen in writing <m>, <n>, <i> and <u> caused readers some difficulty; for instance, <m> + <i> looked like <n> + <u>. Such ambiguous sequences were often broken up by using <o>, which has no down-strokes or minims, instead of <u>. The result is that we can expect to find <o>≡/ʌ/ (*come*) and <o>≡/uː/ (*move*) in a context of <m> or <n>. This general principle of minim avoidance may be lost sight of among the individual correspondence rules.

Graphotactics is also involved in the framing of context-sensitive correspondence rules. Can the context for a correspondence be described more concisely in terms of letter sequences or of phoneme sequences? Traditionally letter sequences have been used, as in McLeod's rules in §2.8.2 (see below), along with occasional feature-defined natural classes of phonemes: 'hissing sounds', 'long vowels', 'short vowels'. In distinguishing between <k> and <c> spellings of /k/, for instance, the context of the following vowel is easier to define in terms of letter sequencing. Graphic specification of contexts is probably more economic overall, since spelling conventions are usually established with the needs of readers, rather than writers, in mind.

For literacy work, it would be useful to employ the term **reference rule** for rules that spellers may consciously quote. These are rules which prevent them from making mistakes in spelling by wrong analogies. The classic example is the '<i> before <e>, except after <c>' rule discussed above. Reference rules are discussed in §2.8.2 (below).

There is a further type of rule that applies to the printed word. **Syllabification rules** show how to map phonetic syllables on to strings of letters. Their effect is to mark places at which a word may be split by the printer at the end of a line of print. They are discussed in §2.8.3 (pp. 76–9).

2.8.2 Classroom spelling rules

Reference rules used by teachers.

Until the advent of 'look and say' methods of teaching literacy, the general public firmly believed that writing and spelling were 'rule'-governed activities. You learned the sound values of letters and combinations of letters, together with a number of 'rules'. The function of the rules was to prevent you making mistakes in writing when you came to put letters together to match the pronunciation of a word. Even more recent generations taught to read by 'look and say' methods may still have a lingering idea that there are rules in existence which help you avoid making mistakes. It is doubtful whether anyone really believed that explicit and recallable 'spelling rules' were a wholly adequate basis for teaching writing. Children have always learnt to spell by making analogies and by subconsciously recognising recurrent patterns (and deviations from them) in carefully graded written material presented to them. So what were the spelling rules that could actually be stated and that could be referred to by a hesitant speller? We shall call them **reference rules**.

The 'spelling' rules offered in junior school textbooks frequently expand into areas of literacy teaching which are not strictly to do with spelling at all, but which are part of vocabulary development. An adaptive rule explaining the alternation between <-y> – <-ies> in *berry–berries* may develop into a general account of how plurals are formed. But there is no spelling problem as such, given the pronunciation, in the pairs *leaf–leaves*, *man–men*, *goose–geese*. Lists of gender pairs such as *monk–nun*, *wizard–witch* or opposites such as *sense–nonsense*, *trust–distrust*, *increase–decrease*, etc. may even come under the rubric of 'spelling'. This extension of 'spelling' usually develops out of adaptation rules. Under the general heading of 'spelling', *W3NID* (p. 25a) describes various ways of dealing with a final vowel in forming an adjective from a proper name. Final <-a> or <-o> is dropped when adding the suffix <-an> or <ian>: *America–American*, *Canada–Canadian, Victoria–Victorian*, *Morocco–Moroccan*. There is /v/ insertion in *Harrow–Harrovian*, /n/ insertion in *Cicero–Ciceronian*. 'Spelling' is here a curiously wide concept and shades off into vocabulary development and word formation. These rules are not simply about spelling the known sound, or reading the known spelling. The questions asked are: How is 'feminine' (or 'negative', or 'plural') realized in the structure of English words? How do you form an adjective from a name? How is a morpheme realized in different contexts?

McLeod (1961) gives an interesting insight into how 'rules' were traditionally used in the classroom. She reports the result of a survey to which 76 teachers in 28 Scottish schools contributed. These teachers had all claimed to make use of explicit rules in teaching spelling. They submitted rules which they had acquired either from their own teaching experience or from textbooks and which they taught to pupils directly. McLeod reproduces 27 of these rules. A further 32 formulae that had been submitted were discarded, since they merely grouped words according to common suffixes. McLeod has several criteria to assess the classroom value of a rule: it should apply to a large number of words, it must have few exceptions, it must be easy to state and understand and it must cover only the appropriate words. It is assumed that the rules will apply within the limits of primary school vocabulary. These requirements may make good sense pedagogically, but they inevitably exclude a great many possible and useful generalizations about English spelling. For instance, one can predict with almost total certainty when to spell final /əʊ/ with <ow> as in *window* and when with <o> as in *tango* (see pp. 172ff). It would not be possible, however, to frame this regularity as an easily stated rule under McLeod's criteria. Learners have to develop their own more or less subconscious awareness of this regularity from graded word lists. It is no wonder then that the number of explicit and easily stated rules that McLeod was able to collect proved to be no more than 27. Her two lists are worth examining carefully to see what kinds of regularity the traditional spelling rules could exploit.

However, one must not be too narrowly academic about McLeod's classroom rules. They are meant as reference rules or reminders for small children; they are not always explicit formulae. Their chief purpose is clearly to trigger a child's awareness of what the teacher had already said about a particular spelling problem. They work, if at all, when the child makes that connection. McLeod was interested in the practicality of the rules in classroom use and she provides detailed comments on this aspect. We can usefully add a few further comments by noting the bearing of the rule: whether it applies to reading, writing or to both. A reading rule may require the correspondence information to be formatted rather differently from a writing rule and vice versa. We can also try to fit the rules into the major categories of correspondence rules, adaptation rules and graphotactic rules.

The first section of McLeod's rules is as follows; the original text of the rule is italicized to separate it from my comments:

A) Rules not derived directly from textbooks:

Rule I – Words ending with a consonant preceded by a single vowel double the consonant before adding an ending.

– an adaptation rule to give *mat – matting*. The terms 'consonant' and 'vowel' evidently will refer to letters, not sounds throughout. Nor is 'an ending' very precise: it would give *<cappful>, *<preferrment>, *<matts>. Presumably <x> has special status to prevent *<boxxing>. The rule should no doubt have read: '. . . before adding an ending beginning with a vowel'.

Rule II – A word ending in 'e' *usually drops it when a syllable beginning with a vowel is added.*

– an adaptation rule. As far as the children are concerned, 'syllable' presumably means 'bit'. What in fact would they be taught to recognize as a syllable? There are exceptions covered by 'usually' (*saleable*).

Rule III – When you hear the name of a vowel add silent 'e' *at the end of the word.*

– a correspondence rule for writing. The wording is slack: we have to assume a monosyllabic word or a final stressed syllable (*make*, *waste*, *partake*). There will be exceptions, such as **poste*. The rule presupposes that only one vowel letter is being used (not **faile*).

Rule IV – After 'w' *and* 'wh', 'a' *sounds* 'o'.

– a reading rule as it stands. The word 'sounds' is unfortunate, since the users of the rule have no direct way of referring to sound (see §2.2 p. 9). What we have is a kind of rewrite-rule with the intention: 'carry on reading as if the <a> were an <o>' and this is expected to prompt either /ɒ/ (*watch*) or /ɔː/ (*water*). The rule does not apply to <e>-marked long vowels, as in *whale*, *wane*, etc.

Rule V – A noun ending in 'y' with a consonant before makes its plural by changing 'y' into 'i' and adding 'es'.

– an adaptation rule.

Rule VI – The last letter of 'full' is dropped when the word is placed at the end of another.

– an adaptation rule.

Rule VII – Pro-, suc-, and ex- take 'ceed'. All the rest take 'cede' except super- which takes 'sede'.

– this is a correspondence rule of sorts but the unit of correspondence is a whole syllable; <ceed> and <cede> are different spellings of the same §Latinate element, but <sede> represents a different element. Spellers can hardly be expected to associate this with a difference in meaning between <cede> and <sede>, so the rule simply states what goes with what.

Rule VIII – 'i' comes before 'e' except after 'c' when the sound of the letters is 'ee'.

– this classic spelling rule was discussed above as a graphotactic rule (p. 68).

Rule IX – Words ending in 'f' with a consonant in front change 'f' into 'v' and add 'es' in the plural.

– in effect *elf – elves*, *shelf – shelves*, *wolf – wolves*, and graphically, *calf – calves*, *half – halves*, but excluding *serf – serfs*. The rule looks like an adaptation rule, but it is hardly a rule of the writing system at all. Plural forms such as *shelves*, *wolves* are spelt by normal correspondences and the <-ves> is in no way peculiar in spelling. The rule simply draws attention to the phonetic variation in the stem between singular and plural: it really comments on the fact that it is rather unusual for a plural ending to alter the stem. The main problem with the <-ves> plural is that it only applies to a closed set of words. We do not get *<reeves> from *reef*.

Rule X – When two vowels are together the first one says its own name and the second one is silent.

– this rule seems to be a classroom favourite for dealing with correspondences using more than one vowel letter: it predicts /əʊ/ in <ough> *though*, <ow> *low*, <oa> *boat*, via the name of the first letter; clearly a reading rule.

Rule XI – After 'n', 'ch' sounds 'sh'.

– this too is a reading rule, though the intention is not very clear. After /n/ within a morpheme the value of <ch> may be either /ʃ/ or /ʧ/, free variants for many SBS speakers (*lunch* as /lʌnʃ/ or /lʌnʧ/). The rule would not apply at a boundary, as in *enchant, unchain.* It may perhaps be meant to avoid the §Greek correspondence <ch>≡/k/, but *anchor* is the only common word. Others would be *bronchitis, melancholy, synchronic.*

Rule XII – 'x' and 's' can never come together.

– a graphotactic rule; presumably it is meant to prevent words such as *exceed* being spelt as *<exseed>.

Rule XIII – When 'all' is in a word it has only one 'l'.

– an adaptation rule; it obviously refers to initial /ɔːl/, identifiable as the morpheme {all}, in *almost, already, always* and not simply to the letter string <all> in *taller*. A writer needs to know when there is one written word (*already*) and when there are two words (*all ready, all right, all aboard*).

Rule XIV – 'w' before 'r' is silent.

– a reading rule; anyone who did attempt a cluster [wɹ-] would probably do no more than pronounce a strongly labialized [ɹ] acceptable as /r/.

Rule XV – Words ending in 'o' with a consonant before it usually form the plural by adding 'es' to the singular.

– an adaptation rule (see p. 19).

The second section of McLeod's rules is as follows. I have omitted some rules that are more or less equivalent to those in section A:

B) Rules given in textbooks:

Rule IV – Words of one syllable ending in a single consonant preceded by a single vowel double the consonant when another syllable is added.

– a correspondence rule; again 'consonant' and 'vowel' can only refer to letters. This is another version of rule A–I.

Rule V – To make the plural of words ending in 'y' change 'y' to 'ie' and add on 's'.

– an adaptation rule (= rule A–V).

Rule VI – Many words ending in 'er' and 'or' drop the 'e' and 'o' in words derived from them.

– this seems to be a general warning to the speller that both /ə/ and its spelling are often elided in words such as *hindrance, hungry, remembrance, actress, doctrine.* These are instances where the writing system does not provide a constant shape for a morpheme.

Rule VII – Words ending in 'y' preceded by a vowel simply add 's'.

– an adaptation rule, presumably to form the plural or 3rd pers. pres. sg.: *boy – boys, say – says, employ – employs.*

Rule VIII – 'e' is kept before 'ful' except in 'awful'.

– an adaptation rule; (*hateful* not **hatful*, etc.).

Rule IX – If you want to add other letters to a word ending in 'y' preceded by a consonant change 'y' into 'i'.

– an adaptation rule; it refers in effect to the correspondence <y>≡/aɪ/ (*deny–denial*); the restriction 'preceded by a consonant' is intended to rule out *betray–betrayal, employ–employer*. McLeod points out that it does not apply before <-ing> (*denying*).

Rule X – 'i' before another 'i' becomes 'y'.
– a graphotactic rule; presumably it refers in an oblique way to examples such as *die–dying* or *carrying–carrier–carried*; the recent loan-word *skiing* is an exception.
Rule XI – Words ending in a hissing sound form their plural by adding 'es' instead of 's'.
– this has the form of an adaptation rule. It is a recognition that <s>, unlike the <ed> of the past tense, does not represent all the allomorphs /s/, /z/ and /ɪz/ of the plural (see p. 19).
Rule XII – Adding of a final 'e' changes a short vowel into a long vowel.
– this is a correspondence rule which treats <e>-marking of vowels as a general process in pairs such as *hop–hope*; the rule is worded as a writing rule ('adding of . . .') but it is valid for both reading and writing. This is also a good example of the necessary inexplicitness of such rules: it is assumed that the short vowel is spelt with a single letter: *<heade> is not a possible spelling of /hiːd/.

It can be safely assumed that the rules collected by McLeod are typical of reference rules in general and, indeed, that her lists are fairly exhaustive. A group of 76 Scottish primary school teachers who used spelling rules in the classroom in the late 1950s, and who firmly believed in their use, might surely be expected to provide a reasonable coverage of what rules were actually available.

The rules we have just seen are chiefly notable for what they do not do. The basic problem of the speller is to select the right correspondence when faced with several choices. Some competing spellings can never be sorted out by rule because there is no variation in context to condition one spelling rather than the other: *bed–head*, *meet–meat*, *grow–though*, etc. There are, nevertheless, many statistically worthwhile generalizations which can be made, and which children undoubtedly do make as they accumulate experience, by using analogy and probability. The extent to which this is possible can only be measured by writing a detailed spelling algorithm, as Hanna (1966) set out to do, though it does not necessarily follow that the rules of a computer algorithm will satisfy McLeod's natural criteria for an exploitable and stateable spelling rule. For the general public a typical spelling rule would be some form of '<i> before <e> except after <c> . . .' (A–VIII above). Fowler (1926: 556) calls this rule 'very useful'. Such rules are warnings against common pitfalls for the unwary. Nevertheless, selection among competing correspondences has never been, and could never be, covered by a set of such aids to memory.

The problems of framing reference rules to use in the classroom are also evident in Clymer (1963). This is a survey of a set of 45 'phonic generalizations' associated with phonic methods of teaching literacy, which assesses their value across the vocabulary of primary-school reading texts. It would be wrong, however, to see the rules examined in this survey as a good implementation of phonic methods. They are a set of reference rules for reading and have little to do with the business of teaching an awareness of phonetic correspondences. In these rules, 'vowel' and 'consonant' ultimately refer to letters (see §2.2 pp. 9ff). This means that there are two 'vowels' in *boat* and that <w> is sometimes a 'vowel' and sometimes a 'consonant'. The rules do not consider a correspondence <ea>≡/iː/ in *bead* or <oa>≡/əʊ/ in *boat*, to be a digraph correspondence, but rather a 'vowel' and a silent letter:

> (1) When there are two vowels side by side, the long sound of the first one is heard and the second is usually silent.

This would apply in *pain*, *bead*, *boat*, but not in *field*.
Similarly, in the case of <ie>≡/iː/:

> (7) In the phonogram *ie*, the *i* is silent and the *e* has a long sound.

This would apply in *field*, but not in *friend*.
The unit of correspondence decides what is an exception and so affects Clymer's efficiency rating of the rule:

> (11) When the letter *i* is followed by the letters *gh*, the *i* usually stands for its long sound and the *gh* is silent.

An example of this would be in *high*. But *neighbour* would be an 'exception' to this rule, simply because the unit of correspondence is not taken to be <ei>≡/eɪ/ (let alone <eigh>). Is it then a true assessment of this rule, that the correspondence <igh>≡/aɪ/ is only '71 per cent efficient'? This is a good practical example of how the 'facts' of literacy can be distorted by inadequate theory. (Segmentation into units is discussed in §2.6 p. 32ff.)

Clymer has no direct way to refer to phonemes, except by association with particular letters. Consider the statement:

> (24) The letter *g* often has *a sound similar to that of j in jump* [my italics] when it precedes the letter *i* or *e*.

An example would be *engine*, but not *give*. This shows scant regard for the alphabetic principle, however battered it may be in English. As far as the writing system is concerned, the /j/ of *jump* and the /j/ of *engine* are simply the same phoneme, not two 'similar sounds'.

It is sad that, in the ebb and flow of fashion in the teaching of literacy, such early versions of phonics are often used as an unreal target to decry all phonetic involvement in initial literacy teaching. In so far as phonics did teach sound-spelling correspondences, it could be viewed as a worthwhile enterprise. As practised in the 1960s, however, it often lacked linguistic and phonetic insight. More recent phonic reading schemes have a greater linguistic awareness. The 'Phonics 44' scheme for initial literacy developed by J.M. Morris (1984) is a good example of a graded presentation of vowel correspondences and consonant clustering that works towards independence in reading and spelling.

Even linguists hesitate to use the term 'rule' for all the regularities that can be found in the writing system, partly because the word 'rule' is pre-empted for classroom reference rules like those discussed above, and partly because they wish to allow for some individual freedom in spelling habits. Certainly there are genres, such as literary dialogue, in which the freedom to spell differently is a stylistic resource and, in the case of proper names (§6.3), idiosyncratic spelling has a strong distinctive function. Witness Sam Weller on the spelling of his surname:

> 'I never had occasion to spell it more than once or twice in my life, but I spells it with a V.'
>
> Here a voice in the gallery exclaimed aloud, 'Quite right too, Samivel, quite right. Put it down a we, my lord, put it down a we'.
>
> (Charles Dickens *Pickwick Papers* ch. XXXIV)

In the present study the term 'rule' is used of any regularity in correspondence that seems to be statistically worth exploiting as a device for describing the present English writing system. These regularities often fall far short of McLeod's criteria for a 'spelling rule', since they may not be 'easy to state and understand' (at least for children). The further criterion that a rule should apply to a large number of words is a matter of judgment, but for practical literacy work one would clearly not want to set up a 'rule' as particular as: '/æ/ is spelt <ai> after /pl/ and before a word-final alveolar plosive' to account for *plait* and *plaid*.

2.8.3 Syllabification rules: splitting words

Variation in usage

Most printed text is 'justified', not 'ragged': all the lines on a page, or in a column, end in exactly the same place. The edge of the print presents a straight vertical line, unlike the ragged edge left by an ordinary typewriter, when each line almost always ends in a complete word. This is done wherever possible by juggling with slightly wider or slightly smaller spaces at the word boundaries so that the line of print expands or contracts to end at a word boundary. Sometimes this cannot be done neatly and a word has to be split over two lines, using a hyphen. How this is achieved is partly a matter of phonetics and morphology, partly a matter of taste and sometimes sheer caprice. The wider the page or column, the less need there will be for word division, so the best place to study this practice under pressure is in a narrow-column layout, or 'narrow measure'.

Good dictionaries, such as *W3NID*, indicate for each entry word the places where it can conveniently be split with a hyphen. Compositors do not, of course, reach for their dictionary at every overlap; general principles almost always point to a natural division. However, the general principles sometimes conflict with each other and decisions can vary. There are many differences, for instance, in the divisions suggested in the first (1948) and third (1974) editions of the *Oxford Advanced Learner's Dictionary of Current English*, a leading authority for foreign learners of English. Here is a small sample:

1st edn: *ge-ra-nium*, *sty-lish*, *jave-lin*, *mo-nas-tic*;
3rd edn: *ger-anium*, *styl-ish*, *jav-elin*, *mon-as-tic*;
1st edn: *de-spise*, *de-spoil*, *de-spond-ent*, *det-o-nate*;
3rd edn: *des-pise*, *de-spoil*, *de-spon-dent*, *det-on-ate*.

There are even apparent discrepancies within one edition: *den-sity*, *tens-ity*; *re-spon-sive*, *de-fens-ive*; *ketch-up*, *kit-chen*; *crud-ity*, *nu-dity* (3rd edn). It is not always easy to deduce the principles from the practice. The 1st edition says that: 'Syllabification has been indicated, partly as a help to pronunciation and partly to guide learners on the question of how to divide words in writing and typing' (1st edn: v). The 3rd edition says that: 'The broad basis for the division is syllabification but other considerations, such as derivation and intelligibility of either part of the divided word, play a part' (3rd edn: ix). The 3rd edition also makes occasional use of a syllable-boundary marker in the phonetic transcription: '*cartridge* /ˈkɑ-trɪʤ/ is so shown to suggest that the junction between the two halves of the word should be pronounced as in *car-trip* and not as in *cart-ride*' (3rd edn: xiii). But this is an instance where the word-division marker printed in the head-word is adequate: *car-tridge*.

Phonetic syllable boundaries

Just as the phonetic terms 'consonant' and 'vowel' have been hijacked to mean 'consonant letter' and 'vowel letter', so the phonetic term 'syllable boundary' has been hijacked to refer to these points of division. There is only a very approximate relationship between printers' sub-strings and a phonetic syllable. There is general agreement that written boundaries should normally coincide with morpheme boundaries and that consonant clusters on either side of the boundary should, as far as possible be those found in monosyllabic words. But there are conflicting views among phoneticians about syllable boundaries in English. Views differ on how to deal with intervocalic consonants after stressed vowels. Wells (LPD 1990: xixf) distinguishes three main views:

	happy	*lady*	*candy*
1	ˈhæ-pi	ˈleɪ-di	ˈkæn-di
2	ˈhæp-i	ˈleɪ-di	ˈkæn-di
3	ˈhæp-i	ˈleɪd-i	ˈkænd-i

The first is common phonetic practice: wherever possible a single intervocalic consonant goes with the following syllable. The second is the basis for most printing practice. The third is Wells' own view of phonetic syllable division, which sets out to provide a syllable within which one can predict phonetic variation due to aspiration, glottalization and cluster simplification: 'consonants are syllabified with which ever of the two adjacent vowels is more strongly stressed; or, if they are equally stressed, with the leftward one'.

General principles and usual practice

Phonetic theory offers a number of different criteria for drawing a syllable boundary in a /-VCV-/ sequence. Syllables beginning with a vowel rather than a consonant are relatively rare, both in English and across human language generally. Indeed, if you start out saying a slow string of VC syllables, such as [. . . ap-ap-ap-ap . . .], you will find that, as the tempo increases, your perception of the sound switches to [. . . pa-pa-pa-pa-. . .]. There is also a common notion of syllable 'weight', whereby a short vowel plus a consonant weighs the same as a long vowel. These factors provide some phonetic basis for splitting the printed word:

1 Whenever possible start each part with a consonant letter – *pal-lid*, *prob-lem*, *sub-li-mate*; but complex letter correspondences other than doublets need to be kept intact: *knick-ers*, *spa-ghetti*.
2 However, a single consonant letter after a stressed short vowel usually goes with the previous vowel letter – *sol-id*, *prod-uct*. Sometimes this happens with an unstressed vowel: *stat-istics* probably occurs as frequently as *sta-tistics.*
3 Do not separate any letter that has a marking function from what it marks – *singe-ing* (not **sing-eing*); *dicta-tion* (not **dictat-ion*); *ra-tional* (not **rat-ional*); *sale-able* (not **sal-eable*).
4 When a consonant letter string spans the point of division, split it as evenly as possible into a final and an initial string that are found otherwise occurring – *laun-dry*, *flim-sy*. With an odd number of consonants, the heavier cluster usually follows the split. Sometimes the split may give unusual letter clusters, such as an initial <dl> in *bun-dle.*
5 In a complex word, it is easier for the reader if the break occurs, if possible, at an element boundary, especially a free-form boundary – *news-paper*, *semi-circle*, *defens-ive*, (cf. *cos-tive*). The inflectional endings <-ed>, <-er>, <-es>, <-est>, <-ing> and the ending <-ish> do not usually attract a previous consonant letter (*whit-ish*, *bak-er*, *lat-est.* But this may override criterion (1), giving *leav-er*, as against *bea-ver.* This may not operate in proper names: *mill-er*, *Mil-ler*. Cf. *W3NID* (p.22a): '*England* and by extension *English* are often divided after the *g* to keep

the *land* intact but we have adopted the decision before the *g*'. This is apparently the obverse of criterion (3), since *En-gland* would ensure the pronunciation of the /g/, but at the expense of not marking <n>≡/ŋ/. Elements in §Latinate or §Greek words that are not free, may or may not be disregarded: *democ-racy* or *demo-cracy*, *pro-duct* or *prod-uct* (overriding criterion (2)). When there is already a hyphen in the spelling of a compound, there is naturally a strong compulsion to make do with that: *ex-king*, *anti-smoking*, *non-violent*, *semi-detached*.

6 A general aesthetic principle of balance requires both parts to be more than one letter long: do not split after or before a single letter (**a-sparagus*, **buffal-o*). This applies even when the single letter may be an element (**a-head*, **frisk-y*, **impediment-a*). There may be some temptation not to observe this in cases such as *mange-y*, where *mang-ey* would shift the <e> marker of <ge>≡/ʤ/. On the other hand, splits such as *strang-er*, *rang-ing* are quite usual.

Whether these orthographic 'syllables' can provide any basis for writing spelling correspondence rules is very dubious. Hanna *et al.* (1966) use the 'syllables' provided by *W2NID* as a unit within which spelling rules operate and their use of 'initial' and 'final' refers to such units. Few people, when presented with such a rule, can easily work out what words would be covered by it. More significantly, the computer which processed the spelling rules did not decide by following some strategy where these boundaries were. The boundaries were given in the input data. For further discussion see §2.8.5. pp. 86ff.

2.8.4 Types of spelling error

Social penalties

The road to literacy is paved with spelling mistakes. The complexity of the English writing system makes this inevitable. Clearly, the mistakes that people make are worth a careful analysis if the teaching of literacy is to be improved. They are certainly of prime interest to spelling reformers, who look to a spelling system that would cut mistakes to a minimum. Although the state played no part in the evolution of traditional orthography, education authorities do require this traditional orthography to be taught and a social stigma attaches to those who cannot cope with it.

Spelling errors have social penalties. If you cannot spell you are thought to be uneducated and, by a further savage twist, unintelligent. That is why the handicap of developmental **dyslexia** is such a burden. There is no evident reason why some otherwise normal intelligent children prove to have severe difficulties in reading, writing and spelling. The consequences of this disability will affect their whole lives:

> Their inability to read, whether for information or pleasure, and their daily failure in their attempts at written work, has a devastating effect upon their ability and motivation to learn. . . . Their poor writing and spelling tends to be viewed as a symptom of educational subnormality or lack of intelligence – or, if the child is known to be intelligent, leads to a charge of laziness or 'not trying', with subsequent punishment at school and increased family tension at home. As a result, it is not surprising to find that many such children become anxious, withdrawn or aggressive – with deteriorating behaviour in some cases leading to them being described as maladjusted. Career prospects, in such cases, are minimal.
>
> (Crystal 1987: 273)

A single spelling mistake can ruin any carefully prepared presentation by distracting the reader from the message itself. In a 1992 pre-election television programme in England by the Labour party, when education policy was, as ever, a crucial issue, a spelling mistake in the subtitles of the film caused ribald comment:

> The impression of intellectual distinction was, however, rather undermined by a howler in the subtitles screened with the broadcast. 'Power carries responsibility', declared the Leader, as he strode masterfully towards a waiting helicopter, 'and unless you are prepared to excercise [*sic*] that responsibility . . .'
>
> (*Observer* 29/9/91)

A spelling mistake for which Kinnock was not even remotely responsible is used to brand him as lacking in education. It serves as a stylistic banana skin to drop him from a carefully contrived peak of rhetoric – *intellectual distinction, power, responsibility, strode masterfully.* The irony is that journalists who feel this to be perfectly ethical, would be horrified to think that their own contributions might ever be devalued by similar slips.

When a politician is publicly seen to be responsible for a spelling mistake, his credibility may suffer lasting ridicule. The American Vice-President, Dan Quayle, arranged to be filmed in a classroom on a school visit in June 1992 as part of his re-election campaign. A child was asked by the teacher to write the word *potato* on the blackboard. This the child did. Quayle, however, went up to the blackboard and 'corrected' the child's spelling to *<potatoe>. The child was much aggrieved. President Bush, Quayle's running-mate, was unavailable for comment. Political opponents were. (See also p. 447.)

On the other hand, as Gillian Brown points out in Stubbs (1986: 3), there are widespread defiant deviations from the standard orthography. She notes the use of apostrophes and other deviant spellings in shops: 'Leave your *trolley's here'; '*Property's in your area'. There may be a reluctance to alter the shape of a morpheme such as <property> by the adaptation rule that turns the final <-y> into <-ie-> when the plural ending is added, since words such as *trolley* keep a final <-y> in the plural. The bold use of an apostrophe, however irregular, seems to be a kind of totem for making a public notice look official. Ringway Golf Club has an unforgiving notice advising the public that '*Trespass's will be prosecuted'. Homophones are a common source of such confident misspellings. My local greengrocer advertises *<naval oranges>, printed on a glossy trade poster. When challenged, he asserts that this is the trade spelling. This freedom to do one's own spelling is inevitably rather limited, though freedom to change irregular spellings by allowing more regular variants to be used is a practicable means of spelling reform. This use of *<naval> for *navel* may ultimately change the orange metaphor to fit the <-al> spelling: the power of vitamin C to prevent scurvy on long voyages may take over from the dimple at the base of the orange.

There have been a number of detailed studies of spelling errors, exploring, for instance, the design of a computerized spelling checker (Yannakoudakis and Fawthrop 1983), or the problems of phonological interference in teaching English as a second language (Brown, A. 1988), or the psycholinguistic processes involved in writing (Nauclér 1980), or simply recording the types of error likely at different stages of learning to read and write. These various interests tend to use different criteria in classifying errors. There is no generally used set of categories. For instance, if you want to help typists by devising a computer program to spot probable spelling errors, simple graphotactic categories such as inversion, doubling, omission, will allow most spelling discrepancies to be picked out by computer, unless the mistake represents some other correctly spelt word. In literacy research, a wider set of categories is obviously needed. We can briefly review here some of the parameters that might prove relevant.

Competence errors and performance errors. Variant errors. Slips

A very basic difference is that between a **competence error**, which is a fairly consistent misspelling, and a **performance error**, which is a temporary lapse. These can only be differentiated if there are statistics available, as when the work of a child is monitored over a period of time.

Casual spelling errors rarely confuse the reader, not only because the wider context helps, as in 'a pair of *shoos'. Most casual errors are simply an error of choice among competing spellings of the phoneme. So, *<compleat> is immediately recognizable as *complete* and *<prefurred> as *preferred*. The correspondence is wrong, but the phoneme can be spelt like that elsewhere. These may be called **variant errors**.

Other performance errors can be referred to as **slips**. These are unintentional errors, not errors of understanding. Nauclér (1980) draws out the psycholinguistic implications from an interesting Swedish database. A common type of slip is when the writer anticipates in the string of letters a later spelling that requires some attention. In a hand-written restaurant menu where 'cooked' appeared several times correctly, I have noticed '. . . *coked with okra and other vegetables'. The exotic spelling of <okra> seems to have been the triggering factor. Doubling of a wrong letter is a very common slip: *<innacuracy> *inaccuracy*, *<ommitted> *omitted*, particularly where there are treacherous analogies such as *innocent*, *committed*. These seem to be more common when a doubled letter follows later in the word; this would account for *<ussually> *usually*. A doubled letter seems to be a memorable graphic feature, but the location of the doubling proves less certain. Similar instances of uncertainty about the placement of a graphic feature are *<whispher> *whisper*, *<realeased> *released*, *<lenght> *length*. I have seen the latter as a persistent misspelling by one student, even in *<lenghten>. In these examples the letters in error are a well-formed string such as <ea>, <ph>, <kh>,<th>. An example of later misplacing, rather than anticipation, is the *Observer* (10/2/91) headline: 'Major dampens hopes of *"kakhi" election'. This is all the more surprising since *khaki* is highlighted in citation marks as new jargon.

Slips in typing are more complex, because we need to discount mere off-target fingering on the keyboard: *<holixay> for *holiday*. What to regard as a slip is not always clear-cut. We might regard the <rr> of *<gorrilla> as a fingering slip, in anticipation of the doubled <ll> to come. On the other hand it could be a perfectly understandable confusion about when to double: cf. /ər/≡<orr> in *horrific*, and the variant spelling of *guer(r)illa*. Finding categories of unintentional performance errors is clearly not an easy task.

Lexical errors. Malapropisms

Not all mistakes in writing a string of letters are simple correspondence errors. A child who was asked to write about the eruption of a volcano, wrote: 'As the helicopter approached, they could see the *creator still smoking'. The string *<creator> is not simply a spelling error for *crater*: it is the right spelling of the wrong word. Simply to say that this contained the wrong correspondences /eɪ/≡<ea> and /ə/≡<or>, would be unhelpful. Similar confusions are: 'He wanted to marry a *devoiced woman' (for *divorced*); 'Cuts and *liaisons should be covered by a clean plaster' (for *lesions*). These are **lexical errors** involving confusion between similar sounding morphemes or words. In literature this kind of error may be used for comic effect as a **malapropism** – so-called after the character Mrs Malaprop in Sheridan's *The Rivals*: 'She's as headstrong as an *allegory on the banks of the Nile'. As a comic device for making fun of the uneducated, it is as old as literature itself. In a play the misfit words have to be spoken as such. When the confusion occurs simply as a child's spelling error, it may simply be a chance confusion of shape, an unthinking visual mix-up between words which the child knows very well. This would presumably be the case with children's errors such as *<changed> for *chased*, *<frighting> for *fighting*. On the other hand, the examples of Black English spelling mistakes given on pp. 61f show that there may be an underlying phonological problem due to the child's accent: this would explain *<brave> for *brother*, *<rise> for *rest*, *<hole> for *hold*, *<when> for *win*, *<wilds> for *wildest*, etc.

When the same kind of error occurs with adults, it may reflect a real confusion over relatively unfamiliar words. Student errors I have noted include writing the name of the sound [ə] as <choix> instead of *schwa*, or to confess that 'teaching was not her *meteor' (for *metier*). Perhaps 'the *anus of proof' was just bad handwriting. We could perhaps include here a restaurant's spelling of the trade name *Nescafé* as *<Nescoffee>.

It is worth distinguishing phonetic near-misses like these from instances where the two words are pure homophones in the speaker's accent and the difference is accordingly a simple correspondence error: 'his *unwaivering support', 'the *course fishing season', or 'the soft *palette is lowered in nasal consonants'. These, too, are spellings of a different word. Misunderstanding of a metaphor is probably responsible for: 'he handed over the *reigns of his business empire to his son'. Medical structures resembling a cord were often spelt with <ch> up to the middle of the nineteenth century as in Latin *chorda*; the modern spelling is <cord>. However, the spelling *<vocal chords> is still seen occasionally, presumably because of the association of voice and musical 'chords'. There seems to be no temptation to write *umbilical *chord*. Also common are 'a *discreet item' for *discrete* and.'in *complimentary distribution' for *complementary*.

This type of confusion may involve a homophonous word element, such as an affix or stem, rather than the whole word. A surprisingly frequent error in student scripts is: 'the *proceeding letter' instead of *preceding*. These are presumably people for whom *proceed* and *precede* are homophones /prə'siːd/, rather than differing by /prə-/ – /prɪ-/. The suffixes <-ant> and <-ent> are frequently confused (**consonent*, **turbulant*); <effect> and <affect> often show prefix confusion (*the *affect was*, *it *effects me*). Consider also: '. . . change which can raise the oppressed from the *affrontery of economic capitalism' (*Guardian* 25/3/91:17). This represents a quite natural confusion between 'to affront' (= 'to shamelessly offend') and 'effrontery' (= 'shameless boldness'). Similar instances, but without any semantic link, are *<descriminate> for *discriminate*, by analogy with *description*, and *<desperse> for *disperse* on the pattern of *despise*. In some instances the error may show an unawareness of some aspect of word structure: *<genious> for *genius*, probably triggered by *ingenious*, is a wrong use of an adjectival suffix; *<neutrilization> may be influenced by *sterilization*; *<occour> for *occur* has an ending usually associated with nouns; similarly *stationary* has an ending typical of adjectives (but cf. *legionary*), and *stationery* has a common noun ending. §Latinate affixes are often misspelt even when there are such indicators to fall back on. Should *correlate* be <cor>+<relate> or *<co>+<relate>? Here the difference between the vowels /ɒ/ – /əʊ/ is marked by the single/double consonant letter and the writing system can bring in a hyphen to underpin the difference (*co-respondent* v. *correspondent*), but this does not prevent the error *<corelate>.

Analogy errors. Jumbling. Splits

Errors which involve confusion between elements of word structure often appear to be **analogy errors**. For instance, *<apostrophy> for *apostrophe* may be a false analogy with *atrophy*, *trophy*, instead of *catastrophe*. Uncertainty about word structure can result in **jumbling**: 'They were *unindated with replies'.

Spelling errors, as such, violate some spelling rule. So, *<feild> for *field* violates the well-known graphotactic rule about the ordering of <i> and <e> as a spelling of /iː/. 'Rule' in this sense does not imply generality: *<lesure> for *leisure* violates a very marginal correspondence rule. Occasionally there are subsystem mistakes: *feasible* is a fairly technical word and, perhaps for that reason, attracts the spelling *<pheasible>.

Mistakenly putting a space boundary in what should be written as a single word can be called a **split**: *<to gether>, *<out side>, *<be fore>, *<in tact>. Very subtle differences of stress and phrase structure need to be observed: 'we went on to a night club' and 'we went onto a yacht'; 'we drove in to the centre' and 'we drove into the hedge'; 'I don't want any more jam' and 'she doesn't go there anymore'. The writing system is sometimes inconsistent, requiring, for instance, *already* but *all right*. Why is *<alright> so stigmatized? Where does the authority come from for statements such as: 'The words should always be written separate' (Fowler 1926:16 on *all right*). The very force of this injunction implies that people persist in following a natural analogy. Forty years later in the 2nd edition, it is suggested that the prejudice against *alright* is a 'recognition of the colloquial levity of the phrase' (Fowler 1965: 18). Writing things down is evidently a serious business.

Articulation or interference errors

A large number of spelling errors are traceable to the particular pronunciation used by the speller. Spellers may forget that the spelling is based on a 'lento' or isolate form of the word. Indeed, an allegro form may be the norm for their particular accent. The processes common in 'allegro' forms, such as consonant cluster simplification, smoothing of two adjacent vowels, elision of /ə/, will produce misspellings such as: *<bankrupcy> *bankruptcy*, *<pumkin> *pumpkin*, *<strick> *strict*, *<reconise> *recognize*, *<goverment> *government*, *<distingtion> *distinction*, *<boundry> *boundary* (cf. *foundry*), *<litrature> *literature*, *<schwar> *schwa* (with 'intrusive' <r>), *<emnity> *enmity* (a common metathesis), *<pome> *poem*, *<vacume> *vacuum*. These are sometimes referred to as **articulation errors** (Sterling 1983). This may, however, give the impression that an allegro pronunciation such as /'baʊndrɪ/ is itself an 'error'. A better term would be **interference errors**. This would also cover spelling errors due to the accent of the speaker. These have already been discussed under dialect in §2.7 (see pp. 53ff.).

A similar type of error is made by foreign learners, due to interference from the phonological system or from the writing system of their native language. Chinese speakers have difficulty in pronouncing final consonant clusters, so they are likely to write '*the vowels *produce by* . . .', or '. . . *can still be *perceive as* . . .', even when their knowledge of grammar should alert them to a further consonant /t/ or /d/, representing the suffix {-ed}. An example of interference from another writing system is *<hot ntoks> in a Greek restaurant for *hot dogs*. In Modern Greek, [d] is spelt <ντ> (<nt>). The *<k>, on the other hand, is from an assimilation of the plosive to an assumed /s/.

When English is learnt by foreigners orally as a second language used in their community (ESL), there is some evidence that they learn word shapes as whole units, as unpredictable strings of graphemes. They do not appear to develop detailed strategies that might include phoneme-grapheme correspondences. Lester (1964) tested a group of native speakers and a group of ESL speakers for misspellings in words of four different categories based on differences in text frequency and differences in the regularity of the spelling:

1 High frequency High regularity (cat, paper)
2 Low frequency Low regularity (tsetse, ghoul)
3 Low frequency High regularity (fen, yak)
4 High frequency Low regularity (of, one).

The results showed that, for ESL speakers, words in group (3) proved more error-prone than words in group (4). The reverse was true for native speakers. This would imply that native speakers might be more able to exploit sound–spelling correspondences.

Brown, H.D. (1970) ran a similar test, but with different words. He found that both the ESL group and the native speakers performed better on high frequency words. There is clearly scope for more research here. The design of the test is critical. *Yak* is a regular spelling only if one recognizes that it is non-§Basic – cf. *back*. Moreover the tests did not ascertain whether the low frequency words had ever been encountered by the subjects. *Ptomaine*, *rhizome* and *palimpsest* had probably not. But the native subjects may well have come across *saccharin* or even *masochist*.

Adaptation rules are frequently not observed. The doubling of a final <r> in a stressed syllable before a vowel-initial suffix often fails, giving *<occured>, *<occurence>. Final <-e> deletion before a vowel causes problems. One reason may be that before <-able> the accepted spelling varies unpredictably: in *OED* both *statable/stateable* are given, but not *<salable> or *<noteable>.

Single errors can usually be classified in an informative way. Sometimes, however, errors pile up on each other, so that it is difficult to imagine what misunderstandings interacted to produce the result. Take for instance *<inaddecatesea> as a spelling of *inadequacy*. There seems to be an association with *inadequate*, but then a despairing resort to §Basic correspondences such as <ea>≡/iː/ in a §Latinate word and an unfamiliarity with noun-forming <-cy> (*immediate – immediacy*). This seems to indicate that the spelling of §Latinate words might usefully be taught by practising paradigms of word formation.

2.8.5 'Phoneme–grapheme correspondences as cues to spelling improvement' (Hanna *et al.* 1966)

The Hanna speech-to-text algorithm

When digital computers first became available in the 1960s as a research tool in the humanities, they were seized on gratefully by those concerned with literacy problems. Controversy was then rife over whether children should be taught to read by 'phonic' methods, in which spelling rules played an important role, or by 'look and say' methods in which a pupil learnt to recognize a word by remembering its overall shape without worrying about sound-to-spelling correspondences. Computers offered an opportunity to set out the facts of the case. Apart from the statistical chore of plotting the deployment of spelling correspondences, a computer can also model systems of spelling rules to see what information is needed as input for the speller and test the efficiency of individual rules. But given that you want to relate speech to writing, computer algorithms can operate in each direction, either modelling writing (speech-to-text) or reading (text-to-speech).

In 1963, the US Office of Education launched 'a massive attack' on the problem by setting up a large-scale funded research project at Stanford University (Hanna *et al.* 1966). The title of the report asserts its educational purpose: *Phoneme–grapheme correspondences as cues to spelling improvement*. Phase I of this project analysed a database consisting of 17,000 words from the Thorndike and Lorge database plus a further 2,000 words from the addenda to the second edition of *Merriam–Webster's New International*

Dictionary (*W2NID*) and produced statistical counts of spelling correspondences and information about the contexts in which different spellings occurred. On the basis of this information, Phase II involved writing an algorithm to spell all the words in the database, using as input only their pronunciation as a string of surface phonemes. The summary result was that 90 per cent of the correspondences made by the program were correct and 50 per cent of the words in the database were spelt wholly correctly.

The 50 per cent regularity rating for English spelling has been quoted time and again ever since the report appeared. It has been accepted without question as being factually 'right'. This 50 per cent result is not only easily memorable, but it achieved a certain notoriety when Simon and Simon (1973: 127) pointed out that a class of 4th grade children performed much better than the Hanna algorithm in spelling a selected list of 268 words. They maintained that the rules of the Hanna algorithm could not conceivably help the children and even that: 'at more advanced levels, consistent use of the algorithm would *degrade* the spelling of all but the poorest human spellers'.

This is rather damning criticism and, ever since then, the 50 per cent Hanna result has usually been presented in the literature along with the Simon and Simon criticism. It certainly makes good copy: little kids beat giant computer. The academic impact of this critique was to reinforce the arguments of those who claim that the regularities of the English spelling system are too meagre to warrant serious consideration in, for example, the teaching of reading. The sheer quotability of the 50 per cent result coupled with the demoralising Simon and Simon claim has also meant that the Hanna project, in escaping serious consideration, has also escaped detailed evaluation.

Spelling rules based on the 'syllable'

One prior assumption of the Hanna approach is that spelling rules in English need to operate largely with syllables and syllable boundaries. Whether this syllable-based approach is necessary or productive is not discussed, yet any acceptance of Hanna's statistics is ultimately based on the validity of these syllable-based rules. The Hanna rules are rarely referred to, so I have quoted them below in §3.3 at the end of each phoneme subsection. In trying them out, one should remember that 'initial', 'medial' and 'final' refer to positions in the syllable.

The syllable boundaries in the Hanna algorithm are not worked out from any general principles by the computer. They are given as part of the data. They represent printing-house conventions for splitting up a word at the end of a line of text (see §2.8.3 pp. 76ff.). A set of such conventions is given in the introduction to the 2nd edition of *Merriam–Webster's New International Dictionary* (*W2NID*), which was used as Hanna's ultimate source of phonetic data. The word *trigonometry*, for instance, is split into graphic 'syllables' by Hanna (ibid.: 48) like this: <trig-o-nom-e-try>. A printer using these boundaries as a guide would presumably allow hyphenation at the end of a line as <trig-onometry>, <trigo-nometry>, <trigonom-etry> or perhaps <trigonome-try>, but not as <trigono-metry>.

The problem for any theory of the syllable is how to allocate intervocalic consonants, the consonants which lie between the syllable peaks. Where do you draw the boundary? Hanna's guidelines for chopping words up, deduced from the examples in the book, seem to be:

1 an intervocalic consonant after a stressed short vowel closes the previous syllable: *bos-om*, *rap-id*, *rec-i-pe*, *sep-a-rate*;
2 an intervocalic consonant after a stressed long vowel goes with the following syllable: *re-gion*, *va-can-cy*, *ro-sette*, *si-ren*;
3 an intervocalic consonant after an unstressed vowel goes with a following syllable: *a-dorn*, *re-venge*, *sa-tan-ic*, *hi-lar-i-ty*;
4 intervocalic clusters are usually split evenly: *neg-lect*, *sus-pect*, *phan-tom*, *lun-cheon*, *lam-poon*;
5 morpheme boundaries are usually allowed to override these divisions: *speak-er*, *beat-er*, *tank-ard*, *greas-y*, *pro-pos-al*, *pleas-ing*, *coat-ing*, etc. (but sometimes not: *spor-tive*, *cra-zy*, *thrif-ty*, etc.)

The purpose of these conventions is simply to indicate where a word might be split up at the end of a line of justified print. See §2.8.3 (pp. 76ff.) for a fuller discussion. Usually this does correspond to a phonetic syllable boundary. Allowing a morpheme boundary to override a syllable boundary can, however, cause hiccups in the spelling rules. This can be seen in the spelling of *beater* and *beaver*. Because of the morpheme boundary after the /t/, the /iː/ in *beater* is 'medial' and *beater* is spelt correctly. The /iː/ in *beaver* is 'final' before a 'syllable' boundary and the word would be spelt *<bever>.

Spelling pronunciations as a mnemonic device

Some traditional methods of teaching spelling do require pupils to 'syllabify' words in order to find the right correspondences. What actually happens when this is done is rather obscure. It seems to be that in the process the pupil is taught a spelling pronunciation of the word, from which a correct spelling follows naturally. For instance if /ə/ in *accountant* is to be spelt correctly the pupil may be taught to 'syllabify' it as /æ/-/kaʊn/-/tænt/. Such a pronunciation is never found in real speech, but given the stress placement and vowel reduction, /əˈkaʊntənt/ follows naturally enough. Taken a step further, this may even open the way to teaching */bɒm/-/bɪŋ/ for *bombing*. Spelling pronunciations may be fostered as a method of teaching literacy. We may quote one traditional training manual (Hook

1976). It devotes several sections to 'faulty pronunciation'. It 'teaches you to hear and say the word in a standard way in order to see and write it in standard spelling' (ibid.: vii). For *describe*, *destroy*, the instructions are: 'say to yourself *de scribe*, *de stroy*. Say the *de* very strongly' (ibid.: 64), that is with /iː/ rather than the usual /ɪ/. Again, '*bargain* may be associated with *entertain* and the like, even though the *ain* in it is less distinctly pronounced' (ibid.: 171). Similarly, *literature* and *miniature* are taught as having five [*sic*] syllables: 'pronounce *lit er a ture* and *min i a ture*, being careful not to omit any syllables' (ibid.: 54). There seems to be more justification for this teaching method than for the use of purely arbitrary memory associations, such as expecting pupils to remember that *occurrence*, *goddess*, *possess*, *committee*, *balloon* are a group of words which have two sets each of doubled letters (ibid.: 106f.).

But is it necessary or desirable to teach special spelling pronunciations? Do we need to specify contexts in terms of graphic-based 'syllables' in writing spelling rules? If 'syllables' could form the basis of a reasonable description of spelling conventions, could the notion of 'syllable' be worked into classroom practice with any efficiency? These are left as open questions. But there is no doubt that few people, when presented with one of the Hanna rules where 'initial' and 'final' refer to 'syllables', can easily work out what words would be covered by it. More significantly, the computer which processed the spelling rules did not itself decide by following some strategy where these boundaries were. The boundaries were given in the input data. Hence the algorithm is hardly a true model of spelling competence, since we do not know whether a human speller can know and use these boundaries. But leaving that aside, do the results represent an accurate picture?

Is English spelling '50 per cent regular'?

The well-publicized 50 per cent success rate of the Hanna algorithm can soon be seen, after even a cursory examination of the records, to be in some doubt. It both understates and overstates the case. We must, of course, remember that this was a relatively early computer project and the team of authors, using commercial computer programmers, must have found liaison rather difficult. It is important to bear these difficulties in mind.

The case for understatement: is it better than 50 per cent?

We can consider first the extent to which the 50 per cent result is an understatement. In their later comments on the project, the Hanna team rightly claimed that the 50 per cent result could easily be improved by refining the algorithm, especially by taking morphology into account. But, even on its own terms of straightforward sound-to-spelling correspondences, the Hanna algorithm is not efficient. Take two of the basic devices of English spelling: <C>-doubling to mark a previous short vowel (cf. *holly*, *holy*) and <e>-marking of long vowels (cf. *mat*, *mate*). These two devices are not dealt with by general rules, but are lost sight of among the detailed rules for individual phonemes where they are not fully and consistently implemented. A large number of words are spelt wrongly because of failure to double a consonant letter:

> *<hoby>, *<rufle>, *<coma>, *<blacen>, *<holy>, *<tater>, *<funel>, *<super>, *<squirel>, *<mosy>, etc. – for *hobby*, *ruffle*, *comma*, *blacken*, *holly*, *tatter*, *funnel*, *supper*, *squirrel*, *mossy*, etc.

The restricted scope and uneven effect of the Hanna rules for <C>-doubling can easily be seen simply by listing them to demonstrate the variability of context:

/p/≡<pp> after a short vowel before syllabic /l/.
/b/≡<bb> final accented before syllabic /l/.
/t/≡<tt> after a short vowel before syllabic /l/.
/d/≡<dd> accented after a short vowel before syllabic /l/.
/k/≡<ck> i) after a short vowel word-final accented; ii) before syllabic /l/.
/g/≡<gg> final before syllabic /l/.
/ʧ/≡<tch> final after a short vowel.
/ʤ/≡<dge> after a short vowel word-final accented.
/m/≡<mm> (no rule given).
/n/≡<nn> (no rule given).
/f/≡<ff> after a short vowel or /ɔː/ word-final.
/s/≡<ss> i) word-final accented after /æ, e, ɒ, ʌ/; ii) after /e/ word-final unaccented.
/z/≡<zz> final before syllabic /l/.
/l/≡<ll> after a short vowel or /ɔː/ word-final accented.
/r/≡<rr> (no rule given).

The gaps in this coverage are fairly obvious. Most of the above categories only represent a single context. The sole context for <pp> is: after a short vowel before syllabic /l/. This gives *apple* correctly, but does not cater for *approve*, *copper*, *happen*, etc., which get single <p> by default. Double <mm>, <nn> and <rr> are not dealt with at all. It is easy enough to find other exceptions to these rules and, conversely, very difficult to understand why they vary so much from consonant to consonant. There is little attempt to generalize.

The percentage success rate of the doubling rules seems to be reasonably good from the figures quoted in Appendix G of the report. For instance, of 23 instances of <bb> to which the rule applies, 18 are correctly dealt with, that is 78 per cent. But a quick trawl through Hanna's database shows a further 44 instances of <bb> to which the doubling rule as given does not apply, so the predictability of getting <bb> spelt correctly by the algorithm is actually 27 per cent. This difference between the quoted efficiency of the doubling rules as they stand and their actual predictive performance is found with other phonemes. A check on the Hanna database reveals discrepancies of the order shown below in table 8.

Table 8 Predictability of doubled consonant letters in Hanna's rules

	Actual	*Claimed*		*Actual*	*Claimed*
<bb>	27%	(78%)	<ll>	26%	(75%)
<ck>	43%	(78%)	<pp>	6%	(75%)
<dd>	25%	(86%)	<ss>	44%	(95%)
<dg(e)>	55%	(94%)	<tch>	65%	(66%)
<ff>	20%	(62%)	<tt>	11%	(85%)
<gg>	22%	(100%)	<zz>	52%	(100%)

The claimed performance figures represent what the Hanna rules get right. The actual performance figures include what the Hanna rules overlooked. Neither figure is a true index of what the predictability of <C>-doubling would be if given better rules. Since <mm>, <nn>, <rr> were not catered for in any rules, their predictability for Hanna is an irrelevant 0 per cent. One important factor in these results is that those doubled spellings which are associated with §Latinate prefixes (e.g. <pp> in *apposite* as well as *hopper*) come out worse in the Hanna rules.

Another general fault in the performance of the Hanna algorithm is the large number of words in which the <e>-marking of a long vowel is not deleted before a vowel-initial suffix:

> *<aleien>, *<aleienate>, *<antiquateed>, *<baseal>, *<baseic>, *<belateed>, *<braveery>, *<debateable>, *<crusadeer>, *<craveing>, etc.

There are also instances where the <e> is wrongly deleted before a consonant at a morpheme boundary:

> *<confinment>, *<liflike>, *<firfly>, *<timly>, *<refinment>, *<firplace>, *<sidlong>, etc.

Some words which are wrongly spelt contain impossible letter strings, indicating that contextual variation was not properly accounted for and exploited:

> *<elc> for else; *<droc> for dross; * <exxama> for eczema; *<butec> for buttock; *<goosy> for juicy; *<goonier> for junior.

These predicted spellings ignore: i) <x> never doubles; ii) the correspondence /s/≡<c> is not found in word-final position; iii) <ec> is rarely found as a final unstressed ending; iv) <g> before <o> cannot represent /ʤ/. Similar examples which show that morpheme boundaries are not properly taken into account are:

<bacuard> for backward;<tianeal> for chenille;*<tialack> for shellac.

Of course there comes a time for anyone engaged in the tedious task of writing such an algorithm when the law of diminishing returns begins to bite. Any algorithm which claims complete success will either have a look-up table of irregular items or a large number of nonce rules. However, most of the above errors are more general and could have been catered for by rule within the framework of the Hanna algorithm. Putting right the lapses in <C>-doubling and <e>-marking, on a rough-and-ready calculation, would alone boost the overall number of correct spellings from 50 per cent to somewhere close to 60 per cent.

The case for overstatement: is it worse than 50 per cent?

Let us now consider the case for overstatement of the results. The evidence is rather tucked away. If we look at the list of words spelt successfully by the algorithm, we find an unrealistically efficient spelling of /ə/ in unstressed syllables. The algorithm appears to distinguish the unstressed endings in the following in spite of the spelling variation:

/-ɪənt/ in *miscre**ant**–luxuri**ant**–nutri**ent***;
/-ərɪ/ in *mast**ery**–merc**ury**–gran**ary**–hist**ory***;
/-ənt/ in *pend**ant**–pend**ent***;
/-əl/ in *candl**e**–scand**al**, avow**al**–vow**el***;
/-əns/ in *avoid**ance**–depend**ence***;
/-ɪəs/ in *aqu**eous**–impecun**ious***;
/-ɪəl/ in *ether**eal**–imper**ial***;
/-ʧər/ in *pic**ture**–pit**cher***.

If the above words were correctly spelt, what was the input? Certainly not a string of surface phonemes. Nor was it intentionally in any way a morphophonemic input. The so-called phonemic transcription derives ultimately from *W2NID* (1957). The much-revised 3rd edition of the dictionary (*W3NID* of 1961) was available and is included in their bibliography, but they did not use it as data. Without going into too much detail, we can easily focus on the source of error. This *W2NID* transcription only showed normal vowel reduction very sparingly. The dictionary-makers were shy of using /ə/ to represent an unstressed vowel. They provided a superfluity of symbols for /ə/ which are evidently designed as an educational device to associate with the variation in spelling. The 3rd edition of the dictionary, on the other hand, has completely revised such transcriptions and represents /ə/ consistently. The old *W2NID* transcription, with no less than 32 different vowel symbols, was taken over by the Hanna team. They reduced these 32 symbols to 22 by cutting out variations due to lower-than-primary degrees of stress. For instance they merged the different symbols provided for the first vowel in *chaos* and the first vowel in *chaotic*. These were a longer (stressed) and a shorter (unstressed) allophone of the same phoneme /eɪ/. They sum up their changes as follows:

> Long and short vowel phonemes are retained and their allophonic variations are assigned to them. In addition all weakened forms of vowel phonemes were grouped together to comprise the vowel phoneme /ə/ (ibid.: 20).

Whatever this wording may mean, it did not mean that vowel reduction was correctly represented in the data, even for slow formal pronunciation. Many polysyllabic words in their phonetic transcription have no reduced vowels at all, for example:

accountant, refusal, epistemology, caravan.

The input transcription was equivalent to:

/æˈkaʊntænt/, /riːˈfjuːzæl/, /iːpɪstiːˈmɒləʊʤɪ/, /ˈkæræværn/.

As here, unstressed suffixes such as <-ant>, <-al>, and unstressed prefixes such as the <ac-> of *accountant* were given a full vowel /æ/. These are forms which no-one ever says, strings of phonemes that never appear on the surface. It is for this reason that the algorithm, using differing phonetic inputs for the weak vowels, was able to spell correctly the pairs such as *pendant* – *pendent* listed above. In each of these word-pairs one instance of /ə/ was transcribed as /ə/, the other was transcribed as a full vowel appropriate to the spelling. Many other common unstressed endings were processed with full vowel quality input showing no reduction to /ə/:

*<-ed>≡/ed/ – *hooded*, *jagged*, *rugged*, *wicked*, etc.;
*<-el>≡/el/ – *enamel* (but *camel* with /ə/);
*<-en>≡/en/ – *chicken*;
*<-es>≡/ez/ – *riches*, *breeches*;
*<-et>≡/et/ – *jacket*, *rocket*, *thicket*, *wicket*, etc.;
*<-ment>≡/ment/ – *embarrassment*, *establishment*, etc.

This treatment of vowel reduction played a very important part in pushing the success rate up to 50 per cent.

The *W2NID* transcription which was fed into the Hanna algorithm is a perfectly valid transcription if you wish to link the stressed realization of a vowel and its unstressed realizations with vowel reduction. The stressed unreduced vowel has to be the underlying form. You can get a fast pronunciation of *Margate* with /ɪ/ from a formal pronunciation with /eɪ/, but as Robert Bridges (1919: 47) pointed out, you cannot do it the other way round. There is an unstressed /ɪ/ which relates to /eɪ/ as in *Margate* and an unstressed /ɪ/ that may only vary by further reduction to /ə/, as in *merit*. Bridges takes Daniel Jones to task for treating the unstressed [ɪ] of *Margate* and *merit* and the stressed [ɪ] of *mirror* as the same phoneme /ɪ/. He calls attention to 'the low standard of pronunciation adopted by our professional phoneticians, and to the falsity of their orthodox teaching' and also to 'the necessity of observing vowel distinctions in unaccented syllables'. Insistence on a purely phonetic transcription:

> has led [Mr. Jones] to assert and teach that an unaccented vowel in English retains no trace of its proper quality . . . and one of his examples, which he advances with the confidence of complete satisfaction, is the name *Margate*,which he asserts is pronounced *Margit*, that is, with a short *i*. The vowel is no doubt short . . . but it is not a short *i*, it is an extremely hastened and therefore disguised form of the original and proper diphthong *ei* (heard in *bait* and *gate*); and the true way to write it phonetically would be *ei*, with some diacritical sign to show that it was obscured. . . . In the second syllable of *Margate* the diphthong is hastened and obscured, but a trace of its quality remains, and will more distinctly appear as you speak the word slower. . . . Mr. Jones introduces the symbol of an *alien unrelated* sound, a sound, that is, which is *distinctly wrong instead of being indistinctly right*: and this fault vitiates all his books. Economy of symbols has led him to perversity of pronunciation.
>
> (ibid.: 43 – Bridges' own italics).

Bridges is wrong, of course, in maintaining that a reduced /eɪ/ always retains some feature which keeps it phonetically different from /ɪ/.

The problem with the data processed by the Hanna algorithm is the converse of this. All reduced vowels were supposedly represented by /ə/, but that was manifestly and significantly not true.

It is very difficult to gauge the overall effect of these peculiarities of the Hanna rules and of their input data. Perhaps all one can say with any certainty is that, taking into account both the overstatement and the understatement in the Hanna algorithm, their 50 per cent success rate of correctly spelt words is probably too generous **for the rules as they stand** rather than, as they claim, an understatement. As for the rules themselves, they are not independent of the 'syllable' boundaries which were provided as part of the input data and they have been lost sight of. What is abundantly clear is that any statistics derived from the Hanna algorithm should be treated with care. They should certainly not be taken, as they have often been, as a sufficiently valid index of the regularity of English spelling.

An unjustified counterclaim? Simon and Simon (1973)

A brief mention must be made of the relevance of the Simon and Simon

(1973) article to all this, partly because they have another type of spelling algorithm to suggest and partly because they propagate further errors by assuming that the Hanna algorithm was an accurate reflection of phonological regularity. This last point is rather subtle so we shall consider it first.

Simon and Simon consider the possibility of whether the Hanna rules, based on surface phonemes, were the right rules. They point out that Chomsky and Halle (1968) have suggested that English spelling often reflects an underlying phonological structure, not always a surface structure. In other words English spelling is often morphophonemic. Those words in their list of 268 that were misspelt by the Hanna algorithm could, in most cases, be spelt correctly by paying attention to morphophonemics. 'We conclude that the Chomsky proposal might have some use in building a spelling program, but probably can play only a quite **minor** role' (ibid.: 127). This is in reality a very doubtful conclusion because it is based on words that Hanna spells **wrongly**. The presupposition is that words spelt correctly by the Hanna algorithm are spelt correctly by **surface** regularities alone. But, as we have just seen, a great many reduced vowels were coded in a manner which pre-determined the spelling. Not by design, but by being overlooked, these vowels were given a quasi-morphophonemic transcription uncannily like the underlying forms used by Chomsky and Halle. The correct spelling of reduced vowels by the Hanna algorithm largely depended on such forms. Consequently, Simon and Simon have no firm basis for dismissing an approach based on the work of Chomsky and Halle. The error data from the Hanna algorithm cannot really be used as evidence for this. Hanna was far closer to Chomsky and Halle than Simon and Simon knew. This is such stuff as myths are made on.

A futuristic algorithm for 'word recognition'

A second aspect of the Simon and Simon article is worth noting. They themselves propose a spelling algorithm of a different kind by anticipating a few leaps in suitable technology. The Hanna algorithm is a simple deterministic algorithm – it produces a spelling which is right or wrong. But algorithms do not have to be deterministic to be useful. The computer facilities which doctors will supposedly have in their surgeries in the near future, so-called 'expert systems', will presumably be much more flexible. They will narrow down the list of possible ailments which could produce the given symptoms and provide the doctor with a best-bet diagnosis. In other words the algorithm will give a narrowed-down choice with probability ratings, rather than a definitive answer. The futuristic algorithm sketched out by the Simons would use phonetic information to provide a set of possible spellings. Then the speller's experience would provide some 'word recognition information' which would select the correct spelling. This is 'information stored in memory that enables a reader to recognize a word when it is presented to him visually'. Such information gradually accumulates with experience and is available indirectly to help a reader to spell. Simon and Simon only discuss how this might work for a couple of example words. One is the word *knowledge.* Here the memory of an initial <kn-> or a final <-dge> would help to reject spellings <no-> or <-age> and select from the list of possible phonetic spellings the right one. This is a radically different approach in that they would be asking the computer to behave like a human speller learning by experience – a performance model. No doubt the current wave of activity in artificial intelligence will eventually make it possible to write such programs, but it is not yet reality.

2.9 SPELLING SUBSYSTEMS AND LITERACY

2.9.1 Native and foreign

English spelling as a system of subsystems

Sooner or later it should dawn on the more successful schoolchild trying to spell English that different spelling rules apply to different sectors of vocabulary: that in foreign/learned words there are correspondences such as /f/≡<ph> in *philosophy* (not *<filosofy>) which are not found in basic vocabulary and, conversely, there are correspondences peculiar to basic everyday words such as /k/≡<ck> in *mock* (not *<moque> or *<mok> or *<moc>). Indeed the same string of sounds can have different spellings depending on which sector of vocabulary the word falls into: *fisher–fissure*, *carrot–carat*, *cash–cache*, *shoot–chute*, *ark–arc*, *peak–pique*, *jellied–gelid*, *root–route*, *meddle–medal*, *mussel–muscle*. It is not just that these spellings have different correspondences. That would be equally true of pairs such as *meat–meet*, *doe–dough*, *wait–weight*. The different correspondences in the *fisher–fissure* pairs may associate with different potential patterns of word-formation, different phonological patterns and, less explicably, with different semantic fields and different ranges of experience. If you want to make a colloquial form of the word *lunatic*, you respell it as *looney* or *loony* rather than **luny*.

If the writing system is viewed as a single system, these differences can only appear as irregularity, or, to be more precise, as 'plurality of symbolization' (Albrow 1972: 14). A polysystemic analysis reduces this apparent irregularity by showing that some alternative spellings are peculiar to, and conditioned by, membership of different sectors of vocabulary. The spelling varies, but the variants are conditioned and subject to rule.

The National Curriculum in England and Wales recognizes various levels of spelling ability. At the higher levels pupils should be aware of the various subsystems in English spelling. They should be able to:

> spell (and understand the meaning of) common roots that have been borrowed from other languages and that play an important role in word-building, e.g. *micro-*, *psych-*, *tele-*, *therm-*. Recognize that where words have been borrowed in the last 400 years, there are some characteristic sound-symbol relationships that reflect the word's origin, e.g. ch- in words like *champagne*, *chauffeur*, *charade*, and *ch-* in Greek words like *chaos*, *chiropody*, *chorus*, compared with *ch-* in long-established English words like *chaff*, *cheese*, *chin*.
>
> (Cox 1989 17.37 level 7)

2.9.2 Subsystem markers

Albrow's (1972) three-system model

Albrow (1972) is the only linguist to have explored in any detail the various subsystems of English orthography. He describes three principal subsystems. System 1 is the 'basic' ('English') system. System 2 largely comprises 'Romance' spellings and the foreign/learned part of the lexicon. System 3 is only sketched briefly as a possible system of more exotic 'non-English' spellings. Labels such as 'English', 'Romance', 'Greek' and 'foreign' used descriptively within the present writing system are only convenient identifiers of recognizable sets of words and spellings. They do not refer absolutely to the origin of a given word but merely indicate that certain conventions tend to be found in words of such origin. Whether their origin is marked by some means which the speller can recognize is another matter. Albrow's 'system 1' and 'system 2' have the merit of being neutral terms. However, it is not words as such which have system membership in Albrow's description:

> It has been suggested to me that it is not symbols which belong to systems, but words; thus a word like *cake* would be in system 1, *philosophy* system 2. I had considered this, and I have thought about it again, but it would not, I think, be practicable. For example, *mice* would be a system 2 word since it has <ce>, which I have assigned to system 2. We now have <m>, <i-e> in system 2 as well as in system 1, and this sort of thing would proliferate until most system 1 symbols were duplicated in system 2 and any distinction would become obliterated – <a>, <n> of *anchor* and *language*, <l> of *language* and *school*, <s>, <oo> of *school* are cases in point. I therefore reject this approach in favour of the one I have adopted, though I would loosely term items containing system 2 symbols system 2 items, and have done so.
>
> (ibid.: 45)

So in his view it is **correspondences** which belong to systems, rather than **words** (or perhaps **morphemes**). A particular word may have correspondences from both systems: '*grant*, *minute* . . . have some consonants of system 1, but vowels of system 2, *mice* has <ce> of system 2, <m>, <i-e> of system 1. *mouse* is entirely system 1' (ibid.: 34).

The advantage of Albrow's stated view is that it allows considerable freedom in description, since there are very few interlocking constraints on how the subsystems operate. This very freedom, however, carries a penalty. The two main subsystems as sketched by Albrow would be difficult to describe explicitly as part of a speaker's competence in handling English orthography. It is difficult to explain the basis on which a writer would make an informed choice of a particular spelling if words may contain a mixture of system 1 and system 2 correspondences.

If there are two principal subsystems in English orthography which literate speakers exploit as part of their competence, we should expect these orthographic subsystems to be connected with other aspects of English structure, particularly with phonology and word-formation. If we only consider individual correspondences to be the units of operation, it is difficult to make such connections. Take the correspondence /s/≡<c>, which came into use with French loan-words and spread from them into native English words such as *ice*. Albrow, not surprisingly, makes it a system 2 correspondence. However, the only way to spell /aɪs/ in an English monosyllable (apart from exotica such as *gneiss*) is as <ice>; <s> cannot be deployed here since <ise> is a regular spelling of /aɪz/. So, if the correspondence <c>≡/s/ is to be restricted to system 2, we are saying that words containing /aɪs/ cannot be wholly spelt by the 'basic' correspondences of system 1; they must also involve system 2. Yet words such as *mice*, *nice*, *twice*, *ice* do not share the word-formation potential of words in which System 2 conventions usually operate. Nor in terms of the phonology of modern English is there anything 'non-basic' about such monosyllables. Presumably Albrow wishes to indicate that, in a more consistent system, *mice* would be spelt **mise* and *rise* would be spelt **rize*, but if this is his intention, it is not explicitly said.

A similar difficulty in linking the regularities of orthography with the regularities of phonology is found, for example, in the treatment of /ɑː/ (as a lengthening of the Middle English short vowel /a/) in *dance*, *path*, *grass*, etc. and the unchanged short vowel in *ample*, *mass*, etc. Albrow (ibid.: 34) appears to divide the resultant spelling correspondences across systems 1 and 2 as shown in table 9.

This does not make for an integrated description. The effect of the sound change was seemingly to put some system 1 correspondences into system 2 and some system 2 correspondences into system 1. It is difficult to see why *ample* and *cancer*, which have Latinate word formation (*amplify*, *cancerous*) should be associated with system 1 and why *lass* (a very ordinary Germanic word) should be associated with system 2.

The use of yet a third system as a convenient home for the more exotic

Table 9 Some examples of /ɑː/ and /æ/ in Albrow's subsystems

	Change	*No change*
Lengthening before nasal + C	<a>≡/ɑː/ *example, dance* SYSTEM 2	<a>≡/æ/ *ample, cancer* SYSTEM 1
Lengthening before fricative	<a>≡/ɑː/ *grass, master* SYSTEM 1	<a>≡/æ/ *lass, aster* SYSTEM 2

spelling correspondences brings further problems. Having three systems at one's disposal means that 'irregularity' may be largely done away with. For instance, the list of complex vowel symbols for system 2 (ibid.: 37) includes <eo>≡/iː/ (*people*) and <oo>≡/əʊ/ (*brooch*). Both these are nonce spellings, outside proper names. Admittedly *people* is Romance in origin and *brooch* may well be, but if <eo>≡/iː/ and <oo>≡/əʊ/ are nonce spellings and if there are no phonological or morphological reasons for putting them in system 2, it is difficult to see why they cannot equally well be in system 3, or purely by default in system 1, or, as nonce forms, in no system at all. This may also be true of minor correspondences, such as <ai>≡/æ/ in *plait*, *plaid*, which Albrow also puts in system 2. On the other hand, why is the correspondence <ch>≡/ʃ/ (*chevron*, *machine*), which is impeccably Romance in origin, in system 3 rather than system 2?

Albrow's suggestion that there is a system 3 of foreign correspondences outside the Romance system was not developed in any detail. We can easily find examples of spellings which suggest the need for such a third subsystem:

(1) <mock> (2) <baroque> (3) <amok>

where *amok* is neither native nor Romance, but is distinctly exotic. Yet even fairly common spellings which seem candidates for system 3 on the basis of non-Romance foreignness rarely lend themselves to systematic treatment, since there appear to be few explicit markers of system 3 membership to exploit other than an intuition that they are: 'small groups of items very obviously borrowed (in many cases quite recently) from various foreign sources' (ibid.: 43).

One advantage of having system 3 was to avoid plurality of correspondence in one of the other two systems. But to follow that through would allow a proliferation of small subsystems.

Albrow's criteria for system 3 membership only seem viable within a reading-oriented description. In an analysis which fits spellings to sounds, an equivalent to system 3 can only be set up as a dump for recurrent spellings not ascribable to systems 1 and 2. We cannot find positive phonological, grammatical, or semantic markers of the word *amok* that would shunt it into a third system. Of course, for the human speller, the word *amok* may have personal associations of non-Romance foreignness (rubber planters, Far East, excitable natives, Somerset Maugham, . . .), but these associations are not common property.

Observable markers

The treatment of subsystems adopted here is different in that it tries to cater more for the writer and speller and not just for the reader. That certainly does not mean that this approach will be more successful. Indeed, it will be much more restricted. It will be assumed that it is whole words (or in some cases, morphemes) that belong to subsystems, rather than individual phoneme-letter correspondences, and we shall try to find explicit phonological and grammatical markers that a human speller might exploit in recognising what sector of vocabulary a word belongs to. We shall not link competence in spelling to non-linguistic cultural or historical information, however striking, since this varies with the 'awareness' of the speller. This is perhaps paradoxical, since one of the design features of the English writing system is the extent to which it preserves such information. Types of awareness are discussed in §2.9.3 (pp. 102f.).

In talking about different sectors of vocabulary, people tend to use etymological labels. It is a small step from saying that '*chauffeur* comes from French' or '*synonym* comes (by way of Latin) from Greek', to saying '*chauffeur* is a French word' or '*synonym* is a Greek word'. But this second kind of statement is not merely absurd, it is unhelpful. You will find the letters <chauffeur> with a different pronunciation (as a string of French phonemes) and a very different range of meanings in French: it includes the meaning 'stoker'. We are referring to an English word pronounced /ˈʃəʊfə(r)/ in SBS (and /ʃoʊˈfɜr/ in AmE) with a different semantic range from the French word and subject to English morphology. As for the word *synonym*, it does not transliterate into any Greek form, old or new. Yet the historical fact that a word was borrowed from French, or made up from Greek elements, is important, because the word joins other such words. Groups of words have an identity because of shared spelling correspondences such as the <eur>≡/ɜː(r)/ and <ch>≡/ʃ/ of *chauffeur*.

We clearly need to use more widely the type of distinction made in the pair 'Latin' and 'Latinate'. I have used the symbol '§' as in '§Greek' for labels which refer to a set of present-day English spelling conventions in words or elements of words that are more or less linked to a particular etymology. The symbol '§' is meant to stand for 'subsystem'. However, the network of subsystems and markers in English spelling results from waves of outside influence over the centuries and can hardly be expected to present a tidy picture. The treatment given here is very tentative.

In addition to a §Basic sector of vocabulary (equivalent to Albrow's system 1), we need to refer to §Latinate word-formation in words such as *appropriate*, *appropriation*, §French conventions as in *chauffeur*, *vignette*, *pique*, and scientific and technical use of §Greek conventions in words such as *philosophy*, *rhododendron*, *chrysalis*. For instance, *rouge* and *route* have the §French correspondence /uː/≡<ou>; *eulogy* and *pseudonym* have the §Greek correspondence /juː/≡<eu>. *Rouge* has an explicit marker, the final /ʒ/, to alert the speller, but *route* is also marked by the <ou . . . e> as different from §Basic *root*. It may be useful to refer to early borrowings from French, such as *measure*, *treasure*, as §Romance to distinguish them from more direct borrowings from Latin, to account for the combination of <ea>≡/e/ with the /ʒ/ and /-ure/, a mix of correspondences that is neither Latin nor French. The main markers of §Greek correspondence are not affixes as such, but lexical morphemes in complex stems. Complex words with the §Greek elements {tele}, {scope}, {phone}, {graph}, etc. are usually all §Greek. The §Basic system also has its own specific correspondences such as /uː/≡<oo> (as in *root*), but the §Basic system also serves as a default system. Words such as *map*, *dot*, which have no correspondences or markers peculiar to other subsystems, can be classified as §Basic by default whatever their origin. *Deacon* is a word of Greek origin, but it has no overt characteristics which reflect that origin and so it may be treated as §Basic along with native *beacon*. *Totem*, on the other hand, is a word of American Indian (Algonquin) origin, but it may be regarded as §Greek because of its phonetic shape and because, by analogy with *system–systemic–systemicity*, it has derived forms *totemic–totemicity*. Some words have mixed elements. *Television* has a §Greek element <tele> and a §Latinate element <vision>; if abbreviated to <telly> it becomes §Basic with characteristic <C>-doubling and final <-y>. We shall use the label §Exotic to refer to non-§Basic spellings that would be in the 'foreign sources' of Albrow's system 3, such as the final <q> of *Iraq* or the <ah> of *pariah*. §Exotic will include Scots Gaelic, Welsh and Irish conventions, more especially in personal names and placenames.

Albrow was right to be wary of allotting whole words or morphemes to subsystems. In some words there is system confusion. This is particularly so in commercial jargon with coinages such as *washeteria*. The base form of some loan-words has been anglicized, while derived forms keep a 'learned' §Latinate or §Greek spelling: *invoke–invocation, joke–jocular, provoke–provocative, pontiff–pontifical*. A *<-voce> spelling would not be valid here, since it would read as <c>≡/s/.

2.9.3 Awareness

Phonological awareness, system awareness and lexical awareness

Successful spelling depends to no small extent on the relative awareness of the speller. There are factors in literacy that cannot be reduced to simple rules for which the only input is the known phonetic form and some grammatical information. The competence of successful spellers exploits more subtle means. The three main aspects of awareness are discussed below.

Phonological awareness is an awareness of the phonology that underlies the writing system when it differs from the accent of the speller. A speller is sometimes aware of how speakers of other dialects would pronounce a word, or, more strongly, of the range of contrasts in another phonological system. An SBS speaker would pronounce *loch* as /lɒk/ (= *lock*), but an awareness that Scots pronounce it as [lɒx] (with a voiceless velar fricative instead of a plosive) would safeguard the spelling <ch>. More useful and more general would be for an SBS speaker to be aware of the distribution of /r/ in "rhotic" accents (such as AmE or Scots) where //r// before a consonant has not been lost. Such awareness can have an indirect effect. Anyone who knows that an American would say *tomato* with their equivalent of /eɪ/, would not be tempted to spell *tomato* as *<tomarto>. An SBS-speaking speller may well be aware of the difference between "linking" /r/ in '*spar is*' and its absence in '*spa is*', but those speakers who have 'intrusive' /r/ and pronounce both as /spɑːr ɪz/ will have difficulty looking beyond the /r/-intrusion process. To a large extent awareness grows as literacy develops. Cockney speakers who, left alone, would have no /h/ phoneme, will sort out the incidence of <h> spellings better if they are exposed to the speech of those who have an /h/. The freely available recorded speech of films, television and radio should help literacy by increasing an awareness of other accents.

System awareness, too, is a question of exposure. In its extreme form it would mean that the speller had been taught languages other than English and would be better able to cope with the spelling of loan-words, even where these were to some extent respelt by English conventions. At the lower end of the scale, system awareness might associate certain sectors of vocabulary with particular spelling conventions. Since fashion and etiquette are dominated by French terminology, this could mean a reluctance to spell *chic* as *<sheek> or *pique* as *<peek>. This type of awareness would include guessing that a particular scientific term may have §Greek conventions (when explicit markers are lacking). For example, if *chrysalis* is suspected of being a §Greek scientific term, this may trigger the correspondences <ch>≡/k/ and <y>≡/ɪ/ and exclude the ending <-ice>.

Lexical awareness is the ability to recognize recurrent elements of word structure and to review the range of possible structures in which a morpheme can occur. This could, for instance, have a bearing on <r>-spellings. If *advertise* /ˈædvətaɪz/ is related to *advert* /ˈædvɜːt/ (where /ɜː/ must have an <r> spelling), or if *allurement* /əˈlʊəmənt/ is related to /əˈlʊərɪŋ/ (where the //r// is realized), the underlying //r// becomes apparent and requires a letter <r> in the spelling. Lexical awareness is chiefly needed, however, in deciding on the spelling of a reduced unstressed vowel by recalling parallel forms where the vowel is stressed and the spelling obvious: *atom* with <o> because of *atomic*, *theatre* with <a> because of *theatrical*, etc. It also involves an awareness of consonant alternations: that <-icity> with /s/ is related to <-ic> with /k/ and that such /s/ – /k/ variants are not spelt with <ss>, <s>, <ck> or <k>, but as *electricity*, *electric*.

Morpheme boundary recognition can distinguish <-id+ly> as /-ɪdlɪ/ in §Latinate words, such as *candidly*, *lucidly*, *vividly*, from <-+ed+ly> in *decidedly*, *devotedly*, *doggedly*, *guardedly*, *hurriedly*, *wickedly*. This will also apply to *advisedly*, *amazedly*, *assuredly*, *avowedly*, *composedly*, *confessedly*, *confusedly*, *markedly*, *supposedly*. Here the form without the <-ly> does not end in /-ɪd/, but in a simple /-d/ (*advised*) or /-t/ (*marked*). If the human speller can distinguish bound stems such as <viv-> from free stems such as <confuse> or <dog>, there is no spelling problem.

Chapter 3

Speech-to-text correspondences: encoding

3.1 A CORPUS-BASED STUDY

3.1.1 The database

The data used are of two kinds: **lexical items** and **proper names**. They have been dealt with differently. For lexical items we need to know how spellings are distributed across the lexicon (lexical frequency) and how frequently they occur in running text (text frequency). For names, this is hardly practicable. Correspondences peculiar to names and patterns of variation found in names were examined by closely sampling the large number of names given in LPD and EPD, but without any quantification.

For studying the distribution of spellings in lexical items and for trying out spelling rules a database was assembled by merging five very large independent word-frequency counts. To the orthographic forms of these counts were added grammatical categories and phonetic forms based on LPD, backed up with EPD. Various keys were then computed from the phonetic forms to allow grouping by syllable structure, number of syllables, stress pattern, etc.

The five frequency counts used were:

1 Thorndike and Lorge (1944) – derived from approximately 18 million words of text (= 'Thorndike' below);
2 The Brown University corpus of American English (Kucera and Francis 1967) – derived from approximately 1 million words of prose text of modern American English (= 'Brown' below);
3 The Lancaster-Oslo-Bergen Corpus (Johansson and Hofland 1989) – a British English analogue of the Brown University corpus (= LOB below);
4 A word frequency count (courtesy computer printout taken from the raw text) of the material collected for one of the Projects in Applied Linguistics conducted at the Catholic University of Louvain under the direction of Professor Engels, (*Analysis of Present-Day English Theatrical Language 1966–1972*), comprising approximately 1 million

words of play texts (= 'Louvain' below);

5 The word frequency count derived from the American Heritage Dictionary project (Carroll, B., Davies, D. and Richman, B. 1971) derived from approximately 5 million words of prose text (= 'Heritage' below).

Although each of the counts is very large and so 'representative' of English, they do differ to some extent in kind, date and format and so they complement each other. Thorndike is lemmatized: it does not list regular inflected forms such as *cleaned*, *cleaning*, *cleans*, *cleaner*, *cleanest*, separately, but adds them to the frequency of the base form *clean*. The other corpora are not lemmatized and treat the inflected forms separately. Brown, LOB and Heritage are more recent surveys and are carefully planned to cover a wide range of different genres, with appropriate weighting and with stringent sampling techniques, and are carefully restricted in time and provenance. Louvain is also recent and adds a genre, modern stage dialogue, not represented in the others. The Thorndike count, a long-standing reference base for educational studies, though very large, is an odd mixture of several word counts dating back half a century. It is firmly centred on narrative prose biased towards literary usage. The addition of the other more recent databases redresses the balance.

We can show the literary bias of Thorndike by comparing the relative frequency of words which have literary connotations with relatively neutral words, using Louvain as a basis of comparison. In Thorndike the word *doom* represents 37 per cent of the combined frequency of *doom* and *punishment*; in Louvain it only represents 12 per cent. Similarly, *fiery*, an adjective with literary connotations, has 70 per cent in Thorndike of the combined total of *fiery* and *cautious* (a neutral adjective), but only 33 per cent in Louvain.

Thorndike, then, represents a very literary database with a distinct 'classical' bias. The stage dialogue of Louvain is a valuable counterweight to the other counts, which are all based on contemporary prose.

The five different counts were pre-edited for the present study as follows.

1 Vocal gestures such as *ah*, *aha*, *ouch*, *tra-la*, *o-ooh-aye* were excluded, but syntactically integrated gestures such as *boo*, giving *booed*, *booing*, *boos,* were included.
2 Manifest archaisms such as *ycleped* and verb forms in *-eth* and *-est* were excluded.
3 Abbreviations which would read as the full orthographic form, such as *cwt*, were included by adding to the frequency of the full form; abbreviations such as *i.e.*, *viz.* were excluded; truncated colloquial forms such as *veg*, *trad*, *meths* were retained.
4 'Unassimilated' words of foreign origin were excluded. The choice made

under this heading is inevitably idiosyncratic, but can be illustrated by the following small sample of excluded words:

bunt, capita, contra, da, de, der, des, donna, du, duc, ecole, exeunt, fait, faubourg, frère, habeas, infinitum, livre, maître, mardi, memoriam, noir, noster, notre, obscura, oyez, padrone, princeps, priori, poilu, prix, sic, siècle, stadtholder, summa, supra, tonneau, un, und, etc.

Some trivial discrepancies may have resulted from the exclusion of part of a foreign tag. No attempt was made to adjust the frequencies for instances of (included) *grand* which may have gone with (excluded) *prix*, or those of *corpus* which went with *habeas*, or those of *in* which went with *memoriam*, or those of *camera* which went with *obscura*.

5 Manipulated jargon and trade names were omitted.

6 Variant spellings (*plow*, *plough*, etc.) were standardized as single entries. American spellings were changed to British. Possessive forms were merged with noun plural/verb 3rd person present singular forms (except in cases like *sheep's*, *woman's*, *postman's*) since the database was only intended for phonological use.

7 Homographs such as *invalid*, *insult*, *bass*, *row*, *tear*, *implement* were split into different entries with the appropriate phonetic forms and syntactic classification and concordance printouts of Lancaster and Brown were inspected to determine the relative frequencies.

8 Compounds made up of free forms which occurred wholly or in part with hyphens were excluded (*eye-lash, beer-barrel,* etc.). This will have affected the raw frequency count of their components, but it was assumed that this effect would be more-or-less proportional to the frequency of the components.

A computer program was written to lemmatize four of the corpora – Brown, LOB, Louvain and Heritage – to bring them into line with Thorndike, adding the frequencies of inflected forms (*carries, carried, carrying*; *potatoes*; *brighter, brightest*) to that of the base form (*carry*; *potato*; *bright*). These editing procedures produced a database of 26,048 words (uninflected forms). Adding the frequencies of these five large word counts together to produce this hybrid would hardly be justified in most applied linguistic studies, but the aim was to provide reasonably acceptable frequency weightings for words which readers and writers of English might encounter in the pursuit of literacy.

Two different computer programs were written to provide relevant data for this study:

1 a **correspondence analysis** program (described in §3.1.2 below) to gather statistics of how spelling correspondences are distributed across the database to provide the material for the survey of speech-to-text correspondences in §3.

2 a **text-to-speech algorithm**, similar to Ainsworth (1973), but some 40 per cent larger, to evaluate simple correspondence rules available to the reader. This is the basis for the treatment of text-to-speech correspondences in §4.

3.1.2 Analysis of correspondences

Getting spelling statistics from any database is not without problems. The guidelines for setting up correspondences suggested in a previous section (§2.6 pp. 32ff.) have been observed as far as possible.

The computer program was written to find an appropriate match for each phoneme with a string of letters; there was no attempt to model the strategies which a human reader/writer might conceivably follow in such a task. The input to the computer program was the string of phonemes in each word of the database and the string of letters in its spelling. As part of the control data the program was given a file of possible letter strings for each phoneme. This file was gradually augmented over a series of trial runs. The computer took each phoneme of a word in sequence and searched the control data for a matching letter string. The possible letter strings for each phoneme were ordered for testing with the longer strings before their substrings to prevent the shorter strings being chosen wrongly. Thus in looking for a string to match /p/, the program was first asked to try <pp> before it tried <p>. In a constantly re-run program this would be a very uneconomic type of search, since one is checking the less frequent spellings before the more frequent spellings. But in a one-off research project it had the advantage of easier programming. If the control file did not contain a suitable letter string, the computer tested the next few letters in the string to see if any of them could be set aside as dummy (empty or inert) letters, so that the string of normal correspondences could be picked up again later. Having found <d>≡/d/ and <e>≡/e/, the computer would not be able to find a letter string to match /t/ in the word *debt*, since <bt> was not given as a possible letter string for /t/, so it would identify the <b> as a dummy letter, <b>≡/Ø/, and then pick up the normal correspondences with <t>≡/t/. Each dummy letter or letter string found in this way was stored for reference to simplify future searches. No prior list of dummy letters was provided; the computer would obviously find dummy letters wherever there was a remainder not covered by adjacent correspondences. If the matching process failed completely, the word was abandoned and the history of the search was recorded on a dump file to allow refinement of the program. The program and control files were adjusted and refined over a series of runs until the matching process and the strings provided could cope with all the data.

In some instances where correspondences could not be found for single phonemes, two-phoneme strings were used:

1 when a single letter formed a correspondence with two phonemes:
<x>≡/ks/ or /gz/ in *box*, *examine*,
<u>≡/juː/ in *cubic*;

2 when the reverse ordering of two letters could be regarded as a better match for the two phonemes:
<gn>≡/nj/ in *poignant*,
<le>≡/əl/ in *bottle*,
<re>≡/ər/ in *acreage*;

3 where one letter correspondence only occurred in the context of the other:
<qu>≡/kw/ in *quite*,
<oi>≡/wɑː/ or /wæ/ in *boudoir*, *bourgeoisie*,
<zz>≡/ts/ in *intermezzo*;

4 for the morphemic spelling of the *-ed* suffix where the word is treated as a separate entry in the corpus:
<ed>≡/ɪd/ in *flabbergasted*.

The two surface diphthongs /ɪə/ and /ʊə/ were provided with an over-kill list of possible strings made up by combining each of the letter strings for /iː/ + /ə/ and similarly for /uː/ + /ə/, since in many cases these surface phonemes can be taken to be a sequence of two underlying vowels. Not all of these hypothetical combinations materialized, of course. A set of restriction rules in the program was used to prevent too large a phonetic string from being hived off at the expense of following correspondences. For instance, <oa>≡/əʊ/ is read in *boat*, but not in *boa* where we need <o>≡/əʊ/+<a>≡/ə/. Cf. *bruise–bluish*.

The phoneme /ə/, including syllabicity of a following consonant, was allowed a zero representation in *sarcasm*, *prism*, *rhythm*, etc.

An arbitrary decision was required in the treatment of <r> in non-prevocalic position in a 'non-rhotic' accent such as SBS. In such accents of English an original pre-consonantal /r/ (*farm*) or pre-boundary /r/ (*far*) has been lost. We could treat this <r>, at least before a boundary, as an inert letter with no phonetic counterpart (<r>≡Ø). Alternatively, we could make it part of the letter string for the preceding vowel (<ar>≡/ɑː/). The latter alternative is better suited to processing and presenting the data. Information about the context of spellings is provided by processing adjacent correspondences as a pair of data points. So to treat <ar> in *farm* (SBS /fɑːm/) as <a>≡/ɑ̣ː/ plus <r>≡Ø would only allow us to show that each of these correspondences occurred in the context of the other. We could not show that, for instance, <ar>≡/ɑː/ occurred before consonants (*farm*) or before a boundary (*far*). A further consideration why the <r> is best taken as part of the vowel spelling is that the usual phonemic analysis of SBS pre-empts it. The phonemes /ɜː/ and /ɛə/ only occur where there is latent //r// and the phonemes /ɪə/ and /ʊə/ largely occur there.

We return now to the earlier problem of how the computer established correspondences. Some types of contextual information are not apparent just from the immediate context. If we compare *tap* and *tape*, the function of the <e> is to mark the previous long vowel and, by default, the unmarked vowel in *tap* is short. In *tapper* the marker of vowel quality is instead the doubling of the consonant letter; the unmarked vowel in *taper* is long by default. If we look only at the immediate context we can make descriptive statements such as:

<a>≡/eɪ/ with <p>≡/p/ in *tape*, *taper*;
<a>≡/æ/ with <p>≡/p/ in *tap*;
<p>≡/p/ with <e>≡ Ø in *tape* and with # (where # represents the word boundary) in *tap*.

By analogy with the treatment of <r> in vowel correspondences, we can make the <e> of *tape* part of a correspondence <a..e>≡/eɪ/ rather than treat the <e> as an empty letter. This allows us to present the above data more accurately as:

<a..e>≡/eɪ/ with <p>≡/p/ in *tape*, *taper*;
<a>≡/æ/ with <p>≡/p/ in *tap*;
<p>≡/p/ with #.

After successive refinements the program was able to deal with the whole corpus and so provide the necessary statistics for the lexical and text frequencies of correspondences.

3.1.3 Text frequency and lexical frequency

Frequency of use is an important parameter in the description of English spelling. Words in the main subsystems of the English writing system certainly differ in potential frequency: the §Latinate vocabulary because of its semantic specialization will tend to have lower frequencies than §Basic words; the subset of §Greek words will tend to have still lower frequencies. These are general distributional tendencies but, of course, there are many words which, either through archaism or through innovation, have atypical frequencies. Aside from such broad tendencies in distribution, we need to know how the different spellings of a phoneme are distributed across words of different frequencies. We can ask how often /k/ is spelt as <ch>, and whether the spelling /k/=<ch> is distributed across words of different frequencies more or less like other spellings of /k/ and other pronunciations of <ch>.

Questions of frequency ought to be easy to answer, since we have a large corpus of counted data. To provide numerical answers is indeed simple enough. It is more difficult to say how significant and insightful these numbers are as descriptors of English spelling conventions. We must first make the bold assumption that the database described earlier in this section is a representative sample of what English speakers might come across in reading and writing. No linguistic database is ever large enough, or new enough, or ideally balanced, but the sources drawn on in this present study are sufficiently comprehensive to present fairly settled statistics at the word level. Given the database, there are two dimensions of frequency to consider: lexical frequency and text frequency (or, in more general terms, type frequency and token frequency). The two can vary quite significantly. A simple phonetic example will make the point. If we are told that /ð/ has a higher 'frequency' than /r/, /m/, /w/ or /k/, we can see immediately, without being told, that this evaluation is based not on lexical frequency but on text frequency. The high value for /ð/ depends on the high text frequency of a small closed set of function words (including *the*, *then*, *that*, *there*, *this* and a few other function words). Similarly the frequency of /h/ in the same way is boosted by several common pronouns and auxiliary verb forms such as *he*, *him*, *have*, *has*.

This highlights the problem of giving an impressionistic picture of the relative text frequency of spellings. Raw text frequencies will be misleading since the overall pattern of frequencies may be dominated by the closed set of a few dozen function words. There are several good reasons why we should deal with function words and lexical words separately. In reading and writing, function words are more likely to be treated holistically. Phonetically each function word is usually very variable, with a range of allegro and lento forms showing different degrees of vowel reduction and consonant elision (Cruttenden 1994: 11.3). For reasons such as these, the percentage figures quoted for the text frequency of spellings have been restricted to lexical words only, with function words (articles, demonstratives, pronouns, auxiliary verbs, conjunctions, and prepositions) excluded. This gives a better indication of how often a given spelling is likely to crop up in the lexical words of a text.

We can take the diphthong /ɛə/ as a critical example. The text frequency of /ɛə/ is dominated by the three function words *where*, *there* and *their*. The relative frequencies of the main spellings of /ɛə/ are very different depending on whether these three words are included or excluded, as shown in table 10.

The three words *where*, *there* and *their* account for more than half the raw text frequency of /ɛə/. In lexical words, however, <ere> and <eir> are very infrequent spellings. Both sets of figures are informative but, if we are considering the way in which spellings are distributed across the lexicon and the problem of reading or writing a new lexical word, the excluded frequencies give a more useful picture of what to expect.

To be fully consistent we ought perhaps to go even further and deal with stems and affixes separately for much the same reasons. Affixes such as <-ion>, <-ly>, <-ness> will, because of their high frequency, dominate the

Table 10 Text frequency of /ɛə/ with and without function words

	Including function words	*Excluding function words*
<are>, <ar>	23.6%	58.5%
<air>	12.3%	28.1%
<ear>	3.9%	9.6%
<ere>, <er>	37.2%	0.2%
<eir>	22.0%	0.3%
other spellings	1.0%	3.3%

frequency distribution of some spellings. The phoneme /ʃ/ is not at all frequent in stems, but the overall text frequency of /ʃ/ is quite high due to its occurrence in common endings, such as <-tion>, <-tial>. However, this variation in distribution can be dealt with by a sufficiently detailed consideration of the context in which the spellings occur. In any case, to abandon the word as our database unit in favour of the morpheme would create a host of problems. Affix-stripping by computer could be simple enough with discrete affixes, but unfortunately, if we are to work with the surface forms of English, there are too many indeterminate boundaries within words. So, although the word is not an ideal unit for studying the frequency of spellings, the task of carving out morpheme units would present its own problems, both practical and theoretical.

The lexical frequency of spellings also involves a problem of accounting and presentation. Ideally, lexical frequency should be based on morphemes rather than words. The correspondence <ayor>≡/ɛə/ only occurs in the morpheme {mayor}, but this can be found in four words: *mayor*, *mayoral*, *mayoress*, *mayoralty*. On the other hand <oo>≡/əʊ/ only occurs in the morpheme {brooch} which in our corpus has no derived forms and only occurs as the word *brooch*. So in one sense {mayor} and {brooch} should count equally in terms of lexical frequency, but in another sense {mayor} does have a different impact in the lexicon because of its spread over different derived forms and should therefore count more. The figures for lexical frequency given here will follow the latter practice and count frequency in words.

The percentages of text frequency and lexical frequency (as defined above) for each of the spellings of a phoneme give an indication of the relative importance of the spelling. The percentages for the spellings of phoneme /f/ are given in table 11.

Table 11 Text and lexical frequencies for spellings of /f/

<f>	TF 83.5%	LF 77.0%
<ff>	TF 3.9%	LF 13.9%
<ph>	TF 10.7%	LF 8.4%
<gh>	TF 1.9%	LF 0.7%

A comparison of text frequency with lexical frequency for any one spelling provides further insight into its distribution. The above figures show that <ff> tends to occur in words of lower frequency than the other spellings. This might seem surprising, but it is due to the <-ff-> found with Latinate prefixes in words such as *effete*, *suffragan*, etc. On the other hand, the rather odd <gh> spelling only occurs in a few words, but these are quite common: *cough*, *draught*, *enough*, *laugh*, *rough*, *tough*, *trough*. Interesting differences of this kind will be marked in the text as 'F+' for a tendency to occur in high-frequency words and 'F-' for a tendency to occur in low-frequency words. These differences should be interpreted against the relative frequency of the phoneme in question. Each phoneme has its own distribution across words of differing frequency: /ʒ/ tends overall to occur in words of lower frequency than does /t/.

3.2 GENERAL FACTORS IN SPEECH-TO-TEXT RULES

3.2.1 Common features of spelling correspondences

One of the curious failings of the Hanna spelling rules (§2.8.5) is that these rules do not capture some obvious general design features of the English writing system. There are rules for individual 'phoneme–grapheme correspondences', but there is no attempt to examine what these correspondences may have in common. Even if their rules for individual phonemes could be considered more or less 'adequate' as a descriptive statement of the facts, these would still not reflect the competence of a literate person. They do not seek to explain that the <pp> of happy has the same function as the double <-CC-> of *hobby*, *fatty*, *eddy*, *lucky*, *baggy*, *jiffy*, *bossy*, *fizzy*, *mammy*, *sunny*, *hurry*, *belly*. Similarly, the <-e> at the end of *tape* has the same function as at the end of *babe*, *late*, *wade*, *bake*, *rage*, *safe*, *base*, *laze*, *tame*, *sane*, *fare*, *male*. Even the shortness of the function words *in*, *or*, *by*, compared with the lexical words *inn*, *ore*, *bye*, is not accidental. If we are to account for the competence of people who use the present writing system successfully, such general design features have to be explained and evaluated. That is the business of the next five subsections.

3.2.2 Consonant-letter doubling

We can begin by exploring in some detail the conventions which regulate the use of 'double' consonant letters in English spelling. This has always been a problem for spellers. One of Addison's 'correspondents' in the *Spectator* writes for advice:

> *SIR*,
> I am a young Woman and reckoned Pretty, therefore you'll pardon me

that I trouble you to decide a Wager between me and a Cousin of mine, who is always contradicting one because he understands *Latin*. Pray, Sir, is Dimpple spelt with a single or a double P?

I am, SIR,

Your very Humble Servant,

Betty Saunter

(*Spectator* No.140, August 10, 1711)

The cousin's Latin would be useful in distinguishing §Latinate words from §Basic words, but it would not have helped with the spelling of §Basic *dimple*. Miss Saunter would have to be told that <C>-doubling does not take place after a previous consonant letter, or that <mpp> is not a possible letter sequence in the spelling of an English morpheme (so excluding instances at boundaries, such as *dampproof*). This advice, one suspects, would not have been welcome.

What little guidance on <C>-doubling there is in the spelling literature is sadly inadequate and falls far short of explicitness. Fowler (1926: 575) singles out letter doubling, impressionistically at least, as the most frequent source of misspelling in English:

> If a list were made of the many thousands of words whose spelling cannot be safely inferred from their sound, the doubtful point in perhaps nine-tenths of them would be whether some single consonantal sound was given by a single letter, as m or t or c, or a double letter, as mm or tt, or two or more, as sc or cq or sch. A*cq*uiesce and a*qu*educt, bivoua*c* and bivoua*ck*ing, Bri*t*ain and Bri*tt*any, co*mm*i*tt*ee and co*m*ity, *c*rystal and *ch*rysalis, i*n*oculate and i*nn*ocuous, insta*ll* and insti*l*, ha*r*ass and emba*rr*ass, leve*ll*ed and unparalle*l*ed, perso*n*ify and perso*nn*el, *sch*edule and *sh*ed, *s*cience and *s*ilence, ti*c* and ti*ck*, are examples enough.
>
> (ibid.: 554)

Fowler has indeed put his finger on some troublesome examples, but it is surprising that consonant-letter doublings are grouped together with other digraphs as simple aberrations from a 'one letter, one phoneme' ideal. The difference between the <tt> and <t> of *latter* and *later* is not of the same order as the difference between the <sc> and <s> of *science* and *silence* and it is different again from the two letters found at the boundary between a §Latinate prefix and stem in *innocuous*, *attention*, etc. It is understandable that Fowler, after looking at the problem in this unrewarding way, comes to the conclusion that 'nothing short of a complete spelling-book will serve the turn of a really weak speller' (loc. cit.).

Here the term 'consonant-letter doubling' (abbreviated as '<C>-doubling') will be used for postvocalic instances of <tt>, <ss>, <pp>, etc., including as 'doubled' letters <tch> <dg(e)> and <ck> for the phonemes /ʧ/, /ʤ/ and /k/ (see #D3 below).

Double letters do not occur initially except in the <Ll> and <Ff> of Welsh names (*Lloyd*, *Llanrwst*, *Ffestiniog*), in the totemic absurdity of *Ffitch*, *Ffolliot* and *Ffoulkes* and in occasional foreign loans, such as *llama*. Indeed, there is a marginal contrast on the fringes of what might or might not be 'English' between *llama* (animal) and *lama* (Tibetan monk). Similarly, the <rr> of a few §Greek medical terms, such as *haemorrhage*, may be regarded as element-initial.

The double-letter problem is chiefly one for the writer, but it does cause difficulty for readers because double letters play a complicated role in determining whether the preceding vowel is long or short. In both reading and writing this may present problems for the foreign learner of English. This is particularly so for speakers of languages which make a phonemic contrast between long and short consonants and write them with two letters and one letter respectively (cf. Swedish: *lada–ladda* (['laːda] – ['ladːa]), *mina–minna*, etc.). The two consonant letters in Swedish spelling represent a geminate consonant with a well-defined syllable boundary running through it. Such a phonetic difference is not of course found in English words such as *banish* and *mannish*, or *tenor* and *tenner*, where both <n> and <nn> represent the same single phoneme. A geminate consonant in English cannot occur within a morpheme but only at word boundaries (cf. the difference between *fine nail* and *fine ale*), or, less frequently at morpheme boundaries within a word (*wholly* may differ from *holy* as /-ll-/ against /-l-/). That there is a phonetic difference underlying the <-CC-> spellings in, for example, *unnerving* compared with *announcing*, is rarely pointed out in spelling books.(cf. Vallins 1965: 53). In accounting for <C>-doubling, it will be necessary to distinguish words such as *stammer*, *apple*, *baffle*, *follow*, etc. from the same consonant letters occurring at what once were §Latinate morpheme boundaries in *command*, *approve*, *offend*, *illicit*, etc. This difference will be discussed later.

Marking short vowels: matting–mating

<C>-doubling appears to have a consistent marking function in that it identifies the previous vowel as short (cf. *latter–later*). On the other hand there are many short vowels not so marked (cf. *cannon–canon*). Our first generalization therefore needs to be put negatively:

Table 12 No <C>-doubling with third-syllable shortening

/eɪ/	*grateful*	/æ/	*gratitude*	(not **grattitude*)
/eɪ/	*sane*	/æ/	*sanity*	(not **sannity*)
/iː/	*obscene*	/e/	*obscenity*	(not **obscennity*)
/ɪə/	*hero*	/e/	*heroine*	(not **herroine*)
/aɪ/	*vile*	/ɪ/	*vilify*	(not **villify*)
/aɪ/	*crime*	/ɪ/	*criminal*	(not **crimminal*)
/əʊ/	*omen*	/ɒ/	*ominous*	(not **omminous*)
/əʊ/	*sole*	/ɒ/	*solitude*	(not **sollitude*)

#D1: Double consonant letters do not normally follow long vowels.
The qualification 'normally' is there because of the special instances of <ff>, <ss>, <ll> and <rr> discussed under #D10.

Before putting together further conditions for the occurrence of <C>-doubling, we can examine those contexts where it does and predictably does not occur. Names will not be included here; <C>-doubling in names is dealt with separately in §6.4.

One category of short vowel which may possibly not be found with <C> doubling, in view of #D1, will be those vowels which vary between long and short in a particular morpheme and where the base form has the long vowel.

A morpheme containing a long vowel in its isolate form may have the equivalent short vowel, for instance, when the vowel happens to fall in the third syllable from the end of the word before certain suffixes. The writing system keeps the spelling constant, as in table 12. There are one or two exceptions: *amenity*, *lenity* have either /iː/ or /e/. Stems with the diphthong /juː/ are usually not affected – *community*, *credulity*, *crudity*, *immunity*, *impunity*, *nudity*, *opportunity*, *purity*, *unity*, etc.

In a process description the long vowel would be taken to be basic (or underlying) and the short vowel would be derived from it by rule. This particular kind of shortening is here referred to as third-syllable shortening. Chomsky and Halle (1968: 180) call it 'trisyllabic laxing' and include it in a complex rule along with similar shortening before the endings <-ic>, <-id>, <-ish>.

Both the endings <-ic> and <-ical> tend to have a short vowel in the previous syllable. Words with <-ical> (*theatrical*, *comical*, *political*, etc.) are already covered by the third-syllable shortening rule. Examples of shortening before final <-ic> are given in table 13.

Pairs of <-ic>/<-ical> forms may both occur (*historic–historical*), sometimes with a semantic difference. In other cases we only find one in common use: *static* but not **statical*, *typical* but not **typic*.

There are a few exceptions where a long vowel occurs before the ending <-ic(al)> such as: *strategic*(*al*), *acoustic*(*al*), *pharmaceutic*(*al*), *heroic*(*al*); in *musical* the <-ic-> is part of the stem. Long vowels before <-ic> where the <-ical> form does not occur include: *cubic*, *paraplegic*, *hydraulic*, *anaemic*,

Table 13 No <C>-doubling before suffix <ic>

/eɪ/	*mania*	/æ/	*manic*	(not **mannic*)
/eɪ/	*state*	/æ/	*static*	(not **stattic*)
/iː/	*athlete*	/e/	*athletic*	(not **athlettic*)
/iː/	*gene*	/e/	*eugenic*	(not **eugennic*)
/aɪ/	*paralyse*	/ɪ/	*paralytic*	(not **paralyttic*)
/aɪ/	*mime*	/ɪ/	*mimic*	(not **mimmic*)
/ɔː/	*euphoria*	/ɒ/	*euphoric*	(not **euphorric*)
/əʊ/	*cone*	/ɒ/	*conic*	(not **connic*)

phonemic, *hygienic*, *scenic*, *runic*, *basic*, *acetic*, *therapeutic*. These exceptions do not, however, affect the value of these suffixes in predicting an absence of <C>-doubling.

The words ending in <-ic> fall into three categories:

1 examples with a single consonant following a short vowel where the stem recurs elsewhere with a long vowel: *sonic*, *tonic*, *osmotic*, *mimic*, *lyric*, etc. (cf. *sonar*, *tone*, *osmosis*, *mime*, *lyre* and for some speakers the pair *splenic* with /e/ and *spleen*);
2 examples with a single consonant following a short vowel where there are no readily apparent long vowel alternants: *comic*, *sporadic*, etc.;
3 examples with <C>-doubling following a short vowel: *attic*, *classic*, *ferric*, *phallic*, *prussic*, *tannic*, *traffic*. The single-morpheme nouns *traffic* and *attic* would be more consistently spelt **traffick* (cf. inflected *trafficking*) and **attick*, like *derrick* and *gimmick*. There is nothing to distinguish them from such §Basic words. The <-ff-> of *traffic* has, however, come from an original Latin *<trans+fic-> and *attic* was originally the Greek *Attic*. Since each is irregular in the context of modern English spelling, they should perhaps be spelt as if they were §Basic words with final <ck>.

The endings <-id> and <-ish> also provide contexts in which a short vowel, if it does occur, is not marked by <C>-doubling. We can judge the effectiveness of these endings as spelling markers by sorting words in which they occur into the same three categories which are evident in the <-ic> examples:

1 There are alternants for *placid*, *vapid*, *florid*, *vivid* (cf. *complacent*, *vapour*, *floral*, *revive*). Some speakers have /æ/ and /eɪ/ in the pair *rabid* and *rabies* , rather than /eɪ/ in both;
2 There are no obvious alternant words for *acid*, *rigid*, *frigid*, *solid*, *stolid*, *timid*, *intrepid*, *tepid*, *arid*, *fetid*, *avid*;
3 The few exceptions with <-CC-> before the <-id> ending – *pallid*, *horrid*, *torrid* – are a small minority. They represent a class of exceptions which no generalization can account for, since the <C>-doubling is a feature of the Latin stem and it does not change with suffixation (cf. *pallescent*, *horrify*, *horrendous*, *torrefaction*). It would have been a nice generalization to say that <C>-doubling is only a feature of §Basic words and does not occur as a marker of short vowels in §Latinate words, but there are in fact quite a number of Latin stems, especially with <-ll->, <-rr->, and <-ss->, which prevent such a broad generalization.

Words which end in <-ish> after a short stressed vowel differ similarly:

1 There are alternants for only one or two: *replenish*, *punish* (cf. *plenary*, *punitive*);
2 *abolish*, *admonish*, *astonish*, *banish*, *blemish*, *cherish*, *finish*, *flourish*, *lavish*, *nourish*, *parish*, *polish*, *radish*, *relish*, *vanish*. All these are either

words in which the <-ish> is added to a bound form (*punish*) or words which are single morphemes (*parish*);

3 The above clearly differ from {-ish} as an adjective-forming suffix added to nouns and adjectives (as free forms): *bullish*, *clannish*, *cloddish*, *donnish*, *foppish*, *hellish*, *hoggish*, *mannish*, *piggish*, *priggish*, *raffish*, *reddish*, *skittish*, *sluggish*, *snobbish*, *sottish*, *waggish*. This suffix does not affect the stem to which it is added either by shortening the vowel or affecting the stress placement. So the long vowel is preserved in *apish*, *mulish*, *whitish*. If we set up (bound form + <-ish>) as a class of words where we would not have <C>-doubling after a short vowel, the only exception seems to be *rubbish*, apparently in origin a variant of *rubble*.

In addition to the <-ic>, <-id>, <-ish> contexts specified in the Chomsky and Halle shortening rule, there do appear to be other word-endings which generally associate with a preceding short vowel that is not marked by <C>-doubling and which has long vowel alternants in other contexts (in some words at least).

The ending <-ule> is restricted to §Latinate words:

1 *globule*, *nodule*, *module*, *granule* (cf. *globe*, *node*, *mode*, *grain*);
2 *schedule*, *stipule*;
3 *gemmule*, *ferrule* have <-CC-> in the Latin stems.

The endings <-it> <-et> (excluding §French <-et>≡/eɪ/ *ballet*) are both pronounced /ɪt/ in SBS, but there is an increasing tendency to hear /ət/ for words with <-et> spellings. We list them separately.

Words ending in <-it>:
1 *spirit*, *posit*, *deposit*; (cf. *aspire*, *pose*, *depose*);
2 *habit*, *debit*, *prohibit*, *inhibit*, *tacit*, *elicit*, *illicit*, *solicit*, *credit*, *edit*, *profit*, *digit*, *limit*, *vomit*, *decrepit*, *inherit*, *merit*, *visit*, *davit*;
3 *rabbit, summit.*

Words ending in <-et>:
1 *brevet*, *closet*, *facet*; (cf. *brief*, *close, face*);
2 *civet*, *claret*, *comet*, *covet*, *planet* (not related to *plane*), *privet*, *tenet*, *trivet*, *valet*;
3 *billet*, *bonnet*, *bracket*, *bucket*, *budget*, *buffet*, *bullet*, *cosset*, *cresset*, *cricket*, *docket*, *drugget*, *ferret*, *fidget*, *fillet*, *gadget*, *garret*, *gibbet*, *gullet*, *gusset*, *jacket*, *jennet*, *lappet*, *linnet*, *locket*, *mallet*, *midget*, *millet*, *mullet*, *nugget*, *packet*, *pallet*, *pellet*, *picket*, *plummet*, *pocket*, *poppet*, *posset*, *pullet*, *punnet*, *puppet*, *quillet*, *rabbet*, *racket*, *rennet*, *rocket*, *russet*, *skillet*, *socket*, *sonnet*, *tappet*, *thicket*, *ticket*, *tippet*, *turret*, *wallet*, *whippet*, *wicket*.

For those SBS speakers who pronounce both <-it> and <-et> in the above words as /ɪt/, there is obviously a spelling problem in deciding between the

<-i-> and <-e-> spellings. There is a minimal spelling contrast in *rabbit–rabbet*. The absence of <C>-doubling in the (1) and (2) groups can often, but by no means always, be associated with a potential for §Latinate word-formation: *elicit–elicitation*, *edit–editorial*, *digit–digital*, *merit–meritorious*, *inherit–inheritance*. This is not much help as a marker where such derived forms are rare or not even found. The examples with <-v-> in groups (1) and (2) are not really a problem, since doubling of <v> is exceptional.

Clearly there can be no unqualified rule to predict <C>-doubling before either <-et> or <-it>. The majority of cases would be covered by saying that <-it> without previous <C>-doubling occurs in forms with §Latinate word-formation potential, but that otherwise one should expect <-et> with <C>-doubling. This means that the exceptional cases would be group (3) for <-it> and groups (1) and (2) for <-et>. So for an SBS speaker with /ɪ/ in both endings, *vomit* would be regular and *comet* exceptional. A speaker who might conceivably distinguish them as /ˈvɒmɪt/, /ˈkɒmət/ would, however, find both spellings relatively predictable.

The long/short vowel relationships we have just explored clearly indicate contexts in which a short vowel, contrary to expectation, will not be marked by <C>-doubling. The simple phonological explanation would be that the underlying vowel in *cave–cavity* and *mime–mimic* and similar alternations, is long and the morphemes have a constant spelling representing the long vowel. There are, however, many examples of short vowels in such contexts where there is no apparent corresponding form available with a long vowel. This would not be a problem in phonology, but in describing spelling regularities we are more constrained by what does and does not occur in actual surface forms. This is particularly so if we base our description on what a normal literate adult can bring to the level of awareness.

An awareness of the relationship between the long and short phonetic values of the simple vowel letters <a>, <e>, <i/y>, <o>, <u> must be assumed to be part of the competence of a literate English speaker. But this does not mean that the alternation of long/short vowels in different forms of the same morpheme is always accessible for use in generalizations about spelling. It is easy to show that in practice speakers are not always aware from introspection that such pairs of allomorphs are in fact related. Speakers may be aware of the link, say, between *crime* and *criminal* or *grateful* and *gratitude*, but not necessarily of the link between *omen* and *ominous*, or *state* and *static*. We cannot simply assume that the elements of Latin and Greek morphology are linked by semantic associations when they are used in English words. Even in deliberate introspection the ordinary English-speaker does not necessarily link the word *oval* with 'eggs' or the word *immense* with 'measuring' or the word *precarious* with 'praying'. Not many people, one suspects, can draw the fine distinction between 'going' in *intercede* and 'sitting' in *supersede* or between 'estimating' in *census* and 'feeling' in *consensus*.

We would be well advised to avoid an assumption of such semantic links in spelling rules. It would be unrealistic as a performance-based rule to suggest: '<C>-doubling does not occur after a short vowel derived from an underlying long vowel', however valid this might be, since this presupposes an awareness of the semantic identity of the morpheme. The speller would be required to know that /ɒmɪn/ in *ominous* and /əʊmen/ in *omen* are in effect the same meaningful chunk.

What we can note with certainty from the above long/short relationships is that a great many short vowels will occur unmarked by <C>-doubling in the antepenultimate syllable of §Latinate words and, as we have seen, before certain suffixes. The opposite process of lengthening an underlying short vowel (as in *manager–managerial*) is not very common in English word-formation, and would not appear to provide a basis for any spelling regularities.

§Latinate prefixes: approve, immerse, offend

Before formulating general statements to predict where <C>-doubling will occur, we must make special provision for some of the §Latinate prefixes. Two identical consonant letters near the beginning of a §Latinate word may represent a fossilized morpheme boundary between prefix and stem. There is little scope here for operational rules based on the current pronunciation. All we can do is note the problem of associating these double letters with the constituent prefixes and stems:

#D2: Two identical consonant letters may occur in words with a §Latinate prefix (ad-, com-, e(x)-, in-, ob-, per-, sub-): as in *adduce*, *command*, *innate*.

The prefix often assimilates to the initial consonant of the stem, as in *approve*, *affect*, *announce*, *immerse*, *illegal*, *occlude*, *offend*. Normally the two letters of the spelling correspond to a single consonant phoneme in the present-day English forms.

Although {ob}+{clude} gives a <-cc-> in *occlude*, and {ad}+{sent} gives a <-ss-> in *assent*, there is one letter-doubling restriction worth noting. If the §Latinate stem begins with an <-sC-> cluster, there is no <-ss->, but only single <-s->. So we have *ascribe*, *aspect*, *ascend*, *dispirited*, *distance*, *transpire*, not **asscribe*, **disstance*, **transspire,* etc. This does not apply to the prefix {mis-}, as in *misspent*, *misstate*, which is different in that it is added to free forms.

The preceding vowel is stressed in some words (*affluent*, *effluent*, etc.) but is frequently unstressed and reduced in others (*offensive*, *sufficient*).

In the underlying §Latinate morphemes there is a boundary between the consonant at the end of the prefix and a consonant beginning the stem {ad+duce}, etc. Phonetically in the spoken English forms there is only a single consonant. In some cases, where the following stem represents a free form (*illegal*, *immodest*, *dissentient*) and where the prefix is clearly additive in terms of meaning, formal pronunciation may produce a geminate consonant. But to take a realistic view of the spelling problem we must assume a single phonetic consonant in all such cases. The <-CC-> letter clusters associated with these §Latinate prefixes resemble the <C>-doubling that marks short vowels, and the vowels of the prefixes are indeed short. Many such clusters will be covered by the rules given below for <C>-doubling (*affix* (n.), *annexe*, etc.), but the <-CC-> found with prefixes does represent a spelling problem because, in many instances, the prefix vowel is reduced to /ə/: *affix* (v.), *commute*, *oppose*, etc. The reduced vowel in the prefix may cause confusion with other reduced syllables followed by a single consonant letter. Spellers (in SBS at least) have to distinguish *allure* from *alight*, *illegal* from *elope*, *affront* from *afraid*, etc. For practical reasons then, it is better to note these prefix <-CC-> clusters separately, as we have done under #D2, rather than try to merge them with a general rule for <C>-doubling.

Though it is clearly impracticable to teach the spelling of all such words through the meaning of the component §Latinate morphemes, anyone who can find recurrent morphs such as <ab->, <ad->, <-err->, <-brev-> might be able to see a reason for the difference in spelling between such pairs as <ab-> and <abb-> in *aberrant* and *abbreviate*. Recognising these recurrent units may or may not involve learning their basic meaning. The strongest form of literacy would involve the ability to make semantic generalizations within the §Latinate vocabulary. The best chance of this is with those words, such as *illegal* or *aberrant*, where the stem is an independent free form, so that prefix and stem are still separable. The effort involved need be no more than that required in some associative techniques for teaching spelling. Hook (1976) uses 'attention to etymology' as a learning technique: 'when you learn, for example, that *colonel* is derived from the Italian *colonello*, you will have a better chance of remembering the spelling' (ibid.: vii). This introductory example is misleading, since he does get down to teaching the meaning of Latin and Greek elements: 'General Grant "sat above" his predecessor when he superseded him' (ibid.: 79). But often he relies on associations which have no general value: 'Notice that *tragedy* starts with *trag*. The word goes back to Greek *tragos*, meaning goat, as some early actors wore goat skins' (ibid.: 58). Hook seems, on the whole, to require an unrealistic academic interest from his bad spellers; witness: 'Scandinavian or Low German influence appears in *guess*' (ibid.: 245). He may prefer a dazzling etymology to a simple association with similar words in English: '*condemn*, *column* and *solemn* each have a silent *n*. These words come from Latin words in which the *n* was pronounced: *condemnare*, *columna*, *solemnis*.' (ibid.: 244). But there is no comparison with English *condemnation*, *columnar*, *solemnity*. Given our present writing system the usual English pronunciation on its own is certainly an inadequate basis for literacy in the §Latinate and §Greek vocabulary, but some markers have to be picked up by the speller for dealing with the §Latinate affixes. Hook's approach demands an unrealistic level of cultural system awareness (see §2.9.3 pp. 102f.).

Consonant letters that double

We can now suggest probabilistic statements for the occurrence of <C>-doubling. These are general but not exhaustive and have to be read in conjunction with the later sections on the spelling of individual phonemes.

#D3: The following 15 simple consonants regularly have <C>-doubling in the appropriate contexts: /p b t d k g ʧ ʤ f s z l r m n/.

The normal default spelling of <C>-doubling is the repetition of the consonant letter (e.g. <pp>, <bb>, etc.) except in the following correspondences:

/k/≡<ck> – (cf. *bake–back*; <cc> is usually associated with /ks/);
/ʧ/≡<tch> – (cf. *beach–batch*);
/ʤ/≡<dge> – (cf. *cage–cadge*).

Doubling does not normally occur before or after another consonant letter in the same morpheme (*hamper, hinder, blister, bomber, salmon*) or when the previous vowel in the morpheme is spelt with more than one letter (cf. *rubble–trouble*). These are graphotactic restrictions. They do not account for *apple, rubble, bottle*, etc. To do that we may instead specify 'another consonant phoneme' (rather than 'letter') in the wording of the conditions if the phoneme sequence is taken to be /ˈrʌbəl/, with /ə/ realized as the syllabicity of the /l/. But then we should have to account for the absence of doubling alongside empty or inert letters in *salmon, bomber*, etc.

The nine consonant phonemes which do not normally have <C>-doubling are a mixed group. They include the glides /w j h/. Of the remainder, /θ ð ʃ ʒ ŋ/ do not have a context-independent single-letter spelling. That, however, is also true of /ʧ/, which has doubling nevertheless. We owe the <tch> spelling to Caxton. The literally 'doubled' spelling <chch> was in use in Middle English, though it was often simplified to <cch> (Vallins 1965: 34). The <t> of Caxton's spelling has some phonetic appropriateness and the longer *<chch> would exceed the general limits on the size of consonant spellings. There is a clear graphotactic constraint on doubling a digraph: *<thth>, *<shsh>, *<ngng>. The remaining consonant is /v/. This only has <C>-doubling in some marginal cases (*flivver, bovver, revving*). The restriction on <-vv-> seems to have been due to the development of <w> as an individual letter. Albrow (1972: 20) regards <ve> as the normal equivalent of <C>-doubling for /v/ in words such as *love, live* [lɪv]. Their structure is <l> <o> <ve>, <l> <i> <ve>, while the structure of *cove, live* [laɪv], is taken to be <c> <o..e> <v>, <l> <i..e> <v>.

The letter <x> does not double since it usually represents a consonant cluster /ks/. Albrow (1972: 21) suggests that the letter shape <x> can be regarded as a 'shorthand' form of the letter string <cs>.

Marking stressed short vowels

#D4: Stressed short vowels in simple base forms with the primary stress on the last or next to the last syllable are normally marked by <C>-doubling: *full*, *miss*, *stiff*, *back*, *badge*, *badger(ing)*, *badger*(*ingly*), *fadd(ist)*, *rubber*(*y*), *shrubb*(*ery*), *spaghetti*, *armadillo*.

<shrubb> is not the isolate form because of #D5. There is no <C>-doubling, naturally enough, of an intervocalic consonant which is initial in a recurrent element: *product*.

<C>-doubling after vowels lacking primary stress

<C>-doubling also affects syllables which do not have primary stress, but with some inconsistencies. Free-form elements of a compound follow the doubling rules: *inputting*, *jitterbugging*, *leapfrogging*. So, too, do final unstressed syllables of minimal free forms if they have full vowel quality and hence some degree of stress: *formatted*, *handicapped*, *hobnobbing*, *kidnapped*. Some such are variable: *combatting–combating*. This does not apply to the /-ʌp/ of *hiccuped*, *hiccuping*, even though the full vowel quality is often cited to show a phoneme contrast in SBS between *hiccup* with /ʌ/ and *syrup* with a reduced /ə/. An /-el/ exception is *parallel* with *paralleled*, *parallelism*, where two double <-ll-> spellings in succession would seem very dense.

The requirement that the previous short vowel is stressed, or at least has unreduced vowel quality means that there is normally no <C>-doubling before a vowel-initial suffix in the final /-VC/ syllable of a free form if that vowel is /ə/ or /ɪ/. So, /ə/≡<a> and a final <C> gives *orphaned* (not *<orphanned>), *toboganer*; /ə/≡<e> and a final <C> gives *banqueting*, *bayoneted*, *blanketing*, *bracketing*, *bitumened*, *carpeting*, *cosseted*, *coveting*, *rocketed*; /ɪ/≡<i> and a final <C> gives *credited*, *gossipy*, *limited*, *orbiting*, *profiting*, *vomiting*; /ə/≡<o> and a final <C> gives *abandoned*, *balloted*, *beckoned*, *bigoted*, *developing*, *galloped*, *imprisoned*, *reckoning*, *summoned*, *walloped*; /ə/≡<u> and a final <C> gives *chirruped*, *chromiumed*, *syrupy*, *talcumed*, etc. *Worship* is an exception: *worshipped*, *worshipper*, *worshipping*. Words ending in <c> double it to <ck> to preserve a /k/ pronunciation before <i, e>: *bivouacked*, *picnicked*, *trafficking*. This would presumably extend to the verb *vac* (*vacked*, *vacking*) as an abbreviation of 'to vacuum-clean'. Similarly, it is clear that *gravelly* (as *gravel+ly*) needs its <ll> to distinguish it from *gravely* (as *grave+ly*).

There is, however, some variation in the treatment of unstressed syllables and some insecurity for the speller. In British, but not in American spelling, there is usually doubling of <l> in *carolling*, *chancellor*, *counsellor*, *duellist*, *equalling*, *labelled*, *levelling*, *marshalled*, *modelling*, *pencilled*, *quarrelling*, *signalling*, *traveller*, etc. The <ll> of *skill*, *will*, may be kept or simplified in *skillful*, *skilful*, *willful*, *wilful*. This variation is not found with

<ss>: *blissful*, *distressful*, *stressful*, *successful*. Some words ending in <s> may or may not double it: *biassed–biased*, *busses–buses*, *bussing–busing*, *focussed–focusing*.

The stress pattern is relevant to verbs ending in <-er>. Those with stress on the last syllable of the base form *confer, defer, prefer, refer*, have <C>-doubling in their inflected forms *conferring, deferred, preferred, referring*, as do *disbarring, abhorring, demurring*. On the other hand, *differ, offer, proffer, suffer,* with stress on the first syllable, do not, as in *differed, offering, proffered, sufferer.*

The abbreviation *cel* from *celluloid*, meaning 'a celluloid still from a cartoon film' (*The Independent* 20/01/92: 12), has a plural *cels*. Doubling would cause confusion by making it identical with *cell.*

Absence of <C>-doubling before a word boundary

#D5: <C>-doubling does not, however, usually occur with /p b t d g m n/ before a word boundary: *rip*, *rib*, *lit*, *lid*, *leg*, *ram*, *ran*.

This may not apply in proper names. Underlying //r// should also be included here, though the vowel in front of it is now long in SBS – cf. *mar –marry*. In effect final <C>-doubling is largely restricted to <ff>, <ss>, <ll>, <ck>, <tch>, <dge>. Monosyllabic VC lexical words may be bulked up to a minimum of three letters by <C>-doubling to set them apart from the smaller function words: *add*, *egg*, *inn*, *err* (the 'short word rule' p. 131).

Absence of <C>-doubling in three-syllable words

#D6: When the primary stress falls on a short vowel which is three or more syllables from the end of a minimal free form, there is usually no <C>-doubling to mark it.

This accounts for the absence of <C>-doubling in words such as *bigamy*, *caravan*, *cataract*, *celery*, *character*, *copula*, *denizen*, *elephant*, *faculty*, *nemesis*, *pelican*, *prodigal*, *strategy.* This is also the case with similar words which, for some speakers, may have final stress, such as *gaberdine* (not *<gabberdine>), but these are a minority. Chomsky and Halle (1968: 77ff) provide an Alternating Stress Rule to ensure antepenultimate stress in most trisyllabic words, but words such as /gæbə'diːn/ would have to be marked as exceptions. We can note that in context such words frequently do have their stress shifted to the first syllable: my *gab*erdine *rain*coat, my *new* gaber*dine*. Jones (1956: §931f) called this 'rhythmical variation'. In recent years the same notion has been developed in the framework of metrical phonology.

§Latinate prefixes, as in *attribute, dissolute, suffragan*, etc., are excluded (#D2, p. 119).

Absence of <C>-doubling before certain endings

#D7: <C>-doubling does not usually occur before the bound-form endings <-ic>, <-id>, <-ish>, <-ule> and §Latinate <-it>.

Cf. *static*, *tepid*, *polish*, *globule*, *debit*. In *mannish*, *reddish*, etc., the <-ish> is an affix added to a free form. §Latinate <-it> words include *credit*, *debit*, *digit*, *edit*, *elicit*, *habit*, *limit*, *merit*, *posit*, *profit*, *spirit*, *tacit*, *visit*, *vomit*. Most of these are marked as §Latinate by word formation: *digital*, *editorial*, *habitual*, *limitation*, *meritorious*. There are very few other words ending in <-CCit>. Of these *rabbit*, in spite of distant French origins, has come to be seen as §Basic. *Summit* misleadingly preserves the <-mm-> of a Latin stem. The association of <C>-doubling with §Basic words is shown in *whodunnit*.

<C>-doubling and the constant morpheme shape

#D8: <C>-doubling persists in the spelling of a morpheme even when the primary stress is shifted by stress-determining suffixes.

This often involves reduction of the vowel before the <-CC-> to /ə/, as in *grammar–grammatical*. Other consonants may change to accommodate suffixes, as in *sabbath–sabbatical*.

<C>-doubling before inverted <le> in §Basic words: mettle, meddle

#D9: Before final /əl/ in a word, a previous short vowel is marked by <C>-doubling and the /əl/ is spelt with inverted <le> in §Basic words: *mettle*, *meddle*, *peddle*, *bubble*, *bottle*, etc.

Final /əl/ is not marked by doubling in §Latinate words and the /əl/ is spelt with a vowel letter (usually <a> or <e>) followed by <l>: *chapel*, *medal*, *metal*, *panel*, *pedal*, *petal*.

<C>-doubling after 'new' long vowels: /ɑː/, /ɔː/ and /ɜː/

#D10: There are several instances in which the general restriction that <C>-doubling does not follow long vowels (#D1) appears to fail in SBS. These involve the 'new' long vowels /ɑː/, /ɔː/ and /ɜː/.

These vowels have developed since early Modern English by the lengthening of original short vowels before certain consonants. From the point of view of the writing system, these SBS vowels have to be regarded as underlying 'short' vowels. They do not enter into contrasting pairs of 'long'–'short' vowels . The following instances of <ff>, <ss>, <ll> and <rr> are relevant:

1 <ff>≡/f/ and <ss>≡/s/ occur after /ɑː/ (*staff*, *class*) marking an original short vowel which was lengthened before these consonants in the eighteenth century in the South of England (Wells (1982) – 'Pre-

fricative lengthening' and 'TRAP–BATH SPLIT'). This left the more conservative Northerners with a more regular system of <C>-doubling;

2 <ll>≡/l/ occurs after /ɔː/ (*small*) finally in monosyllabic free forms;

3 a vowel letter followed by <rr> may represent /ɜːr/ or /ɑːr/ before a vowel (*referral*, *furry*, *starry*), usually at a free form boundary.

Graphotactic restrictions on <C>-doubling

#D11: There are letter-sequencing (graphotactic) restrictions on <C>-doubling. It does not occur:

1 if the previous vowel is spelt with more than one letter (*trouble–rubble*);

2 if the vowel correspondence following the consonant is medial <y>≡/ɪ/ (*onyx*, *larynx*);

3 if a suffix or other morpheme follows beginning with the same letter {full+ly} > *fully*. Compare *shrilly*, *stilly*.

This means that, although we can write a compound *pondlife* as one word, we have to put a hyphen in *still-life*. Compare 'a skull-less skeleton' with 'a headless skeleton'.

A trial run: instances of <bb>

We can now try these generalizations on a sample group of words by taking those words which have a stressed short vowel followed by phoneme /b/, to see how far they predict the spellings <bb> and <b>.

Free forms consisting of one or two syllables are easily identified as the whole word or as part of the word in:

> *abbe*, *abbey*, *abbot*, *abbess*, *babble*, *blubber*, *bobbin*, *bobby*, *bubble*, *cabbage*, *cabby*, *chubby*, *clobber*, *cobble*, *crabbed*, *cribbage*, *cubby-hole*, *dabble*, *dibble*, *dribble*, *drubbing*, *dubbing*, *fibber*, *flabby*, *gabble*, *gibber*, *gibberish*, *gibbet*, *gibbon*, *gobble*, *grubby*, *hobble*, *hobby*, *hubbub*, *jabber*, *lobby*, *lubber*, *nibble*, *nobble*, *pebble*, *quibble*, *rabbi*, *rabbit*, *rabble*, *ribbon*, *robber*, *rubber*, *rubble*, *sabbath*, *scabbard*, *scrabble*, *scribble*, *shabby*, *shrubbery*, *shrubby*, *slobber*, *snobbery*, *snobbish*, *squabble*, *stubble*, *stubborn*, *tabby*, *wobble*, *yobbo*, etc. The final <bb> of *ebb* is also regular (the 'short word rule' p. 131).

As one would expect, final <bb> does occur irregularly in names as padding – *Chubb*, *Cobb*, *Robb*, *Webb*, and *Dobbs*, *Gibbs*, *Hobbs*, *Stubbs*, *Tibbs*.

A shortening marker is identifiable in the endings of *aerobic* (some speakers have /əʊ/ anyway), *globule*, *rabid*, *debit*, and *habit*, (#D7), so there is no <bb>. As for *snobbish* and *rubbish*, /snɒb/ is a free form and we expect the <bb>. *Rubbish*, however, is irregular; it does not relate to any meaning of *rub*. If we look at minimal free forms of more than two syllables with stress on the antepenultimate, we find one example with doubling: *shibboleth*. There is, however, quite a large group of forms without doubling:

abatis, *abacus*, *bobolink*, *ebonite*, *ebony*, *gaberdine*, *habergeon*, *cabaret*, *labyrinth*, *liberate*, *liberal*, *liberty*, *libertine*, *obelisk*, *plebiscite*, *probable*, *sabotage*, *sibilant*, *sybarite*, *subaltern*, *tibia*.

These bear out the expectation in #D6 that, when the primary stress is three syllables from the end of a word, the short vowel is most frequently not marked by <C>-doubling. This is the context for third-syllable shortening, though in the above examples there is no evidence of other forms with underlying long vowels. There are also *haberdasher*, *prebendary*, and *tabernacle*, which have stress on the fourth syllable from the end.

It would evidently be difficult to sort out the above <bb> and <b> spellings on the tempting hypothesis that doubled letters occur in §Basic words. Pure etymology would certainly produce numerous exceptions. There would be some conflict with correspondences such as /ʤ/≡<g> in *gibbet*, an early borrowing from French.

What we now have left is rather a mixture. *Double* and *trouble* have no <C>-doubling because the short vowel is spelt with a digraph (#D11). The words *gobbledygook*, *flabbergasted*, and *flibbertigibbet* are typical of invented or onomatopoeic words which phonetically have all the appearance of compounds. If they are taken to be pseudo-compounds, then *gobble-*, *flabber-*, *flibber-*, and *-gibbet* can be treated as free forms with the expected <bb> spelling. *Cupboard* is not now recognizable as a compound and would be better spelt **cubbard*. The words *rabbinical*, *sabbatical*, and *sabbatarian* are covered by #D8. Here, because of the stress shift and vowel reduction and the change in the final /θ/ of *sabbath*, the speller has somehow to identify the stem morpheme to get the <-bb-> spelling. In *abbreviate*, *abbreviation*, the unstressed /əb/ has to be identified as a prefix before the stem <-brev-> (#D2). This is asking rather a lot of our normal literate English adult, especially since assimilation of the underlying *ad-* to the following /b/, makes it confusingly like the prefix *ab-*, which has a very different meaning, and also because of the many words with initial <a-> (*abreast*, etc.).

What still remains unaccounted for is a small group of exceptions, where <C>-doubling is not found after the stressed short vowel in disyllabic words: *cabin*, *rebel* (n.), *ribald*, *riband*, *robin*, *suburb*, *tabard*, *treble*. Some shreds of explanation are still extractable for various individual words: *rebel* is derived from the underlying verb, where the stress is on the second syllable; *suburb* has the prefix *sub-*, but it is by no means certain that a speller would make the link with *urban* and regard <sub-> as a prefix here; *riband* does have an alternative spelling *ribband* in engineering usage. *Treble* is exceptional beyond all hope. Present-day spellers can hardly be expected to know the etymological reason for the single <b>: that it goes back to an original cluster /-pl-/, which is now split by /ə/. In earlier centuries the spelling of some of these words was often regularized to <-bb-> (e.g. **ribbald*). From a teaching point of view they clearly form a group of exceptions, since the regular <-bb-> occurs in many similar words: *scabbard–tabard*, *bobbin–robin*, *pebble–treble*.

There are, no doubt, other strategies to predict <C>-doubling. At the expense of learning a list of Latin stems with doubled letters (as in *horrid*, *ferric*, etc.), one might follow through the hypothesis that <C>-doubling is a feature of §Basic words and not of §Latinate and §Greek words. One could explain the doubling in *reddish* as a feature of a §Basic system word *red*, while *replenish* belongs to a §Latinate system and its stressed vowel is linked to forms such as *plenary*, where the vowel is long. Shortening of underlying long vowels is largely confined to §Latinate vocabulary, though it does occur in §Basic words: *wise–wisdom*, *South–Southern*, *know–knowledge*, *holy–holiday*. On the other hand, the generalization in #D4 simply requires the speller to recognize the free form /red-/ within *reddish* and to recognize that there is no similar free form within *replenish*. Recognising /red-/ as {red} in *reddish* does, of course, involve semantic identity, but the phonetic form is constant. This is different from the difficulty which a normal adult speller might have in handling the semantics of Latin and Greek morphology.

Doubling, in spite of its importance in the present writing system, does not find favour with most spelling reformers as a convenient way of marking the 'short' quantity of a previous vowel. Reformers usually operate on the principle, stated or unstated, that a vowel should be fully represented by a string of one or more vowel letters. The guiding principles of 'New Spelling', the scheme favoured by the Simplified Spelling Society of Great Britain include: '(5) Each symbol (letter or digraph) to be self-contained, that is, its significance not to depend on any other letter in the sequence' (MacCarthy 1969a: 95). He points out that this precludes 'the doubling of consonant letters to indicate the (short) value of the preceding vowel'. The scheme does, however, include the use of <rr> to distinguish:

/ɑː/ in *starry* *<stari> from /æ/ in *carry* *<karri>;
/ɜː/ in *furry* *<furi> from /ʌ/ in *hurry* *<hurri> (*fury* is *<fueri>);
/ɔː/ in *story* *<stori> from /ɒ/ in *sorry* *<sorri>.

Wijk (1959), who tries as far as possible to preserve the regularities of the present system, retains <C>-doubling as a vowel marker, extending its use to spellings such as: **reddy*, **shaddoe*, **sammon*, **wimmen*, **munney*, etc. These respellings are clearly recognizable to any reader. But Wijk does not do this throughout and presents a rather ill-defined compromise:

> It will evidently be a very difficult problem to decide exactly how far one should go in this respect. On the whole it would seem preferable not to

> make any changes except where they are definitely desirable . . .
>
> (Wijk 1959: 106)

What exactly is desirable and why, is not explored.

From the purely descriptive point of view, <C>-doubling is not regarded as an important regularity by all linguists. Hall (1961: 45) puts it into a curious category of ‘regular irregularities’:

> . . . even our irregular spellings are by no means wholly random; they fall, to a large extent, into certain sub-sets which are consistent within themselves . . . which we might call ‘regular irregularities’, such as *ee* and *ea* for /iy/, *oa* and *oe* for /ow/, etc. Another type of ‘regular irregularity’, this time in the writing of consonants, is the use of double consonant letters at the end of words, and after vowel letters in their ‘short’ values in the middle of words: e.g. *muff*, *till*, *mitt* etc.; *sitting*, *hatter*, *kidded* and so on. With spellings of this type, their phonemic interpretation is still quite clear, and the normal speaker of English will read off *spreat* as /spríyt/, *toak* as /tówk/, or *diff* as /díf/. Going the other way, however, these ‘regular irregularities’ offer alternate ways of writing down what one hears, and it is quite likely that a person who hears such a word as /níyk/ may write as *neak* or *neek* instead of *neke*, or may write /lə́rt/ as either *lurt*, *lert* or *lirt*. This type of alternate possibility, within the framework of our ‘regular irregularities’, is responsible for a large proportion of the naive and harmless misspellings we get all the time from so many children (and adults!). . . . [Note. Hall’s /iy/, /ow/, /ərt/≡SBS/iː/, /əʊ/, /ɜːt /]
>
> (Hall 1961: 45)

Hall evidently sees less predictability in <C>-doubling than we have suggested, since he puts the difference between pairs such as <tt> and <t> as spellings of /t/ on a par with the difference between <ea> and <ee> as spellings of /iː/. Even at the level of mere predictability this is clearly uninformative, but it also ignores the marking function in the <tt> and <t> difference. Anyone familiar with English conventions who hears */zætə/ will certainly not spell it as *<zater>. The two spellings *<zatter> and *<zater> are not ‘alternate possibilities’.

<C>-doubling is part of a more regular graphotactic pattern in present-day English orthography. A single vowel letter before any <CC> cluster tends to represent a short vowel; the complex historical developments which brought this about are reviewed in Cummings (1988: 96ff). The spelling <th> behaves as a letter cluster in this respect since, within a morpheme and without <e>-marking, it is usually preceded by a short vowel – *bother*, *gather*, *mother*, *wither*, or by the ‘new’ long vowel /ɑː/ – *father*, *lather* (var.), *rather*. Occasional exceptions occur in §Greek words – *ethos*, *pathos*, etc. Similarly, the spelling <sh> rarely has a preceding long vowel (as /əʊ/ in *kosher*). Some consonant letter clusters, however, may allow a previous long vowel: <-mb>

(*climb*, *tomb*), <-nd> (*find*), <-ld> (*cold*, *mild*), <-lt> (*bolt*), <-st(e)> (*waste*), <-gh> (*night*, *sigh*), <-gn> (*sign*), <-ng(e)> (*change*). These are discussed in the following sections under individual vowels. Clusters containing /f, θ, s/ and some clusters of nasal + consonant, such as <sp>, <st>, <ft>, <nt>, have the 'new' long vowel /ɑː/ (*clasp*, *fast*, *aft*, *plant*, etc.) in SBS. The spelling <-Cle> (*noble*, *staple*) is not really an exception to the general rule since <-le>, like the <-re> of *fibre*, *ogre*, is essentially a vowel + consonant spelling in which the letters are conventionally switched round (metathesis).

3.2.3 <e>-marking functions

Marking long vowels

Equally important as <C>-doubling in showing the quality of the preceding vowel is the <e>-marking of long vowels. The two processes are often complementary: <e>-marking in *mate* makes it unnecessary (#D4) to have <C>-doubling in *mat*; <C>-doubling in *latter* makes it unnecessary to have <e>-marking before the vowel-initial suffix in *later*. On the face of it this alternation between the two markers represents economy of effort. But there are other factors. A constant, and hence sometimes redundant, marking of long vowels with <e> would produce spellings of /eɪ/ such as *take*, **takeing*, **takeer*, which would make the interpretation of vowel digraphs such as <ei>, <ee>, more difficult. This is not a problem in 'New Spelling', where the marking <e> forms a digraph with the previous vowel letter: *<taek>, *<taeking>, *<taeker>. As with <C>-doubling, the <e>-marking of vowels in names is discussed separately in §6.4 pp. 454ff.

An <e>-marking rule cannot simply operate on a phonological class of long vowels; it also requires to know whether the vowel is spelt with a single letter or not.

#E1: Long vowels (spelt with a single vowel letter) followed by a single consonant (spelt with a single consonant letter) and a free-form boundary are marked by an <e> after the consonant.

Examples: *late, debate, mete, deplete, rise, confide, rope, atone, tune, repute*.

In recent §French loan-words, such as *charade* and *latrine*, the stressed <a> and <i> may have their closest English equivalents /ɑː/ and /iː/, rather than /eɪ/ and /aɪ/. Exceptionally, there may be no <e>-marking, as in *corral*, *motif*.

Marking stem-final /s/, /z/ *and* /ð/

The marking function of <-e> may also serve to indicate differing word-structure:

#E2: Stem-final /s/, /z/ and /ð/ are marked by an <e> after long vowel

digraphs, as in *crease*, *house*, *browse*, *maize*, *praise*, *parse*, *freeze*, *breathe*, **and after short vowel plus consonant**, as in *else, tense, adze*, *bronze*, *cleanse*.

This extension of <e>-marking differentiates the /z/ of inflected forms from stem-final /z/: *prays–praise*, *frees–freeze*, and differentiates final /θ/ in nouns and adjectives from final /ð/ in verbs: *bath–bathe*, *loath–loathe.* The verb *to mouth* is an exception.

Marking word-final stressed <-CCe> in French loan-words

We also find <e>-marking of stress in §French stressed endings such as <-ette>, <-enne>:

#E3: Stressed endings consisting of a short vowel and a single consonant in §French loan-words tend to have double <-CCe>.

The §French loan-words are usually recognizable as such by the final stress. The most common are words ending in <-ette>: *brunette*, *cassette*, *chiffonette*, *coquette*, *corvette*, *croquette*, *gazette*, *marionette*, *pipette*, *pirouette*, *rosette*. The <-ette> has become, by analogy, a diminutive suffix that can be added to free forms to form new coinages: *flannelette*, *kitchenette*, *launderette*, *novelette*. Frequently used words may have the stress shifted to the first syllable, as in *cigarette*, *etiquette*, *omelette, vaudeville*. The stress shift in *kilogramme*, *programme* has probably encouraged a change of <-amme> to <-am>. This is the usual form in American spelling. In British English the <-amme> spelling is still used, but *program* is the form required in computer applications and increasingly elsewhere. In computer operating systems the spelling <program> is frequently a reserved word.

Other examples are: *giraffe*, *gazelle*, *cayenne*, *comedienne*, *cretonne*, *bizarre*, *parterre*, *pelisse*, *crevasse*, *finesse*, *impasse*, *lacrosse*, *largesse, gavotte*. There are also some monosyllables with a final <-CCe> spelling which, as such, have no stress marker: *gaffe*, *tulle*, *grippe*, *steppe*, *mousse*.

3.2.4 Deletion of the final <e> marker in derived forms

Spellers are often very uncertain about when to delete the final <-e> of a word if an ending is added. The basic rule is simple enough: the <-e> is deleted if the ending begins with a vowel. The <e> that marks long vowels, as in *mate*, is regularly deleted before the inflections {-ed}, {-ing}, as in *mated*, *mating*. This is no confusion since <C>-doubling takes over the task of marking the vowel length: *mate* and *mat* become *mated* and *matted*, *mating* and *matting*. Before a consonant, there is no deletion: *hateful*, *finely*, *elopement*, *paleness*. The <e> that marks a stem-final /z/, /ð/ or /v/ is also deleted: *teasing*, *loathing*, *loving*, *festivity*. This makes {bathe} and {bath} homographs in *bathing*, *bathed*, *bather* (which can conceivably also mean 'one who baths someone'). The deletion also affects the empty <e> of *come*, to give *coming*. The suffix <-ine> also loses its <e>: *alkalinity*, *salinity*, where the vowel is shortened to /ɪ/ by third-syllable shortening.

The <-e> has to be kept when it is a marker of the pronunciation of the previous consonant as in *gaugeable*, *manageable*, *noticeable*, *traceable*. A spelling *<noticable> would invite <c>≡/k/ before the <a> as in *practicable*. So, *singeing* with /nʤ/ is kept different from *singing* with /ŋ/. It has to be said that present spelling does not do this with any consistency and with advantage could be regularized. We have *change*, *changing*, *hinge*, *hinging*, *whinge*, *whinging*, where a regularized *<changeing> would be a vast improvement. Again, if dictionary makers already allow some undeleted forms before <-able> such as *likeable*, *saleable*, there is no good reason why the freedom could not be extended to other words with <-able>, allowing *<deleteable>, *<wipeable>, etc.

The <e> in the vowel digraphs <-ee> and <-oe> is not deleted before <-i->, giving *agreeing*, *seeing*, *canoeing*, *shoeing*, *toeing*, etc. The reason is no doubt that the loss of <e> would cause confusion between <ei> and <oi> if we had **seing*, **shoing*. The <e> of the digraph <-ue> is usually deleted, as in *arguing*, *accruing*, *barbecuing*, *construing*, *continuing*, *ensuing*, *issuing*, *pursuing*, *queuing*, *rescuing*, *ruing*, *subduing*, *valuing*, and in *truism*. On the other hand, there is free variation between *blueish*, *bluish*, *clueing*, *cluing*, *cueing*, *cuing*, *glueing*, *gluing*, *trueing*, *truing*. The spelling *blueish* preserves the written shape of the morpheme, whereas *bluish* begins to look uncomfortably like *blush*. Nor is the <-e> deleted in *bluey*, *gluey*, since *<bluy>, *<gluy>, begin to resemble the <uy> spelling in *buy*, *guy*. The <-e> of final <-gue> is deleted in *cataloguing*, *fatiguing*, *haranguing*, *intriguing*, *monologuist, plaguing*, *tonguing*, as with <-que> in *cliquish*, . The <e> of final <-ie> is deleted, with a change of <i> to <y> to avoid <-ii->, in *lying*, *tying*. This gives the same spelling *dying* for both *die* and *dye*, though *dieing* is found in the sense 'cutting with a die'. This last example is like the rare <-ieing> forms noted by Cummings (1988: 157), *birdieing*, *sortieing*. The use of the nouns *die*, *birdie*, and *sortie* as verbs is evidently so novel that the orthography draws attention to it by ignoring the usual graphotactic change and here, too, preserving the shape of the morpheme. A further example would be the forms *marbleing* and *marbleize*, where the verbal forms are uncommon compared with *tabling*, *troubling*.

3.2.5 The 'short word rule'

Lexical words usually have a minimum of three letters

Both <e>-marking and <C>-doubling have another function in that they are used to bulk up the spelling of monosyllabic lexical words to a minimum of three letters (Jespersen 1909: 4.96). This is referred to as 'the short word rule' or 'the three letter rule'. Albrow cites this as one of the factors differentiating the main subsystems of lexical words from the subsystem of function words, in which the rule does not apply. Jespersen himself interprets the convention as essentially a marking of phonetic 'quantity' in that *be*, *by*, *in*, *an* (compared with *bee*, *bye*, *inn*, *Ann*) usually occur as unstressed syllables and are physically reduced compared with the equivalent stressed forms. Jespersen also notes that, in the seventeenth century, some authors used differential spelling to indicate [+/- stress] with variants such as *hee–he*, *shee–she*, etc. Whether the printing houses or the individual authors were responsible for this convention is not always clear (Brengelman 1980), but certainly Milton exercised a tight control over his text. He exploits this and other orthographic devices to show metrical intentions. Compare *me* and *mee* in:

so besides
Mine own that bide upon me, all from mee
Shall with a fierce reflux on mee redound,
On mee as on thir natural center light . . .
Did I request thee, Maker, from my Clay
To mould me Man, did I sollicite thee
From darkness to promote me, or here place
In this delicious Garden?

(Milton *Paradise Lost* X, 737ff.)

The pronoun *thee* cannot vary in this way because of potential confusion with the definite article *the*. Similarly Milton's text is careful to show how the {-ed} suffix is to be pronounced: 'with linked Thunderbolts' (PL I, 328); 'High overarch't' (PL I, 304); 'and darken'd all the Land' (PL I, 343). It is evidently intended that 'linked' should be pronounced /ˈlɪŋkəd/ or /ˈlɪŋkɪd/ in the above context.

John Donne uses the same stressed and unstressed forms of pronouns, with perhaps less consistency than the text of Milton, but certainly to good stylistic effect:

For every man alone thinkes he hath got
To be a Phoenix, and that then can bee
None of that kinde, of which he is, but hee.

(Donne *An Anatomie of the World*: 216ff.)

With our present standardized spelling we can no longer show allomorphic variation in stress in the function words by varying the vowel spelling, any more than we can show adequately the allomorphic variation between long and short vowels, as in *mime/mimic* or the different allomorphs of {-ed}. We can only show unstressed forms by using an apostrophe (*I've*, *I'm*, *they'll*, *aren't*, etc.) where the vowel is reduced (/aɪəv/) or completely lost /aɪv/. In 'New Spelling', consistent use of their reform criteria would give

*<mee>, *<hee>, *<shee>, *<wee>, *<bee>, but the present spellings are in fact retained to reflect the usual status of these function words as reduced forms (MacCarthy 1969a: 100). A viable alternative would be to take up Milton's usage with stressed *<shee> and unstressed <she> etc.

Albrow simply refers to the convention for the length of lexical monosyllables as 'the three letter rule'. If this is taken literally, it would seem that *ox* is an exception (Sampson 1985: 202, Stubbs 1980: 67), since it is a lexical word spelt with two letters. However, this need not be the best way of looking at it. In using the short word rule, we are in fact marking the long vowels of /CV/ lexical monosyllables with <-e> (*bye*, *lie*, *bee*, *toe*, *rue*) and the short vowels of /VC/ monosyllables with <C>-doubling (*ebb*, *add*, *inn*, *egg*) to show that, unlike function words, they are normally stressed. In that case, *ox* could be regarded as regular since phonetically it is a /VCC/ monosyllable. In any case <x> is not a consonant letter that can be doubled (#D3). The spelling <ox> is perfectly regular if we consider the 'three-letter rule' to be the normal exploiting of <e>-marking and <C>-doubling. The placename *Exe* is not a good analogy because <e> is often used as mere padding in the spelling of names (see §6.4). What does seem irregular then is the spelling of *axe* and *go*. The limited use of *go* as a borderline auxiliary, as in *I'm going to do it*, hardly makes it grammatical. However, there is no denying that *ox* does stand out as somewhat peculiar. It is worth noting that, in *OED*, Murray gives the spelling <ax> preference over <axe>, since it is 'better on every ground, of etymology, phonology, and analogy, than *axe*, which has of late become prevalent' (*OED* under *ax*, *axe*). The 1972 Supplement to *OED*, however, deletes the <ax> spelling as 'now disused in Britain'. *W3NID* gives both *ax* and *axe* with no stated preference. It may well be that the spelling *axe* derives from a reanalysis of the plural *axes* as <axe>+<s> rather than <ax>+<es>.

We can formulate the Short Word Rule just discussed as:

Lexical monosyllables are usually spelt with a minimum of three letters by exploiting <e>-marking or vowel digraphs or <C>-doubling where appropriate.

This means, for instance, that /V/ monosyllables must combine, irregularly, both a vowel digraph and <e>-marking (*eye*, *owe*); the long vowels of /CV/ monosyllables must have either at least a vowel digraph or <e>-marking (*nigh*, *low*, *die*, *bye*); short vowels in /VC/ monosyllables must be marked by <C>-doubling if the consonant letter is one which doubles elsewhere (*ebb*, *egg*). The <e> marker is kept in the suffixed forms *ageing*, *ageism*, *ageist*, unlike the regular *raging*, *staging*.

Abbreviations such as *bo* 'hobo', *ma*, *pa*, do not observe the rule, though *OED* does cite a variant *pah*, which did not catch on. The early names of some musical notes did not observe the rule: *do*, *re*, *mi*, *fa*, *so*, *la*, *ti*. Later spellings changed some of these: *doh*, *ray*, *fah*, *soh*, using <h>, untypically for English, to indicate a long vowel. Some consonant letters have 'names' spelt *ef*, *el*, *em*, *en*, in *OED*, which are exceptions; *ess* is not. There is doubling in the inflected form 'effing and blinding' to mean swearing. The word *hum*, which basically refers to the sound [m], has been bulked up with an initial <h>. Occasional exotic <CV> words such as *ti* 'tropical plant' and *bo* 'Senghalese tree' are exceptions that prove the rule. For the reader, they are clearly marked as §Exotic by the spelling.

3.3 SPEECH-TO-TEXT CORRESPONDENCES PHONEME BY PHONEME

Note: the phonemes are grouped phonetically. Traditional names, as in Cummings (1988), are associated with the vowels in addition to the IPA phonetic symbol.

In the following phoneme-by-phoneme survey of spelling regularities, the phonemes are grouped into phonetically convenient sections. The grouping and ordering of these sections is phonetic rather than 'alphabetical'. This is not often done in literacy work but, if we are to describe speech-to-text correspondences, it would seem sensible to start with natural phonetic classes.

1 short vowels: /ɪ, e, æ, ʊ, ʌ, ɒ/ (§3.3.1),
– these are sometimes referred to as 'checked' vowels since they cannot occur finally in an open syllable such as */pæ/, */nʊ/. For SBS, in the case of /ɪ/ this may have to mean in a stressed open syllable (if the speaker has /ɪ/ in *happy*, etc.). Conversely, long vowels are sometimes called 'free', since they do not have this restriction.
2 long phonological counterparts of the short vowels: /aɪ, iː, eɪ, aʊ, əʊ/ (§3.3.2),
3 long vowels associated (always or in part) with postvocalic //r//: /ɑː, ɔː, ɜː, ɪə, ɛə, ʊə, jʊə/ (§3.3.3),
4 other long vowels: /uː, juː, ɔɪ/ (§3.3.4),
5 /ə/ and vowel reduction (§3.3.5),
6 stops: /p, b, t, d, k, g, ʧ, ʤ/ (§3.3.6),
7 fricatives: /f, v, θ, ð, s, z, ʃ, ʒ, h/ (§3.3.7),
8 nasals: /m, n, ŋ/ (§3.3.8),
9 liquids: /l, r/ (§3.3.9),
10 semivowels: /w, j/ (§3.3.10).

The range of contexts in which each phoneme occurs is explored to find any regularities – either absolute or statistically worthwhile. Lists of examples are given to illustrate the range of words involved. How many words are actually given is a matter of judgement and relative interest. Derived forms with a given stem are not usually listed: *bawd*, *dawdle* and *tawdry* are given to illustrate /ɔː/≡<aw> before /d/ leaving out *bawdy* and *tawdriness*. Lists of words which are potentially much longer are left open with an 'etc.'. The lists derive from the database described in §3.1.1, so occasionally there may well be further possible examples of minority spellings in the fringes of archaic or technical vocabulary or in those foreign tags whose sheer foreigness, *bien entendu*, is their main attraction.

The description of the spelling of each phoneme ends with a summarized reference to the rules of the Hanna (1966) algorithm, since that project is responsible for widely-held views on the relative regularity of English spelling. Few of those who have inherited these views have actually seen the rules on which they are based. The Hanna rules are given with the necessary symbol translations. It is essential when gauging the effect of these rules to remember that most of the contexts 'initial', 'medial' and 'final' refer to positions in what Hanna regards as a 'syllable' (see §2.8.5 p. 87 for details). The rules for drawing these syllable boundaries were not made explicit; boundaries were given to the algorithm as part of the input. A few keywords are cited to illustrate each Hanna rule; these are taken from Hanna's output lists; in some cases they may appear distinctly odd to anyone who has a different concept of 'syllable'. The rules are numbered for reference purposes.

3.3.1 Short vowels: /ɪ, e, æ, ʊ, ʌ, ɒ/

3.3.1.1 /ɪ/ as in bit *('short <i>')*

The SBS phoneme corresponds to AmE /ɪ/. There is, however, a difference of distribution in unstressed syllables. AmE and an increasing number of younger SBS speakers would have a closer [i]-like quality in the final unstressed vowel of *hankie*, *happy*, *monkey*, and would assign it to phoneme /iː/ rather than /ɪ/. On the other hand, many Northern speakers of British English have /ɪ/ as in SBS. Traditional phonemic analysis requires the vowel to be lumped either with /ɪ/ or with /iː/. The contrast between /ɪ/ and /iː/ is effectively neutralized in this final unstressed context.

AmE has /aɪ/ rather than /ɪ/, as in SBS, in the prefixes *anti-*, *multi-*, and *semi-*, and in a number of words such as *dynasty, endive, hilarious, short-lived, simultaneous, vitamin.*

Distribution of variant spellings

/ɪ/ has some spelling divergence since it occurs not only in stressed syllables but also in unstressed syllables, where it is linked in morphology to several different stressed vowels and so to a range of different minority spellings. This linkage makes it difficult to provide statistics. The figures given in table 14, below, lump together occurrences of /ɪ/ in both stressed and unstressed syllables. They relate to uninflected forms, so the regular adaptation of final <y> to <ie> as in *carry, carried, carries* is not included. The figures given in brackets include all those instances of unstressed /ɪ/ which are in free variation with /ə/ in words such as *private*, *goodness*, *forest*, *furnace*, *mountain*. These bracketed figures represent a maximal use of /ɪ/ in preference to /ə/ in unstressed syllables (excluding inflections as in *watches*, *wanted*), but the

Table 14 Spellings of /ɪ/

spellings of /ɪ/	*TF*		*LF*	
<i>	61 %	(60 %)	61 %	(58 %)
<y>	20 %	(19 %)	21 %	(19 %)
<e>	16 %	(18 %)	16 %	(20 %)
<a>, <a..e>	2 %	(2 %)	<1 %	(2 %)
other spellings	2 %	(2 %)	1 %	(1 %)

difference between the two sets of figures is hardly significant.

AmE would differ in the percentage of <y>≡/ɪ/, since the many instances of final unstressed <-y> in *happy* etc. would be transferred to /iː/.

The inclusion of function words *him*, *his*, *in*, *is*, *it*, *will*, which have /ɪ/≡<i> would increase the text frequency of <i> spellings to 64%. The above figures also assume that the final vowel in words such as *happy*, *easy*, is equated with /ɪ/ rather than with /iː/. Three instances of /ɪ/ which cause spelling problems in homophonous affixes are discussed in detail in §5.5: the endings <-ied> and <-id> in *sullied–solid* (see p. 430), the endings <-y>, <-ie> and <-ey> as in *hanky*, *hankie*, *monkey*, *Freddy*, *Freddie* (see p. 431), and stem-final /ɪ/ as either <e> or <i> in *stupefy*, *putrify* (see p. 438).

In morphology /ɪ/ is the shortened alternant of /aɪ/ in pairs such as *agile–agility*, *analyse–analytic*, *mime–mimic*, *sign–signature*.

<y> spellings

In SBS, <y>≡/ɪ/ occurs both in unstressed and stressed syllables. It is the default spelling of unstressed /ɪ/ word-finally: *carry*, *city*, *country*, etc. A regular adaptation rule converts this final <y> to <ie> to form the plural of nouns (*cities, dollies*, etc.) and the third person singular present of verbs (*carries, sullies*, etc.). The possessive singular is *city's*; the possessive plural is *cities'*. The plural of the abbreviation *poly*, for *polytechnic*, is *polys*. Compare also *the two Germanys*.

Some suffixes do not change a preceding <y> spelling (*ferryman*, *babyhood*); others have <i-> instead (*fanciful*, *happiness*). A boundary has to be recognized in names such as *Barrymore*, *Eddystone*, *Gettysburg*, *Hollywood*, *Holyrood*, *Lillywhite*, *Prettyman*. On the other hand, with most names ending in <-man> such as *Elliman*, *Harriman*, *Horniman*, *Merriman*, *Runciman*, the first part is not spelt as if it were a free-form. This is also true of names in <-son>: *Davison*, *Edison*, *Harrison*, *Margerison*, *Morrison*.

<y> is also commonly found in §Greek words and names:

- (stressed) – *asphyxiate*, *cryptic*, *crystal*, *cyclamen*, *cygnet*, *cylinder*, *cynic*, *dynasty*, *glycerine*, *gymnast*, *gypsum*, *hieroglyphic*, *hymn*, *hypnotism*, *lymph*, *nymph*, *polygamy*, *salicylic*, *strychnine*, *sybarite*, *sycamore*,

sycophant, *symbol*, *sympathy*, *syndicate*, *syphilis*, *tyranny*, etc.; in names – *Cyril*, *Lycidas*, etc.;
- (unstressed) – *acetylene*, *apocrypha*, *beryl*, *bicycle*, *calyx*, *caryatid*, *chlorophyl*, *cotyledon*, *etymology*, *hydroxyl*, *onyx*, *oryx*, *oxygen*, *pachyderm*, *pharynx*, *phylactery*, *polyandry*, *polyanthus*, *polygon*, *pterodactyl*, *triptych*, etc.; in names – *Beryl*, etc.

Even when a §Greek word is marked in some way so that the speller knows it is '§Greek', there is still the need to select between <y> and <i> spellings. §Greek morphemes which have /aɪ/ – /ɪ/ variation will have a <y> spelling: *cycle–bicycle*, *tyrant–tyranny*. Some words which have come into English by way of French have been given a <y> by reviving the Greek etymology: *gryphon* is simply a respelling of *griffin*. *Pigmy* has the variant spelling *pygmy*. *Gipsy* has a variant *gypsy*, which seems more common in the plural *gypsies*; it relates to *Egypt*, thought to be their country of origin. A few words with stressed <y>≡/ɪ/ have no valid Greek connection: *gymkhana*, *gyp*, *lynch*.

Welsh names may also have <y>≡/ɪ/ spellings: *Aberystwyth*, *Brynmawr*, *Colwyn*, *Dilys*, *Dylan*, *Glynis*, *Llewellyn*, etc.

An antiquarian <y> spelling of stressed /ɪ/ is often found in §Basic names such as *Aldwych*, *Brooklyn*, *Byng*, *Collyns*, *Conyngham*, *Hylton*, *Lydgate*, *Lyly*, *Lyndhurst*, *Prynne*, *Pym*, *Smyth*, *Thynne*, *Wycliffe*, *Wyndham*.

Minority spellings in stressed syllables

There are a number of minority and nonce spellings for stressed /ɪ/, which figure prominently in the spelling literature:

- <e> : *England, English, pretty*;
- <ee> : *breeches*;
- <ie> : *sieve*;
- <o> : *women*;
- <u> : *business*, *busy*;
- <ui> would belong here, too, unless *build*, *built* is analysed with <bu>≡/b/, parallel with <gu>≡/g/ in *guild*, etc.

Unstressed syllables

There is further spelling divergence for /ɪ/ in unstressed syllables. <a>≡/ɪ/ only occurs in unstressed syllables. No less than TF 78%, LF 91 per cent of instances of this correspondence occur in either the ending <-age> (with bound or free stems) or the ending <-ate> (nouns or adjectives, but not verbs, which would have full vowel quality /eɪt/).

Examples of <-age> : (with a bound stem) *advantage*, *average*, *courage*, *damage*, *image*, *language*, *manage*, *message*, *village*, etc.; (added as a suffix to free-forms) *breakage*, *cleavage*, *leakage*, *orphanage*, *passage*, *pilgrimage*, *poundage*, *roughage*, *sewerage*, etc. Examples in names are *Armitage*, *Burbage*, *Carthage*, *Cranage*, *Gamage*, etc. In *marriage* and *carriage* the /ɪ/ at the end of the stem and the /ɪ/ of the suffix merge into one; the <i> of the stem can be regarded as an inert letter. There is scope for spelling confusion with the ending <-age> in the final syllables of *college*, *privilege*, *sacrilege*; *vestige*; *cartridge*, *partridge*, *porridge*; *knowledge*, *selvedge*.

Examples of <-ate> (with either /ɪ/ or /ə/): *delicate*, *climate*, *private*, *estimate* (n.), *accurate*, *temperate*, etc. In compound names, unstressed {gate} often has /eɪ/ reduced to /ɪ/: *Aldgate*, *Ludgate*, *Margate*, *Ramsgate*, etc. This ending has a certain interest since *Margate* was an example used by Robert Bridges to object to Daniel Jones' phonetic transcriptions of unstressed vowels. Bridges insisted that the phonetic [ɪ] of *Margate* could only usefully be regarded as a recognizable /eɪ/ and remained functionally different from the /ɪ/ of *bit* (Bridges 1919: 43). Jones for his part lamented the growth of spelling pronunciations: 'Margate trippers now generally speak of /ˈmɑːgeɪt/ instead of /ˈmɑːgɪt/' (EPD 1st edn 1917: v). The issue is really one of phonological theory and both views are 'correct', but at the time the issue was 'the beauty of the language'.

Other instances of <a>≡/ɪ/ in SBS are: *shillelagh*; *literature*, *signature*, *temperature*; *spinach*; *character*; *orange*; *furnace*, *necklace*, *palace*, *pinnace*, *preface*, *surface*; *purchase*. Many speakers will have /ə/ in some of these. *Wallace* has a variant *Wallis*.

Apart from a few exceptional spellings such as *England*, *English* and *pretty*, <e>≡/ɪ/ only occurs in unstressed syllables. Most instances occur in affixes such as <de->, <re->, or in recurrent bound morphemes such as <tele->:

- <be-> : *become*, *befriend*, *befuddle*, *behalf*, *beloved*, *besiege*, *betray*, *bewildered*, etc.;
- <de-> : *deliver*, *demand*, *depart*, *depend*, *describe*, *derogatory*, *design*, *desire*, *detract*, *develop*, etc.;
- <e-> : *effect*, *eject*, *elope*, *emerge*, *emotion*, *erode*, etc.;
- <ex-> : *exhibit*, *expect*, *explode*, *extinguish*, *extreme*, *exuberant*, etc.; this prefix has /e/ even when unstressed in some accents;
- <pre-> : *predict*, *prepare*, *preponderant*, *preserve*, *pretend*, *prevent*, etc.;
- <re-> : *receive*, *refresh*, *remember*, *respectable*, *result*, etc.;
- <-ed> : *avowedly*, *blessed*, *ragged*, *sacred*, *wicked*, etc.;
- <-et> : *blanket*, *brisket*, *budget*, *gusset*, *market*, *pocket*, *poet*, *puppet*, *trumpet*, *whippet*, etc. This common ending <-et> differs from the others in not being a morpheme. In names the doubled spelling <-ett> is equally common: *Blackett*, *Garnett*, *Jarrett*, *Smollett*, *Tippett*, etc. compared with *Becket*, *Bridget*, *Dorset*, *Somerset*, etc. There are occasional spelling variants with <i>: *Jowett–Jowitt*;
- <-ety> : *anxiety*, *moiety*, *notoriety*, *piety*, *propriety*, *sobriety*, *variety*, etc. – this is a variant of <-ity> used after a letter <i> to prevent the minim

sequence *<ii>.

In polysyllabic stems there are frequent instances of unstressed <e>≡/ɪ/. These cannot be catered for by simple correspondence rules, since it is difficult to specify any context. In some cases there is nothing in the morphology to point to an <e> spelling rather than <i>:

- *anecdote*, *antelope*, *apothecary*, *arquebus*, *category*, *consecrate*, *eczema*, *elephant*, *fuselage*, *hallelujah*, *isosceles*, *mannequin*, *ocelot*, *peregrine*, *vaseline*, *vehement*, *vinegar*, etc.

In many other instances, however, the /ɪ/ is a reduction of a vowel /e/ or /iː/ and this morphological relationship indicates the <e> spelling. The /nɪg/ of *negation* need not be a spelling problem if associated with the /neg/ of *negative*; the /rɪg/ of *regalia* (some *rig*!) associates with the /riːg/ of *regal*. Possible examples where, for some speakers at least, this type of relationship might be evident, are:

- (unstressed /ɪ/ related to stressed /e/) – *alchemist*, *allegation*, *celebrity*, *crescendo*, *integration*, *medicament*, *negation*, *neglect*, *rebellion*, *subject* (n.), *tremendous*, etc.;
- (unstressed /ɪ/ related to stressed /iː/) – *barometer*, *regalia*, *renegade*, *sequential*, *theatrical*, etc.

The stem-final /ɪ/ before some endings may have <e> rather than <i> (see §5.5, pp. 438f.): *stupefy–typify*, *permeate–calumniate*, *rodeo* (as /ˈrəʊdɪəʊ/)–*studio*, *lineage–foliage*.

Speakers who have /ə/ rather than /ɪ/ in the diminutive noun suffix {-icle} (as in *follicle*, *radicle*, *testicle*, etc.) will find it difficult to distinguish from the noun ending <-acle> in *barnacle*, *spectacle*, *tentacle*, etc. The stressed vowels of *spectacular*, *testicular*, may help.

In final open unstressed syllables in free-forms (where some accents may have /iː/ rather than /ɪ/), the default spelling of /ɪ/ is <-y>, but <-ey>, <-ie> and <-e> also occur; <-ey> and <-ie> are restricted to this context:

- <-ey> in nouns: *abbey*, *alley*, *attorney*, *barley*, *chimney*, *chutney*, *coney*, *covey*, *donkey*, *flunkey*, *galley*, *hackney*, *hockey*, *honey*, *jersey*, *jockey*, *journey*, *kersey*, *kidney*, *lackey*, *lamprey*, *medley*, *money*, *monkey*, *motley*, *palfrey*, *parley*, *parsley*, *pulley*, *storey*, *tourney*, *trolley*, *turkey*, *valley*, *volley*; *osprey* is perhaps more usual with final /eɪ/; §Basic names often have <-ey>:*Alderney*, *Anglesey*, *Camberley*, *Courtney*, *Helmsley*, *Hennessey*, *Kearsley*,*Olney*, *Trelawney*, *Whalley*, *Whiteley*, etc., more than half of which have <-ley>;
- <-ey> in adjectives derived from nouns ending in <e> or occasionally in <y>: *acey*, *cagey*, *clayey*, *dopey*, *gamey*, *homey*, *jokey*, *matey*, *nosey*, *skyey*; but *poky* and *wavy* are exceptions;
- <-ey> in humorous words: *ballyhooey*, *baloney*, *blarney*, *blimey*, *gooey*,

malarkey; *cockney* may belong here, too;

- <-ie> as a diminutive or familiar suffix (see §5.5, p. 431): *auntie*, *birdie*, *bolshie*, *bookie*, *brassie*, *budgie*, *chappie*, *commie*, *conshie*, *cookie*, *coolie*, *darkie*, *dearie*, *girlie*, *hippie*, *laddie*, *lassie*, *movie*, *nightie*, *rookie*, *quickie*, *sweetie*, *talkie*; *Aussie*, *Louie* (= *Louis*), *Susie*;
- <-ie> in recent French loans: *calorie*, *camaraderie*, *coterie*, *curie*, *gaucherie*, *lingerie*, *menagerie*, *organdie*, *reverie*;
- <-ie> in other words: *aerie*, *boogie*, *bowie*, *cowrie*, *eyrie*, *genie*, *gillie*, *pixie*, *prairie*, *zombie*;
- <-e> : in §Greek words (often marked as such with prefixes such as {cata-}, {apo-}, {epi-}) and in some §Exotic words: *acme*, *acne*, *adobe*, *agave*, *anemone*, *apostrophe*, *bonafide*, *catastrophe*, *cicerone*, *dilettante*, *epitome*, *extempore*, *facsimile*, *finale*, *forte*, *furore*, *hyperbole*, *karate*, *machete*, *nepenthe*, *posse*, *recipe*, *reveille*, *sesame*, *simile*, *strophe*, *tsetse*, *ukelele*, *vigilante*; but the spelling *trophy* comes via French, though marked as §Greek by the <ph=/f/;
- <-i> : in §Italian and §Exotic words: *bikini*, *broccoli*, *chilli*, *confetti*, *graffiti*, *khaki*, *literati*, *macaroni*, *mufti*, *nazi*, *safari*, *salami*, *salmagundi*, *scampi*, *spaghetti*, *taxi*, *vermicelli*, *yogi*; those with three or more syllables and penultimate stress are more easily identifiable.

There are occasional minimal pairs: *caddie* (in golf) – *caddy* (tea-container), *storey* (Br. 'floor') – *story*. Many of the <-ie> words may also be found with <-y> : *organdy*, *pixy*, etc. The <-ie> spelling of diminutive nouns may contrast with instances of final <-y>: *carry* (v.) – *Carrie* (dim. of *Caroline*), *pinky* ('fairly pink') – *pinkie* ('a lukewarm socialist' or Scots for 'little finger').

Unstressed /ɪ/ also has a variety of occasional spellings, though in some of the following examples speakers may have /ə/ rather than /ɪ/; some speakers, too, may not have vowel reduction in all of these words but may retain an /iː/, /aɪ/, or /eɪ/ unreduced in some words:

- <u> : *minute* (n.), *missus* (alt. *missis*);
- <ae> : *anaesthetic*, *gynaecology*;
- <ai> : *captain*, *chamberlain*, *chaplain*, *murrain*, *porcelain*; *portrait*; *reconnaissance*;
- <ay> : *Barclay*, *Billericay*, *Biscay*, *Bungay*, *Finlay*, *Moray*, *Murray*; in unstressed {day}: *Monday*, *Tuesday*, etc. (but usually /eɪ/ in *birthday*); *Halliday* seems to have /eɪ/ because of strong-weak-strong rhythm, though this does not always apply to *holiday*;
- <ea> : *guinea*;
- <ee> : *coffee*, *committee*, *toffee* and in unstressed *been*; also stressed in the nonce spelling *breeches*;
- <ei> : *forfeit*, *surfeit*; *mullein*, *villein*;
- <oe> : *oesophagus*.

The Hanna (1966) spelling rules (for '/I3/') are:
1 <y> in word-final position(*happy*);
2 <a..e> syllable-initial or syllable-medial before word-final /t/ (*e-lec-tor-ate*, *cor-po-rate*);
3 <a..e> syllable-initial before /ʤ/ (*cabb-age* , *man-age*, *par-son-age*, *sav-age-ry*);
4 <a..e> syllable-medial before word-final /ʤ/ (*her-mi-tage*, *pil-gri-mage*, *pos-tage*);
5 (default) <i>.

Unless internal free-form boundaries could be recognized, rule 1) would produce *<babihood>, *<ferriman>. This could be avoided largely by selective affix-stripping, distinguishing *babyhood*, *ferryman*, from *fanciful*, *happiness*. The next three rules try to capture particular suffixes: <-ate> in nouns and adjectives and <-age> in nouns. Rule 2) wrongly covers all words ending in <-it> as well, giving *<gambate> and *<bate> for *gambit*, *bit*.

The lexical frequencies given by Hanna (for phoneme '/I3/') are slightly different: <i> 68 per cent, <y> 23 per cent and <e> <1 per cent. This peculiarly low figure for <e> spellings is partly due to accent difference and partly due to the lack of normal vowel reduction in their phonetic input. For instance, in *elevation*, *elegant*, *elope*, the Hanna algorithm has /iː/ as input for the unstressed <e>, not /ɪ/; in *ellipse*, *employ*, *enamel*, it has /e/ as input, not /ɪ/.

3.3.1.2 /e / *as in* bet *('short <e>')*

The equivalent AmE phoneme also covers the SBS phoneme /ɛə(r)/ and to some extent /ær/, since *merry* /er/, *marry* /ær/ and *Mary* /ɛər/ may well be identical in AmE as [ˈmeri]. The AmE phoneme often has the symbol /ɛ/. Some words have variation in SBS between /e/ and /iː/: *crematorium*, *premier*, *zebra*, *zenith*. In these words AmE generally has /iː/. On the other hand, AmE may have /e/ in some words where SBS has /iː/ – in *aesthete, anaesthetist*, *breve*, *centenary*, *Daedalus*, *devolution*, *ecumenical*, *febrile*, *lever*, *methane*, *oestrogen*, *Oedipus*, *penalize*, *pyrethrin*, *Semite*, *systemic*, *senile*. The <ae> and <oe> digraphs are simplified to <e> in American spelling.

Distribution of variant spellings
/e/ has only slight spelling divergence:

Table 15 Spellings of /e/

spellings of /e/	*TF*	*LF*	
<e>	84 %	96 %	
<ea>	6 %	3 %	F+
<ai>	4 %	<1 %	F+
<a>	4 %	<1 %	F+
other spellings	1 %	<1 %	

'F+' : tends to occur in high frequency words

The different TF and LF values indicate that <ea>, <ai> and <a> spellings must occur in some very common words. The /e/≡<a> spelling is usual in SBS *ate* – but some speakers have a regularized pronunciation /eɪt/. It also occurs in the two high frequency words *any* and *many*. Some people may have <a>≡/e/ in the suffixes <-ary> and <-arily> (*necessary*, *necessarily*). This is the usual AmE pronunciation.

In morphology /e/ is the shortened alternant of /iː/ in pairs such as *deceive – deception*, *metre–metric*, *plenary–replenish*, *redeem–redemption*.

The <ai>≡/e/ correspondence occurs in *again*, *against* and *said*, where the long vowel of *gain* and *say* has been shortened, presumably by frequent use. The long vowel is still used by some SBS speakers in *again*, *against*, but /e/ in *said* is standard.

In the correspondence <ea>≡/e/ the following consonant is restricted to:

- —/p/ : *weapon*; from //iː// – *leapt*;
- —/t/ : *sweat*, *threat*;
- —/d/ : *ahead*, *already*, *bread*, *breadth*, *dead*, *dread*, *head*, *instead*, *lead* (n.), *meadow*, *read* (past), *ready*, *spread*, *stead*, *steady*, *thread*, *tread*;
- —/k/ : from //eɪ// – *breakfast*;
- —/ʧ/ : *treachery*, *treacherous*; (cf. *lechery*, *lecherous*);
- —/f/ : *deaf*;
- —/v/ : *endeavour*, *heaven*, *heavy*, *leaven*;
- —/θ/ : *death*; from //iː// – *breath*;
- —/ð/ : *feather*, *heather*, *leather*, *weather*;
- —/st/ : *breast*;
- —/z/ : *peasant*, *pheasant*; from //iː// – *pleasant*;
- —/ʒ/ : *measure*, *pleasure*, *treasure*;
- —/m/ : from //iː// – *dreamt*;
- —/n/ : from //iː// – *cleanliness*, *cleanse*, *leant*, *meant*;
- —/l/ : *jealous*, *realm*; from //iː// – *dealt*, *health*, *stealth*, *wealth*, *zealous*.

There is no <ea>≡/e/ before the single consonants /b, g, ʤ, s, ʃ, ŋ/, but this set is hardly definable as a natural class.

Many of the above words are in a morphophonemic relationship with /iː/≡<ea>: *mean–meant*, etc. This long/short pairing of vowels is usually found in §Latinate words and with the default spelling <e> (*serene–serenity*). Except for *pleasant*, the alternating morphemes with <ea> are, surprisingly, not Romance in origin but native Germanic. Less immediately, *wealth* relates to *weal* and *health* to *hale*. The <ea> spelling is difficult to fit into any subsystem structure. It is usually found in §Basic words (*head*, *leather*, etc.). It also occurs in the *measure*, *treasure* group, which are marked by the /ʒ/ and the ending <-ure> as possible members of a §Romance subsystem. These may have /eɪ/ in AmE.

The most common context for <ea>≡/e/ is before /d/, with TF 52 per cent, LF 36 per cent (F+) of this correspondence.

The other spellings of /e/ are rather a mixed group of very varying frequency:

- <ei> : *heifer*; *leisure* (AmE /iː/)
- <eo> : *jeopardy*, *leopard*; *Geoffrey*, *Leonard*;
- <ie> : *friend*, and more or less in *lieutenant* (Br. /lefˈtenənt/, AmE /luː-/); in AmE the <ie> may represent a hiatus in *hygienic* as /haɪʤiˈenɪk/;
- <oe> : *asafoetida*;
- <u> : *bury, burial.*

Third-syllable shortening gives <ae>≡/e/ in *haemorrhage*, *haemorrhoid*; there is also a variant <ae>≡/e/ in *aesthetic.*

Looking at other phonemes which may have the spelling <e>, we find that <e>≡/e/ only accounts for TF 39 per cent, LF 37 per cent. Over a third of the instances of simple <e> represent a reduced vowel in an unstressed syllable, either /ɪ/ (TF 21 per cent, LF 30 per cent) or /ə/ (TF 17 per cent, LF 23 per cent). Simple <e> without <e>-marking also represents long /iː/ (TF 7 per cent, LF 7 per cent) and to a lesser extent /eɪ/ (TF <1 per cent, LF <1 per cent). These figures do not include the /ɪ/ of past tense or the /ə/ of comparative inflections, which would increase the proportion of reduced vowels considerably.

The Hanna (1966) spelling rules (for '/E3/') are:

1 <a> syllable-initial before /r/ (*sanc-tu-ar-y*)

– in the ending <-ary>; but the American /e/ of this suffix is syllable-medial rather than initial after the /t/ in *san-i-tar-y* and similar words, given the syllable boundaries provided in the input data;

2 <ea> syllable-medial before /θ/ (*breath*);

3 (default) <e>.

Neither of the first two rules is particularly relevant. The ending <-ary> usually has /ə/ in SBS. The <ea> spelling before /θ/ applies only to *breath* and *death.* It is the §Basic correspondence before /θ/. Non-§Basic words (*method, stethoscope, ethics*, etc.) have the default /e/≡<e>.

3.3.1.3 /æ/ *as in* bat *('short <a>')*

In AmE, as in Northern accents of British English, the phoneme /æ/ is also found in words such as *path, after, class, dance* (see table 6, p. 59). In SBS the original /æ/ of such words has been lengthened and retracted to /ɑː/ before /f, θ, s/ and nasal+consonant. So SBS *path* /pɑːθ/ is AmE /pæθ/, SBS dance /dɑːns/ is AmE /dæns/. This does not in itself affect spelling since <a> is the default spelling for both /æ/ and /ɑː/. Australians and New Zealanders both have pre-fricative lengthening like SBS. New Zealand and South African English resemble SBS more closely in also having lengthening before nasal+consonant, as in *advance*, *dance*, *demand*, *example*, which Australians on the whole do not.

Distribution of variant spellings

/æ/ has virtually no spelling divergence: /æ/≡<a>.

In morphology /æ/ is the shortened alternant of /eɪ/ in pairs such as *cave–cavity*, *depraved–depravity*, *mania–manic*, *explain–explanatory*. There is variation between /æ/ and /eɪ/ across accents in some words. SBS usually has /æ/ in *palaeography, patriot, phalanx, ration* and /eɪ/ in *apricot, patent*. In AmE there is usually the reverse.

In the database the only alternative spellings to <a> occur in a few low frequency words mostly of recent French origin: <i> – *timbre*, *timbale*, *impasse*, *meringue*, *lingerie*, where the nasalized /ɛ̃/ of French is usually anglicized to /æ/ + nasal consonant. In 1920 the Society for Pure English suggested that *timbre* should be fully anglicized as *tamber* /ˈtæmbə/ (*OED* 2nd edn). The <ei> in *reveille* (/rɪˈvælɪ/) is quite exceptional. Two other words have an equally idiosyncratic /æ/≡<ai>: *plaid* (from Gaelic) and *plait* (a semantic split from *pleat* /iː/).

In other dialects of English /æ/ (or the equivalent front open short vowel) may occasionally have other spellings. AmE and speakers in the North of England have /æ/≡<au> in *aunt*, *laugh* (no lengthening as in SBS).

The proportion of simple <a> spellings corresponding to /æ/ in lexical words is only (TF and LF) 36 per cent. Rather more <a> spellings (TF 38 per cent, LF 42 per cent) represent a reduced /ə/. Many of these are associable with an underlying //æ// through derivation (cf. *special* with a reduced vowel and *speciality* with stressed /æ/). The remainder of simple <a> spellings mainly refer either to /eɪ/ (in the absence of <e>-marking) – TF 8 per cent, LF 15 per cent, or to /ɑː/ – TF 5 per cent, LF 3 per cent. The letter <a> is also found in a large number of high-frequency function words which would have /æ/≡<a> if the function word happened to be stressed: *am*, *an*, *and*, *as*, *at*, *can*, *had*, *has*, *have*, *shall*, but usually they occur unstressed and the vowel is reduced to /ə/.

In the Hanna (1966) rules, <a> is the default spelling and no variant rules are offered. The predictability is virtually total, apart from the §French words cited above (*timbre*, etc.) and *plaid, plait*. The successful <a> spelling of some unstressed suffixes is unnaturally bolstered by giving an /æ/ as input (e.g. *pendant*). See §2.8.5.

3.3.1.4 /ʊ/ as in put *('short <u>')*

In AmE /ʊ/ also covers the SBS diphthong /ʊə/, in so far as it survives, so SBS *cure* /kjʊə/ (or /kjɔː/) is AmE /kjʊr/.

Distribution of variant spellings

This rounded /ʊ/ has a different distribution in SBS and in AmE, as compared with the more conservative Northern dialects of British English. It is found partly in words which escaped the change of /ʊ/ to /ʌ/ in Early Modern English (called by Wells (1982: 196) 'the FOOT-STRUT split') and partly in words where it goes back to Middle English /oː/. These origins are reflected in its distribution across the two principal spellings <u> and <oo> (Table 16).

Table 16 Spellings of /ʊ/

spellings of /ʊ/	*TF*	*LF*	
<u>	32 %	54 %	F-
<oo>	64 %	35 %	F+
minority spellings <o, ou>	4 %	11 %	F-

'F-' : tends to occur in low frequency words; 'F+' : tends to occur in high frequency words

The figures exclude adjective-forming <-ful> as in *hateful* and adverbial <-fully>, where /ʊ/ only occurs in lento forms and /ə/ usually occurs in allegro forms. Compound nouns such as *spoonful* keep an unreduced /ʊ/. All the spellings of /ʊ/ are shared by other phonemes.

<oo> occurs in monosyllabic free forms before /t, d, k, m/: *foot*, *soot*; *good*, *stood*, *wood*, *hood*; *look*, *book*, *took*, *shook*, *hook*, *brook*, *rook*; *room*, *groom*, *broom*. It also occurs in the suffix *-hood* (*womanhood*, etc.). *Put* is an exception. The *look* and *room* sets have long /uː/ in Northern British English. Before /m/ there is some free variation between /ʊ/ and /uː/ (e.g. /rʊm/ – /ruːm/) within SBS; AmE has /uː/. Abbreviations such as *pud* (*pudding*) naturally have the spelling of the full form.

Given this distribution of stressed <oo>, we can predict <u> by default:

- before consonants other than /t, d, k, m/: before /ʃ/ in *push*, *bush*, *cushion*, *bushel*, *ambush*, *cushy*; /ʧ/ in *butcher*; /s/ in *pussy*, *brusque* (if not /uː/ or as in AmE /ʌ/); /z/ in *hussar*; /f/ in *buffet*; /g/ in *sugar*; /l/ (ignoring *wool* for a moment) in *full*, *pull*, *bull*, *bullet*, *bulletin*, *bully*, *pulley*, *pullet*, *bullion*;
- in polysyllabic words where the syllable containing /ʊ/ is unstressed (and reducible to /ə/ in quick speech): *adjutant*, *century*, *educate*, *erudite*, *instrument*, *prejudice*, *quadruped*;
- in an occasional polysyllabic §Basic word (*cuckoo*, *pudding*);
- in the common suffixes <-ful> and <-fully>.

The words *wool* and *woof* may appear to be nonce forms but they are in fact quite regular since the selection of <oo> after <w>, to avoid sequences of vertical pen-strokes or minims, overrides the selection of <u>. This is also the reason for single <o> spellings in *wolf*, *wolverine*, *woman*, and *worsted* and in names such as *Wollaston*, *Wollstonecraft*, *Wolmer*, *Wolsey*. These can be included with <oo> in a common statement: after /w/ we have <o> except in CVC monosyllabic words where we have <oo>. Anglo-Saxon names keep their <u> spelling: *Beowulf*, *Ethelwulf*.

A minority spelling of /ʊ/ is <ou> in *courier* and for some speakers in *camouflage*. The word *bosom* is odd in that there is no motivation in the shape of the adjacent letters <b> and <s> for minim avoidance. Conversely, in technical terms with <wu> formed from foreign proper names, there is no minim avoidance where one would expect it: *wulfenite*, *wurtzite*. In non-§Basic words these <wu> spellings are in fact regular, since the minim-avoiding <o(o)> spellings after /w/ are a feature of §Basic words. The <wu> of *Wuthering Heights* is an oddity: the usual pronunciation is /ʌ/, for which one would expect *<Wothering>. Some §Basic names have an <o..e> spelling as an alternative to <oo>: *Broke*, *Pembroke*, *Wodehouse*; *Boleyn* also has <o>, with an alternative spelling *Bullen*.

Foreign names, particularly German, tend to have an /ʊ/ pronunciation of <u>: *Bruckner*, *Buddha*, *Gluck*, *Grundig*, *Innsbruck*, *Irkutsk*, *Kuwait*, *Ulrik*, *Yoruba*. There is some free variation: *Bunsen*, *Gustavus*, *Humboldt*, *Krupp*, *Lund*, *Mogul*, *Muslim*, *Mustapha*, *Uppsala*, may have /ʊ/ or /ʌ/. The /ʌ/ variant is the anglicized pronunciation, so it is to be expected in *Humperdinck* as a British pop-singer and *Bunsen* of burner fame. Words and names borrowed in India sometimes adopted an /ʌ/ pronunciation and a <u> spelling for a fully open [a] vowel, which is perceptually quite close to some pronunciations of English /ʌ/, as in *Punjab*. There may be occasional variation between SBS and AmE in the lexical distribution of /ʊ/ and /uː/. Only small numbers of words are affected. The /ʊ/ pronunciation in *Buddha, cuckoo, sputnik,* for instance, may be long /uː/ in AmE.

Phonetically there is variation between /ʊ/ and /uː/ before a further vowel, largely in non-§Basic words such as *bivouac*, *pirouette*, *actuarial*, *ruin*, *altruistic*.

The conventional representation of the sound of cheering in earlier centuries was *huzza*. From this has developed *hurrah* or *hooray*. 'The form *hurrah* is literary and dignified; the popular form *hooray*' (*OED*). It is interesting to note that here the <u> – <oo> difference in spelling correlates with 'literary' – 'popular', a correlation with §Exotic and §Basic.

The need to differentiate function words from lexical words in describing the writing system is well-illustrated by the correspondence /ʊ/≡<ou>. It occurs in the three common auxiliary verbs *could*, *should* and *would* and thereafter only in recent §French borrowings at the low-frequency end of the lexicon such as *courier*.

The Hanna (1966) spelling rules for '/O7/', which would also cover SBS /ʊə/, are:

1 <u..e> syllable-medial accented before word-final /r/ (*sure*);
2 <u> syllable-medial accented before syllable final /r/ (*jur-y*);
3 <u> syllable-medial accented before /l/ (*pull*);
4 <u> syllable-medial unaccented (*fulfil*);
5 <u> syllable-final (but not of course when final in a free form, where /ʊ/ would not be found) (*conjugal*, *prejudice*, *hussar*, *buffet*);
6 <oo> syllable-medial accented (by default).

3.3.1.5 /ʌ/ as in putt *('low short <u>')*

SBS and AmE agree closely in the distribution of /ʌ/. Some American phoneticians have suggested merging /ʌ/ and /ə/ into a common phoneme, since /ʌ/ occurs almost entirely in stressed syllables and the phonetically similar /ə/ in unstressed syllables. This would not offer any advantage in the description of spelling correspondences.

Distribution of variant spellings

/ʌ/ shows spelling divergence similar to that of /ʊ/. This is not surprising since present-day /ʊ/ and /ʌ/ both originate from Middle English /ʊ/ by what Wells (1982: 196) has described as 'the FOOT-STRUT split'. All the spellings of /ʌ/ are shared by other phonemes. The main divergence is between <u>, <o> and <ou> (Table 17).

Table 17 Spellings of /ʌ/

spellings of /ʌ/	*TF*	*LF*	
<u>	63 %	91 %	F-
<o>	27 %	7 %	F+
<ou>	8 %	2 %	F+
minority spellings	2 %	<1 %	

'F-' : tends to occur in low frequency words; 'F+' : tends to occur in high frequency words

These figures exclude the function words *done*, *one*, *but*, *thus*, *must*, *up*. The discrepancy between text and lexical frequency shows that the <o> and <ou> spellings will include other high frequency words. In addition to these we have the minority spelling /ʌ/≡<oo> in *blood* and *flood*, which adds to the spelling divergence considerably, since <oo> also represents /uː/ (*food*, *fool*, etc.), /ʊ/ (*good*, *foot*, etc.) and even /əʊ/ in *brooch*.

In morphology /ʌ/ is the shortened alternant of /aʊ/ in pairs such as *abound–abundance*, *profound–profundity*, *pronounce–pronunciation*, with a difference in spelling. It is also an alternant of /(j)uː/ in pairs such as *reduce–reduction*, *resume–resumption*.

The context of a following consonant is not very helpful in predicting the spellings <u>, <o> and <ou>. If we ignore the pair *blood* and *flood*, only <u> occurs before /d, k, g, ʤ, ʃ/ as a spelling of /ʌ/:

- *bud*, *buddy*, *cuddle*, *fuddled*, *mud*, *muddle*, *scud*, *shudder*, *spud*, *stud*, *study*, *sudden*, *suds*, *thud*, *udder*, etc.;
- *buccaneer*, *bucket*, *buckle*, *buxom*, *conduct*, *crux*, *ducat*, *duck*, *fluctuate*, *flux*, *fructify*, *juxtapose*, *knuckle*, *luck*, *luxury*, *product*, *reluctance*, *struck*, *structure*, *succour*, *succulent*, *suck*, *suction*, *truck*, *truculent*, *yucca*, etc.;
- *bug*, *bugger*, *buggy*, *chug*, *drug*, *dug*, *hug*, *jug*, *juggernaut*, *juggle*, *jugular*,

lug, *luggage*, *lugger*, *luxuriate*, *mug*, *nugget*, *plug*, *repugnant*, *rug*, *rugby*, *rugged*, *shrug*, *slug*, *smug*, *smuggle*, *snug*, *struggle*, *thug*, *tug*, *ugly*, etc.;
- *bludgeon*, *budge*, *budget*, *budgie*, *cudgel*, *drudge*, *grudge*, *gudgeon*, *judge*, *nudge*, *sludge*, *smudge*, *trudge*, etc.;
- *blush*, *brush*, *crush*, *flush*, *gush*, *hush*, *lush*, *mush*, *plush*, *rush*, *shush*, *slush*, *thrush*, *usher*, etc.

These account for TF 11 per cent, LF 11 per cent of all instances of /ʌ/ as a whole and TF 18 per cent, LF 12 per cent of /ʌ/≡<u>.

Only <o> occurs before /θ/ (in the single word *nothing*) and before /v/: *covenant*, *cover*, *covet*, *covey*, *dove*, *glove*, *govern*, *love*, *lovely*, *oven*, *plover*, *shove*, *shovel*, *slovenly*, etc. These account for TF 6 per cent, LF 2 per cent of instances of /ʌ/ correspondences and TF 24 per cent, LF 32 per cent of /ʌ/≡<o>. AmE speakers may have /ʌ/ in *grovel, hovel.* The abbreviation of *governor* is usually spelt *guv*. This is perhaps an attempt, like *<woz> for *was*, to mark illiteracy in the speaker.

A few common words have <ou>, including *country*, *couple*, *cousin*, *double*, *touch*, *trouble*. These prevent some possible generalizations about <o> and <u> spellings. Apart from *touch*, only <u> occurs before /ʧ/ (*clutch*, *crutch*, *duchess*, *escutcheon*, *much*). Apart from *double*, *doubloon*, *trouble*, only <u> occurs before /b/ (*blub*, *chub*, *club*, *cub*, *drub*, *dub*, *grub*, *gubernatorial*, *hub*, *hubbub*, *public*, *publish*, *republic*, *scrub*, *shrub*, *snub*, *stub*, *tub* and all words beginning with the common prefix *sub-*). Apart from *southern*, in which the <ou> derives from the base form *south*, only <o> occurs before /ð/ (*brother*, *mother*, *other*, *smother*). Apart from *couple* and *hiccough* and the obsolescent *twopence*, *twopenny*, only <u> occurs before /p/ (*abrupt*, *corrupt*, *cup*, *supper*, *supple*, *supplement*, *upholster*, etc.). The remaining <o> and <ou> spellings seem to offer no worthwhile generalizations.

The use of <o> spellings seems to be dictated by minim avoidance, at least in §Romance words (Scragg 1974: 44). Certainly, TF 90 per cent, LF 76 per cent of /ʌ/≡<o> spellings occur before <v>, <m> or <n>. Typical <om> and <on> spellings are:

- *become*, *come*, *comfort*, *company*, *compass*, *somersault*, etc.; *conjure*, *front*, *frontier*, *ironmonger*, *Monday*, *money*, *mongrel*, *monk*, *monkey*, *month*, *son*, *sponge*, *ton*, *tongue*, *wonder*, etc.

On the other hand there are equally common words with <u> spellings before <m> and <n>:

- *drum*, *jump*, *lumber*, *mumble*, *mumps*, *munch*, *mundane*, *number*, *pump*, *slum*, *sum*, *thump*, *trumpet*, etc.; *fun*, *fund*, *gun*, *hundred*, *hunt*, *lunch*, *punch*, *run*, *sun*, etc.

There are also a few <o> spellings where adjacent letters do not have minim strokes: *brother*, *colour*, *colander*, *thorough*, *borough*, *other*, *dozen*. In the absence of context-based rules, such spellings can only be taught by sample lists, which can exploit a statistical preference. For instance, though <om> and <um> spellings are both quite common, only <um> appears before <b>: *jumbo*, *lumbar*, *mumble*, *number*, etc.

AmE speakers may have /ʌ/ in *condom*, *donkey* (making it rhyme with *monkey*). On the other hand, some words which in SBS have /ʌ/, tend to have AmE /ɑ/ (the equivalent of SBS /ɒ/), as in *accomplice, colander, compass, conjurer, constable, fishmonger, mongrel, monetary*. AmE may have /oʊ/ rather than /ʌ/ in *covert, plover*. AmE tends to have /ɜːr/ in *borough, burrow, courage, currant, currency, curry, flourish, furrow, hurricane, hurry, nourish, occurrence, worry,* and in names such as *Durham, Murray, Surrey*, with no contrast between *flurry* (SBS /ʌr/) and *furry* (SBS /ɜːr/).

The complex spelling <ough>≡/ʌf/ occurs in three high-frequency words *enough*, *rough*, *tough*, and in *slough* ('to shed skin').

See under /ʊ/ for free variation between /ʌ/ and /ʊ/ in foreign names such as *Gustavus*, *Krupp*.

The Hanna (1966) spelling rules (for '/U3/') naturally have the default spelling <u> and the only predicted variant is <o> after /k, w/ (*come*, *won*). In words such as *company*, *conjurer*, the <o> spelling was originally motivated by the vertical pen-strokes of the <m> and <n>, not the <c>. However, a rule based on a following <m> or <n> would not be viable because of the frequency of remaining <um> and <un> spellings.

3.3.1.6 /ɒ/ as in pot *('short <o>')*

There is no simple direct equivalent of /ɒ/ among the vowels of most speakers of AmE (see p. 59). Through loss of lip-rounding it is subsumed largely under AmE /ɑ(ː)/. Witness the ancient phonetic joke:

American immigration officer: Profession?
British would-be immigrant: I'm a clerk.
American immigration officer: You go tick-tock, tick-tock??

The low back vowels of American English have a complex distribution across American speakers, so a comparison with British English is difficult. There are two main groups of words affected by the lack of a single equivalent to SBS /ɒ/ in AmE:

1 The set of words with AmE /ɑ(ː)/ includes not only *father, palm, sonata, spa,* and words with /ɑːr/ such as *star, start,* but most of the words which in SBS have /ɒ/≡<o>, such as *bomb, cot, job, volley*.
2 AmE shares with some Southern British speakers a vowel /ɔ(ː)/ instead of the more open vowel before voiceless fricatives /f θ s/, as in *cough, cross, froth, loss, off, soft, trough*. AmE extends this /ɔ(ː)/ to words such as *coffee, office, glossy*, and often to words in which SBS has /ɒ/ followed by /r/, such as *orange, porridge, sorrow*.

Apart from this, some American speakers keep the lip-rounding as /ɔ(:)/ before /g/, /ŋ/, in words such as *dog*, *fog*, *long*, *strong*.

Distribution of variant spellings

For SBS speakers /ɒ/ has very little divergence and that is largely predictable (table 18).

Table 18 Spellings of /ɒ/

spellings of /ɒ/	*TF*	*LF*
<o>	92 %	95 %
<a>	6 %	4 %
minority spellings	2 %	1 %

All the spellings of /ɒ/ are shared by other phonemes.

In morphology /ɒ/ is the shortened alternant of /əʊ/ in pairs such as *atrocious–atrocity*, *cone–conic*, *neurosis–neurotic*, *verbose–verbosity*. Some words, such as *onerous, scone*, may have either vowel in SBS.

The <a> occurs regularly after /w/ (<w>, <qu>): *want*, *warrant*, *warrior*, *wash*, etc.; *quality*, *quarrel*, *squabble*, *squash*, etc. *Wobble*, *wonky*, are exceptions. <a> also occurs in the common function word *what* (after <wh>) and in stressed *was*. These are not included in the text frequency figures, which are meant to reflect incidence in lexical words. If *what* and *was* had been included in the text frequency figures (even along with the inclusion of *from*, *of*, *on* and *not*), the proportion of <a> spellings would have been much higher at the expense of the <o> spellings. That would have given the false impression that <a>≡/ɒ/ was a relatively common correspondence across lexical items.

Exceptional instances of <a>≡/ɒ/ are: *blancmange*, *yacht*. *Scallop* has an alternative spelling *scollop*. Some speakers have /ɒ/ rather than /ɔː/ in some words spelt with <al> such as *alder*, *almanac*, *alter*, *balsam*, *falcon*, *false*, *malt*, *salt*, *walrus*, *waltz* (see under /ɔː/ p. 182). In AmE *quaff, scallop, wrath*, may have /æ/. Some Canadian and AmE speakers may also have their 'short *o*' /ɑ/, instead of /ɔː/, in words such as *almost*, *auction*, *author*, *bald*, *broad*, *cause*, *false*, *gaunt*, *hydraulic*, *ought*, *precaution*, *scrawny*, *small*, *walk*, so that *dawn* and *don* are homophones.

Disyllabic names in which stressed <o> is followed by a single consonant letter sometimes have /ɒ/, where one might have expected /əʊ/: *Bonar*, *Grocott*, *Hosack*, *Mashona*, *Ronald*, *Ronuk*, *Sodom*; or, alternatively /ɒr/, where one might have expected /ɔːr/: *Gorell*, *Horace*.

The minority spellings are:

- <e> : before a nasal in French loan-words – *detente*, *encore*, *ensemble*, *entente*, *entourage*, *entree*, *entrepreneur*, *rendezvous*;

- <au> : *cauliflower*, *laurel*, *sausage*, *Aussie*, *Laurence*, *Maurice*, and, alternating with /ɔː/, in *austerity*, *laudanum*, *Australia*, *Austria*; /ɒ/ is the usual pronunciation in SBS *because*;
- <aw> is only found in names, such as *Lawrence;*
- <ou> : *cough*, *trough*, *hough*; *Gloucester*;
- <ow> : *knowledge*, *rowlock*;
- <eau> : *bureaucracy*, *bureaucratize*.

The spelling of *bureaucracy* is rather interesting. The <eau> represents long /əʊ/ in the base form *bureau* and the spelling is preserved in the third-syllable shortening. Usually these long/short vowel alternations are the result of the Vowel Shift and are restricted to the default spelling, here <o>. The French loan-words in these lists are all well established and some of them are quite common. *Knowledge* and *rowlock* are also unusual examples of vowel shortening in §Basic words; the base forms *know* and *row* have /əʊ/.

AmE speakers may have /ʌ/ in a number of words where SBS has /ɒ/ such as *condom*, *donkey, grovel, hovel, hover*, and /əʊ/ in *shone*. They have 'short *o*' as /ɑ/ in a number of words where SBS speakers have the long vowel, such as *codify*, *phonetician*, *processor*, *Soviet*.

The Hanna (1966) rules for '/O3/' as in *job*, *plot*, and '/O5/' as in *cross*, *long*, naturally have <o> as the default spelling. The only predicted variant is <a> after /(k)w/ (*wand*, *squash*). /hw/ should have been included as a further context for *what*, *whatever*.

3.3.2 Long phonological counterparts of the short vowels: /ɑɪ iː eɪ ɑʊ əʊ/

3.3.2.1 /aɪ/ *as in* like *('long <i>')*

This vowel has much the same lexical distribution in stressed syllables in AmE as in SBS.

Distribution of variant spellings

/aɪ/ shows less spelling divergence than appears at first sight, if <e>-marking and the rule-governed alternation of <i>/<y> spellings are taken into account (table 19).

The default spelling in both §Basic and §Romance words is <i> or <i..e>. As a long vowel, /aɪ/ has regular <e>-marking (see #E1, p. 129) in words such as *mile*, *oblige*, *size*, *time*, etc.

There are some differences of lexical distribution between SBS and AmE to take into account. The unstressed ending <-ile> in *agile*, *docile*, *facile*, *fissile*, *fragile*, *futile*, *infantile*, *prehensile*, *projectile*, *puerile*, *reptile*, *servile*, *sterile*, *tensile*, *versatile*, *volatile*, has a full vowel /aɪ/ in SBS. In AmE this ending usually has a syllabic /l/ so that *fertile* rhymes with *turtle* and the

Table 19 Spellings of /aɪ/

spellings of /aɪ/	*TF*	*LF*	
<i>, <i..e> and final <-ie>, <-y>	80 %	82 %	
Non-final <y>	2 %	9 %	F-
<igh>	13 %	4 %	F+
minority spellings ‡	5 %	5 %	

‡ <eigh>, <ei>, <ey>, <ai>, <ay>, final <-i>

'F-' : tends to occur in low frequency words; 'F+' : tends to occur in high frequency words

pair *hostel–hostile* are homophones. AmE has /aɪ/ rather than /iː/ (as in SBS) in *albino*, *geyser*, *migraine*, *strychnine*, and *quinine* /'kwaɪnaɪn/. LPD reports an American military pronunciation of *oblique* with /aɪ/. On the other hand, AmE usually has /iː/, where SBS has /aɪ/, in *adamantine, bovine, carbine, crystalline, elephantine, labyrinthine, philistine, serpentine*, and in *mercantile*. This, too, is the usual preference in that familiar pair *either, neither*. AmE also has /aɪ/ in the prefixes *anti-*, *multi-*, and *semi-*, and in *dynasty, endive, idyll* (as /aɪdl/=*idle*, *idol*), *short-lived, simultaneous, vitamin,* where SBS has short /ɪ/.

Regular <ie> and <y> spellings

Where /aɪ/ occurs finally, there appears at first sight to be some plurality of correspondence due to competing forms with <ie> and <y>. This variation in spelling proves, however, to be fairly regular. In monosyllables we have on the one hand words such as *die*, *fie*, *hie*, *lie*, *pie*, *tie*, *vie*, which form a minority group, and on the other hand a larger group of words such as *cry*, *dry*, *fly*, *fry*, *ply*, *pry*, *shy*, *sly*, *sty*, *try*, *wry*. There is an obvious difference between the two groups. The latter all have an initial consonant cluster or a single consonant spelt with a digraph such as <sh>. The former only have one consonant letter; so the <ie> spelling in these words is clearly used to bulk up the words to a minimum of three letters (the 'short word rule', p. 131). The <ie> of the inflected forms *lies, lied, tries, tried*, is common to both groups. Final <-y> of longer words also changes to <ie> in inflected forms: *magnified, magnifies*. There is good reason to treat *buy*, *guy*, as having initial <bu>≡/b/, <gu>≡/g/, rather than set up <uy>≡/aɪ/.

Other <i> and <y> spellings

Among the non-default spellings which we need to account for are <i> in final position and <y> in non-final positions. Final <i> occurs in a few rather odd words: *alibi* (a Latin adverb used as a noun), *alkali* (from Arabic), *rabbi*. Its use as an anglicized pronunciation of the Latin masculine plural ending in §Latinate technical vocabulary may be considered regular: *alumni*, *alveoli*, *foci*, *fungi*, *gladioli*, etc., but the suffix also has a more purist pronunciation with /iː/ (dodging the English vowel shift to /aɪ/). Male *alumni* and female *alumnae* are distinguished as /aɪ/ and /iː/. There is frequent confusion of the Latin genders, as in *<streptococchae> (*Guardian* 5/9/91: 38). Some of the minority spellings dealt with below, notably <igh>, may also occur in final position.

Final <-ye> occurs irregularly in a few §Basic words. *Dye, lye* ('soda'), *rye*, compared with *sky*, *dry*, *wry*, etc. are bulked up with <e> to three letters (the 'short word rule', p. 131). Similarly lexical *bye* is differentiated from the function word *by*. *Dye* and *lye* are differentiated from the much more common *die* and *lie* in present-day spelling, but in earlier centuries there was some free variation between the <ie> and <ye> spellings. Other §Basic words are: *dyke*, *tryst* (or /ɪ/), *tyke*. Apart from these, the non-final <y> spellings are almost entirely to be found in §Greek words:

- *acolyte*, *analyse*, *anodyne*, *asylum*, *aureomycin*, *cryostat*, *cyanide*, *cycle*, *cyme*, *dialyse*, *dryad*, *dynamic*, *enzyme*, *formaldehyde*, *glycogen*, *gynaecologist*, *gyroscope*, *heterozygous*, *hyacinth*, *hyaline*, *hybrid*, *hydrogen*, *hyena*, *hygiene*, *hygrometer*, *hymeneal*, *hyperbole*, *hyphen*, *hypothesis*, *lyre*, *myopic*, *neophyte*, *papyrus*, *paralyse*, *phagocyte*, *proselyte*, *psychology*, *pylon*, *pyre*, *pyrites*, *syenite*, *syne*, *thyme*, *thymus*, *thyroid*, *type*, *typhoid*, *tyrant*, *tyro*, *xylophone*.

Some of these words are relatively recent coinages direct from Greek roots to serve scientific needs: *phagocyte*, for example, dates from the 1880s. Others go back to the early Renaissance: *type* was used as a technical term in late medieval theology (as a term in printing it only dates from the eighteenth century). Early borrowings came via Latin and sometimes via medieval French. The difference between early and late loans is sometimes reflected in spelling. Present-day *rhyme*, spelt with <rh> and <y>, was frequently spelt *rime* in earlier centuries in a completely anglicized spelling. The re-association with Latin *rhythmus*, itself borrowed from Greek, was deliberate scholarly interference. However, *rhyme* still shows itself to be an early borrowing by not having the word-formation potential of a §Greek loan-word compared with *rhythm–rhythmic*.

Not every exotic word with /aɪ/≡<y> can be regarded as §Greek. *Typhoon* may be of Arabic origin and *nylon* is an invented name. We must draw the line at *forsythia* in spite of the intervocalic /θ/, since <f> is not §Greek; similarly *lychee* (Chinese) would not fit because <ch> as /ʧ/ is not §Greek. Apart from the /aɪ/≡<y> spelling, there is nothing else, phonological or morphological, to mark these words as §Greek.

In §Basic names <y> is often used as a variant of <i> as in *Wilde–Wylde*, or, as /ɪ/, two South Manchester place-names *Withington* and *Wythenshawe*, where the common element is 'withy', meaning 'willow'.

Minority spellings of /aɪ/

The other spellings of /aɪ/ are relatively minor. <igh> is very restricted in contexts:

- finally in *high*, *nigh*, *sigh*, *thigh*;
- before /t/ in *alight*, *bight*, *blight*, *bright*, *delight*, *fight*, *flight*, *fright*, *knight*, *light*, *might*, *night*, *plight*, *right*, *sight*, *slight*, *tight*, *wright*.

The <gh> of <igh> reflects a Germanic velar consonant which has been lost, though it survives in some Scottish accents. The spelling *delight* came about by a false association with *light* but the word is Romance in origin. This is not the usual direction of spelling manipulations, which usually try to impose a false Latinity. /aɪ/≡<eigh> is also Germanic and only occurs in *height* and *sleight*.

The survival of the <igh> spelling before /t/ has been ensured by its occurrence in quite common monosyllabic words. One less drastic spelling reformer was quite happy to keep it (see pp. 482f.). Table 20 shows the relative frequencies of <-ite> and <-ight> spellings in monosyllabic words.

Table 20 Distribution of <ite>≡/aɪt/ and <ight>≡/aɪt/ in monosyllabic words

spellings	*TF*	*LF*	
<-ite>	29 %	39 %	F-
<-ight>	71 %	61 %	F+

'F-' : tends to occur in low frequency words; 'F+' : tends to occur in high frequency words

So, although there are high-frequency words with <-ite> spellings (*write*, *quite*, *white*), the <-ight> spellings are the dominant group in monosyllabic words. In polysyllabic words, apart from *delight*, <-ight> spellings only occur in forms derived from the monosyllables and a good number of <ite> spellings are accounted for by the suffix <-ite>.

- <ae> is found in *maestro* and an occasional classical name such as *Maecenas*.
- <ai>≡/aɪ/ is found in the database only in a very small mixed group of words: *aisle*, *assegai*, *naiad*, *shanghai*. <ay> only occurs in *cayenne*, *papaya* and in names such as *Bayeux*, *Bayreuth*.
- <ei> occurs in *eider*, *gneiss*, *kaleidoscope*, *poltergeist*, *seismic* and in one pronunciation of *either*, *neither*. It also occurs in German and other foreign names, such as *Beira*, *Brunei*, *Fahrenheit*, *Geiger*, *Heidelberg*, *Heinz*, *Holbein*, *Holstein*, *Leiden*, *Reilly*, *Steinbeck*, *Steinway*, *Transkei*, *Zeiss*. <ey> only occurs in *eye*; *geyser* has variants /aɪ/ – /iː/.
- <oy> occurs as a nonce spelling in the AmE pronunciation of *coyote*.

There are various oddities in the spelling of names with /aɪ/. The usual conventions of <C>-doubling and <e>-marking may be ignored: *Argyll*, *Bridson*, *Hinde*, *Wilde*, *Wylde*. There is free variation in the spelling of many personal names: *Ballantine–Ballantyne*, *Carlile–Carlisle–Carlyle*, *Crighton–Crichton*, etc. Nonce spellings include *Aneurin* /əˈnaɪərɪn/, *Ardingly* /-laɪ/.

The short vowel counterpart of /aɪ/ in derived forms is /ɪ/: *agile–agility*, *crime–criminal*, *describe–description*, *mime–mimic*, *private–privy*, *sign–signatory*, etc.

The spelling of /aɪ/ in the present-day system is undoubtedly very complex, but within that complexity there is more regularity than at first appears. The less common spellings are firmly entrenched in high-frequency words. Only the spelling <igh> is peculiar to /aɪ/.

The Hanna (1966) spelling rules are:

1 <i..e> syllable-initial (*re-al-ize, quartz-ite*);
2 <igh> syllable-medial before /t/ (*night*);
3 <i..e> syllable-medial before word-final phoneme (*time*);
4 <i> syllable-medial before syllable-final phoneme (*re-cit-al*);
5 <y> word-final (*try*);
6 <i> syllable-final (*i-tem*).

3.3.2.2 /iː/ *as in* leak *('long <e>')*

This vowel has much the same lexical distribution in stressed syllables in AmE as in SBS. If the final unstressed vowel of *happy*, *laddie*, *monkey*, is taken to be phoneme /iː/ rather than /ɪ/ in accents such as AmE, this adds spellings such as <y> and <ey>, which (apart from *key*) would not otherwise correspond to /iː/.

<e> as the default spelling of /iː/

Hall (1961: 42) in a listing of the 'regular graphemic representations' of each phoneme (one per phoneme) cites the <e>-marked spelling for the five long vowels /iː eɪ aɪ əʊ juː/ in *mete*, *hate*, *kite*, *mote*, *cube*, and claims that this is the default spelling that you would get if you asked people to spell nonsense syllables. This would demonstrate, if true, an awareness of the regularity of <e>-marking as a process, an awareness of design in the system as a whole which clearly overrides the bare statistics in the case of /iː/.

Though <e> is overall the default spelling, and indeed the spelling which in the jargon of literacy teaching 'says its name', its distribution is very peculiar. One striking peculiarity of /iː/ spellings is in fact the very restricted use of <e>-marking. The following table shows the relative frequency of <e>-marked vowel correspondences in the spelling of five long vowel phonemes: i) as a proportion of the spellings of the phoneme, ii) as a proportion of unmarked letter plus marked letter (e.g. <a..e> as a percentage of <a> plus <a..e>) and iii) as a proportion of the spelling of the phoneme in monosyllables.

Table 21 Percentage of <e>-marked spellings for long vowels

	% of phoneme		*% of <V>+<V..e>*		*% of monosyllables*	
	TF	*LF*	*TF*	*LF*	*TF*	*LF*
mete <e..e>≡/iː/	3	4	9	9	27	14
mate <a..e>≡/eɪ/	38	28	59	34	76	18
mite <i..e>≡/aɪ/	40	31	36	39	70	19
mote <o..e>≡/əʊ/	16	15	21	18	72	34
mute <u..e>≡/(j)uː/	17	15	45	24	48	16

We can see that the <e>-marked spelling of the simple vowel letter is usually an important variant in the case of <a>, <i>, <o> and <u>, and one that may be associated with high-frequency words. This is not true for <e..e>. When we look at the actual words spelt with <e..e>, we find that there are surprisingly few monosyllables when compared with other <e>-marked spellings: *breve*, *cede*, *eke*, *eve*, *gene*, *glebe*, *grebe*, *mete*, *scene*, *scheme*, *theme*. Of these, the three §Basic words: *eke*, *eve* and *mete* are archaic. The rest are Latin, Romance or Greek in origin. It is somewhat surprising then that Albrow should regard <e..e>≡/iː/ as a system 1 correspondence, or, in our terms, §Basic. The major and competing spellings in monosyllables are <ee> and <ea> along with half a dozen minority spellings, of which <e..e> is but one. The extent to which these spellings compete is illustrated by the number of homophones such as *beech–beach*; some 30 per cent of monosyllables containing /iː/ have a differently-spelt homophone. The great majority of these words can be regarded as §Basic and, in spite of the odd §Romance word spelt with <ee> or <ea>, the correspondences <ea>≡/iː/ and <ee>≡/iː/ are very decidedly §Basic. Albrow puts them in system 1.

Distribution of variant spellings

The default spelling of /iː/ has nevertheless to be <e>, but even so Table 22 shows that half the instances of /iː/ are divided equally between <ee> and <ea> (the figures refer only to lexical words and exclude the high-frequency function words *be*, *he*, *me*, *she*, *the*, *we*).

There are some differences of lexical distribution between SBS and AmE to take into account. AmE has /aɪ/ rather than /iː/ (as in SBS) in *albino*, *geyser*, *migraine*, strychnine, and *quinine* /ˈkwaɪnaɪn/. On the other hand, AmE usually has /iː/, where SBS has /aɪ/, in *adamantine,*

Table 22 Spellings of /iː/

spellings of /iː/	*TF*	*LF*	
<e>, <e..e>, final <-ee>	38 %	49 %	
<i>, <i..e>, final <-ie>	2 %	7 %	F-
<ea>	25 %	20 %	
non-final <ee>	26 %	15 %	F+
non-final <ie>	5 %	4 %	
minority spellings ‡	4 %	4 %	

‡ <ei>,<ae>,<oe>, <eo>, <ey>, <ay>)

'F-' : tends to occur in low frequency words; 'F+' : tends to occur in high frequency words

bovine, carbine, crystalline, elephantine, labyrinthine, philistine, serpentine, and in *mercantile*. This, too, is the usual preference in that familiar pair *either, neither*. Some words have variation in SBS between /iː/ and /e/: *crematorium, premier, zebra, zenith*. In these words AmE generally has /iː/. On the other hand, AmE has /e/ in some words where SBS has /iː/ – in *aesthete, anaesthetist, breve, centenary, Daedalus, devolution, ecumenical, febrile, lever, methane, oestrogen, Oedipus, penalize, pyrethrin, Semite, systemic, senile*. The <ae> and <oe> digraphs are simplified to <e> in American spelling.

/iː/ in monosyllables

We can look at <ea> and <ee> spellings, together with any minority spellings, in monosyllables to see whether the vowel spelling is restricted by the context of the following consonant; the few words which have §Latinate word-formation potential are labelled 'L'.

The only decisive contexts are:

- —/b/ : *glebe, grebe*;
- —/ʃ/ : *leash*;
- —/g/ : *league*;
- —/ld/ : *field, shield, wield, yield* (ignoring *weald* as archaic);
- —/θ/ : *heath, sheath, wreath*;
- —/nd/ : *fiend*.

In other contexts there is quite often a minority spelling adding more divergence to the competing <ea> and <ee> spellings:

- final : *flea, lea, pea, plea, sea, tea*; *bee, flee, free, glee, knee, lee, pee, see, tee, three, tree, twee, wee*; minority spellings: *key*; *quay*;
- —/p/ : *cheap, heap, leap, neap, reap*; *beep, bleep, cheep, creep, deep, jeep, keep, peep, seep, sheep, sleep, steep, sweep, weep*;
- —/t/ : *beat, bleat, cheat, cleat, eat, feat, meat, neat, peat, pleat, seat, teat, treat* (L), *wheat*; *beet, feet, fleet, greet, meet, sheet, skeet, sleet, street, sweet,*

tweet; minority spelling: *mete*;

- —/d/ : *knead*, *lead*, *mead*, *plead*, *read*; *bleed*, *breed*, *creed* (L), *deed*, *feed*, *greed*, *heed*, *meed*, *need*, *reed*, *seed*, *speed*, *tweed*, *weed*; minority spelling: *cede* (L);
- —/k/ : *beak*, *bleak*, *creak*, *freak*, *leak*, *peak*, *sneak*, *speak*, *squeak*, *streak*, *teak*, *tweak*, *weak*, *wreak*; *cheek*, *creek*, *leek*, *meek*, *peek*, *reek*, *seek*, *sleek*, *week*; minority spellings: *eke*; *shriek*; *chic*; *clique*, *pique*;
- —/ʧ/ : *beach*, *bleach*, *breach*, *leach*, *peach*, *preach*, *reach*, *teach*; *beech*, *breech*, *leech*, *screech*, *speech*;
- —/f/ : *beef*, *reef*; *leaf*, *sheaf;* minority spelling: *brief*, *chief*, *fief*, *grief*, *lief*, *thief*;
- —/v/ : *cleave*, *eaves*, *greave*, *heave*, *leave*, *reave*, *sheaves*, *weave*; *reeve*, *sleeve*; minority spellings: *breve*, *eve*; *grieve* (L), *thieve*;
- —/ð/ : *breathe*, *sheathe*, *wreathe*; *seethe*, *teethe*;
- —/s/ : *cease* (L), *crease*, *grease*, *lease*, *peace* (L); *fleece*, *geese*; minority spelling: *niece*, *piece*;
- —/st/ : *beast*, *East*, *feast*, *least*, *yeast*; minority spelling: *priest*;
- —/z/ : *ease*, *pease*, *please* (L), *tease*; *breeze*, *cheese*, *freeze*, *lees*, *sneeze*, *squeeze*, *wheeze*; minority spellings: *seize*; *frieze*;
- —/m/ : *beam*, *bream*, *cream*, *dream*, *gleam*, *ream*, *scream*, *seam*, *steam*, *stream*, *team*; *deem*, *seem*, *teem*; minority spelling: *scheme* (L), *theme* (L);
- —/n/ : *bean*, *clean*, *dean*, *glean*, *jeans*, *lean*, *mean*, *quean*, *wean*; *been*, *green*, *keen*, *preen*, *queen*, *screen*, *seen*, *sheen*, *spleen*, *teens*, *ween*; minority spellings: *gene* (L); *mien*;
- —/l/ : *deal*, *heal*, *leal*, *meal*, *peal*, *seal*, *squeal*, *steal*, *teal*, *veal*, *weal*, *zeal* (L); *creel*, *eel*, *feel*, *heel*, *keel*, *kneel*, *peel*, *reel*, *steel*, *wheel.*

The words marked with (L) in the above lists have some §Latinate, §Romance or §Greek word-formation potential if we look at derived forms such as *treat–treatise*; *cede–cession*; *creed – credence*, *credential*; *grieve – grievance*, *grievous*; *cease–cessation*; *peace – appeasment*, *pacify*; *scheme–schematic*; *theme–thematic*; *gene–genetic*; *scene–scenic*; *zeal–zealous*. Unfortunately they do not always conform to the usual convention that long/short vowel variants should be spelt by the same (default) vowel letter, in this case <e>. If it were decided to regularize these words within present conventions, spellings such as **plese* – **plesure*, **zele* – **zelous* would be in order. Some of the above words, such as *peace–pacify* have much more complex phonological relationships.

/iː/ in disyllabic words with initial stress

There is further competition between alternative spellings of /iː/ in disyllabic words – that is in minimal free-forms of two syllables, not including derived forms of monosyllabic words (*breeding*, *sneaky*, *weaker*). Since the proportion of §Basic words is much less than in monosyllables, the role of <ea> and <ee> overall is reduced. As with monosyllables, however, we do find <ea> and <ee> in some §Romance words. We can consider, first of all, disyllabic words with stress on the first syllable and reduced vowel quality in the second. This stress pattern is typically §Basic, so <ea> and <ee> still dominate:

- <ea> : *beacon*, *beadle*, *beagle*, *beaker*, *beaver*, *creature*, *deacon*, *eager*, *eagle*, *easel*, *feature*, *heathen*, *meagre*, *measles*, *queasy*, *reason*, *season*, *sleazy*, *treacle*, *treason*, *weasel*;
- <ee> : *beetle*, *cheetah*, *feeble*, *freesia*, *geezer*, *needle*, *teeter*, *wheedle*;
- <e> : *betel*, *cedar*, *decent*, *demon*, *edict*, *equal*, *ether*, *even*, *evil*, *fever*, *frequent*, *legal*, *legion*, *lethal*, *lever*, *metre*, *negus*, *pecan*, *penal*, *penis*, *recent*, *regal*, *regent*, *region*, *schema*, *secret*, *sedum*, *semen*, *sequel*, *sequent*, *velum*, *venal*;
- <ae> : *aegis;*
- <ey> : *geyser;*
- <i> : *litre*, *piquant*, *visa.*

This is indeed an odd mixture. *Deacon* is pure Greek in origin but is wholly assimilated as a §Basic word (cf. *beacon*) and only takes §Basic suffixes: *deaconhood*, *deaconship. Cheetah* has the <-ah> to mark it as exotic and as a single morpheme (not *<cheet>+<er>), but it also contains §Basic <ee>≡/iː/. *Metre* (cf. *metric*) is entirely regular, but it must seem strange to children that two similar-sounding words such as *metre*, *litre*, found in the same area of experience, should have a different vowel spelling, all the more so when metrication is in the interests of regularity. However, most of the <e>-spelt words are predictable from word formation potential or their own ending.

It is difficult to see how many of these <e> spellings would fit into Albrow's analysis: 'Before single consonants in polysyllables *simple* vowel symbols in system 2 correspond to *short* vowels. (In system 1 they correspond to long vowels, as we have seen)' (Albrow 1972: 34). The 'system 2' example given is *merit*, the 'system 1' example is *mete.* These assignments are difficult to justify for the disyllabic words listed above and even more so for longer words (see p. 156 above).

/iː/ in the final syllable of polysyllabic words

We must now examine minimal free-forms of two or more syllables which either have stress or full vowel quality on the final syllable. This is not a typical §Basic pattern except with the prefixes <be-> and <for-> (*believe*, *forgive*). Hence most of the words will be non-§Basic and the incidence of <ee> and <ea> spellings will be a great deal less. Since the final syllable tends to be a recurrent element, either a root such as <cede>, <ceive>,

<vene>, or an ending such as <-ene>, <-ese>, minimal free-forms longer than two syllables need also to be considered here. (Final /iː/ will be considered separately later.)

- <ea> : *impeach; anneal, appeal, conceal, congeal, repeal, reveal; demean; decrease, increase, release; bereave*; *defeat, entreat, retreat;*
- <ee> (excluding the suffix morpheme <-ee>) : *exceed, proceed, succeed; genteel; esteem, redeem; canteen, careen, colleen, lateen, nankeen, sateen, tureen; discreet;*
- <e..e> : the root <cede> with *ac-, con-, inter-, pre-, re-, se-; centipede, stampede, supersede, velocipede; blaspheme, extreme, phoneme, supreme, trireme;* the suffix <-ene> (see §5.5, pp. 432) in *acetylene, anthracene, benzene, ethylene, kerosene, methylene, phosgene, polythene, styrene, terylene, toluene;* the root <vene> with *con-, contra-, inter-, super-; gangrene, obscene, serene; obese;* the root <plete> with *com-, de-, re-; aesthete, athlete, compete, concrete, discrete, effete, excrete, exegete, obsolete, secrete; journalese* (see §5.5, pp. 433), *manganese, trapeze;*
- <ei> : the roots <ceit> or <ceive> with *con -, de -, per -, re -*; others – *caffeine, codeine, protein*; the word *casein* has /iːɪ/, a clear candidate for smoothing to /iː/;
- <ie> : the ending <ieve>/<ief> in *achieve, aggrieve, believe, belief, relieve, relief, reprieve, retrieve; besiege* is from the free form *siege; hygiene* would be better spelt **hygene;*
- <i..e> : *automobile, chenille, imbecile; regime;* the suffix <-ine> (see §5.5, pp. 432) in *glycerine, morphine, nicotine, phosphine, strychnine, tyrosine* and numerous chemical terms; *brilliantine, crinoline* (also /ɪ/), *cuisine, dentine, figurine, gabardine, guillotine, latrine, limousine, machine, magazine, margarine, marine, mezzanine, opaline, quarantine, ravine, routine, sardine, submarine, tambourine, tangerine, trampoline, vaccine, vaseline; artiste, modiste; caprice, pelisse, police; elite, marguerite, petite; naive, recitative; cerise, chemise, expertise, valise; prestige; fatigue, intrigue; antique, boutique, critique, mystique, oblique, physique, technique, unique;*
- <i> : *ambergris, massif, motif.*

There is potential confusion here in using the suffixes <-ine> and <-ene> correctly, more so because either spelling may be used in pseudo-technical words: *gasolene/gasoline.* There is also a problem with <-ese> and <-ise>, where *expertise* is exceptional (cf. *journalese, Chinese*, etc.). See §5.5, p.433, for both these pairs of suffixes. There are occasional homophones: *discreet, discrete.* Whether an ending can be added to a bound-form or a free-form may be a guide: <-ine> but not <-ene> can be added to free-forms: *figurine, opaline.* On the whole <e> associates with recurrent stems such as <plete>, <vene>, <crete>, while <i> associates more with suffixes; <ee> and <ea>

do not occur in morphemes larger than two syllables. The AmE spelling <technic> for the noun (SBS *technique*) makes it look more §Greek-like and a better match for the adjective *technical.* With the change in spelling, the stress shifts forward to give /ˈteknɪk/.

'<i> before <e> except after <c>'

A familiar phonotactic rule (discussed in §2.8.2, p. 69) tries to sort out the distribution of <ei> and <ie> spellings of /iː/ relative to each other – '<i> before <e> except after <c>'. After <c> we find *ceiling* and a group of words with variants of the §Latinate stem {ceive}: *conceit*, *conceive*, *deceit*, *deceive*, *perceive*, *receipt*, *receive.* There are some exceptions with <ei> as a spelling of /iː/ without a <c> immediately before it: *caffeine*, *codeine*, *counterfeit*, *inveigle*, *protein*, *seize* and the AmE pronunciation of *either, neither, leisure.* As one might expect of any rule, there are likely to be even more exceptions in names, many of which are Scottish:

- *Beith*, *Bernstein*, *Bulleid*, *Dalgleish*, *Feilden*, *Feist*, *Geikie*, *Keig*, *Leila*, *Leitch*, *Leishman*, *Leichtenstein*, *MacNeice*, *Menteith*, *Neil*, *Reid*, *Reims*, *Reith*, *Seigel*, *Sheila*, *Teign*, *Veitch*, etc.

Final /iː/

We turn now to word-final position. Final /iː/ corresponds to simple <e> in the stressed pronunciation of *be*, *he*, *me*, *she*, *the*, *we;* function words are not required to have a minimum of three letters as are lexical items (the 'short word rule' p. 131). For some speakers there is an unstressed final /iː/≡<e> in words such as *aborigine*, *acme*, *epitome*, *psyche;* other speakers will have /ɪ/. A similar minority group are the final iː <i> spellings in *kiwi*, *ski* and *potpourri.* Final unstressed /iː/ is also the purist pronunciation of the Latin masculine plural ending along with the anglicized /aɪ/ (in *cacti*, *fungi*, *stimuli*, *etc.*); this is discussed more fully under /aɪ/ (see pp. 152f.).

Final /iː/, usually stressed, as the passive suffix <-ee> is added to verbs to form nouns. These usually represent the notional animate object of the verb in the stem (direct as in *employee*, or indirect as in *grantee*, or reflexive as in *devotee*):

- *addressee*, *appointee*, *assignee*, *conferee*, *consignee*, *debauchee*, *deportee*, *devotee*, *divorcee*, *draftee*, *employee*, *enrollee*, *grantee*, *inductee*, *internee*, *interviewee*, *invitee*, *legatee*, *lessee*, *licensee*, *mortgagee*, *nominee*, *parolee*, *patentee*, *payee*, *referee*, *trainee*, *transferee*, *trustee*, *vestee.*

Frequency of use may shift the stress away from the suffix in a few of these. For *employee* LPD prefers /ɪmˈplɔɪiː/ to /emplɔɪˈiː/, but for *divorcee* it prefers /dɪvɔːˈsiː/ to /dɪˈvɔːsiː/, while *devotee* only has final stress. There is no object relationship in *escapee*, *refugee*, *truckee*. The verb may be truncated: *nominee* rather than **nominatee*. In spite of the rather variable syntax of these words, the suffix is immediately recognizable and presents no spelling problem.

Similarly, <ee> is the regular spelling for final stressed /iː/ in polysyllabic words where it does not represent a suffix: *agree*, *buckshee*, *chickadee*, *chimpanzee*, *decree*, *jamboree*, *marquee*, *repartee*, *rupee*, *settee*. These words have primary or secondary stress on the final syllable in their citation forms. This should prevent confusion between the /iː/≡<y> of some speakers in *easy*, *happy*, etc. (cf. *refugee* – *effigy*).

There are also words with initial stress which have final <-ee>. They are more likely to show confusion with <-y>: *apogee*, *banshee*, *filigree*, *jubilee*, *lychee*, *pedigree*, *topee*, *trochee*. I have seen a greengrocer's spelling *<lychies> for *lychees*, which points to a singular form *<lychy> or *<lychie>.

Other spellings of /iː/

We can now say that <e> is the default spelling elsewhere, but even this very limited claim has some exceptions:

- *cliche*, *kilo*, *milieu*, *albino*, *ballerina*, *bikini*, *casino*, *concertina*, *farina*, *graffiti*, *incognito*, *maraschino*, *merino*, *mosquito*, *scarlatina*, *semolina*.

In this last group we might be tempted to salvage a further regularity from among these exceptions. Words of three or more syllables with penultimate stress on /iː/ followed by a single consonant and a final vowel seem to have <i>≡/iː/. This takes a lot of saying, but the rhythm is an immediately apparent fact and for many people there will be some vaguely Italian association. Alas, there are exceptions even here: *hyena*, *torpedo*, *tuxedo*, *verbena*.

In names, <eigh> is a minority spelling of /iː/ – *Deighton*, *Eastleigh*, *Fairleigh*, *Hatherleigh*, *Keighley* (as /ˈkiː(θ)lɪ/), *Leigh*, *Meighen*, *Weighton*. In names <ey> occurs medially as an archaic spelling of /iː/ in *Alleyn*, *Eyam*, *Eyton*, *Heysham*, *Keyes*, *Keymour*, *Keyne*, *Keyte*, *Sneyd*, *Steyne*.

The sheer length of this account of /iː/ is a measure of the divergence in spelling. Would that there had been more striking regularities to find. It is ironic that many demands for a reform or tidying up of English spelling tend to cite irrelevant minority spellings such as *gauge* or *people*. The larger-scale divergence we have just seen requires quite complex explanation and would be difficult to regularize.

We have almost sliced away enough identifiable categories to be able to say that the default <e> is found in all other instances, but not quite. Before another vowel in a minimal free-form we find <i> as the default spelling: *inebriation*, *insomniac*, *liaison*, *orgiastic*, *orient*, *psychiatric*, *serviette*, *trio*, *vitriolic*, etc. The form <psychi-> differs from the free form *psyche.* Some §Greek and one or two §Latinate words have <e>, including the common prefixes <neo-> and <geo->: *beatitude, create, creole, ideology, osteopath, protease, spontaneity* (also with /eɪ/), *theology, trachea.* Exceptional spellings are *aeon* and *plebeian.* The §Latinate prefixes <de->, <pre->, <re-> (*deactivate, preamble, reactor*) are easily recognized. In some of these contexts, before a vowel the /iː/ may be in free variation with /ɪ/. There is potential confusion between <i> and <e> spellings, unless the speller learns to recognize recurrent morphs.

Ligature spellings <æ> and <œ> were used in some §Latinate and §Greek words and names in the eighteenth and nineteenth centuries, but in recent decades they have fallen into disuse and have been replaced by digraphs <ae> and <oe>:

- *aegis, aeon, mediaeval, Aegean, Aeneas, Aesop, Caesar, Daedalus, Judaea; diarrhoea, foetus, oesophagus, Croesus, Oedipus, Phoebe, Phoebus, Phoenix,* etc., or in some cases, especially in American spelling, simply by <e> – *medieval, esophagus.*

The common word *people* has a nonce spelling which may go back to an early attempt to link the spelling to Latin *populus* or may represent a Middle English front rounded vowel. Whatever the source of the spelling, it is a striking example of how irregularity can persist as an institution in a very high-frequency word. A couple of names have this same correspondence: *Peover*, and one pronunciation of *St. Neot's*, which also has a regular /ɪə/.

By default, then, we would expect <e> in §Latinate words of three or more syllables:

- *abbreviate, abstemious, accretion, adhesion, alleviate, analgesia, appreciate, arena, camellia, cathedral, cohesive, comedian, crematorium, demarcation, deviate, elongate, expedient, facetious, frequency, genius, helium, lenient, magnesium, medium, obsequious, plenary, tedious, verbena,* etc.

These are usually marked by suffixes as §Latinate, so there is some indication to the speller that a spelling *<creamatorium> might well be wrong.

The short vowel counterpart of /iː/ in derived forms is /e/: *species–special, medium–medieval, genus–genera, convene–convention, discreet–discretion,* etc.

The Hanna (1966) spelling rules have no overall default spelling but the contexts catered for are:

1 <ea> syllable-initial (*ea-sy, coll-eague*);
2 <ei..e> syllable-medial after /s/ and before /v/ (*de-ceive*) – this in effect identifies the §Latinate stem <ceive>;
3 <ie..e> syllable-medial before /v/ (*be-lieve, re-prieve*);
4 <ie> syllable-medial before /f/ (*re-lief, shield*);
5 <ee> syllable-medial after /t/ (*teeth, six-teen*);
6 <ee> syllable-medial before /p, d/ (*deep, feed*);

7 <ea> syllable-medial elsewhere (*lean, squeam-ish*);
8 <ee> word-final (*flee, decree, jamboree*);
9 <e> syllable-final (*o-be-di-ent, le-gion*)

Hanna does not cater for <i> or <i..e> spellings. The <ee> after /t/ context would be very minor if the suffixes <-ee> and <-teen> were dealt with by affix-stripping.

3.3.2.3 /eɪ/ *as in* lake *('long <a>')*

This vowel has much the same lexical distribution in stressed syllables in AmE as in SBS. There are only small groups of variants to take into account. AmE may have /eɪ/ in a few words where SBS has /iː/, such as *beta, devotee, quay, repartee, theta, zeta*, and in some §Romance names and words where SBS has /ɑː/, such as *El Dorado, Titania, charade, cicada, desiderata, desperado, gala, praline, pro rata, stratum, tomato, vase, virago*. /eɪ/ is sometimes quoted as a possible AmE pronunciation of *measure, pleasure, treasure*. This seems to have re-formed /e/ and its palatal off-glide to /ʒ/ as phoneme /eɪ/. AmE also has /eɪ/ where SBS has /æ/ in a few §Greek words: *phalanx, satrap, satyr*.

Distribution of variant spellings

/eɪ/ has a number of divergent spellings (table 23), but, apart from the group of <ai> and <ay> spellings, the divergence is restricted to relatively small groups of words. The default spelling is <a>, which has regular <e>-marking as <a..e>.

Table 23 Spellings of /eɪ/

spellings of /eɪ/	*TF*	*LF*	
<a>, <a..e>	65 %	82 %	F-
final <-ay>	18 %	4 %	F+
<ai>	12 %	10 %	F+
minority spellings ‡	5 %	5 %	

‡ <e..e>, <-e>, <-ee>, <-er>, <-et>, <-ay->, <ei>, <ey>, <aigh>, <eigh>.

'F-' : tends to occur in low frequency words; 'F+' : tends to occur in high frequency words

<ai> and <ay> spellings of /eɪ/

The spelling <ay> is the final variant of <ai> in §Basic free forms: *stay, stayed, staying*, but *staid, stain*; *bray, brayed, braying*, but *braid, brain*, etc. The high text frequency of words with final <-ay> is largely due to some very common words, such as *away, day, lay, pay, play, say, stay, today, way*. It may occur at internal free-form boundaries: *always, layman, maybe, waylay*. This accounts for some medial <ay> spellings in two-element §Basic names such as *Drayton* but, in names generally, medial <ay> is common: *Aylesbury*, *Ayling*, *Aylward*, *Ayton*, *Bayley*, *Baynes*, *Blaydes*, *Brayley*, *Clayton*, *Mayne*, *Payne*, *Paynter*, *Raynes*, *Taylor*, *Wayne*. Some of these use an anomalous <e> for padding, as do *Maine*, *Paine*, *Thwaite*, *Vaile*, etc.

Since <ai> spellings make up 12 per cent of instances of /eɪ/, any evidence of complementary distribution between <ai> and <a> would be valuable. It is, however, obvious from the number of homophones that any regularities found will be statistically weighted rather than clear-cut. We have, for instance, *bale–bail*, *made–maid*, *male–mail*, *maze–maize*, *plane–plain*, *waste–waist*, *wave–waive*, etc. Moreover, any statements about what does not occur will be limited to the present database. If we were to probe into the remoter fringes of the English lexicon, we might find words such as *aiguillesque* or *aikinite* which take us outside the normal run of words and introduce sequences peculiar to foreign writing systems or to proper names. The general distribution of <ai>≡/eɪ/ and <a>≡/eɪ/, with these reservations, is as follows:

<a> occurs before vowels and before /b k g ʤ ð ʃ ʒ/: *aorta, labour, take, bagel, agent, lathe, acacia, erasure*. Only <ai> occurs before the cluster /nt/ (*acquaint*, *paint*, etc.); only <a> occurs before the cluster /n(d)ʒ/ (*change*, *range*, *strange*, etc.).

Before / p f v θ s ʧ/, <ai> only occurs in a relatively few words and <a> is more common:

- —/p/ : *traipse;* but *escape*, *scrape*, *taper*, etc.;
- —/f/ : *waif;* but *chafe*, *safe*, *wafer*, etc.;
- —/v/ : *waive;* but *brave*, *rave*, *wave*, etc.;
- —/θ/ : *faith*, *wraith* and the name *Galbraith;* no monosyllables with <a>, but *atheist*, *bathos*, *pathos;*
- —/s/ : *plaice*, *waist* and the names *Aisgill*, *Gaisford*; but *place*, *race*, *waste*, etc.;
- —/ʧ/ : *aitch;* but *nature*, *legislature* and one or two other palatalization forms.

The final <s> of the French names *Beaujolais*, *Calais*, *Millais*, *Rabelais*, is empty (or inert: *Rabelaisian*).

There is, however, significant competition between <ai> and <a> before /t d z l m n/. The <ai> spellings are usually in a minority except before /l/ and /n/ where they are more frequent than <a> spellings. Table 24 below shows the percentage text frequency and lexical frequency of each of the two correspondences <ai>≡/eɪ/ and <a>≡/eɪ/ (including <a..e>) in the six contexts and the proportion of <ai> spellings in each context.

Table 24 <ai> and <a> spellings of /eɪ/

	% of <ai>≡/eɪ/		*% of <a>≡/eɪ/*		*<ai> as % of <a>+<ai>*	
	TF	*LF*	*TF*	*LF*	*TF*	*LF*
‡—/t/	7 %	5 %	18 %	30 %	7 %	2 %
—/d/	9 %	7 %	7 %	4 %	19 %	18 %
—/z/	5 %	7 %	1 %	2 %	41 %	28 %
—/l/	19 %	24 %	2 %	2 %	64 %	55 %
—/m/	5 %	5 %	7 %	2 %	11 %	20 %
—/n/	52 %	49 %	6 %	5 %	63 %	57 %

‡ words ending in the suffix <-ate>≡/eɪt/ (e.g. the verb *advocate*) are excluded

The following table 25 shows the same figures but only for monosyllabic words.

Table 25 <ai> and <a> spellings of /eɪ/ (for monosyllabic words)

	% of <ai>≡/eɪ/		*% of <a>≡/eɪ/*		*<ai> as % of <a>+<ai>*	
	TF	*LF*	*TF*	*LF*	*TF*	*LF*
—/t/	8 %	7 %	14 %	10 %	10 %	22 %
—/d/	12 %	10 %	10 %	6 %	19 %	42 %
—/z/	8 %	8 %	2 %	7 %	50 %	33 %
—/l/	19 %	27 %	3 %	9 %	57 %	58 %
—/m/	7 %	4 %	12 %	6 %	10 %	21 %
—/n/	43 %	35 %	7 %	10 %	56 %	61 %

The two tables show that the same relative distribution holds in monosyllabic words as in longer words. The following examples show the extent to which the two spellings compete in these contexts:

- —/t/ : *bait, caitiff, distrait, gait, gaiter, strait* (cf. also *straight*), *traitor, wait; data, date, gate, mate, status*, etc.;
- —/d/ : *afraid, aid, aide, braid, maid, raid, staid*; and the two inflected forms *laid, paid; blade, cradle, fade, lady, made, shade, stadium*, etc.;
- —/z/ : *baize, braise, chaise, complaisant, daisy, liaison, maize, malaise, mayonnaise, praise, raise, raisin; amaze, blaze, brazen, craze, daze, erase, gaze, glaze, graze, gymnasium, haze, hazel, laser, laze, maze, phase, phrase, raze, razor*, etc.;
- —/l/ : *ail, aileron, assail, avail, bail, braille, curtail, detail, entail, entrails, fail, flail, frail, grail, hail, jail, mail, nail, pail, prevail, quail, rail, raillery, retail, sail, snail, tail, travail, wail, wassail; ale, alias, alien, azalea, bale, calyx, dale, exhale, female, gale, hale, halide, halo, impale, kale, male, pale, regale, regalia, salient, saline, scale, shale, stale, tale, vale, valence, whale*, etc.;

- —/m/ : *aim*, *claim*, *exclaim* (*de-*, *pro-*, etc.), *maim; chamber*, *flame*, *game*, *name*, *stamen*, *tame*, etc.;
- —/n/ : *brain*, *chain*, *cocaine*, *contain*, *disdain*, *drain*, *entertain*, *explain*, *gain*, *grain*, *maintain*, *migraine*, *moraine*, *obtain*, *ordain*, *pain*, *plain*, *quatrain*, *rain*, *remain*, *sprain*, *stain*, *strain*, *train*, *vain*, *wainscot*, etc.; *ancient*, *arrange*, *bane*, *butane*, *cane*, *change*, *chicane*, *crane*, *danger*, *germane*, *humane*, *hurricane*, *lane*, *mane*, *mania*, *membrane*, *pane*, *plane*, *profane*, *range*, *sane*, *strange*, *thane*, *vane*, *wane*, etc.

The two inflected words *paid* and *laid* are unnecessarily irregular, since the past tense morpheme does not have its usual <ed> spelling as in *prayed*, *delayed*, etc. There is no advantage to be gained from odd variants such as these, though they are sometimes cited with approval as being 'more phonetic'.

Other spellings of /eɪ/

We can now consider the minority spellings of /eɪ/. The conveniently round figure of 5 per cent for the minority spellings conceals some variation between text frequency and lexical frequency. For instance, <ea> is found in a few very common words such as *break*, *great*, *steak;* <ei> is found in twice as many words but they are on the whole much less common.

A curious correspondence <e..e>≡/eɪ/ is found in a few §French words: *cortege*, *crepe* (also anglicized as *crape*), *fete*, *suede*, where an English /e/ rather than /eɪ/ would have been a better phonetic match for the French /ɛ/. The final <-e> spelling seems to be the reason for choosing the long vowel /eɪ/ instead. This is yet another example of English spelling conventions overruling purely phonetic considerations in anglicizing foreign loan-words.

Final /eɪ/ in polysyllabic words indicates French loan-words spelt with <-e>, <-ee>, <-er>, <-et>. The <t> and <r> are empty letters; the <r> does not provide 'linking /r/' in *a dossier on* . . ., *the atelier of* . . ., simply because /eɪ/ is not followed by //r// in SBS. Examples:

- *atelier*, *dossier*, *foyer;*
- *ballet*, *beret*, *bouquet*, *buffet*, *cabaret*, *cachet*, *chalet*, *crochet*, *croquet*, *gourmet*, *parquet*, *ricochet*, *sachet*, *soubriquet*, *tourniquet.* Stress may vary on some of these words: a more 'French' pronunciation has final stress. If stress is on an earlier syllable, as in /ˈbæleɪ/, the /eɪ/ may reduce to /ɪ/. The word *valet* has traditionally been /ˈvælɪt/, but there is a 'French' pronunciation with /eɪ/. As an empty letter, the <-t> of this ending does not double in the rare inflected forms: *ricocheted, tourniqueted.* There is an obsolete spelling *ricochetted*, *ricochetting*, going back to an anglicized /-et/ pronunciation. Both are probably now out of use (LPD).
- *entree*, *fricassee*, *matinee*, *melee*, *puree*, *soiree*, *toupee;*

- *abbe*, *attache*, *blase*, *cafe*, *canape*, *cliche*, *communique*, *consomme*, *decollete*, *emigre*, *fiance*(*e*), *glace*, *habitue*, *naivete*, *neglige*, *protege*(*e*), *recherche*, *resume* (n. /'rezjumeɪ/), *retrousse*, *roue*, *saute*, *souffle*.

There are no indications available to the English speller, other than some knowledge of French, to indicate which spelling <-e>, <-ee>, <-er>, <-et> to adopt. Misspellings are therefore quite likely. French accents (as in <-é>, <-ée>) have not been considered an English convention; if they are used within an English text, then they mark a switch to French orthographic conventions for a particular word or for a longer insert of French text.

Other minority spellings:

- <ay> : non-final in *bayonet*, *cayenne*, *crayon*, *layette*, *mayonnaise*. In *rayon*, the <ay> falls at an opaque free-form boundary: the word is a deliberate coinage from the noun *ray*. The boundaries in words such as *layman, wayfarer, waylay*, are more obvious;
- <ea> : *break*, *great*, *steak*, *yea;*
- <ei> : *beige*, *deign*, *feign*, *feint*, *heinous*, *nonpareil*, *obeisance*, *reign*, *rein*, *reindeer*, *seine*, *sheik* (also /iː/), *skein*, *surveillance*, *veil*, *vein*, *vermeil;*
- <ey> : occurs finally in: *bey*, *convey*, *fey*, *grey* (has alternative *gray*), *hey*, *obey*, *prey*, *purvey*, *survey*, *they*, *whey;* the *abey-* of *abeyance* is clearly not a free-form, so this is an exception;
- <aigh> : *straight;*
- <eigh> : *eight*, *freight*, *neigh*, *neighbour*, *sleigh*, *weigh*, *weight;* to these we must add *inveigh*, which is a singularly perverse spelling in view of *con-*, *pur-* and *sur-* + <vey>, and since the etymologies of all four are completely obscure in their present spellings;
- oddities: <ae> in *brae* (Scottish), *Gaelic*, *sundae*, *maelstrom* (Dutch); <ao> in *gaol;* <au> in *gauge.*

These last two words probably have the distinction of being the most derided fossil spellings in English. In US spelling they are very sensibly normalized as *jail* and *gage.* Over the centuries these two words have generated a wide range of spelling variants (see *OED*). There is even a medieval spelling of *gaol* as **gayhole.*

Names have some nonce spellings: *Graham* is best analysed with an empty <h>; *Blackie* has /æ/ – /eɪ/ variation in spite of the <C>-doubling, but the /eɪ/ can also be spelt *Blaikie.*

The short vowel counterpart of /eɪ/ in derived forms is /æ/: *sane–sanity*, *mania–manic*, *nature–natural*, *grateful–gratitude*, *navy–navigate*, *nation–national*, etc. There is variation between /æ/ and /eɪ/ across accents in some words. SBS usually has /æ/ in *palaeography*, *patriot*, *phalanx*, *phosphatic*, *ration* and /eɪ/ in *apricot, patent.* AmE speakers may have the reverse.

The only spelling peculiar to /eɪ/ is <aigh>.

The Hanna (1966) spelling rules have no overall default spelling but:

1 <a..e> syllable-initial (*lem-on-ade*, *lib-er-ate*);
2 <a..e> syllable-medial unaccented (*fe-male*, *em-i-grate*);
3 <ai> syllable-medial accented before /l, m, n/ (*fail, claim, train*);
4 <a..e> syllable-medial accented (*wage*, *waste*);
5 <ay> word-final (*dismay*);
6 <a> syllable-final (*i-mag-i-na-tive*, *la-dy*).

The Hanna algorithm does not cater for any of the minority spellings <e..e>, <e>, <er>, <et>, <ei>, <ey>, <aigh> or <eigh>. The instances of <ai> before /m/ do not seem to be significant: /eɪ/ before /m/ is spelt more frequently with <a>.

3.3.2.4 /aʊ/ *as in* clown

This vowel has much the same lexical distribution in stressed syllables in AmE as in SBS.

Distribution of variant spellings

/aʊ/ shows scarcely any spelling divergence. The default spelling in both §Basic and §Romance words is <ou>, which has the variant <ow> in final position and before vowels:

Table 26 Spellings of /aʊ/

spellings of /aʊ/	*TF*	*LF*	
<ou>/final <ow>	93 %	83 %	
Pre-consonant<ow>	6 %	13 %	F-
<ough>	<1 %	2 %	
<au>	<1 %	2 %	

'F-' : tends to occur in low frequency words

A general graphotactic constraint against having <u> in word-final position is responsible for the final <ow> spelling of /aʊ/, instead of <ou>. The archaic pronoun *thou* is an exception.

The only peculiarity about /aʊ/≡<ou> is that the digraph <ou>, borrowed from French, is the spelling across both §Basic and §Romance words. This predates the Vowel Shift: <ou> became used as a spelling for early modern English /uː/, which shifted into present-day /aʊ/. The result is that the long/short variation between /aʊ/ and /ʌ/ (*pronounce–pronunciation*, *profound–profundity*) displays a difference in spelling: <ou> – <u>. Other long/short pairs: /eɪ/ – /æ/, /iː/ – /e/, /aɪ/ – /ɪ/, /əʊ/ – /ɒ/ share the same spelling for both phonemes in allomorphic variation: <a>, <e>, <i>, <o>.

<ow> occurs in final position instead of <ou> (*allow*, *bow*, *brow*, *chow*, *cow*, *endow*, *now*, *prow*, *scow*, *trow*, *vow*, *wow*) and before a vowel letter

(*bowel*, *bower*, *coward*, *cower*, *dowager*, *dowel*, *flower*, *glower*, *howitzer*, *power*, *prowess*, *rowel*, *shower*, *towel*, *tower*, *trowel*, *vowel*). This is essentially a graphic (not a phonetic) constraint since the homophones *flower* – *flour* both have a following /ə/.

Both <ow> and <ou> occur before the following consonants:

- —/d/ : *crowd* and disyllabic *chowder*, *dowdy*, *powder*, *rowdy; aloud*, *cloud*, *loud*, *proud*, *shroud.* Names spelt with <owd> include *Bowdler*, *Cowdray*, *Dowd*, *Dowden*, *Frowde*, *Plowden*, and with <oud> *Froud* and *Stroud.* So, in monosyllables, *crowd*, *Dowd*, would seem to be irregular;
- —/l/ : *cowl*, *fowl*, *growl*, *howl*, *jowl*, *owl*, *prowl*, *scowl*, *yowl; foul;*
- —/n/ : *brown*, *clown*, *crown*, *down*, *drown*, *frown*, *gown*, *renown*, *town; noun;* before clusters /nt/, /nd/, /ns/ only <ou> occurs – *count*, *ground*, *bounce*, *etc.*;
- —/z/ : *blowsy*, *browse*, *drowse; blouse*, *carouse*, *house* (v.), *lousy*, *rouse*, *spouse*, *thousand*, *tousled*, *trousers.*

Before all other consonants within a morpheme only <ou> occurs, as in *couch*, *doubt*, *flout*, *grouse*, *mouth*. This is not entirely true of names, where we have spellings such as *Crowther*, *Bowker*, *Howson*, *Lowther.* The obscure words *cowrie*, *frowsty*, *frowzy* are also exceptions. The infrequency of <w> before other consonant letters can be explained as avoidance of complex consonant-letter strings.

<ough> occurs, with the exception of disyllabic *doughty*, in monosyllabic Germanic (§Basic) words: *bough*, *drought*, *plough*, *slough*, *sough.* This spelling is a frequent target of spelling reformers and has a high citation rating. It also illustrates a reluctance to abandon odd spellings which serve to distinguish homophones. In AmE the more regularly spelt *plow* is already established, but no-one has yet adopted **bow*, **slow*, or **sow* as alternatives to *bough*, *slough* and *sough* simply because these spellings would then be homographs with /bəʊ/, /sləʊ/, /səʊ/. Before the place-name element <-ton>, an <ough> spelling frequently corresponds to /aʊ/: *Boughton*, *Broughton*, *Houghton*, *Loughton*, *Oughton*, *Sloughton*, *Troughton*, but as always there is possible variation with /əʊ/, /ɔː/ and even /ʌf/.

<au>≡/aʊ/ may occur in §Greek *claustrophobia*, *glaucoma* and *tau* and in the hybrid *aureomycin.* It also occurs in German *ablaut*, *sauerkraut*, *umlaut*, and in German names such as *Audi*, *Bauer*, *Breslau*, *Faust*, *Gauss*, *Nassau*, *Strauss*, *Tauchnitz.* Both §Greek and German loan-words with <au> present a problem for the English reader and tend to have the spelling pronunciation /ɔː/ rather than /aʊ/ if they are in common use, as with *trauma.* The /aʊ/ pronunciation appears to be more common than /ɔː/ in AmE. *Sauerkraut* is saved by the semantic link with {sour}. *Nassau* in the Bahamas and as the name of the aristocratic family has /ɔː/.

From a purely phonetic point of view it seems highly perverse to give a

German name, such as *Braun*, a 'French' spelling pronunciation /brɔːn/, when the available English phoneme string /braʊn/ is a straightforward match for the German pronunciation. The Braun company apparently encourages the /brɔːn/ pronunciation because they wish to avoid confusion with §Basic *Brown.* Other languages adopt a different strategy to the spelling and pronunciation of loan-words. Swedish stays as close as possible to a foreign pronunciation using native correspondences, so the Swedish word *poäng* is a graphically unrecognizable phonetic approximation [pu'eŋ] to the French original *point* [pwɛ̃] (where the nasalization of [ɛ̃] is mapped as a velar nasal consonant). What is peculiar in the case of *Braun* is that German /aʊ/ is given a pure vowel pronunciation as /ɔː/, phonetically not far from French /o/, a slightly closer vowel, whereas French loans with this /o/, such as *gauche*, usually end up with English /əʊ/.

When /aʊ/ occurs before underlying //r//, an /ə/ glide links the two: both *flour* and *flower* represent /'flaʊə(r)/. In the <ower> spellings (*bower*, *cower*, *dower*, *flower*, *glower*, *power*, *shower*, *tower*) the spelling is split over two correspondences <ow>≡/aʊ/ plus <er>≡/ə(r)/. In the <our> spellings (*devour*, *flour*, *hour*, *lour*, *scour*, *sour*), we have to take the whole string as the correspondence: <our>≡/aʊə(r)/. Welsh *Brynmawr* is anglicized with /-maʊə(r)/.

In names there may be an irregular <e> as padding (§6.4): *Browne*, *Clowes*, *Cowes*, *Downe*, *Frowde*.

There are no spellings peculiar to /aʊ/.

In the Hanna (1966) spelling rules, the default spelling is <ou> and the only other contexts catered for are: <ou..e> before /s, z/ (as in *louse*, *rouse*) and <ow> syllable-finally (as in *now*, *flow-er*). The first of these two contexts applies to minimal free-forms and not to inflected forms such as *cows*, *allows.*

3.3.2.5 /əʊ/ *as in* clone *('long <o>')*

This vowel has much the same lexical distribution in stressed syllables in AmE as in SBS. In AmE the vowel is more usually a pure rounded vowel, usually given the symbol /o(:)/ or /oʊ/. The symbol /əʊ/ reflects an absence of rounding at the beginning of the SBS glide.

Distribution of variant spellings

/əʊ/ has less spelling divergence than the number of minority spellings would suggest, since the second most common spelling <ow> has a fairly predictable distribution (table 27).

Table 27 Spellings of /əʊ/

spellings of /əʊ/	*TF*	*LF*	
<o>,<o..e>,<-oe>	75 %	85 %	
<ow>	18 %	7 %	F+
<oa>	4 %	5 %	
minority spellings ‡	4 %	3 %	

‡ <ou>, <eau>, <au>, <oh>, <eo> <ol>, <ough>, <ew>, <oo>
F+' : tends to occur in high frequency words

Final <ow> and <o>

<ow> is almost exclusively found in morpheme-final position in §Basic words:

- (monosyllables) *blow*, *bow*, *crow*, *flow*, *glow*, *grow*, *know*, *low*, *mow*, *row*, *show*, *slow*, *snow*, *sow*, *stow*, *throw*, *tow;* these compete with a smaller group consisting of *doe*, *floe*, *foe*, *hoe*, *roe*, *sloe*, *throe*, *toe*, *woe; sew; beau; dough*, *though;* but not perhaps competing with two-letter *go*, *no*, *so*, *lo*, or with *fro* (as in *to and fro*), which can be regarded as more or less grammatical rather than lexical;
- (disyllabic words with intervocalic liquid (/l/ or /r/)) *arrow*, *barrow*, *bellow*, *billow*, *borrow*, *burrow*, *callow*, *fallow*, *farrow*, *fellow*, *follow*, *furrow*, *hallow*, *harrow*, *hollow*, *mallow*, *marrow*, *mellow*, *morrow*, *narrow*, *pillow*, *sallow*, *shallow*, *sorrow*, *sparrow*, *swallow*, *tallow*, *wallow*, *willow*, *yarrow*, *yellow* and the names *Gillow*, *Jarrow;*
- (other disyllabic words) *elbow*, *meadow*, *minnow*, *shadow*, *widow*, *window*, *winnow;*
- (more than two syllables) *bungalow* – which can be regarded as exceptional.

Competition between <ow> and other spellings is effectively restricted to the monosyllables, since the disyllabic words ending in <-ow> are a well-marked class of §Basic words. None of these disyllabic <-ow> words has stress on the second syllable, or a long vowel in the first syllable, or medial consonants outside the range /d, n(d), l, r/, which have the phonetic similarity of all being voiced alveolar phonemes. The only exception with <ow> rather than <o> is *elbow*. It could be saved by allowing alveolar-initial clusters, but that would only serve to make other exceptions, such as *salvo*. The only exceptions with <o> rather than <ow> are *burro* and *cello*, but this is an abbreviation of *violoncello. Furlough* has a nonce spelling.

These may seem to be a complex set of criteria, but one has only to look at the above lists to appreciate that the words do have a distinct and very striking profile. Predictably, then, <ow> will not occur in the following words, giving the default spelling <o>; some words share several excluding factors:

- long vowel: *beano, bravo, cargo, dado, dido, gyro, halo, hero, hobo, judo, kilo, largo, lido, maestro, negro, photo, polo, quarto, rhino, sago, shako, solo, sumo, tyro, veto, zero*, etc.;
- medial consonants which are not alveolar (among them palato-alveolar /ʧ/ and /ʤ/): *banjo, bingo, blanco, bravo, bronco, cargo, dingo, echo, ego, fresco, gecko, hobo, jingo, jumbo, largo, limbo, lingo, mango, memo, negro, recto, sago, salvo, servo, shako, stucco, tango, tempo, yobbo*, etc.;
- voiceless consonants: *alto, blanco, blotto, bronco, canto, ditto, echo, fresco, gecko, ghetto, gusto, maestro, motto, photo, poncho, presto, pronto, quarto, recto, scherzo, shako, stucco, tempo, torso, veto*, etc.;
- no medial consonant: *trio*;
- /lC/ clusters: *alto, dildo, salvo*, etc.; *elbow* has already been noted as an exception;
- stress potentially on last syllable: *bravo, hello; bestow* is not a single morpheme.

The final <-o> of names is similarly predictable: *Banquo, Batho, Bisto, Castro, Cato, Como, Congo, Dido, Dodo, Douro, Elmo, Fargo, Fido, Giro, Hugo, Marco, Nero, Oslo, Otto, Plato, Pluto, Sappho, Sligo, Shinto, Tasso, Tito, Volvo.* Most of these will be recognizably not §Basic. Some names, however, have <-ow> without the restrictions found in words: *Barlow, Benbow, Bristow, Chepstow, Dunmow, Harlow, Hounslow, Ludlow, Moscow, Onslow, Wilmslow. Rollo* is a converse exception. Some of these, such as *Chepstow* (= 'market' + 'place'), are compound §Basic names in which the elements have been obscured. There are also one or two §Basic names with final <-ough>≡/əʊ/ – *Bullough, Greenough, Myerscough, Whatmough; Burroughs* is a variant of *Burrows.* The spelling <ow> sometimes has an <e> for padding (§6.4) in names: *Barlowe, Blencowe, Bowes, Bowles, Bristowe, Crowe, Fellowes, Henslowe, Knowles, Lowe.*

Simple words of three or more syllables have final <-o> (the only exception being *bungalow*): *alfresco, archipelago, avocado, bravado, buffalo, calico, casino, contralto, desperado, domino, embryo, falsetto, flamingo, impetigo, indigo, manifesto, merino, momento, mosquito, mulatto, oratorio, patio, piccolo, pimento, potato, proviso, rodeo, scenario, sombrero, studio, tomato, virago, volcano*, etc. These are all nouns and are markedly non-§Basic in origin. Indeed if a minimal free form has three or more syllables, final /əʊ/ itself marks the word as §Exotic.

The default spelling <-o> for final /əʊ/ does not occur in *cocoa, oboe*, some French names and some recent French loan-words. These are spelt either with an empty final consonant (*apropos, argot, depot, tricot, sabot*) or with the ending <-eau> (*bandeau, bureau, chateau, flambeau, plateau, portmanteau, rondeau, tableau, trousseau*). If an unlikely association is made between *sabot* and *sabotage, saboteur*, the <t> of *sabot* would be an inert letter. French names with empty final <C_1> include

Bordeaux, *Diderot*, *Gounod*, *Peugeot*, *Renault*, *Rievaulx*, *Vaux*.

There is some uncertainty about the spelling of the plural of nouns ending in <-o> (see §2.4, p. 19); we usually find:

- only <-os> : *concertos*, *contraltos*, *quartos*, *radios*, *solos*, *sopranos*, etc.;
- only <-oes> : *dominoes*, *heroes*, *potatoes*, *tomatoes*, *torpedoes*, etc.;
- either <-os> or <-oes> : *cargo(e)s*, *commando(e)s*, *halo(e)s*, *tornado(e)s*, *volcano(e)s*, etc.

People are very willing to be dogmatic about this, but usage varies and there are no firm guidelines. The <-oes> form is not found in decidedly §Exotic words (*generalissimos*, *mulattos*) or in words where the plural is unusual (*indigos*, *impetigos*) or in words with the colloquial ending <-o> in *boyos, buckos, dipsos, winos*. The only phonetic criterion is that, if there is a vowel before the final /əʊ/, the <-oes> form does not occur (*radios*, *cameos*). The monosyllables *goes* and *noes* (cf. *does* aux.) have the <e>-marked form. Insecure spellers frequently derive a singular spelling **pota-toe*, **tomatoe* from the <-oes> plural form (p. 80).

Medial /əʊ/ in monosyllables

Not all instances of <ow> occur in morpheme-final position, so we need to look again at monosyllables to assess the competition between <o>, <o..e>, one or two remaining examples of <ow> and various minority spellings. A few contexts are modestly diagnostic:

- <o..e> occurs before /b/, /g/, /z/ as in *globe*, *lobe*, *probe*, *robe; brogue*, *rogue*, *vogue; close* (vb.), *doze*, *froze*, *hose*, *nose*, *pose*, *prose*, *rose*;
- <oa> occurs before /f/, /ks/ as in *loaf*, *oaf; coax*, *hoax;*
- <o> occurs before /nt/ as in the adjective *wont* and the two abbreviations *don't*, *won't*.

In other monosyllables the following consonant is not a deciding factor and there is competition to varying degrees between the <o..e>/<o> and <oa> vowel spellings, though in some contexts a clear majority allows a qualified generalization:

- —/p/ : *cope*, *dope*, *grope*, *hope*, *lope*, *mope*, *pope*, *rope*, *scope*, *slope*, *trope; soap;*
- —/t/ : *cote*, *dote*, *mote*, *note*, *quote*, *rote*, *smote*, *tote*, *vote*, *wrote; bloat*, *boat*, *coat*, *float*, *gloat*, *goat*, *groat*, *moat*, *oat*, *stoat*, *throat;*
- —/d/ : *bode*, *code*, *lode*, *mode*, *node*, *ode*, *rode*, *strode; goad*, *load*, *road*, *toad*, *woad;*
- —/k/ : *bloke*, *broke*, *choke*, *coke*, *joke*, *poke*, *smoke*, *spoke*, *stoke*, *stroke*, *woke*, *yoke; cloak*, *croak*, *oak*, *soak;* minority spellings: *folk*, *yolk; toque;*

- —/ʧ/ : *broach*, *coach*, *loach*, *poach*, *roach;* minority spelling: *brooch;* which in AmE has a regular /uː/;
- —/v/ : *clove*, *cove*, *drove*, *grove*, *hove*, *rove*, *stove*, *strove*, *trove*, *wove;* we can presumably take *loaves* (pl.) as predictably <oa> given the base form with <oa>; minority spelling: *mauve;*
- —/θ/ : *both*, *quoth*, *sloth*, *troth*, *wroth; oath; loth/loath* are variants;
- —/ð/ : only in derived forms – *clothe; loathe*, *oaths;*
- —/st/ : *ghost*, *host*, *most*, *post; boast*, *coast*, *roast*, *toast;*
- —/ʃ/ : *cloche* (alt. /ɒ/); minority spelling: *gauche;*
- —/m/ : *chrome*, *dome*, *gnome*, *home*, *tome; comb; foam*, *gloam*(*ing*), *loam*, *roam;* minority spellings: *ohm* – the only instance of <oh>≡/əʊ/ apart from *doh*, *soh; holm;*
- —/n/ : *bone*, *cone*, *crone*, *drone*, *hone*, *lone*, *phone*, *prone*, *stone*, *throne*, *tone*, *zone; groan*, *loan*, *moan*, *roan;* minority spelling: *own* (plus a group of past participles – *blown*, *flown*, *grown*, *known*, *shown*, *sown*, *thrown*, which are not single morphemes);
- —/l/ : *bole*, *dole*, *hole*, *mole*, *pole*, *role*, *sole*, *stole*, *thole*, *vole*, *whole; boll*, *droll*, *knoll*, *poll*, *roll*, *scroll*, *stroll*, *toll*, *troll; coal*, *foal*, *goal*, *shoal;* minority spellings: *soul; bowl;*
- —/lt/ : *bolt*, *colt*, *dolt*, *jolt*, *volt;* minority spellings: *moult;*
- —/ld/ : *bold*, *cold*, *fold*, *gold*, *hold*, *old*, *scold*, *sold*, *told*, *wold;* minority spelling: *mould;*

Among the minority spellings, there are some irregularities that apply in the text-to-speech direction only and present no reading problems. The spelling <oh> in *ohm* can only be /əʊ/. Albrow observes that <ou> corresponds to /əʊ/ and not to /aʊ/ :

> in such items as *soul*, *moult*, *mould.* All such items end in *l*, *lt* or *ld*, however; that is to say, in such items *oul* – corresponds consistently to [əʊl]. [aʊl] is regularly written – *owl*, e.g. *owl*, *cowl*, *prowl*, *fowl.* The one exception to both groups is *foul*, in which [aʊl] is written *oul.* This, however, provides visual differentiation of *foul* from *fowl* .
>
> (Albrow 1972: 17)

This reading regularity does not have much importance in the other direction, where such spellings represent a very small group of exceptions.

Other instances of /əʊ/

In the first syllable of disyllabic words, <ou> occurs in: *boulder*, *coulter*, *poultice*, *poultry*, *shoulder*, *smoulder* (cf. *bolster*, *holster*, *soldier*) and <ow> in *bowie*, *rowan.* When /əʊ/ occurs in a final syllable followed by /ʧ/ there is <oa>, as in monosyllables, in *reproach*, *approach*, *encroach.*

In the verbs *control*, *enrol* (but var. *enroll*), *extol*, *patrol*, there is somewhat annoyingly an <o> without <e>-marking (cf. *console*, *parole*). The inflected forms have double <ll> in British spelling as *controlled, patrolling*, but often have single <l> in American spelling. A single <l> in *controling* may seem a better indication of the previous long vowel, but we have in any case to distinguish elsewhere between *rolling* with /əʊ/ and *lolling* with /ɒ/. Apart from this small group, in final syllables where the /əʊ/ is followed by a single consonant we have <o..e>: *anecdote*, *baritone*, *bellicose*, *console*, *creosote*, *electrode*, *envelope*, *episode*, *heliotrope*, *juxtapose*, *lachrymose*, *provoke*, *rigmarole*, *suppose*, *tadpole*, *trombone*, etc.

There are a few recent French loan-words with <au> (*chauffeur*, *hauteur*) and /əʊ/ is a common pronunciation for French /o/ in names such as *Daudet*, *Lausanne*, *Tussaud*, though /ɔː/ would be a better phonetic match. Some old anglicized French names such as *Beaufort*, *Beaumaris*, *Beaumont*, have /əʊ/.

The nonce spelling *yeoman* and the names *Yeo*, *Yeovil* come from an eroded Germanic etymology rather than any exotic source. It is particularly out of step with other spellings in that the first vowel letter, <e> does not 'say its name'. Albrow puts this isolated <eo>≡/əʊ/ in system 1. Isolated archaic spellings such as *yeoman* have the totemic value of irregularly spelt proper names. For the yeomanry regiments of the British Army <eo>≡/əʊ/ must be a valued asset. In names there are also <ew>≡/əʊ/ in *Shrewsbury* and <ol>≡/əʊ/ with no /l/ in *Axholm*, *Colne*, *Colney*, *Folkestone*, *Holborn*, *Rolfe*, *Stockholm.* EPD, however, has *Folkes* with an /l/.

We have almost cleared the way for <o> as the default spelling for the remainder of §Exotic spellings, but there are one or two small groups still to account for. The less common of these spellings show un-English conventions for writing a long vowel, in this case /əʊ/. They include using <h> as an auxiliary letter to mark the long value of <o> (as /əʊ/ in *ohm*) or indicating /əʊ/ by doubling the vowel letter (as in *brooch*). These are frequently-used devices to represent length in other writing systems but, as such, are foreign to English. Admittedly we do have the common spelling <ee>≡/iː/ for the long value of <e>, but spellings such as *<ii>, *<uu> cannot represent a single vowel in English; <aa>, which can occasionally do so, is distinctly §Exotic (*aardvark*, *Haakon*). The final <e> in *gauche* and *toque* is also un-English.

§Exotic conventions can be found in foreign names: <aoh>≡/əʊ/ in *Pharaoh*; <oh>≡/əʊ/ in *Beerbohm*, *Cohen*, *Lohengrin*, *Shiloh*, *Tulloh;* <oo>≡/əʊ/ in *Boog*, *Loos*, *Roosevelt;* <eou>≡/əʊ/ in *Seoul.*

The short vowel counterpart of /əʊ/ in derived forms is /ɒ/: *sole–solitude*, *globe–globule*, *joke–jocular*, *mode–module*, *provoke–provocative*, *telephone–telephonic*, etc.

The Hanna (1966) spelling rules have <o> as the default spelling and:

1 <oa> syllable-initial accented (*oak*);
2 <o..e> syllable-initial unaccented (*cath-ode, gran-di-ose*);
3 <oa> syllable-medial before /t, d/ (*goat, goad*);
4 <o..e> syllable-medial accented before word-final phoneme (*con-voke, ex-plode*);
5 <o> syllable-medial accented before syllable-final phoneme (*dis-pos-al, up-hol-ster*);
6 <o..e> syllable-medial unaccented (*glu-cose, i-so-tope*);
7 <ow> word-final accented (*snow, swallow*).

No provision is made for minority spellings such as <ou>, <eau>, <ough>, <ew>. Hanna's '/O/' also occurs before //r// in *explore, more*, etc.

3.3.3 Long vowels associated with //r//: /ɑː ɔː ɜː ɪə ɛə (j)ʊə/

Note: in a 'rhotic' accent, such as AmE or Scottish, the vowels /ɜː/, /ɪə/, /ɛə/, /(j)ʊə/ are the equivalent of some other vowel phoneme(s) followed by //r//.

The vowels in this section are /ɑː/ as in *cart, calm*, /ɔː/ as in *court, caught,* /ɜː/ as in *curt*, /ɪə/ as in *leer*, *idea*, /ɛə/ as in *lair* and /(j)ʊə/ as in *lure*. These vowels are partly (in the case of /ɑː/, /ɔː/, /ɪə/) or wholly (in the case of /ɜː/, /ɛə/, /ʊə/, /jʊə/), associated with an original //r//. This //r// was lost before a consonant and before a phrase boundary in SBS and many regional accents of British English, but many 'rhotic' accents, including those of South West England, Scottish, Irish and American English keep it in all contexts. The //r// was lost in SBS by becoming a mere glide [ə] or simply a lengthening of the previous vowel. This phonetic merger produced new vowel phonemes such as /ɜː/ and added to the scope of existing phonemes such as /ɔː/. These are the vowels dealt with in this section. The pronunciation of English in Australia, New Zealand and South Africa resembles SBS significantly in also being non-rhotic.

Since traditional spelling reflects the vowel system of early modern English before the //r// was lost, all these vowels will have some spellings consisting of vowel-letters followed by <r>. Needless to say, it is very difficult to compare these new vowel phonemes directly with the vowels of a conservative rhotic accent. SBS /ɜː/ covers a range of words in which some Scottish accents have no less than three contrasting pronunciations – /ɛr/ *heard*, /ɪr/ *bird*, /ʌr/ *word* (Wells 1982: 407). Conversely, many American speakers do not contrast *Mary–merry*.

3.3.3.1 /ɑː/ *as in* cart, calm

Distribution of variant spellings

/ɑː/ has divergence which is more apparent than real. This present-day SBS vowel does not fit into the historical relationships between long/short vowels. The long/short pair of vowels associated with the spelling <a> are /æ/ – /eɪ/ (*mat*, *mate*). SBS /ɑː/ derives almost entirely from the lengthening of Middle English short /a/ in two main contexts:

1 before //r//; as part of the process the /r/ was lost in SBS except before a vowel in a word or close-knit phrase as 'linking r' (cf. *bar*, *barred* with *barring*, *bar it*) (Wells, 1982: 3.2). In rhotic accents /ɑː/ is followed by /r/ in all these contexts; see p. 290;

2 before the fricatives /f, θ, s/ and occasionally /v, ð/, or before nasal + consonant (Wells, 1982: 3.1.9): as in *after, laugh, daft, draught, staff, bath, path, brass, class, glass, dance, plant, ranch* (see pp. 291ff.). In Northern British English the short vowel remains. In AmE the vowel may be phonetically lengthened, but it still belongs to the 'short *a*' phoneme /æ/. The alternation is also found in some words where Northern British English would, like SBS, have a long vowel. So we have SBS /ɑː/ – AmE /æ/ in *Americana, banana, calf, can't, cascara, drama, finale, impala, Java, khaki, Lana, morale, Nagasaki, Nevada, nirvana, Pakistani, palaver, plaza, Sahara, scenario, tiara*, etc.

A further difference of distribution between SBS and AmE needs to be noted:

3 words with 'short *o*' such as *bother, got, stop, watch*, are in a separate phoneme /ɒ/ in SBS, but belong here under /ɑ(ː)/ for AmE speakers. The relative length of the vowel is not critical for describing AmE, hence the American preference for 'free' – 'checked', or 'tense' – 'lax' rather than the traditional 'long' – 'short'. Since the merger of short /ɒ/ (*bomb*) with /ɑː/ (*balm*), AmE /ɑ/ is not strictly a 'checked' vowel, since it occurs finally in *bra, spa*.

Examples of <C>-doubling to mark the original short vowel (see #D10, p. 124): *brass*, *class*, *grass*, *pass*, *surpass*; *chaff*, *distaff*, *staff*. In accents where the vowel lengthening did not take place, as in Northern English, these examples represent regular short vowel spellings.

Hence, taking <ar> to be a complex spelling, the divergence in SBS is largely between <a> with following <r>, /ɑː/≡<ar> TF 60 per cent, LF 60 per cent, and <a> without <r>, /ɑː/≡<a> TF 34 per cent, LF 32 per cent.

Adult competence will not always find this divergence a spelling problem since the underlying //r// may still be realized as 'linking r' before a vowel in a close-knit phrase and there may be awareness of other accents, Scottish, Irish or American, which have kept an original //r// in all contexts (the so-called 'rhotic' accents; see Wells 1982: 75f.). Rhotic accents, unlike SBS, have /r/ before a consonant (*farm*) and before a word boundary (*far*). Also relevant is the fact that in some morphemes we have alternation between /ɑː/ and /æ/ (*class* and *classify*, *graph* (if pronounced with /ɑː/) and *graphic*, etc.). Such alternations clearly indicate a spelling without <r>. Similarly, any following consonant which would *not* in itself occasion lengthening will usually indicate a spelling with <r>: *marl*, *barb*, *cart*, etc.

§Exotic /ɑː/

Some recent French, Italian and exotic borrowings have <a>≡/ɑː/ before consonants which do not cause lengthening in §Basic words. In AmE some of these words may have /æ/. Many of the following words are recognizable in some way as phonetically or semantically exotic:

- —/ p / : *gestapo*;
- —/ b / : *macabre*, *candelabra*;
- —/ t / : *cantata*, *karate*, *legato*, *literati*, *nazi*, *sonata*, *staccato*, *toccata*, *tomato*, and for some speakers *stomata*, *stigmata*; §Latinate *stratum* also belongs here. Some of these, *tomato, stratum*, have /eɪ/ in AmE;
- —/ d / : *charade, cicada, desperado, El Dorado, facade, incommunicado*; some of which have /eɪ/ in AmE;
- —/ k / : *debacle*, *khaki*, *plaque* (see p. 219); AmE *khaki* has /æ/, which unfortunately makes it homophonous with *cacky*;
- —/ g / : *saga*, *lager*, *virago*, *farrago*;
- —/ ʤ / : *adagio*;
- —/ v / : *lava*, *bravo*, *grave* ('accent'), *Graves* ('wine'), *guava*, *balaclava*, *cassava*, *palaver*. In *cadaver* /æ/ is more common than /ɑː/ or /eɪ/ (LPD);
- —/ z / : *plaza*, *blase*;
- —/ ʃ / : *moustache* (AmE /'mʌstæʃ/); in *panache* /æ/ is more common;
- —/ l / : *corral*, *gala*, *finale*, *praline*;
- —/ m /+/V/ : *salami*, *diorama*, *cyclorama*, *cinerama*, *lama*;
- —/ n /+/V/ : *banana* (AmE /æ/), *iguana*, *guano*, *gymkhana*, *liana*, *marijuana*, *sultana*, *soprano* (AmE /æ/).

One of the most marked contexts for an <r>-less spelling in such examples is a word of three or more syllables with penultimate stress and ending in a vowel. To attract the primary stress in such a context before a single consonant, /ɑː/ must be treated phonologically as a long vowel, so giving /ges'tɑːpəʊ/ not */'gestəpəʊ/ (cf. *dynamo*).

Other spellings of /ɑː/

The remaining spellings of /ɑː/ outside the two main groups (LF 6 per cent, TF 8 per cent) are very mixed. Older fossilized spellings with <r> occur in a few words, some of very high frequency:

- <ear> : *heart*, *hearth*;
- <er> : *clerk*, *derby* (both of which have /ɜr/ in AmE); *sergeant* (cf. the name *Sargent*); and in a few words where a following /l/ was lost by merging with the vowel:
- <al> : *half*, *calf*; *halve*, *calve*; *calm*, *palm*, *almond*, *psalm*, *balm*, *alms*, *qualm*, *malmsey*.

The pronunciation of *napalm* as /ˈneɪpɑːm/ is curious. This word was concocted from the first part of *naphtha* and the first part of *palmitate* (/pælm/), but it reassociated with the pronunciation of underived {palm} as /pɑːm/.

Final /ɑː/≡<ah> in exclamations: *ah!*, *hurrah!* exploits <h> as a length marker, but otherwise, in spite of its phonetic transparency, <ah> is not used as a spelling of /ɑː/ except in exotic words and names (see p. 286).

It follows from the historical development of /ɑː/, largely from an original short vowel, that it will not have <-e>-marking in §Basic words. However, relatively recent loan-words often retain a §French-type <a..e> spelling:

- *promenade*, *facade*, *ballade*, *charade*, *pomade*; *strafe*; *morale*, *locale*, *rationale*, *chorale*, *timbale*; *suave*; *caste*; *vase*; *garage*, *collage*, *massage*, *camouflage*, *barrage*, *espionage*, *entourage*, *sabotage*, *fuselage*, *mirage*, *menage*, *badinage*, *corsage*, *montage*, *dressage*, *decolletage*, etc.

Several words have exceptional <e>-marking of /ɑː/ after two consonant letters: *moustache*, *panache*; *giraffe*; *impasse*, but they do have alternative pronunciations with short /æ/ instead. The double <-ff-> of *giraffe*, where French in fact has <-f->, presumably reflects a short vowel pronunciation. The word *corral* (cf. *chorale*) is exceptional in not having <e>-marking. There is, surprisingly, no tendency to generalize the pronunciation of the ending <-age> in the recently borrowed nouns listed above to /-ɪʤ/, as in early borrowings (*village*, *advantage*, etc.), with the partial exception of *garage*. Final unreduced /-ɑːʒ/ appears to be a desirable marker of French association. An interesting example of this <e>-marking for prestige, culled from a circus poster, is: 'full *caste of 36 artistes'. The writer was no doubt confused by *half-caste*.

Late borrowings from French may have the correspondence /wɑː/≡<oi>: *boudoir*, *bourgeois*, *chamois*, *coiffure*, *memoir*, *patois*, *repertoire*, *reservoir*, *soiree*.

/ɑː/ in names

The common variation between /ɑː/ and /æ/ in names such as *Cleopatra*, *Damascus*, *Padua* is discussed in §6.5, p. 458. The /ɑː/ variants no doubt seemed a good approximation to a short, fully open foreign [a] when SBS /æ/ was much less open than it is nowadays (Wells 1982: 291); they seem now to be in retreat. Some of the /ɑː/ pronunciations mentioned as variants in earlier editions of EPD are decidedly archaic. Does anyone still have /ɑː/ in *Cincinnati*?

In AmE, there is greater use of /ɑ(ː)/ in foreign names and loans. Examples where SBS would have /æ/ are the names *Bangladesh, Calvados, Caracas, Casals, Datsun, Davos, Dvorak, Fernando, Franco, Galapagos, Gdansk, Golan, Gulag, Hambro, Hanoi, Kafka, Kant, Latvia, Luganda, Mombasa, Nansen, Nassau, Natasha, Navaho, Onassis, Pablo, Plassey,*

Raquel, Rashid, Slovak, Sri Lanka, Tamil, Uganda, Vivaldi, Yasser, and the words *bagnio, chianti, grappa, kebab, pasta, pastiche, pilaf, samba.*

Regularized spellings of the <er>≡/ɑː/ correspondence such as *Barkley, Clark, Darby, Harvey, Sargeant,* exist alongside *Berkeley, Derby, Hervey, Sergeant.* Non-§Basic spellings of /ɑː/ which occur in names include <aa>, as in *Afrikaans, Baal, Saab* (an acronym), and <ah>, as in *Ahmed, Bahrein, Brahma, Mahdi, Mahler, Shah.* These exploit duplication and <h> as natural markers of vowel length.

Stressed /ɑː/ frequently occurs in the penultimate syllable of polysyllabic names of widely differing origin: *Chicago, Colorado, Eldorado, Guatemala, Juliana, Kampala, Mikado, Nevada, Santiago, Uppsala.* There are also many examples of foreign names with stressed /ɑː/ before a final consonant which is not lengthening in §Basic words: *Amman, Aswan, Iran, Iraq, Islam, Khan, Koran, Punjab.*

This phoneme has no direct single equivalent in the Hanna rules but, insofar as it overlaps the Hanna '/A3/' and '/A5/', the only spelling provided is <a>. The problem of differentiating spellings with and without <r> did not arise since Hanna's American English retains //r// in all positions.

3.3.3.2 /ɔː/ as in court, caught

Distribution of variant spellings

/ɔː/ has considerable divergence in non-rhotic accents such as SBS (table 28). As with /ɑː/, we need to distinguish two main groups of spellings. One group involves postvocalic //r// and the other group comes mostly from an earlier [aʊ] diphthong or from [a] + [l] (with the [l] being lost).

SBS no longer has a contrast between a diphthong /ɔə/, associated with //r//, and a pure vowel /ɔː/ independent of //r//. Pairs such as *court–caught, pour–paw* have become homophones. Peters (1985: 20) seems to be unaware of this lack of contrast in SBS-type accents. She finds it difficult to explain why a sizeable group of children have misspelt *saucer* as *<sorser> and suggests that it may be due to 'faulty auditory perception'. 'The child hears the spoken word in a distorted way and reproduces this'. But the children are not 'distorting' anything. They simply find it difficult to perform the memory task of sorting out the <r> spellings from the spellings without <r>, since both sets of words probably have, for them, the same phoneme /ɔː/.

Speakers may, to some extent, be able to distinguish the two main groups of /ɔː/ spellings if they are aware of the underlying //r// as a potential 'linking /r/' in *pour* and of its absence in *paw*: *pour it* as /ˈpɔːr ɪt/, *paw it* as /ˈpɔː ɪt/. This does not apply when the //r// occurs before a consonant: both *board* and *bawd* are /bɔːd/ in SBS. However, an 'intrusive /r/' is becoming increasingly common by analogy with linking /r/ as a means of preventing

Table 28 Spellings of /ɔː/

spellings of /ɔː/	*TF*	*LF*	
<r>spellings	39 %	43 %	
<or>,<ore>,<ar>	25 %	35 %	F-
<aur>	<1 %	2 %	F-
<oar>	2 %	2 %	
<oor>	3 %	<1 %	F+
<our>	8 %	4 %	F+
non-<r>spellings	61 %	57 %	
<a>(before/l/)	29 %	14 %	F+
<al>(empty<l>)	5 %	1 %	F+
<aul>(empty<l>)	<1 %	<1 %	
<au>	9 %	25 %	F-
<aw>	9 %	12 %	
<oa>	<1 %	<1 %	
<augh>	2 %	2 %	
<ough>	6 %	2 %	F+

'F-' : tends to occur in low frequency words; 'F+' : tends to occur in high frequency words

vowel hiatus. For such speakers *paw it* becomes /ˈpɔːr ɪt/ equivalent to *pour it*. Wells (1982: 285) expects intrusive /r/ from 'mainstream RP' speakers. Speakers with accents which have not lost the //r// or have preserved the contrast as /ɔə/ – /ɔː/ will not have the spelling problem of possible confusion between these two main groups.

The low back vowels of North American English vary considerably in their distribution. Some Canadian and AmE speakers may have their 'short *o*' /ɑ/, instead of /ɔ(ː)/, in words such as *almost, auction, author, bald, broad, cause, false, gaunt, hydraulic, ought, precaution, scrawny, small, walk,* so that *dawn* and *don* are homophones. This means that, for these speakers, spellings such as <augh>, <au> and <aw> are competing with <o> as variant spellings.

Conversely, the SBS short /ɒ/ before /r/ in *Boris, coral, Dorothy, Florida, forest, horrid, lorry, origin, porridge, quarantine, quarrel, sorry, warrant*, may have /ɔ(ː)/ in AmE. This takes away any short vowel marking effect of the double <rr> spellings.

/ɔː/ in final position

Final /ɔː/ with underlying //r// has the following spellings:

- <ar> : *war* (the <a> is regular after /w/ instead of <o>, unless there is <e>-marking – *wore*);
- <or> : *abhor*, *cantor*, *condor*, *corridor*, *cuspidor*, *decor*, *humidor*,

matador, *mentor*, *realtor*, *tor*, *toreador*, together with a probable /ɔː/ rather than /ə/ in *grantor*, *lessor*, *mortgagor*, *vendor* (which have a contrast with the suffix <-ee>); there are empty final consonants in *corps*, *rapport*, which do not prevent linking /r/ (*the corps of journalists* /ˈkɔːr əv/);
- <aur> : *centaur*, *dinosaur*;
- <oar> : *boar*, *hoar*, *oar*, *roar*, *soar*;
- <oor> : *door*, *floor*;
- <ore> : *bore*, *core*, *explore*, *galore*, *ignore*, *more*, *score*, *semaphore*, *shore*, *sore*, *spore*, *store*, *swore*, *sycamore*, *tore*, *whore*, *wore*, etc.;
- <our> : *four*, *pour*.

The default spelling is <ore>, with <or> where the ending is more-or-less agentive. *Abhor* is irregular in not having an <-e>-marker. The <a> spelling in *war* is what one would expect after /w/ by analogy with /ɒ/ spellings, but there are apparent exceptions: *swore*, *wore* are inflected forms (cf. *swear*, *wear*; *sworn*, *worn*). The <w> in *whore* /hɔː/ is an empty letter and the <ore> is quite regular, as is the <or> of *sword*.

The spellings <or> and <aur> also occur when the //r// is realized before a following vowel within a minimal free-form:

- <or> : *borax*, *chlorine*, *corporeal*, *decorum*, *euphoria*, *floral*, *glory*, *oral*, *orient*, etc.;
- <aur> : *aura*, *aural*, *auriferous*, *aurora*, *laureate*, *thesaurus*.

The phonetic identity of *oral* and *aural* is so inconvenient that *aural* is increasingly pronounced with /aʊ/.

Final /ɔː/ without //r// is regularly spelt <aw>: *caw*, *claw*, *draw*, *flaw*, *gnaw*, *guffaw*, *haw*, *jackdaw*, *jaw*, *law*, *macaw*, *maw*, *paw*, *raw*, *rickshaw*, *saw*, *slaw*, *squaw*, *straw*, *thaw*, *yaw*, with an occasional exotic exception such as *landau*.

Awe is an example of <-e>-marking used to make up a three-letter lexical word (the 'short word rule', p. 131). The <e> is dropped in *awful* but not usually in *awesome*, *aweless* (?). Cf. also the function word *or* and the lexical word *ore*.

/ɔː/ in association with <l>

It is worth considering separately the spelling of /ɔː/ before /l/ (where <r> spellings of /ɔː/ do not occur) and also before an empty <l> in the correspondence /ɔː/≡<al>. The latter correspondence is found in a small group of monosyllabic words ending in /k/: *balk*, *chalk*, *stalk*, *talk*, *walk*, two of which are high frequency words. Before clusters of /l/ plus a consonant, /ɔː/ is in free variation with /ɒ/ within a morpheme: *alder*, *alderman*, *almanac*, *altar*, *alter*, *baldric*, *balsam*, *falcon*, *false*, *falter*, *halt*, *halter*, *malt*, *palfrey*, *palsy*, *paltry*, *salt*, *walrus*, *waltz*; *assault*, *cauldron*, *fault*, *vault*. In *jackal* the /ɔː/ alternates with /ə/. Words such as *walnut* where the cluster is split by a morpheme boundary, and *bald* only have /ɔː/ in SBS.

Final /ɔːl/ rather oddly has <C>-doubling (see #D10, p. 124) in monosyllabic words spelt <all>: *all*, *ball*, *call*, *fall*, *gall*, *hall*, *mall* (alt. /æ/), *pall*, *small*, *squall*, *stall*, *tall*, *thrall*, *wall*. In isolation *instal*(*l*) and *appal*(*l*) may have <l> or <ll>, but only <ll> with {-ed} and {-ing} (*appalled*, *installing*). The <ll> does have a function in that it differentiates /ɔː/ from /eɪ/ in *palled–paled*, *stalled–staled*. This <ll> is clearly not the same departure from normal <C>-doubling that we find in occasional Latin stems (as in *bellicose*). One way of dealing with it would be to regard the first <l> as part of a vowel digraph, giving: <al>≡/ɔː/, <l>≡/l/. We already need <al>≡/ɔː/ in *talk* and there is the nonce correspondence <al>≡/æ/ in *salmon*. The final <all> spelling competes with <aul> and <awl>: *haul*, *maul*; *awl*, *bawl*, *brawl*, *crawl*, *drawl*, *scrawl*, *shawl*, *sprawl*, *trawl*, *yawl*.

/ɔː/ in other contexts

There is potential confusion between spellings with and without <r> before a consonant in the following contexts:

- —/ʃ/ : with <r> *abortion*, *extortion*, *portion*, *torsion*, etc.;
  without <r> *caution*;
- —/p/ : with <r> *absorption*, *corporal*, *corporation*, *corpse*, *porpoise*, *scorpion*, *torpedo*, *torpid*;
  without <r> *pauper*; *gawp*;
- —/b/ : with <r> *absorb*, *morbid*, *orb*, *orbit*;
  without <r> *auburn*, *bauble*, *daub*;
- —/t/ : with <r> *cavort*, *chortle*, *cohort*, *consort*, *fort*, *horticulture*, *important*, *mortal*, *mortar*, *portico*, *portrait*, *report*, *resort*, *short*, *sort*, *sport*, *support*, *tortoise*, *vortex*, etc.; *court*; *quarter*, *quarto*, *quartz*, *thwart*, *wart*;
  without <r> *bought*, *brought*, *fought*, *nought*, *ought*, *sought*, *thought*, *wrought*; *caught*, *daughter*, *distraught*, *fraught*, *haughty*, *onslaught*, *slaughter*, *taught*; *water*; *astronaut*, *autistic*, *autograph*, *automobile*, *autonomy*, *autumn*, *cauterize*, *flautist*, *juggernaut*, *nautical*, *taut*;
- —/d/ : with <r> *afford*, *border*, *chord*, *cord*, *horde*, *lord*, *mordant*, *ordeal*, *order*, *ordinary*, *ordnance*, *ordure*, *record*, *sordid*, *sword*, etc.; *board*, *hoard*; *reward*;
  without <r> *applaud*, *audacious*, *audience*, *caudal*, *fraud*, *gaudy*, *laud*, *marauder*, *maudlin*, *plaudit*; *bawd*, *dawdle*, *tawdry*; *broad*;
- —/k/ : with <r> *porcupine*; *cork*, *fork*, *port*, *snorkle*, *stork*; *torque*; *orchestra*, *orchid*;
  without <r> *auction*, *caucus*, *glaucous*, *raucous*; *auk*; *bauxite*; *awkward*, *hawk*, *mawkish*, *squawk*, *tomahawk*; *caulk*; *chalk*, *stalk*, *talk*, *walk*;

balk and *baulk* are alternative spellings (p. 410);

- —/g/ : with <r> *morganatic*, *organ*, *organdie*, *organize*, *orgasm*; *sorghum*; *morgue*;
  without <r> *auger*, *augment*, *augur*, *august*, *inaugurate*; *auxiliary*;
- —/ʧ/ : with <r> *fortune*, *orchard*, *porch*, *scorch*, *torch*, *torture*;
  without <r> *debauch*;
- —/f/ : with <r> *forfeit*, *orfe*; *dwarf*, *wharf*; *morphine*, *orphan*, *porphyry*;
  without <r> *dauphin* (also /əʊ/);
- —/θ/ : with <r> *forth*, *north*, *orthodontist*, *orthodox*;
  without <r> *authentic*, *author*, *authority*;
- —/s/ (excluding <sC> clusters) : with <r> *corset*, *divorce*, *endorse*, *exorcize*, *force*, *forsythia*, *gorse*, *horse*, *morse*, *morsel*, *porcelain*, *remorse*, *sorcerer*, *torso*, etc.; *coarse*, *hoarse*; *course*, *source*;
  without <r> *faucet*, *mausoleum*, *paucity*, *sauce*, *saucer*;
- —/m/ : with <r> *corm*, *dormitory*, *enormous*, *form*, *gormandise*, *gormless*, *hormone*, *inform*, *normal*, *perform*, *platform*, *storm*, *torment*, *uniform*, etc.; *swarm*, *warm*;
  without <r> *haulm*;
- —/n/ (excluding <nC> clusters) : with <r> *adorn*, *born*, *borne*, *corn*, *corner*, *cornice*, *forlorn*, *horn*, *hornet*, *morning*, *scorn*, *suborn*, *sworn*, *thorn*, *torn*, *tornado*, *worn*; *mourn*;
  without <r> *awning*, *brawny*, *dawn*, *drawn*, *fawn*, *lawn*, *pawn*, *prawn*, *spawn*, *tawny*, *yawn*; *faun*, *fauna*, *sauna*.

Only spellings with <r> occur in the following contexts:

- —/ʤ/ : *disgorge*, *forge*, *gorge*;
- —/nj/ : *lorgnette*;
- —/v/ : *corvette*;
- —/ð/ (derived from /θ/) : *northerly*, *northern*.

Only spellings without <r> occur in the following contexts; there are, of course, inflected forms such as *adorned*, *coursed*, *cores*, where a morpheme boundary intervenes:

- —/nd/ : *jaundice*, *laundry*;
- —/nt/ : *dauntless*, *flaunt*, *gaunt*, *haunt*, *jaunt*, *saunter*, *taunt*, *vaunt*;
- —/nʧ/ (or /nʃ/) : *haunch*, *launch*, *paunch*, *staunch*;
- —/sp/ : *auspicious*;
- —/st/ : *austere*, *caustic*, *exhaust*, *holocaust*;
- —/z/ : *cause*, *clause*, *gauze*, *nausea*, *pause*, *plausible*; *hawser*.

Though there is clearly scope for spelling confusion here between spellings with and without <r> and within these two main groups, the number of homophones is not as large as one might expect: *court–caught*, *source–sauce*, *sore–soar–saw*, *roar–raw*, *floor–flaw*, *pore–pour–paw*, *lore–law*, *bawl–ball*, *horde–hoard*, *board–bawd*, *torque–talk*, etc. There should be no such confusion between the spelling of single morphemes and inflected forms in pairs such as *pause–paws*, *clause–claws*.

/ɔː/ in names

The wide divergence of /ɔː/ spellings is also reflected in names. Some names have variants with an irregular final <-e> as padding (§6.4) – *Bagshawe*, *Brawne*, *Dawes*, *Hoare*, *Horne*, *Thorpe*, *Yorke*. Some names with <augh> have a regularized variant – *Bradlaugh*, *Bradlaw*. The names *Braughan*, *Brahan, Maugham*, are monosyllables. In compound names, <aw> may occur medially – *Crawford*, *Crawley*, *Hawthorn*. Some names with no apparent element boundary may have <au> – <aw> variation as in *Fawcett*, *Faucett*, *Fawssett* and *Faulkner*, *Fawkner*. The §Basic element <all> in compound names often retains its double <ll> before a consonant (cf. the fate of <ll> in *almost*, *already*, *walnut*) – *Allbright*, *Allcroft*, *Allworthy*. *Bengal* and *Nepal* are marked as exotic names by the final stress and have single <l>. An <ar> spelling is not found in some names after /w/ – *Quorn*, *Worman*, *Worple*. *Utah* has an exceptional /ɔː/≡<ah> spelling. *Arkansas* has an exceptional <as>≡/ɔː/. LPD records a spelling pronunciation /ɑːˈkænzəs/ for the Arkansas River.

The Hanna (1966) spelling rules (insofar as /ɔː/ matches the Hanna '/O2/') have <au> as the overall default spelling and:

1 <au..e> before /z/ (*cause*); – there are no competing <or> spellings in this context;
2 <a> syllable-initial before /l/ (*al-most*);
3 <o> syllable-initial before /r/ (*dis-or-der*, *or-gan-ic*);
4 <au> syllable-initial elsewhere (*aug-ment, aux-il-ia-ry*);
5 <a> syllable-medial after /(k)w/ (*quar-ter*, *walk-er*);
6 <o> syllable-medial before /r/ (*dis-tor-tion*, *re-form*);
7 <au> syllable-medial elsewhere (*ex-haust*, *un-daun-ted*);
8 <aw> word-final (*claw*);
9 <au> syllable-final (*plau-dit*, *tar-pau-lin*).

3.3.3.3 /ɜː/ as in curt

Distribution of variant spellings

/ɜː/ shows considerable divergence. With the exception of an occasional French loan-word such as *milieu*, or a German name such as *Koestler*, where SBS /ɜː/ stands for the foreign front rounded [ø], all the spellings involve <r> (table 29).

Since the realization of //r// in SBS as /r/ or as zero is predictable, it is best to treat /ɜː/ and the potential following /r/ as one spelling unit. This also helps when comparing different accents.

Table 29 Spellings of /ɜː/

spellings of /ɜː/	*TF*	*LF*	
<er(r)>	39 %	54 %	F-
<ur(r)>	17 %	24 %	F-
<ir(r)>	18 %	11 %	F+
<or(r)>	17 %	4 %	F+
<ear>	8 %	4 %	F+
<our>	<1 %	2 %	
<eur>	<1 %	<1 %	
<yr(r)>	<1 %	<1 %	

'F-' : tends to occur in low frequency words; 'F+' : tends to occur in high frequency words

As an SBS phoneme, /ɜː/ has only come about through the loss of original //r// before consonants or word-finally. Its counterparts in rhotic accents, which have kept //r// intact, consist of a simple vowel plus /r/ (as a consonant segment or as retroflexion of the vowel). In these rhotic accents the spellings <er>, <ur>, <ir>, <or>, etc. may reflect a range of different contrasting vowels, so there is much less divergence than in SBS. The merger of the different simple vowels reflected in the spelling has inevitably produced a few (but perhaps surprisingly few) homophones in SBS: *berth–birth*, *earn–urn*, *fir–fur*, *heard–herd*, *serf–surf*, *tern–turn*. Some of these homophones may well be distinct in other accents.

The <irr> and <urr> spellings, as in *whirr*, *purr*, are onomatopoeic and the <rr> doubling is irregular. The phonetic basis of the onomatopoeia is not obvious from the present SBS pronunciation. It presumably goes back to an original trill [r]: all these words are associated with an iterative noise of some kind. The final <C>-doubling here can perhaps be regarded as a graphic representation of iterative sound. Onomatopoeia seems also to govern spellings with <ir> and <ur>, as distinct from <er>. The letter <i>, by association with high-resonance ('acute') vowels, is appropriate for rapid movement or high-frequency noise: *chirp*, *swirl, twirl, skirmish, squirt, whirl, whirr*. The letter <u>, by association with low-resonance ('grave') vowels, is appropriate for slow movement or low-frequency noise: *burble, burp, burr, gurgle, purr*.

We may take <er> to be the default spelling, but we need to examine the phonetic contexts of /ɜː/ to find regularities, absolute or statistical, in the distribution of the other spellings.

Stressed final /ɜː/

Stressed and in final position we find:

- <ere> : the function word *were*, which when unstressed reduces to /wə/;
- <err> : *err* (making a lexical item of at least three letters by the 'short

word rule', p. 131);

- <er> : (only verbs) *aver*, *confer*, *defer*, *deter*, *disinter*, *infer*, *inter*, *prefer*, *refer*, *transfer*;
- <ir> : *fir*, *sir*, *stir*;
- <ur> : *blur*, *concur*, *cur*, *demur*, *fur*, *incur*, *occur*, *recur*, *slur*, *spur*;
- <eur> : *connoisseur*, *entrepreneur*, *hauteur*, *poseur*, *provocateur*, *raconteur*, *restauranteur*;
- <irr> : *chirr*, *shirr*, *whirr*;
- <urr> : *burr*, *purr*; final <rr> also occurs in names such as *Burr*, *Kerr*, *Spurr*;
- <yrr> : *myrrh*.

The /ɜː/ spellings <or> <ear> <our> are not found finally. The <-eur> words are polysyllabic recent French loans and in most cases the {eur} is agentive. The SBS pronunciation of *milieu* is /-jɜː/, which might well have 'intrusive /r/' before a vowel. AmE has /-juː/.

The <er> and <ur> words include a number of recurrent Latin elements {fer}, {ter}, {cur}, so the learning task is less than the lists might indicate. The {cur} spelling cannot be *<cer> in any case, since that can only represent /sɜː(r)/.

/ɜː/ after various consonants

In a large number of words /ɜː/ occurs unreduced in a recognizable stressable prefix: <per-> (*perfect*, *permanent*), <inter-> (*intercalate*, *interpolate*), <super-> (*superfluous*, *superlative*), <sur-> (*surcharge*, *survey* (n.)), <circum-> (*circumflex*, *circumvent*), <hyper-> (*hyperbole*, *hypertrophy*). There are also recurrent elements in the §Latinate words such as {vert}, {cern}, {fer}, which can serve as a basis for association. There is a spelling problem with <per->, however, since quite a number of words begin with <pur-> (*purblind*, *purchase*).

The Hanna rules for /ɜː/ are based on the preceding consonant as a useful spelling indicator. Initial /w/ selects the <or> spelling: *liverwort*, *whorl*, *whortleberry*, *word*, *work*, *world*, *worm*, *worse*, *worsen*, *worship*, *worst*, *worth*, *worthy* and in §Basic names *Ainsworth*, *Bosworth*, *Galsworthy*. This is another instance of minim avoidance (avoiding <w> + <i> or <w> + <u>). Exceptions: *were* (a function word); *whirl*, *whirr* (onomatopoeia); the names *Wearn*, *Wurlitzer*. After /Cw/ clusters we find <er> (*swerve*, *twerp*, *Antwerp*; *quern*, *Puerto-Rico*) and <ir> (*swirl*, *twirl*, *quirk*, *squirm*, *squirt*).

The Hanna rules predict <ur> after /b/, /k/ and /ʧ/:

- after /b/ – in *burble, burden, burdock, burgess, burgher, burglar, burgeon, burnet, burgoo, burgundy, burly, burlap, burlesque, burn, burnish, burp, burr, bursar, burst, disburse, hamburger, laburnum, suburb,* with only a few exceptions, such as *berg, berth, birch, bird, birth*;

- after /k/ – in *curse, concur, cur, curb, curd, curdle, curfew, curl, curlew, curse, cursor, curt, curtail, curtain, curtsey, curve, excursus, incur, occur, recur, scurf, scurvy,* with some exceptions: *colonel, courteous, kerchief, kernel, kersey, kirtle*, and /sk-/ clusters *skirl, skirmish, skirt;* it is worth noting that *curtsey* with <ur> is a regularization of *courtesy*;
- after /ʧ/ – in *church, churl, churn,* with exceptions *chirp, chirr, concerto*.

They also predict <ir> in smaller groups after /g/, /θ/, /hw/ and /kw/:

- after /g/ – in *gird, girder, girdle, girl, girt, girth,* with exceptions *gherkin, gurgle, regurgitate*;
- after /θ/ – in *third, thirst, thirteen, thirty,* with exceptions *thermal, thermos, Thursday*;
- after /hw/ – in *whirl, whirr,* with exceptions *whorl, whortleberry*;
- after /kw/ – in *quirk, quirt, squirm, squirt,* with no exceptions.

The default is then <er>, to which there are a number of exceptions:

- with <ur> – *absurd*, *appurtenance*, *blurt*, *disturb*, *diurnal*, *expurgate*, *frankfurter*, *furbish*, *furl*, *furlong*, *furlough*, *furnace*, *furnish*, *furniture*, *furtive*, *furze*, *hurdle*, *hurl*, *hurtle*, *insurgent*, *laburnum*, *liturgical*, *lurch*, *lurk*, *metallurgical*, *murder*, *murky*, *murmur*, *nasturtium*, *nocturnal*, *nurse*, *nurture*, *purchase*, *purgatory*, *purge*, *purl*, *purlieu*, *purloin*, *purse*, *purvey*, *regurgitate*, *return*, *splurge*, *spurn*, *spurt*, *sturdy*, *surf*, *surface*, *surge*, *surgeon*, *surgery*, *spurn*, *surly*, *taciturn*, *turban*, *turbid*, *turbine*, *turbot*, *turbulent*, *turd*, *turf*, *turgid*, *turkey*, *turmoil*, *turn*, *turnip*, *turquoise*, *turtle*, *urban*, *urchin*, *urge*, *urgent*, *urn*;
- with <ir> – *besmirch*, *chirp*, *circle*, *circus*, *cirque*, *dirk*, *dirt*, *firm*, *firmament*, *first*, *firth*, *flirt*, *irk*, *mirth*, *shirk*, *smirk*, *virtual*, *virtue*, *virtuous*, *zircon*;
- with <yr> – *myrtle*, and a few names: *Byrd, Byrne, Kyrle, Smyrna*;
- with <ear> – *earl*, *early*, *earn*, *earnest*, *dearth*, *earth*, *heard*, *hearse*, *learn*, *pearl*, *rehearse*, *search*, *yearn*;
- nonce spellings : *colonel*, *attorney*.

The early antecedents of present-day SBS /ɜː/ were usually a short vowel followed by //r//. Consequently we have <C>-doubling in *preferred*, *referral*, *transferring*, etc., where the underlying short vowel is stressed and a suffix with an initial vowel letter follows.

Since spellings of /ɜː/ reflect this earlier short vowel plus <r>≡//r//, there is no <-e>-marking of the vowel as long. Any final <-e> will be a marker for the consonant following the <r>. The <-e> of *curse*, *disperse*, *immerse*, *purse*, *rehearse*, *verse*, *worse*, indicates /s/ and not /z/ (cf. *curse–curs*); *coerce*, *commerce*, also show a final /s/ rather than /k/; *dirge*, *merge*, *purge*, *scourge*, *serge*, *surge*, show final /ʤ/ rather than /g/; more redundantly, *nerve*, *serve*, *swerve*, *verve*, follow the general avoidance of final <v>; the <-e> of *furze* is redundant, but prevents final <-z>, which is a distinctly exotic spelling. In names there is frequent use of an irregular <-e> for padding (§6.4): *Aherne*, *Byrne*, *Fearne*, *Kirke*, *Searle*.

The Hanna (1966) spelling rules for '/U2/' with following /r/ preserved are:

1) <ea> syllable-initial (*earth*, *earn*);
2) <o> syllable-medial after /w/ (*word*, *worship*);
3) <u> syllable-medial after /b, k, ʧ/ (*burn*, *curt*, *church*);
4) <i> syllable-medial after /g, θ, hw, kw/ (*girl*, *third*, *whirl*, *squirt*);
5) <e> syllable-medial (*de-ter-mine*, *ser-vile*).

In AmE //r// has not been lost in these cases, but the phonetic nature of the V + //r// is a constant retroflexed vowel [ɜ˞]. There is not the diversity of vowel found in some Scottish English accents (Wells 1982: 407), where *pert*, *heard* have /ɛr/, *dirt*, *bird* have /ɪr/ and *hurt*, *word* have /ʌr/ and where, consequently, there are reliable cues to the vowel letter of the spelling.

3.3.3.4 /ɪə/ as in leer, idea

Distribution of variant spellings

/ɪə/ is very divergent. This reflects its peculiar status as a surface phoneme of SBS. Unlike /ɛə/ this phoneme does not only derive from a vowel variant before //r// as in *clear*, *beard*, as a variant of underlying //iː//. It may also represent a blend of two phonologically separate vowels as in *idea*, *congenial*. In other forms such as *ideology*, *congeniality*, the second part of the glide is clearly a discrete vowel. In unstressed syllables there is a marked tendency to move from [ɪə] to [jə], from a glide with falling prominence to a glide with rising prominence.

/ɪə/ reflecting two underlying vowels

We can begin with instances of /ɪə/ which reflect two phonologically independent vowels that happen to have merged into a single syllable in SBS, but which for some speakers may still represent disyllabic /iː/+/ə/. This is more likely in stressed syllables, as in *museum*, *homogeneity*. The great majority of the examples below are unstressed. In either case, the spelling will be a combination of one of the spellings of /iː/ plus a spelling of /ə/. This might seem to offer an enormous range of possibilities, but in practice a few common spellings account for most of the variants:

<ia> spellings represent TF 10 per cent, LF 31 per cent , F-

- final <-ia> – *ammonia*, *bacteria*, *begonia*, *camellia*, *criteria*, *hernia*, *hysteria*, *insignia*, *media*, *millennia*, *myopia*, *salvia*, *sepia*, *trivia*, *utopia*, etc.; spellers may not be aware that some such words are Latin plurals with a singular in <-ium> as in *bacterium–bacteria*;
- <-ial> – *editorial*, *industrial*, *jovial*, *material*, *memorial*, *radial*, *remedial*, *serial*, etc.;

- <-ian> – *barbarian, comedian, grammarian, guardian, historian, pedestrian, reptilian, ruffian*, etc.;
- <-iant>, <-iance>, <-iancy> – *brilliant, dalliance, luxuriance, radiancy, suppliant, variance, variant*, etc.;
- <-iable> – *amiable, enviable, variable*, etc.;
- <-iary> – *auxiliary, incendiary, intermediary*, etc.;
- <-iar> – *familiar, peculiar*;

<ea> spellings represent TF 12 per cent, LF 6 per cent, F+

- final <-ea> in nouns – *area, azalea, cochlea, cornea, idea, nausea, panacea, rhea, urea*; medial in single morpheme – *pancreas, real, theatre*;
- <e> plus a suffix – *malleable, permeable*; *lineament*; *roseate*; *epicurean*; *linear, nuclear*;
- <ei> occurs in *homogeneity*;
- <eo> occurs with common §Greek elements {geo-} and {theo-} (*geographic, theocratic*) and with the <-o-> representing a linking vowel in *choreographic, mimeograph, stereophonic, teleological*; other instances of <eo> – *chameleon, creosote, galleon, melodeon, meteor*;
- <eu> occurs in the endings <-eum> and <-eus> – *coleus, linoleum, malleus, mausoleum, museum, nucleus, petroleum*;
- <ie> occurs in the ordinal numbers *twentieth, thirtieth*, etc.; in the endings <-ier> *happier*, <-iest> *happiest*, <-ient> *salient*, <-ience> *salience*; other examples of <ie> – *alien, soviet, spaniel*;
- <io> occurs with the <-o-> as a linking vowel in *physiological, sociological*; other examples of <io> – *period*; *vitriol*; *axiom, idiom*; *bastion, bullion, centurion, clarion, million, minion, opinion, pinion, union*, etc.; *chariot, idiot, patriot*;
- <iu> occurs in the endings <-ius> and, more commonly, <-ium> – *genius, radius*; *compendium, delirium, gymnasium, medium, opium, potassium, radium, stadium, tedium*, etc.;
- <eou> occurs in the ending <-eous> – *courteous, hideous*, etc.;
- <iou> occurs in the ending <-ious> – *fastidious, previous*, etc.

Less common spellings occur in *halcyon*; *archaeological*; *diahorroea, gonorrhoea, pyorrhoea*.

Most of the above examples involve suffixes attached to bound stems. Stressed /ɪə/ can occur occasionally across a free-morpheme boundary: *agreeable, foreseeable*.

For unstressed /ɪə/ the problem in most cases is first to choose between <i> or <e> as the first letter. This is not always easy, witness <-eous> and <-ious>. The second problem is to choose the letter(s) representing the [ə] part of the glide, but this is from a wide range. However, the difficulty is not a very real one since it usually involves recognition of a particular suffix. The problem of finding a spelling for the [ə] part of /ɪə/ is solved if in word-formation the same syllable may occur with stress: *patriot–patriotic*, *theatre–theatrical*, etc.

This type of association does not usually help with names. The difference between, say, final stressed <ea> in *Caesarea*, *Chaldea*, *Crimea*, *Dorothea*, *Hosea*, *Medea*, *Thea*, and stressed <ia> in *Maria*, *Nicosia*, *Tanzania*, simply has to be learnt.

/ɪə/ as a merger of underlying //iː// plus //r//

Before //r// the vowel //iː// developed a glide to [ə] as a single syllabic [ɪə]. In a surface phonemic analysis this is hived off as the separate phoneme /ɪə/ in SBS with the loss of postvocalic //r//. So both *dear* and *idea* come to end in the same surface phoneme /ɪə/. A similar glide has developed before postvocalic 'dark' /l/ (a velarized allophone [ɫ]) for many Southern speakers so that *reel* and *real* are homophones, with /ɪə/. This second main group of spellings of /ɪə/ includes most spellings of /iː/ plus the letter <r>:

- <er> and <ere> – TF 12 per cent, LF 10 per cent, F+ (of /ɪə/) – but excluding *here*, as grammatical – *era*, *hero*, *inherent*, *managerial*, *perseverance*, *series*, *serum*, *zero*, etc.; *austere*, *interfere*, *mere*, *revere*, *severe*, *sincere*, *sphere*, etc.;
- <ear> – TF 28 per cent, LF 7 per cent, F+ (of /ɪə/) – in a good many very common words – (stressed) *appear*, *clear*, *dear*, *ear*, *fear*, *gear*, *hear*, *near*, *rear*, *smear*, *tear*, *year*, etc.; (unstressed) *linear*, *nuclear*;
- <eer> – TF 4 per cent, LF 5 per cent (of /ɪə/) – *beer*, *career*, *cheer*, *leer*, *peer*, *queer*, *sheer*, *sneer*, *steer*, etc.; in the suffix <-eer>: *auctioneer*, *mountaineer*, *pamphleteer*, *privateer*, *profiteer*, etc.;

Less common spellings with <r> occur in *weird*; *meteor* (also as /ɪɔː/).

The Hanna (1966) spelling rules for '/E2/' with following //r// preserved are:

1 <ea> syllable-initial (*ear*);
2 <e..e> syllable-medial unaccented (*cash-mere*, *strat-o-sphere*);
3 <ea> syllable-medial accented after /l, w, j, r, b/ (*clear*, *weary*, *year*, *real*, *beard*);
4 <ee> syllable-medial accented after /n, ʧ/ before word-final phoneme (*do-mi-neer*, *cheer*);
5 <ea> syllable-medial accented before word-final phoneme (*a-ppear*, *shear*);
6 <e> syllable-medial accented before syllable-final phoneme (*cer-e-al*, *her-o*).

These rules are not easy to interpret because of the indeterminate Hanna 'syllable'.

3.3.3.5 /ɛə/ as in lair

Distribution of variant spellings

/ɛə/ has some divergence, largely between the default <a> spellings and <ai> spellings (table 30).

Table 30 Spellings of /ɛə/

spellings of /ɛə/	*TF*	*LF*	
<ar>,<are>	59 %	64 %	
<air>	28 %	15 %	F+
<aer>	<1 %	6 %	F-
<ear>	10 %	6 %	F+
<er>,<ere>	<1 %	3 %	
<aire>	<1 %	3 %	
<eir>	<1 %	1 %	
minority spellings ‡	2 %	3 %	

‡ <erre>, <ayer>, <ayor>

'F-' : tends to occur in low frequency words; 'F+' : tends to occur in high frequency words

This phoneme of SBS is entirely a product of the loss of an original //r//. Consequently all the spellings involve <r>, which may or may not be realized as /r/ (*rare*, *rareness*, *rarity*) in predictable contexts. A surface phonemic analysis has to set up two different phonemes /eɪ/ and /ɛə/ because of minimal surface contrasts such as *pay–pair*, but effectively *pair* contains the same vowel unit as *pay*, with //r// as a final consonant. In *pay*, *pain*, *pair* we have in effect //pA//, //pAn//, //pAr//, using //A// to represent the common underlying vowel.

In final syllables <are> and <air> are in direct competition and there are homophones such as *flare–flair*, *fare–fair*, *pare–pair*, *stare–stair*, *hare–hair*. Other monosyllables with <air> are *air*, *chair*, *lair* and the Scottish words *bairn*, *cairn*, *laird*. Disyllables ending in <air> are *affair*, *despair*, *corsair*, *impair*, *mohair*, *eclair*. The only base form in which /ɛə/≡<ar> occurs before a consonant is *scarce*. There is little here to serve as a specific context for <ai>.

Examples of the default spelling <ar(e)>:

- in monosyllables – *bare*, *blare*, *care*, *dare*, *fare*, *flare*, *glare*, *hare*, *mare*, *pare*, *rare*, *share*, *snare*, *spare*, *square*, *stare*, *sware*, *tare*, *ware*;
- in disyllables – *aware*, *beware*, *compare*, *prepare*, *warfare*, *welfare*;
- in common §Latinate endings – *egalitarian*, *librarian*; *gregarious*, *multifarious*; *commissariat*, *proletariat*;
- in §Latinate stems – *barium*, *parent*, *rarefy*, *variegated*.

We turn now to the minority spellings:

- /ɛə/≡<aer> only occurs as a graphic bound form of {air} in *aerate*, *aeration*, *aerator*, *aerial*, *aerobacter*, *aerobic*, *aerodrome*, *aeronautics*, *aeroplane*, *aerosol*, etc. The free form <air> is found in §Basic-type compounds (cf. *airfield–aerodrome*). *Airplane* and *aeroplane* are synonyms, but *airspace* and *aerospace* have distinct meanings. /ɛə/≡<aire> (from Latin <-arius>) occurs as a final stressed syllable in §French words of three or more syllables. This context is sufficient to identify it in the absence of any common semantic features: *commissionaire*, *concessionaire*, *doctrinaire*, *millionaire*, *questionnaire*, *secretaire*, *solitaire*. *Debonair* (from French *de bon air*) is different in having no final <e>.

The other minority spellings of /ɛə/ are rather mixed in origin and none accounts for many words:

- <ear> – *bear*, *pear*, *swear*, *tear*, *wear*;
- <er> – *bolero*, *recherche*, *scherzo*, *sombrero*;
- <ere> – *ampere*, *compere*, *premiere*;
- <eir> – *heir*;
- <ayer> – *prayer* (one morpheme);
- <ayor> – *mayor*;
- <erre> – *parterre*.

All the monosyllables in these minority spellings (except *prayer*) form homophones with one of the two main spellings: *bear–bare*, *heir–air*, *mayor–mare*, *pear–pair*, *swear–sware*, *tear–tare*, *wear–ware*.

In names there are still further minority spellings: *Aaron*, *Ayre*, *Behrens*, *Caerphilly*, *Eyre*. There may be variation between /ɛə/ and /ɜː/ in foreign names such as *Auvergne*, *Bergen*, *Berlioz*, *Berne*, *Cherbourg*, *Hertz*, *Palermo*, *Sauterne*, *Verner*, *Versailles*, where /ɛə/ would seem closer to a foreign /er/ and the /ɜː/ is a more anglicized form. This variation is reflected in LPD, where *Hertz*, a familiar company name, gets only /ɜː/, while *Bergen* has /ɜː/ in preference to /ɛə/ and *Palermo* also has both but with the reverse preference.

The Hanna (1966) spelling rules (for '/A2/') with following //r// preserved:

1 <ai> syllable-initial (*air-*);
2 <e..e> syllable-medial after /hw/, /ð/ (*where, there*);
3 <a..e> syllable-medial before word-final /r/ (*care*);
4 <a> syllable-medial before syllable-final /r/ (*ca-nar-y*, *par-ent*).

The first rule reflects the greater text frequency of *air* and derived forms over *area*. There is no rule to cater for all the words with <air> after a consonant (*fair, flair, hair*, etc.). The second rule applies only to the two function words and derived forms (*thereby*, *whereabouts*).

3.3.3.6 /ʊə/ as in lure, /jʊə/ as in cure

Distribution of variant spellings

The diphthong /ʊə/ as a single syllable peak in SBS will occur partly in words such as *actual*, *fluent*, *incongruous*, *mutual*, *usual*, where stem and suffix join. The spelling will vary considerably. It usually consists of <u> plus a further vowel spelling representing the merged /ə/. The diphthong also occurs in words such as *cruel*, *gruel*, *jewel*, where there is no such apparent internal boundary. With underlying //r// the diphthong occurs finally or before consonants in words such as: *boor*, *moor*, *poor*, *spoor*; *amour*, *bourgeois*, *dour*, *gourd*, *gourmet*, *tour*, *tournament*, *velour*; *abjure*, *sure*. With the //r// realized as /r/ it occurs before vowels in words such as: *boorish*, *insurance*, *juror*, *moorings*, *pleurisy*, *rural*, etc. From a spelling point of view this glide can be regarded as a variant of //uː// before //r//, or in the previous examples as a variant of //uː// plus a further vowel.

However, there is a growing spelling problem here in SBS. The four centring diphthongs /ɪə/, /ɛə/, /ʊə/, /ɔə/, which resulted from the loss of //r// except before a vowel, have been gradually eroded. /ɔə/ has already merged with /ɔː/ in SBS and, for many speakers, so has /ʊə/ before //r// (/pʊə/ has become /pɔː/ in *poor*). A loss of phonemic contrast will inevitably produce spelling difficulties. The words *Shaw*, *shore*, *sure* instead of being distinct as /ʃɔː/, /ʃɔə/, /ʃʊə/ have become homophones for many speakers as /ʃɔː/, and so the spellings <aw>, <ore>, <ure> are divergent spellings of /ɔː/.

The status of /(j)ʊə/ in spelling rules

In spelling rules /(j)ʊə/ is best treated not as a separate phoneme but as /(j)uː/+/ə/. This means that, for instances without a following //r//, the spelling is made up of two separate parts: <u>≡/juː/+<a>≡/ə/ in *gradual* <u>≡/juː/+<ou>≡/ə/ in *arduous*, etc. In *boor* (when it is /ʊə/ and not /ɔː/ as in *bore*) we have <oo>≡/uː/+∅≡/ə/+<r>≡//r//.

The triphthong /jʊə/ is usually pronounced in SBS as a single syllable peak rather than a sequence of two independent vowels. It occurs in words such as: *annual*, *puerile*, *valuable*, etc., where the spelling will vary considerably as <u> plus a further vowel spelling representing the merged /ə/.

/jʊə/≡<ur(e)> occurs with underlying //r//, which is only realized in SBS in pre-vowel contexts in a close-knit phrase: *cure-all*, *secure it*, etc., or within a word: *furious*, *curing*, *security*, etc. In SBS the /ə/ part of the glide persists even when the /r/ is realized (as in *furious*). In some other non-rhotic accents, when the /r/ is realized there is no /ə/ glide at the end of the previous vowel (cf. Northern England [ˈfjuːrɪəs] rather than [ˈfjʊərɪəs]); this trivial transcriptional difference does not, however, affect spelling.

The Hanna (1966) rules treat /ʊə/ as a variant of /ʊ/ (/O7/) before /r/, giving <u..e> before word-final /r/ and <u> before syllable-final /r/ (accented in both cases).

3.3.4 OTHER LONG VOWELS: /uː juː ɔɪ/

3.3.4.1 /uː/ *as in* booty *('simple long <u>')*

Distribution of variant spellings

We shall treat complex /juː/ and simple /uː/ separately. They both show considerable divergence across much the same range of spellings. The difference in the incidence of /juː/ and /uː/ across different accents is discussed under /juː/ in the next section §3.3.4.2.

There are three main spellings (table 31), which account for four-fifths of the total of simple /uː/ (excluding function words *do*, *to*, *you*, *who* and the numeral *two*). Of these, the <oo> spelling is not found with /juː/. These figures include instances with and without <e>-marking. The remaining fifth of instances of /uː/ are spread over a number of minority spellings.

Table 31 Spellings of /uː/

spellings of /uː/	*TF*	*LF*	
<u>, <u..e>, <ue>	27 %	42 %	F-
<oo>	39 %	33 %	F+
<o>, <o..e>, <oe>	15 %	7 %	F+
<ew>	9 %	5 %	
<ou>	7 %	8 %	
<ui>	2 %	2 %	
<eu>	<1 %	1 %	

'F-' : tends to occur in low frequency words: 'F+' : tends to occur in high frequency words

With such a spread it is not surprising that there are few restrictions to particular contexts. To have included the function words *do*, *to*, etc., would have given <o> a text frequency covering almost 70 per cent of spellings of /uː/, while <ou>, with the inclusion of *you*, would then have 9 per cent.

The incidence of simple /uː/ in correspondences varies in different accents. Compared with SBS, AmE has many fewer instances of /juː/, which is losing ground to the /j/-less vowel (see p. 200). The proportion of <oo> spellings would be correspondingly less in AmE.

Monosyllables with /-uːC/

Though there are no immediately apparent generalizations to be made, it does seem that the distribution of spellings differs significantly in SBS between monosyllables and longer words. These generalizations are loosened up a little in AmE by the dropping of /j/ in some contexts. We shall look first of all at monosyllabic words to see if the postvocalic consonant is a predictive context and then separately at longer words:

- —/p/ – with <oo> *coop*, *droop*, *hoop*, *loop*, *poop*, *scoop*, *sloop*, *snoop*, *stoop*, *swoop*, *troop*, *whoop*; with <ou> *croup*, *group*, *soup*, (*re*)*coup*, *troupe*; with <u..e> in AmE *dupe*;
- —/b/ – with <oo> *boob*; with <u..e> in AmE *tube*;
- —/t/ – with <oo> *boot*, *coot*, *hoot*, *loot*, *moot*, *root*, *scoot*, *shoot*, *toot*; with <ou> *route*; with <u..e> *brute*, *chute*, *flute*, *jute*, *lute*; with <ui> *bruit*, *fruit* and, for AmE and most SBS speakers, *suit*;
- —/d/ – with <ew> *lewd*, *shrewd*; with <oo> *brood*, *food*, *mood*, *rood*; with <u..e> *crude*, *prude*, *rude*, and in AmE *dude, nude*;
- —/k/ – with <oo> (*gobbledy*)*gook*, *snook*, *spook*; with <u..e> *fluke* and in AmE *duke*; *nuke;*
- —/ʧ/ – with <oo> *hooch*, *mooch*, *smooch*; and in AmE *brooch* (SBS has /əʊ/);
- —/ʤ/ – with <oo> *stooge*;
- —/m/ – with <eu> *rheum*; with <o> *tomb*, *womb*; with <o..e> *combe* (as in names such as *Ilfracombe*); with <oo> *bloom*, *boom*, *broom*, *doom*, *gloom*, *groom*, *loom*, *room*, *zoom*; with <u..e> *plume*;
- —/n/ – with <oo> *boon*, *coon*, *croon*, *loon*, *moon*, *noon*, *soon*, *spoon*, *swoon*; with <ou> *wound*; with <u..e> in AmE *dune, tune;*
- —/f/ – with <oo> *goof*, *hoof*, *poof*, *proof*, *roof*;
- —/v/ – with <o..e> *move*, *prove* (and *approve*, *improve*, *reprove*); with <oo> (*be*)*hoove*, *groove*;
- —/θ/ – with <eu> *sleuth*; with <oo> *sooth*, *tooth*; with <ou> *youth*; with <u> *ruth*(*less*), *truth*;
- —/ð/ – with <oo> *booth* (AmE /θ/), *smoothe*, *soothe*;
- —/s/ – with <oo> *boost*, *goose*, *loose*, *moose*, *noose*, *roost*; with <ou> *mousse*; with <u..e> *spruce*, *truce*; with <ui> *juice*, *sluice*; with <e..u> in AmE *deuce;*
- —/z/ – with <o..e> *lose*; with <oo> *booze*, *choose*, *ooze*, *snooze*; with <u..e> *cruse*; with <ui> *bruise*, *cruise*; with <ew> in AmE *news*;
- —/ʃ/ – with <ou> *douche*;
- —/ʒ/ – with <ou> *rouge*;
- —/l/ – with <oo> *cool*, *drool*, *fool*, *pool*, *school*, *spool*, *stool*, *tool*; with <ou> *ghoul*; with <u..e> *rule.*

A few generalities can be drawn from this. The <oo> spellings are in a majority and <u..e> is especially common after /l/ and /r/. What is chiefly striking about the §Basic spelling correspondence /uː/≡<oo> is the large proportion of slang words: *boob*, *booze*, *coon*, *drool*, *goof*, *gook*, *hooch*, *poof*, *smooch*, *snook*, *snooze*, *spook*, *toot*, and perhaps *croon*. This may well be a function of the vowel independently of the spelling. The ageing American slang expression *a zoot suit* has the §Basic <oo> for *zoot*, but *suit* is not changed to <soot> for obvious reasons.

French loan-words usually have <ou> but the French connections must surely be lost to most people in a word as common as *group*, which is §Basic by default. In *troop* and *troupe* we have a medieval and a nineteenth century borrowing of the same word. §French spelling conventions often accompany exotic loan words such as *ghoul* (from Arabic).

In names an irregular <e> is often added for padding (see §6.4: p. 454): *Boone*, *Broome*, *Crewe*, *Croome*, *Doone*, *Goole*, *Looe*, *Toole*. §Basic names often have monosyllabic elements with <oo>: *Blackpool*, *Bloomfield*. *Ffoulkes* has an empty <l>.

Final /uː/

The commonest spelling for final /uː/ is <ew>: *brew*, *cashew*, *chew*, *crew*, *eschew*, *screw*, *shrew*, *strew*, *view* (*inter-*, *pre-*, *pur-*, *re-*), *yew* and the small group of past tense forms *blew*, *drew*, *flew*, *grew*, *slew*, *threw*. The <i> and <y> of *view* and *yew* are taken to be separate spellings of the /j/. In names there are *Andrew, Hebrew, Renfrew*.

Other final /uː/ spellings are:

- <-ue>: *accrue*, *blue*, *clue*, *construe*, *flue*, *glue*, *imbrue*, *true*, *rue* and the nonce form *grue*(*some*);
- <-eu>: if we take <i> to be a spelling of /j/, then we can also include here the French loans *adieu*, *lieu* and *purlieu*; and in AmE *milieu*, where SBS has /-jɜː/;
- <-oe>: *canoe*, *shoe*;
- <-oo>: as the stressed final syllable of polysyllabic words: *ballyhoo*, *bamboo*, *buckaroo*, *cockatoo*, *hullaballoo*, *kangaroo*, *kazoo*, *shampoo*, *taboo*, *tattoo* (but without primary stress in *cuckoo*, *hoodoo*, *voodoo*); in names such as *Bakerloo*, *Timbuctoo*, *Waterloo*; in monosyllables *goo*, *loo*, *too*, *woo*, *zoo* including the onomatopoeic words *boo*, *coo*, *moo*, *shoo*; *pooh* untypically has a final empty <h>;
- <-ou>: *caribou*, *maribou*, *sou*;
- <-u>: *flu*, *gnu*, *guru*, *juju*, *jujitsu*, *ormolu*.

Final <-o> characterizes the function words *do*, *to*, *who* and the number *two*. The function word *through* is the only example of final <ough>≡/uː/, apart from a variant AmE pronunciation of slough (n.) as /sluː/.

/uː/ in other polysyllabic words

In polysyllabic free-forms, <u> is much more common; <oo> does not usually feature in §Latinate or §Greek words. So, in words with §Latinate affixes we can predict <u> as the default spelling: *absolute*, *abstruse*, *alluvial*, *aluminum* (AmE), *cerulean*, *crucify*, *exclusive*, *frugal*, *glucose*, *hallucinate*, *judicial*, *juvenile*, *lucid*, *lucrative*, *luminous*, *peruse*, *prudent*, *recluse*, *rubicund*, *ruminate*, *salubrious*, *scrutiny*, *seclusion*, *solution*, *suture*, etc. An <ou> spelling occurs in some §Greek words such as *acoustic*, but the <ou> may be Latinized to <u>, as in *plutocrat.*

This leaves us with a very mixed group of polysyllabic single morphemes with the default spelling <u>: *guru*, *judo*, *jujitsu*, *juju*, *julep*, *lupin*, *peruque*, *rhubarb*, *ruby*, *rupee*. There are some §Romance words in the group but they neither have a French <ou> spelling nor §Latinate word-formation potential. The word *recruit* is exceptional. The obscure pair *boogie* and *googly* are best regarded as derived from non-existent *<boog> and *<google>. In contrived words such as this, one feels that the spelling marks some feature of the meaning; so much for the arbitrariness of the linguistic sign.

Apart from the two rare technical terms *caisson* and *canton(ment)*, final stressed /-uːn/ is spelt with <oo>: *baboon*, *bassoon*, *buffoon*, *cartoon*, *cocoon*, *doubloon*, *dragoon*, *festoon*, *harpoon*, *lagoon*, *lampoon*, *macaroon*, *maroon*, *monsoon*, *octoroon*, *pantaloon*, *platoon*, *poltroon*, *pontoon*, *racoon*, *spittoon*, *tycoon*, *typhoon*, and in the names *Cameroon*, *Kowloon*, *Rangoon*, *Sassoon*, *Walloon*. The spelling <oo> also occurs medially in a very few other polysyllabic words – *bazooka*, *booby*, *boomerang*, *booty*, *coolie*, *loony*.

The §Romance <ou> spelling is found in: *accoutrement*, *barouche*, *boudoir*, *boulevard*, *boutique*, *cantaloupe*, *cartouche*, *cougar*, *coulomb*, *coupon*, *croupier*, *denouement*, *douche*, *goulash*, *insouciance*, *louvre*, *mousse*, *oubliette*, *ragout*, *rendezvous*, *rouble*, *rouge*, *roulette*, *routine*, *silhouette*, *soubrette*, *souffle*, *souvenir*, *toucan*, *toupee*, *troubadour*, *trousseau* and, possibly with vowel reduction, *bouquet* (also /əʊ/), *carousel.* Most of these can be identified as §French by endings or by particular phoneme sequences (e.g. /uːʃ/, /wɑː/). <ou> also occurs in a variety of names: *Foulger*, *Froude*, *Goulden*, *Houdini*, *Houston*, *Khartoum*, *Outram*, *Poulson*, *Souza*, *Zouche.*

<eu>≡/uː/ occurs after /l/ or /r/ in a few §Greek words – *leukaemia*, *rheumatism*, etc.; and in names such as *Aleutian*, *Buccleuch* (with <ch>≡Ø), *Reuben.*

There may be occasional variation between SBS and AmE in the lexical distribution of /ʊ/ and /uː/. Only small numbers of words are affected. The /ʊ/ pronunciation in *Buddha, cuckoo, sputnik, Yakut,* for instance, may be long /uː/ in AmE; it also has /luː-/ in *lieutenant*, where British English has /lef-/.

The Hanna (1966) spelling rules are:

1 <oo> syllable-initial (*ooze*);
2 <o..e> syllable-medial before word-final /v/ (*move*);
3 <o> syllable-medial before syllable-final /v/ (*approval*);
4 <u..e> syllable-medial after /l, r/ and followed by word-final /d/ (*interlude*, *rude*);
5 <oo> syllable-medial elsewhere (*moon*, *ty-phoon*);

6 <ew> word-final (*chew*);
7 <u> syllable-final (*ru-by, flu-ent*).

3.3.4.2 /juː/ *as in* beauty *('complex long <u>')*

Distribution of variant spellings

It is convenient to treat /juː/ as a single spelling unit, even though it represents a string of two phonemes in the kind of phonemic analysis adopted here. In unstressed contexts we find reduced /jʊ/ or /jə/ and, either before //r// or in a merger with /ə/, we find /jʊə/. This phonetic variation is dealt with very clumsily by any surface phonemic analysis, but would fall into place quite neatly in a process description based on a single underlying vowel.

The incidence of the diphthong /juː/ and the pure vowel /uː/ varies considerably across different accents. The /j/ has been, and is being, lost in various contexts, most notably in AmE. By no means all instances of SBS /juː/ do have /uː/ as a counterpart in AmE. The contrast between /juː/ and /uː/ is maintained in contexts such as *beauty–booty, cute–coot, feud–food, hew–who*, *mute–moot*, *mew–moo*. So, /juː/ generally remains after labials /p b m f v/, velars /k g/ in AmE: *computer, puberty, puerile*; *abusive, bugle, rebuke*; *amuse, music, mute*; *feud, funeral, refuse, nephew*; *ovule, review*; *barbecue, cumulative, cuticle*; *argue, contiguous, legume*. The /j/ also survives after /h/: *exhume, hew, huge, human, humid, humility, humour*. Simple /uː/ is not found initially except in its own <oo> spelling, as in *ooze*. So we have /juː/ initially in *eulogy, union, unique.*

After the liquids /l r/, the /j/ has been generally lost: *include, lubricate, ludicrous, lukewarm*; *crucial, rubric, ruby, truth*. Some words, however, have kept the /j/ after /l/, at least for some speakers: *deluge, prelude, value, volume*, *where* /l/ is the coda of the stressed syllable and the /j/ as the onset of the second syllable: /ˈdel – juːʤ/ etc. This is a favourable context for retaining the /j/, since here it clearly has a consonantal function.

It is after the alveolars /t d n s z/ and an occasional /θ/ that /j/ is most frequently lost. The majority of AmE speakers do not have /j/ in these contexts:

> after /t/ in *astute*, *attitude, costume, destitute, impromptu, institute, intuition, mature, multitude, Neptune, obtuse, opportunity, petunia, prostitute, restitution, solitude, steward, studio, student, substitute, Teutonic, tube, Tudor, tune,* etc.;
> after /d/ in *adduce, deuce, dubious, dude, duplicate, duty, introduce, mildew, produce, residue, subdue,* etc.;
> after /n/ in *annuity, avenue, Canute, knew, minute* (adj.), *neutral, news, nuclear, nude, numerous, nutrition, pneumatic, revenue,* etc.;

after /s/ in *assume, consume, hirsute, pseudo, pursue, sewer*, etc.
after /z/ in *exhume, exuberance, exude, presume, resume,* etc.

For the /j/ to be dropped, however, there is a necessary condition that the syllable must have some degree of stress. So in *avenue* there is a rhythmical stress on the last syllable and the /j/ may be dropped, but there is no degree of stress on the /juː/ of *continue* and the /j/ is kept.

/juː/ is the normal tense vowel value of the letter <u> and represents the 'name' of the letter. The spelling <u>, with or without <e>-marking, accounts for TF 81.6 per cent, LF 93.2 per cent (F-) instances of /juː/, reduced /jʊ/, and, in conjunction with underlying //r//, /jʊə/. The spelling <oo>, which is quite a common spelling for /uː/, is not found as a spelling for /juː/. *Hulme* has an empty <l>.

In SBS allegro forms the /j/ will tend to form an affricate /ʧ/ or /ʤ/ with a preceding /t/ or /d/: *attitude*, *substitute*, *costume*, *statue*, etc.; *reduce*, *nodule*, *duke*, etc.

Reduced /jʊ/, reducible still further to /jə/, usually occurs as part of the regular metrical pattern after a stressed vowel. The vowel following the /jʊ/ may have full vowel quality (*stimulate*, *immunize*) or may also be reduced (*nebulous*, *angular*). As with /juː/, the /j/ will tend to form an affricate /ʧ/, /ʤ/ with a preceding /t/, /d/ in allegro forms: *congratulate*, *petulant*, *fistula*, *pendulum*, *modular*, *glandular*.

Only TF 18 per cent, LF 7 per cent (F+) of /juː/ spellings other than plain <u> are found (based on SBS forms). Of these the most common is /juː/≡<ew>. The discrepancy between the text and lexical frequencies is a consequence of some very common words with the <ew> spelling, notably *new*, *few* and *knew*. Other words are: *curfew*, *curlew*, *dew*, *ewe*, *hew*, *mew*, *mews*, *mildew*, *nephew*, *newel*, *newt*, *pew*, *pewter*, *sinew*, *skew*, *spew*, *stew*, *thews*; *ewer*, *skewer*, *steward*; *sewage* and *sewer* may have /juː/ or /uː/. All these are §Basic words; they represent TF 81 per cent, LF 38 per cent (F+) of the minority spellings of /juː/. In *view* and *yew* we have taken the <i> and <y> to be separate spellings of /j/ and the vowel is dealt with under /uː/. Names with <ew> include *Agnew, Bartholomew, Bewicke, Clerihew, Dewey, Dewsbury, Ewart, Newton, Tewkesbury, Whewell.*

The correspondence /juː/≡<eu> when non-final belongs to the §Greek system. It occurs in two prefixes: <pseudo> – 'fake', which may also have /suː/: *pseudonym*, *pseudostoma*, etc., and <eu> – 'good': *eulogy*, *euphonic*, *euphoria*, *euthanasia*, etc. Other examples are *Europe*, *eunuch*, and in technical and scientific vocabulary: *neurology*, *therapeutic*, *pneumonia*, etc. *Neuter* derives from Latin, but looks §Greek. The spelling <eu>≡/uː/ also occurs finally in French loans *adieu*, *lieu*, *purlieu*, if the <i> is taken to be /j/. Names with <eu> include *Beulah, Deuteronomy, Eugenie, Eunice, Euston, Odysseus, Prometheus, Teuton, Zeus* and anglicized *Devereux, Molyneux,* with final /juː/.

Two other minor spellings are:

- /juː/≡<ui>: in *suit* this is a rather old-fashioned pronunciation – 72 per cent of Wells' poll for the LPD preferred /suːt/; LPD has a preference for /juː/ in *pursuit* and *nuisance*;
- /juː/≡<eau> in *beauty*.

The spelling /juː/≡<ui> is particularly odd, since in terms of phonetic appropriateness the two letters are the wrong way round. A child who writes *<siut> for *suit*, assuming the pronunciation /sjuːt/, is being quite reasonable.

The Hanna (1966) spelling rules are:

1 <u..e> syllable-initial before word-final phoneme (*leg-ume*, *prel-ude*);
2 <u> syllable-initial all other cases (*un-ion*, *fig-ur-a-tive*);
3 <u..e> syllable-medial (*a-ssume*, *in-duce-ment*);
4 <ue> word-final (*due*);
5 <u> syllable-final (*mu-tu-al*, *pos-tu-late*).

These rules also cover /jʊə/.

3.3.4.3 /ɔɪ/ as in boy

Distribution of variant spellings

/ɔɪ/ has no real divergence (table 32).

Table 32 Spellings of /ɔɪ/

spellings of /ɔɪ/	*TF*	*LF*	
<oi>	61 %	71 %	F-
<oy>	39 %	29 %	F+

'F-' : tends to occur in low frequency words; 'F+' : tends to occur in high frequency words

The <oy> variant occurs finally in free-forms: *destroy*, *employ*, *joy*; *destroyer*, *employed*, *joyful*, etc. Instances of non-final <oy> are: *boycott*, *foyer*, *gargoyle*, *hoyden*, *loyal*, *oyster*, *royal*, *soya*, *voyage*, and *coyote*, which has /aɪ/ in AmE. These are single morphemes. Some of them have an ending which resembles a class-marking suffix, such as <-ster> (a noun ending), or <-al>, (an adjective ending), but the remainder <oy->, <voy-> or <roy-> are nonce forms. The verb *to boycott* is derived from a personal name.

Names have non-final <oy> much more frequently than <oi>, even when there is no suggestion of an element boundary: *Ackroyd*, *Boyce*, *Boyd*, *Boyle*, *Burgoyne*, *Croydon*, *Doyle*, *Floyd*, *Foyle*, *Hoylake*, *Holroyd*, *Joyce*, *Lloyd*, *Loyola*, *Moya*, *Moynihan*, *Poynton*, *Royce*, *Royston*, *Samoyed*, *Saroyan*, *Toynbee*, *Toyota*, etc. The commonness of <-oyd> in names may have influenced the *OED* spelling of the recent loan *sloyd* ('Swedish carpentry' from Sw. <slöjd>). *Hanoi* has an unusual final <oi>.

The spelling <oy> is peculiar to /ɔɪ/, but the spelling <oi> occasionally represents /wæ/ or /wɑː/ in unanglicized loan-words from French: *boudoir*, *bourgeois*, *chamois* (anglicized as /'ʃæmɪ/), *coiffure*, *memoir*, *patois*, *repertoire*, *reservoir*, *soiree*. The pair *toilet* with /ɔɪ/ and *toilette* with /wɑː/ represent an early and a late borrowing.

The word *buoy* is often /buːi/ rather than /bɔɪ/ in AmE.

The Hanna (1966) spelling rules are:

1 <oy> word-final (*employ*);
2 (default) <oi> (*noisy*).

The 'word-final' context, however, should also apply in derived forms. The Hanna algorithm gives *<boihood>, *<enjoiable>, *<flamboiant>, *<joious>, etc.

3.3.5 /ə/ and vowel reduction

Distribution of variant spellings

/ə/ shows more divergence than any other phoneme. This is only to be expected since it represents the reduced form of a wide range of underlying vowels in unstressed syllables. In the stress-timed rhythm of English, vowel reduction naturally accompanies absence of stress. Proponents of reformed, more consistent, alphabetic spelling find the divergence of /ə/ to be one of their main problems. Yet they have to come to terms with the fact that the present morphophonemic spelling is not by any means inefficient:

> there is no vowel letter in the roman alphabet that could regularly and uniquely stand for the neutral, central or schwa vowel that occurs in such a high proportion of weakly stressed syllables in English. The compilers of the Simplified Spelling Society's 'New Spelling' gave much thought to this difficult problem and decided that vowels in unstressed syllables should in general be represented by the letters now used in those syllables (thus *sister*, *begar*, *aktor*, etc.). This means that the proper New Spelling of the vowels in such syllables cannot be deduced from pronunciation, and a certain amount of arbitrary memorization of spellings is inevitable. A minor compensatory advantage is that the relation between a number of cognate words is still able to be shown (thus *foetograaf*, *fotografer*, *foetografik*), in cases where the shift of stress is in speech accompanied by altered vowel qualities
>
> (MacCarthy 1969:103ff; for 'New Spelling' see §7.3.2)

Phonetically /ə/ is found either as a separate segment [ə] or as syllabicity of a sonorant /l/, /m/, /n/. Syllabic consonants will be dealt with here as phonetic variants of /ə/ plus consonant.

The text frequency percentage figures below refer only to the occurrence of /ə/ in lexical words. The raw text frequency of /ə/ would be a great deal higher because of its frequent occurrence in function words: *to*, *at*, *as*, *and*, *the*, *a/an*, etc. Their inclusion would not, however, make much difference to the relative proportions of /ə/ spellings because they have the same spread of variation. The actual incidence of /ə/ in the lexical words of the database depends to some extent on how one assigns the unstressed vowel in words such as *goodness*, *forest*, – whether to /ə/ or /ɪ/. In this study the /ə/-/ɪ/ variation has been counted towards /ə/ (see p. 135). This will tend to increase slightly the proportion of <a> and <e> spellings of /ə/. The principal spellings of /ə/ are shown in table 33.

Table 33 Spellings of /ə/

spellings of /ə/	*TF*	*LF*	
<a>	35 %	30 %	F+
<o>	19 %	24 %	F-
<ou>	<1 %	2 %	F-
<or>≡/ə(r)/	2 %	2 %	
<e>	13 %	13 %	
<er>≡/ə(r)/	15 %	12 %	
<le>≡/əl/	6 %	6 %	
<u>	3 %	3 %	
<ure>≡/ə(r)/	2 %	<1 %	
<i>	1 %	1 %	
other spellings	5 %	6 %	

'F-' : tends to occur in low frequency words; 'F+' : tends to occur in high frequency words

The pronunciation of English in Australia, New Zealand and South Africa shows a growing use of /ə/ at the expense of /ɪ/ in unstressed syllables, as in *forest, solid, village*. This is carried furthest in Australian English. The plural ending after sibilants is /-əz/ rather than /-ɪz/, which makes for homophones such as *dances–dancers, boxes–boxers, offices–officers*. The grammatical words *it* and *is* also have /ə/ rather than /ɪ/, so *sell it once* = *sell at once*, *Bruce is well* = *Bruce as well*. In SBS, too, /ə/ is becoming more common in the <-ed>, <-es> inflections of *wanted*, *offices*. This may underlie spelling errors such as 'Realism by vendors has persuaded some *purchases to enter the market' (*Independent* 19/8/92: 2).

Formal pronunciations as a spelling aid

The spelling of /ə/ is the most difficult problem that faces a normal adult speller. In many instances, especially in technical vocabulary, spellers may actively adopt the strategy of storing a spelling pronunciation with full vowel quality such as */ˈsɪlɪkɒn/ (for *silicon*). In ordinary spoken registers the word is usually said as /ˈsɪlɪkən/, but the hyperformal spelling register may be called on when the word has to be written. In some cases these spelling pronunciations may see actual use in formal or deliberate speech: */ˈæktɔː/ (rather than /ˈæktə/) and */əʊˈpres/ (rather than /əˈpres/) for *actor* and *oppress*. The old-fashioned teaching method of getting pupils to 'syllabify' words seems to have been a cloak for teaching pupils to remember such hyperformal pronunciations. The unstressed syllables, plucked out of a normal spoken context, were pronounced with full vowel quality: /æ/, /kaʊn/, /tænt/ for *accountant*. To be sure of the spelling, one had to be taught a special pronunciation. These deliberately contrived pronunciations should be unnecessary if shifting stress patterns can betray the quality of the 'underlying' vowel in the normal processes of word formation (*atom–atomic*, *theatre–theatrical*, etc.). Yet we cannot always rely on the speller being aware of the semantic identity of morphemes in the foreign/technical sectors of vocabulary, and semantic identity is essential to the matching process.

The spellings of /ə(r)/

Final /ə(r)/ is spelt with various vowel letters followed by <r> in suffixes (*lunar*, *runner*, *actor*, *stupor*, *splendour*, *pressure*). The identification of these suffixes is discussed under homophonous affixes in §5.5, pp. 426ff.

Final /ə(r)/ after a consonant may be spelt with <-re> in British English in single-morpheme words in the following contexts:

- after /b/ – *calibre*, *fibre*, *sabre*, *sombre*, *timbre*; but there are also *amber*, *ember*, *lumber*, *number*, *sober*, *timber*, etc.;
- after /t/ – *accoutre*, *centre*, *goitre*, *litre*, *lustre*, *metre*, *mitre*, *reconnoitre*, *saltpetre*, *sceptre*, *spectre*, *theatre*; but there are also *hamster*, *water*, etc.;
- after /k/ – *ochre*, *sepulchre*; *acre*, *chancre*, *lucre*, *massacre*, *mediocre*, etc.;
- after /g/ – *meagre*, *ogre*; but there are also *auger*, *eager*, *lager*, etc.;
- after /v/ – *louvre*, *manoeuvre*; but there are also *clover*, *lever*, etc.

It is clear that this <-re> spelling is peculiar to §Romance or §Greek words. Some of them, but by no means all, are marked by word-formation potential as non-§Basic. There are, for instance, §Latinate or §Greek suffixes in *central*, *lucrative*, *metric*, *sepulchral*, *spectral*, *theatrical*, etc. The earlier loans do not necessarily have this potential. Both *meagre* and *eager* are early Romance loans, but, as adjectives, they do not share this word-formation potential.

The above instances were of /ə(r)/ following a consonant; the /ə/ serves to split what would otherwise be an un-English final cluster //-br//, //-tr//, //-kr//, //-gr//, //-vr//. The greater prominence of the //r// is bound to give an extra syllable phonetically. In English this is done by splitting the consonants (/ˈluːvə(r)/, *louvre*) not, as in French, by adding [ə] as a voiced off-glide ([luːvrə]).

The on-glide [ə] to //r// also occurs after vowels, which has brought about the diphthongs /ɪə/ *mere*, /ʊə/ *tour*, /ɛə/ *pair*, taken to be unit phonemes in SBS. The similar glide in other cases is usually analysed as two phonemes /aɪ/+/ə/ in *fire*, /aʊ/+/ə/ in *hour*, but for SBS speakers these may be monosyllabic. From the spelling point of view the [ə] glide is subsumed in the <r> spelling, so we have *fire*, *file*, *fine*; *pair*, *pail*, *pain*. In the case of /aʊ/+/ə/ we find *scour*, *scout*, *scowl* but more usually a spelling which reflects the presence of the /ə/: *power*, *tower*, etc.

The spelling of any particular /ə/ may be apparent because it occurs in a recurrent string, initially or finally, in words of a particular category. Spellings of /ə/ plus //r// in strings which the speller might treat as wholes are:

- <-ar> – as an irregular agent suffix in *beggar*, *burglar*, *liar*, *pedlar*; as a §Latinate adjective suffix in *columnar*, *polar*, *popular*, *regular*, *titular*, etc.;
- <-arch-> (unstressed; in §Greek words) – *anarchy*, *monarch*, etc.;
- <-ard> – as the ending /-əd/ in nouns: *bastard*, *custard*, *mustard*, *scabbard*, etc.; *mallard* is more likely to be /ˈmælɑːd/;
- <-er> as the common agent suffix – *knocker*, *settler*, *viewer*, etc.; as the comparative suffix – *better*, *brighter*, *colder*, etc.;
- <-eur> – in recent French loans *amateur*, *chauffeur*, *grandeur*; in the latter case there is clear morpheme boundary <grand>+<eur> and the word might well be reanalysed and respelt as *<grandure>;
- <for-> – *forbid*, *forget*, etc.;
- <hyper-> – *hyperactive*, *hypermarket*, etc.;
- <inter-> – *interactive*, *intercede*, etc.;
- <-our> – is largely found as a noun ending: *colour*, *favour*, *labour*, *neighbour*, etc.;
- <per-> – *perform*, *peroxide*, etc.;
- <super-> – *supermarket*, *superordinate*, etc.;
- <sur-> – *surprise*, *survive*, etc.;
- <-ur> – *murmur*, *femur*, *sulphur*, *augur*, *lemur*;
- <-ure> – this §Romance ending is found in some very common nouns; some of the more frequent are: *adventure*, *capture*, *creature*, *culture*, *failure*, *feature*, *figure*, *furniture*, *future*, *gesture*, *literature*, *manufacture*, *measure*, *nature*, *picture*, *pleasure*, *pressure*, *procedure*, *structure*, *temperature*, etc.;
- <-ward(s) > – *afterward(s)*, *backward(s)*, *forward(s)*, etc.;
- <-yr> – in the §Greek words *martyr*, *satyr*, *zephyr*.

/ə/ (without //r//) in common elements

Common elements of word structure containing /ə/, irrespective of whether there is sufficient semantic identity to make them morphemes, include:

- <a-> – as a §Basic prefix (derived historically from {on}) in *aboard*, *abreast*, *abroad*, *ahead*, *away*, etc., but with potential confusion from §Latinate prefixes as in *address*, *assign*;
- <-a> – as a learned plural form for some §Latinate and §Greek nouns: *data*, *erotica*, *memoranda*, *phenomena*, etc.; with /ɪə/ in *criteria*, *media*, etc.; the relation of these plurals to their singular forms (e.g. *criterion*, *medium*) is often not apparent to our normal adult speller and in some cases the plurality is lost (*an agenda*);
- <-a> as an exotic noun ending, in words of three or more syllables stressed on the penultimate – *abscissa*, *alfalfa*, *anaconda*, *bonanza*, *concertina*, *cyclorama*, *enigma*, *farina*, *gymkhana*, *magenta*, *pianola*, *persona*, *regatta*, *vendetta*, etc. Indeed word-final /ə/ without latent //r// is spelt <a> almost without exception. The only exception in the data was *macabre* /mə'kɑːbrə/ (cf. *candelabra*). Final <-a>, however, may be followed by an 'intrusive' /r/ before another vowel as an anti-hiatus device: *data input* /'deɪtər ɪnpʊt/;
- <-able>/<-ible> (see §5.5, p. 424) – *capable*, *notable*, *suitable*, etc.; *possible*, *terrible*, *visible*, etc.;
- <-ace> – this ending marks nouns but is not a morpheme; it is found in *furnace*, *menace*, *palace*, *pinnace*, *populace*, *solace*, *surface*, *terrace*; *carcase* and *purchase* are spelt with <s>; for some speakers the vowel may be /ɪ/;
- <-acle> – as a noun ending – *coracle*, *oracle*, *tentacle*, etc.;
- <ad-> and its assimilated forms : *account*, *admire*, *affiliated*, *aggression*, *alliteration*, *announce*, *apply*, *arrive*, *assign*, *attend*, etc.;
- <-al> – as a §Romance adjective ending: *central*, *liberal*, *loyal*, etc.;
- <-ance>/<-ence> – *appliance*, *science* (see §5.5, p.422);
- <-ant>/<-ent> – *elephant*, *element* ;
- <-ary>/<-ery> – *salary*, *artery* (see §5.5, p. 431);
- <-ate> (in nouns and adjectives) – *advocate*, *articulate*, *delicate*, *duplicate*, *intricate*, etc.; a few ending in <-iate> (*associate* n.) come under /ɪə/; the verbs ending in <-ate> have an unreduced /eɪ/;
- <com-> and assimilated forms – *command*, *committee*; *connect*, *connubial*; *collect*, *collide*; *corrosive*, *corruption*;
- <-dom> – *dukedom*, *fiefdom*, *freedom*, *kingdom*, *wisdom*, etc.;
- <-ess> – *actress*, *countess*, *heiress*, etc. and in words where the <-ess> does not constitute a morpheme: *cypress*, *witness*; for some speakers the vowel may be /ɪ/ in this and <-less> (*endless*, *helpless*, *regardless*, etc.); <-ness> (*darkness*, *fitness*, *happiness*, etc.);
- <-ile> in *docile, facile, fissile, fragile, futile, infantile, prehensile, projectile,*

puerile, servile, sterile, tensile, versatile, volatile, has a full vowel /aɪ/ in SBS, but only a syllabic /l/ in AmE, so that *fertile* rhymes with *turtle* ;

- <ob-> and assimilated forms – *obligatory*, *obscene*, *obscure*, *observe*, *obsession*, etc.; *offend*, *official*; *occasion*, *occur*;
- <-ock> – *bullock*, *buttock*, *hassock*, *hillock*, *mattock*, etc.;
- <-od> – *method*, *synod*;
- <-ology> – *biology*, *pathology*, etc.;
- <-om> – *blossom*, *bosom*, *custom*, *phantom*, *venom*, etc.; discussed in more detail under homophonous affixes, §5.5, p. 438.
- <-op> – *bishop, collop, develop, dollop, envelop, gallop, hyssop, lollop, scallop, shallop, trollop, wallop;* this is not a suffix proper, but the most common spelling by far of final /əp/ and the only one after <l>; the only competitor is <-up> in *catsup, chirrup, ketchup, stirrup, syrup*;
- <pro-> – *procure*, *production*, *profane*, *professor*, *proficient*;
- <-some> – *bothersome*, *gruesome*, *irksome*, *toothsome*, *winsome*, etc.;
- <to-> : *today*, *tomorrow*.

Other simple <V>-letter correspondences for /ə/

The correspondence <o>≡/ə/ relates to a stressed <o>≡/əʊ/ or a stressed <o>≡/ɒ/ in words such as *abdomen* (*abdominal*), *colloquy* (*colloquium*), *custody* (*custodial*), *prolong* (*prolongation*), *sobriety* (*sober*). <o>≡/ə/ is often found as the linking vowel in §Greek-type compounds: *cellophane*, *chlorophyl*, *microphone*, *monolith*, *phonograph*, *saxophone*.

There are, however, many polysyllabic words where there are no apparent guides to the <o> spelling: *acrobat*, *broccoli*, *daffodil*, *exodus*, *iodine*, *kaolin*, *lobelia*, *mandolin*, *parody*, *police*, *purpose*, *ricochet*, *tobacco*, *violate*, etc.

- –medial <ur> occurs in *auburn*, *expurgate*, *jodhpurs*, *liturgy*, *metallurgy*, *pursue*, *Saturday*, *saturnine*, *surmise*, *surmount*, *surpass*, *surprise*, *survey* (v.), *survive*.

- <y> would normally be associated with /ə/ only where /ɪ/ was a possible alternant; there are a few words such as *pyjamas* where one would not expect /ɪ/; there is greater likelihood of /ə/ when an unstressed /ɪ/ follows in the next syllable: *analysis*, *labyrinth*.

Complex spellings of /ə/

Complex spellings of /ə/ include:

- <ah> – finally in §Exotic names, many of them Arabic or Hebrew – *Abdullah*, *Allah*, *Basrah*, *Beulah*, *Brahmah*, *Deborah*, *Delilah*, *Dinah*, *Elijah*, *Hannah*, *Isaiah*, *Jeddah*, *Jehovah*, *Messiah*, *Nkrumah*, *Norah*, *Rajah*, *Sarah*, *Uriah*. Some of them may drop the final <h>, as in *Basra*, *Nora*.

- <ai> – *chieftain*, *villain*; *caisson*;
- <au> – *epaulet*, *meerschaum*, *restaurant*;
- <eau> – as a vowel reduction of /əʊ/≡<eau> in *bureaucrat*, *bureaucratic*;
- <oi> – *connoisseur*; *porpoise*, *tortoise*; the latter is the basis for one of Alice's problems in Wonderland (= *taught us*);
- <ou> – very common in the ending <-ous> (*anxious*, *famous*, *nervous*, *religious*, etc.); other instances – *limousine*, *moustache*, *vermouth*;
- <ow> – is rather doubtful as a spelling of /ə/ for SBS speakers; the final /əʊ/ of *barrow*, *hollow*, *narrow*, *sorrow*, *window*, etc. tends not to be reduced and /ə/ in such words is a marker of stigmatized speech, as against 'educated' speech, for speakers of many different accents.

> "This is the first class in English spelling and philosophy, Nickleby," said Squeers. . . . "C-l-e-a-n, clean, verb active, to make bright, to scour. W-i-n, win, d-e-r, der, winder, a casement. When the boy knows this out of the book, he goes and does it".
>
> (Charles Dickens *Nicholas Nickleby*, Ch. VIII)

The only likely context in which <ow> would represent /ə/ is in derived forms in a metrically weak syllable, as in *sorrowful*;

Uncommon spellings of /ə/ may occur in compounds where the unstressed element has suffered vowel reduction and often a blurring of its semantic identity:

- <o..e> – *brimstone*; *welcome*;
- <oar> – *cupboard*, *larboard*, *starboard*;
- <ar> – *halyard*.

The Hanna (1966) spelling rules for /ə/ may be rather misleading since the incidence of /ə/ in the input data is unrealistic (see §2.8.5, pp. 92f.). So, 'syllable-initial before /b/' would not include *abandon*, which is input with initial /æ/, not /ə/. Another reason is that syllabic /əl/, /əm/, /ən/ are treated as separate phonemes ('/L1/', '/M1/', '/N1/') with the spellings <le>, <m>, <en>. With these restrictions, their rules for /ə/ are:

1 <o> syllable-initial after /ʃ/ and before /n/ – in effect the ending <-tion>;
2 <ou> syllable-initial before /s/ – in effect the ending <-ous>;
3 <u> syllable-initial before /m/ – in effect the ending <-um>;
4 <o> syllable-initial before /b/ (*observe*);
5 <i> syllable-initial other instances;
6 <eou> syllable-medial after /ʤ/ or /ʧ/ (*cou-ra-geous*, *righ-teous*);
7 <u> syllable-medial after /s/ (*con-sul*, *sus-tain*);
8 <o> syllable-medial after /k/ – in effect the prefix <com->;
9 <o> syllable-medial after /ʃ/ or /ʒ/ and before /n/ – in effect the endings <-tion>, <-sion>;
10 <e> syllable-medial after /m/ and before /n/- in effect the endings <-men>, <-ment>;
11 <e> syllable-medial before /n/ (*car-pen-ter*, *dil-i-gent*, *wo-ven*);
12 <u> syllable-medial before /m/ (*dic-tum*, *cir-cum-flex*);
13 <ou> syllable-medial before /s/ – in effect the ending <-ous>;
14 <o> syllable-medial (*gam-bol*, *pi-lot*);

15 <o> syllable-final after /k/ – in effect the prefixes <com->, <con-> (*co-mmerce*, *co-nnect*);
16 <i> syllable-final before /t/ or /k/ (*sim-plic-i-ty*, *u-ni-corn*);
17 <ɑ> all other instances.

It is extremely difficult to assess the effect of these rules, but it is evident that to a large extent they work by targeting specific affixes. That being so, simple affix-stripping would be a better parallel of what a speller might do, instead of these highly specific phoneme rules.

3.3.6 Stop consonants: /p b t d k g ʧ ʤ/

3.3.6.1 /p/ *as in* pan

Distribution of variant spellings

/p/ has no real divergence: <p> 95 per cent; <pp> 5 per cent. The proportion of <pp> would be higher if we were to include the many inflected forms in {-ed},{-ing}, such as *dropped, dropping,* from *drop*. Apart from its use in the correspondence /f/≡<ph>, the letter <p> only serves as a spelling of /p/.

<p> is an empty letter in *cupboard*, *raspberry*, and in some §Greek digraphs such as <pn> (*pneumonia*), <ps> (*psychology*) and <pt> (*pterodactyl*). The fact that the §Greek root {pter} also occurs with /pt/ in *helicopter* is hardly enough to suggest that the <p> is inert rather than merely empty. Before <th>≡/θ/, <ph> is often pronounced /p/ rather than /f/ in *diphtheria*, *diphthong*, *naphtha*.

The notorious word *hiccough* gets its peculiar spelling from a contrived etymology. It was thought to be some form of *cough*. A common alternative spelling is *hiccup* but an earlier recorded spelling *hickup* would be more in line with §Basic conventions.

Distribution of <pp>

(For general rules of <C>-doubling (#D1 to #D11), see §3.2.2, pp. 114ff.).
There are no #D4 exceptions with final <pp> except in proper names (cf. *lap–Lapp*) – *Alsopp*, *Capp*, *Chipp*, *Krupp*. A single <p> is usual in final unstressed syllables – *Bacup*, *Dunlop*, *Gallup*, *Glossop*, *Harrap*, *Hindlip*, *Hyslop*, *Inskip*, *Jessop*, *Mendip*, *Philip*, *Ruislip*, *Worksop*, etc. An unusually large proportion of <-pp-> spellings are due to the Latin prefixes *ad-*, *ob-*, *sub-* with assimilation. In some cases the Latin stem is unrecognizable as a recurrent form because the word has undergone major changes in French, from where it was borrowed. For instance *approach* goes back eventually to *ad+propiare* and *apply* to *ad+plicare* (cf. *application*).

Examples of <pp> with prefixes:

- (reduced vowel): *appear*, *approach*, *appeal*, *apply*, *apparent*, *appoint*, *approve*, *appropriate*, *applause*, *applicable*, *append*, *appal*, *appreciate*,

apprentice, *approximate*, *appraise*, *apportion*, *appendix*, *appurtenance*; *oppose*, *opponent*, *oppress*, *opprobrium*; *suppose*, *supply*, *support*, *suppress*, *supplant*;
- (unreduced vowel): *application*, *apparatus*, *appetite*, *apprehension*, *applicant*, *apprehend*, *apparition*, *appointee*, *appetizing*, *approbation*; *opportune*, *opposite*; *supplement*, *supposition*, *supplication*, *suppuration*.

Since some of these §Latinate forms do not always have an obvious structure with a recognizable recurrent stem and prefix, there is scope for spelling confusion in other words such as: *apartment*, *apology*, *apostrophe* (unless *apo-* is recognized as a recurrent unit), or (in non-rhotic accents) with *surprise*, *surpass*.

There is regular absence of <C>-doubling after a stressed short vowel before certain non-§Basic endings (#D7, p. 123). This accounts for the single <p> before the ending in the following:

- <-ic(al)> (adj.) – *adipic, epic, myopic, philanthropic, telescopic, topical, tropical;*
- <-id> (adj.) – *insipid, intrepid, rapid, tepid, vapid*;
- <-it> (in §Latinate words) – *decrepit*;
- <-ule> – *stipule.*

Exceptional spellings with single <-p->: *chapel*, *copy*, *jalopy*, *leper*, *proper*, *rapine*, *triple*.

Exceptional spellings with <-pp->: *hippodrome*, *hippopotamus*. These would not be exceptional for the above rules if *hippo* were regarded as a free-form. French /i/ is usually matched with the long /iː/ rather than short /ɪ/ in English so if *grippe* ('influenza') is borrowed as /griːp/ we have a clearly anomalous <C>-doubling. The spelling *steppe* ('plains') is usefully distinguished as foreign or technical from ordinary *step* by a fairly common convention <-eCCe> (cf. <-ette>, <-enne>).

The Hanna (1966) spelling rules: <p> is the default spelling and:

1 <pp> after a short vowel and before syllabic /l/ (*apple*).

This is a patently inadequate rule for the incidence of <pp>.

3.3.6.2 /b/ as in ban

Distribution of variant spellings

/b/ has virtually no divergence (table 34).

The occurrence of <bb> has already been discussed in showing the application of #D1 to #D11 (see pp. 124ff. The proportion of <bb> would be higher if we were to include the many inflected forms in {-ed} and {-ing}, such as *robbed, robbing,* from *rob*.

Table 34 Spellings of /b/

spellings of /b/	*TF*	*LF*
<b>	98 %	96 %
<bb>	<1 %	3 %
<bu>	1 %	<1 %

There is regular absence of <C>-doubling after a stressed short vowel before certain non-§Basic endings (#D7, p. 123). This accounts for the single <b> before the ending in the following:

- <-ic(al)> (adj.) – *aerobic, syllabic;*
- <-id> (adj.) – *rabid;*
- <-it> (in §Latinate words) – *debit, exhibit, habit, inhibit, prohibit*;
- <-ule> – *globule, lobule.*

Since the <-ish> of *rubbish* is not a suffix as in *snobbish* (#D7), the <C>-doubling is irregular (cf. *parish, polish, radish, vanish,* etc.).

The spelling <bu> occurs in *buy*, *build* and *buoy* and their derived forms. The first two are extremely common lexemes. The <u> is best taken to be part of the consonant spelling rather than as part of vowel spellings *<uy>, *<ui> and *<uoy>. This is justified by overall economy and by analogy with the <gu> spelling of /g/. However, <gu> is functional in distinguishing between spellings of /g/ and /ʤ/, whereas <bu> has no such use. We can note, however, that <buy> as a lexical word satisfies the 'short word rule' (see p. 131); cf. the function word *by*.

Apart from its occurrence as an empty letter in *debt*, *doubt*, and in final <-mb> as in *bomb, comb*, *lamb*, <b> is unique to /b/.

The Hanna (1966) spelling rules: <b> is the default spelling and:

1 <bb> syllable-final accented before syllabic /l/ (*dabble*).

This is a patently inadequate rule for the incidence of <bb>.

3.3.6.3 /t/ *as in* tame

Distribution of variant spellings

/t/ has virtually no divergence: <t> 96 per cent; <tt> 3 per cent. The proportion of <tt> would be higher if we were to include the many inflected forms in {-ed} and {-ing}, such as *batted, batting,* from *bat,* or in {-er}, {-est}, such as *hotter, hottest*, from *hot*. The letter <t> is also involved in the regular doubled <tch> spelling of /ʧ/ and the regular <th> spelling of /θ/ and /ð/.

In consonant clusters //t// is elided in words such as *hasten*, *soften*, *Christmas*, but when this occurs at morpheme boundaries, the //t//≡<t> may be semantically recoverable by the speller from *haste*, *soft*, etc. This is presumably not so for *potpourri* and *mortgage*.

The <tw> of *two* is best analysed as /t/≡<t> and Ø≡<w>: an inert letter which surfaces in the semantically related *twenty*, *twain*, *twin*. The <p> of *receipt* is also an inert letter (cf. *reception*, *receptacle*). It would be misleading to set out the correspondences as /t/≡<tw> in *two* and /t/≡<pt> in *receipt*. One or two other irregular spellings involve <t>≡/t/ in conjunction with purely empty letters: Ø≡<b> in *debt*, *doubt*, *subtle*; Ø≡<c> in *indict*; Ø≡<d> in *veldt*; Ø≡<p> in *ptarmigan*, *pterodactyl*, *ptomaine*. *Yacht* not only has Ø≡<ch> but an irregular /ɒ/≡<a> (after /j/). These are all firm favourites with those who wish to highlight the irregularities of the system. But since they are at the remote edge of the frequency distribution, they hardly dent the overriding regularity of /t/ spellings.

The cluster /ts/ is best treated as a unit in the following instances:

- /ts/≡<z> : *schizophrenia*, *scherzo*, *nazism*, *bilharzia*;
- /ts/≡<tz> : *quartz*, *chintz*, *blitz*, *howitzer*;
- /ts/≡<zz> : *mezzotint*, *intermezzo*, *mezzanine*, *pizza*.

The <tz> in final position has the limited advantage of preventing confusion with plural {-s}: *quarts–quartz*.

The correspondence <th>≡/t/ occurs in *posthumous*, *thyme* and is quite common in names – *Anthony*, *Esther*, *Goethe*, *Hindemith*, *Lesotho*, *Mathilda*, *Neanderthal*, *Pathan*, *Thailand*, *Theresa*, *Thames*, *Thomas*, *Thompson*. Many of these have variants with simple <t>≡/t/ (*Antony*, etc.). Since <-ham> is a recognizable place-name element and since //h// is frequently elided in unstressed syllables, names such as *Chatham*, *Streatham*, *Trentham*, have <t>≡/t/ and <h>≡Ø rather than <th>≡/t/.

Palatalization with the suffixes <-ion>, <-ious> means that in an analysis of the surface correspondences <ti> may correspond to /ʃ/ or /ʧ/.

Distribution of <tt>

(For general rules of <C>-doubling (#D1 to #D11), see §3.2.2, pp. 114ff).

#D4 exceptions with final <tt> – *watt*, *boycott* (both derived from personal names); *butt*, *putt*, *matt* (competing in each case with higher-frequency *but*, *put*, *mat*); *mitt*, *mutt* (slang). *Net* in the sense 'final, remaining' as in *net profit*, has a variant *nett*. Final <-tt> is extremely common in names: in monosyllables – *Mott*, *Pitt*, *Platt*, *Pratt*, *Trott*, *Watt*, etc., before final <-s> – *Coutts*, *Kitts*, *Letts*, *Potts*, etc.; and in final unstressed syllables – *Bartlett*, *Blackett*, *Boycott*, *Cobbett*, *Elliott*, *Gauntlett*, *Hazlitt*, *Pigott*, *Westcott*, *Wyatt*, etc.

Examples of <tt> with prefixes – #D2 (reduced vowel): *attempt*, *attend*, *attach*, *attack*, *attain*, *attract*, *attire*, *attest*, *attrition*, *attenuate*, *attaint*, *attribute* (v.).

Examples of <tt> with prefixes – #D2 (unreduced vowel): *attitude*, *attribute* (n.), *attestation*.

The §Latinate {mit(t)} is usually stressed and either final as in *permit* (v.) or as the stressed penultimate syllable in *admittance, committal, committee, intermittent, transmitter, unremitting*, in which case the <C>-doubling is normal.

The suffix <-ette> with <C>-doubling is dealt with in §5.5, p. 429 under homophonous affixes and under doubling generally p. 130: *brunette*, *cassette*, *cigarette*, *gazette*, *kitchenette*, *roulette*, etc.

There is regular absence of <C>-doubling after a stressed short vowel before certain non-§Basic endings (see #D7, p. 123). This accounts for the single <t> before the ending in the following:

- <-ic(al)> (adj.) – *aesthetic, dramatic, erotic, erratic, exotic, fanatical, frenetic, idiotic, magnetic, narcotic, neurotic, operatic, pathetic, patriotic, rheumatic, sadistic, static, sympathetic, synthetic,* etc.;
- <-id> (adj.) – *carotid, caryatid, fetid*;
- <-ish> (not as a suffix) – *fetish.*

Exceptional spellings with double <-tt->: *battalion* (unless it is associated with *battle*), *rattan* (/rə'tæn/), and *tattoo* (/tə'tuː/). The last two have alternative pronunciations with a full /æ/, but the stress makes them exceptional. *Buttress* and *mattress* have <tt> before another consonant letter within the same morpheme.

Exceptional spellings with single <-t->: *atoll*, *atom*, *baton*, *city*, *matins*, *metal*, *paten*, *petal*, *pity*, *plateau*, *satin*. *Potash* is a compound, though this may not be apparent to those who use it as simply an alternative term to *potassium*. *Satyr*, with medial <y>≡/ɪ/, has no <C>-doubling because of the following <y> (#D11).

The Hanna (1966) spelling rules: <t> is the default spelling and:

1 <tt> after a short vowel and before syllabic /l/ (*battle*).

This <C>-doubling rule is inadequate.

3.3.6.4 /d/ *as in* dame

Distribution of variant spellings

/d/ has no real divergence: <d> 98 per cent; <dd> 2 per cent. The proportion of <dd> would be higher if we were to include the many inflected forms in {-ed} and {-ing}, such as *added, adding,* from *add,* or in {-er}, {-est}, such as *sadder, saddest* from *sad*. The letter <d> is also involved in the <dg>, <dge> and <dj> spellings of /ʤ/ (*lodging*, *bridge*, *adjutant*).

Elision of /d/ regularly occurs to simplify the medial cluster in *grandson*, *granddaughter*, *grandfather*, *grandpa*, etc., *handkerchief*, *handsome*, *landscape*, *sandwich*. In some of these the speller could retrieve the <d> from the meaning. In kinship terms containing {grand-}, the omission of the /d/ is so usual that *gran* and *granny* are the familiar forms of *grandma*, and *grandad* is not spelt *<granddad>.

Some §Exotic borrowings may have <dh>≡/d/ – *dhobi*, *dhoti*, *dhow*, *sandhi*, *Buddha*. An empty <b>≡Ø occurs alongside <d>≡/d/ in *bdellium*, *lambda*.

Distribution of <dd>

(For general rules of <C>-doubling (#D1 to #D11), see §3.2.2, pp.114ff.).

VC monosyllables with final <dd> by the 'short word rule' (p. 131): *add*, *odd*. An exception is the abbreviation *ad* for *advertisement* ('*small ads*').

Examples of <dd> with a prefix – #D2 (reduced vowel): *address*, *addicted*, *adduce*, etc.

Examples of <dd> with a prefix – #D2 (unreduced vowel): *addressee*, *addict* (n.), etc.

Doubled <dd> is relatively rare in single morpheme words such as *sudden*, *shudder*, *saddle*, *fodder*, etc. Most examples of <dd> are in derived words: *shredder*, *redden*, *goddess*, *muddy*, etc. Spellings in <-ddle> seem to have a pejorative sound-symbolism effect in about one third of such words: *addled*, *diddle*, *fiddle*, *fuddled*, *huddle*, *meddle*, *muddle*, *puddle*, *tiddly*, *toddle*, *twiddle*, *waddle* as against neutral words such as *middle*, *paddle*, *saddle*, etc.

In names final <-dd> occurs – *Budd*, *Dodd* (and *Dodds*), *Judd*, *Kidd*, *Lydd*, *Rudd*, *Todd*, etc.

There is regular absence of <C>-doubling after a stressed short vowel before certain non-§Basic suffixes (see #D7, p. 123). This accounts for the single <d> before the ending in the following:

- <-ic(al)> (adj.) – *episodic, melodic, methodic, nomadic, periodic, prosodic, spasmodic, sporadic*;
- <-it> (in §Latinate words) – *credit, edit;*
- <-ule> – *module, nodule, schedule.*

Exceptional spellings with single <-d->: *adage*, *adult*, *bodice*, *body*, *medal*, *model*, *modern*, *pedal*, *pedant*, *shadow*, *study*, *widow*. The nouns *produce* and *product* are not exceptional if the prefix boundary is identified (see #D4, p. 121).

The Hanna (1966) spelling rules: <d> is the default spelling and:

1 <dd> after a short vowel before syllabic /l/ (*paddle*).

This <C>-doubling rule is inadequate.

3.3.6.5 /k/ *as in* came

Distribution of variant spellings

/k/ is the most divergent of the consonants (table 35).

Table 35 Spellings of /k/

Spellings of /k/	*TF*	*LF*	
<c>	59 %	69 %	F-
<k>	21 %	10 %	F+
<ck>	6 %	5 %	
<ch>	2 %	3 %	
<cc>	1 %	1 %	
<x>≡/ks/	5 %	6 %	
<qu>≡/kw/	4 %	4 %	

'F-' : tends to occur in low frequency words; 'F+' : tends to occur in high frequency words

The above figures do not include the function words *can* and *could*, which if included would increase the proportion of <c> spellings by about 2 per cent. The letter <k> only serves in spellings of /k/; <c> serves in the <ch>and <tch> spellings of /ʧ/ and the <c>, <ce> spellings of /s/.

Distribution of <c>and <k>

Much of the divergence found in spellings of /k/ can be explained in terms of subsystems. The <k>≡/k/ spelling has a restricted distribution in terms of the following vowel and in some consonant clusters. It is quite clearly a §Basic, native spelling in *king*, *think*, *make*, and after <oo> in *book*, *look*. This means, effectively, that it is not a §Romance or §Latinate correspondence. It does, however, occur in some §Greek words (e.g. *krypton*, *kaleidoscope*), rather than the more common /k/≡<ch> (from Greek <χ>), and it also occurs in §Exotic words such as *amok*, *kapok*. The early spelling *kinema* has been replaced by *cinema* with /s/≡<c> under French influence, but the <k> remains in scientific terms such as *kinetic*.

Though the incidence of <k>, <c>, <ch> and some of the minority spellings is bound up with native, Romance or Greek origins and so explicable in terms of subsystems, we can also look for general constraints of context.

There is a common {voc} §Latinate element in *revocation*, *vocal*, *vocation*, *vociferous*. But since <c>≡/k/ cannot be used with <e>-marking, we cannot have *<revoce>, which would spell /-vəʊs/. Hence we have an anomalous <k> in an otherwise §Latinate word *revoke*.

Final <c> is almost entirely found in the suffix <-ic>. Other examples:

bloc (in the diplomatic sense), *disc*, *maniac*, *manioc*, *sac*, *talc* and abbreviations such as *choc*, *doc*. Some of these words, such as *sac*, are semantically specialized forms of words which otherwise have a <k> or <ck> spelling. *Arc* is §Latinate, from the same root (meaning 'bow') as *arch*, while *ark* is §Basic (from Old English); but there are no clues for the ordinary speller.

Final <k> is much more common and is usually found in monosyllabic words after <VV> or <C>: *break*, *brink*, *clank*, *croak*, *dunk*, *shank*, *shirk*, *shriek*, *skulk*, *task*, *took*, *walk*, *yolk*, etc. Polysyllabic words with final <k> are either quasi-compounds, such as *bobolink*, *chipmunk*, *honkytonk*, *tomahawk*; or are in some respects non-§Basic, as *kiosk, obelisk*.

Before /əl/ there is <k> only in disyllabic words: *ankle*, *crinkle*, *rankle*, *snorkle*, *sparkle*, *sprinkle*, *tinkle*, *twinkle*, *winkle*, *wrinkle*; *shekel*, *yokel*. These are all nouns or verbs. In the same context we find <c> in *circle*, *cycle*, *treacle*, *uncle*. In polysyllabic words (three or more syllables) we have largely the ending <-icle>, which in some instances may be identifiable as a diminutive noun suffix: *article*, *cubicle*, *chronicle*, *curricle*, *cuticle*, *follicle*, *icicle*, *radicle*, *testicle*, *ventricle*.

A <k> spelling seems at first sight to be largely conditioned by the following vowel, but the phonetic facts are untidy:

- —/aɪ/ – *kibosh*, *kind*, *kine*, *kite*, *skive*, *sky*; <c>≡/k/ does not occur before /aɪ/, only exceptionally in one pronunciation of *foci*, *menisci*;
- —/e/ – *kelp*, *ken*, *kennel*, *kept*, *kerosene*, *ketch*, *ketchup*, *kettle*, *skeleton*, *sketch*, *unkempt*;
- —/eɪ/ – *skein*; *kale*, *kapok*, *kaolin*, *okay*, *skate*; the latter are rare examples of <k> before <a>, where <c> is more usual (*cane*, *escape*);
- —/ɪ/ – *kidney*, *king*, *kiss*, *kitten* and in a few endings alternating with /ə/ such as <-et> in *basket*, *blanket*, *brisket*, *casket*, *gasket*, *junket*, *market*, *musket*, *trinket*, and <-ey> in *donkey*, *flunkey*, *malarkey*, *monkey*, *turkey*; <c>≡/k/ does not occur before /ɪ/; in *biscuit*, *circuit*, the /k/ is spelt <cu> (cf. <gu> marking the velar /g/ in *guinea*, and the <bu> of *build*, which has no marking function);
- —/iː/ – *keel*, *keen*, *keep*, *key*; *bikini*, *ketosis*, *kilo*, *kiosk*, *kiwi*, *leukaemia*, *nankeen*, *parakeet*, *ski*; <c>≡/k/ does not occur before /iː/;
- —/əʊ/ – *gingko*, *koala*, *kodak*, *kohl*, *kola, shako* are all §Exotic; <c>≡/k/ is the normal correspondence before /əʊ/ as in *coat, cone*;
- —/ɜː/ – *kerb*, *kerchief*, *kern*, *kernel*, *kersey*; *kirtle*, *skirl*, *skirmish*, *skirt*; <c>≡/k/ does occur before /ɜː/ but only with the spellings <ur> (*curb*, *curl*, *curlew*, *curtain*, *curve*, etc.), or <our> (*courtesy*, *scourge*), and in the nonce spelling *colonel*;
- —/ʌ/ – the only <k> spellings are in the cluster <sk> – *skulk*, *skull*, *skunk*; in place-names the <sk> spelling usually indicates a Scandinavian origin, but of these three words only *skulk* is so; in present English they are clearly exceptional and <sc> is the norm: *scud*, *scuffle*, *scull*, *sculptor*, etc.

<c>≡/k/ occurs unusually before /e/ in *Celts, Celtic*; these are pronounced with a regular <c>≡/s/ in Scotland, as in the Scottish football team *Celtic*. The regular spelling *Kelts, Keltic*, is also used by historians.

It is clear that the incidence of <k> can be more directly explained in terms of the following letter than in terms of the following sound: <k>≡/k/ normally occurs before <i> and <e>, where <c>≡/k/ does not occur. It is a matter of letter sequencing, or graphotactics. One should not draw false conclusions from this about the relative importance of the phonetic and graphic sides of correspondences. It simply reflects the underdifferentiation of English vowel phonemes by the Roman alphabet. If we took whole spellings into consideration rather than the first letter of the spelling, the range of contexts is then wider graphically than it is phonetically: <e>, <ey>, <ei>, <ee>, <er>, <i>, <i..e>, <ir>.

There are also restrictions on <k>≡/k/ in consonant clustering within a minimal free-form. Only <scr> is found in non-names – *scrap*, *screw*, *script*, *scroll*, *scruple*, etc.; an occasional <skr> occurs in names – *Skrimshaw*, *Skrine*. <sc> and <sk> are largely conditioned by the following vowel letter – *alfresco*, *biscuit*, *descant*, *escalate*, *fiasco*, *masculine*, *rascal*, *rescue*, *scaffold*, *scale*, *scar*, *telescope*, etc. and *askew*, *basket*, *brisket*, *casket*, *dusky*, *gasket*, *musket*, *whisker*, *whisky*, etc. Exceptions are *askance*, *sceptic* (AmE spelling *skeptic*). The clusters /kl/ and /kr/ are normally <cl> and <cr> (*clean*, *cream*) with only occasional §Exotic or §Greek exceptions – *klaxon*, *kleptomania*, *krypton*.

Whether a <k> or <c> occurs as /k/ in medial consonant-letter clusters is still largely a function of the following vowel. We have medial /lk/ as <lc> in *alcohol*, *alcove*, *balcony*, *calculate*, *falcon*, *talcum*, *volcano*, and as <lk> in *welkin*. Exceptions are *alkali*, *polka*. Similarly we have <rc> in *arcade*, *barcarole*, *circus*, *circuit*, *mercantile*, *mercury*, *narcotic*, *porcupine*, *tuberculosis*, and <rk> in *gherkin*, *jerkin*, *jerky*, *turkey*. An §Exotic exception is *mazurka*.

Both <k> and <c> occur after /ŋ/, but in very different sets of words. <k> occurs in monosyllabic words – *bank*, *drink*, *honk*, *mink*, *monk*, *plonk*, *swank*, *think*, etc.; the only <c> examples in the database were *franc* and *zinc*. The relatively few disyllabic morphemes with <k> after /ŋ/ have §Basic endings and initial stress: *blanket*, *canker*, *flunkey*, *hanker*, *monkey*, *tinkle*, *trinket*, *winkle*, *wonky*, etc. <c> occurs in words with §Latinate affixes: *distinct*, *function*, *punctual*, *sanctity*, *tincture*, *unctuous*, etc. The only other polysyllabic words which have <c> are *blanco*, *bronco*, *carbuncle* and *uncle*. The two sets of words, those with <nk> and those with <nc>, may well have a distinct profile for the speller, but to set down explicitly what the phonological and morphological features of each set are would make for a very complex 'rule'.

In clusterings with consonants other than /ŋ/, <k> is decidedly §Exotic – *klaxon*, *kleptomaniac*; *blitzkrieg*, *okra*, *sauerkraut*; *plankton*, *tektite*. The

<cl>, <cr>, <ct> clusters are the usual spellings, as in *cloud*, *crowd*, *elect*.

There are also a few morphemes in which <k> occurs before a vowel letter other than <i/y> or <e> – *askance*, *hokum* (cf. *locum*), *kaolin*, *kale*, *kangaroo*, *kapok*, *kappa*, *kaput*, *leukaemia*, *okay*, *paprika*, *skate*, *skulk*, *skull*, *skunk*, *ukulele*. The spelling *oakum* looks more native, as indeed it is, than the contrived word *hokum*, by having the §Basic correspondence <oa>≡/əʊ/.

Distribution of <q>

The phoneme string /kw/ is usually spelt <qu> in both §Basic words (*quake*, *queen*, *quick*, *squint*, etc.) and in §Latinate words (*adequate*, *colloquial*, *consequent*, *equestrian*, *sequester*, etc.). In some contexts a former /kw/ has been pared down to /k/, so we have the correspondence <qu>≡/k/. The same correspondence also occurs in French loans, where <qu>≡/k/ is necessary before <i> or <e>, since <ci> or <ce> would be spellings of /s/. Examples of <qu>≡/k/ – *bouquet*, *communique*, *conquer* (but there is <qu>≡/kw/ in *conquest*), *croquet*, *exchequer*, *liqueur*, *liquor*, *mannequin*, *marquee*, *marquetry*, *masquerade*, *mosquito*, *palanquin*, *parquet*, *piquant*, *piquet*, *quoits*, *sobriquet*, *tourniquet* and words ending in <-ette>: *coquette*, *croquette*, *etiquette*; *mannequin*, *quoits*, may also be pronounced with /kw/.

As final <-que>≡/k/ this spelling also occurs in *baroque*, *barque*, *bisque*, *brusque*, *casque*, *catafalque*, *cheque*, *cirque*, *clique*, *marque*, *masque*, *opaque*, *peruque*, *pique*, *plaque*, *toque*, *torque*; *antique*, *boutique*, *critique*, *mystique*, *oblique*, *physique*, *technique*, *unique*; *arabesque*, *burlesque*, *grotesque*, *painteresque*, *picturesque*, *statuesque*. The stressed endings <-ique> and <-esque> are easily identified.

The only exceptions to the <qu> spelling of /kw/ are found in recent French loans: *coiffure*, *cuisine*. In native *awkward* we must assume that /wəd/ is a separable element. The letter <q> may occur without its <u> as <q>≡/k/ in Arabic names such as *Qatar, Iraq*. It is interesting that the acronym of the Australian airline *QANTAS* is pronounced with /kw/.

Distribution of <ch>

The <ch> spelling of /k/ is restricted almost entirely to §Greek words: *archaeology*, *archaism*, *archangel*, *architect*, *archive*, *bronchial*, *catechism*, *chaos*, *character*, *charisma*, *chasm*, *chemist*, *chiropody*, *chlorine*, *choir*, *cholesterol, chord*, *chorus*, *christian*, *chromium*, *chronic*, *cochlea*, *echo*, *epoch*, *eunuch*, *hierarchy*, *lichen*, *malachite*, *matriarch*, *mechanic*, *monarch*, *ochre*, *oligarch*, *orchestra*, *orchid*, *pachyderm*, *patriarch*, *psyche*, *schematic*, *stochastic*, *stomach*, *strychnine*, *technical*, *trachea*, *triptych*, etc. This is by no means a complete list, but it serves to show the problems of using subsystems in deterministic procedures. Some words with <ch>≡/k/ have been in common use in English for centuries (*anchor*, *school*) and came by way of Latin rather than directly from Greek. *Lachrymose* and *sepulchre* are strictly Latin in origin, but were mistakenly thought in antiquity to have a Greek connection. Many words with <ch>≡/k/ are highly technical complex words used by scientists for whom the constituent §Greek morphemes, such as {pachy} or {derm}, have a separate semantic identity. In some cases the Greek meanings are irrelevant to the technical use of the words since they involve obscure metaphors. One does not normally need to know that orchids have anything to do with testicles – it's actually the shape of the roots. There appear to be no explicit phonological markers of §Greek-ness in the words listed above. The morphological criterion of word-formation potential is the best marker, but this works best with the technical end of the range. We can hardly cue the <ch> in *school* by calling up *scholastic*.

One or two non-§Greek words have <ch>≡/k/: *ache*, *cinchona*, *loch*, *masochism*. The verb and the noun now spelt <ache> did not develop like other pairs that had an underlying //k//, such as *bake–batch, speak–speech, wake–watch.* The two merged in an odd compromise: we have the verb pronunciation with /k/ and a noun spelling meant for a vanished /ʧ/. There is every reason for undoing this and spelling *ache* as *<ake>. The derived noun is no problem: cf. *the wake, the *ake.*

The spelling of /ks/

The phoneme string /ks/ within a morpheme is usually spelt as <x> in §Basic, §Latinate and §Greek words:

(§Basic) – *axe*, *axle*, *ox*, *six*, *vixen*, etc.;
(§Latinate) – *extract*, *influx*, *laxative*, *maximal*, *reflex*, etc.;
(§Greek) – *climax*, *lexicon*, *orthodox*, *oxygen*, *pharynx*, *thorax*, etc.

The ending <-ics> in *physics*, *heroics*, etc. contains a morpheme boundary, as of course do words such as *frolicsome*. Whole-word recognition may prevent *ecstasy* from being misspelt *<extasy>; we can hardly expect a boundary to be noticed. The same is true of *tocsin* ('alarm') and *toxin* ('poison').

Where //s// has been palatalized after /k/, the correspondence <x>≡/kʃ/ has arisen, as in *flexure*, *luxury* and similarly <xi>≡/kʃ/ in *complexion*, *connexion* (or <-cti>), *crucifixion*, *fluxion*, *noxious*.

Spellers must also be aware of the <cc>≡/ks/ spelling. This occurs largely in §Latinate prefixes:

(reduced vowel) – *accelerate*, *accentuate*, *accept*; *eccentric*; *succeed*, *success*, *succinct*;
(unreduced vowel) – *access*, *accident*; *occident*.

At an abstract level, this is exactly like the <-pp->, <-tt->, <-rr->, <-gg-> of *support*, *attend*, *irresolute*, *aggressive*, but the underlying //k// has become /s/ before the following close or mid front vowel. Compare the alternation in *electric–electricity*. The <cc> continues to represent two phonetic segments, but this is not so for <-pp-> etc. The correspondence <cc>≡/ks/ is also found in or or two stems: *flaccid*, *vaccine*. The nonce spelling *eczema* /ˈeksɪmə/ is irregular from the point of view of present English, though it accurately reflects the etymology. It comes from the §Greek prefix /ek-/+/z-/, which assimilated to /eks/. A further complication in the spelling of /ks/ is due to the reduction of /eks/ + /s-/ giving <xc>≡/ks/: *exceed*, *excel*, *except*, *excerpt*, *excess*, *excise*, *excite*. Since there is no geminated /-ss-/ in these words, spelling errors such as *<exerpt> are very likely.

There are various other minor spellings of /k/:

- <kh> – *astrakhan*, *gymkhana*, *khaki*, and scarcely assimilated *khan*, *khedive*;
- <cqu> – *lacquer*.

Distribution of <ck>, <cc> and <kk>

(For general rules of <C>-doubling (#D1 to #D11), see §3.2.2, pp. 114ff.).

<C>-doubling with /k/ takes the form <ck> in §Basic words. Since <ck> is not a §Romance spelling, there is for once a clear difference in spelling between <C>-doubling to mark a previous short vowel and the <C>-doubling associated with the §Latinate prefixes. These have <cc> or, before /w/, <cq>.

Examples of <cc> and <cq> with prefixes:

- (reduced vowel) – *acclaim*, *acclimatize*, *acclivity*, *accommodate*, *accompany*, *accomplice*, *accomplish*, *accord*, *accost*, *account*, *accredit*, *accretion*, *accrue*, *acculturate*, *accumulate*, *accursed*, *accuse*, *accustom*; *occasion*, *occlusive*, *occur*; *succumb*; *acquaint*, *acquiesce*, *acquire*, *acquit*;
- (unreduced vowel) – *acclamation*, *accolade*, *accurate*, *accusation*; *occult*, *occupy*; *succour*, *succulent*.

There are, however, some instances of <cc> in stems after a short (or reduced) vowel. These come from a variety of sources: Latin (directly), Italian and from various exotic languages, often at second or third hand. From the point of view of the English writing system it is of no relevance that the name of a popular houseplant, the *yucca*, was borrowed at a long remove from the Carib Indians. What is of interest is that, if this word is considered in some way to be exotic, one would hardly expect a spelling *<yucker> and might then take <cc> as the exotic alternative. The snag is that what begins as exotic may become a part of daily life. Tobacco and potatoes are as basic as bread nowadays. The word *tobacco* has no markers of its exotic origin; phonologically /tə'bækəʊ/ is no different from, say, /tə'mɒrəʊ/. So, if we take a list of words with <cc>, we cannot expect associative markers of exoticness for all of them: *broccoli*, *buccaneer*, *coccus*, *coccyx*, *desiccate*, *ecclesiastic*, *felucca*, *flocculate*, *hiccough*, *mecca*, *meccano*, *moccasin*, *peccadillo*, *peccary*, *piccaninny*, *piccolo*, *staccato*, *streptococci*, *stucco*, *tobacco*, *toccata*, *yucca*. On the other hand *gecko*, which is undoubtedly exotic, has <ck>. In *bacchanal*, *saccharine*, *zucchini*, we presumably have <cch>≡/k/, since no purpose is served by regarding the <h> or the first <c> as an empty letter. The <cc> spelling does not occur in word-final position.

The most interesting word with <cc> is *soccer*, an abbreviation derived from 'association football'. The slang abbreviation *revving*, from 'revolutions', involves a similar exception to the normal conventions for <C>-doubling. There is, however, no <C>-doubling in *chocs* (from *chocolates*) and it is a matter of speculation how /'ʧɒkɪz/ might be spelt: *chockies*, or *choccies*. Since single <c> would never represent /s/ finally in a monosyllabic word, *<chocies> might well be a viable spelling. The diminutive of *biscuit* is usually spelt *biccy*.

An exceptional <kk> occurs in names – *Akkad*, *Dekker*, *Habakkuk*, *Rikkitikitavi*, *Sikkim* – quite a mixed bag. It also occurs in inflected forms of *trek*: *trekked*, *trekker*, *trekking*. An exceptional form of <C>-doubling with <cqu> is also found in *lacquer*, *picquet*, *racquet*.

Examples of regular <C>-doubling (#D5): *beckon*, *block*, *chicken*, *freckle*, *neck*, *quack*, *shackle*, *slick*, *sprocket*, etc.

Pickerel, meaning a young pike, has had third-syllable shortening in the stem. <C>-doubling would not normally occur in such a three-syllable word (#D6 p. 123).

The native English diminutive suffix {-ock}, like {-ness} has <C>-doubling even though the vowel is always /ə/: *bollock*, *bullock*, *buttock*, *hillock*. The <-ock> spelling is also found in disyllabic words where the ending <-ock> is not always identifiable as a suffix: *bannock*, *cassock*, *haddock*, *hammock*, *hassock*, *hummock*, *mattock*, *paddock*, *pollock*, *tussock*. In several of these words the etymology turns out, however, not to be native.

Other instances of <C>-doubling in unstressed and indeed unstressable syllables: *barrack*, *derrick*, *gimmick*, *limerick*, *maverick*, *niblick*.

Words with single <c> after an unreduced short vowel are: *ducat*, *jocund*, *maniac*.

Words with single <k> after an unreduced short vowel are: *amok*, *kapok*, *kodak*, *trek*, *yak*, *yashmak*.

Quasi-compounds with an element containing <ck> include *bailiwick*, *buckaroo*, *buckshee*, *burdock*, *chickadee*, *cockatoo*, *cockatrice*, *fetlock*, *haversack*, *hemlock*, *hollyhock*, *jackanapes*, *lackadaisical*, *ramshackle*, *ransack*, *rowlock*, *shamrock*, *wedlock*.

Exceptional <C>-doubling in antepenultimate syllables of simple words (see #D6 p. 123): *hickory*, *mackerel* (cf. *cockerel*, which is complex), *mackintosh* (derived from a name; interestingly abbreviated to *mac*). Some words such as *mackerel*, which appear from the spelling to have three syllables, are effectively disyllabic (/ˈmækrəl/).

The <ck> of *hackney, cockney* and *huckster*, violates the condition to #D3 (see pp. 120f.) that doubling does not normally occur before a consonant letter other than <l>. The first two are derived from names; cf. *Beckton, Bicknell, Bruckner, Flecknoe, Hucknall, Icknield*, etc. *Huckster* derives from {hawk (v.)}+{-ster}.

<C>-doubling occurs when the suffixes <-y>, <-ed>, <-ing> are added to any form ending in <-ic>, presumably to prevent confusion with <c>≡/s/: *colicky*, *finicky*, *panicky*, *picnicking*, *rheumaticky*, *trafficking*. This is a morpheme boundary problem: *<paniced> rather than *panicked*, could so easily be misread as 'pan-iced' */ˈpænaɪst/. The suffix <-ic> was often spelt <-ick> before the nineteenth century. The Church of England's 1662 *Book of Common Prayer* has 'one Catholick and Apostolick Church'. The present <-ic> spelling marks such words as §Greek. *Bivouac* also has doubled <ck> in *bivouacked, bivouacking*. Words which end in a consonant letter plus <-c>≡/k/, such as *arc*, *zinc, talc*, have variation before §Basic suffixes both in British and American spelling, as in *arced, arcked, arcing, arcking* and similarly *talcy*, *talcky*, *zinced, zincked, zincy, zincky* (and even *zinky*).

The Hanna (1966) spelling rules treat /k/, /ks/ and /kw/ as separate units though all three could easily be accommodated under a single /k/. Hanna's rules (for '/K/'):

<c> is the default spelling and:

1 <k> after /ŋ/ (*sink*);
2 <ck> before syllabic /l/ (*tackle*);
3 <k> syllable-initial before /iː, ɪ, aɪ, e/ (*keep, kill, kite, kettle*);
4 <k> syllable-final after /ʊ/ and //r// (*look, fork)*;
5 <x> syllable-final accented followed by /s/ (*box*);
6 <ck> word-final accented after a short vowel (*tack*);
7 <k> word-final accented all other cases (*take*).

Hanna's rules for ('/KS/'):
<x> is the default spelling (duplicating one of the rules for /k/) and:
1 <cs> syllable-final unaccented after /ɪ/ (*hysterics*) – this rule virtually specifies a particular suffix.
Hanna's rules (for '/KW/'):
<qu> is the default spelling.

3.3.6.6 /g/ *as in* game

Distribution of variant spellings

/g/ shows very little divergence in itself (table 36), but the letter <g> plays an important part in the spelling of /ʤ/ and /ʒ/ and in a few very minor correspondences.

Table 36 Spellings of /g/

spellings of /g/	*TF*	*LF*	
<g>	92 %	86 %	
<gg>	2 %	6 %	F-
<gu>	3 %	4 %	
<gh>	<1 %	<1 %	
/gz/≡<x>	4 %	4 %	

'F-' : tends to occur in low frequency words

The proportion of <gg> would be higher if we were to include the many inflected forms in {-ed} and {-ing}, such as *bagged, bagging,* from *bag,* or in {-er}, {-est}, such as *bigger, biggest*, from *big*. The <gh>≡/g/ spelling is found in a few exotic loan-words and a couple of native Germanic words: *aghast*, *burgher*, *dinghy*, *ghastly*, *ghat*, *ghee*, *gherkin*, *ghetto*, *ghost*, *ghoul*, *sorghum*, *spaghetti*, *yoghurt*. In earlier centuries *ghost* and *-ghast-* were frequently spelt just with <g>. The survival of the <gh> spelling in these two words may be more than just loyalty to Caxton, who seems to have brought the <gh> with him when he came from the Netherlands, where it was used to represent a velar fricative (Jespersen 1909: 2.314). The association with the supernatural was reinforced by *ghoul*, an eighteenth century Arabic borrowing.

The <gu> spelling is a device to prevent confusion between /g/≡<g> and /ʤ/≡<g>. Its use is fairly restricted. In final position we have <gue> in: *catalogue*, *colleague*, *demagogue*, *dialogue*, *fatigue*, *fugue*, *intrigue*, *league*, *monologue*, *morgue*, *plague*, *prorogue*, *rogue*, *synagogue*, *vague*, *vogue*. In initial position we have <gu> in: *guarantee*, *guard*, *guess*, *guest*, *guide*, *guild*, *guilder*, *guile*, *guillemot*, *guillotine*, *guilt*, *guinea*, *guise*, *guitar*, *guy*. The letter <u> is here used as a kind of buffer to show that we have a velar ('hard') /g/ rather than a palato-alveolar ('soft') /ʤ/ before the letters <i/y> and <e> representing an original front vowel or, in the case of final <e>, a long-vowel marker (cf. *vague–wage*). The use of <gu> in the present spelling system is far from consistent. It is redundant in words such as *guard* (before a back vowel) and *demagogue* (finally after a short vowel), where *<gard> and *<demagog> would be perfectly explicit. Moreover there are quite a few words in which /g/≡<g> occurs before <i/y> and <e> without the benefit of the <u>: *begin*, *bogy*, *boogie*, *fogy*, *fungi* (/-giː/ or /-gaɪ/), *gear*, *gecko*, *geese*, *geezer*, *gelding*, *gestapo*, *get*, *geyser*, *gibbon*, *giddy*, *gift*, *giggle*, *gild*, *gill* ('of fish'), *gillie*, *gilt*, *gimlet*, *gimmick*, *git*, *give*, *hegemony*, *target*, *together*, *yogi*. There are homophones: *guild*, *gild*; *guilt*, *gilt*. Jespersen (1909: 2.313) has a convincing explanation of why some of these words did not acquire <gu>: it would have been inappropriate for other forms of the word with a different vowel such as *got–get*, *gave–give*, *began–begin*. The spelling difference **beguin–began* would be too great, while **beguin–*beguan* would have little to recommend it.

All one can profitably say about the words with <gu> in present-day English is that they largely represent a French spelling convention designed to differentiate French /g/ and /ʒ/ before front vowels. Albrow (1972: 38) puts <gu>≡/g/ into his system 2. Some of the words, however, are actually Germanic in origin: *guess*, *guest*, *guild*, *guilt*, and the group as a whole shows surprisingly few §Romance features, either phonological or morphological. The <gu> of *demagogue, pedagogue, monologue, synagogue,* remains before the suffix <-ery> *demagoguery*, preserving the /g/. Before suffixes beginning with /ɪ/, the <u> is lost and the pronunciation is usually with /ʤ/ in *monologist* /mə'nɒləʤɪst/, *pedagogic*. It varies between /g/ and /ʤ/ with the suffix <-y> as in *pedagogy*. The simplified spelling <-og> is mainly found in *monolog*.

The <x>≡/gz/ correspondence rather than the more common <x>≡/ks/ occurs after a vowel or voiced consonant in a weakly-stressed syllable before a stress – *Alexander*, *anxiety*, *auxiliary*, *exaggerate*, *exalted*, *examiner*, *exasperated*, *executor* (cf. <x>≡/ks/ in *execute*), *exemplary*, *exempt*, *exhaust*, *exhilarating*, *exist*, *exonerate*, *exuberant*, etc.

Distribution of <gg>

(For general rules of <C>-doubling (#D1 to #D11), see §3.2.2, pp. 114ff.)

Because /g/ does not normally have <C>-doubling in final position (#D4), the percentage of <gg> spellings is relatively low. Final <-gg> does occur in names – *Askrigg*, *Bragg*, *Brigg* (and *Briggs*), *Brownrigg*, *Clegg*, *Cragg*, *Fogg*, *Gregg*, *Grigg*, *Hogg*, *Kellogg*, *Sprigg*, *Twigg*, etc. Final <-gge> is also quite common; the final <-e> is not, however, a marker of palatalization to /ʤ/ – *Bigge*, *Fagge*, *Legge*, *Pegge*, *Snagge*.

VC monosyllable with final <-gg> by the 'short word rule' (p. 131): *egg*.

Examples of <gg> with prefixes – #D2 (see p. 119):

- (reduced vowel) – *agglomeration*, *agglutination*, *aggrandizement*, *aggressive*, *aggrieved*;
- (unreduced vowel) – *aggravate*, *aggregate*.
- (quasi-compounds) – *juggernaut*, *skullduggery*.

Exceptional spellings with single <-g-> – *dragon*, *flagon*; *agate*, *frigate*, *legate*; *legume*; *figure*; *rigour*, *vigour*; *brigand*; *bigot*, *spigot* (cf. *maggot*); *sugar*. *Faggot* and *waggon* have variants *fagot*, *wagon*.

The Hanna (1966) spelling rules: <g> is the default spelling and:

1 <gg> before syllabic /l/ (*giggle*);
2 <x> before /z/ (*exact*).

These do not cope with <gu> or most <gg> spellings.
Prefix merger, as in *aggressive, aggrieved*, could have been dealt with by affix-stripping. <C>-doubling after short vowels could be done by a more general rule.

3.3.6.7 /ʧ/ as in chest

Distribution of variant spellings

/ʧ/ shows some divergence, but it is more apparent than real. The default spelling is <ch> (TF 65 per cent, LF 62 per cent); its doubled form is <tch> (TF 10 per cent, LF 12 per cent). Although the doubled spelling <tch> is unique to /ʧ/, <ch> is very divergent since it frequently represents /k/ and /ʃ/. The palatalization spelling <ti> (*question*) may also represent /ʃ/ (*dictation*, *conscientious*, etc.).

Distribution of <tch>

(For general rules of <C>-doubling (#D1 to #D11), see §3.2.2, pp. 114ff.).

The letter-name *aitch* is one of the few exceptions to the rule that long vowels do not precede <C>-doubling (#D1). There is no <C>-doubling in *bachelor*, *cochineal* and *treachery*, but this can be considered regular (#D6) since these are minimal free-forms. Exceptional spellings without <C>-doubling are: *attach*, *duchess*, *duchy*, *lecher*, *macho*, *much*, *rich*. Of these, the <duch-> allomorph shows shortening compared with *duke*, but that scarcely helps.

Other spellings of /ʧ/

Almost all the remaining spellings (TF 25 per cent, LF 26 per cent) reflect palatalization of an original /t/ before /i/ or /j(uː)/ with various endings:

- <-ion> – *combustion*, *exhaustion*, *question*, *suggestion*, etc.;
- <-ue> – *statue, virtue*;
- <-ure> – *departure*, *fixture*, *furniture*, *structure*, etc.;
- <-ual> – *factual*, *mutual*, *ritual*, *virtual*, etc.;
- <-uous> – *virtuous*, *voluptuous*;
- <-ury> – *century*;
- <-uate> – *perpetuate.*

The minority spelling /ʧ/≡<c> is found in *cello* and *concerto*, which are well-established loan-words from Italian, and in very marginal borrowings such as *cicerone* as /ʧɪʧə'rəʊnɪ/ rather than /sɪsə'r../.

In the Hanna (1966) spelling rules the default spelling is <ch> and:

1 <t> syllable-initial unaccented before /juː/ (*actual, culture*);
2 <ti> syllable-initial unaccented before /ə/ (*suggestion*);
3 <t> syllable-final before /juː/ (*fatuous*);
4 <tch> syllable-final after a short vowel (*ratchet*).

The first of these rules relies on an unreduced /juː/.

3.3.6.8 /ʤ/ *as in* jest

Distribution of variant spellings

The letter <j> is in many ways rather a peculiar spelling. It is not in origin a separate letter of the Roman alphabet but was simply a cursive variant of <i> until the seventeenth century, when the two letters began to take on different functions. The words in which <j> occurs are, therefore, rather a mixed group. Those words which do not share the §Latinate suffixes or other §Romance markers go by default into the §Basic system. They tend to have word-initial <j>. In spite of their various and usually obscure origins they include many very common words: *jaw*, *job*, *jar*, *jug*, etc., which show no peculiarities not shared by the Germanic word stock. §Romance words containing <j> (for Latin <i>) include some very common Latin roots: <jac>, <ject>, <judic>, <junc>, <jur>, <juv>, <maj>, which recur in a great many derived forms (*ejaculate*, *inject*, *judicial*, *conjunction*, *perjury*, *rejuvenate*, *majesty*, *major*, *majority*, etc.). Medial <j>≡/ʤ/ otherwise occurs only in a small group of words, some vaguely §Romance, some distinctly §Exotic – *cajole*, *enjoy*, *marjoram*, *sojourn*; *banjo*, *jujitsu*, *juju*, *pyjamas*, *rajah*. Though people very clearly regard <j> as the default spelling of /ʤ/, it only accounts for TF 29 per cent (LF 22 per cent) of instances. <g>, either alone or as <ge> accounts for TF 61 per cent (LF 70 per cent) of the other spellings of /ʤ/. These figures include /ʤ/ in the very common suffix <-age>, which alone accounts for TF 10 per cent (LF 10 per cent) of the instances of /ʤ/.

If we look at word-initial /ʤ/ we find the proportion of <j> to <g> is rather different. This context accounts for TF 29 per cent, LF 22 per cent of /ʤ/. Of these, <j> represents TF 73 per cent, LF 62 per cent, and <g> represents TF 27 per cent, LF 38 per cent. These figures also indicate that <j> tends to occur in words of higher frequency than <g> (as a spelling of /ʤ/). The correspondence /ʤ/≡<g> clearly belongs to the §Romance system. Albrow (1972: 11, 38) compares /g/≡<g> in *get* with /ʤ/≡<g> in *gem*, as representing systems 1 and 2 respectively.

Some speakers have final /ʤ/ rather than /ʧ/ in *sandwich* and *spinach*; these are the only examples of /ʤ/≡<ch>.

Palatalization gives /ʤ/≡<di> only in *soldier*. The correspondences /ʤ/≡<dj> (TF <1 per cent, LF 2 per cent) only occurs in §Romance and §Latinate words with the prefix {ad-}:

- (unreduced vowel) – *adjective*, *adjutant*, *adjunct*, *coadjutor*, *adjuration*;
- (reduced vowel) – *adjust*, *adjudge*, *adjoin*, *adjacent*, *adjourn*, *adjudicate*.

The correspondence /ʤ/≡<gg> only occurs in two very common words *suggest* and *exaggerate* and some marginal Italian loan-words such as *loggia* and *arpeggio*.

Distribution of <dg(e)>

(For general rules of <C>-doubling (#D1 to #D11), see §3.2.2, pp. 114ff.).

Only a relatively small proportion of words with /ʤ/ show <C>-doubling (TF 5 per cent, LF 5 per cent). The doubled representation of /ʤ/ is <dg(e)> (Albrow 1972: 21), cf. *cage–cadge*. The <C>-doubling occurs after five of the six short vowels; /ʤ/ is not found after /ʊ/:

- /ɪ/ – *bridge*, *fridge*, *midget*, *ridge*, *widgeon*, etc.;
- /e/ – *dredge*, *edge*, *hedge*, *ledger*, *pledge*, etc.;
- /æ/ – *badge*, *badger, cadge*, *gadget*; etc.;
- /ʌ/ – *budgie*, *cudgel*, *grudge*, *judge*, *trudge*, etc.;
- /ɒ/ – *dodge*, *lodge*, *lodger, splodge*, *stodgy*, etc.

Exceptions with no <C>-doubling: *agile*, *digit*, *fragile*, *imagine*, *pageant*, *pigeon*, *vigil*, some of which are marked as non-§Basic (*digital*, *fragility*, *imagination*). Regular absence of <C>-doubling (#D7) before <-ic(al)>: *biological, geological, magic*, *logical*, *tragic*.

The Hanna (1966) spelling rules are:

1 <j> syllable-initial before /eɪ, æ, əʊ, ɔː, ɒ, ɜː, ʌ, ɔɪ, aʊ/ (*jail, ejaculate, jovial, jaw, majority, sojourn, jungle, rejoice, jowl*);
2 <g> syllable-initial all other cases (*giant, gypsum*);
3 <d> before /juː/ (*arduous, verdure*);
4 <dge> word-final accented after a short vowel (*badge*);
5 <ge> word-final all other cases (*village, hinge*);
6 <g> syllable-final (*imagine, digit*).

3.3.7 Fricative consonants: /f v θ ð s z ʃ ʒ h /

3.3.7.1 /f/ *as in* ferry

Distribution of variant spellings

/f/ has very little divergence if /f/≡<ph> is regarded as regular within a §Greek subsystem (table 37).

Table 37 Spellings of /f/

spellings of /f/	*TF*	*LF*	
<f>	84 %	77 %	
<ff>	4 %	14 %	F-
<ph>	11 %	8 %	
<gh>	2 %	<1 %	F+

‘F-’ : tends to occur in low frequency words; ‘F+’ : tends to occur in high frequency words

The unit spellings <f>, <ff> and <ph> are all unique to /f/ in lexical morphemes. This excludes <f>≡/v/ in *of* and <ph> at boundaries, as in *haphazard* and *shepherd*, where admittedly the boundaries are rather opaque.

The <gh> spelling is found in a few very common words after /ʌ, ɒ, ɑː/: *enough*, *rough*, *tough*; *cough*, *trough*; *draught*, *laugh*. The earlier Germanic velar fricative which prompted the <gh> spelling seems to have become a labio-dental fricative in an acoustic reinterpretation rather than in an articulatory drift from the back of the mouth to the very front. /f/≡<gh> is therefore a highly inappropriate spelling from a phonetic point of view; nor can it find much support from a wish to preserve the etymology. The spelling <gh> is not even peculiar to /f/, since, apart from initial <gh>≡/g/ (*ghost*), <gh> forms part of complex vowel spellings (/ɔː/ in *caught*, /əʊ/ in *though*, /aʊ/ in *plough*). Clearly the spellings of these words can only be acquired by rote learning. Needless to say they are high on the hit-list of all spelling reformers. If there were a citation rating for irregular spellings, the /f/≡<gh> correspondence would outstrip all others in notoriety.

In dealing with <ph>, we need to look briefly at its origin in Roman orthography. The digraph spelling <ph>≡/f/ is found in words borrowed from Greek, either directly or indirectly through Latin. The Romans themselves used <ph> from the second century BC as a spelling of Greek /p^{h}/≡<ϕ> an aspirated plosive, later a fricative, that contrasted with unaspirated /p/≡<π> (Allen 1978: 26). The point of this little digression is that the Romans did not merge Greek /p^{h}/≡<ϕ> with their own /f/≡<f> (*facio*, *flumen*, etc.), so the two different spellings <ph> and <f> were institutionalized in written Latin and preserved the etymology of the words.

If we know a word to be of Greek origin, then we can use the spelling <ph> with confidence. The most usable markers of §Greek words (see §2.9.2 p. 101) are a number of common elements: {anthrop}, {apo}, {dia}, {epi}, {geo}, {graph}, {oid}, {ortho}, {phil}, {phon}, {photo}, {phys}, {soph}, {syn}, {tele}, etc. Given one of these elements in a word, we can use the correspondence /f/≡<ph>: *apocrypha*, *diaphragm*, *epitaph*, etc. The only basis for literacy in technical and learned vocabulary is to recognize a §Greek subsystem on the basis of such markers. However, there are occasional snags. Scientific terminology often blends Latin and Greek, so one may find a §Greek affix attached to a §Latinate stem to give a spelling such as *fucoid*, where, given {oid}, one would expect **phucoid*. Such cases are obviously rare and only affect a few technical users.

A reformer who wished to reduce plurality of symbolization at any price would obviously wish to respell <ph> as <f>. This would not, as we have seen, result in any loss of contrast within the §Greek word stock. It would, however, remove a common orthographic marker of Greek-based words. The advantages of having such a marker are difficult to assess, but they should not be dismissed lightly.

The spelling <pph> in *sapphire* is irregular; the first <p> is best regarded as an empty letter. Similarly the <h> in *shepherd*, a hoary old example in the spelling literature, should be regarded as an inert letter in an unstressed {herd}. The string <ph> is not a unit in *shepherd* and should not be cited as an example of plurality of correspondence along with <ph>≡/f/.

Distribution of <ff>

(For general rules of <C>-doubling (#D1 to #D11), see §3.2.2, pp. 114ff.)
The double <ff> is essential to distinguish *off* with /f/ from *of* with /v/. As a function word, *of* does not require a minimum of three letters (the 'short word rule', p.131).

Examples of <ff> with prefixes – #D2:

- (reduced vowel) – *affair*, *affect*, *affection*, *affiance*, *affirm*, *affix* (v.), *afflict*, *afford*, *affray*, *affright*, *diffuse*, *efface*, *effect*, *effeminate*, *effete*, *efficient*, *effrontery*, *effulgent*, *effusive*, *offend*, *official*, *sufficient*, *suffuse*;
- (unreduced vowel) – *affable*, *affectation*, *afferent*, *affidavit*, *affirmation*, *affix* (n.), *affluent*, *different*, *difficult*, *diffident*, *effervescent*, *efficacious*, *effigy*, *efflorescence*, *effluent*, *effort*, *suffer*, *suffix*, *suffragan*, *suffragette*.

Examples of regular <C>-doubling – *baffle*, *caffeine*, *chaffinch*, *draff*, *gaff*, *gaffer*, *raffle*, *saffron*, *scaffold*; *cliff*, *griffin*, *jiffy*, *miff*, *piffle*, *skiff*, *sniff*, *sniffle*, *stiff*, *tiff*, *whiff*; *coffee*, *coffer*, *coffin*, *doff*, *offal*, *offer*, *office*, *proffer*, *quaff*, *scoff*, *toff*, *toffee*, *waffle*; *bluff*, *buff*, *cuff*, *duffer*, *fluffy*, *gruff*, *guffaw*, *muffin*, *muffle*, *puffin*, *puffy*, *ruffle*, *scruffy*, *shuffle*, *snuff*, *stuff*, *truffle*. In *chaff*, *distaff*, *giraffe*, *staff*, the original short vowel was lengthened in SBS but not in Northern England or AmE.

There is regular absence of <C>-doubling after a stressed short vowel before certain non-§Basic endings (#D7, p. 123). This accounts for the single <f> before the ending in the following:

- <-ic(al)> (adj.) – *beatific, pacific, prolific, scientific, soporific, specific, terrific.* The noun *traffic* has regular <ff>.
- <-it> (in §Latinate words) – *profit.*

In *raffish*, the *raff* as a free form is archaic.

Final /f/ in an unstressed syllable has <C>-doubling in *bailiff*, *caitiff*, *mastiff*, *midriff*, *plaintiff*, *sheriff*, *tariff*; *dandruff*. This is so in *pontiff*, but it has a single <f> in derivations: *pontificate, pontifical.*

Exceptional <C>-doubling in the antepenultimate syllable of morphemes (see #D6 p. 123): *buffalo*, *daffodil*, *raffia*, *ruffian*, *taffeta*.

Various oddities: *buffoon*, *chauffeur*, *coiffure*, *graffiti*, *paraffin*, *souffle*.

Quasi-compounds: *fisticuffs*, *ragamuffin*, *riffraff*.

In the Hanna (1966) spelling rules, <f> is the default spelling and:

1 <ff> word-final after a short vowel (*stiff*). For SBS this would include lengthened /ɑː/ (*staff*). This one context is clearly inadequate.

3.3.7.2 /v/ as in very

Distribution of variant spellings

/v/ has virtually no divergence. The one peculiarity is that <ve>, rather than <vv> is arguably the doubled form (Albrow 1972: 20). The letter <v> is exclusive to the spelling of /v/.

There is one nonce spelling of /v/ as <ph> in some pronunciations of *nephew*. Among function words we have the nonce spelling <f> in *of*.

Distribution of <vv> and <ve>

(For general rules of <C>-doubling (#D1 to #D11), see §3.2.2, pp. 114ff.)

We only find medial <vv> or final <v> in slang, humorous forms, or abbreviations: *navvy*, *flivver*, *civvy*, *skivvy*, *revving*, *bovver*; *gov* or *guv*, *lav*, *rev*, *spiv*. When, quite rarely, /v/ is final after a long vowel in an abbreviation, <e>-marking is required: *fave* (from *favourite*), *Dave* (from *David*).

Albrow (1972: 20) regards <ve> as the normal equivalent of <C>-doubling in the case of /v/ in words such as *love*, *live* [lɪv]. Their structure is <l> <o> <ve>, <l> <i> <ve>, while the structure of *cove*, *live* [laɪv], is <c> <o..e> <v>, <l> <i..e> <v>. The 'doubled' <ve> spelling is not very common compared with the doubled spellings of other phonemes, if we exclude the common §Latinate suffix <-ive> (*active*, *positive*, *restive*, etc.). However it does occur in some very common words: *have*, *live* (v.), *give*; *love*, *glove*, *shove*, *dove*. This use of <ve> cannot be regarded as a particularly effective spelling for several reasons. It clearly conflicts with <e>-marking of long vowels: *wave*, *hive*, *rave*. It does not persist as much as ordinary <C>-doubling, because the <e> is usually elided before vowels: *lover*, *loving* (though *loveable*) compared with *winner*, *winning*, *winnable*. The final <e> is also used as a general orthographic device to prevent <v> occurring finally when the /v/ ends a consonant-letter cluster, as in *serve*, *valve*.

With /v/, then, there is no <C>-doubling after the short vowel in: *cavern*, *cavil*, *gavel*, *gravel*, *havoc*, *ravage*, *ravel*, *ravin*, *savage*, *savant*, *slaver* (/æ/), *spavin*, *tavern*, *travail*, *travel*, *traverse* (n.); *bevel*, *bevy*, *clever*, *crevice*, *devil*, *ever*, *level*, *levy*, *never*, *revel*, *seven*, *sever*; *chivy*, *civil*, *deliver*, *drivel*, *liver*, *privy*, *quiver*, *river*, *shiver*, *shrivel*, *sliver*, *snivel*, *swivel*; *grovel*, *hovel*, *hover*, *novel*, *novice*, *proverb*, *province*, *provost*; *coven*, *cover*, *covert*, *covet*, *covey*, *govern*, *oven*, *plover*, *shovel*, *sloven*.

#D7 examples: *avid*; *lavish*, *ravish*; *civic*; *livid*, *vivid*; *trivet*, *privet*, *rivet*.

The Hanna (1966) spelling rules are:

1 <v> syllable-initial or -medial (*advance, thieves*);
2 <v> syllable-final preceded by a long vowel (*a-pprov-al*, *cleav-age*, *cove*);
3 <ve> word-final (*love, swerve, valve*);
4 <v> syllable-final (*e-quiv-o-cal, liv-id*).

3.3.7.3 /θ/ as in thigh *and /ð/ as in* thy

Distribution of variant spellings

/θ/ and /ð/ have no divergence. They are both represented by the digraph <th>. This is also used as a minority spelling for /t/ (*thyme*, *Thomas*). Spelling reformers have suggested that /θ/ and /ð/ should be differentiated by writing /θ/ as <th> and /ð/ as <dh>. From a writer's point of view there is no spelling problem. Nor does the reader have much of a problem, since there is very little actual contrast between /θ/ and /ð/. The function words *the*, *this*, *these*, *that*, *those*, *thine*, *thy*, *then*, *thence*, *there*, *thither*, have /ð/, otherwise there is /θ/ in initial position: *thigh*, *think*, *thread*, etc. Medially there is /ð/ in native words (*blather*, *bother*, *brother*, *lather*, *wither*, etc.) and /θ/ in §Greek words (*orthodox*, *method*, *ether*, *cathode*).

In final position /θ/ and /ð/ alternate in noun/adjective and verb forms: *bath–bathe*, *loath–loathe*, with <e>-marking of the final /ð/.

In *eighth* there is <th>≡/tθ/. A graphotactic rule reduces the potential string <tth> at the morpheme boundary to <th>. The string <th> may be split by a boundary in compounds such as *pothook*.

There are /θ/ variants for *thence* and *thither* (LPD) and occasionally for *booth, lithe, loathsome, zither, Scythia.*

The Hanna (1966) spelling rules simply have <th> as the default spelling of both phonemes.

3.3.7.4 /s/ *as in* seal

Distribution of variant spellings

/s/ is involved in a two-way divergence: not only does /s/ have divergence between <s> and <c> and some minor spellings, but <s> also has to serve in the commonest spelling of /z/ (*easy*) and /ʒ/ (*vision*). The morphemic spelling of {plural} (*cats*, *dogs*), {possessive} (*Pete's*, *John's*) and {third person singular present tense} (*barks*, *howls*), where simple <s> varies in context between /s/ and /z/, reinforces the frequency with which <s> may correspond to /z/. Various orthographic devices are available to help to separate 'lexical' <s> from 'grammatical' <s> as in *tax–tacks*, *lapse–laps*. <s> is also involved in the spelling of /ʃ/ as <sh> (*short*) and several minor spellings such as <sch> (*schnozzle*), <sc> (*fascist*).

Including <C>-doubling, we find <s> spellings in TF 79 per cent (LF 78 per cent) and <c> spellings in TF 15 per cent (LF 15 per cent) of instances of lexical /s/.

Distribution of <ss>

(For general rules of <C>-doubling (#D1 to #D11), see §3.2.2, pp. 114ff.)
The doubled form of <s> is, of course, <ss>; the spelling <cc> represents either /ks/ (*accident*) or /k/ (*acclaim, broccoli*).

Examples of normal <C>-doubling: *ass*, *bass* ('fish'), *crass*, *lass*, *macassar*, *mass*, *morass*; *distress*, *dress*, *essay*, *less*, *press*; *bliss*, *hiss*, *kiss*, *miss*, etc.; *abyss*, *hyssop*; *wassail*; *cross*, *gossip*, *loss*, *possum*, *toss*; *pussy*; *discuss*, *fuss*, *mussel*, *truss*, etc. The previous vowel may be /ɑː/ in *brass*, *class*, *surpass*, etc., where lengthening of an original short vowel has taken place before /s/ in SBS. The vowel remains short in Northern England and AmE.

Examples of exceptional <C>-doubling in non-§Basic words after a long vowel or a vowel spelt with two letters: *bass* (with /eɪ/, 'singer'), *caisson*, *connoisseur*, *gneiss*, *mousse*, *pelisse*, *reconnaissance*, *renaissance*, *trousseau*. Similar non-§Basic examples after an unstressed short vowel: *alyssum* (as SBS /'ælisəm/), *bassoon*, *canvass* (cf. *canvas*), *cassava*, *cassette*, *compass*, *cutlass*, *embarrass*, *embassy*, *fricassee*, *lasso*, *masseur*, *masseuse*, *messiah*, *trespass*, *windlass*. *Carcass* has a more common but irregular variant *carcase*. The spelling of *harass* fits the American pronunciation /hə'ræs/ with the double <ss> marking the stressed short vowel. This pronunciation has been gaining ground in Britain since the word came into vogue in the 1970s (LPD). The original British pronunciation /'hærəs/ frequently attracts a mistaken spelling *<harras(s)>. This may be influenced by the spelling of *harry*, a verb with similar meaning, or of *embarrass*. §Latinate {-miss-} needs to be recognized as a recurring element in *admissible, commissar, emissary, permissible, promissory,* though hardly by meaning. In *classic* and *prussic* the double <ss> is unusual before the ending <-ic> (see #D7 p. 123).

The need to recognize a free base form within a polysyllabic word can be seen in *classification–pacification*; *essential* has to be related to *essence*. Longer words with no apparent one- or two-syllable free base are: *ambassador*, *brassica*, *brassiere*, *bassinet*, *casserole*, *lassitude*, *massacre*, *potassium*, *sassafras*.

Exceptional instances of final single <s>: *alas*, *bus*, *gas*, *plus*, *yes* and the two function words *this*, *thus*. Inflected forms of these words may or may not have <C>-doubling: *bussed*, *bussing*, *busses*, *gassed*, *gassing*, *gasses*. There is no doubling in the §Latinate forms *gaseous, gasify*.

Most examples of <ss> are found in the common suffixes <-ess>, <-less> and <-ness>. The vowel of <-ess> varies rhythmically between /ə/ as in *actress, tigress*, *waitress*, and /e/ as in *lioness* and discriminatory gender terms which are now avoided, such as *poetess, shepherdess*. The <-ess> of *cypress* and *prowess* is not a suffix, but the <ss> is necessary to distinguish them from inflected forms in <-es>. The unstressable suffix <-less> derives, of course, from the stressed free-form <less> and retains its spelling. The suffix <-ness>, a bound form, has no such justification for a double <ss>

and was often spelt <-nis> or <-nes> before 1700. By comparison, there is no retention of <C>-doubling like that of <-less> in the suffix <-ful>.

Many examples of <ss> occur in §Latinate prefixes: *assail*, *assault*, *assembly*, *assent*, *assess*, *asseverate*, *assiduous*, *assign*, *assist*, *assizes*, *associate*, *assorted*, *assuage*, *assume*; *dissect*, *dissemble*, *disseminate*, *dissension*, *dissent*, *dissimilar*, *dissimulate*, *dissipate*, *dissociate*, *dissolute*, *dissonance*, etc.

The §Latinate ending <-it> precludes <C>-doubling (see #D7 p. 123), so there is a single <c> rather than <ss> in *elicit, explicit, illicit, implicit, solicit, tacit.*

<s> and <c> spellings

We can discuss the divergence between <s> and <c> spellings of /s/ by taking <s> to be the default spelling and trying to account for the instances of <c>. Albrow takes a similar approach by putting <s> into system 1 and <c> into system 2 as spellings of /s/, but this does not help matters much if we are treating words and morphemes, rather than individual correspondences, as the units which belong to subsystems. Within the §Romance/§Latinate vocabulary <s> frequently occurs in much the same contexts as <c>.

In consonant clusters the spelling is almost entirely with <s> not <c>: *span, stay, skin, scheme, smile, snow, slope, sphere, despot, master, escape, dismay*. This is true of final clusters *laps, cats, backs*, but those where the /s/ is part of the stem have <e>-marking *apse, tense, else.* /ks/ has the special spelling <x>. Words spelt with <-nce> are an exception, such as *dance, once, ponce, pounce,* and the suffixes <-ance> and <-ence>, as in *defiance, diffidence.*

There is one notable restriction on the occurrence of /s/≡<c> before vowels; it only occurs before what were originally close or mid front vowels. This is easier to express now in graphic terms (a graphotactic rule) than in phonetic terms, since the vowels have changed their phonetic quality in some cases. The original front close vowels are reflected in the spellings <i>, <y> and <e>, which now, in modern English, may have taken on the values /iː, ɪ, e, aɪ, ɪə, ɜː, ə/. The same contexts limit the occurrence of /s/≡<sc> (as in *science*). There is only the odd exception, such as *facade*, where we have no device similar to the French cedilla <ç> to relate the <c> to /s/. In *caesura*, *caeca*, *coelacanth,* the <e> of the digraph has a similar marking function.

Consequently, /s/ before a consonant or any other vowel spelling than the above will be spelt <s> by default. This refers to contexts such as: *aerosol*, *dinosaur*, *esophagus*, *masquerade*, *persuade*, *pestilence*, *sample*, *sardine*, *slide*, *smoke*, *snarl*, etc. Since <c> is not found as a final letter in prefixes attached to free-forms, the above generalization also covers words such as *disgust*, *dishonour*, *mishap*, *misjudge*, etc. There are other restrictions which follow from the limited distribution of <c>≡/s/. For instance, the agent suffix cannot be <-or> in words such as *artificer*, *bouncer*. The choice of spellings of /ɜː/ after <c> does not include <ur>. These restrictions on the <c> spelling of /s/ are predictable from the phonetic context or the word structure.

If suffixes are identified as whole spellings, then <-icity>, <-ices>, <-ence/-ance>, <-ency/-ancy> will account for a large number of <c> spellings. A phonological regularity in such suffixes is that morphologically related /k/ will give /s/≡<c> as in <-ical> – <-icity> (*electrical*, *electricity*; *genetic*, *geneticist*, etc.). There are, however, problems with the simple endings <-cy> and <-sy>. Many forms with <-sy> relate to other forms with /t/≡<t>: *apostasy*, *controversy*, *ecstasy*, *heresy*, *hypocrisy*, *idiosyncrasy* (cf. *apostate*, *heretic*, etc.). But then so do many words with <-cy>: *secrecy*, *primacy* (cf. *secret*, *primate*). It is not always possible then to distinguish <-cy> and <-sy> spellings by way of underlying forms. There are, however, a few very modest generalizations which a speller may become aware of in these words. Free-forms are followed by <-cy>: *colonelcy*, *normalcy*, etc.; *minstrelsy* is an exception. In *jealousy* there is a differently-placed boundary. Small groups of words can be found to support sequencing restrictions. Since *<pc> will not spell /ps/ we have *autopsy*, *biopsy*, *dropsy*, *epilepsy*, *gipsy*, *necropsy*. *Atrocity* is likely to be confused with the group *animosity*, *curiosity*, *generosity*, *verbosity*.

Recognition of some of the common §Latinate stems will also identify a great many <c> spellings:

- <cede> – *recede*, *precede*, *concede*, etc.;
- <ceive> – *receive*, *deceive*, *conceive*, etc.;
- <cept> – *receptor*, *deception*, *concept*, etc.;
- <cess> – *recessive*, *concession*, *procession*, etc.;
- <cide> – *decide*, *coincide*, *suicide*, etc.;
- <cise> – *incise*, *decisive*; though *exercise* has a different etymology.

Within the §Latinate and §Greek vocabulary there are obvious problems in knowing when to expect <s> or <c>. The ordinary person can hardly know the semantic reasons for the different spellings of /s/ in *intercede* and *supersede* or in cases such as *session–cession*, *sensor–censor–censer*, *census–consensus*, *counsellor–councillor*, *exercise–synthesize*.

<se> and <ce> spellings

Two notorious spelling pairs are *licence–license* (which either as noun or verb are free variants in British English) and *practice–practise* (which, as strictly noun and verb respectively, are not).

Albrow (1972: 22) makes the generalization that /s/≡<se> belongs to his system 1 and /s/≡<ce> to his system 2 along with /z/≡<se>. The <e> marks the <s> as the end of a lexical item and not a suffix morpheme (cf. *lapse–laps*, *browse–brows*). For practical spelling purposes, this deployment in different systems is not very helpful. The speller may not have any firm criteria for putting pairs such as *lease* and *peace* in different systems.

For /z/ it makes good sense to say that the normal spelling after long vowels is <s> with <e>-marking: *lose*, *choose*, etc. However, the spelling of /s/ is not so clear-cut after a long vowel and does vary in predictability as <c> or <s> with the vowel:

- after /aɪ/ and /ɔɪ/, <ce> is regular – *advice*, *device*, *ice*, *nice*, *price*, *slice*, *twice*; *choice*, *rejoice*, *voice*;
- after /eɪ/ we have – *face*, *place*, *race*, *space*, *trace* and also *plaice*, but *base*, *case*, *chase* are exceptions. There are some more or less related derived forms such as *basal*, *casual*, *casuist* (with shortening), though it is a little far-fetched to point out that you have <s> rather than <c> in *case* because *<cacual> (instead of *casual*) could not be a spelling for /ʒ/;
- after /iː/ in §Romance words we have <ce> – *caprice*, *police*, where the final stress is a marker; they are clearly different from *fleece*, *niece*, *piece*, *peace*. Examples of /iː/ followed by <se> are *geese*, *cease*, *crease*, *grease*, *lease*, *release*;
- after /uː/ we have, on the one hand, *spruce*, *truce*, *juice*, *sluice*, *deuce,* and, on the other, *goose*, *loose*, *moose*, *noose*. The <oo> is a §Basic spelling of /uː/ and prompts a §Basic <s>;
- after /aʊ/ and /əʊ/ there are only <se> spellings of /s/: *douse*, *house* (n.), *grouse*, *louse*, *mouse*, *scouse*, *souse*; *close* (adj.), *dose*. The spelling <-oce#> does not occur;
- after /ɔː/ without <r> we have *sauce*. Vowel spellings with <r> do not present a clear-cut choice: <s> in *arse*, *sparse,* but <c> in *farce*; *scarce*; *fierce*, *pierce*; <s> in *gorse*, *horse*, *endorse*, *remorse*, *coarse*, *hoarse*, *course,* but <c> in *source*, *force*, *divorce*; <s> in *asperse*, *curse*, *disburse*, *hearse*, *nurse*, *purse*, *terse*, *verse*, *worse*, etc. but <c> in *commerce*, *coerce*.

The <ce> and <se> spellings of /s/ also follow a short vowel plus a consonant /n/, /l/ or /p/: *tense*, *chance*, *pulse*, *lapse*, etc.. For /ns/ clusters <nc(e)> is the majority spelling, as in *dance*, *once*, *pounce*, *renounce*, etc. and the suffixes <-ance> and <-ence>. The <ns(e)> spelling is found in: *condense*, *dense*, *dispense*, *expanse*, *expense*, *immense*, *incense*, *intense*, *manse*, *recompense*, *response*, *rinse*, *sense*, *suspense*, *tense*. A few of these are related to forms with /d/: *response–respond*, *expanse–expand*. It is interesting that new coinages have <nce>: *bonce*, *ponce*.

American spelling has changed some <-nce> spellings to <-nse> as in *defense*. There is no real impediment to such a reform since the <c> spelling is not required in these words to represent an alternation between /s/ and /k/ as in *electricity–electric*. In a case such as *lapse–laps* the <e> has the sole function of marking a lexical item as distinct from an item with a plural ending. After <c> it marks the /s/ value of <c> as distinct from its /k/ value. Indirectly, however, the <e> is also helping to distinguish /s/ – /z/ pairs such as *pence–pens*, *since–sins*, (as also in *lease–leas*).

<sc>≡/s/ and other minor spellings

It is very difficult to find specific indications of when to expect the minority spelling <sc>≡/s/ rather than simple <s>≡/s/. Most examples have §Latinate word formation. A few common §Latinate elements account for a large number of instances:

- <-esce>, <-escence>, <-escent> : *acquiesce*, *acquiescence*, *acquiescent*, *adolescence*, *coalesce*, *convalescence*, *crescent*, *effervescence*, *excrescence*, *fluorescence*, *luminescence*, *reminiscent*, etc.;
- <-scend>, <-scent> : *ascend*, *ascent*, *condescend*, *descend*, *descent*, *reascend*, *transcend*, and derived forms.

Other instances of <sc>≡/s/ are: *abscess*, *abscissa*, *ascetic*, *ascertain*, *corpuscle*, *discern*, *disciple*, *discipline*, *fascicle*, *fascinated*, *isosceles*, *lascivious*, *miscellany*, *muscle*, *nascent*, *obscene*, *omniscient*, *oscillate*, *plebiscite*, *prescient*, *proscenium*, *rescind*, *resuscitate*, *scenario*, *scene*, *scent*, *sceptre*, *sciatica*, *science*, *scimitar*, *scintillate*, *scion*, *scissors*, *susceptible*, *scythe*, *viscid*, *viscera.*

There are a few very minor spellings of /s/. The word *schism* is either /'sɪzm/ (with an exceptional <sch>≡/s/), or /'skɪzm/. A number of §Greek technical and scientific terms have initial <ps>≡/s/: *pseudonym*, *psoriasis*, *psychology*. *Psalm* and *psalter* did originally come from Greek, but very early by way of Latin into Old English. Apart from this <ps>≡/s/, they have related forms such as *psalmodic* which show thwm to be §Greek <z>≡/s/ occurs in *chintz*, *eczema*, *howitzer*, *quartz*, and, with or without the /t/, in *waltz*. <sw>≡/s/ has an empty <w> in *answer*, *sword.* Due to cluster simplification there is no actual /t/ in *chasten*, *christen*, *fasten*, *glisten*, *hasten*, *moisten*; *apostle*, *bristle*, *bustle*, *castle*, *epistle*, *gristle*, *hustle*, *jostle*, *nestle*, *pestle*, *rustle*, *thistle*, *throstle*, *trestle*, *wrestle*, etc. The <t> is inert, rather than empty, in some of these, since there are related forms such as *apostolic*, *chaste, fast, haste, nest.* The examples with <-en> mostly have a free-form stem. There are only one or two competing forms with <ss>: *hassle*, *lessen*, *tussle*.

The string /ks/ is usually spelt <x> within a morpheme; see under /k/.

The Hanna (1966) spelling rules have <s> as the default spelling and:

1 <x> syllable-initial with /k/ (*flex-i-ble, prox-y*);
2 <ce> syllable-final after /ɔɪ/ (*voice*);
3 <se> syllable-final after /aʊ/ (*mouse*);
4 <ce> word-final after /n, r, ɪ, iː/ (*dance, force, office, caprice*);
5 <ss> word-final accented after /æ, e, ʌ/ (*mass, mess, fuss*);
6 <c> word-final accented all other cases (*place*);

– this rule presumably relies on the <e> of *place* being provided by the long vowel spelling. In other contexts it gives in error a word-final <c> *<looc> *loose*, *<mumpc> *mumps*, *<toc> *toss*, etc.

7 <ss> word-final unaccented after /e/ (*actress, careless, goodness, process*).

The first rule refers to the merger of /k/ and /s/ into <x>. The rules for <ss> after short vowels do not cater for <ss> in *hiss, kiss, miss*, etc. As is often the case in Hanna, the suffixes dealt with by the seventh rule are assumed to have full vowel quality as input.

3.3.7.5 /z/ as in zeal

Distribution of variant spellings

/z/ shows divergence between <s> and <z> spellings which cannot always be accounted for by context. Although the form of the Roman alphabet which we have adopted for English makes available the two letters <s> and <z>, these are not used in simple direct correspondence with /s/ and /z/. Instead there is a complex interplay of <c>, <s> and <z> where <z> is very much the minority spelling of /z/. The commonest spelling of /z/ is, in fact, an <s> (TF 93 per cent, LF 69 per cent, F+). Spellings with <z>, including <C>-doubling, only account for TF 5 per cent and LF 27 per cent (F-). These figures also show another important difference: <z> spellings tend to occur in low-frequency words.

In initial position <s>≡/z/ does not occur, so we find <z>≡/z/ in *zeal*, *zebra*, *zenith*, *zero*, *zest*, *zigzag*, *zinc*, *zip*, *zodiac*, *zombie*, *zoo*, *zoom*, etc. One or two words have a §Greek correspondence <x>≡/z/ initially (or for some speakers <x>≡/gz/) – *xenon*, *xenophobia*, *xerox*, *xylophone*.

It is otherwise extremely difficult to find phonetic or structural contexts which clearly differentiate between <s> and <z> spellings. The §Latinate prefixes require the <s> spelling to follow: *absolve*, *designate*, *observe*, *present*, *preside*, *reside*, *resolute*, *resonate*, *resurrect*, etc. The /z/ in *seedsman*, *woodsman*, etc. has the morphemic spelling <s>. Sometimes, as in the cluster /nz/, the spelling <z> characterizes marked foreign loans: *bronze*, *enzyme*, *influenza*, *chimpanzee*, *benzene*, *stanza*, *cadenza*, *bonanza*, *extravaganza*. Against these we have *pansy*, *quinsy*, *tansy*, which are equally foreign in ultimate origin but have a §Basic phonetic shape. Words with /mz/ have <ms>: *clumsy*, *damsel*, *crimson*, *flimsy*, *whimsy*, *damson*.

In addition to the simple spellings <s> and <z>, there are also <se> and <ze> spellings to complicate the picture. It seems that one function of the <e> is to distinguish word-final /z/ and /s/ from the morphemic spelling <s>. So we have *browse–brows*, *please–pleas*, *praise–prays*, *freeze–frees*, *furze–furs*. Albrow (1972: 22) calls this 'lexical e' and puts the /z/≡<se> correspondence into his system 2 along with /s/≡<ce> (*please*, *fleece*). This does not have much practical use since there are no other system markers available to the speller to predict an <-se> spelling in words such as *parse*, *blouse*, *browse*, *drowse*, *tease*, *pause*, *bruise*, *cruise*, *choose*. Some such words do have §Latinate derivation as an indicator that they are not §Basic: *arouse–arousal*, *please–pleasure*, *ease–easement*, but this is not extensive.

The lexical function of <-se> is clearly quite important to the reader in helping to distinguish pairs such as *pause–paws*, *praise–prays*, even though the <aw> or <ay> spellings themselves indicate a morpheme boundary. But, since the <-se> and <-ze> spellings are usually found in conjunction with a long vowel, it is best treated as an extension of the usual <e>-marking rule (#E2 p. 129). This extends the <e>-marking of long vowels before /z/ to those represented by digraphs: *parse*, *turquoise*, *house* (v.), *rouse*, *blouse*, *spouse*, *carouse*, *browse*, *drowse*, *raise*, *praise*, *malaise*, *braise*, *please*, *ease*, *tease*, *disease*, *cheese*, *pause*, *cause*, *clause*, *applause*, *noise*, *poise*, *choose*, *bruise*, *cruise*, *masseuse*. Examples with <z> are: *maize*, *baize*, *freeze*, *breeze*, *squeeze*, *sneeze*, *wheeze*, *seize*, *frieze*, *gauze*, *ooze*, *booze*, *snooze*, *furze*. The only apparent exceptions to #E2 are mostly where /z/≡<s> is explicable as a morphemic spelling: *always*, *nowadays*; *species*, *series*; *gallows*, *bellows*, *mews*.

The <se> spelling of /z/ is occasionally found after long vowels which have undergone shortening in isolated instances: *because* (/ɒ/), *cleanse* (/e/), *gooseberry* (/ʊ/), *chastisement* (/ɪ/).

The endings <-ise>, <-ize> and <-yse> are discussed under homophonous affixes (§5.5 p. 433).

Distribution of <zz>

(For general rules of <C>-doubling (#D1 to #D11), see §3.2.2, pp. 114ff.)

Doubled <zz> represents only a small proportion (TF <1 per cent, LF 2 per cent) of spellings of /z/. Examples: *dazzle*, *frazzle*, *jazz*, *snazzy*; *embezzle*; *blizzard*, *dizzy*, *drizzle*, *fizz*, *fizzle*, *frizzle*, *gizzard*, *grizzly*, *mizzen*, *sizzle*, *whizz*; *nozzle*, *schnozzle*; *buzz*, *buzzard*, *fuzz*, *guzzle*, *muzzle*, *muzzy*, *nuzzle*, *puzzle*. The list leaves one with an impression that there is very strong symbolism here and that the spelling plays an important role in it. Absence of <C>-doubling in final position is exceptional: *quiz*, *fez*. Other exceptions are: *hazard*, *bezel*, *lizard*, *wizard*, *wizen*(*ed*), *vizard*. The ending <-ard>, in spite of the few examples here, normally does not prevent <C>-doubling (cf. *buzzard*, *blizzard*, *gizzard* and *scabbard*, *haggard*, *niggard*, etc.). There are no exceptional spellings with /z/≡<zz> in the antepenultimate syllable of a free-form. Double <zz> only represents /z/, except in one or two Italian loans such as *mezzanine*, *pizza*, where we have /ts/≡<zz>.

Double <ss> represents /z/ only occasionally, though in some quite common words (TF <1 per cent, LF <1 per cent): *possess*, *dissolve*, *scissors*, *dessert* and the less common *hussar*. Single <s> spellings in contexts where <C>-doubling would be normal are: *basil*; *present*, *presence*, *desert*, *resin*;

visit, *prison*; *posit*, *closet*, *rosin*; *bosom*. Only the function words *as*, *has*, *is*, *was* have final /z/≡<s>. This is consistent with the usual purpose of <C>-doubling as a marker of stressed vowels, since these function words are almost always unstressed.

In the Hanna (1966) spelling rules, <s> is the default spelling and:

1 <x> syllable-initial after /g/ (*examine*);
2 <z> syllable-initial accented before /eɪ/ (*a-zal-ea, or-gan-i-za-tion*);
3 <se> syllable-final after /aʊ/ (*blouse*);
4 <z> syllable-final after /aɪ/ (*capsize, baptize*);
5 <zz> syllable-final before syllabic /l/ (*drizzle*).

3.3.7.6 /ʃ/ as in shop

Distribution of variant spellings

/ʃ/ shows considerable divergence. The spelling <sh> in *shop* is unique to /ʃ/, but <ch>, as in *chef,* also frequently represents /k/, as in *chemist*, and /ʧ/, as in *chain*. The palatalization spelling <ti> may also represent /ʧ/ (*question*, *mutual* etc.).

However, the various spellings of /ʃ/ do fall into distinct and recognizable groups. Rather surprisingly, perhaps, the most common group consists of spellings where /ʃ/ is the result of palatalization (TF 55 per cent, LF 64 per cent, F-). An earlier /t/, /s/ or /k/ has become /ʃ/ by assimilation to a following close front vowel. Hence the spellings usually involve <t> (*dictate–dictation*), or <s> (*repulse–repulsion*), or <c> (*logic–logician*) together with a following <i>. Some common §Latinate stems ending in <-ss> also have palatalization: *depression*, *obsession*, *passion*, *percussion*, *possession*, *profession*, *recession*, *transgression*, etc. There are also <sci> spellings in: *conscience*, *conscious*, *fascia*, *luscious*, and quite exceptionally <chsi> in *fuchsia.* It is convenient to regard the <i> in such words as part of the consonant spelling: /ʃ/≡<ti> *partial*, /ʃ/≡<ssi> *recession*, etc. In *ocean* and in *cretaceous*, *crustacean*, *herbaceous*, *sebaceous*, *siliceous* and a few other technical terms, the vowel letter is <e>: /ʃ/≡<ce>.

In a few instances the palatalization results not from a following front vowel but from the semivowel glide beginning /juː/: *censure* (cf. *censor*), *tonsure*, *commensurate*. The correspondence here is /ʃ/≡<s>, since the <u> is required for the following vowel. Two common words have similar palatalization of //sj// to /ʃ/ in the stem: *sugar* (Albrow 1972: 19), *sure*.

The apparent complexity of these spellings does not, however, constitute a major problem for the speller. Such spellings largely occur where §Latinate suffixes are added and the required consonant letter is usually apparent in the base form (as above in *dictate*, *repulse*, *depress*, *logic*). Occasionally this fails, as in *spatial–space*, *palatial–palace*, (rather than as in *racial–race*). As we have already noted, we cannot be sure that the speller will necessarily associate the derived form with its base, as, for example, in *officiate–office*. For some words there is no related form to provide the right consonant letter for spelling the /ʃ/: *appreciate*, *negotiate*, etc.

In assessing spelling errors, there is a clear difference to be drawn between spelling *discretion* wrongly as *<discresion> or *<discrecion> and, on the other hand, spelling it wrongly as *<discreshion> or *<discrechion>. The latter spellings are decidedly less literate since they show that the speller is not fully aware of the subsystems involved.

Apart from §Latinate suffixes, the two most important spellings of /ʃ/ are <sh>, the default §Basic spelling, and <ch>, the default §Romance spelling (which Albrow surprisingly prefers to put in system 3). <sh> is much more common (TF 37 per cent, LF 28 per cent, F+) than <ch> (TF 1 per cent, LF 2 per cent, F-). A comparison of the text frequencies and lexical frequencies indicates that <ch> is not only a minority spelling but also that it tends to be found in low-frequency words. <sh> is found both in stems (*shot*, *shed*, *brush*, *rash*, etc.) and in the common suffix <-ish> (*sluggish*, *greenish*, etc.). Many early borrowings from French have <-ish> as an integral part of the stem: *finish*, *establish*, *publish*, *punish*, *flourish*, *vanish*, *nourish*, *varnish*, *garnish*, etc.

Words with /ʃ/≡<ch> are clearly exceptional from the initial teaching standpoint, but they do have characteristics which can aid recall. The spelling /ʃ/≡<ch> is a clear marker of French origin. For a common word such as *machine* the cultural link is probably no longer evident in spite of the additional marking by final stress. But, when a word is clearly a technical term in areas of French interest, the cultural association may serve as a valid reminder of the spelling: *brochure*, *cachet*, *chagrin*, *chaise*, *chalet*, *chamois*, *champagne*, *chancre*, *chandelier*, *chaperon*, *charade*, *charlatan*, *chassis*, *chateau*, *chauffeur*, *chef*, *chemise*, *chenille*, *cheroot*, *chevron*, *chic*, *chicane*, *chiffon*, *chivalry*, *cliche*, *crochet*, *echelon*, *gauche*, *machine*, *marchioness*, *nonchalance*, *parachute*, *recherche*, *ricochet*, *sachet*.

Such a range, however, defies any neat semantic summary, covering as it does areas of culture as widely different as manners, warfare, fashion and venereal disease. Many such words are also marked by particular suffixes or final stress. Final /ʃ/≡<ch> is always associated with final stress and with <e>-marking: *barouche*, *cache*, *cartouche*, *cloche*, *creche*, *douche*, *gauche*, *moustache*, *panache*. *Avalanche* increasingly has initial stress.

Minority spellings of /ʃ/ in stems are also found:

- /ʃ/≡<sch> in *seneschal*, *schedule*, *schist*, *maraschino*, *schnapps*, *schnozzle*, *meerschaum*;
- /ʃ/≡<sc> in *conscientious*, *crescendo*, *fascist*.

The Hanna (1966) spelling rules have <sh> as the default spelling and:

1 <t> syllable-initial unaccented before <ɪ> (*ter-ti-a-ry, ne-go-ti-ate*);
2 <ti> syllable-initial unaccented all other cases (*cre-a-tion, tan-gen-tial*);
3 <ti> syllable-final before /ə/ (*am-biti-on, con-diti-on*).

These rules put rather a strain on the idea of the 'syllable' as a convenient unit for the description of English spelling conventions.

3.3.7.7 /ʒ/ as in measure

Distribution of variant spellings

/ʒ/ is a phoneme which is entirely restricted to §Romance and §Latinate lexical items. Though lexically the least frequent consonant phoneme of English, its phonetic survival may be due to the paired symmetry of the system of fricatives: /f/ – /v/, /θ/ – /ð/, /s/ – /z/, and /ʃ/ – /ʒ/. Its fortis counterpart, /ʃ/, is much more common and occurs across the whole of the lexicon. /ʒ/ often occurs as the result of assimilation of /z/ by palatalization across word boundaries in allegro forms (e.g. *these yachts* /ˈðiʒ ˈjɒts/). Within a word it frequently represents a similar palatalization across morpheme boundaries, as in *composure*.

The spelling of /ʒ/ is largely based on <s> (TF 91 per cent, LF 74 per cent, F+) and to a much smaller extent on <g> (TF 4 per cent, LF 23 per cent, F-). These figures also indicate that <g> spellings tend to occur in low-frequency words.

The <s> spellings of /ʒ/ only occur with certain endings, where the /ʒ/ results from palatalization, as in:

- <-ion> : *allusion*, *conclusion*, *decision*, *division*, *occasion*, *protrusion*;
- <-ual> : *casual*, *usual*;
- <-ure> : *closure*, *composure*, *erasure*, *exposure*, *leisure*, *measure*, *pleasure*, *treasure*;
- <-ury> : *treasury*, *usury*;

The <-sion> words relate to base forms ending in /-d/, //-r//, /-s/, /-z/, as in:

- /-d/ : *conclusion–conclude*, *protrusion–protrude*, *division–divide*;
- //-r// : *adhesion–adhere*;
- /-s/ or /-z/ : *profusion–profuse*, *incision–incise*, *pleasure–please*.

<g> is only involved as a spelling of /ʒ/ before an <e>, with the sole exception of *regime*. Most instances are in the suffix <-age> in fairly recent French loans: *badinage*, *barrage*, *camouflage*, *collage*, *corsage*, *decolletage*, *dressage*, *entourage*, *espionage*, *fuselage*, *garage*, *massage*, *menage*, *mirage*, *montage*, *sabotage*. These words clearly vary in frequency of current use; some of them are quite common. They also differ in the extent to which a French connection persists as part of their associations. Consequently their pronunciation is unstable: stress may shift away from the last syllable and

the /ʒ/ may become /ʤ/. Where the French association persists this may even involve a zero {plural}: *collages* /kɒ'lɑːʒ/. Some speakers have *barrage* /'bærɑːʒ/ – *barrages* /'bærɑːʤɪz/, rather than /'bærɑːʒɪz/. This may show some reluctance to use a plural /-ʒɪz/, since it combines a powerful marker of §Frenchness with a non-§French plural inflection.

Other instances of /ʒ/≡<ge> are: *beige*, *blancmange*, *bourgeois*, *cortege*, *litharge*, *macrophage* (where <age> is not a suffix), *prestige*, *protege*, *neglige*, *regime*, *rouge*. The masculine/feminine difference of *protege–protegee* (with or without the French acute accents) is not usually maintained in English.

A very curious correspondence of /ʒ/≡<ti> occurs for many speakers in *equation*. Among the large number of words ending in <-ation>, this appears to be a single exception.

<z> is involved as a spelling of /ʒ/ only in *azure*, *crozier* and *seizure*.

In the Hanna (1966) spelling rules, <s> is the default spelling and:

1 <si> before /ə/ (*con-fu-sion, di-visi-on*).

With the exception of *amnesia*, *fantasia*, this rule only seems to deal with the suffix <-sion>.

3.3.7.8 /h/ *as in* head

Distribution of variant spellings

/h/ has virtually no divergence. The only exceptions to the normal /h/≡<h> correspondence are a few words with /h/≡<wh>: *whole*, *whoop*, *whore* and the function words *who* and *whose*. For American, Irish and Scottish speakers of English who contrast [ʍ] and [w] in *wheel* – *weal* etc., the [ʍ] is best analysed as /hw/≡/wh/. This is then one of the very few spellings where the order of letters does not match the order of phonemes. Phonologically, the order has to be /h/ + /w/, with increasing prominence. The reversed spelling <wh> developed in Middle English; the Old English spelling was <hw>: *hwelp* (Mod. E. *whelp*), *hwil* (Mod. E. *while*).

The letter <h> also forms part of the common digraphs <ch>, <ph>, <sh>, <th> and some minority spellings such as <gh>, <kh>, <rh>.

Those who have accents of English with no /h/ phoneme have to become aware of one in the process of acquiring literacy. This involves rote-learning of individual words, since there are no rules for the incidence of /h/ in words. The difficulty is highlighted by minimal pairs such as *heart–art*, *harm–arm*, *hair–air*, *hill–ill*, etc. Another source of difficulty is that <h> occurs occasionally as an empty or auxiliary letter (TF 1 per cent, LF 6 per cent, of <h> spellings) in words such as: *annihilate*, *catarrh*, *cheetah*, *cirrhosis*, *dahlia*, *diarrhoea*, *gonorrhea*, *haemorrhage*, *jodhpurs*, *messiah*, *myrrh*, *pariah*, *pooh*, *posthumous*, *pyorrhoea*, *rajah*, *savannah*, *silhouette*, *vehe-*

ment, *yeah*, and initially in the very common words *heir*, *hour*, *honour*, *honest*. The <h> is inert rather than empty in the common place-name element <-ham> (*Clapham*, *Streatham*, etc.), and in *exhibit* (cf. *inhibit*), *exhilarate* (cf. *hilarious*), *forehead* (cf. *head*), *philharmonic* (cf. *harmony*), *vehicle* (cf. *vehicular*), and, more remotely, in *shepherd* (cf. *herd*).

In unstressed syllables, /h/ is very unstable; hence we find weak forms of function words *he*, *her*, *him*, *his*, where the /h/ is dropped when they are unstressed in connected speech. Similarly, the initial /h/ of polysyllabic lexical words beginning with an unstressed syllable may not always be pronounced – as in *habitual*, *heredity*, *historical*, *hospitable*, *hotel*, etc. If there is no /h/, the indefinite article will have its pre-vocalic variant: *an hotel*, *an habitual drunkard*, etc. and the definite article will similarly be /ðiː/ or /ðɪ/ rather than pre-consonantal /ðə/.

In addition to /h/≡<h>, the Hanna (1966) spelling rules cater for a separate phoneme /ʍ/≡<wh> (*wheel, white,* etc.) and an 'artificial phoneme' /H9/ used to cater for the zero correspondence /Ø/≡<h> in *hour, honest, vehement,* etc.

3.3.8 Nasal consonants: / m n ŋ /

3.3.8.1 /m/ *as in* sum

Distribution of variant spellings

/m/ has virtually no divergence: <m> TF 96 per cent; <mm> TF 3 per cent. The proportion of <mm> would be higher if we were to include the many inflected forms in {-ed} and {-ing}, such as *jammed, jamming,* from *jam,* or in {-er}, {-est}, such as *trimmer, trimmest,* from *trim.* Minority divergent spellings are the strings <mb>, <mn> and <gm>. The letter <m> is only involved in the spelling of /m/.

<mb> occurs morpheme-finally in: *aplomb*, *bomb*, *catacomb*, *climb*, *comb*, *coulomb*, *crumb*, *dumb*, *jamb*, *lamb*, *limb*, *numb*, *plumb*, *succumb*, *thumb*, *tomb*, *womb*, and in names derived from them, such as *Lambton, Plumbe, Wombwell.* It also occurs with final <e> in *combe*, 'a deep valley', which is a frequent component of placenames (*Edgecombe*, *Ilfracombe*). The US county *Buncombe* is immortalized without the <b> in *bunkum* ('nonsense'). The <b> is clearly an inert letter in *bomb* because of *bombard*, but this seems to be an isolated instance. It requires a long etymological reach to associate *plumb* and *plumber* with technical terms for the metal lead, such as *plumbeous*, *plumbic*, *plumbiferous* or to relate *succumb* to *succumbent.* Hence the <b> of <mb> in words other than *bomb* is effectively an empty letter.

Within a morpheme, <mb> represents /mb/ – *chamber*, *clamber*, *emblem*, *member*, *symbol*, *timber*, etc. So, *number* is graphically ambiguous – /ˈnʌmə/ 'more numb', /ˈnʌmbə/ 'numeral'; so, more remotely, is *comber* /ˈkəʊmə/

from *to comb* and *comber* /ˈkɒmbə/ ‘fish’. *Crumby* has been respelt *crummy* for its figurative slang meanings; *dummy* similarly comes from *dumb*.

<mn> is very different. It occurs initially with an empty <m>, but only in a few learned terms, such as *mnemonic*. Otherwise, in morpheme-final position the <n> is clearly an inert rather than an empty letter – *autumn*, *column*, *condemn*, *damn*, *hymn* and *solemn*. All of these have reasonably familiar derived forms where the /n/ surfaces (*autumnal*, *columnar*, *condemnation*, *damnation*, *hymnal*, *solemnity*).

In the much less common <gm> the <g> is also inert: *apothegm*, *diaphragm*, *paradigm*, *phlegm*, *syntagm*; they have derived forms with <gm>≡/gm/ – *paradigmatic*, *phlegmatic*.

Distribution of <mm>

(For general rules of <C>-doubling, see §3.2.2, p. 114ff.)

Examples of <mm> with prefixes (#D2):

- (reduced vowel): *command*, *commemorate*, *commence*, *commend*, *commercial*, *commingle*, *commiserate*, *commission*, *commit*, *committee*, *commodious*, *communicate*, *communion*, *community*, *commuter*;
- (unreduced vowel): *accommodate*, *commandeer*, *commendation*, *comment*, *commerce*, *commissar*, *commune* (n.), *commutator*; *immanent*, *immaterial*, *immature*, *immeasurable*, *immediate*, *immemorial*, *immense*, *immerse*, *immigrant*, *imminent*, *immobilize*, *immoderate*, *immodest*, *immolate*, *immoral*, *immortal*, *immovable*, *immune*, *immutable*.

The prefix *in-* meaning either ‘in’ (as in *immerse*) or ‘not’ (as in *immutable*) assimilates to /ɪm/≡<im-> before labials /p/, /b/ and /m/ and this is reflected in the spelling. Before the labio-dental consonants /f/ and /v/, English speakers may produce a labio-dental nasal [ɱ] for either an expected /n/ or /m/ (cf. [ˈɪɱfənt] *infant*, [ˈtraɪʌɱf] *triumph*). Unless they can associate the [ɪɱ] with {in-}, there is every possibility that they will produce spellings such as *imform, *imvade.

British spellers are allowed variants in the spelling of the ending /-græm/. It may have the original French spelling <gramme> or the simplified American spelling <gram>: *gram, gramme, kilogram, kilogramme*. The two spellings may even associate with different meanings. For instance, the spelling *program* is invariably used in the sense of ‘computer program’ and usually in computer languages the string <program>, with that spelling, is a reserved word. As long as the spelling *programme* is allowed, there is always the danger of **telegramme*.

Exceptional spellings with double <-mm->: *inflammable*, *inflammatory*, *ammonite,* and before <-ule> *gemmule* (#D7). The <-flamm-> stem reflects the Latin spelling, but since English *flame* has a long vowel with a single <m>, spellers might expect that single <m> to persist even when the vowel was in a shortening context.

There is regular absence of <C>-doubling after a stressed short vowel before certain non-§Basic endings (#D7). This accounts for the single <m> before the ending in the following:

- <-ic(al)> (adj.) – *academic, anatomical, atomic, ceramic, comic, dynamic, economical, epidemic, mimic, panoramic, polemic;*
- <-id> (adj.) – *timid*;
- <-ish> (not as a suffix) – *blemish, famish*;
- <-it> (in §Latinate words) – *limit, vomit*, but not *summit*.

Exceptional spellings with single <-m->: *damage*, *gamut*, *camel*, *chemist*, *tremor*, *lemon*, *image*, *woman*, *women*, *promise*, *homage*, *pumice*.

The Hanna (1966) spelling rules have the single correspondence /m/≡<m> and no provision is made for <C>-doubling (*summer, stammer*, etc.). Prefix merger is sometimes catered for by providing a geminate consonant as input (e.g. two phonemes /-mm-/ as a pronunciation for *immoral*). Syllabic /m/ is treated as a separate phonemic unit '/M1/' with the one spelling <m>, largely in the suffix <-ism> and *sarcasm, microcosm*, etc.

3.3.8.2 /n/ *as in* sun

Distribution of variant spellings

/n/ has virtually no divergence: <n> TF 97 per cent; <nn> TF <1 per cent. The proportion of <nn> would be higher if we were to include the many inflected forms in {-ed} and {-ing}, such as *banned, banning,* from *ban,* or in {-er}, {-est}, such as *thinner, thinnest*, from *thin*. Minority divergent spellings are <gn>, <kn>, <pn>; <mn> has been dealt with under /m/. Of these minority spellings, <kn> is the most common at TF 1 per cent, LF <1 per cent. Some of its occurrences are in quite common words; it occurs in: *knack*, *knave*, *knead*, *knee*, *knell*, *knickers*, *knife*, *knight*, *knit*, *knob*, *knock*, *knoll*, *knot*, *know*, *knowledge*, *knuckle*. This is clearly a §Basic spelling; all the words are Germanic in origin. It also has a highly restricted distribution since it only occurs initially in free forms. The <k> can be regarded as an empty letter, though presumably it is inert in *know* because of *acknowledge.*

The spelling <gn> occurs initially in a few §Basic words: *gnarled*, *gnash*, *gnat*, *gnaw* and also in *gneiss*, *gnome*, *gnomon*, *gnu*. A preliminary attempt to decode <gn-> as */gn-/ would alert the reader to a non-English cluster. The same applies to initial <kn-> and <pn->. Occasional spelling pronunciations occur. Since *agnostic* is in fairly common use compared with *gnostic*, the latter may be heard with a spelling pronunciation of initial /gn-/ instead of /n-/. Curiously, the <g> of <gn> does not surface as /g/ in *physiognomy* though it occurs after a vowel. Such empty letters are, however, always a problem for the writer.

The acronym <Gnu> is used as a noun in computer jargon for a facility which is 'not'+'Unix', where *Unix* is a trade name. The <G> is included as mere padding, presumably because <nu> did not seem like a lexical word in only having two letters.

The non-initial instances of <gn>≡/n/ are all in §Romance and §Latinate words. Most of them occur in the context of a previous letter <i> in the spelling of /aɪ/, /eɪ/, /ɔɪ/ and opinions differ on how the string of letters representing the vowel and the /n/ should be analysed. The <g> is clearly an inert letter in *assign*, *benign*, *design*, *malign*, *reign*, *resign*, *sign* (cf. *assignation*, *benignant*, *designate*, *malignant*, *regnant*, *resignation*, *signify*). The present spellings of *align*, *non-aligned*, *alignment* are purely graphic variants of an earlier *aline* due to a false analogy with the previous group. Here the <g> in consequence is purely an empty letter. It is curious that analogy should so cloud common sense and make {line} less recognizable in these words.

The remainder are a small mixed group: *arraign*, *campaign*, *champagne*, *cologne*, *campaign*, *deign*, *ensign*, *foreign*, *impugn*, *sovereign*. The similarity of *sovereign* to *reign* is a contrived spelling which dates back to Middle English. In all these <g> is an empty letter.

<gn> is a spelling for the cluster /nj/, from the French palatal nasal [ɲ], medially in loan-words such as *cognac*, *lorgnette*, *mignonette*, *vignette*; *poignant* has /n/ or /nj/. Italian *Bologna*, *Campagna* also have <gn>≡/nj/. These have to be distinguished from the /gn/ of names such as *Agnew, Bagnall, Magnus, Wagner*. In final position in a name, <gn(e)> is just /n/, since /nj/ is not a possible final cluster in English: *Auvergne*, *Charlemagne*, *Cockaigne, Gascoigne*, *Presteign*, and similarly in *Paignton*. In *Boulogne*, the palatal feature has been shifted into the vowel as /-ɔɪn/.

The spelling <pn> is restricted to words of Greek origin: *pneumonia*, *pneumatic* and the <p> is clearly an empty letter.

Elision of /n/ is fairly usual in *government*, making the <n> an inert letter.

Distribution of <nn>

(For general rules of <C>-doubling, see §3.2.2, p. 114ff.)

There is a VC monosyllable with final <nn>: *inn* (by the 'short word rule' p. 131).

Examples of <nn> with prefixes (#D2):

- (reduced vowel): *announce*, *annoy*, *annihilate*, *annex* (v.), *annul*, *annunciate*; *connect*, *connive*, *connubial*, *connote*, *connumerate*;
- (unreduced vowel): *annotate*, *annexe* (n.); *innocent*, *innate*, *innuendo*, *innocuous*, *innovation*.

The word *anneal* resembles the above words, but it is in fact Old English in origin; the *an-* is related to {on}. There is also a resemblance in words containing Latin *annus* ('year'), where the <-nn-> is part of the stem: *annual*, *annals*, *annuity*, *perennial*, *centennial*.

The §Latinate <in-> prefix is a particularly difficult problem for the speller because there is normally no phonetic difference between <in-> before /n/, as *innocuous, innovative*, and before a vowel, as in *inebriated*, *ineffable*, *ineptitude*, *inexorable*, *iniquity*, *inoculate*, *inundate*. It is difficult to see how this can be taught other than by rote learning or by drawing attention to the meaning of §Latinate stems in groups of similar words. Even this approach may be found wanting. A colleague confesses that for years she spelt *inoculate* as **innoculate*, wrongly thinking that it meant 'to make not harmful' (cf. *noxious*). The real etymology is far from obvious: from the Latin *inoculare* 'to graft'; *oculus* meant an 'eye' or bud.

There is regular absence of <C>-doubling after a stressed short vowel before certain non-§Basic endings (see #D7 p. 123). This accounts for the single <n> before the ending in the following:

- <-ic(al)> (adj.) – *actinic, botanical, bubonic, chronic, clinic, conic, harmonic, ironic, laconic, mechanic, organic, sonic, symphonic*; but *tannic*, *tyrannical* are exceptions;
- <-ish> (not as a suffix) – *admonish, astonish, banish, diminish, finish, punish, replenish, vanish*;
- <-ule> – *granule*.

Exceptional spellings (see #D6 p. 123) with double <-nn->: *binnacle*, *cannibal*, *cinnabar*, *cinnamon*, *tintinnabulation*, *zinnia*.

Exceptional spellings (see #D4 p. 121) with single <-n->: *anode*, *manor*, *manage*, *tenet*, *honour*, *honest*, *money*, *honey*.

The Hanna (1966) spelling rules have the single correspondence /n/≡<n> and no provision is made for <C>-doubling (*dinner, kennel*, etc.). Prefix merger is sometimes catered for by providing a geminate consonant as input (e.g. /-nn-/ as a pronunciation for *innate*). Syllabic /n/ is treated as a separate phonemic unit (/N1/) with the one spelling <en> (*wooden, begotten*).

3.3.8.3 /ŋ/ *as in* sung

Distribution of variant spellings

/ŋ/ shows complete regularity. It is spelt with the digraph <ng> (TF 75 per cent, LF 60 per cent, F+) unless /k/ or /g/ follows. In that case the <n> alone suffices. These figures are based on a lemma count and do not include the common *-ing* inflection. 'Conservative' dialects of English, typically in Northern England, will have no loss of morpheme-final /g/. For them, *singing* is ['sɪŋgɪŋg] (not as SBS ['sɪŋɪŋ]) and *singer* rhymes with *finger* as ['sɪŋgə] (see p. 57).

When a prefix-final /n/ precedes a stem beginning with /k/ or /g/, the velar nasal varies with /n/: *income* as either /'ɪŋkʌm/ or /'ɪnkʌm/, *synchronic* as as either /sɪŋ-/ or /sɪn-/. In *anxiety*, *anxious* the /k/ or /g/ may disappear by cluster simplification.

The Hanna (1966) spelling rules are:

1 <ng> syllable-medial before /θ/ (*length, strength*);
2 <n> syllable-medial all other cases (*drunk, juncture*);
3 <n> syllable-final before /kw/ (*delinquent, banquet*);
4 <ng> word-final (*evening, sting*);
5 <n> syllable-final before /k, g/ (*canker, dingle*);
6 <ng> syllable-final all other cases (*kingdom, lengthy*).

3.3.9 Liquids: / l r /

3.3.9.1 /l/ as in lamp

Distribution of variant spellings

The divergence of /l/ is largely predictable (table 38).

Table 38 Spellings of /l/

spellings of /l/	*TF*	*LF*	
<l>	75 %	81 %	
<le> (for /əl/)	8 %	9 %	
<-ll->	18 %	10 %	F+

'F+' : tends to occur in high frequency words

<l> is an empty letter in the three function words *could*, *should* and *would*. In *should* and *would* the original /l/ of ME *sholde*, *wolde* was lost in early Modern English, and *could*, which never had an /l/, acquired its current spelling by analogy. So, this group of modals came to have a uniform spelling.

The string <al> is found as a spelling of /ɑː/ (*half*, *calm*, etc.) and of /ɔː/ (*talk*, *walk*, etc.) in some very common words. It is also a nonce spelling of /æ/ in *salmon*. The <l> in *palm* can only be considered an inert representation of /l/ (as both 'part of hand' and 'tree'): cf. *palmary*, *palmic*, *palmiferous*.

Apart from instances of /Ø/≡<l> and the vowel spelling <al>, the spellings <l> and <ll> are peculiar to /l/.

The problem of distinguishing <-le> spellings of /əl/ from <-al>, <-el>, <-il>, <-ol> and <-ul> is discussed under homophonous affixes in §5.5 pp. 433ff.

Distribution of <ll>

(For general rules of <C>-doubling, see §3.2.2, pp. 114ff.).

There is more difficulty in accounting for the occurrence of double <-ll-> than for the double spelling of any other consonant. This is partly due to the frequency of <-ll-> in Latin and Greek stems and partly because §Latinate words borrowed by way of French may no longer have recognizable constituents.

Normally, <l> would double after a short vowel in a monosyllable (*bell, cell, doll, mill*, etc.), but there are some exceptions. They are all marginal in various ways, usually by abbreviation: technical loan *col* ('gap between hills' < French); *gal* (< *girl*), *pal* (< Romany); technical abbreviations *bel* (< the name '(A.G.) Bell', = 'unit of power comparison'), *cel* (< *celluloid*, see p. 122), *gel* (< *gelatine*), *mel* ('perceptual unit of pitch'), *mil* (< *millimetre*), *nil* (contraction of Latin *nihil*); short names *Hal* (< *Henry*), *Sal* (< *Sally*) (p. 458).

Examples of <-ll-> with prefixes (see #D2 p. 119):

- (reduced vowel): *alleviate*, *alliteration*, *allude*, *allusion*, *ally* (v.); *collate*, *collateral*, *collect* (v.), *collide*, *collision*.
- (unreduced vowel): *allocate*, *ally* (n.); *collect* (n.), *colleague*, *college*, *collimate*, *colloquy*; *illegal*, *illegible*, *illicit*, *illimitable*, *illuminate*, *illusion*, *illustrate*; *pellucid*.

There are quite a few words which resemble the above and in which the <-ll-> is not covered by other doubling conventions: *allegory*, *allergy*, *alligator*. There is some etymological uncertainty about *allot*, *allow*, and *allure*. *Allay* has come to have a §Latinate appearance in spite of its Old English origin (*a* + *lecgan*). To the average reader these spellings must seem to belong with the §Latinate prefixes.

A good many words, contrary to #D6 (see p. 123), have <-ll-> in the third syllable from the end of a free-form after a stressed short vowel. The ending <-ion> seems to require this spelling, but not in all instances: *billion*, *bullion*, *galleon*, *million*, *mullion*, *pillion*, *postillion*, *stallion*, but also *battalion*, *pavilion*, *vermilion*. Compare doubled and single <r> in *carrion–clarion*.

Other examples of <-ll-> unaccounted for are: *ballerina*, *ballistic*, *balloon*, *bellicose*, *brilliant*, *bulletin*, *calligraphy*, *calliopsis*, *camellia*, *colliery*, *ebullient*, *ellipse*, *embellish*, *fallacious*, *fallacy*, *fallible*, *gallery*, *gallium*, *hallelujah*, *hallucinate*, *hellebore*, *intellect*, *intelligent*, *mellifluous*, *miscellany*, *palliate*, *pallium*, *parallel*, *pollute*, *shallot*, *shillelagh*, *tellurium*.

Pseudo-compounds are: *ballyhoo*, *bulldozer*, *hullaballoo*, *lollipop*, *scallywag*.

There is regular absence of <C>-doubling after a stressed short vowel before certain non-§Basic endings (see #D7, p. 123). This accounts for the single <l> before the ending in the following:

- <-ic(al)> (adj.) – *alcoholic, angelic, carbolic, diabolical, italic, symbolic, vocalic,* but not *metallic* and *phallic*;
- <-id> (adj.) – *solid, squalid, stolid, valid,* but not *pallid*;
- <-ish> (not as a suffix) – *abolish, demolish, polish, relish,* but not *embellish*;
- *cellule* is unusual in having <CC> before <-ule>.

Exceptional spellings with single <-l-> – *balance*, *chalet*, *choler*, *column*, *develop*, *felon*, *lily*, *malice*, *palace*, *palate*, *salad*, *salon*, *scholar*, *solemn*, *talent*.

The endings <-ally> and <-ically> have a single /l/ in pronunciation in spite of the latter's morpheme boundary with underlying //l// on either side. In practice both <-icly> and <-ically> are often pronounced /ɪklɪ/ with a non-syllabic /l/, so that *stoicly* and *stoically* and such pairs are usually indistinguishable except in very deliberate speech.

Unlike the suffixes <-less> and <-ness>, which have double <ss>, there is no doubling in <-ful>. Spelling errors such as *<spoonfull> are likely in the absence of a general pattern.

To some extent, British and American spelling differ in the use of <-l-> and <-ll->. The most common case is the group of final-stressed two-syllable words *distil, enrol, enthral, fulfil, instal, instil,* which have this single <l> in British spelling, but which usually have <ll> in American spelling.

In British spelling the <-l> at the end of the final unstressed syllable of words such as *signal, bevel, cavil, carol,* is doubled before the endings {-ed}, {-ing}: *signalled, signalling, travelled, cavilling, carolling*. This doubling sometimes occurs in American texts, but a single <-l-> is more usual: *signaled, signaling, traveled, caviling, caroling*. Other words of this type are: *apparel, barrel, bevel, cancel, channel, chisel, counsel, cudgel, devil, dial, dishevel, drivel, duel, enamel, equal, fuel, funnel, gambol, grovel, jewel, kennel, label, libel, shovel, shrivel, snivel, spiral, stencil, tassel, towel, trowel, tunnel, victual*. The American single <-l-> spelling would only occasionally invite a wrong reading, such as <due-led> for *dueled*. The <-ll-> of *gravelly* (from *gravel*) keeps it different from *gravely* (from *grave*).

In the Hanna (1966) spelling rules, <l> is the default spelling and:

1 <ll> word-final accented after /ɔː/ or a short vowel (*tall, mill, bell, pull, hull*).

Prefix merger is sometimes catered for by providing a geminate consonant as input (e.g. /-ll-/ as a pronunciation for *illegal*). Syllabic /l/ is treated as a separate phonemic unit (/L1/) with the one spelling <le>.

3.3.9.2 /r/ *as in* ramp

Distribution of variant spellings

/r/ has virtually no divergence (table 39).

The complete loss of //r// before consonants in SBS and other 'non-rhotic'

Table 39 Spellings of /r/

spellings of /r/	*TF*	*LF*
<r>	94 %	95 %
<rr>	4 %	4 %
<wr>	2 %	<1 %
<rh>	<1 %	<1 %

accents of English means that the <r> is best considered as part of the vowel spelling <ar>, <ir>, <or>, etc. in words such as *farm, firm, form*. Apart from this, <r> is confined to the spelling of /r/.

The <wr> spelling is always initial in monosyllabic minimal free-forms and a few frequentative words ending in <-le>. Examples: *wraith*, *wrangle*, *wrath* (var. *wroth*), wreak, *wreath*, *wren*, *wrestle*, *wriggle*, *wrinkle*, *wrist*, *writhe*, *wrong*, *wrought, wry*. There are some homophone pairs differing only in <wr->, <r->: *wrack*, *wrap*, *wreck* (*reck* is, however, archaic), *wretch*, *wright*, *wring*, *write*, *wrote*, *wrung*.

<rh> occurs in §Greek words and names: *rhapsody*, *rhea*, *rheostat*, *rhetoric*, *rheum*, *rheumatism*, *rhinoceros*, *rhizome*, *rhodium*, *rhododendron*, *rhyme* (see also under /aɪ/ p. 153), *rhythm*; *Rhoda, Rhodes*. It also occurs in other non-English names: *Penrhyn*, *Rheims*, *Rhine*, *Rhondda, Rhyl*. The etymology of *rhubarb* is rather obscure, but the scientific §Greek spelling <rh> indicates the esteem in which it was held by herbalists. In *catarrh*, *myrrh*, the <h> is presumably an empty letter.

Distribution of <rr>

(For general rules of <C>-doubling, see §3.2.2, pp. 114ff.).

Examples of <rr> with prefixes: *arrange*, *array*, *arrest*, *arrogant*, *arrogate*; (negative {in-}) *irrational*, *irredeemable*, *irregular*, *irrelevant*, *irresistible*, etc.; ({in-} 'in') *irradiate*, *irradicate*, *irrigate*, *irrupt*; *correct*, *correlation*, *correspond*, *corroborate*, *corrode*, *corrugated*, *corrupt*; *interrogate*; *surreal*, *surreptitious*, *surrogate*. There is frequent confusion between the homophones *irruption* and *eruption* in spite of the extreme difference of meaning (see §5.3, p. 405).

Exceptional spellings with double <-rr->: *barricade*, *barrister*, *carraway*, *carrion*, *corridor*, *farrier*, *garrison, garrulous*, *harridan*, *horrify*, *narrative*, *parricide*, *terrapin*, *terrier*. Some of these are derived from base forms with <-rr-> (e.g. *horror*). In others the <rr> appears to be deliberate short-vowel marking in English: *garrison* is related to French *garer* ('to protect') as is the later loan *garage*.

There is regular absence of <C>-doubling after a stressed short vowel before certain non-§Basic suffixes (see #D7 p. 123). This accounts for the single <r> before the ending in the following:

- <-ic(al)> (adj.) – *allegoric, atmospheric, barbaric, clerical, empirical, euphoric, generic, historic, hysterical, mesmeric, meteoric, rhetorical, satiric, tartaric;*
- <-id> (adj.) – *arid, florid,* but not *horrid, torrid;*
- <-ish> (not as a suffix) – *cherish, parish, perish;*
- <-it> (in §Latinate words) – *inherit, merit, spirit;*
- <-ule> – *spherule* but not *ferrule.*

Exceptional spellings with single <-r->: *apparel, baron, beret, bury, carat, carob, carol, cherub, claret, coral, florin, florist, forage, foray, foreign, forest, garage, gerund, herald, heron, mirage, moral, orange, peril, seraph, serif, sheriff, syrup, tariff, very, virile.*

The Hanna (1966) spelling rules have the single correspondence /r/≡<r> and no provision for <rr>. Prefix merger is sometimes catered for by providing a geminate consonant as input (e.g. /-rr-/ as a pronunciation for *irresponsible*).

3.3.10 Semivowels: /w j/

3.3.10.1 /w/ *as in* well

Distribution of variant spellings

/w/ shows some divergence, but this is largely explicable from contexts (table 40).

Table 40 Spellings of /w/

spellings of /w/	*TF*	*LF*	
<w>	64 %	59 %	F+
<qu>≡/kw/	27 %	31 %	F-
<wh>	5 %	5 %	
<u>	4 %	4 %	
<oi>≡/wɑː/	<1 %	1 %	

'F+' : tends to occur in high frequency words; 'F-' : tends to occur in low frequency words

The above figures do not include function words: *one, what, why, where, which, whether, when, while,* etc.

The grapheme <w>, either as a single letter shape or literally as <uu>, 'double <u>', was intended by medieval scribes to separate the consonantal and syllabic uses of <u>. However, §Latinate words, such as *anguish*, continued to have <u> and, on the other hand, the new <w> came to be used in vowel digraphs such as <aw>, <ew>, <ow>.

Words with <wh> which have homophones spelt with <w> are: *whale–wail; wheel–weal; whet–wet; whey–way, weigh; whig–wig; whit–wit;*

whoa–woe.

There are several onomatopoeic words with <wh>: *whack*, *wham*, *wheeze*, *whimper*, *whine*, *whinny*, *whirr*, *whisper*, *whistle*, *whizz*, *whoopee*.

Other words with <wh> are: *overwhelm*, *wharf*, *wheat*, *wheedle*, *whelk*, *whelp*, *wherry*, *whiff*, *whim*, *whimsy*, *whip*, *whippet*, *whirl*, *whisk*, *whisker*, *whisky*, *whist*, *white*, *whopper*, *whopping*, *whorl*, *whortleberry*.

A common feature of these words is that the <wh> occurs initially in a minimal free-form. Scottish, Irish or American speakers, who contrast /hw/ with /w/, have a distinct spelling advantage here.

The string /kw/ is normally spelt <qu> within a morpheme (see under /k/ for details). This <u> spelling is also found elsewhere, notably in §Latinate words after /g/ and /s/, following the Latin convention that <u> (and <i>) represented both a vowel and a semi-vowel. Words with <u>≡/w/:

- after /g/ : *anguish*, *distinguish*, *extinguish*, *guano*, *guava*, *iguana*, *language*, *languid*, *languish*, *linguist*, *penguin*, *sanguine*, *unguent*;
- after /s/ : *assuage*, *persuade*, *suave*, *suede*, *suite*;
- others: *cuisine*, *marijuana*, and in one of several pronunciations of *conduit*.

Words with <oi>≡/wɑː/ are recent French loan-words: *boudoir*, *bourgeois*, *chamois*, *coiffure*, *escritoire*, *memoir*, *patois*, *repertoire*, *reservoir*, *soiree*, *toilette*. Some speakers have /wæ/ when it is non-final.

In the Hanna (1966) spelling rules, <w> is the default spelling and:

1 <u> after /k, g/ (*quite, sanguine*).

3.3.10.2 /j/ *as in* yell

Many American writers use the phoneme symbol /y/.

Distribution of variant spellings

/j/ is not easy to deal with as a unit of spelling correspondence. We may distinguish three main groups:

1 contexts in which /j/ appears to function as an independent consonant which is not subsumed under the spelling of a following //u//: *yet*, *yacht*, *youth*, *yard*, etc.
2 contexts in which the /j/ is bound up with an underlying //u//, appearing as surface /juː/, /jʊ/, /jʊə/ or /jə/, and where there is no independent 'consonantal' spelling of the /j/: *use*, *presume*, *cute*, *mule*, etc. This /j/ will not appear in related allomorphs with short /ʌ/: *presume* /zjuːm/ – *presumption* /zʌm/.
3 contexts in which the /j/ represents a reduction of an underlying //iː// or //ɪ// as in *saviour*, *behaviour* (where /jə/ is the only phonetic form) or *envious*, *cordial* (where the lento form is /ɪə/ and an allegro form is /jə/).

Phonetically these two variants represent the same high front to mid central glide; the only difference is in the prominence pattern: decreasing in /ɪə/ and increasing in /jə/ (Jones 1956: §442f). Such instances of /j/ usually occur at the junction of stem and suffix in §Romance or §Latinate vocabulary.

The /j/≡<y> correspondence, rather surprisingly, accounts for only a relatively small proportion of instances of /j/ (TF 19 per cent, LF 4 per cent, F+). Since the distribution of /j/ is restricted to syllable initial position, given the type of phonemic analysis used here, /j/≡<y> is usually found in word-initial position, often in very common §Basic words: *yacht*, *yard*, *year*, *yell*, *yellow*, *yes*, *yet*, *yield*, *yoga*, *yoke*, *yolk*, *young*, *youth*, etc. It is initial in a variant <-yer> of {-ier} in *bowyer*, *lawyer*, *sawyer*; the variant seems to be conditioned by the previous <w>. Only occasionally is /j/≡<y> found medially in a single morpheme: *canyon*, *banyan*. In *carillon* /kəˈrɪljən/, there is the marginal correspondence <ll>≡/lj/. These medial examples are clearly exotic, as are words with the spelling /j/≡<j>: *majolica* (also with /ʤ/), *hallelujah*.

The correspondence /j/≡<y> is generally thought of as the normal 'consonantal' spelling. However,<y> is one of the letters which do not 'say their name', presumably because of its complex history. It came into the Roman alphabet to represent Greek upsilon <υ> (cf. French 'i grec') and in English came to have both consonant and vowel values (*yet*, *sky*). In consequence it is a prime source of confusion for the layman in distinguishing sounds and spellings.

/juː/ as a unit of correspondence is examined separately under long vowels (see p. 200).

The Hanna (1966) spelling rules are:

1 <y> accented (yellow, youth);
2 <i> unaccented (brilliant, junior).

/j/ is subsumed in a phoneme '/U/' (new) and there is a different phoneme '/O6/' for plain /uː/ (threw).

Chapter 4

Text-to-speech correspondences: decoding

4.1 SCALE AND COMPLEXITY IN TEXT-TO-SPEECH SPELLING RULES

Text-to-speech technology

Since the Renaissance many descriptions of English spelling conventions have been written, with varying degrees of explicitness, in a text-to-speech format. The teaching of reading required them. Today, in man-machine communication, the same body of knowledge has to be available in a fully explicit form for information processing. Information can be switched between the written and the spoken medium for various practical purposes. A spoken message can alert a computer operator more directly than a written message, which may linger unnoticed on the screen. An optical character reader has been linked to a speech synthesizer to provide the Kurtzweiler reading machine for the blind. Listening to a speech-converted written text has been shown to be an efficient method of proof-reading. Written text can be sent automatically to a recipient in the form of an ordinary spoken telephone call. All these facilities for reading text evidently have a built-in strategy for dealing with English spelling conventions. So, one would think that to find a full and friendly account of the spelling rules of English, one need only look inside such a system. This is only partly true.

The way in which such machines deal with spelling conventions is not necessarily analogous to human reading processes at the level of conscious awareness. The nature of the built-in rules varies with the computer power available for running them, and with the level of naturalness required in the synthetic speech produced. For instance, an algorithm which has enough computer power to build some of the syntactic and morphological competence of a human speaker into the reading process will be more accurate than one that crudely tries to turn letters into phonemes in ignorance of syntactic categories and morpheme boundaries. A computer which can afford to store a large look-up list of relatively irregular spellings can do without rules which operate only in a very few words. Consequently, the rules we find in such systems will vary in form, complexity and coverage. One difference between such rules and ordinary correspondence rules which a human being might employ as reference rules, is that the computer rules often have a complex hierarchical structure, with the output from any one rule feeding down through layers of other rules. The effect of a single rule cannot always be read off in isolation.

Computers also check the spelling as a facility in word processing systems. This does not involve text-to-speech relationships and is largely done with comprehensive and expandable look-up dictionaries. Even here there may be some scope for rules as graphotactic rules, which can spot mistakes by noting irregular letter sequences. So, for instance, a three-letter sequence in English cannot normally consist of three identical letters, so *<happpy> can be corrected to <happy>. These spelling checkers can suggest an alternative spelling for a suspected mistake, but their suggestions have to be based on orthographic resemblance. Homophone errors are difficult to deal with. The system would have to have some grammar to cope with *their–there*, or *scene–seen* confusion.

In quest of spelling rules, we can now look briefly at three text-to-speech computer algorithms of varying scale and complexity to see how they cope with the irregularities of English spelling.

4.1.1 Modelling human cognitive ability in spelling

The MITalk system (Allen, J., Hunnicutt, M. S. and Klatt, D. 1987)

The MITalk system, one of the most elaborate text-to speech conversion systems (Allen *et al.* 1987), has been more than 25 years in the making. Even in the early 1960s it was apparent that computers might ultimately be capable of natural synthetic speech output from ordinary written text input and the basic research into text-to-speech conversion started then, long before the technology for rapid low-cost conversion was available. Speech synthesis-by-rule requires a fairly detailed allophonic transcription as input to the synthesizer device. This is provided in MITalk by a comprehensive linguistic analysis of the text at phonemic, syllabic, morphemic and syntactic levels, eked out by whatever semantic and pragmatic information can be deduced. The system was designed as a cognitive model: 'it seeks to mirror the human cognitive capability for reading aloud' (ibid.: 12).

If this model is a valid one for what the human reader does, then it comes down heavily in favour of a holistic model of the reading process. After some initial tidying up of numbers and abbreviations such as 'Mr', the words in the text are broken down into morphs (affixes and stems), or left as whole words. Each recognized morph or word is then looked up in a dictionary containing no less than 12,000 morphs to find the corresponding pronunciation – the word *carelessness* would be looked up as three chunks.

So the system can obviously cope with several times as many words as the 12,000 entries in the look-up list, indeed no less than 95 per cent on average of running text. Within a known subject area, say economics or botany, this performance figure could no doubt be increased by adding to the dictionary other forms used in the jargon of that subject. Only when a word or morph cannot be found in the dictionary, is the pronunciation assembled by using a set of correspondence rules. The very size of the dictionary shows that it contains not only irregular words and minority spellings, but also words that are quite regularly spelt. It indicates that, for the computer running the system, it is more economical to look up such a word than to process the individual spelling correspondences.

Since writing English is a left-to-right linear process, reading is popularly thought to be a left-to-right scan of the printed words. This is not so in the MITalk system. When a word not in the dictionary is processed by rule, there are three distinct stages. The example word given is *caribou*. Any affixes would be first stripped off. Then the consonant letters are dealt with to give #/k/-?-/r/-?-/b/-?-# and then, using this as a framework, the vowels are slotted in. Doing the consonants first, it is claimed, makes sure that you get <a>≡/æ/ after the /k/ and before the /r/. After a /w/ you would get /ɔː/. This can obviously be done just as well by context-sensitive ordered rules, but the MIT research team obviously found some processing economy in dealing with consonants first.

4.1.2 Two early miniature systems with 'readable' rules

McIlroy (1974)

There have been much simpler systems than MITalk and other present-day state-of-the-art systems. The two we shall now examine were written in the 1970s and designed to run on small computers with restricted storage space. They are valid systems on the assumption that a large look-up table cannot be accommodated. They aim to produce acceptable speech from a cheap synthesizer rather than wholly natural speech. Since the input to the synthesizer is essentially just a string of phonemes, their spelling rules can be read directly by the human speller. Whether or not these systems are still valid for today's technology is irrelevant for our purpose. They are interesting because they try to account for English spelling as far as possible with simple correspondence rules. We can look in some detail first at a system of medium complexity, and then at a system of maximum simplicity, to see what regularities they find worth exploring and what eludes them.

McIlroy (1974), working at Bell Laboratories, describes a relatively compact program, requiring a minimum of storage, for producing synthetic speech by rule using a cheap votrax speech synthesizer. This was to cater for amateur computer users who wished to add spoken output to their computer games, or for a limited range of spoken messages that the computer might wish to tell the operator. For that purpose less than perfect speech is quite acceptable. 'Neither the program nor the output device pretend to produce natural speech, but it is intelligible to everybody who has heard much of it' (ibid.: 1). On the other hand, the quality of the speech would have to be reasonably good, because once produced it vanished. Unclear speech cannot be re-read like unclear printed output.

Input to the synthesizer takes the form of a string of acoustic segments from a set of 64, which are used singly and in combination to represent phonemes, with some allophonic variation. The section of McIlroy's algorithm that contains recognizable spelling rules to produce this input is referred to as the 'word fragment rules'. It is interesting to note where McIlroy got them from. They came partly from *Webster's New International Dictionary* and partly from Venezky (1970b), but, inevitably for a pioneering project, from two other sources: 'off the top of the head' and after 'intensive interactive experimentation . . . with word lists' (ibid.: 7). Before these rules operate, however, the raw text has to be processed in various ways.

An algorithm for text-to-speech conversion in English needs to work with the printed word as its operational unit. A necessary first step is to identify word boundaries marked by a space or a punctuation mark and to merge capitals with lower case letters. After this, McIlroy is able to re-use capital letters later on in the algorithm to represent recognizable long vowels in the output of various rewriting rules. The next step in McIlroy's algorithm is to find the complete pronunciation of any word stored in his look-up list. In McIlroy's case this list is very small; it could hardly be called a 'dictionary' as in the MITalk system. It is strictly for unacceptable irregularities. Moreover the items in the list are whole words; it does not include affixes. It is for the writer of such an algorithm to decide when it would pay to look up the whole pronunciation of a particular word in a list rather than add new rules to cover what happens to be irregular. What is or is not cost-effective depends on many factors and is a matter of hunches rather than strict calculation. McIlroy's look-up table of irregular words is very modest, with a mere 103 entries. It would, however, be misleading to cite this '103' as an index of irregularity, since the 'word fragment rules' which follow often refer, in effect, to a single free form such as *bear, break, certain, death, foreign, laugh, place, private, react* or to a single bound form such as *beaut-, creat -, exagg-, prett -*. McIlroy's look-up list is perhaps worth quoting in full:

a, alkali, always, any, april, are, as, because, been, being, below, body, both, busy, copy, do, does, doesn't, doing, done, dr, early, earn, eleven, enable, engine, etc, evening, every, everyone, eye, february, finally, friday, gas, guest, has, have, having, heard, his, imply, into, is, island, john, july, live, lived, living, many, maybe, meant, moreover, mr, mrs, nature, none, nothing, nowhere, nuisance, of, on, once, one, only, over, people, read, reader, refer, says, seven, shall, someone, something, than, that, the, their, them, there, thereby, these, they, this, those, to, today, tomorrow, tuesday, two, upon, very, water, wednesday, were, who, whom, whose, woman, women, yes. (103 words)

The list includes common abbreviations, irregular names (whose capital letters have been made small in the preprocessing stage), and well-known irregular words such as *one, people, women.* Initial <th>≡/ð/ in deictic or 'pointing' words (*there, those,* etc) is evidently not ascribed by rule. *Gas* and *has* are here, McIlroy says, to prevent them from rhyming with *was.* What this means is not immediately apparent. It turns out that *was* is processed by following the rules as /wəz/, which is a reasonable compromise, since most instances of *was* are unstressed in running text. Two rules produce this /wəz/: <a>≡/ə/ before final <s> (*Americas,* etc.) and final <s>≡/z/ by default (*his, bans,* with exceptions *antics, pops, cats,* etc.). This snippet highlights one main reason why these more compact rule systems are difficult to relate to human literacy. The test of success is the intelligibility of the synthetic speech output. It pays to make sure that *was* gets its /ə/. It is perceptually less important to worry about the difference between *pigs* /z/ and *picks* /s/. Though this is a common phonemic contrast, it is effectively neutralized after a previous obstruent. Obstruent clusters in English are all lenis ('voiced' is phonetically inaccurate) or all fortis ('voiceless'). We have /gz/ and /ks/ but not */gs/ and */kz/. Moreover, the phonetic difference between the /z/ and /s/ in this context is reduced, since /z/ has final devoicing. In these circumstances any rough-and-ready burst of high frequency noise might well do: '*naturalness* was not a pre-requisite' (ibid.: 1). As a further consequence of this approach, there is a premium on getting words with high text frequency right, rather than seeing how a particular rule would perform across the lexicon as a whole. The human reader, on the other hand, is more likely to want rules which are reliable for unfamiliar words.

The next stage, after checking a word against the look-up list, is to strip off various affixes. The inflectional and derivational suffixes are particularly important. However, McIlroy's deliberately-restricted approach only allows affix identification in terms of simple letter strings. There is no differentiating, for instance, between the endings of *waiter–water, bomber–lumber,* which all end in <-er>, but which have different word-structure. Some of the strings stripped off may not be discrete affixes at all, but part of the root morpheme.

An <-s> is stripped off unless preceded by another <s> or by <u> (*miss,* *minus*). The <s># is then pronounced /z/, or, more precisely, it is given the VOTRAX synthesizer code for [z] followed by the code for [s] (ibid. rule 22.2: A17). This would presumably have the effect of a devoiced allophone of /z/, but phoneme /z/ it must be. *Yes* would fail and so is in the look-up list, but *his, bans,* are correct. Why then *his* and *has* are in the look-up list is unclear. If the stem ends in a letter indicating a voiceless consonant, <c,f,k,p,t>, the <s> is processed as /s/, but for some unexplained reason the synthesis of *antics, puffs, ticks, pops, cats,* is marked as 'a poor but intelligible pronunciation'. One reason for stripping off a final <-s> is so that any <ie> in front of it can then be rewritten as <y>, whether or not such a form exists (*laddies* now becomes *laddy* + /z/ and *series* becomes **sery* + /z/).

Suffix stripping is part of the process of identifying long vowels. If the suffix or a final <-e> is preceded by a single consonant letter apart from <x>, it is assumed that the previous vowel is long. The endings *-able, -ably, -ed, -en, -er, -ery, -est, -ey, -ic, -ical, -ing, -less, -ly, -ment, -ness* and *-or* are marked with '|' to indicate a potential <e>-marked boundary. So *mating* is rewritten as <mAt|ing>. Capital letters are now used to indicate long vowels and these are treated separately in the rules. Some vowels inevitably come to be wrongly marked, as in *hyperbole, gone, risen.* The endings <-al>, <-le>, <-re>, <-us> and <-y> are treated as equivalent to final <-e> for identifying long vowels (<mOdal>, <bUgle>, <fIbre>, <stYlus>, <spIny>). Similarly in other stems a single vowel letter followed by only one consonant letter is taken to represent a long vowel (<fUgue>, <rElay>).

The obvious exceptions to these rules for identifying long vowels (*canal* as */keɪnl/, *metal* as */miːtl/, etc.) could have been included in the look-up list of exceptional words, if there had been storage space available. Alternatively they could be regarded as a 'corrigible' mispronunciation. The listener would presumably be able to treat the VOTRAX synthesizer used by McIlroy as a speaker with a different and unusual incidence of phonemes in some words, just as speakers differ in saying *scone* with /əʊ/ or with /ɒ/. A human says /kə'næl/; the VOTRAX has its own idiolect and says */keɪnæl/.

Free-form boundaries within words cause problems when there is a morph-final <-e>. The <-e-> in *cockleshell, bumblebee, thistledown* is clearly part of <le>≡/əl/ after a consonant letter. A similar boundary in *latecomer, takeaway, fencepost, horseback, linesman* is not so easily identified. Here the human reader scanning from left to right can identify the completion of a known free form, but in a relatively simple algorithm like McIlroy's, there is little scope for modelling this aspect of linguistic competence by other means.

It is here, perhaps, that the computer algorithm ceases to be reader-friendly. To solve this problem of medial 'silent <e>', McIlroy provides three rules of 'considerable reliability', but however well they may work in practice, their effect is scarcely obvious to the human reader. The first of these in McIlroy's notation and bracket-use (which need not concern us unduly) is:

¬[#] ¬[#][bcdfgmnprst][bdfgkpt]*le* ¬[aeiouy |] ¬[|]*[aeiouy]⇒ ...*le* |...
(McIlroy 1974: 6)

– where the sign '¬' complements the set, so that '¬[aeiouy]' means any non-vowel letter including '#'. This rule will insert a silent <e> marker in *bumble |bee, cockle |shell, thistle |down,* (roughly) when the <le> is preceded by two consonant letters which are not at the beginning of the word and which are followed by a consonant letter (excluding <y>) and a vowel letter. It is quite straightforward for a computer to see whether the first of two consonant letters is in the set <bcdfgmnprst> and the second in the set <bdfgkpt>, in spite of the fact that barely a quarter of such combinations would actually occur. A human reader, however, could only visualize the possibilities in terms of natural, definable classes. These are in effect:

1 <C> doublings, as in *cobblestone, huckleberry, saddlebag, dufflecoat, gogglebox, applewood, battlefield*;
2 spellings of homorganic nasal and plosive, as in *tumbledown, simpleton, candlestick, mantlepiece, anklesocks, stranglehold*;
3 <st>, as in *mistletoe*;
4 <rC> clusters, as in *warblefly, girdlecake, whortleberry.*

The ability to recognize the boundary in these is partly based on phonetic competence that McIlroy's computer could not have.

A further rule recognizes a 'silent <e>' which marks a preceding long vowel and which is followed by a free form boundary when the string <V> <C> <e> <C> is preceded by a word boundary or consonant letter, but the <V> may not be <e>. The third rule recognizes a 'silent <e>' preceded by a consonant letter and one of the strings <oa>, <oi>, <oo>, <ou>, <oy>. In both of these rules there are two conditions:

1 the <C> before the <e> is not <w>, <x>, <y>;
2 the <C> after the <e> is not <n>, <r> or <y>.

These rules seem to be too complex and amorphous for a human speller to follow consciously. Yet they are an index of the competence otherwise effortlessly shown by human readers in coping with the structure of complex words.

Words not found in McIlroy's look-up list of irregularities are then put through some 580 'word fragment rules' for conversion into the acoustic segments of synthesizer input. Effectively they can be read as rules which map letters on to phonemes. The rules are not all simple direct correspondence rules; they include a large number of rewriting rules. To show how they operate, here is one small section – that for <c>-strings. I have made one or two minor alterations in layout to make the extract more readable.

I have changed the synthesizer codes to phoneme symbols. The arrow ⇒ means 'rewrite as'. The rewritten string then continues its processing through any further rules that apply to it. At each stage, any phoneme symbols produced by a rule go straight to the synthesizer. Symbols in curly brackets are alternative contexts. The symbol '|' has been inserted by the pre-processing rules to mark a potential 'silent <e>'. The rules are printed here in the order in which they apply and should be read.

> 4.4 cy /s/ ⇒ y (Which means that an /s/ is sent to the synthesizer and the <y> is left for further processing, as in: <decency>).
> 4.3 ck /k/ (As in: <check|ing>, <acknowledge>).
> 4.2.8 mech ⇒ mek (As in: <mechaniSm>. This simply respells <mech>).
> 4.2.7 machIn /məʃ/ ⇒ En (As in: <machIne|ry>. This sends /məʃ/ to the synthesizer and respells the <In> as <En>, so that it comes out with /iː/, not /aɪ/).
> 4.2.6 arch {iy} ⇒ ark {iy} (As in: <architect>, <hierarchy>).
> 4.2.5.2 ch|or ⇒ k|or (As in: <anch|ore|d>, <parach|or>).
> 4.2.5.1 chor ⇒ kor (As in: <chordAte>). It does not apply to a marked long vowel as in: chOre, chOrus.
> (4.2.4 is not printed).
> 4.2.3 ch {lnr} /k/ ⇒ {lnr} (As in: <chlorIde|>, <technique|>, <achromat|ic>). It does not apply to match|less, rich|ness.
> 4.2.2 chem ⇒ kem (As in: <chem|ical>). Exception: chemISe.
> 4.2.1 charact /kærɪkt/ (As in: <characterIze>).
> 4.2 ch /ʧ/ (church). Exceptions: <ache|>, <cache|>, <chaSm>, <chef>, <choir>, <chthOnian>, <drachm>, <echo>, <fuchsia>, <parachUte|>,<stomach>, <yacht>.
> 4.1.3 ci {aeo} /ʃ/ ⇒ {aeo} (As in: <fAcial>, <efficient>, <vicious>).
> 4.1.2 c|i ⇒ si (As in: <fenc|ing>).
> 4.1.1 ce {ao}⇒ ci {ao} (As in: <Ocean>, <herbAceous>).
> 4.1 c {EeIiY} ⇒ /s/ {EeIiY} (As in: <precEde|>, <success>, <placid>, <incIte|>, <cYcle>).
>
> (ibid.: A5)

There is no real advantage in framing rules as rewriting rules rather than as direct correspondence rules. Rule 4.2.8 might just as well send the whole string /mek/ direct to the synthesizer. The rewriting format makes it difficult for a human reader to follow a particular word through the rules. On the other hand, rewriting may indicate a natural spelling reform by showing how best to regularize an irregularity.

The smallest practicable text-to-speech algorithm? Ainsworth (1973)

The smallest practicable text-to-speech algorithm in publication appears to be Ainsworth (1973). It is designed to provide rules for a modest speech synthesizer operating at the limit of acceptability and making minimal demands on computer time and memory. It does not make use of stored irregularities, but relies entirely on correspondence rules. This does not really mean that it is a different type of algorithm, since some 'rules' inevitably deal with a single word or morpheme. As a working system it seems to have been overtaken by events, since 'small' computers nowadays are much more powerful. But as an attempt to write a maximally simple spelling algorithm it retains its interest. In this artificial speech system, the information supplied to the synthesizer is in the form of phoneme strings with a simple stress assignment rule and division of the text into apparent breath groups. The 159 correspondence rules of the algorithm are quoted in table 41 below. A quarter of these correspondence rules effectively relate to single words or morphemes (*a, are, able, ever, have, here, shoe, the, their, there, -tion, upon, were, what, where, who,* etc.) and to very small sets of irregular spellings. Seven rules are devoted to sorting out <ough>, six rules to <ow>.

Since the original rules take up very little space, we can quote the whole set more or less as published. The rules were printed with no commentary or evaluation in the format given below in table 41. In his short presentation, Ainsworth did not cite examples or exceptions and did not comment on the efficiency of any individual rule. Here I have numbered the rules and changed the phoneme symbols to those used in this book. Ainsworth's formal notation for these rules is explained as meaning:

'-' = a word boundary;
'V' = one or more vowel letters;
'C' = one or more consonant letters;
'E' = a single consonant followed by <e> or <i>;
'Xv' = a voiced consonant;
'SUF' = suffixes <-e, -ed, -es, -er, -ing>.

The letter(s) of the correspondence are enclosed in round brackets, with the context outside the brackets. One consequence of this presentation is that alternative contexts with some identity as a group are shown in separate rules. No rules are provided for double consonant letters <pp>, <bb>, etc.: they become two phonemes in the output and the second of these is simply deleted by a simplification rule.

It cannot be stressed too often that the number of rules, or the size of a look-up table, in algorithms such as these cannot be quoted as a single unqualified index of the complexity of the English writing system. What do we count as a single 'rule'? In dealing with speech on its own, a single phonological rule may apply to a whole 'natural class' of phonemes. The class can be defined by features and other conventions. We can assume that the easiest way for speech-processing to operate is to recognize and exploit such classes. These notions of 'naturalness' and of definable classes are not

Table 41 Ainsworth's text-to-speech correspondence rules

Rule	Sound	Rule	Sound	Rule	Sound
1 -(a)-	/ə/	54 (g)SUF	/g/	107 (oo)	/uː/
2 -(are)	/ɑː/	55 (g)i	/ʤ/	108 sh(oe)	/uː/
3 (a)E	/eɪ/	56 (g)et	/g/	109 (oe)	/əʊ/
4 (ar)	/ɑː/	57 (g)e	/ʤ/	110 c(ow)	/aʊ/
5 (a)sk	/ɑː/	58 (gh)	/g/	111 h(ow)	/aʊ/
6 (a)st	/ɑː/	59 (g)	/g/	112 n(ow)	/aʊ/
7 (a)th	/ɑː/	60 w(h)	Ø	113 v(ow)	/aʊ/
8 (a)ft	/ɑː/	61 (ha)v	/hæ/	114 r(ow)	/aʊ/
9 (ai)	/eɪ/	62 (h)	/h/	115 (ow)	/əʊ/
10 (ay)	/eɪ/	63 -(i)-	/aɪ/	116 g(o)-	/əʊ/
11 (aw)	/ɔː/	64 (i)ty	/ɪ/	117 n(o)-	/əʊ/
12 (au)	/ɔː/	65 (i)E	/aɪ/	118 s(o)-	/əʊ/
13 (al)l	/ɔː/	66 (ir)	/ɜː/	119 (o)-	/uː/
14 (a)ble	/eɪ/	67 (igh)	/aɪ/	120 (o)	/ɒ/
15 (a)ngSUF	/eɪ/	68 t(io)n	/ʌ/	121 (ph)	/f/
16 (a)	/æ/	69 (i)nd	/aɪ/	122 (psy)	/saɪ/
17 (b)	/b/	70 (i)ld	/aɪ/	123 (p)	/p/
18 (ch)	/ʧ/	71 -C(ie)	/aɪ/	124 (q)	/kw/
19 (ck)	/k/	72 VC(ie)	/iː/	125 (r)-	Ø
20 (c)y	/s/	73 (i)	/ɪ/	126 (rho)	/rəʊ/
21 (c)e	/s/	74 (j)	/ʤ/	127 (r)	/r/
22 (c)i	/s/	75 -(k)n	Ø	128 (sh)	/ʃ/
23 (c)	/k/	76 (k)	/k/	129 (ss)	/s/
24 (d)	/d/	77 (le)-	/əl/	130 (sch)	/sk/
25 VC(e)-	Ø	78 (l)	/l/	131 Xv(s)	/z/
26 th(e)-	/ə/	79 (m)	/m/	132 V(s)-	/z/
27 -C(e)-	/iː/	80 (n)g	/ŋ/	133 (s)	/s/
28 -C(e)d-	/e/	81 (n)	/n/	134 (there)	/ðɛə/
29 VCd(e)d-	/ə/	82 (or)	/ɔː/	135 (their)	/ðɛə/
30 VCt(e)d-	/ə/	83 (o)E	/əʊ/	136 (th)r	/θ/
31 VC(e)d-	Ø	84 (oa)	/əʊ/	137 (th)	/ð/
32 (e)r-	/ə/	85 (o)ld	/əʊ/	138 (t)ion	/ʃ/
33 wh(ere)	/ɛə/	86 (oy)	/ɔɪ/	139 (t)	/t/
34 h(ere)	/ɪə/	87 (o)ing	/əʊ/	140 (u)pon	/ʌ/
35 w(ere)	/ɜː/	88 (oi)	/ɔɪ/	141 (u)V	/uː/
36 (ere)	/ɪə(r)/	89 y(ou)	/uː/	142 (u)C-	/ʌ/
37 (ee)	/iː/	90 (ou)s	/ʌ/	143 r(u)	/uː/
38 (ear)	/ɪə(r)/	91 (ough)t	/ɔː/	144 l(u)	/uː/
39 (ea)	/iː/	92 b(ough)	/aʊ/	145 (u)	/juː/
40 (e)ver	/e/	93 t(ough)	/ʌf/	146 (v)	/v/
41 (eye)	/aɪ/	94 c(ough)	/ɒf/	147 (w)r	Ø
42 (e)E	/iː/	95 -r(ough)	/ʌf/	148 (wh)o	/h/
43 c(ei)	/iː/	96 r(ough)	/uː/	149 (wha)t	/wɒ/
44 (ei)	/aɪ/	97 (ough)	/əʊ/	150 (wa)	/wɒ/
45 (e)r	/ɜː/	98 (oul)d	/ʊ/	151 (wo)r	/wɜː/
46 (eo)	/iː/	99 (ou)	/aʊ/	152 (w)	/w/
47 (ew)	/juː/	100 (oor)	/ɔː/	153 (x)	/ks/
48 (e)u	Ø	101 (oo)k	/ʊ/	154 -(y)	/j/
49 (e)	/e/	102 f(oo)d	/aː/	155 VC(y)	/ɪ/
50 (f)-	/v/	103 (oo)d	/ʊ/	156 -C(y)	/aɪ/
51 (f)	/f/	104 f(oo)t	/ʊ/	157 (y)E	/aɪ/
52 (g)e-	/ʤ/	105 s(oo)t	/ʊ/	158 (y)	/ɪ/
53 (g)es-	/ʤ/	106 w(oo)	/ʊ/	159 (z)	/z/

easy to apply to the letters of the English writing system. Suppose we have a rule such as:

<c>≡/s/ before {<e>,<i>,y>}

meaning: '<c> corresponds to /s/ before <e>, <i> or <y>'. Do <e>, <i>, <y>, form a 'natural class' of letters? Only in the sense that they are the first letter of spellings that represent a front vowel phonologically, as in *centre, cease, deceive, cipher, decency,* etc. The fact that a computer language such as PASCAL allows us to define sets of entities, such as a set of employees or holiday resorts, and then to process them as sets, does not alter this. At some stage we have to tell the computer what constitutes the set by providing it with a simple list. The set is not defined by its attributes. We cannot, of course, use a defining feature external to the program. This should be borne in mind in comparing two algorithms such as McIlroy's and Ainsworth's. We cannot measure their relative complexity by simply counting the printed rules. McIlroy would write the above <c>-rule as one rule; Ainsworth would write it as three.

In Ainsworth's algorithm, as in McIlroy's, the deliberate aim was less-than-perfect synthesis. Comprehensibility of the synthetic speech output was judged by listeners. The best results naturally came from the more experienced listeners who were used to listening to synthetic speech. The best of these could identify 90 per cent of synthesized words correctly; the poorest listeners could only manage 50 per cent. McIlroy claimed 97 per cent adequacy. But, since the performance of the synthesizer itself is built into these results, the figures obviously underrate the efficiency of the algorithm as a letter-to-phoneme translation device. Indeed, the range of Ainsworth's results for 'good' and 'poor' listeners indicates this. Interpreting the figures is also made difficult by the fact that Ainsworth used a more sophisticated synthesizer than McIlroy.

If Ainsworth's 159 correspondence rules set out to perform the task of McIlroy's look-up table of 103 words and 580 'word-fragment rules', then some very trenchant economies will have been made. Ainsworth is proposing to make 80 per cent–90 per cent of words in a text identifiable using only a quarter of the rules that would make 97 per cent identifiable with McIlroy's algorithm. Even if we know that the listeners will be making informed guesses by exploiting redundancy, this result is still surprisingly good. An indication of the difference between the two can be gauged from Ainsworth's six <c>-rules, compared with McIlroy's quoted above:

18 (ch) /ʧ/;
19 (ck) /k/;
20 (c)y /s/;
21 (c)e /s/;

22 (c)i /s/;
23 (c) /k/.

This treatment does not find it worthwhile to attempt two quite common correspondences:

<ch>≡/k/ in §Greek words (*chloride, technical,* etc.);
<ch>≡/ʃ/ in §French words (*parachute, chauffeur,* etc.)

which McIlroy partly catered for. The rationale seems to be that redundancy will make a synthesized */ˈʧlɔːraɪd/ or */ˈpærəʧuːt/ identifiable.

Not much detail is given by Ainsworth on the limits of tolerance apart from the following:

> Consonant errors tended to be the substitution of a voiced consonant for its unvoiced equivalent (e.g. /ð/ for /θ/) or vice versa. Such errors are fairly unimportant perceptually, and though they detract from the quality of the speech produced, they rarely change the meaning of a word. Errors in unstressed vowels are also relatively unimportant, especially if the substituted vowel is a near neighbour in the vowel chart of the correct one.
>
> (ibid.: 289)

The voicing errors mentioned are almost entirely confined to /s/ – /z/ and /θ/ – /ð/.

Ainsworth's rules have been adapted in a later section (§4.3 below), as a basis for exploring the regularity of grapheme-phoneme correspondences. For this purpose, the number of rules has been increased by more than 40 per cent to account for definable sets of words which fell outside the strictly limited scope of the original rules.

While the simpler 'readable' computer algorithms for text-to-speech conversion have considerable interest for anyone concerned with the dynamics of the English writing system, they do have a built-in bias, which should not be overlooked. They put a very high premium on text frequency. Human readers who are past the initial learning stage tend to require spelling rules (reference rules) to sort out unfamiliar words in the foreign/learned sector of the lexicon. The lexical frequency of a correspondence rather than its text frequency is a more important consideration for them.

4.2 GENERAL FACTORS IN TEXT-TO-SPEECH RULES

4.2.1 Letter-to-phoneme correspondences

For a detailed examination of correspondences in the text-to-speech direction, our approach will be rather different from the description of speech-to-text correspondences in §3.3 above. We shall start with a set of rules and consider their adequacy. The correspondence rules which follow are based on the set of 159 rules given in Ainsworth (1973) and listed above in table 41 p. 265, but the set is larger by 42 per cent at 225 rules. There is no look-up table. These rules are employed purely as a descriptive device to explore the effectiveness and inadequacies of direct correspondence rules of this type across the lexicon. This is rather different from the purpose of Ainsworth's rules, which was to be cost-effective in getting an acceptable standard of synthetic speech from a small synthesizer.

This larger set of 225 rules has been applied to the corpus of data described in §3.1.1, pp. 104ff., to show the range of their application lexically and to provide some statistical evaluation of the individual rules. It is not suggested that such rules necessarily represent the best strategy for a human reader, or that the notation has been honed to perfection. The rules are used here merely as a convenient test-bench for exploring the limited adequacy of simple spelling correspondence rules. For this purpose, it is often more convenient to look at two separate rules and their separate performance, even when the formal notation could have merged them into a single more complex rule by using some formal device. Readers may certainly notice for themselves adjustments that would achieve greater delicacy and greater compactness, but the law of diminishing returns soon bites.

About one fifth of these 225 rules refer to specific words or affixes. In more complex algorithms these would be catered for by direct look-up facilities. A rough-and-ready index of spelling divergence can be seen in the distribution of the rules. Vowel spellings show more divergence than consonants. Of the consonant letters, <s, c, t, d> in decreasing order show most divergence. The relative divergence of vowel letter correspondences is <o, a, e, i, u, y>, in decreasing order.

The rules are divided into sections for each string-initial letter and numbered within each section. So <air>, <ay>, <aw>, will all be found under the <a>-rules section. Similar rules are grouped together as far as possible in each section. Rules should be read in the order given, because to some extent the rules are critically ordered within such a section. Longer strings must obviously be dealt with before shorter strings which form part of them: <aer>≡/ɛə(r)/ must come before <ae>≡/iː/. A few rules which are optional are marked 'OPT'.

The notation resembles that currently used in phonology, and explanations of the more complex rules are added in the text. An example of the notation is:

I.8 <ig>≡/aɪ/ | — {<m>,<n>} #

This is rule 8 for strings beginning with the letter <i>. The symbol '≡' means 'corresponds to'. The symbol '|' means 'in the context . . .' and the slot '—' is the place in which the letter string <ig> must occur for the rule to apply.

The curly brackets { } contain a list of alternatives. The symbol '#' indicates a free-form boundary: '— #' is used to mean 'word-finally' and '# —' means 'word-initially'. So, the above rule, the 8th <i>-rule, reads:

> 'the letter string <ig> corresponds to the phoneme /aɪ/ when followed either by the letter <m> (*paradigm*), or the letter <n> (*align*), and then by a word boundary'.

A subscript number refers to a **minimum** number of letters: '<C_1>' means 'at least one consonant letter'; that could be, for instance, <C>, <CC>, or <CCC>. '<C_0>' 'means any number of consonant letters, including zero'. Ordinary round brackets contain optional items: '/n(t)s/' means 'either /nts/ or /ns/'.

Some rules are not limited to a particular context:

F.1 <f(f)>≡/f/

– this is the default rule, indeed the only rule, for the letters <f> and <ff> and it applies in any context. It simply means that a single or double <f> letter corresponds to the phoneme /f/.

The symbol '#' as a free-form boundary allows suffixation with <-dom> *dukedom*, <-ful> *fateful*, <-hood> *statehood*, <-ish> *apish*, <-less> *homeless*, <-let> *platelet*, <-like> *gnomelike*, <-ling> *hireling*, <-ly> *homely*, <-man>, <-men> *iceman*, <-ment> *elopement*, <-most> *foremost*, <-ness> *lateness*, <-ship> *comradeship*, <-some> *lonesome*, <-ward(s)> *homewards*, <-wise> *likewise*, <-y> *shaky*, and the inflections <-ed>, <-er>, <-est>, <-(e)s>, <-ing>. These are suffixes that can be added without restriction, more or less, after a free-form boundary. Those beginning with a vowel letter absorb any <-e> marker. So, as part of a rule, the free-form boundary symbol '#' means either 'word final' or 'followed by one of these listed suffixes'. Notice that in rule I.8 above, the rule would apply to *align* followed by <-ment>, as one of these allowed suffixes, but not to *sign* followed by <-al>, or *paradigm* followed by <-atic>. A similar check list of prefixes could have been built in, but in general, initial boundary and prefix recognition is less critical.

A second group of endings is involved in one of the general rules for long vowel prediction, largely in §Latinate words. For instance:

A.28 <a>≡/eɪ/ | #<C_0>— <C>* ENDING

– where 'ENDING' refers to a group of endings which can be added to stems that are not free-forms (i.e. bound stems). The <-al> of *nasal*, *natal*, is added to the bound stems <nas-> and <nat->. That they 'can' be so added to bound forms is the criterion here. Some of them can also be added to free-forms There are also words, such as *basal*, *fatal*, which are derived from the free-forms *base* and *fate*. The endings in this group are listed in §4.2.4, p. 279, in the discussion of long vowel rules.

Common words and affixes which are so irregular that they would virtually each need a separate correspondence rule are mentioned at the beginning of each section.

The rules only have access to the letter strings of the spelling. Occasionally a rule may assume that the reader can identify a word as a potential monosyllable by its shape. Stress patterns are not known to the algorithm and so cannot be used to control vowel reduction to /ə/.

How many examples to give of the workings of a rule has to be a matter of judgement. When a rule is gratifyingly regular, such as <f(f)>≡/f/, only a few examples need be given. Rules which have a range of exceptions are exemplified more fully. For very minor rules, all the examples in the database may be given. The full range of derived forms cannot usually be cited: if *care* is given as an example of <are>≡/ɛə/, there is no need to add *careful*, *carefully*, *carefulness*, *careless*, *carelessly*, *carelessness*, etc. However, in the statistics of lexical incidence, all the lexical forms in the database are counted; only the inflected forms with <-s>, <-ed>, <-er>, <-est>, <-ing> are excluded.

Foreign names are dealt with only if usually anglicized as a string of English phonemes, e.g. *Soares* /səʊ'ɑːrɪz/.

Under the heading 'Exceptions:' are given those words for which a particular rule does not work. These frequently include sub-groups recognizable to a human reader sensitive to orthographic subsystems, with which the crudity of the algorithm used cannot cope. Since exceptions are of special interest, they are usually listed quite generously. The exception list for the final rule of a set, the default rule, is effectively an exception list for all the preceding rules in the set. Those exceptions to the final default rule which are best seen as 'near misses', due to inadequate framing of an earlier rule, may be brought forward and mentioned with the earlier rule. The exception list to the default rule is then a more concentrated list of hard cases. Because of this flexibility in giving examples, it will not serve as a valid index of the effectiveness of a rule simply to balance the size of the given exception list against the given example list. Performance statistics of a rough-and-ready nature are quoted for rules which cover more than just a few examples.

4.2.2 Rule evaluation

The performance of a rule can be judged by various criteria. The most accessible is its **efficiency**: the percentage of correct results; this will be quoted separately for ordinary words and for names. That is straightforward enough. The problem is that, in literacy work, rules vary in 'importance'. There are some rules that you must have in the early stages of literacy in English, and there are some rules you only need at a later stage for technical and literary vocabulary. The correspondence rule <aer>≡/ɛə/

is a perfectly viable rule and is virtually 100 per cent efficient, but it is restricted to fairly technical words: *aeration*, *aerial*, *aerobic*, *aerosol*, etc.

Even so, it is not easy to quantify whether a rule plays a major or a minor role in the writing system, since several factors are involved.

- If we try to calculate the workload of a particular rule in a database of English text, we ought to distinguish text frequency use from lexical frequency use: how much the rule would figure in running text, how much in covering the words in the lexicon.
- If we rank rules simply on the basis of frequency of use, we ignore the varying frequency of phonemes. The rules for common phonemes such as /t/, /d/, /n/ will, for that very reason, have a greater workload than rules for less common phonemes such as /ʒ/, /ɔɪ/.
- How do we quote the use of a rule? Rather than count its use right or wrong, it is probably best to quote figures for the successful use of a rule as a contribution to the successful prediction of a phoneme.

For a preliminary classification into three broad categories: **core** rules, **minor** rules and **marginal** rules, we have taken into account the extent to which a rule is responsible for the successful prediction of a phoneme in lexical words. Arbitrary limits were set for marginal and minor rules: a **marginal** rule contributes less than 2.5 per cent to the successful prediction of the phoneme and a **minor** rule less than 5 per cent but at least 2.5 per cent. On this basis the 225 rules break down into 106 (47 per cent) marginal, 26 (12 per cent) minor and 93 (41 per cent) core rules. These terms are not based on the share of the overall workload, but on the share of successfully representing the target phoneme. The core rules will include default rules and rules which deal with important divergent spellings.

We ignore names in assigning the classification into core, minor and marginal rules, though what is a core rule in words is usually a core rule in names. To take a simple example, /ɔɪ/ is successfully predicted by rule in 89 per cent of cases. This is done by rule O.3 <oi>≡/ɔɪ/ and rule O.30 <oy>≡/ɔɪ/. The O.3 rule contributes 62 per cent of the overall 89 per cent successful spelling of /ɔɪ/ and the O.30 rule contributes the other 27 per cent. These are clearly **core** rules, since they play such a significant role in the spelling of /ɔɪ/. The fact that /ɔɪ/ is a relatively rare phoneme is irrelevant to this classification. These aspects of a rule's performance are essentially proportions: 62/89 and 27/89. The two figures of the proportion are kept intact and are reported in the text, rather longwindedly, as '62 percentage points of 89 per cent successful /ɔɪ/ predictions'. This preserves the information that the rules for /ɔɪ/ are 89 per cent efficient and that the contribution to this by the O.3 rule is 62 per cent. These figures are only quoted for the principal competing spellings of a phoneme, such as the <oi> and <oy> spellings of /ɔɪ/.

This /ɔɪ/ example can also serve to show how words and names may differ in the balance between different spellings of the same phoneme. The corresponding figures for names are: for the O.3 rule 21/78 and for the O.30 rule 57/78. The number of cases involved are shown in table 42.

Table 42 Relative success in predicting /ɔɪ/ in words and names

	right (in words)	*wrong (in words)*	*right (in names)*	*wrong (in names)*
Rule (O.3) <oi>≡/ɔɪ/	200 (62 %)	34 (11 %)	28 (21 %)	25 (19 %)
Rule (O.30) <oy>≡/ɔɪ/	88 (27 %)	0	77 (57 %)	4 (3 %)

So, in the 322 words, the rules successfully predict /ɔɪ/ in 288 instances (89 per cent), to which O.3 contributes a 62 per cent slice. In the 134 names, the rules successfully predict 105 instances (78 per cent), to which O.3 only contributes a 21 per cent slice.

We can now consider other measures of the work done by a particular rule. This can be shown by approximate statistics based on ranking. Three different aspects of the words to which a rule applies can be quantified, though the three are not entirely independent:

1 **text frequency workload**. The work done by a rule can be related to the text frequency of the words which are successfully spelt by the rule. Text frequency adds a further dimension to the notion of 'work done'. For this, the words of the database were ranked by text frequency and then divided up into ten arbitrary sections. The sections were not equal in size, but a 'slope' was built to allow for the increasing number of tied ranks as frequency decreases. When a frequency spanned a section boundary, the words with that frequency were allocated randomly to make up the numbers on either side of the boundary. This gave a rough frequency weighting of 1 to 10 for each word. All the rules were then ranked by the sum of these weightings for the words in which the rule successfully applied. The top 75 rules for text frequency are referred to in the text as either a 'very heavy workload' (ranks 1 to 25), a 'heavy workload' (ranks 26 to 50), or a 'fairly heavy workload' (ranks 51 to 75). The highest ranked rules are, not surprisingly, the default rules for the most common phonemes. This gives some idea of the **quantity** of work done.

2 **text frequency bias**. This is not an indicator of the quantity of work done, but reflects the **balance** of high frequency words or low frequency words. Using the same arbitrary word frequency bands, we can find the mean text frequency of the words covered by a rule by dividing the text frequency weighting by the number of words involved. If the words involved prove not to be balanced in their distribution over the ten categories, this mean frequency would, assuming a more or less smooth distribution, show some bias, either towards low frequency words or

towards high frequency words. All the rules, except those covering fewer than 10 words, were ranked by the mean text frequency of the words in which the rule successfully applied. The extreme 15 rules at the top end of the distribution were labelled 'very strong bias towards high TF words', the next 15 'strong bias . . .', and the next 15 'some bias . . .'. The same three tranches were taken at the opposite end of the ranking scale: 'very strong bias towards low TF words', etc.

3 **word length**. It may be useful for literacy work to know whether a rule tends to apply more of the time in short words or in long words. Rather than measure word length for this purpose in letters or phonemes, it seems best to measure it by the number of syllables in the word. That is because native compounds, which tend to be 'consonant-heavy' both in phonemes and even more so in letters, are then better differentiated from Latinate polysyllabic words: cf. *lengthways* (10 letters, but 2 syllables) and *legibility* (10 letters, but 5 syllables). Here, too, the statistic is based on ranking. All the rules, except those covering fewer than 10 words, were ranked by the mean length in syllables of the words in which the rule successfully applied. The extreme 15 rules at the top end of the distribution were labelled 'very strong bias towards longer words', the next 15 'strong bias . . .', and the next 15 'some bias . . .'. The same three tranches were taken at the opposite end of the ranking scale: 'very strong bias towards shorter words', etc.

Descriptive statistics usually state the obvious, but it is useful even for native speakers to have an intuitive judgement confirmed. The few instances where the statistics do not seem to match one's intuitive judgement, are often due to a mismatch between SBS and the earlier pronunciation for which the writing system was intended. For instance, the classification of <aw>≡/ɔː/ before a consonant or boundary (A.11) as a minor rule rather than a core rule is due to the loss of contrast between a phoneme /ɔː/ and a phoneme /ɔə/ (*paw–pore*) in present-day SBS; *paw* and *pore* both have /ɔː/. This makes the <aw> spellings a smaller proportion of /ɔː/ than previously.

4.2.3 Problems in correspondence matching

The identification of a word in reading is here taken to be an informed guess, with several channels more-or-less simultaneously bringing relevant information to bear, including, if necessary, the monitoring of spelling-to-sound correspondences. Making an informed guess means, in effect, that you exploit redundancy. The most striking general feature of phonetic redundancy in English is that the vowel system shows more variability across individual speakers, across stylistic registers and across regional and social accents than the consonant system. Vowels also vary more than consonants with the morphological structure of the word. An awareness of the ways in which vowels may vary is part of the competence of a literate person and may be brought to bear in handling spelling-phoneme correspondences.

Vowels vary with stress. If a reader comes across a word spelt **catapa*, denoting an unfamiliar fruit, there would be several alternative likely pronunciations involving different correspondences for the <a>s. There are four possible vowel phonemes involved: /æ/, /eɪ/, /ɑː/ and /ə/. But these can certainly not occur freely in the 4 x 4 x 4 = 64 permutations of the three vowel positions ..V..V..V. We are only likely to find a mere five: /ˈkætəpə/, /ˈkætəpɑː/, /kəˈteɪpə/, /kəˈtɑːpə/, /kætəˈpɑː/. The choice is restricted for various reasons: the stress pattern dictates the vowel reduction of unstressed syllables; an antepenultimate vowel tends to be short, which probably rules out /eɪ/ and /ɑː/ in the first syllable (*/keɪtəpə/); final <a> cannot be /eɪ/ or /æ/.

The consequences of these restrictions must be reflected in any account of how a reader might cope with vowel reduction. Take the correspondence <or>≡/ɔː(r)/. This correspondence occurs in stressed syllables. (The /r/, incidentally, is totally predictable: in SBS it occurs before a vowel (*choral*), but not before a consonant or boundary (*short*, *shore*). In AmE the /r/ occurs in all contexts.) If we took the extreme position of only allowing readers the one stressed correspondence <or>≡/ɔː/ without admitting /ə/ as a natural rhythmical variant linked to the stress pattern, then the correspondence rule would only be 63 per cent efficient. In words of n-syllables this breaks down as:

Table 43 Distribution of <or>≡/ɔː/ spellings in n-syllable words

no. of syllables in word	1	2	3	4+
% of correct <or> in n-syll.words	97%	77%	61%	54%

In monosyllables the efficiency is almost total, since these are stressable. This drops to three-quarters in disyllabic words because of the common unstressed suffix <-or> (*author*, *captor*). In long polysyllabic words only about half have the stressed vowel correspondence, because the <or> frequently falls in an unstressed syllable. But, since this vowel reduction is predictable from the stress pattern, we can hardly count /ɔː/ for /ə/ as a 'mistake' in *aborigine*, *actor*, *aphorism*, *carnivorous*, *collaborate*, *decorous*, *defamatory*, *factory*, *humorist*, etc. It is not surprising that someone learning to transcribe English speech in phonetic detail will quite happily put an unreduced /ɔː/ in such words, in spite of having heard /ə/. Consequently, in assessing the efficiency of some vowel correspondence rules, it will be sensible to make explicit allowance for vowel reduction as a process automatic to the reader.

Vowel reduction is but one example of a general relationship (or process) which reflects a reader's competence, but which cannot be treated concisely by general correspondence rules. Another such general relationship can be seen in <r> spellings. Long vowels in SBS and many other English accents have glides to /ə/ before an underlying //r//. The spelling correspondences before other consonants and before //r// in SBS are shown in table 44. Clearly, one might say that these are effectively pairs of variants of the same vowel correspondence with a predictable glide before //r// (Wells 1982: 289f). Realizing this relationship is part of literacy. In the case of <o>, the value before //r// in SBS has changed fairly recently to /ɔː/ from /ɔə/, merging *pour* and *paw*. Many accents, however, have retained the /ɔə/-/ɔː/ contrast.

Table 44 SBS vowel correspondences before consonants and before //r//

<a>	/eɪ/	*mate*	/ɛə/	*mare*
<ai>	/eɪ/	*paid*	/ɛə/	*pair*
<e>	/iː/	*mete*	/ɪə/	*mere*
<ea>	/iː/	*heat*	/ɪə/	*hear*
<i>	/aɪ/	*mite*	/aɪə/	*mire*
<o>	/əʊ/	*mote*	/ɔː/	*more*
<u>	/juː/	*mute*	/jʊə/	*demure*
<u>	/uː/	*lute*	/ʊə/	*lure*

A similar relationship holds between /juː/ and /uː/: they can be treated for most practical purposes as conditioned variants. The [j] glide is not found after the liquids /l/ and /r/ (*lunar*, *rune*) and is merged into preceding palatals such as /ʤ, ʃ/ (*June*, *chute*).

4.2.4 Long values of single vowel letters

There are also some general criteria which determine whether a single vowel letter has its short or long value, but these would be difficult to formulate in any concise form and they vary somewhat for different vowels. The use of <C-letter>doubling as a marker of a short vowel (cf. *matting–mating*), and the rarity of a long vowel before a consonant cluster, may suggest that in a <VCV> sequence the first <V> will generally represent a long vowel. This is by no means so, and it is difficult in the absence of stress rules to predict the exceptions which have a short vowel. A trial run of this simple VCV generalization to predict the long value of the letter <a> had a success rate of only 20 per cent in words such as *apparatus*, *caterer*, *complacent*, *crazy*, *labour*, *ultimatum*. If stress patterns had been available, some of the contexts where a long vowel would not appear might have been ruled out. A stressed short vowel frequently occurs in the third syllable from the end, a tendency known as third-syllable shortening: *calico*, *charity*, *fatuous*, *humanity*, *manager*, *maritime*, etc. An unstressed short vowel reduced to /ə/ also occurs frequently in the second syllable from the end: *catapult*, *cyanide*, *equalize*, *mahogany*, etc.

The only general provision for long vowel correspondences such as <a>≡/eɪ/ in the original Ainsworth rules was in the form: '(a)E /eɪ/'. The context 'E' meant: before a single consonant letter followed by the letters <e> or <i>. Parallel rules were provided for the other vowel letters. The main function of such a rule was evidently to capture the <e>-marking of a stressed vowel such as <a>≡/eɪ/ and the inflected forms (*grade*, *grades*, *graded*, *grader*, *grading*; *sane*, *saner*, *sanest*).

This is a fairly robust generalization, but for all the vowels there are numerous subsets of exceptions. Ainsworth's long vowel <a> rule does not provide, as we have seen, for a phonetic variant <ar>≡/ɛə(r)/ in the analogous forms *care*, *cares*, *cared*, *carer*, *caring*, *bare*, *barer*, *barest*, where the single consonant letter in the rule happens to be <r>. It does not allow <Cl>, <Cr>, <th>, <st> or <ch> as intervening consonants, as in *staple, acre, bathe, waste, ache*. Nor does it exclude stems with short vowels in the antepenultimate syllable such as *camera*, *calendar*, *javelin*, etc. It would give */ˈkeɪmərə/ for *camera*. It also fails when there is a short vowel before <-ic>, <-id>, <-ish>, <-it> as in *manic*, *placid*, *vanish*, *habit*.

The default pronunciation for each single vowel letter <a, e, i/y, o, u> is here taken, as in the original rules, to be the short value – /æ, e, ɪ, ɒ, ʌ/. Instead of Ainsworth's single '(a)E' type of rule, the normal long values of the vowel letters <a>≡/eɪ/, <e>≡/iː/, <i>≡/aɪ/, <o>≡/əʊ/, <u>≡/(j)uː/, <y>≡/aɪ/, are captured in five different contexts which seem to give a reasonable return, though there will inevitably be a residue of exceptions requiring further comment and for which there may well be other spelling strategies. There is certainly no simple, easy strategy for reading off a vowel letter as long or short. The five long vowel contexts in the augmented set of rules apply when complex vowel spellings such as <ai>, <ou>, <eau> have been dealt with. They are as follows.

Penultimate — <C> <V>

A long vowel is predictable in the penultimate syllable of non-§Basic words such as *panorama*, *magneto*, *neutrino*, *carcinoma*. For <e> and <o> the value is normal /iː/ and /əʊ/, but <a> and <i> have their other long values /ɑː/ and /iː/. This rule is hardly worth applying to <u> or <y>, though there are a few examples, such as *Profumo*, *Montezuma*.

<e>-marking

A long vowel is predictable before a single <C> followed by a marking <-e>, as in *take*, *scene*, *kite*, *hope*, *rule*. The <e>-marker may occur finally in a word, or before a suffix (as in *elopement*, *hopeless*, *lateness*, *saleable*, *spaceman*, *spiteful*, *stately*), or merged with a vowel initial suffix (*baked*, *baker*, *baking*, *later*, *latest, flaky*). This means not only that the vowel is marked as long in these contexts, but also that the <e> itself is read as an empty letter unlike the medial <e> of *malefactor, maverick, tenement*, *supplement*. Words which end in the same string of letters as a suffix are treated as if the ending were a suffix. There is no way for the algorithm input to distinguish *father* or *gather* as single morphemes from *bather*, which is two. The words *shyly*, *truly*, *duty*, are treated by analogy as if their structure were *<shyle>+<-y>, *<trule>+<-y>, *<dute>+<-y>. This is not unrealistic since any exceptions show where the reader has a potential problem.

There is one general <e>-marking rule for each vowel letter, for instance:

A.27 <a>≡/eɪ/ |— (<C>*) <e>#

The other such rules are E.25, I.15, O.37, U.4 and Y.4. The asterisk in such rules refers to restrictions on the <C>; these are printed as a set of conditions along with the rule. In all cases the <C>* may not be <x>. The letter <x> represents a /CC/ cluster, which usually dictates a previous short vowel. The <C>* may be <Cl> or <Cr>, excluding doubled <ll>and <rr>, as in *table, rifle, noble, bugle, cycle* and *acre, metre, mitre, ogre, lucre*. Here the <-Cle> and <-Cre> strings are really inverted spellings of <-Cel> and <-Cer> and represent a syllable. American spelling has reordered <-Cre> to <-Cer>, as in *center*, but keeps the <-Cle> of *table*. The string <-eble> occurs occasionally in names: *Keble*, but there seems to be no <-yCre>. The <C>* may be <th>, as in *bathe, lithe, scythe*. The absence of <-ethe>, <-othe>, <-uthe> seems an accidental consequence of the rarity of medial <th> and the rarity of <-eCe> (see pp. 155). This leaves us with three instances where the <C>* is peculiar to the <a>-rule: <st> *waste*, <ch>≡/k/ *ache*, <ng>≡/nʤ/ *strange*. The correspondence <ng>≡/nʤ/ was thought to be worth a separate rule (here A.26) by Ainsworth.

The '( )' brackets in the rule allow a final <-ae> (*brae*), as in the parallel rules for the vowel letters <o>, <u>, and <y> (O.37, U.4, Y.4), catering for *toe*, *rue*, *dye*, as well as *tone*, *rule*, *dyke*. However, <ee> (E.14) and <ie> (I.4 to I.7) in *see*, *lie*, are pre-empted as digraph spellings.

The <e>-marking is restricted to the last syllable of a minimal free form partly to allow for third-syllable shortening in words such as *maverick*, *sanity*. These would get a long /eɪ/ by Ainsworth's rule '(a)E', where the 'E' envisaged any single consonant followed by <e> or <i>. That strategy would be fairly productive in terms of text frequency because of the <e> and <i> in the inflectional affixes <-ed>, <-en>, <-er>, <-es>, <-est>, <-ing>, but it would prove far from reliable across the lexicon.

Hyphens are not always used to separate the constituents of a compound word. That makes it difficult to account for the <-e> marker in compounds such as *alehouse*, *baseball*, *homespun*, *smokestack*, *stagecraft*. Such boundaries need to be recognized for two good reasons:

- to identify the long vowel value marked by the <-e>;
- to avoid taking the <-e> itself as a vowel.

The writing system is reluctant to use hyphens for commonly used compounds such as *baseball*. Limiting ourselves as we do, to simple correspondence recognition, we need some rule-of-thumb strategy to recognize a marking <-e> stranded in the middle of a compound without a hyphen. This will inevitably require more of the reader than a simple left-to-right correspondence scan. With the limited input available here, we can only construct a very simple compound-guesser.

The majority of compounds written without hyphens have monosyllabic first elements, so we can content ourselves with assuming a marking <-e> in strings with the structure:

$$\# <C_0> <V> <C> <e> + <C_1>^* <V_1> <C> \ldots \#$$

– where the $<C_1>^*$ represents a possible word-initial consonant or cluster. This assumes that the reader can judge that the word is long enough to be a compound and can check that the letters which follow the <-e> are pronounceable as an initial consonant or possible initial consonant cluster. If they are not, then the reader will have to backtrack to read the <e> as a vowel, while realizing that the previous vowel may not now be marked as long. The most likely clusters of consonant letters to occur initially are:

- <b, c, f, g, p> followed by <l, r>;
- <c, g, k, p, s, t> followed by <h>;
- <d, t> followed by <r>;
- <g, k, s> followed by <n>;
- <s, t> followed by <w>;
- <s> followed by <c, k, l, m, p, t>.

The underlying phonetic clusters are, of course, much more patterned than this statement of the corresponding letter strings.

A further rule-of-thumb criterion can be added to this compound-guessing strategy. If the word ends in the kind of suffix which is only added to bound forms, as in *valedictory*, *malevolent*, the word is unlikely to be a compound with a first element **vale* or **male*. One of the characteristics of compounds is that the elements are short and the first element especially tends to be monosyllabic.

A compound-guesser along these lines was incorporated into the testing of the <e>-marking rules of the algorithm. This allows the <a> of *baseball* to be /eɪ/ by the <e>-marking rule A.27 and treats the <e> as empty by E.2.

Hiatus: — <V>

Most strings of two vowel letters in English are the complex spelling of a single vowel as in *chain*, *bead*, *reins*, *coin*, *goat*, *zoom*. They can also represent the spelling of two separate vowels in sequence, a hiatus. Hiatus can sometimes be indicated by a hyphen, as in *re-enact*, *co-exist*, *de-escalate*, usually when the second element is a free form. Unmarked examples are far more common: <ai> in *prosaic*, <ea> in *react*, <ei> in *reinstate*, <eo> in *theory*, <eu> in *museum*, <ie> in *science*, <oa> in *coaxial*, <oe> in *coexist*, <oi> in *soloist*, <oo> in *zoology*, etc. The first vowel in such cases is the normal long vowel value of the letter, so this regularity ought to be represented in the long vowel rules. But, since the complex spellings of single vowels, such as <ai>, <oa>, are dealt with in earlier rules, many instances end up in the exception list to such a rule. There are, however, letter strings such as <ia>, <ao>, which can only be spellings of a hiatus, so the hiatus rule is needed to cater for them.

— <C> <i> <V>

A long vowel is predictable for most accents of English before the string <-CiV> as in the /eɪ/ of *aviary*, *radial*, *stadium*.

Suffix-marked long vowels

These are long vowels separated from a particular suffix by a single consonant letter other than <x> (*notary*, *votive*), or by <th> (*pathos, lethal*), or by a <Cr> cluster (*vagrancy*, *matron*). For this purpose a 'suffix' is taken to be one of the following: <-acy> *papacy*, <-age> *dotage*, <-al#> *fatal*, < -an#> *pagan*, <-anc(e/y)> *fragrance*, <-ant> *fragrant*, <-ar> *radar*, <-ary> *notary*, <-enc(e/y)> *potency*, <-ent> *potent*, <-ian> *Asian*, <-ide> *bromide*, <-iness> (for {y}+{ness}) *holiness*, <-ir> *nadir*, <-is> *thesis*, <-ite>, <-ive> *votive*, <-on> *mason*, <-os> *pathos*, <-our> *flavour*, <-um> *serum*, <-ur> *lemur*, <-ure> *nature*, <-us> *bonus*. This rule tries to capture analogies that the reader might make between words with the same ending. Those marked with '#' may not retain the previous long vowel medially: *fatality*, *sadistic*. These suffixes are referred to in the rule notation as 'ENDING'.

The context for these suffixes has been limited in this algorithm to stems of one syllable. It might seem that longer stems could have been included to cater for words such as *abrasive*, *adjectival*, *anecdotal*, *apparatus*, *cathedral*, *detritus*, *digitalis*, *doctrinal*. That would only be possible for an algorithm that knew the stress pattern, since otherwise a large number of exceptions would be let in with a short unstressed vowel before the suffix: *abdominal*, *ablative*, *assonance*, *cardinal*, *cerebral*, *chrysalis*, *countenance*, *decimal*, *elegance*, *episcopal*, *festival*, *optimal*, etc.

One might think, then, that the rule should be made more general to take in any disyllabic word with a single intervocalic consonant letter or <-Cr-> as a good predictive context for a long vowel in the first syllable. This is unfortunately not so. There are many words with short vowels, such as *carol*, *chapel*, *cherub*, *chisel*, *comet*, *cretin*, *drivel*, *fathom*, *level*, *panel*, *planet*, *privet*, *rosin*, *salad*, *spigot*, *vigil*. Short and long vowels occur in similar spellings: *basin–cabin*, *label–chapel*, *navel–gavel*, *major–manor*, *Mavis–Travis*, *fecund–gerund*, *fibrous–citrous*, *pilot–pivot*, etc.

4.2.5 Suffix-marked short vowels

If a single vowel letter does not occur in the long vowel contexts, it will be assumed to represent the short vowel by default. Some of these vowels, however, will be explicitly marked as short by certain suffixes. This is worth noting, even though no extra rule is needed to capture them. The §Latinate and §Greek endings <-ic(al)>, < -id>, <-it> mark a short vowel in words such as *titanic*, *historical*, *placid*, *habit*. This applies to morphemes which in other contexts may have a long vowel variant: *complacent–placid*, *volcano–volcanic*, etc. The ending <-ish> within a morpheme also marks a short vowel: *lavish*, *finish*, *parish*, *polish*, *relish*, *vanish*, *punish*. This should not be confused with the adjective-forming suffix <-ish> of *modish, slavish, Danish*, *Polish*, *Swedish*, from *mode*, *Dane*, etc. One of these two groups is bound to be wrongly dealt with here, since this algorithm does not know an internal morpheme boundary. The *modish* group will be correct, since the <e>-marking rules know that <-ish> is a possible suffix, leaving the *lavish* group to figure as exceptions to those rules.

4.3 TEXT-TO-SPEECH SPELLING RULES

Before looking at the rules in detail, we should again note that they are optimistic generalizations of varying validity which are being tested as much for what they fail to do, as for what they can do. It is important in reading them to remember that they form an algorithm in which the word is decoded by rule from left to right. Some rules, but not all, depend upon the prior application of other rules. For instance, rule U.1 for <ui>≡/uː/ is read after the <bu> of *build* has already been hived off as a spelling of /b/ by rule B.1. Rule U.1 is not a statement to be read independently of that rule, since with a different ordering of the two, we should get */buːld/.

<a>-rules

Correspondences are dealt with in rules numbered as follows.

A.1 <age>≡/ɪʤ/ A.2 <a>≡∅ A.3, 4, 24 <a>≡/ə/

A.5 <aer>≡/ɛə(r)/	A.6 <ae>≡/iː/	A.7 <ai>≡/eɪ/
A.8 <ay>≡/eɪ/	A.9 <augh>≡/ɔː/	A.10 <au>≡/ɔː/
A.11 <aw>≡/ɔː/	A.12 <ah>≡/ɑː/	A.13 <al>≡/ɔː/
A.14 <al>≡/ɑː/	A.15 <al>≡/ɔːl/	A.16 <ar>≡/ɔː(r)/
A.17 <a>≡/ɒ/	A.18 <ar>≡/ɑː(r)/	A.19–23, 25 <a>≡/ɑː/
A.26–30 <a>≡/eɪ/	A.31 <a>≡/æ/ – default correspondence.	

Function words with irregular <a>-spellings, which would ideally go to a look-up table, include:

- the indefinite article *a* with /eɪ/ when stressed, but usually unstressed as /ə/;
- *are*, *aren't* with /ɑː/ when stressed; the regular correspondence would be /ɛə/ by part of A.27 (cf. *care*, *stare*); usually unstressed with /ə/;
- *have*, *having*, *haven't* with /æ/ – not with /eɪ/ by A.27 (cf. *cave*, *stave*); the auxiliary *have* is usually unstressed with /(ə)v/.

The reduced vowels of the suffixes in the next four rules are also difficult to fit into simple correspondences if there is no parallel information about stress patterns.

A.1 <age>≡/ɪʤ/ | <V> <C$_0$> — #
– the context requires a previous syllable, to exclude stressed /eɪʤ/ in monosyllabic free forms *cage*, *sage*, etc. These would still have to be recognized in derived forms such as *enraged, outraged, interstage*. Many accents have /ə/ rather than /ɪ/ in this suffix.

Examples: *average*, *bandage*, *cabbage*, *courage*, *envisage*, *frontage*, *garbage*, *haulage*, *image*, *lineage*, *manage*, *mortgage*, *pillage*, *roughage*, *sewage*, *silage*, *usage*, *village*; *Alsager*, *Armitage*, *Swanage*, etc.

Exceptions:

- Fairly recent French loan-words with /ɑːʒ/ or /ɑːʤ/ – *barrage*, *camouflage*, *collage*, *corsage*, *entourage*, *espionage*, *fuselage*, *massage*, *menage*, *montage*, *sabotage*;
- There is a full vowel /eɪ/ in the last syllable of verbs (and derived nouns) where the <-age> is stressed as /eɪʤ/ and is not a suffix: *assuage*, *engage*, *enrage*, *interstage*, *outrage*, *rampage*.

Efficiency: in words 81 per cent; in names 70 per cent; a marginal rule.

A.2 (OPT.) <a>≡∅ | <V> <C$_0$> — <lly>
A marginal rule.

Examples: *artistically, critically, dramatically, drastically, emphatically*, etc.

The suffix <-ally> may lose its first vowel in the normal process of vowel reduction, especially after <-ic->, as in *critically* /ˈkrɪtɪklɪ/. There is naturally very strong bias towards longer words.

Since this algorithm has no basic grammatical information to distinguish verbs and nouns, the suffix <-ate> may be tentatively read as /eɪt/, reducible in nouns to /-ət/. Cf. *advocate* as verb and noun. This can be quite subtle. Some speakers have /ət/ for *advocate* (= lawyer) and /eɪt/ for *advocate* (= one who advocates) – hence the written form '*She is an advocate of wider experience*' could be ambiguous. The suffix <-ative>, however, always has reduced vowels in SBS . For this, the next rule prevents a long <a>≡/eɪ/.

A.3 <ative>≡/ətɪv/ | <V> <C_0> — #
Examples: *affirmative*, *argumentative*, *appreciative*, *comparative*, *decorative*, *evocative*, *figurative*, *formative*, *generative*, *indicative*, *laxative*, *lucrative*, *sedative*, *talkative*, *tentative*, etc.

Exceptions and potential misreadings: *creative*, *recitative* (/resɪtə'tiːv/).

Efficiency: in words 99 per cent; a marginal rule. There is naturally very strong bias towards longer words.

A.4 <a>≡/ə/ |<V> <C_0> — <bl> {<e>, <y>} #
– this distinguishes the suffix with unstressed /ə/ as in *capable*, from disyllabic words such as *able*, *ably*, *cable*, *table*, with stressed /eɪ/. Ainsworth's global rule gives /eɪ/. Stressed <-abl-> with /eɪ/ is dealt with below in A.27, the normal <e>-marking rule.

Examples: *available*, *capably*, *durable*, *eatable*, *enjoyable*, *habitable*, *inflammable*, *liable*, *notably*, *parable*, *reliably*, *syllable*, etc.

Exceptions: only where there is an internal boundary in words such as *disable*, *enable*, *timetable*, *unstable*.

Efficiency: in words 99 per cent; a marginal rule with a fairly heavy workload. There is naturally very strong bias towards longer words and strong bias towards low TF words.

The above rules have been concerned with suffixes. The general correspondence rules for strings beginning with <a> are as follows:

A.5 <aer>≡/ɛə(r)/ (AmE /ɛr/)
Examples: *aeration*, *aerial*, *aerobic*, *aerodrome*, *aeronaut*, *aerosol*, *anaerobic*, etc. Almost all involve a §Greek spelling of {air}. *aerie* has the alternative pronunciation /'ɪərɪ/, preferred by LPD. The names *Faerie*, *Faeroes* also follow this rule. *Braeriach*, *Phaer* have /eɪə/, which is virtually homophonous with /ɛə/ (cf. *payer–pair*).

Exceptions:

- Welsh names with <caer> (*Caerleon*, *Caernarvon*, etc.) have /ɑː(r)/; so too has *Stranraer*;
- *Laertes* /eɪ'ɜː/ has hiatus.

Efficiency: in words 100 per cent; in names 31 per cent; a marginal rule with very strong bias towards low TF words .

A.6 <ae>≡/iː/
Conditions: excluding final <-ae> in monosyllables, such as *brae*, which come under the general <e>-marking rule A.27.

Examples:

- in §Greek words – *aegis*, *aeon*, *aesthetic*, *anaemia*, *anaesthetist*, *archaeology*, *encyclopaedia*, *leukaemia*, *paean*, etc.;
- in classical names – *Aegean*, *Aeneas*, *Aesop*, *Athenaeum*, *Caesar*, *Judaea*, *Bacchae*, *Mycenae*, *Thermopylae*;
- the Latin feminine plural in scientific terms – *alumnae*, *aortae*, *lacunae*, *lamellae*, *ulnae*, etc.

There is a very strong bias towards low TF words. The digraph <ae> has been simplified to <e> in American spelling (*esthetic*).

Exceptions:

- with medial /eɪ/ – *Disraeli*, *Gaelic*, *Jaeger*, *Praed*;
- with /eɪə/ – *Graeme*, *Ishmael*, *Israel*, *Raphael*;
- with /æ/ in Anglo-Saxon names – *Aelfric*, *Caedmon*;
- with /ə/ – *Michael*;
- with /aɪ/ – *maelstrom*, *maestro*, *Baedeker* (or anglicized to /eɪ/);
- *Danaë* is usually marked with a diaeresis to show that the <ae> is disyllabic.

Efficiency: in words 89 per cent; in names 63 per cent; a marginal rule with very strong bias towards low TF words and strong bias towards longer words.

A.7 <ai>≡/eɪ/ (before //r// the vowel is /ɛə/)
Examples: *abstain, acquaint*, *ail*, *bait*, *baize*, *campaign*, *claim*, *dainty*, *entrails*, *faint*, *malaise*, *plaintiff*, *rainy*, *sailor*, *terrain*, *waiver*, etc.; *Abigail*, *Adelaide*, *Adlai*, *Adonais*, *Aiken*, *Aileen*, *Ailsa*, *Aitchison*, *Aquitaine*, *Bahrain*, *Bailey*, *Blaikley*, *Braille*, *Cain*, *Calais*, *Cockaigne*, *Daimler*, *Douai*, *Elaine*, *Haigh*, *Jamaica*, *Kuwait*, *Paignton*, *Sainsbury*, *Ukraine*, etc. The surname *Brittain* (sic) may have /eɪn/ rather than /ən/.

With /ɛə(r)/, AmE /ɛr/ – *air*, *cairn*, *clairvoyant*, *commissionaire*, *corsair*, *dairy*, *debonair*, *despair*, *eclair*, *fair*, *flair*, *hair*, *laird*, *lair*, *pair*, *prairie*, *repair*, *solitaire*, *stairs*, etc.; *Adair*, *Airedale*, *Airey*, *Baird*, *Blair*, *Cairngorm*, *Gairdner* (also /ɑː/), *Lothair*, *Sinclair*, etc.

Exceptions:

- the <ai> part of *straight* is regular, but the <gh> are empty letters. If we follow Ainsworth in taking the whole string as a unit, as with <augh>, <igh>, <ough>, then *straight* would require a separate marginal rule. The name *Haight* is either /haɪt/ or /heɪt/;
- the <ai> forms a hiatus /eɪ-ɪ/ in *algebraic*, *archaic*, *formulaic*, *mosaic*, *prosaic*, etc. and *dais*.

- vowel reduction to /ə/ or /ɪ/ only applies in less than 1 per cent of instances, mainly in the unstressed endings <-ain>, <-ait>: *bargain*, *captain*, *certain*, *chamberlain*, *chaplain*, *chieftain*, *curtain*, *mountain*, *murrain*, *plantain*, *porcelain*, *villain*; *portrait*;
- the words *sail* (as in *topsail*, *foresail*) and *saint* (as in *Saint John*) may also have vowel reduction to /ə/;
- with /e/ in the common words *again*, *against*, *said*;
- with /æ/ – *plaid*, *plait* and *Plaistow* as a family name; as a place-name, *Plaistow* has /ɑː/ (LPD);
- with /aɪ/ – *aisle*, *naiad*, *shanghai*; and exotic names *Achaia*, *Aglaia*, *Ainu*, *Caius*, *Cairo*, *Chaim*, *Dai*, *Dalai*, *Dairen*, *Gaisberg*, *Geraint*, *Haifa*, *Hawaii*, *Isaiah*, *Ismail*, *Jaipur*, *Jairus*, *Kaiser*, *Mainz*, *Masai*, *Menai*, *Nairobi*, *Ngaio*, *Sinai*, etc. *Stainer* as an English name is /ˈsteɪnə/, but as a version of the German name has /aɪ/. As the name of an American town, *Cairo* has been anglicized with /ɛər/;
- the <ain> of *Louvain* elicits a variety of approximations to the French nasalized vowel /ɛ̃/: [æ̃, æ̃ŋ, eɪn, æŋ] (the mark over the vowel symbol represents nasalization); LPD anglicizes it as /luːˈvæn/;
- in *Alastair*, *Alistair*, /ɛə/ may be reduced to /ə/;
- *Zaire* is disyllabic /zɑːˈɪə/, shown sometimes in spelling with a diaeresis <Zaïre>;
- *MacDaire* is /məkˈdɑːrə/.

Efficiency: a core rule with some bias towards high TF words and towards shorter words;

in words – 95 per cent (= 9 percentage points of 80 per cent correct /eɪ/ predictions);
in names – 76 per cent (= 12 percentage points of 62 per cent correct /eɪ/ predictions).

For /ɛə(r)/ the efficiency is 95 per cent in words and 81 per cent in names.

A.8 <ay>≡/eɪ/
Examples: *affray*, *astray*, *away*, *bayonet*, *betray*, *carraway*, *day*, *delay*, *essay*, *mayhem*, *mayonnaise*, *pay*, *popinjay*, *play*, *portray*, *pray*, *say*, *stay*, *way*, etc.; *Aylesford*, *Aylmer*, *Bayard*, *Biscay*, *Braynes*, *Halliday*, *Malaya*, *Norway*, *Rayleigh*, *Tebay*, *Tokay*, etc.

Exceptions:

- *always* usually has unstressed /ɪ/;
- <-day> as a suffix is reduced to /dɪ/ in SBS, but not in all accents: *holiday*, *yesterday*, *Monday*, etc.; *workaday* keeps the stressed /eɪ/;
- merged into /ɛə(r)/ – *mayor*, *prayer*;
- with /iː/ – *quay* (sometimes regular with /eɪ/ in AmE);
- with /aɪ/ – *papaya*; on the other hand *cayenne* is usually anglicized with

/eɪ/. French and other foreign names such as *Bayeux*, *Lafayette*, *Tokay*, have either /aɪ/ or /eɪ/, but markedly exotic names have /aɪ/ – *Bayreuth*, *Cetewayo*, *Guayaquil*, *Khayam*, *Paraguay*, *Uruguay*, *Ysaye*. The English or Welsh surname *Haydn* has /eɪ/, the Austrian composer /aɪ/.

Efficiency: a core rule with some bias towards shorter words;

in words – 93 per cent (= 5 percentage points of 80 per cent correct /eɪ/ predictions);
in names – 72 per cent (= 10 percentage points of 62 per cent correct /eɪ/ predictions).

A.9 <augh>≡/ɔː/
Examples: *aught*, *caught*, *daughter*, *distraught*, *fraught*, *haughty*, *naught*, *naughty*, *onslaught*, *slaughter*, *taught*; *Baugh*, *Bradlaugh*, *Connaught*, *Haughton*, *Laughton*, *McNaught*, *Shaughnessy*, *Waugh*. The names *Baughan*, *Maugham*, *Vaughan* are single syllables (/bɔːn/, etc.). This correspondence is one straightforward part of the name *Featherstonehaugh*, pronounced /ˈfænʃɔː/.

Exceptions: with /ɑːf/ (AmE /æf/) in *draught*, *laugh* and derived forms.

Efficiency: in words 89 per cent; in names 77 per cent; a marginal rule with very strong bias towards high TF words and strong bias towards shorter words.

This rule would not be needed if there were a general rule for empty letters <gh>, since the regular <au> part is catered for by A.10.

A.10 <au>≡/ɔː/
Examples: *applaud*, *astronaut*, *auburn*, *audible*, *authentic*, *author*, *auxiliary*, *bauble*, *caucus*, *cauldron*, *flautist*, *haunt*, *laundry*, *nausea*, *nautch*, *nautical*, *paunch*, *raucous*, *saucer*, *taut*, etc.; *Aubrey*, *Auchtermuchty*, *Auden*, *Augustus*, *Aurelius*, *Chaucer*, *Claude*, *Esau*, *Faulkner*, *Lauder*, *Maud*, *Maureen*, *Nassau*, *Nautilus*, *Paul*, *Saunders*, *Shaun*, *Taunton*, *Vaux*, etc. §Greek scientific terms such as *claustrophobia*, *glaucoma*, *tau*, *trauma*, have /ɔː/ – /aʊ/ variation. This does not apply to all words of Greek etymology. Those which have come into English by way of Latin and French and are not specifically 'scientific' only have /ɔː/ – *authentic*, *autograph*, *nausea*, *nautical*, etc. The /aʊ/ variant also may also occur by analogy in *aural* (not from Greek), which is often pronounced with /aʊ/ to prevent confusion with *oral*.

Exceptions:

- with /ɑː/, AmE /æ/, in *aunt*;
- with /eɪ/ – *gauge*;
- with /ɒ/ – *cauliflower*, *laurel*, *sausage*;
- with /əʊ/ – *chauffeur*, *gauche*, *mauve*, *saute*;
- with /aʊ/ – *meerschaum*, *sauerkraut*, *Nauru*;
- French names with <au> may have /əʊ/ rather than /ɔː/, though the latter

would be a better phonetic match: *Auvergne*, *Boucicault*, *Briault*, *Daudet*, *Desvaux*, *Lausanne*, *Sauterne*;

- German names are not usually anglicized to /ɔː/ and have /aʊ/: *Bauer*, *Breslau*, *Faust*, *Schopenhauer*, *Strauss*, but the commercial name *Braun* is pronounced /ɔː/ as a matter of policy and *Audi* sometimes is;
- Welsh <au> is usually /ɪ/: *Blaenau*, *Dolgellau*;
- in classical names the <au> may represent a hiatus with /eɪ-ə/: *Archelaus*, *Capernaum*, *Menelaus*; similarly with /ɑː-ʌ/ in *Kaunda*.

Efficiency: a core rule;

in words – 89 per cent (= 11 percentage points of 82 per cent correct /ɔː/ predictions);
in names – 58 per cent (= 11 percentage points of 84 per cent correct /ɔː/ predictions).

A.11 <aw>≡/ɔː/ |— {<C>, # }
That is, not before a vowel letter, except when a vowel-initial suffix follows, such as <-ed>, <-ing>, <-y> in *overawed*, *drawing*, *strawy*, etc. The context prevents a misreading of <aw> when the <w> has its consonantal value in *awake*, *award*, *aware*, *carraway*, *megawatt*; *Bulawayo*, *Chataway*, *Chaworth*, *Gawain*, *Haworth*, *Malawi*, *Okinawa*, *Rawalpindi*, *Sarawak*, etc.

Examples: *awful*, *awning*, *bawl*, *claw*, *crawl*, *dawdle*, *gawky*, *gnaw*, *guffaw*, *hawker*, *jaw*, *lawn*, *macaw*, *pawn*, *prawn*, *raw*, *saw*, *scrawl*, *squawk*, *trawl*, *yawn*, etc.; *Bradshaw*, *Cawnpore*, *Dawlish*, *Fawcett*, *Hawkins*, *Micawber*, *Skiddaw*, *Trelawny*, *Warsaw*, etc.

Exceptions:

- where the <w> is part of a consonant digraph – *awhile*, *awry*;
- some irregular names – *Blawith* /ˈblɑːɪθ/, *Boscawen* /-əʊ-/, *Hawarden* /ˈhɑːdn/, *Hawick* /hɔɪk/, *Wroclaw* /ˈvrɒtslɑːf/.

Efficiency: in words 98 per cent; in names 89 per cent; a minor rule with strong bias towards shorter words.

A.12 <ah>≡/ɑː/ |— {<C>, #}
This marginal rule largely applies to foreign names. Since it is unambiguously a long open vowel spelling, <ah> is used to represent [ɑː] in respelling dialect forms – Cockney **abaht* (*about*), **tahn* (*town*), and similarly in foreign language pronunciation guides for English speakers.

Examples: *Ahmed*, *Bahrain*, *Brahmin*, *Brahms*, *Dahl*, *Fahy*, *Kahn*, *Mahdi*, *Mahler*, *Mahmud*, *Shah*, etc. *Fahrenheit* has /ɑː/ – /æ/ variation in SBS, but often /er/ in AmE.

There are also vocal gestures with stressed /ɑː/, such as *ah!*, *bah!*, *hurrah!*.

Exceptions:

- the only notable exception is *dahlia*, with /eɪ/; this is derived from the name *Dahl* /dɑːl/, but with popular use has become anglicized; AmE keeps the /ɑː/ or has /æ/;

- final unstressed <-ah> is usually /ə/, a natural reduction – *ayah*, *cheetah*, *hallelujah*, *hookah*, *loofah*, *maharajah*, *messiah*, *pariah*, *rajah*, *savannah*; *Basrah*, *Beulah*, *Deborah*, *Delilah*, *Hannah*, *Jeddah*, *Jonah*, *Norah*, *Sarah*, *Uriah*, etc;
- *Utah* has /ɔː/ in its AmE pronunciation.

A.13 <al>≡/ɔː/ |— {<k>, <l>} {<C>, # }
– this deals with <all> and <alk> before a consonant or free-form boundary.

Examples:

- most of the instances are in monosyllabic words:

before <k> – *balk*, *chalk*, *stalk*, *talk*, *walk*;
before <l> – *all*, *ball*, *call*, *fall*, *gall*, *hall*, *mall*, *pall*, *small*, *squall*, *stall*, *tall*, *thrall*;

- in polysyllabic derived forms such as: *allspice*, *ballroom*, *baseball*, *befall*, *downfall*, *gallstone*, *hallmark*, *overalls*, *pitfall*, *smallpox*, etc.; and similarly in names – *Allcroft*, *Allworthy*, *Goodall*, *McAll*. There is /ɔː/ – /ɔːl/ variation in *Dundalk*, *Falklands*, *Falkner*. Some names with <All-> have /ɒ/ variants (e.g. *Allcroft*, *Allsopp*).

Exceptions:

- with /æ/ – the common function word *shall*; *Pall Mall* in London has two /æ/ vowels;
- with unstressed /ə/ where final <l> is doubled before a vowel-initial suffix in British, but not American spelling – *signalled*, *signalling*, *teetotaller*, etc.; these are not strictly exceptions since the <-ll-> spelling is not that of the free-form *signal*, *teetotal*;
- final /əl/ in names – *Furnivall*, *Marshall*, *Meynall*, *Randall*, *Rossall*, *Tyndall*; but *Udall* has /ɔː/ – /æ/ – /ə/ variation. This unstressed <all> is an example of misleading padding in names, since <-al> is the more usual spelling: cf. *Kendal–Kendall*, *Marshal–Marshall*.

The contexts – finally and before a consonant – exclude *alkali*, *allegation*, *allegro*, *ballad*, *ballistic*, *challenge*, *dally*, *gallery*, *infallible*, *medallion*, *palliative*, *rally*, *shallow*, *valley*, etc., the common suffix <-ally> and names such as *Allerton*, *Chalkis* /ˈkælkɪs/, *Dalkeith*, *Halkett*, *Malkin*, *Valkyrie*. These get their /æ/ by the default rule A.31. So, but wrongly instead of /ɒ/, does *Balkan*.

The free-form boundary should be recognizable to readers in derived forms such as *falloff*, *fallout*, *smallish*, *talkative*, *talkie*, *walkout*, *walkover*, etc., otherwise they would wrongly go to the default rule as exceptions. So do *albeit*, *already*, *also*, *always*. The <alc> of *falcon* is an exceptional spelling that might be brought under the rule, though the word has several pronunciations: /-ɔːlk-/, /-ɔːk-/, /-ɒlk-/, /-ælk-/.

Efficiency: in words 79 per cent; in names 57 per cent; a minor rule with some bias towards high TF words and strong bias towards shorter words.

A.14 <al>≡/ɑː/ | — <m>
Examples: *almond*, *almoner*, *alms*, *balmy*, *becalm*, *calm*, *embalmer*, *malmsey*, *napalm*, *palm*, *psalm*, *qualm*, and some, but not all, derived forms; *Almesbury*, *Chalmers*, *Malmesbury*, *Palmer*, *Palmerston*, and as a variant of the name *Salmon* (EPD).

Exceptions:

- with /æ/ – *salmon*;
- with /æl/ – *halma*, *opthalmia*, *palmate*, *psalmodic*, *salmagundi*, *Almack*, *Alma*, *Almeria*, *Balmoral*, *Dalmatian*, *Falmouth*, *Malmaison*, *Palma*, *Talmud*; in *almanac* there is /ɔːl/, /ɒl/, /æl/ variation;
- with /ɔːl/ – *almighty*, *almost*, *instalment*, which have clear boundaries within the <alm>. The reduction of <ll> to <l> here seems unjustified, as in the previous rule.

Again, this is a marginal rule which works best for monosyllabic roots and which cannot be relied on in names.

Efficiency: in words 67 per cent; in names 29 per cent; a marginal rule with strong bias towards shorter words and some bias towards low TF words.

A.15 <al>≡/ɔːl/ | — {<d>, <t>}
Examples: *alder*, *alderman*, *altar*, *alternate*, *bald*, *baldric*, *basalt*, *cobalt*, *exalt*, *falter*, *halt*, *halter*, *malt*, *paltry*, *salt*, *scald*, and derived forms; *Aldbury*, *Aldgate* (and many other names containing the Old English element <ald>), *Alton*, *Altrincham*, *Archibald*, *Baldwin*, *Baltic*, *Baltimore*, *Caldecott*, *Calder*, *Caldwell*, *Dalton*, *Galt*, *Gibraltar*, *Haldane*, *Maldon*, *Malta*, *Spalding*, etc.

Some of these forms have free variation in SBS between /ɔːl/ and /ɒl/. EPD has variants for *Spalding* but not for *Baldwin*, but LPD has the opposite. Regional accents may have /ɒl/ in most of these words and names.

Exceptions:

- with /æl/ – *alto*, *altitude*, *altruism*, *asphalt*, *contralto*, *formaldehyde*, *heraldic*, *peristaltic*; *Aldebaran*, *Altaic*, *Balthazar*, *Esmeralda*, *Yalta*; there is a boundary in *maltreat* and in the name *Maltravers*;
- less than 2 per cent will have reduction to /əl/ in the absence of stress, as in *subaltern*, and the endings <-alty> (*casualty*, *loyalty*, *penalty*, *royalty*) and <-ald> (*emerald*, *herald*, *ribald*; *Donald*, *Dugald*, *Reginald*, *Ronald*, *Theobald*).

In reading an unfamiliar name there is bound to be some uncertainty between /ɔːl/, /ɒl/ and /æl/. For instance, EPD has *Yalding* with /ɔːl/ as a place-name (excluding /ɒl/), but with /æl/ as a surname.

Efficiency: in words 83 per cent; in names 74 per cent; a minor rule with some bias towards low TF words.

This last rule only prescribed <al>≡/ɔːl/ before <d> and <t>. Other following consonant letters may equally well have <al>≡/æl/: cf. /ɔːl/ or /ɒl/ in *Albany* and /æl/ in *Albert*. Examples with /ɔːl/ or /ɒl/ which, in the absence of any further rule for <al>, would wrongly end up as /æl/ in the default list of exceptions include: *already*, *also*, *always*, *appal*, *balsam*, *jackal*; *Albrow*, *Alford*, *Alfreton*, *Balkan*, *Bengal*, *Donegal*, *Falstaff*, *Galway*, *Halford*, *Halstead*, *Malvern*, *Nepal*, *Palgrave*, *Senegal*, *Talbot*.

The tendency to avoid doubling of consonant letters in a string with other consonant letters is unhelpful here; *always*, *appal*, etc. might be better spelt *<allways>, *<appall>. The Marquess of Donegall [*sic*] does just this with his name (EPD).

Before dealing with <ar>≡/ɛə(r)/ (as part of A.27) and <ar>≡/ɑː(r)/ (A.18), we have to foresee some contexts which select a rounded vowel.

A.16 <ar>≡/ɔː(r)/ | {<qu>, <w>, <wh>} — {<C>, #}
Conditions:

- in SBS not before a further non-final <r> as in *warrior*, *quarry*, etc., which have a short vowel /ɒ/ in SBS. Inflected forms (*warring*) are an exception.

The /r/ in the rule does occur before a consonant and finally in rhotic accents, such as AmE, but only before a vowel in derived forms in SBS. The righthand context prevents the rule applying before a vowel. Words such as *wary*, with a following vowel are dealt with by A.27.

Examples: *quart*, *quarto*, *quartz*, *thwart*, *sward*, *swarm*, *swarthy*, *war*, *warble*, *warden*, *warder*, *warm*, *warp*, *wart*, *wharf*, etc.; *Warbeck*, *Warburg*, *Warburton*, *Wardle*, *Warsaw*, *Warton*, etc.

Exceptions:

- with /ə/ – *bulwark*, *coward*, *stalwart*, *steward*; the suffix <-ward(s)> (*backwards*, *heavenward*, *onward*, etc.), except in *towards*, where it is stressed;
- others – *Warwick* /ˈwɒrɪk/; *Hawarden* /ˈhɑːdn/; *Southwark* /ˈsʌðək/.

Efficiency: in words 53 per cent; in names 41 per cent; a minor rule with some bias towards high TF words and strong bias towards shorter words.

Allowing vowel reduction to /ə/ in the common suffix <-ward(s)> would increase the efficiency rating in words to 96 per cent.

This rule has an obvious phonetic basis: the rounding of /w/ is passed on to the following vowel. We can now conveniently deal with a similar rounding effect in the short vowel /ɒ/.

A.17 <a>≡/ɒ/ | {<qu>, <w>, <wh>} — <C> {<C>, #}
In AmE the vowel is /ɑ/.

The righthand context prevents the rule applying before <(C)V>. So, *equation*, with a following <CV> is dealt with by A.30; *squaw*, *squawk* have already been dealt with under A.11; *aquatic* gets /æ/ by default. The rule is ordered after A.16 which deals with <ar> rounding.

Examples: *quaff*, *quandary*, *quantity*, *quarrel*, *quarry*, *quash*, *quatrain*, *squabble*, *squad*, *squander*, *squash*, *squat*, *swab*, *swamp*, *swan*, *swap*, *swash*, *swastika*, *swat*, *twaddle*, *wad*, *waddle*, *waffle*, *waft*, *wallaby*, *wallet*, *wallop*, *wampum*, *walrus*, *waltz*, *wan*, *wander*, *want*, *wanton*, *wash*, *wasp*, *was*, *watch*, *wattle*, *watt*, *what*.

Exceptions:

- with /æ/ – *quack*, *scallywag*, *swag*, *swagger*, *swam*, *swank*, *thwack*, *twang*, *twat*, *waft*, *wag*, *waggle*, *wangle*, *wank*, *wax*, *whack*, *wigwam*, *wrap*, *wrangle*; among these exceptions with /æ/, the majority have a following velar consonant /k, g, ŋ/; they could be excluded by adding a further condition to the rule;
- with /ɔː/ *walnut*; this shows a tendency to avoid <ll> before another consonant letter; **wallnut*, like *wallwort*, is clearly a more regular spelling (even though they have nothing to do with walls) and would follow A.13.

The /ɒ/ pronunciation of *wrath* is unusual, so <wr-> is not included as a context. AmE usually has /ae/, in *wrath* as do generally *wrangle*, *wrap*, *wrasse*. Unlike the words in the present rule, there is no actual /w/ in *wrath*.

The words *qualify*, *quality*, *squalid*, and derived forms, also have /ɒ/, but they are not captured by the rule since there is a single <l> after the vowel. They would be included if the boundary in the rule were made a morpheme boundary: that is, if the speller recognized the suffix. There is a similar problem with *quarantine*.

Efficiency: in words 69 per cent; in names 58 per cent; a minor rule with some bias towards shorter words.

A.18 <ar>≡/ɑː(r)/ | — {<C>,#} (AmE /ɑr/)
Conditions:

- not before a further non-final <r> (*arrive*, *marry*, etc.), though inflected forms such as *scarred*, *sparring*, keep the /ɑː/ of the base form.

Examples: *arm*, *bar*, *barn*, *carbon*, *cigar*, *guardian*, *large*, *leotard*, *pharmacy*, *star*, *yard*, etc.; *Arthur*, *Bartok*, *Braemar*, *Clarke*, *Darjeeling*, etc.

Exceptions:

- *scarce* and derived forms;
- *Barham*, *Barwick*, *Marham* when pronounced with /ær/.

Vowel reduction to /ə/ is assumed in unstressed syllables: *burglar*, *coward*, *lunar*, *margarine*, *scholarship*, etc. The ending <-ard> in names may be /ɑːd/ or /əd/, with varying probability in a given name: /ɑːd/ seems to be more usual in *Hansard*, /əd/ in *Gerrard* (but LPD prefers /ɑː/ in both).

Efficiency: a core rule with a heavy workload;

in words – 94 per cent (= 52 percentage points of 67 per cent correct /ɑː/ predictions);
in names – 95 per cent (= 51 percentage points of 62 per cent correct /ɑː/ predictions).

In the next four rules, Ainsworth tries to capture the lengthening of an original short //æ// in SBS to /ɑː/ before a voiceless fricative /f, θ, s/ followed by another consonant or a boundary as in *after*, *bath*, *past*. Wells (1982: 232ff) refers to this as the 'TRAP-BATH' split. In many accents of English, notably Northern British English and AmE, these rules would not apply and a short /æ/ would remain by default.

A.19 <a>≡/ɑː/ | — <sk> (default /æ/ in AmE)
Examples: *ask*, *bask*, *basket*, *cask*, *casket*, *flask*, *mask*, *task*; the names in the database do not follow this rule. A marginal rule with very strong bias towards high TF words and towards shorter words.

Exceptions:

- with /æ/ – *gasket* and a number of names: *Alaska*, *Aske*, *Askew*, *Askrigg*, *Askwith* (and *Asquith*), *Baskerville*, *Gaskell*, *Gaskin*, *Maskell*, *Maskelyne*, *Nebraska*, *Saskatchewan*, *Tasker*, *Tregaskis*, *Trevaskis*;
- with unstressed initial <a> as /ə/ – *askance*, *askew*.

A.20 <a>≡/ɑː/ | <C> — <st> (default /æ/ in AmE)
Conditions: not before a final <-e> and derived forms: *basting*, *chaste*, *hasty*, *lambaste*, *paste*, *tasteful*, *waster*. These are accommodated in A.27 by allowing <st> as a further possible cluster with long <a..e>≡/eɪ/. If this condition were simply met by changing the order of the two rules (to Ainsworth's), there would still be a problem. The <e>-marking rule would have wrongly taken out *alabaster*, *caster*, *disaster*, *fasten*, *flabbergasted*, *ghastly*, *master*, *nasty*, *plaster*, with /eɪ/. You have to know the structure of *master* and *waster* to read them. *Caste* is an exception to the conditions.

The <C> of the context precludes initial <ast->, which would otherwise give a number of exceptions such as *aster*, *asterisk*, *asthma*, *astir*, *astonish*, *astray*, *astrology*, *astute*; *Aston*, *Astor*.

Examples: *aghast*, *alabaster*, *blast*, *cast*, *caster*, *castle*, *castor*, *contrast*, *contrastive*, *disaster*, *fast*, *fasten*, *flabbergasted*, *ghastly*, *last*, *mast*, *master*, *nasty*, *pastime*, *pastor*, *pasture*, *plaster*, *vast*; *Belfast*, *Hardcastle*, *Holdfast*, *Newcastle*, etc.

Exceptions: with /æ/ – *bast*, *bastion*, *bombast*, *chastise*, *dynast*, *gymnast*, *mastic*, *mastiff*, *mastoid*, *pasta*, *pastel*, *pastern*, *pastille*, *spastic*; *Bastille*, *Brasted*, *Castille*, *Pasteur*, *Paston*, *Shasta*.

In some words there is free variation in SBS between /æ/ and /ɑː/: *drastic*, *pasteurize*, *plastic*. A poll conducted by Wells for LPD found only 8 per cent of the Southerners had /ɑː/ in *drastic* and only 6 per cent in *plastic*. The reason for a general preference for a short vowel in these words is no doubt the suffix <-ic>. This minority will no doubt have /æ/ in *mastic* and *spastic*.

There is vowel reduction in *ballast*, *breakfast*.

Efficiency: a marginal rule with very strong bias towards shorter words and strong bias towards low TF words;

in words – 36 per cent (= 6 percentage points of 67 per cent correct /ɑː/ predictions); even less successful in names – 28 per cent.

A.21 <a>≡/ɑː/ |— <th> (default /æ/ in AmE)
Conditions:

- not followed further by <e>: as in *bathe*, *lathe*, which have /eɪ/, and derived forms *bathes*, *bathing*, etc;
- only in free monosyllables such as *bath* and derived forms. Cf. /æ/ in *mathematics*, *pathology*, etc., or abbreviations of such words: *maths*, *path lab* (for *pathology laboratory*).

Examples: a marginal rule: just *bath*, *lath*, *path* and derived forms and, for some speakers, *aftermath*; *Bath*, *McGrath*.

Exceptions: with /æ/ – *Gath*, *Rath*; *wrath* has variants /ɒ/, /ɔː/ or /æ/;

This is a very slight rule with the added conditions, but without them the unconditioned <ath>≡/ɑːθ/ rule would only be 11 per cent effective in words and 8 per cent in names. Presumably for the Ainsworth set of rules, */fɑːðəm/ for *fathom* or */sɪmpɑːðɪ/ for *sympathy* from the synthesizer was thought decipherable enough.

A.22 <a>≡/ɑː/ |— <ft> (default /æ/ in AmE)
Examples: a marginal rule: *abaft*, *aft*, *after*, *craft*, *graft*, *haft*, *raft*, *rafter*, *shaft* and derived forms; *Grafton*, *Shaftesbury*, *Taft* (also /æ/).

Efficiency: 100 per cent; with some bias towards shorter words and some bias towards low TF words.

These last four /ɑː/ rules do not account for some groups of words with similar lengthening before fricatives, or before a nasal plus consonant as part of the same process. Without extra rules to cater for them, they would end up with /æ/ by default (which would be correct for AmE). It is convenient to note these other instances of /ɑː/ here, rather than with the other exceptions to the default rule.

Where <a> is followed by a nasal plus consonant :

/-ns/ – *advance*, *chance*, *chancel*, *chancery*, *dance*, *enhance*, *glance*, *lance*, *prance*, *trance*; *France*, *Francis*, *Lancelot*; and with /s/≡<s> in *answer*;
/-nd/ – *command*, *commando*, *countermand*, *demand*, *remand*, *slander*; *Sanders*, *Sanderson*;
/-nt/ – *can't*, *chant*, *enchant*, *grant*, *plant*, *shan't*, *slant*;
/-mp/ – *example*, *sample*;
/-n(t)ʃ/ – *avalanche*, *ranch*; *Blanche*.

The name *Franck* (also with /ɒ/ in LPD) may have /ɑː/ as a vestige of French pronunciation, but *franc* has /æ/.

- monosyllables with <-ass> – *brass*, *class*, *glass*, *grass*, *pass*, (cf. *lass*, *mass*, with /æ/) and derived forms. *Ass* itself is usually /æs/, presumably because as /ɑːs/ it would be homophonous with *arse*. Used as a term of contempt it may well be /ɑːs/, since this restraint does not then apply. *Grasmere* has the usual reduction of a doubled letter in a string of consonant letters – an unhelpful economy. Both pronunciations of *bass* are irregular – /eɪ/ 'singer', /æ/ 'fish' and the name *Bass*;
- with <-asp> – *clasp*, *exasperate*, *gasp*, *grasp*, *rasp*;
- with <-aff>, <-alf> (and related <-alve>) – *chaff*, *distaff*, *staff*; *calf*, *calve*, *half*, *halve*.

There is free variation between /ɑː/ and /æ/ for <-aph> – *autograph*, *cenotaph*, *epitaph*, *graph*, and in *giraffe* (but *gaffe* has /æ/). The poll by Wells in LPD found 77 per cent of the Southerners had /ɑː/ in *graph*, 23 per cent had /æ/.

- before <th>≡/ð/ – *father*, *rather*, which come out as exceptions to the <e>-marking rule A.27, where *bather* (from *bathe*) is regular. The poll by Wells in LPD found 88 per cent of the Southerners had /ɑː/ in *lather*, 12 per cent had /æ/.

From the reader's point of view, the relative success of these last four rules in selecting /ɑː/ rather than /æ/ is a matter of no great concern. There is variation between /ɑː/ – /æ/ across regional accents in the words covered by these rules and, in some words, free variation within SBS. These same two vowels also occur in SBS in variant allomorphs (*class–classify*; *demand–mandatory*). This close relationship must form part of native speaker competence and so must allow easy corrigibility in reading. Misreadings, say, of *chaffinch* with /ɑː/, or *remand* with /æ/, can easily be adjusted.

A.23 <a>≡/ɑː/ | # <C_1> — #
Examples: – a marginal rule: lexical monosyllables *bra*, *ma*, *pa*, *spa* and derived forms.

This only affects a few words and is fairly self-evident from other rules: a short stressed vowel cannot appear word-finally and, of the two long values of <a>, /eɪ/ would need <e>-marking (*brae*).

A.24 <a>≡/ə/ |— #

Otherwise in final position <a> represents an unstressed /ə/.

Examples: *abscissa, agenda, alfalfa, algebra, alpha, antenna, armada, aroma, aspidistra, asthma, balaclava, banana, bonanza, camera, cantata, charisma, cinema, cobra, comma, delta, data, dogma, drama, enigma, era, fauna, flora, manna, opera, panda, polka, quota, saga, silica, soda, tuba, vista*, etc.; *Alexandra, Burma, Canada, Jamaica, Matilda, Odessa, Riga, Sparta, Yoruba*, etc.

Exceptions: with /ɑː/ – the compounds *grandma, grandpa*, and *hoopla, papa.*

Efficiency: in words 99 per cent; in names 99 per cent; a minor rule with very strong bias towards low TF words.

We now try to deal with the other long values of <a>. In A.25 we try to capture an easily recognized group of exotic words which end in <a>, <i> or <o> and which have stressed <a>≡/ɑː/ in the previous syllable.

A.25 <a>≡/ɑː/ |— <C> {<a>, <i>, <o>} #

Examples: *armada, avocado, balaclava, banana, bravado, bravo, cantata, cascara, cicada, cinerama, cyclorama, desperado, drama, farrago, gala, gestapo, guano, guava, gymkhana, iguana, incommunicado, lava, legato, liana, llama, marijuana, mascara, meccano, panorama, pyjama(s), plaza, saga, sonata, soprano, staccato, strata, sultana, tiara, toccata, tomato, virago*, etc. Examples with final <i> are less common – *khaki, literati, pastrami, safari, salami.* Quite a number of foreign names are naturally covered by this rule: *Abaco, Atbara, Bahama(s), Bechuana, Bokhara, Bratislava, Carrara, Chicago, Colorado, Connemara, Gaza, Ghana, Granada, Guatemala, Iago, Java, Juliana, Kampala, Kilimanjaro, Lhasa, Luciano, Lugano, Lusaka, MacNamara, Mikado, Nagasaki, Pakistani, Sahara, Santiago, Scala, Svengali, Yokohama*, etc. *Karachi* differs in having a two-letter spelling of the consonant.

The plurals *schemata* and *stigmata*, if faithful to their Greek origin, would be expected to have stress on the first syllable as in /ˈskiːmətə/, but pronunciations by analogy with the above are now commonly used: /skiːˈmɑːtə/, /stɪgˈmɑːtə/ (LPD).

Some words, such as *data, desperado,* have variation across accents between /ɑː/ and /eɪ/. The difference for SBS is between the exotic and familiar long counterparts of /æ/. More familiarity gives /eɪ/. Presumably, for British English, *potato* with /eɪ/ is more anglicized than *tomato* with /ɑː/. AmE has /eɪ/ for both these and may also have /eɪ/ in some §Romance words such as *El Dorado, cicada, desiderata, desperado, gala, pro rata, strata*. LPD gives *bastinado* with /eɪ/ as more common than /ɑː/, though as yet it is scarcely part of the English experience. *Ava, Clara* and some other personal names also have /ɑː/ – /eɪ/ (/ɛə/) variation. One tends to choose the vowel to fit the person's background: *Ava Gardner* with /eɪ/, *Clara Schumann* with /ɑː/.

Exceptions:

- with stressed /æ/ – *alpaca*, *piano*; the American placenames *Alabama*, *Indiana*, *Louisiana*, *Montana*, *Urbana* usually have /æ/ (but British speakers may say them with /ɑː/);
- with /ə/ – *ado*, *ago*, *archipelago*, *buffalo*, *dynamo*, *papa*; *Akaba*, *Ankara*, *Canada*, *Idaho*, *Ithaca*, *Kerala*, *Magdala*, *Malaga*, *Monaco*, *Panama*, *Smetana*;
- with /eɪ/ – *dado*, *halo*, *lumbago*, *octavo*, *plumbago*, *potato*, *sago*, *tornado*, *volcano*; *Asa*, *Cana*, *Cato*, *Jago*, *Plato*, *Strabo*, *Tobago*. In the poll conducted by Wells for LPD, British speakers had 92 per cent /eɪ/, 6 per cent /ɑː/ and 2 per cent /æ/ in *data*;
- with /ɛə/, the pre-/r/ variant for /eɪ/ – *Demerara*.

Efficiency: in words 66 per cent; in names 58 per cent; a minor rule with some bias towards low TF words.

The next rule is provided by Ainsworth as a special long vowel context for <a>. It has the same effect as adding a context, peculiar to <a>, to the <e>-marking rule A.27.

A.26 <a>≡/eɪ/ |— <ng> <e> #
Examples: *arrange*, *arrangement*, *change*, *changeful*, *danger*, *exchange*, *grange*, *mange*, *manger*, *range*, *strange*, *stranger*, etc.; *Granger*, *Sprange*, and, if we are to believe it, in some people's pronunciation of the name *Banger* (EPD).

Exceptions:

- with /æ/ – *anger*, *banger*, *flange*, *hanger*, *tangerine*; *Clayhanger*, *Ganges*, *Northanger*, *Sanger*, *Stavanger*, *Vange* /vændʒ/;
- with /ɒ/ – blancmange;
- with unstressed /ɪ/ – *orange*.

Efficiency: in words 79 per cent; in names 41 per cent; a marginal rule with very strong bias towards high TF words.

The next four rules deal with the more general conditions for a long vowel, beginning with the main <e>-marking rule (§4.2.4 pp. 276ff.).

A.27 <a>≡/eɪ/ |— (<C>*) <e>* #
Conditions:

- the <C>* is not <x> (*taxing*);
- the <C>* may be a <Cl> or <Cr> cluster other than <ll>, <rr> (*table*, *sabre*), or it may be <th> (*bathe*). Exceptionally for <-aC*e>, the <C>* may be <st> (*waste*), or <ch> (*ache*, see p.220). When the <C>* is <r>, the vowel is /ɛə/;
- the <e>* may be elided before the initial vowel of a suffix as in *shaker*, *shaky* (p. 269).

Examples: with /eɪ/ – *ache, acre, advocate, agitate, amazement, amazingly, awaken, bravery, butane, cable, cage, cave, celebrated, chafe, chaser, comrade, cradle, crazy, crusade, drake, draper, elated, elongate, estate, fateful, flaky, gravy, instigate, knavish, lading, ladle, landscape, lathe, paste, rating, sable, scathingly, shamelessly, slavery, slavish, space, stable, taste, wafer, wager, waster*, etc.; *Allandale, Applegate, Avery, Belgrade, Blake, Caterham, Danish, Drake, Euphrates, Faber, Frazer, Hamish, Haslemere, Lestrade, Strachey*, etc.

With /ɛə/ – *aware, bare, careful, daring, fanfare, garish, glaring, prepared, rarest, spares, square, tare, wares*, etc.; *Adare, Baring, Kenmare, Kildare, Waring*, etc.; *Yare* in Norfolk is regular with /ɛə/, but *Yare* on the Isle of Wight locally has /ɑː/ (EPD).

In monosyllables /eɪ/ occurs finally in Scottish words – *brae, tae* (= *to*), *Rae*, and in the compound names *Braemar, Raeburn*. In terms of the regularity of the whole system, however, these few words represent the normal <e>-marked spelling, as in *lie, toe, sue, bye*.

Exceptions:

- words which have no <e>-marking because what appears to be a suffix is actually part of the stem: for instance, *to slaver* (v.) /ˈslævə/ is not {slave}+{er}. There is a parallel problem with *banish, lavish, parish, ravish, vanish* (cf. *apish, slavish*). The place of the boundary has to be recognized in *sapling* (cf. *stapling*); *cellarer, pillared*; *nasaled, orphaned, turbaned* (cf. *profaned*).
- polysyllabic loan-words from French with stressed /ɑː/ in the final syllable – *ballade, carafe, charade, chorale, facade, locale, morale, pomade, promenade, rationale, timbale*; but *finale,* from Italian, is slightly different, since the <e> is not just a marker.
- other words with /ɑː/ – the common function word *are(n't)*; *amen* (AmE /eɪ/), *cadaver, cadre, father, grave* ('accent'), *lager, karate, macabre, padre, palaver, rather, rationale, strafe, suave, vase*; *Aberdare, Graves* ('wine'), *Sade*.
- with /æ/ – *cache, detached, forebade, gather, majesty, maverick, panache, paten, platen, slaver* ('spittle'), *tapestry, travesty*; *Abingdon, Cader, Cather, Catherine, Lavington, Mather, McTavish, Sadler* (cf. *saddler*), *Spanish, Tapling, Tatler* (cf. *tattler*), *Valery*. There is good reason for writing *attach* and *detach* and their inflected forms with <-atch>, like *despatch*. The same applies to *bachelor*; the name *Batchelor* usually has <-tch->.
- with /ə/ – *abed, aver, flamingo, malinger, sesame*.
- loan-words from French with a final <e>≡/eɪ/ – *cafe, glace*, which are usually spelt with an accent <é>.
- unstressed <-ace> – *furnace, menace, necklace, palace, pinnace, populace, preface, solace, surface, terrace*, and <-ase> – *carcase, purchase*. In the <-ace> spelling, the <e> also marks the /s/ value of <c>.

- the suffix <-ary>, as in *capillary*, is /-ərɪ/ in SBS, but /-ɛəri/ in AmE;
- the Latin plural <es> – *emphases* /ˈemfəsiːz/ and the <es> ending of Greek names – *Aristophanes*, *Cyclades*, *Socrates*;
- *water* has rounded /ɔː/ after /w/; this is exceptional for the long vowel <a> (*wafer*, *wager*, *waver*), but regular for the short vowel (*squad*, *wallet*, *wasp*). /wɔː/ requires a following //r//. See A.16, 17.

The spellings *pastry*, *wastrel*, lose the <e>-marker, so they are not in every respect an improvement on a regular *<pastery>, *<wasterel>.

Traps for the unwary reader, where a medial <e> is not a marker at the end of a morpheme, are: *facetious*, *lateral*, *malefactor*, *malevolent*, *planetoid*, *tapestried*, *valedictory*, and similar words. These can be misread as compounds: **male-factor*. Those which have a non-§Basic suffix such as <-oid>, <-ory>, are unlikely to be misread.

Efficiency: a core rule with a heavy workload;

in words – 89 per cent (= 37 percentage points of 80 per cent correct /eɪ/ predictions);
in names – 61 per cent (= 18 percentage points of 62 per cent correct /eɪ/ predictions).

These figures assume that the suffix <-ate> in nouns and adjectives such as *advocate*, *celibate*, *corporate*, may be read as /eɪt/ and reduced to /ət/ as part of the reader's competence.

A.28 <a>≡/eɪ/ | # <C_o>— <C>* ENDING
Conditions:

- the <C>* may be a <Cr> cluster (*apron*), or <th> (*bathos*);

Examples and exceptions:

with <-al> – *basal*, *fatal*, *nasal*, *natal*, *naval*, *papal*, but not in *cabal*, *canal*, *sacral*;
with <-an> – *pagan*; *Satan*;
with <-ar> – *planar*, *scalar*;
with <-ir> – *nadir*, *tapir*;
with <-is> – *stasis*, which, like *thesis*, originally had a short vowel, was clearly under some analogical pressure to have a long vowel;
with <-on> – *apron*, *bacon*, *blazon*, *capon*, *mason*, *matron*, *natron*, *patron*, but not in *baron*, *baton*, *canon*, *dragon*, *flagon*, *salon*, *talon*, *wagon*. There is a curious difference here. All the examples except *blazon* have a following voiceless consonant and all the exceptions except *baton* have a following voiced consonant.
with <-os> – *bathos*, *pathos*;
with <-us> – *flatus*, *status*, *vagus*;
with <-acy> – *papacy*;

with <-ant, -ance, -ancy> – *blatant*, *flagrant*, *fragrance*, *vacant*, *vagrancy*, but not in *balance*, *savant*;
with <-ary – *vagary*, but not in *canary*, *granary*, *salary*;
with <-ent, -ence, -ency> – *cadence*, *latent*, *parent*, *patent*, but not in *lament*, *talent*;
with <-ine> – *canine* (also /æ/), *saline*, but not in *famine*, *latrine*, *marine*, *rapine*, *ravine*;
with <-ite> – *barite*, but not in *granite*;
with <-ive> – *dative*, *native*;
with <-our> – *favour*, *flavour*, *labour*, *savour*, *vapour*, but not in *clamour*, *glamour*, *valour*.

Efficiency: in words 56 per cent; in names 40 per cent; a marginal rule.

The endings <-ic(al)>, <-id>, <-it> have a complementary function in that they mark a short vowel (the default) in *acid*, *agaric*, *acrobatic*, *aquatic*, *arid*, *avid*, *davit*, *dynamic*, *fanatic*, *habit*, *manic*, *rabid*, *rapid*, *sporadic*, *tacit*, *valid*, *vapid*, *volcanic*; *Adriatic*, *Titanic*. *Affidavit* and *David* with /eɪ/ are exceptional.

A.29 <a>≡/eɪ/ |— <C>* <i> <V>
Conditions:

• the <C>* is not <x>.

This captures a large number of §Latinate words; the many words ending in <-tion>, <-sion> regularly have a long preceding vowel if it is spelt <a>, <e>, <o>, or <u>.

Examples: *alias*, *amiable*, *contagion*, *cranium*, *equation*, *evasion*, *facial*, *fantasia*, *gymnasium*, *invasion*, *labial*, *maniac*, *occasion*, *plagiarism*, *radiate*, *radio*, *stadium*, *uranium*, etc.; *Adriatic*, *Albania*, *Arabia*, *Baliol* (but not *Balliol)*, *Canadian*, *Fabian*, *Pygmalion*, *Scandinavia*, etc.

Exceptions:

• with /æ/ – *battalion*, *caviar*, *companion*, *gladiator*, *manioc*, *tapioca*, *valiant*, *Casio*, *Traviata*;
• unstressed with /ə/ – *Tanzania*;
• with /ɑː/ – *Anastasia*, *Ghanian*.

Restricting the first of the two vowel letters to <i> ignores a few similar instances, such as *azalea*.

Efficiency: a core rule with a heavy workload; since the examples usually involve a §Latinate suffix, there is naturally a very strong bias towards longer words;

in words – 77 per cent (= 23 percentage points of 80 per cent correct /eɪ/ predictions);

in names – 63 per cent (= 10 percentage points of 62 per cent correct /eɪ/ predictions).

A.30 <a>≡/eɪ/ |— <V>
Examples – a marginal rule; <ao> is the only combination not pre-empted as a single vowel spelling: *aorta*, *chaos*, *kaolin*.

Exceptions: the archaic spelling *gaol*; *extraordinary*.The exotic <aa>≡/aː/ in *bazaar*, *Afrikaans*, *Haarlem*, would require an extra rule.

Examples of hiatus previously mentioned in the <a>-rules as exceptions to the complex spelling of a single vowel include: *Laertes*; *algebraic*, *archaic*, *dais*, *formulaic*, *mosaic*, *prosaic*; *Capernaum*, *Menelaus*, *Kaunda*. These could only be dealt with by rule if they were to be marked as belonging to an appropriate non-§Basic subsystem.

A.31 <a>≡/æ/ – the default rule for <a>
Examples: *apple, astronaut, band, channel, crack, extract, invalidate*, etc.

Efficiency – a core rule; in words 80 percentage points of 86 per cent correct unreduced /æ/ predictions and in names 80 percentage points of 81 per cent; a very heavy workload with some bias towards low TF words.

Vowel reduction to /ə/ will naturally occur in unstressed syllables, as in: *abandon*, *abolish*, *accuse*, *botany*, *citadel*, *coolant*, *cutlass*, *ecstasy*, *feudal*, *human*, *lilac*, *marauding*, *mythical*, *orator*, *rival*, etc. Allowing for this, the efficiency of the default rule is 91 per cent (with just /æ/, 85 per cent); the parallel figures for names are 85 per cent including /ə/ and 76 per cent with just /æ/. These figures are rather pessimistic, since there are some recognizable classes of words in the exceptions which remain.

Exceptions to the default rule (and hence to the <a>-rules as a set) which have not been dealt with earlier:

- instances of long /ɑː/ before fricatives or before nasal plus consonant that are not catered for in the contexts of A.19–22 have already been discussed after A.22. Instances of /ɑː/ unaccounted for are – *bazaar*, *bizarre*, *catarrh*, *corral*, *debacle*, *fracas*, *moustache*, *saki*. In these words /ɑː/ is clearly an exotic marker; this is borne out in names – *Afrikaans*, *Allahabad*, *Amman*, *Armagh*, *Bach*, *Braque*, *Haarlem*, *Iran*, *Iraq*, *Islam*, *Prague*, *Sinatra*, *Slav*. Other exotic names with /ɑː/, such as *Anastasia*, come out as exceptions to the /eɪ/ rules above. AmE may have /ɑ(ː)/ rather than /æ/ in *Bangladesh, Calvados, Caracas, Casals, Datsun, Davos, Dvorak, Fernando, Franco, Galapagos, Gdansk, Golan, Gulag, Hambro, Hanoi, Kafka, Kant, Latvia, Luganda, Milan, Mombasa, Nansen, Nassau, Natasha, Navaho, Onassis, Pablo, Plassey, Raquel, Rashid, Slovak, Sri Lanka, Tamil, Uganda, Vivaldi, Yasser,* and in the words *bagnio, chianti, grappa, kebab, pasta, pastiche, pilaf, samba.* The reason for this apparent mis-match is that AmE /æ/ is much less open than SBS /æ/, so the fully open /ɑ/ seems, in terms of AmE, a better approximation.

- the little group *cambric*, *chamber*, *Cambridge* (cf. *Cam* with /æ/); these latter have a long vowel before nasal plus consonant, but it is /eɪ/ instead of /ɑː/ as in *remand*, etc.
- other examples with /eɪ/ which escape the long vowel rules, as given, include *acorn*, *ague*, *ancient*, *apex*, *aphid*, *apricot*, *area*, *azalea*, *basin*, *bass*, *calyx*, *halfpenny*, *hazel*, *matriarch*, *navel*, *patriarch*, *patriot*; *razor*, *April*, *Atchison*, *Balliol*, *Chaffey*, *Charlemagne*, *Jacques*, *Nasmyth*. No doubt many of these could be accommodated by further fine-tuning. AmE, however, does have /eɪ/ in some §Greek words *phalanx, satrap, satyr.*

<b>-rules

B.1 <bu>≡/b/ | — <V>
A marginal rule.

Examples: *build*, *buoy*, *buy* and derived forms; *Builth*.

Exceptions: the rule usually does not work in names, where the <u> represents /w/ or /juː/ - *Buenos Aires*, *Buesst*, *Buick*, *Buisst*, *Cimabue*, *Labuan*.

Any practical system would opt for putting *build*, *buoy*, *buy* in the look-up list, but they have been put into this very marginal rule to draw attention to the analogy with <gu> in *guild*, *guy*, etc.

B.2 <b>≡∅ | <m> — (e) #
Examples: a marginal rule – *bomb*, *catacomb*, *climb*, *comb*, *coulomb*, *crumb*, *dumb*, *jamb*, *lamb*, *limb*, *numb*, *plumb*, *succumb*, *thumb*, *tomb*, *womb*, and derived forms; a number of names ending in <-combe> (*Ilfracombe* etc.).

Exceptions: the rule is exceptionless unless the free-form boundary is not recognized in derivations of the above and a /b/ is wrongly read – *bombing*, *climber*, *crumby*, *dumbfounded*, *dumbly*, *entombment*, *lambkin*, *limbless*, *numbness*, *plumber*, *unplumbed*, etc. This is more likely to happen as a reading error if a vowel follows in cases such as *climber–clamber*.

There is a contrast between *number* (comp. adj.) with no /b/ and *number* (n.) with /b/. The /b/ occurs before endings for bound stems: *bombast*, *bombard*, *plumbic*, *plumbous*, and before the <-le> of *crumble*. *Crumby* has a variant slang spelling *crummy*.

B.3 <b(b)>≡/b/ – the default rule for <b>.
Examples: *about*, *babble*, *bus*, *robbery*, etc.

Exceptions: the empty <b> of *debt*, *doubt*, *redoubt*, *subtle*, and derived forms; but since */bt/ is not an allowed phoneme sequence within an English morpheme, the spelling declares itself to be an irregularity.

Efficiency: a core rule with a very heavy workload;

in words – 99 per cent (= 90 percentage points of 91 per cent correct /b/ predictions);

in names – 99 per cent (= 95 percentage points of 96 per cent correct /b/ predictions).

<c>-rules

Correspondences are dealt with in rules numbered as follows:

C.1 <che>≡/ʃ/ C.2 <ch>≡/k/ C.3 <ch>≡/ʧ/
C.4 <ck>≡/k/ C.5 <cc>≡/ks/ C.6, 8, 11, 12 <c>≡/s/
C.7 <ce>≡/ʃ/ C.9 <c>≡/ʃ/ C.10 <ci>≡/ʃ/
C.13 <c>≡∅ C.14 <c(c)>≡/k/ – the default rule.

C.1 <che>≡/ʃ/ | — #
Examples: barouche, *cache*, *cartouche*, *cloche*, *creche*, *douche*, *gauche*, *moustache*, *niche*, *panache*; *Roche*, *Tollemache*, *Zouche*. There is /ʃ/ – /ʧ/ variation after the /n/ in *avalanche*, *Blanche*.

Exceptions:

- *attache*, *cliche*, *recherche*, which are usually spelt with an accent to show the <é>≡/eɪ/ correspondence;
- with /k/ – *ache* (and its compounds – *backache*, *headache*, etc.);
- with /kɪ/ – *psyche*, *Andromache*, *Didache*;
- with /ʧ/ – EPD has the names *Bache* /beɪʧ/, *Derviche* /ˈdɜːvɪʧ/, *Dyche* /daɪʧ/, *Lutwyche* /ˈlʌtwɪʧ/. *Apache* (American Indian) is /əˈpæʧɪ/, but the former slang term for a Paris ruffian was /əˈpæʃ/.

The boundary recognition is not difficult here, because these words generate few derived forms.

Efficiency: in words 54 per cent; in names 37 per cent; a marginal rule with very strong bias towards low TF words and towards shorter words.

C.2 <ch>≡/k/ | — {<l>, <r>}
Examples: *chlorate*, *chloroform*, *chromatic*, *chronicle*, *chrysalis*, *cochlea*, *lachrymose*, *sepulchre*, etc.; *Chloe*, *Christ*, *Christabel*, *Chrysler*, *Cochran*, *Pitlochry*, etc.

Exceptions: the rule does not apply across obvious boundaries in *speechless*, *suchlike*, etc. and in some names with a similar boundary between elements: *Finchley*, *Hinchliffe*, *Inchrye*, *Lechlade*.

This is one of the few phonetic/orthographic contexts in which it is possible to separate §Greek <ch>≡/k/ from §French <ch>≡/ʃ/ and §Basic <ch>≡/ʧ/, neither of which cluster with <l>, <r>.

Efficiency: in words 89 per cent; in names 91 per cent; a marginal rule with very strong bias towards low TF words and some bias towards longer words.

C.3 <ch>≡/ʧ/ – the default rule for <ch>.
Examples: the default is correct for words of English origin – *beech*, *bench*,

beseech, *birch*, *cheap*, *cheese*, *child*, *church*, *leech*, *teach*, etc., but also for words of Romance origin which have been in use since Middle English – *achieve*, *approach*, *archer*, *attach*, *avouch*, *chair*, *chalice*, *chamber*, *chancellor*, *chapter*, *chaste*. There is free variation between /ʧ/ and /ʃ/ after the /n/ in *lunch*, *luncheon* (cf. C.1). Later loans have <ch>≡/ʃ/ and need to be recognized as §French.

Exceptions:

- the most common group are the many §Greek learned and scientific terms and Greek names with <ch>≡/k/ – *anarchy*, *architect*, *archives*, *bronchitis*, *catechism*, *chameleon*, *chaos*, *character*, *chemistry*, *chiropodist*, *cholera*, *dichotomy*, *epoch*, *mechanic*, *melancholy*, *orchestra*, *parochial*, *psychology*, *technical*, etc.;
- Scottish and Irish names with <ch>≡[x] (a voiceless velar fricative) are usually anglicized with /k/, which puts them on a par with §Greek words and names – *Auchindachie*, *Brechin*, *Buchanan*, *Buchan*, *Carnochan*, *Cuchulinn*, *Leuchars*, *Lochiel*, *Ochiltree*, *Tulloch*, etc.;
- German names with <ch> also have /k/ – *Bach*, *Munich*;
- more recent (i.e. seventeenth century and later) French loan-words with <ch>≡/ʃ/ – *brochure*, *cachet*, *chagrin*, *chaise*, *chalet*, *chamois*, *champagne*, *chancre*, *chandelier*, *charlatan*, *cheroot*, *chevron*, *chic*, *chivalry*, *echelon*, *machine*, *nonchalant*, *parachute*, *ricochet*, *sachet*, etc.

Readers may guess that a word belongs to the §Greek subsystem, and so has <ch>≡/k/, if it contains one of the common §Greek elements used to make up technical terms in science – {logy}, {ism}, {ical}, etc. There is similar marking for some §French words: *sachet* would be **satchet* (cf. *ratchet*) if it had been anglicized with /ʧ/, but words with initial <ch> are more of a problem. It requires some skill to negotiate between the different correspondences in cases such as *archbishop* – *archiepiscopal* /ʧ/ – /k/, *machine* – *machination* /ʃ/ – /k/.

Efficiency: a core rule with a fairly heavy workload;

in words – 67 per cent (= 54 percentage points of 91 per cent correct /ʧ/ predictions);
in names – 54 per cent (= 70 percentage points of 85 per cent correct /ʧ/ predictions);

with a strong bias towards shorter words.

C.4 <ck>≡/k/

Examples: *acknowledge*, *attack*, *barracks*, *black*, *crackle*, *duck*, *hijack*, *hockey*, *mock*, *packet*, *rack*, *stickler*, etc.; *Ackroyd*, *Auckland*, *Blackpool*, *Brocklehurst*, *Eyck*, *Mackenzie*, *Patrick*, etc.

Exceptions: only when the <ck> has become empty in isolated cases: *blackguard* /ˈblægɑːd/, *Cockburn* /ˈkəʊbɜːn/.

If we regard <ck> as the <C>-doubling of <c>, this is really part of the default rule C.14.

Efficiency: a core rule with a heavy workload;

in words – 100 per cent (= 6 percentage points of 90 per cent correct /k/ predictions);
in names – 99 per cent (= 11 percentage points of 89 per cent correct /k/ predictions);

with a strong bias towards shorter words.

C.5 <cc>≡/ks/ | <a> — {<e>, <i>}
Examples: *accelerate*, *accent*, *accept*, *access*, *accident*, *flaccid*, *vaccine*, etc. and derived forms.

Exceptions: a few names of Italian origin have /ʧ/ – *Boccaccio*, *Pagliacci*, *Puccini*, *Riccio*.

Efficiency: in words 100 per cent; a marginal rule with strong bias towards high TF words and, since the examples usually involve a §Latinate suffix, there is naturally a strong bias towards longer words.

C.6 <c>≡/s/ | — <ae>
Examples: a marginal rule: *caecum*, *caesura*; *Alcaeus*, *Caesar*, *Nicaeus*.

Exceptions: *Caen*, *Caerleon* and other Welsh names with {caer}.

This is perhaps trivial, but it is one of four contexts for <c>≡/s/ – before {<ae>, <e>, <i>, <y>}. The rules have in common that <c>, which would be /k/ by default, is 'softened' to /s/ before original front vowels corresponding to present-day /ɪ/, /e/, /iː/ and /aɪ/.

C.7 <ce>≡/ʃ/ | — {<an>, <ous>} #
Examples: a marginal rule: *crustacean*, *ocean*(*ic*); *cretaceous*, *herbaceous*, *sebaceous*, *siliceous*.

This is a small class of exceptions to the next rule. It would clearly best be catered for as part of an optional assimilation process whereby unstressed //siːV// becomes /ʃV/. Stress preserves the /iː/ in *oceanic*. This process is also the basis of C.9, 10.

C.8 <c>≡/s/ | — <e>
Examples: *absence*, *accomplice*, *ace*, *acetic*, *acetone*, *adduce*, *adjacent*, *advanced*, *advice*, *ancestor*, *announce*, *antecedent*, *appendices*, *avarice*, *balance*, *bonce*, *bounce*, *cancel*, *cease*, *cedar*, *celebrate*, *cell*, *census*, *centre*, *century*, *cervical*, *deceit*, *decent*, *deuce*, *divorce*, *glycerine*, *lance*, *matrices*, *police*, *sluice*, *wince*, etc.; *Alice*, *Barcelona*, *Bruce*, *Cecily*, *Ceylon*, *Cicero*, *Fawcett*, *Nice*, *Wallace*, etc.

Exceptions:

- with /ʧ/ – *cello*, *cellist*, *concerto*, and Italian names such as *Botticelli*, *Francesca* and operatic *Berenice* /beriˈniːʧeɪ/ (classical /berɪˈnaɪsɪ/ or /-naɪkɪ/);

- those who do not distinguish /nts/ and /ns/ in *mints, mince*, but have /nts/ in both, will need a further rule to insert the /t/.

In *MacEldowney* etc. the use of the capital letter within the word marks a boundary.

Efficiency: a core rule with some bias towards high TF words; heavy workload;

in words – 99 per cent (= 8 percentage points of 78 per cent correct /s/ predictions);
in names – 91 per cent (= 5 percentage points of 76 per cent correct /s/ predictions).

C.9 <c>≡/ʃ/ | — <iat> <V> (OPT.)
Examples: *appreciate*, *appreciation*, *appreciative*, *appreciator*, *depreciation*, *dissociation*, *emaciated*, *enunciate*, *glaciation*, *noviciate*, *officiate*, etc., with varying probability; it does not apply to *pronunciation*, *renunciation*, etc.

Efficiency: a marginal rule. There is naturally a very strong bias towards longer words.

C.10 <ci>≡/ʃ/ | — <V>
Examples: *ancient, artificial*, *atrocious*, *beneficial*, *commercially*, *delicious*, *efficient*, *electrician*, *financial*, *gracious*, *malicious*, *official*, *politician*, *social*, *special*, *vicious*, and a large number of other words with these suffixes; *Cistercian*, *Confucius*, *Galicia*, *Grecian*, *Patricia*, *Valencia*, etc.

Exceptions:

- inflected forms of words ending in <-cy> – *fancied*, *fancier*, *fancies*, *fanciest*, etc.;
- other words with unassimilated /s/ – *calcium*, *glacial*, *glacier*, *insouciance*, *society*, *sociology*, etc.

The /s/ may assimilate to /ʃ/ in some of these (e.g. *glacial*, *sociology*) without absorbing the following [i] vowel, as the rule does.

Efficiency: a core rule;

in words – 93 per cent (= 5 percentage points of 89 per cent correct /ʃ/ predictions);
in names – 48 per cent (= 3 percentage points of 79 per cent correct /ʃ/ predictions).

There is some bias towards high TF words and a very strong bias towards longer words.

C.11 <c>≡/s/ | — <i>
Examples: *acid*, *anticipate*, *boracic*, *city*, *crucible*, *decide*, *excise*, *icing*, *fanaticism*, *fencing*, *incisive*, *lucid*, *precinct*, *precise*, *publicity*, *recite*, *saucily*, *suicide*, *tenacity*, etc.; *Cecil*, *Cibber*, *Cicero*, *Cilla*, *Cinderella*,

Felicity, *Lycidas*, *Runciman*, *Sicily*, etc.
Exceptions:

- with /k/ – *foci*;
- some Italian names with /ʧ/ – *Cenci*, *Medici*, *Vinci*;
- as in C.8: *MacInnes*, *McIntosh*, etc.

Efficiency: in words virtually 100 per cent; in names 83 per cent; a minor rule with a fairly heavy workload. Since the examples usually involve a §Latinate suffix, there is naturally a very strong bias towards longer words and and some bias towards low TF words.

C.12 <c>≡/s/ | — <y>
Examples: *agency*, *bouncy*, *celibacy*, *currency*, *cyanide*, *cyclamen*, *cycle*, *cygnet*, *cylinder*, *cymbals*, *cynic*, *cynosure*, *cypress*, *leucocyte*, *mercy*, *salycylic*, etc.; *Crecy*, *Cyclades*, *Cymbeline*, *Cynthia*, *Cyprus*, *Cyril*, *Halcyon*, *Lucy*, *Scylla*, *Tracy*, etc.
Exceptions: with /k/ – *Cymru*, *Cynewulf*, *Hecyra*.
Efficiency: in words 100 per cent; in names 92 per cent; a minor rule. Since many of the examples have the suffix <-cy>, there is naturally a very strong bias towards longer words and and a strong bias towards low TF words.

C.13 <c>≡∅ | — <qu>
Examples: – *acquaint*, *acquiesce*, *acquire*, *acquit*, *lacquer*; *Jacqueline*, *Jacques*. A marginal rule with strong bias towards high TF words and towards longer words.

C.14 <c(c)>≡/k/ – the default rule for <c>
Examples: *abstract*, *academic*, *acclaim*, *acclimatize*, *accolade*, *accommodate*, *accompany*, *accomplice*, *according*, *accost*, *account*, *accredit*, *accurate*, *accuse*, *acme*, *actor*, *alcohol*, *balcony*, *cable*, *car*, *casket*, *cavil*, *cliff*, *crude*, *duct*, etc.; *Alec*, *America*, *Cadillac*, *Cain*, *Clacton*, *Macon*, *Meccano*, *Mecca*, *Morocco*, *Pinocchio*, etc.
There are a number of exceptions to the default rule (and hence to the <c>-rules as a set):

- with /s/ – *coelacanth* /siː/, *facade*, *Curacao* /səʊ/, *Provencal* (unless spelt with <ç>);
- with <c>≡∅ – *blancmange*, *indict*, *victuals*, *Connecticut* /-net-/, *Tucson* /'tuːsɒn/, *Czar*;
- exotic – *Czechoslovakia* /ʧ-/, *Gollancz* /-ænts/, *Wroclaw* /'vrɒtslɑːf/.

Efficiency: a core rule with a very heavy workload;

in words – 99 per cent (= 62 percentage points of 90 per cent correct /k/ predictions);
in names – 98 per cent (= 46 percentage points of 89 per cent correct /k/ predictions).

<d>-rules

D.1 <dg>≡/ʤ/ | — {<e>, <i>, <y>, #}
Examples: *abridge*, *badger*, *bludgeon*, *budgie*, *dodgy*, *dredge*, *drudgery*, *fridge*, *gadget*, *judgement*, *knowledge*, *lodging*, *porridge*, *stodgy*, etc; *Aldridge*, *Bainbridge*, *Bridgewater*, *Bridget*, *Claridges*, *Coolidge*, *Edgley*, *Goodge, Hodges, Rodgers*, etc.

The context is a front vowel spelling. An empty <e> is used as a marker for /ʤ/ when it occurs finally as in *bridge*. When <dg> occurs before letters other than <e>, <i>, <y>, there is usually an element boundary between the <d> and <g>, as in the names *Aldgate*, *Edgar*, *Gradgrind*, *Ludgate*, *Lydgate*, *Redgrave*, *Snodgrass*, etc. Some names dispense with the <e> marker in <dge>≡/ʤ/ in contexts where <dg> would be unlikely, except as /d/ + /g/. The name *Dodgson* can only have /ʤ/ because in English /dg/ cannot end a syllable and /gs/ cannot begin one. Other name spellings which may make do without any <e> are *Bridgwater*, *Edgley*, *Hodgkin*, *Sidgwick*. Some words may similarly lack the <e> before a <C> as in *judgment*. EPD notes that *Lydgate* may have /-ʤɪt/ as a street name.

Efficiency: a core rule with some bias towards shorter words;

in words – 95 per cent (=7 percentage points of 80 per cent correct /ʤ/ predictions);
in names – 90 per cent (= 15 percentage points of 89 per cent correct /ʤ/ predictions).

D.2 <dj>≡/ʤ/
Examples: a marginal rule: with §Latinate prefixes – *adjacent*, *adjective*, *adjoin*, *adjourn*, *adjudge*, *adjudicate*, *adjunct*, *adjure*, *adjust*, *adjutant*, and derived forms; in foreign names (an exotic marker) – *Djakarta*, *Djibouti*.

The phonetic difference between /ʤ/ and /dʤ/, from reading <d>≡/d/ and <j>≡/ʤ/ medially in a word such as *adjunct*, is quite trivial, so the rule is for all practical purposes unnecessary.

D.3 <d(d)>≡/d/ – the default rule for <d>.
There are a number of exceptions to the default rule (and hence to the <d>-rules as a set):

- the /d/ may assimilate with /ju:/ to give /ʤu:/ in *educate*, *gradual*, *verdure*, etc.;
- *soldier* has an exceptional <di>≡/ʤ/;
- the <d> is an empty or inert letter in *grandson*, *grandpa*, *handkerchief*, *handsome*, *landscape*, *sandwich*, *veldt* etc. and in the names *Arendt*, *Darmstadt*, *Grundtvig*, *Guildford*, *Rembrandt*, *Sandford*, *Sindbad*, *Windsor*. Some names may have a variant spelling which gets rid of the empty <d>: *Sanford*, *Winsor*.

The <d> of the suffix <-ed> is dealt with under the <e>-rules.

Efficiency: a core rule with a very heavy workload;

in words – 99 per cent (= 83 percentage points of 88 per cent correct /d/ predictions);
in names – 99 per cent. (= 94 percentage points of 95 per cent correct /d/ predictions).

<e>-rules

Correspondences are dealt with in numbered rules as follows:

E.1, 24–28 <e>≡/iː/	E.2 <e>≡∅	E.3 <es>≡/ɪz/
E.4 <es>≡/s/	E.5 <es>≡/z/	E.6 <ed>≡/ɪd/
E.7 <ed>≡/t/	E.8 <ed>≡/d/	E.9 <er>≡/ə(r)/
E.10 <er>≡/ɜː(r)/	E.11 <ear>≡/ɜː(r)/	E.12 <eaux>≡/əʊ/
E.13 <ea>≡/iː/	E.14 <ee>≡/iː/	E.15 <eigh>≡/eɪ/
E.16 <ei>≡/iː/	E.17 <ei>≡/aɪ/	E.18 <eur>≡/ɜː(r)/
E.19 <eu>≡/(j)uː/	E.20 <ew>≡/(j)uː/	E.21 <ey>≡/ɪ/
E.22 <ey>≡/eɪ/	E.23 <e>≡/e/	

E.29 <e>≡/e/ – the default rule.

Common words with idiosyncratic <e>-spellings, which would ideally go to a look-up table, include: with /ɛə/ – *there*, *where* and derived forms *thereof*, *therefore*, *wherever*, *whereupon*, etc.; with /ɜː/ – *were*; with /iː/ – *people*; with /aɪ/ – *eye*, *eyeful*, *eyeless*, etc.

We begin with three rules to deal with final and pre-suffix <e>.

E.1 <e>≡/iː/ | # <C_1> — #
Examples: a marginal, but important rule: stressed forms of the function words *be*, *he*, *me*, *she*, *the*, *we*, and archaic *ye*. These are usually unstressed in connected speech with reduced forms (e.g. /ɪ 'went/ for *he went*).

E.2 <e>≡∅ | — #
Final <e> is usually an empty letter.

Conditions: the free-form boundary is recognized before suffixes such as <-ful>, <-less>, <-liness>, <-ly>, <-man>, <-ment>, <-ship>, <-some>, where <-e> is not elided and at the end of a compound, such as *baseball*, identified in the compound-guesser described in §4.2.3, p. 278.

Examples: *avenue*, *blameless*, *careful*, *clue*, *comedienne*, *corpse*, *dye*, *forceful*, *hopefully*, *indorsement*, *judgement*, *judgeship*, *league*, *lonely*, *lye*, *management*, *noiselessly*, *peacefully*, *rogue*, *serviceman*, *stateliness*, *timeliness*, *tissue*, *wholesome*, *vague*, etc.; *Arne*, *Bourne*, *Donne*, *Osborne*, *Skye*, etc.

Exceptions:

- when the ending <-ment> is not preceded by a free-form – *complement*, *excrement*, *implement*, *supplement*, etc., and indeed *inclement*. There is clearly a danger of reading the <le> of *supplement* as /əl/ to give *<sup-ple>+<-ment>.

- with /ɪ/ – *acme*, *acne*, *hyperbole*, *psyche*; *Daphne*, *Esme*;
- with /eɪ/ and probably an acute accent mark – *protegé, roué,* and similar French loans.

Final <-e> usually has a marking function, indicating the value of a preceding consonant (*bathe, rage, lace, tense*) or the previous vowel as long, but in names it is often mere padding. The <e> of final <-ae>, <-oe>, <-ue> and <-ye> falls under this rule because, unlike <ee> and <ie>, these strings have not been dealt with as complex vowel spellings.

Efficiency: in words 98 per cent; in names 89 per cent; a core rule.

The next group of rules deals with <-es> and <-ed> endings and their different phonetic correspondences. A general condition for all six rules is that the word is not a monosyllable such as *bed*, *fed*, *led*, *wed*, *yes; Les*, *Ted*. These were pre-empted by a separate Ainsworth rule, but instead we can simply specify a previous vowel in the context. The efficiency of these inflectional rules is virtually 100 per cent and, since they apply potentially to all inflected lexical words, they are all core rules.

E.3 <es>≡/ɪz/ | <V> <C_0> {<c>, <ch>, <sh>, <g>, <s>, <z>} — #
These are the possible spellings of sibilant consonants, after which the <-es> ending is pronounced as /ɪz/. Some speakers have /əz/ rather than /ɪz/ (p. 204). For them, *watches* and *watchers* may be homophones.

Examples: *races*, *churches*, *matches*, *wishes*, *ages*, *losses*, *loses*, *gazes* etc.; similarly in names – *Daiches*, *Devizes*, *Hodges*, *Moses*, etc.

Exceptions:

- §Latin/§Greek plurals <-es>≡/iːz/ from a base-form ending in <-is> – *amanuenses*, *antitheses*, *apotheoses*, *crises*, *emphases*, *hypotheses*, *oases*, *parentheses*, *synopses*, *syntheses*, etc.;
- /iːz/ in some names – *Anchises*, *Boanerges*, *Cambyses*, *Ganges*, *Rameses*, *Ulysses*, etc.;
- §French <-ges>≡/ʒ/ *collages*, *Bruges*, *Limoges*, *Vosges*.

There are some ambiguous spellings: *bases* (/ˈbeɪsiːz/ – /ˈbeɪsɪz/) from *basis* or *base*; *analyses* (/əˈnæləsiːz/ – /ˈænəlaɪzɪz/) from *analysis* or *analyse*.

The rule also applies to the possessive <e's> – *George's*, etc.

E.4 <es>≡/s/ | <V> <C_0> {<f>, <k>, <p>, <qu>, <t>} — #
These are the spellings for a preceding voiceless non-sibilant. Except in names, the <e> is usually the marker of a previous long vowel; in names it may be mere padding. A word such as *testes* is hardly to be read as */tests/, since this <e> would not be marking a long vowel; *litotes*, however, is more of a trap.

Examples: the regular inflections *chafes*, *plaques, rakes*, *ropes*, *writes*, etc.; *Brookes*, *Cleethorpes*, *Coates*, *Fawkes*, *Noakes*, *Oates*, *Sykes*, *Weekes*, etc.

Exceptions: with /iːz/ – *diabetes*, *litotes*, *testes*; *Agonistes*, *Cervantes*, *Ecclesiastes*, *Euphrates*, *Laertes*, *Socrates*, etc.

E.5 <es>≡/z/ | <V> <C_0> — #
The default rule for <-es> after E.3 & 4.

Examples: the regular inflections *archives*, *besides*, *clothes*, *homes*, *knives*, *measles*, *planes*, *rogues*, *tales*, etc.

E.6 <ed>≡/ɪd/ | <V> <C_0> {<t>, <d>} — #
The <-ed> suffix is /ɪd/ after /t/ or /d/, for which the spelling is always <t(t)> or <d(d)>.

Examples: *bearded*, *crowded*, *guarded*, *jaded*, *outmoded*, *secluded*, *wooded*; *addicted*, *antiquated*, *besotted*, *bigoted*, *devoted*, *matted*, *stilted*, etc. Some names may have a similar unstressed ending – *Berkhamsted*, *Binsted*, *Brasted*, *Felsted*.

E.7 <ed>≡/t/ | <V> <C_0> {<c>, <f>, <ch>, <sh>, <k>, <p>, <Cs>, <x>} — #
Listing all possible spellings of the voiceless consonant other than /t/ is decidedly awkward.

Both single <s> as /s/ or /z/ (*chased* – *erased*) and <th> as /θ/ or /ð/ (*bath+ed* – *bathe+d*) are ambiguous contexts. They are not included here, but get the default /d/ (E.8).

Examples: *laced*, *glanced*, *chafed*, *chaffed*, *watched*, *hushed*, *baked*, *hoped*, *hopped*, *missed*, *boxed*, etc.

Exceptions:

- attributive <-ed>≡/ɪd/ – *accursed*, *blessed*, *crooked*, (which might also have /-t/ as attributives) and *naked*, *wicked*, *wretched* and derived forms *crookedly*, *wickedness*, etc.;
- not a suffix – *biped*, *quadruped*.

Ainsworth did not make any provision for this /t/ allomorph, presumably thinking that the choice between /t/ and /d/ is not distinctive in this context and probably allowing for less than adequate synthesizer output.

E.8 <ed>≡/d/ | <V> <C_0> — #
The default rule for {-ed} after E.6 & 7, that is, after vowels or voiced consonants other than /d/.

Examples: *armoured*, *ashamed*, *bedraggled*, *begged*, *civilized*, *concerned*, *deformed*, *framed*, *freckled*, *panelled*, *perturbed*, *reserved*, *tattered*, *wedged*, *wreathed*, etc.

Exceptions: attributively with <-ed>≡/ɪd/ – *aged*, *beloved*.

We can now examine complex vowel spellings with <e> as the first letter of the string.

E.9 <er>≡/ə(r)/ | <C> — #

This syphons off the common unstressed ending <-er> before dealing with stressed values of <er>.

Examples: *after, canister*, *cooler*, *diameter*, *draper*, *driller*, *lesser*, *outer*, *planter*, *poorer*, *soccer*, etc.; *Bolinger*, *Dorchester*, *Esther*, *Khyber*, *Mather*, *Rockefeller*, *Slazenger*, etc. The <ier> ending of *carrier*, *happier*, is dealt with by I.18 <i>≡/iː/ before a vowel letter plus R.1 <r>≡/ə(r)/.

Exceptions:

- verbs with final stress have /ɜː/ – *aver*, *confer*, *deter*, *disinter*, *infer*, *inter*, *prefer*, *refer*, *transfer*;
- /eɪ/ in *foyer*, a recent French loan-word cannot have 'linking /r/' before a following vowel: *the foyer emptied* */ðə 'fɔɪeɪr 'emtɪd/.

Efficiency: in words 98 per cent; in names 97 per cent; a core rule with a very heavy workload.

E.10 <er>≡/ɜː/ | — <C> (AmE /ɜr/)

Conditions:

- not before a further <r> (*merry*, *terrible*, etc. have /er/).

Examples: *adverse*, *assert*, *berth*, *certain*, *certify*, *commercial*, *concern*, *conservatism*, *converge*, *converse*, *dessert*, *determine*, *ermine*, *eternal*, *exertion*, *exterminate*, *ferment*, *germ*, *herb*, *hermit*, *inertia*, *jersey*, *merge*, *observe*, *permanent*, *persecute*, *person*, *pervert*, *reserve*, *revert*, *serpent*, *thermal*, *university*, *verger*, *vertigo*, etc.; *Bergen*, *Bermuda*, *Berlin*, *Bernstein*, *Erskine*, *Germany*, *Gilbertian*, *Hercules*, *Mercury*, *Mersey*, *Minerva*, *Palermo*, *Percival*, *Sterne*, *Traherne*, etc.

Exceptions:

- with /ɑː/ – *clerk*, *derby*; *Berkeley*, *Berkshire*, *Hertford*, *Hervey* (these usually follow E.10 in AmE); *sergeant*; *Cherwell*; *Bertie* as a surname may have /ɑː/;
- irregular – *Beauclerc* /'bəʊklɛə/; *Berwick* is /'berɪk/, since the <w> is empty.

Efficiency: a core rule with a heavy workload with some bias towards shorter words;

in words – 98 per cent (= 41 percentage points of 90 per cent correct /ɜː/ predictions);
in names – 83 per cent (= 35 percentage points of 96 per cent correct /ɜː/ predictions).

If reduction to /ə/ is allowed, the figures are virtually 100 per cent and 92 per cent.

E.11 <ear>≡/ɜː/ |— <C> (AmE /ɜr/)
This rule could have been merged with E.10 by bracketing the two as <e(a)r>≡/ɜː/.

Examples: *dearth*, *earl*, *early*, *earn*, *earnest*, *earth*, *heard*, *hearse*, *learn*, *pearl*, *rehearse*, *research*, *search*, *yearn*; *Eardley*, *Earp*, *Fearn*, *Hearne*, *Hearst*, *Searle*, *Stearne*, *Shearme*, *Strathearne*, etc.

Exceptions:

- with /ɪə/ – *beard*;
- with /ɑː/ (AmE /ɑr/) – *hearken*, *heart*, *hearth*; *Liskeard*, etc.;
- with a boundary in *forearm*, *rearm*, *rearrange*.

Since the /ɪə/, /ɜː/ and /ɑː/ pronunciations of <ear> are all found in quite common words, it is not surprising to find free variation in names: for example, /ɜː/ or /ɪə/ in *Shearman*, *Shearn*; /ɜː/ or /ɑː/ in *Kearney*; /ɜː/ or /ɛə/ in *Bearstead*.

Word-final <-ear>≡/ɪə/ (*clear, year*) is dealt with by the <ea>≡/iː/ (E.13) and <r>≡/ə(r)/ (R.1) rules.

Efficiency: a minor rule with very strong bias towards high TF words and towards shorter words.

E.12 <eau(x)>≡/əʊ/
Examples: *bandeau*, *beau*, *beaux*, *bureau*, *chateau*, *flambeau*, *plateau*, *portmanteau*, *rondeau*, *tableau*, *trousseau*; *Beauclerc*, *Beaumaris*, *Beaumont*, *Beaune*, *Furneaux*, *Prideaux*, *Rousseau*, *Watteau*, etc.

These are all French names or loan-words. The singular-plural difference in spelling between <eau> and <eaux>, both pronounced /əʊ/, is now archaic in English; normal plural forms are usual, such as *plateaus*, with /əʊz/.

Exceptions:

- with /juː/ – the common word *beauty* and derived forms *beautiful*, *beautify*, etc. A similar anglicization to /juː/ is found in *Beaulieu* /ˈbjuːlɪ/;
- with third-syllable shortening to /ɒ/ – *bureaucracy*;
- with /ə/ when unstressed – *bureaucrat*;
- others – *Beauchamp* /ˈbiːʧəm/ also has the conformant spelling *Beecham*; *Réaumur* /ˈreɪəmjʊə/ without the accent may well be said as */ˈrəʊ-/.

Efficiency: in words 60 per cent; in names 84 per cent; a marginal rule with strong bias towards low TF words.

E.13 <ea>≡/iː/
Examples: *appeal, beam*, *beach*, *beano*, *breathe*, *cheap*, *clean*, *creature*, *deal*, *dream*, *defeat*, *eagle*, *entreat*, *feature*, *flea*, *heathen*, *increase*, *league*, *measles*, *pea*, *peace*, *plea*, *please*, *reason*, *retreat*, *sea*, *sheath*, *squeak*, *stream*, *tea*, *treacle*, *weak*, *wreath*, etc.; *Battersea*, *Beamish*, *Beattie*, *Beavis*, *Cheatham*, *Creaghan*, *Ealing*, *Eames*, *Greatham* (in Durham, elsewhere /e/),

Hargreaves, *Heanor*, *Keating*, *Lea*, *Leahy*, *Longleat*, *Meath*, *Nuneaton*, *Skeat*, etc. With reduction to /ɪ/: *guinea*, *Chelsea*.

This rule also covers <ear>≡/ɪə(r)/ before a vowel or word-finally (the [ə]-glide comes from R.1 <r>≡/ə(r)/): *appear*, *arrears*, *bleary*, *clear*, *dear*, *ear*, *fear*, *gear*, *hear*, *rear*, *shear*, *smear*, *tear*, *weary*, *year*; there is a boundary in *Pearson*, *Shearson*, etc. Though the <e> and <a> are split by a morpheme boundary, *linear* and *nuclear* are also covered here.

Exceptions:

- with /e/ – *abreast*, *ahead*, *already*, *breadth*, *bread*, *breakfast*, *breast*, *breath*, *cleanliness*, *cleanse*, *dead*, *deaf*, *dealt*, *dread*, *dreamt*, *endeavour*, *feather*, *head*, *health*, *heather*, *heaven*, *heavy*, *instead*, *jealous*, *lead* ('metal'), *leant*, *leapt*, *leather*, *leaven*, *meadow*, *meant*, *measure*, *peasant*, *pheasant*, *pleasant*, *pleasure*, *read* (past), *ready*, *realm*, *seamstress* (with alternative spelling *sempstress*), *spread*, *steady*, *steadfast*, *stealth*, *sweat*, *thread*, *threat*, *treachery*, *tread*, *treadle*, *treasure*, *wealth*, *weapon*, *weather*, *zealous*, *zealot*, etc.; similarly in English names with these as elements – *Armistead*, *Fairweather*, *Headingley*, *Holyhead*, *Leadenhall*, *Leatherhead*, *Whitbread*, etc. and also with /e/ – *Beaminster*, *Beavan*, *Breadalbane*, *Breamore*, *Cleather*, *Heagarty*, *Jeaner*, *Leamington*, *Reading*, *Streatham*, *Trileaven*, *Yeading*;
- with /eɪ/ – *break*, *great*, *steak*, *Culzean* /kə'leɪn/, *Fleay*, *Jeakes*, *McBean*, *McCrea*, *McVeagh*, *Preager*, *O'Shea*, *Seamas*, *Sheaffer*, *Yeats*;
- with /ɛə/ (AmE /ɛr/) – *bear*, *forbear*, *pear*, *swear*, *tear*, *wear*; *Cearns*, etc.

There is, as one might expect, considerable free variation in some names – for instance, *MacLean* has /iː/ – /eɪ/, *Dealtry* has /ɔː/ – /iː/-/e/, *Rea* has /eɪ/ – /ɪə/ – /iː/, *Yeatman* has /iː/ – /eɪ/ – /e/. *Beaconsfield* as the old place-name has undergone third-syllable shortening to /e/ (cf. *cleanliness*), but as the relatively recent title given to Disraeli, it has the default /iː/. There are also a number of nonce spellings in names involving <ea> – *Finzean* /'fɪŋən/, *Meagher* /mɑː/, *MacFadzean* /mək'fædjən/, *Sean* /ʃɔːn/, *Speaight* /speɪt/, *Yealmpton* /'jæmptən/.

One important source of confusion is hiatus, giving <ea>≡/ɪə/ (in some cases disyllabic /iː-ə/) – *area*, *azalea*, *cereal*, *cornea*, *creativity*, *fealty*, *idea*, *laureate*, *miscreant*, *nausea*, *panacea*, *urea*; *Anthea*, *Boadicea*, *Crimea*, *Korea*, etc., or if the <a> has some degree of stress, /iː-æ/ – *beatitude*, *caveat*, *genealogy*, *meander*, *oleander*, etc. and /iː-eɪ/ – *create*, *delineate*, *nauseate*, etc. Prefix boundaries need to be seen in *deactivate*, *preamble*, *react*, *readopt*, *reagent*, *realign*, etc.; a boundary also needs to be seen in *likeable*, *debateable* (where the <e>-marker is optional) and in *noticeable*, *serviceable*, etc. *Lineage* with /iː-ɪ/ is quite a trap (cf. *mileage*). *Eritrea* has /eɪ-ə/. *Yeah* has /ɛə/.

This is all very complex. Yet, amid all the variation, /iː/ is clearly the default correspondence for <ea>.

Efficiency: a core rule with a heavy workload;

in words – 69 per cent (= 18 percentage points of 74 per cent correct /iː/ predictions);
in names – 69 per cent.(= 12 percentage points of 94 per cent correct /iː/ predictions).

E.14 <ee>≡/iː/
Before //r//, there is an [ə] glide, giving /ɪə/ (R.1).

Examples: *agree*, *aniseed*, *apogee*, *asleep*, *beef*, *breeze*, *cheek*, *cheese*, *degree*, *feeble*, *jubilee*, *mortgagee*, *parakeet*, *reel*, *refugee*, *speech*, *sweep*, *teeth*, *tweezers*, etc.; *Aberdeen*, *Beeton*, *Deedes*, *Eileen*, *Halloween*, *Maureen*, *Rees*, *Tweedledee*, *Weekes*, etc.; before //r// – *beery*, *career*, *cheerful*, *deer*, *eerie*, *engineer*, *peerage*, *racketeer*, *seersucker*, *sneer*, *steer*, *veneer*, etc.; *Beersheba*, *Geering*, *Mynheer*, *Sheerness*, *Vermeer*, etc.

Exceptions:

- French loan-words and names ending in <ee>≡/eɪ/, which may or may not carry an accent when anglicized – *entree*, *fiancee*, *fricassee*, *matinee*, *melee*, *puree*, *soiree*; *Desiree*, *Dobree*, etc.;
- also with /eɪ/ – *Beethoven*, *Zeeland*;
- rather perversely, the surnames *Cheesewright* and *Fleeming* may have /e/.

Efficiency: a core rule with a fairly heavy workload and a strong bias towards shorter words;

in words – 98 per cent (= 10 percentage points of 74 per cent correct /iː/ predictions);
in names – 97 per cent (= 6 percentage points of 94 per cent correct /iː/ predictions).

E.15 <eigh>≡/eɪ/
Examples: *eight*, *freight*, *inveigh*, *neigh*, *neighbour*, *sleigh*, *weigh*, *weight*; *Deighton*, *Heighton*, *Leighton*, *Speight*.

Exceptions:

- with /aɪ/ – *height*, *sleight*; *Creighton*, *Heighway*, *Sleights*;
- with /iː/ – *Leigh*, *Weighton*;
- variable names – *Deighton* with /iː/ – /eɪ/ – /aɪ/, *Keighley* (surname) and *Keightley* with /iː/ – /aɪ/; *Keighley* (Yorks.) is quite unexpectedly /ˈkiːθlɪ/.

Efficiency: in words 92 per cent; in names 36 per cent; a marginal rule with very strong bias towards high TF words and some bias towards shorter words.

E.16 <ei>≡/iː/ | <c> —
Examples: *ceiling*, *conceit*, *conceive*, *deceit*, *deceive*, *perceive*, *receipt*, *receive*.

These represent the main exceptions in the '<i> before <e> except after <c>' spelling rule (p. 67f.).

Efficiency: in words 100 per cent; a marginal rule.

E.17 <ei>≡/aɪ/ – the default rule for <ei>

Examples: *eider*, *either*, *gneiss*, *kaleidoscope*, *neither*, *seismic*; *Bechstein*, *Beira*, *Beit*, *Bernstein*, *Brunei*, *Eifel*, *Eiger*, *Eileen*, *Einstein*, *Epstein*, *Feisal*, *Freiburg*, *Geiger*, *Heinz*, *Holbein*, *Holstein*, *Leiden*, *Leipzig*, *Mannheim*, *Meier*, *Pleiad*, *Reichstag*, *Stein*, *Weimar*, *Zeiss*, *Zeitgeist*, etc. Names containing <stein> may also have <iː>.

The spelling <ei> is very divergent. This original Ainsworth rule was evidently meant to capture the /aɪ/ pronunciation of the common words *either*, *neither*, which in any case have variants with /iː/ (as in AmE). Across the lexicon as a whole, however, <ei>≡/eɪ/ would be a marginally better default. The exceptions to /eɪ/ as the default would largely be German names, which in many cases are marked by endings or letter sequences as §German.

Exceptions:

- the main alternative correspondence with /eɪ/ – *beige*, *deign*, *feign*, *feint*, *heinous*, *reign*, *rein*, *reindeer*, *seine*, *sheik* (also /iː/), *skein*, *surveillance*, *veil*, *vein*; *Bahrein*, *Beirut*, *Peiping*, and before //r// with /ɛə(r)/ – *heir*, *Eire*;
- with /iː/ – *caffeine* (also /eɪ/), *casein*, *codeine*, *plebeian*, *protein*, *seize*; *Beith*, *Bodleian*, *Dalgleish*, *Dalkeith*, *Harleian*, *Keith*, *Keiller*, *Leif*, *Leila*, *Leishman* (also /ɪ/), *Leith*, *MacNeice*, *Monteith*, *Neill*, *Reid*, *Reims*, *Reith*, *Veitch*; and before //r// with /ɪə(r)/ – *weir*, *weird*; *Deirdre*, *Keir*;
- with /e/ – *heifer*, *leisure*; *Leinster*, *Leicester* (assuming an empty <ce>);
- with stressed /ɪ/ – *Teignmouth*;
- with unstressed /ɪ/ – *counterfeit*, *foreign*, *forfeit*, *mullein*, *sovereign*, *surfeit*; *Blenheim*;
- with hiatus as /iː-ɪ/ or /eɪ-ɪ/ in words such as *albeit*, *atheist*, *atheism*, *atheistic*, *deify*, *deification*, *homogeneity*, *nucleic*, *pantheism*, the reader is required to recognize the boundary or simply to recognize a polysyllabic word as §Latinate/§Greek, since <ei> is seldom found in these subsystems of English as a single vowel spelling. Prefix hiatus is perhaps less of a problem since a hyphen may be used (*pre-invasive*) to show the hiatus, though not always (*reinforce*, *reinstate*). *Cuneiform* may have /kjuːˈneɪɪfɔːm/ or /ˈkjuːnɪfɔːm/, taking the <e> as a simple marker.

Efficiency: in words 9 per cent; in names 37 per cent; a marginal rule with very strong bias towards low TF words. Because of the large divergence of <ei> spellings, changing the default to /eɪ/ would only show a change to 22 per cent and 12 per cent.

E.18 <eur>≡/ɜː(r)/ | — # (AmE /ɜr/)
Conditions:

- the /ɜː/ is reducible to /ə/ if unstressed.

Examples: a marginal rule – *amateur*, *amateurism*, *chauffeur*, *connoisseur*, *entrepreneur*, *poseur*, *provocateur*, *raconteur*, *restaurateur*; *Pasteur*, *Tourneur*, etc. In some of these AmE may have /ʊər/.

Exceptions: *grandeur* /jə/, *liqueur* /lɪˈkjʊə/.

Efficiency: a marginal rule with very strong bias towards low TF words and some bias towards longer words.

E.19 <eu>≡/(j)uː/
Examples:

- with no /j/ after <l> or <r>: *leukaemia*, *sleuth*, *rheumatism*, etc.; *Aleutian*, *Buccleuch*, *Reuben*;
- with /j/ in SBS but not usually in AmE: *deuce*, *neuter*, *neutral*, *neutron*, *pharmaceutical*, *pneumatic*, *pneumonia*, *pseudonym*, *zeugma*; *Deuteronomy*, *Heptateuch*, *Teutonic*, *Zeus*;
- with /j/ in both SBS and AmE: *eucalyptus*, *eucharist*, *eugenic*, *eulogy*, *eunuch*, *euphemism*, *euphoria*, *euthanasia*, *feud*, *feudal*, *therapeutic*; *Beulah*, *Euclid*, *Eugene*, *Eunice*, *Euphrates*, *Eustace*, *Euston*, *Herstmonceux*, *Molyneux*.

The ending <-eus> in classical names follows this rule in familiar instances – *Theseus* /ˈθiːsjuːs/, and similarly *Morpheus*, *Odysseus*, *Perseus*, *Prometheus*.

<eu> is not a §Basic spelling. It does not, for instance, occur after <j>, <sh> or <ch>, as does <ew> (E.19).

Exceptions:

- with hiatus as /ɪə/ – *coleus*, *linoleum*, *mausoleum*, *museum*, *nucleus*, *petroleum*; *Lyceum*, *Maccabeus*, *Timotheus*; as /aɪə/ – *Aneurin*. *Ceuta* is /s(j)uːtə/ in SBS as a spelling pronunciation, but usually has hiatus in AmE as /eɪ – uː/, closer to the Spanish [eu].
- with /ɔɪ/ in some German names – *Bayreuth*, *Breughel*, *Euler*, *Freud*, *Neuchatel*, *Reuter*;
- with /ɜː/ in SBS (/uː/ in AmE) for some French loan-words and names – *masseuse*; *Chartreuse*, *Montreux*, *Peugeot*;
- with /jə/ – *pasteurize*.

Efficiency: in words 74 per cent; in names 72 per cent; a minor rule with very strong bias towards low TF words.

E.20 <ew>≡/(j)uː/ | i) # <C_0> —
ii) — <C_0> # – the default rule for <ew>

The /j/ glide predictably does not occur after /r/, and palatals /ʃ/, /ʧ/, /ʤ/ and usually not after /l/ (*lewd* can have either /juː/ or only /uː/). The contexts require the <ew> to be in the first or last syllable of a free-form. They prevent examples of medial <ew> split by a boundary as in *causeway*, *forewarn*, *homeward*, *housewife*, *likewise*, *lukewarm*, *sidewalk*, etc. There are similar instances in names – *Bridewell*, *Chuzzlewit*, *Cynewulf*, *Erewhon*, *Hereward*, *Inglewood*, *Ridgeway*, etc. There are also medial instances in exotic names with no apparent boundary – *Cetewayo*, *Saskatchewan*.

Examples:

- without /j/ in both SBS and AmE after <l>, <r> and palatals: *blew*, *brew*, *cashew*, *chew*, *crew*, *drew*, *eschew*, *flew*, *grew*, *jewel*, *lewd*, *lewisite*, *screw*, *shrew*, *shrewd*, *slew*, *strew*, *threw*, *yew*; *Andrew*, *Hebrew*, *Jew*, *Killigrew*, *Lewes*, *Lewin*, *Pettigrew*, *Renfrew*;
- with /j/ in SBS but not usually in AmE: *dew*, *knew*, *mildew*, *newel*, *new*, *newt*, *renew*, *sewage*, *stew*, *steward*; *Agnew*, *Cardew*, *Dewar*, *Dewey*, *Newark*, *Stewart*, *Tewfik*, *Tewkesbury*;
- with /j/ in both SBS and AmE: *askew*, *curfew*, *ewer*, *ewe*, *few*, *mew*, *mews*, *nephew*, *pew*, *pewter*, *sinew*; *Askew*, *Bartholomew*, *Bewick*, *Bewley*, *Ewart*, *Kew*; *hew* is /hjuː/ in SBS, /juː/ in AmE.

Exceptions:

- with /əʊ/ – *sew*, *Shrewsbury* and archaic *shew*;
- with hiatus – *bewail*, *beware*, *bewildered*, *prewar*, *reward*, *rewind*; *Seward* /ˈsiːwəd/.

Efficiency: a core rule with a very strong bias towards shorter words;

in words – 89 per cent (= 4 percentage points of 76 per cent correct /(j)uː/ predictions);
in names – 91 per cent (= 7 percentage points of 51 per cent correct /(j)uː/ predictions).

E.21 <ey>≡/ɪ/ | <V> <C_0> — #
– the vowel is /iː/ rather than /ɪ/ for many speakers.

The effect of the context is to limit the rule to the final syllable of polysyllabic words; monosyllables usually have <ey>≡/eɪ/.

Examples: *abbey*, *alley*, *attorney*, *ballyhooey*, *barley*, *blimey*, *chimney*, *chutney*, *clayey*, *donkey*, *dopey*, *galley*, *gooey*, *hockey*, *honey*, *jersey*, *jockey*, *journey*, *kidney*, *lackey*, *malarkey*, *malmsey*, *matey*, *medley*, *money*, *monkey*, *parley*, *pulley*, *storey*, *trolley*, *valley*, *volley*, etc.; *Airey*, *Ashley*, *Bailey*, *Barnsley*, *Berkeley*, *Bradley*, *Cockney*, *Crawley*, *Finney*, *Godfrey*, *Humphrey*, *Morley*, *Rodney*, *Trelawney*, *Wolsey*, etc.

Exceptions: with stressed /eɪ/ – *convey*, *disobey*, *obey*, *purvey*, *survey*.

These polysyllabic words with stressed final /eɪ/ are verbs or nouns derived from those verbs. They could be identified by grammar and stress patterns, but these are not known by the algorithm.

Efficiency: in words 91 per cent; in names 99 per cent; a core rule with some bias towards shorter words.

E.22 <ey>≡/eɪ/ – the default rule for <ey>
After E.21, these must be non-final or in monosyllables. The non-final instances are relatively few and are usually derived from monosyllables.

Examples: *abeyance*, *conveyance*, *fey*, *grey*, *greyish*, *greylag*, *greyness*, *hey*, *heyday*, *prey*, *purveyor*, *they*, *whey*, etc.; *Bey*, *Beyrout*, *Beyts*, *Cheyne*, *Dreyfus*, *Fonteyn*, *Frey*, *Grey*, *Heywood*, *Leyland*, *Peyton*, *Reykjavik*, *Reynaldo*, *Seychelles*, *Spey*, *Weymouth*, etc. The variant of /eɪ/ before //r// is /ɛə/ as in *Eyre*, but it is uncommon with the spelling <eyr>.

Exceptions:

- with /iː/ – *eyrie*, *geyser*, *key*; *Eyam*, *Heysham*, *Keynes*, *Leys*, *Seymour*, *Sneyd*, *Steyne*;
- with /e/ – *Reynard*, *Reynolds*;
- with /aɪ/ – the common word *eye* and the names *Eyck*, *Eyles*, *Freyberg*;
- with /ɪ/ at an internal boundary – *journeyman*; *Barleycorn*, *Merseyside*, *Wensleydale*, *Humphreys*, *Jeffreys*, etc.; *vineyard* also has an internal boundary and presumably also *beyond*.

There is variation in some names – *Alleyne* /eɪ/ – /iː/ – /ɪ/, *Eyton* /aɪ/ – /eɪ/ – /iː/.

Efficiency: in words 37 per cent; in names 44 per cent; a marginal rule with very strong bias towards high TF words and strong bias towards shorter words.

We can now deal with the long vowel value of <e> as /iː/. The only provision in the original Ainsworth rules was the following:

<e>≡/iː/ | — C {<e>, <i>}

That is before a single consonant followed by the letters <e> or <i>. This context is inadequate for the reasons given in the <a>-rules (p. 276). The <e>≡/iː/ correspondence is explored here in rules E.24 to E.28, which are parallel to A.27 to A.31. Before this, however, Ainsworth prevents a long vowel by default in words such as *ever*, *several*:

E.23 <e>≡/e/ | — <ver>
Examples: *asseverate*, *beverage*, *clever*, *dissever*, *every*, *ever*, *leveret*, *never*, *reverend*, *reverent*, *sever*, *several*; *Beveridge*, *Beverley*, *Eversley*, *Everton*, *Sacheverell*, *Severn*, etc.

Exceptions:

- with stressed /iː/ – *cantilever*, *fever*, *lever*, *leverage*; *Devers*, *Hever*, *Leverhulme*; AmE *lever* usually has /e/;
- with unstressed /ɪ/ – *persevere*, *revere*, *reversal*, *reverse*, *severe*; *Guinevere*.

This Ainsworth rule is motivated by the high text frequency of *ever*, *every*, *never*.

Efficiency: in words 64 per cent; in names 76 per cent; a marginal rule with very strong bias towards high TF and some bias towards longer words.

E.24 <e>≡/iː/ | — <C> {<a>, <i>, <o>} #
Examples: *edema*, *ego*, *emphysema*, *eta*, *hyena*, *magneto*, *schema*, *torpedo*, *tuxedo*, *verbena*, *veto*, *zeta*, etc.; *Abednego*, *Alfreda*, *Athena*, *Eva*, *Geneva*, *Greta*, *Lena*, *Leno*, *Levi*, *Pasadena*, *Philomena*, *Reno*, *Rowena*, *Sheba*, etc.

Exceptions:

- with unstressed /ə/ or /ɪ/ when the stress is on the previous syllable – *anathema*, *cinema*, *eczema*, *enema*, *omega*, *phenomena*, *taffeta*; *Adela*, *Andromeda*, *Angela*, *Bathsheba*, *Drogheda* /ˈdrɔɪɪdə/, *Hobbema*, *Seneca*, *Shilleto*;
- with /eɪ/ – *Sarajevo*, *Toledo*.

Some names have variants in addition to /iː/: unstressed /ɪ/ in *Helena*, *Modena*, /e/ in *Greta*.

For <e> this pattern has the usual §Basic long vowel value /iː/. The same rule for <a> and <i> had non-§Basic values <a>≡/ɑː/ (*panorama*) and <i>≡ /iː/ (*albino*).

Efficiency: in words 49 per cent; in names 56 per cent; a marginal rule.

E.25 <e>≡/iː/ | — <C>* <e>* #
Conditions:

- the <C>* is not <x> (*vexing*);
- the <C>* may be <Cr> (*metre*) or <th> (*ether*). There are no <-eCle> forms other than the name *Keble*. Where the <C>* is <r>, the vowel is /ɪə/;
- the <e>* may be elided before the initial vowel of a suffix as in *competing*, *schemer* (p. 269). Spellings which simply resemble suffixed forms, such as *diabetes, Thebes*, are covered.

Examples: *athlete*, *atmosphere*, *austere*, *benzene*, *cashmere*, *cede*, *centipede*, *compete*, *complete*, *diabetes*, *extreme*, *here*, *impede*, *insincere*, *interfere*, *intervene*, *journalese*, *merest*, *meter*, *obscene*, *obsolete*, *persevere*, *phoneme*, *polythene*, *revere*, *scheme*, *secrete*, *severe*, *sincere*, *sphere*, *stampede*, *supreme*, *theme*, *these*, *trapeze*, etc.; *Bede*, *Burmese*, *Congreve*, *Ebenezer*, *Gadarene*, *Magdalene*, *Peking*, *Steve*, *Swedish*, *Thebes*, etc.; in some names the final <e> is pronounced as /ɪ/ or /iː/ – *Athene*, *Irene*, etc., but it still marks a previous long vowel.

Exceptions:

- some words ending in <-ish> as part of the stem, not a suffix: *relish*, *replenish*. The rule would also wrongly give a long vowel in *Flemish*, *Rhenish*. The /e/ pronunciation of *fetish* is more usual than /iː/;
- the function words *there*, *where* /ɛə(r)/ and *were* /ɜː(r)/;

- with /e/ – *allege*, *bevy*, *celery*, *clientele*, *emery*, *leper*, *levy*, *machete*, *seven*, *tether*, *very*; *Abergele*, *Baedeker*, *Fleming*;
- with /eɪ/ – *fete*, *suede*, *ukelele*, and in German names – *Marlene*, *Weber*, *Weser*; §French *crepe* and *cortege* have /eɪ/ – /e/ variation;
- with unstressed /ɪ/ in some prefixes – *prefer*, *refer*;
- with /ə/ in unstressed syllables – *frightener*, *opener*; with /ɪ/ – *college*, *cricketer*, *hexameter*, *integer*, *parameter*; *Chichele*, *Exeter*.

The wood *sapele* is /səˈpiːlɪ/, following the rule, but the Nigerian town it comes from is /ˈsæpɪlɪ/ (EPD).

Efficiency: in words 32 per cent; in names 44 per cent; untypically, the <e>-marking rule in the case of <e> is only a minor rule.

This relatively poor performance is peculiar to <e..e>≡/iː/ among the long values of single vowel letters. The equivalent rule for other letters performed better: (in words) <a> 90 per cent, <i> 80 per cent, <o> 72 per cent, <u> 94 per cent, <y> 72 per cent. This may well be because the spelling of /iː/ is largely done by <ea>, <ee> and other digraphs. See the discussion of this correspondence under /iː/ in §3.3.2, p. 155f.

E.26 <e>≡/iː/ | <C_0> — <C>* ENDING
Conditions:

- the <C>* may be <th> (*lethal*); there are no examples in the data of <Cr> as the <C>*.

Examples and exceptions:

with <-al> : *legal*, *lethal*, *penal*, *regal*, *renal*, *venal*, but not in *medal*, *metal*, *pedal*, *sepal*;
with <-an> : *pecan*;
with <-ar> : *cedar*;
with <-is> : *penis*, *thesis*, but not in *debris*;
with <-on> : *demon*, but not in *heron*, *lemon*, *melon*, *tenon*, *xenon*;
with <-os> : *ethos*;
with <-ur> : *femur*, *lemur*, but not in *recur*, where the <re-> is a §Latinate prefix;
with <-us> : *genus*, *negus*, *rebus*;
with <-ant, -ance, -ancy> : *secant*, but not in *pedant*, *penance*, *tenant*;
with <-ary> : *plenary*;
with <-ent, -ence, -ency> : *decent*, *recent*, *regent*, but not in *clement*, *present*, *prevent*, *repent*;
with <-ine> : *feline*, but not in *refine*.

As in other types of long vowel context, <e>≡/iː/ is not very predictable.

Efficiency: in words 31 per cent; in names 47 per cent; a marginal rule.

The suffixes <-ic(al)>, <-id>, <-it> have a complementary function in that they mark a short vowel (the default) in *academic*, *athletics*, *credit*, *debit*, *decrepit*, *edit*, *fetid* (or /iː/), *genetic*, *inherit*, *intrepid*, *merit*, *tepid*, etc. *Enid* is an exception.

E.27 <e>≡/iː/ | — <C>* <i> <V>
Conditions:

- the <C>* is not <x>.

This captures a large number of §Latinate words; the many words ending in <-tion>, <-sion>, regularly have a long preceding vowel if it is spelt <a>, <e>, <o>, or <u>. The vowel glides on to a following //r// to give /ɪər/ (*bacteria* /-tɪərɪə/).

Examples: *abbreviate*, *anterior*, *appreciable*, *arterial*, *bacteria*, *cafeteria*, *cohesion*, *comedian*, *completion*, *congenial*, *criteria*, *deteriorate*, *diphtheria*, *experience*, *facetious*, *heliotrope*, *immediate*, *imperial*, *ingenious*, *lesion*, *magnesium*, *material*, *mediocre*, *mysterious*, *posterior*, *remedial*, *senior*, *sepia*, *series*, *wisteria*, etc.; *Armenia*, *Bohemian*, *Celia*, *Cornelius*, *Glaswegian*, *Indonesia*, *Venetian*, etc.

Exceptions:

- with /e/ – *discretion*, *geriatric*, *special*; *Spezia*;
- with /eɪ/ – *Comenius*, *Sibelius*, *Xenia* (also /e/).

There are also instances of unstressed /ɪ/ – *dandelion*, *defiant*, *denial*, *elegiac*, *reliable*, etc.

The rule applies regularly in adjectives freely formed from surnames, where a short vowel spelt <e> is stressed and lengthened – *Brunelian*, *Handelian*.

Efficiency: in words 65 per cent; in names 67 per cent; a minor rule with some bias towards longer words.

E.28 <e>≡/iː/ | — <V>
The usual provision for hiatus; but since <ea>, <ee>, <ei>, and <eu> are dealt with as complex spellings for simple vowels, this applies in effect only to <eo>. Ainsworth's set of rules included one for <eo>≡/iː/, which must have been motivated by the common, but exceptional word *people*. Across the lexicon, the string <eo> occurs most frequently as a hiatus. What value the <o> has depends on whether it is stressed or not; in most cases there is no stress, so there is smoothing to <eo>≡/ɪə/. Occasionally the second vowel is stressed and we get /iː-ɒ/ (*geography*) or /iː-əʊ/ (*apotheosis*).

Examples: *alveolar*, *aqueous*, *choreographic*, *creosote*, *cutaneous*, *erroneous*, *geodetic*, *leonine*, *instantaneous*, *meteor*, *mimeograph*, *neon*, *osteopath*, *peony*, *rodeo*, *theory*, etc.; *Borneo*, *Cleopatra*, *Creole*, *Leonardo*, *Leonora*, *Leontes*, *Theodore*, etc.

Exceptions:

- with <eo>≡/iː/ – *people*; *Peover*, *St. Neots*;

- with <eo>≡/e/ – *jeopardy*, *leopard* (cf. *leotard* /'lɪətɑːd/); *Leominster*, *Leonard*;
- with <eo>≡/əʊ/ – *yeoman*; *Yeo*, *Yeovil*;
- with <eo>≡/ə/ in the ending <-cheon> – *escutcheon*, *luncheon*, *puncheon*, *scutcheon*, *truncheon*, (other than after <ch>, the rule applies – *chameleon*, *galleon*, *melodeon*);
- with <eo>≡/eɪ-əʊ/ – *Beowulf*, *Galileo*, *Montevideo*;
- others – *Macleod* /mə'klaʊd/; *Theobald*(*s*) often has <eo>≡/ɪ/.

Examples of hiatus previously mentioned in the <e>-rules as exceptions to the complex spelling of a single vowel include: smoothed to /ɪə/ – *cereal*, *coleus*, *cornea*, *creativity*, *fealty*, *idea*, *laureate*, *linoleum*, *mausoleum*, *miscreant*, *museum*, *nausea*, *nucleus*, *panacea*, *urea*; *Anthea*, *Boadicea*, *Crimea*, *Korea*, etc.; with /iː-æ/ – *beatitude*, *caveat*, *deactivate*, *genealogy*, *meander*, *oleander*, *preamble*; *Balearic*, etc.; with /iː-eɪ/ – *create*, *delineate*, *nauseate*, etc.; with /iː-ɪ/ – *albeit*, *casein*, *homogeneity*, *lineage*, *nucleic*, *pantheist*, *reinforce*, *reinstate*, etc.

Efficiency: in words 85 per cent; in names 61 per cent; a minor rule with very strong bias towards low TF words and strong bias towards longer words.

E.29 <e>≡/e/ – the default rule for <e>
Examples: *bed, credit, enter, mend, pendulum, terrify*, etc.

There are a number of exceptions to the default rule (and hence to the <e>-rules as a set):

- with final <et>≡/eɪ/ in French loans – *ballet*, *beret*, *bouquet*, *cabaret*, *cachet*, *chalet*, *crochet*, *croquet*, *gourmet*, *parquet*, *ricochet*, *sachet*, *soubriquet*, *tourniquet*, *valet*; cf. §French *buffet* /-eɪ/ and §Basic *buffet* /-ɪt/;
- with /iː/ – *camellia*, *cathedral*, *demesne*, *egret*, *inebriated*. In SBS *febrile* has /iː/ and *zebra*, *zenith* usually have the default /e/; in AmE, the reverse is so;
- with /eɪ/ – *allegro*;
- with /ɒ/ (AmE /ɑ(ː)/ – fully anglicized *encore*, *ensemble*, *entourage*, *entente*, *entree*, and for some speakers *envelope*;
- the prefixes {de-}, {e-}, {pre-} and {re-} when stressed with /iː/ need to be identified, when they occur before recognizable elements (*dethrone*, *egress*, *preschool*, *rephrase*).

Efficiency: a core rule with a very heavy workload;

in words – 82 per cent (= 77 percentage points of 80 per cent correct /e/ predictions);

in names – 76 per cent (= 81 percentage points of 83 per cent correct /e/ predictions).

Allowing for reduction to /ə/ or /ɪ/ in unstressed syllables would increase the efficiency to 91 per cent and 85 per cent.

<f>-rules

F.1 <f(f)>≡/f/ – the default rule for <f>
Examples: *affable*, *affair*, *afflict*, *baffle*, *bailiff*, *benefit*, *bluff*, *buffoon*, *comfort*, *confine*, *dandruff*, *diffident*, *factor*, *fish*, *feeble*, *float*, *frisky*, *gratify*, *pitiful*, *suffocate*, *toffee*, *wife*, etc.; *Africa*, *Bedford*, *Clifford*, *Duffy*, *Falstaff*, *Ferranti*, *Fitzroy*, *Formosa*, *Fyffe*, *Kafka*, *Sheffield*, *Wolffe*, etc.
Exceptions:

- the common preposition *of* /ɒv/;
- the old currency terms *halfpenny* /ˈheɪpnɪ/, *halfpence* /ˈheɪpəns/;
- the Welsh names *Dyfed*, *Ifor*, *Myfanwy*, *Trefor*, have /v/.

Efficiency: a core rule with a very heavy workload;

in words – 100 per cent (= 74 percentage points of 87 per cent correct /f/ predictions);
in names – 99 per cent (= 80 percentage points of 94 per cent correct /f/ predictions).

<g>-rules

Correspondences are dealt with in rules numbered as follows:

G.1 <gg>≡/g/ G.2 <gh>≡/g/ G.3 <gu>≡/gw/
G.4 <gu>≡/g/ G.5, 6 <g>≡∅ G.7 <g>≡/g/
G.8 <ge>≡/ʤ/ G.9, 10, 12 <g>≡/ʤ/ G.11 <gi>≡/ʤ/
G.13 <g>≡/g/ – the default rule.

These rules are rather discursive. Their main task is simply to distinguish /ʤ/ before a front-vowel spelling from /g/ in other contexts.

G.1 <gg>≡/g/
The reason for bringing the doubled <gg> spelling forward from the default rule is to recognize that, with only one or two exceptions, it does not usually represent /ʤ/ and so does not get caught up in the rules for <g>≡/ʤ/ before front vowels.

Examples: *aggressive, buggy*, *ciggy*, *digger*, *druggist*, *egg*, *haggard*, *haggle*, *juggernaut*, *luggage*, *maggot*, *niggardly*, *nugget*, *straggly*, *thuggery*, *wriggle*, etc.

Exceptions: with /ʤ/ – *exaggerate*, *loggia*, *suggest.*

Efficiency: a core rule with strong bias towards low TF words;

in words – 95 per cent (= 5 percentage points of 87 per cent correct /g/ predictions);
in names – 97 per cent (= 4 percentage points of 81 per cent correct /g/ predictions).

G.2 <gh>≡/g/
Examples: *aghast*, *burgher*, *ghastly*, *gherkin*, *ghetto*, *ghost*, *ghoul*, *sorghum*, *spaghetti*, *yoghourt*; *Afghan*, *Allegheny*, *Baghdad*, *Balogh*, *Breughel*, *Creaghan*, *Dergh*, *Diaghilev*, *Ghana*, *Ghent*, *Ghibelline*, *Ghurka*, *Hooghly*, *Lindbergh*, *Pittsburgh*, etc. *Haigh* /heɪg/ as a family name, untypically for <aigh>, follows this rule, but the place-name *Haigh* /heɪ/ has the more usual empty final <gh>.

Exceptions:

- in English names where the <gh> straddles an element boundary – *Egham*, *Coghill*. If no /h/ is pronounced, we have <gh>≡/g/ here too in effect. This does not apply if <n> precedes as in *Birmingham*, where /ŋ/ corresponds to the <ng> and the <h> is inert (though pronounced in AmE);
- *Callaghan* and other Irish names with medial <gh> usually have /h/;
- in British names, the element <-burgh> is usually /-bərə/ – *Edinburgh*, *Jedburgh*, and <-bergh> is /-bə/ – *Sedbergh;* the Texas *Edinburgh* has /-bɜːrg/ (LPD);
- final <-lgh> in a few names represents /-lʃ/ or /-lʤ/ – *Greenhalgh*, *Ridehalgh*;
- otherwise, final <-gh> in names usually has a zero correspondence – *Castlereagh*, *Cavanagh*, *Hugh*, *Fermanagh*, *Vanbrugh*, etc.

The spellings <aigh>, <augh>, <eigh>, <igh>, <ough> are best treated as whole vowel correspondences. Apart from Irish names ending in <-agh>, these instances of <gh> only follow <i> and <u>.

Efficiency: in words 93 per cent; in names 32 per cent; a marginal rule with strong bias towards shorter words.

G.3 <gu>≡/gw/ | <n> — <V> <C>
The <V> <C> of the context excludes final <-ngue>≡/ŋ/ (*harangue*, *meringue*, *tongue*).

Examples: *anguish*, *distinguish*, *extinguish*, *language*, *languid*, *languish*, *lingual*, *linguist*, *penguin*, *sanguine*, *unguent*, etc.

Exceptions:

- with only /g/ – *languor*;
- the prefix <un-> has to be excluded in *unguarded*, *unguided*, etc.

Efficiency: in words 98 per cent; a marginal rule with some bias towards longer words.

G.4 <gu>≡/g/ | — <V>
Examples: *beguile*, *beleaguer*, *daguerreotype*, *demagogue*, *disguise*, *fugual*, *fugue*, *guarantee*, *guard*, *guardian*, *guerrilla*, *guess*, *guest*, *guide*, *guild*, *guilder*, *guile*, *guinea*, *guise*, *guitar*, *intrigue*, *league*, *marguerite*, *plague*,

rogue, *vague*, etc.; *Antigua*, *Guernsey*, *Guiana*, *Guildenstern*, *Guildford*, *Guinness*, *Guisborough*, *Guiseley*, *Huguenot*, *Portuguese*.

Exceptions:

- *harangue*, *meringue*, *tongue*, end up with a final /g/;
- with /gw/ – *guano*, *guava*, *iguana*; *Guadalquivir*, *Guadeloupe*, *Guaira*, *Guarani*, *Guatemala*, *Guido*, *Guillim*, *Guinevere*, *Maguire*, *Paraguay*, *Uruguay*. These exceptions with <gw> are exotic.
- with the <u> representing a full vowel – *Aguecheek*, *ambiguity*, *argue*, *arguable*, *contiguous*, *jaguar*; *Montague*, etc.

Efficiency: in words 97 per cent; in names 89 per cent; a minor rule.

A major problem for this simplistic algorithm is that the string <ng> may vary as /nʤ/ in *stranger*, *angel*, /ŋg/ in *anger*, *longer*, *angry*, and /ŋ/ in *banger*, *banged*. These cannot be distinguished without knowing where the internal morpheme boundaries, if any, are: {strange}+{er}, {bang}+{er}, {anger}, and whether the {er} is comparative as in *longer* or agentive as in *banger*. In SBS <ng> is a spelling for /ŋ/ without /g/ at morpheme boundaries: /g/ occurs within a morpheme in *finger* ({finger}) and *singly* ({singl(e)}+{(l)y}), but not at the boundary in *singer* ({sing}+{er}), *kingly* ({king}+{ly}). The comparative *longer*, *stronger*, etc. is exceptional in keeping /g/, unlike the agent suffix in *banger*, *ringer*. So, some of these are bound to end up as errors in our simple correspondence scan. Any attempt at <g> deletion or at distinguishing /g/ – /ʤ/ after <n> will leave exceptions. G.5 deletes <g> word-finally (*king*), and in the suffix <-ingly> (*engagingly*, but not *singly*), and before a consonant (*amongst*, *innings*, *kingdom*) other than <l>, <r> (*singly*, *tingle*, *angry*). In the rules that follow, /ʤ/ is given precedence over /g/ before front vowels.

G.5 <g>≡∅ | <n>* — { #, <C>* }
Conditions:

- the <C>* is not <l> or <r> (*single*, *angry*), but the boundary # takes precedence over the <C>* to include <-ing-ly>;
- the <n>* is not that of a prefix *con-*, *en-*, *in-*, *on-*, or *un-* (as in *congress*).

Examples: *accordingly*, *amongst*, *hangman*, *kingdom*, *lengthwise*, *oblong*, *provoking*, *sling*, etc.; *Bangkok*, *Byng*, *Kennington*, *Kingsway*, *Nottingham*, *Tring*, etc.

The conditions exclude *single*, *angry*, etc. and names such as *Anglesea*, *Congleton*, *Dingle*, *Ingle*, *Ingleby*, *Pringle*, *Tanglewood*. The rule fails to apply medially to prevent a /g/ in *clangour*, *hangar*, *harangue*, *tongue*. There are also a number of compounds where the boundary must be recognized: *hangout*, *hangover*, *ringleader*, *strongroom*, *strongly*.

From the reader's point of view, <g> zeroing is a triviality. There is in fact no contrast between /-ŋg/ and /-ŋ/, given the morpheme boundaries. Many Northern accents of English realize underlying //ng// as [ŋg] in all contexts.

Efficiency: in words 97 per cent; in names 94 per cent; a core rule with some bias towards high TF words; heavy workload.

G.6 <g>≡∅ | i) — {<m>, <n>} (<e>) #
ii) # — <n>

– in initial and final <gn> and final <gm> clusters, the <g> is zeroed.

Examples: *alignment*, *apothegm*, *arraign*, *assignee*, *campaign*, *champagne*, *champaign*, *coign*, *cologne*, *consign*, *deign*, *designedly*, *diaphragm*, *feigning*, *gnarled*, *gnash*, *gnat*, *gnaw*, *gneiss*, *gnome*, *gnomon*, *gnu*, *impugn*, *paradigm*, *phlegm*, *reign*, *sign*, *sovereignty*, etc. The rule also applies to a few names: *Gnossall*, *Presteigne* /pres'tiːn/, *Teign* /tɪn/.

Efficiency: in words 100 per cent; a marginal rule with very strong bias towards shorter words.

Other instances of <gn> get /gn/ by default. The nature of any suffix is important. Before §Latinate suffixes which can be added to bound forms, the default gives the right result in words such as *indignant*, *pregnant*, *pragmatic*, *designate* and, even though <sign> and <phlegm> are free graphic forms, in *signatory*, *signal*, *phlegmatic*.

There is no rule for <gn>≡/nj/ in some French loan-words – *cognac*, *lorgnette*, *mignonette*, *poignant*, *vignette*, which wrongly get /gn/ by default.

G.7 <g>≡/g/ | — <et> {<C>, #}
Examples: *altogether, beget*, *forget*, *get*, *target*, *together*; *Gethsemane*, *Getty*, *Gettysburg*.

Exceptions:

- with /ʤ/ – *georgette*, *suffragette*; *Paget*;
- with /ʒ/ – *Roget*.

Efficiency: in words 83 per cent; in names 64 per cent; a marginal rule with very strong bias towards high TF words.

Ainsworth clearly wanted this highly marginal rule to capture a few very common words which lacked palatalization to /ʤ/ before <e>. Even with no higher expectation than very rough speech synthesis, a confusion of /get/ – /ʤet/ would have been awkward. The added context prevents the rule applying before a vowel as in *apologetic*.

G.8 <ge>≡/ʤ/ | — <V>*
Conditions:

- the <V>* is not <e>.

This rule prevents the <e> used to mark the <g> as 'soft' (i.e. /ʤ/) from being read as a vowel before vowel-initial suffixes; the condition prevents the break-up of final <ee> (*refugee*).

Examples: *advantageous*, *cagey*, *changeable*, *courageous*, *dungeon*, *gorgeous*, *hydrangea*, *largeish*, *orangeade*, *pageantry*, *pigeon*, *sergeant*, *sturgeon*, *vengeance*, etc.; *Geoffrey*, *George*, *Scrymgeour*, *Spurgeon*, etc.

However, the following vowel correspondence is ruined when the <e> is part of a vowel spelling as in *congeal*, *oesophageal*; *Aegean*, *Egeus*.

Exceptions:

- with /g/ – *gear*, *geyser*, *Angear*, *Geiger*, *Haringey*, *Tingey*, *Tregear*, *Zeitgeist*;
- with /ʒ/ – *bourgeois*; *Peugeot*.

Efficiency: in words 83 per cent; in names 59 per cent; a minor rule with some bias towards longer words.

G.9 <g>≡/ʤ/ | — <e>
Examples: *age*, *aged*, *algebra*, *angel*, *apologetic*, *arrange*, *avenge*, *barge*, *bulge*, *caged*, *challenge*, *change*, *cogent*, *cringe*, *digest*, *divergent*, *emergency*, *engaged*, *eugenic*, *gelatine*, *gem*, *gender*, *genius*, *genus*, *germ*, *gesture*, *longevity*, *magenta*, *oxygen*, *progeny*, *rage*, *refugee*, *regent*, *stratagem*, *stringent*, *tragedy*, *urgency*, *vegetable*, *waged*, *wager*, etc.; *Algeria*, *Angela*, *Argentina*, *Bagehot*, *Burgess*, *Diogenes*, *Dungeness*, *Egerton*, *Eugene*, *Gemini*, *Genesis*, *Geneva*, *Genevieve*, *Genoa*, *Germany*, *Imogen*, *Nigel*, *Nigeria*, *Rogers*, *Tintagel*, *Whittingeham*, etc.

Exceptions:

- with /ʒ/ – *genre*, *negligé*, *protegé*;
- with /g/ – *auger*, *burger*, *eager*, *gecko*, *geese*, *geezer*, *gelding*, *hegemony*, *lager*, *tiger*; *Abergele*, *Armageddon*, *Augener*, *Beddgelert*, *Bergen*, *Bigelow*, *Copenhagen*, *Dolgellau*, *Engedi*, *Geddes*, *Gellan*, *Gennesareth*, *Geraint*, *Gershwin*, *Gertrude*, *Gestapo*, *Hegel*, *Ingersoll*, *Spitzbergen*, *Volkswagen*, etc.

Some names have /ʤ/ – /g/ variation – *Geeson*, *Gerontius*.

Efficiency: a core rule with some bias towards high TF words;

in words – 88 per cent (= 26 percentage points of 80 per cent correct /ʤ/ predictions);
in names – 58 per cent (= 19 percentage points of 89 per cent correct /ʤ/ predictions).

The haphazard use of final <-e> in names destroys its marking value. We find /ŋ/ not /nʤ/ in *Bunge* /ˈbʌŋɪ/, *Hardinge*, *Keatinge*, *Synge*, *Yonge* /jʌŋ/. The family name *Inge* is either /ɪŋ/ or /ɪnʤ/. /g/ occurs in *Eiger*, *Geiger*, *Kruger*, *Ladefoged*, *Trager*. Either /ʤ/ or /g/ occurs in *Foulger*, *Lalage*. The name *Stringer* as an agent form has /ŋ/; *Younger* as a comparative form has /ŋg/; *Northanger* is opaque and has either.

G.10 <g>≡/ʤ/ | — <iat>
This very marginal rule differs from the next since the <i> stays as a vowel.

It is only included to parallel similar rules for <c> C.9 and <t> T.10. The only examples in the data are *collegiate* and *intercollegiate*.

G.11 <gi>≡/ʤ/ | — {<a>, <o>}
Here the <i> can be taken as part of the /ʤ/ spelling in a number of §Latinate suffixes.

Examples: *allegiance*, *collegian*, *contagious*, *legion*, *neuralgia*, *nostalgia*, *prodigious*, *regional*, *religion*, *vestigial*, etc.

Exceptions: with <i> as a vowel – *adagio*, *elegiac*, *giant*, *orgiastic*.

Efficiency: in words 96 per cent; in names 73 per cent; a minor rule with some bias towards low TF words and strong bias towards longer words.

G.12 <g>≡/ʤ/ | — {<i>, <y>}
Conditions:

• not before a further <rC> (*girl*, *girder*).

Examples: *aborigine*, *aegis*, *agile*, *agitated*, *angina*, *biology*, *clergy*, *digit*, *dingy*, *elegy*, *engineer*, *exchanging*, *forging*, *fragile*, *fugitive*, *giblets*, *gibberish*, *ginger*, *gymnastics*, *gyroscope*, *hygiene*, *imagine*, *legible*, *legitimate*, *magic*, *origin*, *plunging*, *pugilist*, *virgin*, etc.; *Agincourt*, *Algiers*, *Belgium*, *Giles*, *Magi*, *Pugin*, *Reginald*, *Sagittarius*, *Tangier*, etc.

Exceptions: with /g/ – *begin*, *bogy*, *boogy*, *fogy*, *forgive*, *fungi*, *gibbon*, *giddy*, *gift*, *giggle*, *gig*, *gild*, *gillie*, *gill*, *gilt*, *gimlet*, *gimmick*, *gimp*, *git*, *give*, *gizzard*, *gynaecology*, *yogi*, – a strange mixture of some very common words with some technical words and some slang; *Argyle*, *Burgin*, *Cargill*, *Carnegie*, *Elgin*, *Fagin*, *Gibbon*, *Gibbs*, *Giblett*, *Gibson*, *Gielgud*, *Gifford*, *Gilbert*, *Gilliat*, *Ginn*, *Ginsberg*, *Gissing*, *Hengist*, *Magyar*, *Porgy*, etc.

Some names have /ʤ/ – /g/ variation – *Burgin*, *Gifford*, *Gimson*, as does the Latin plural *fungi*, *sarcophagi*.

Efficiency: a core rule with a fairly heavy workload with strong bias towards low TF words and very strong bias towards longer words;

in words – 89 per cent (= 21 percentage points of 80 per cent correct /ʤ/ predictions);
in names – 38 per cent (= 7 percentage points of 89 per cent correct /ʤ/ predictions).

G.13 <g>≡/g/ – the default rule for <g>
Double <gg> has been dealt with separately and taken forward to G.1.

Examples: *agog*, *anagram*, *beg*, *bogus*, *cargo*, *drug*, *fragrant*, *gaudy*, *glisten*, *glad*, *growl*, *gurgle*, *jig*, *keg*, *log*, *zigzag*, etc.; *Agnes*, *Algol*, *August*, *Figaro*, *Gadsby*, *Gaza*, *Glasgow*, *Grieg*, *Margot*, *Rugby*, *Tagalog*, *Uganda*, etc.

There are a number of exceptions to the default rule (and hence to the <g>-rules as a set) apart from those mentioned earlier:

• with /ʤ/ – *gaol*, *syringa*, *veg* (abbrev.);

Efficiency: a core rule with a very heavy workload;

in words 97 per cent (= 74 percentage points of 87 per cent correct /g/ predictions);

in names 96 per cent (= 70 percentage points of 81 per cent correct /g/ predictions).

<h>-rules

H.1 <h>≡/h/ – the default rule for <h>
Examples: *ahoy*, *alcohol*, *behind*, *behold*, *boyhood*, *enhance*, *habit*, *hair*, *half*, *help*, *herring*, *horrid*, *hymn*, etc.; *Ahab*, *Bahamas*, *Bihar*, *Bohemia*, *Brocklehurst*, *Cahill*, *Copenhagen*, *Doherty*, *Galahad*, *Goonhilly*, *Haakon*, *Hackney*, *Halifax*, *Hamish*, *Helen*, *Holland*, *Hythe*, *Idaho*, *Mohawk*, *Peterhead*, *Soho*, *Solihull*, *Tahiti*, *Yehudi*, etc.

Exceptions:

- with initial <h>≡∅ – *heir*, *honest*, *honour*, *hour*, and derived forms; one or two other words may occasionally have <h>≡∅ – many people say 'an hotel' with no /h/ and with the pre-consonantal form of the article;
- with <h>≡∅ in most words after the prefix <ex->, but varying from speaker to speaker (see p. 377): *exhale*, *exhaust*, *exhibit*, *exhilarate*, *exhort*, *exhume*;
- final <h> occurs as a marker of vowel length in some exclamations – *ah*, *oh*, *pooh*, *whoah*, *yeah*;
- final <h> occurs in some non-§Basic names – *Anouilh*, *Gizeh*, *Jahveh*, *Oudh*, *Pharaoh*, *Shiloh*, *Sindh*, *Noah*, *Shenandoah*, etc.; after a vowel letter and <d, l> it represents zero. The <bh> of *Cobh* is /v/.

In unstressed syllables the /h/ of a placename element may disappear – the ending <-ham> in names is usually /əm/ (*Birmingham*, *Hexham*, etc.) – this is not true of some accents of English including AmE, where the <-ham> often has a secondary stress as /-hæm/.

Efficiency: a core rule with a heavy workload;

in words – 99 per cent (= 74 percentage points of 75 per cent correct /h/ predictions);

in names – 93 per cent (= 86 percentage points of 87 per cent correct /h/ predictions).

The clusters <ch>, <ph>, <sh>, <th>, <wh>, are treated as spelling units. So are the clusters <gh>, <kh>, <rh>, but there is a difference. In the first group, the <h> has the natural function of indicating the features 'voiceless and fricative' in representing [ʧ], [f], [ʃ], [ʍ]; <th> represents only 'fricative' for both voiceless [θ] and voiced [ð]. In the group <gh>, <kh>, <rh>, the <h> is empty and arbitrary; there is some marking, however: <rh> is §Greek, <kh> is exotic.

<i>-rules

Correspondences are dealt with in numbered rules as follows:

I.1 <i>≡/ə/ I.2 <i>≡/iː/ I.3 <i>≡/ɪ/
I.4, 5 <ie>≡/aɪ/ I.6 <ie>≡/ɪ/ I.7 <ie≡/iː/
I.8 <ig>≡/aɪ/ I.9 <igh>≡/aɪ/ I.10 <ir>≡/ɜː(r)/
I.11, 12, 15–17 <i>≡/aɪ/ I.13 <i>≡/ɪ/ I.14, 18 <i>≡<iː>
I.19 <i>≡/ɪ/ – the default rule.

In some <i>-initial strings of more than one vowel letter, the <i> has caused palatalization of the previous consonant: *dictation*, *partial*, *spacious*, etc. Ainsworth's rules deal with the <io> of the suffix <-tion>, the commonest of these, as a vowel digraph. Here, to get a more general coverage, the <i> is taken to be part of the palatalized consonant spelling: <ti>≡/ʃ/, <ci>≡/ʃ/, etc. Either method is awkward. A generative description in which an underlying //tiən// becomes /ʃən/ would better reflect this aspect of spelling competence.

The vowels of some other common endings need special attention:

I.1 <i>≡/ə/ | <V> <C_0> — <bl> {<e>, <y>}
Examples: *audibly*, *compatible*, *contemptible*, *crucible*, *digestible*, *fallible*, *feasibly*, *flexible*, *gullible*, *horribly*, *invincible*, *legibly*, *mandible*, *plausible*, *possibly*, *sensible*, *terribly*, etc. There is free variation between /ə/ and /ɪ/ in this ending.

Efficiency: in words 100 per cent; a minor rule with very strong bias towards longer words.

I.2 <i>≡/iː/ | — <que> #
Examples: *antique*, *boutique*, *clique*, *critique*, *mystique*, *oblique*, *obliquely*, *physique*, *piqued*, *technique*, *unique*, *uniqueness*, etc.; *Henriques*, *Martinique*, *Mozambique*.

Communiqué is usually differentiated by an accent <é>. A marginal rule.

I.3 <i>≡/ɪ/ | <V> <C_1> — {<c>, <v>} <e> #
– that is, in the unstressed endings <-ice> and <-ive>.
Examples:

- <-ice> – *apprentice*, *armistice*, *artifice*, *auspice*, *avarice*, *bodice*, *chalice*, *cowardice*, *crevice*, *dentrifice*, *edifice*, *jaundice*, *justice*, *lattice*, *liquorice*, *malice*, *notice*, *novice*, *office*, *poultice*, *practice*, *service*, *solstice*, etc.; *Alice*, *Eunice*, *Lettice*, *Prentice*, *Venice*;
- <-ive> – *active*, *adhesive*, *aggressive*, *endive*, *extensive*, *festive*, *forgive*, *fugitive*, *imperative*, *massive*, *missive*, *olive*, *passive*, *positive*, *responsive*, *sensitive*, *vindictive*, etc.

Exceptions:

- <-ice> – with <aɪ> – *advice*, *allspice*, *device*, *dormice*, *entice*, *sacrifice*, etc.; with /iː/ – *police*;
- <-ive> – with /aɪ/ – *alive*, *archive*, *arrive*, *beehive*, *connive*, *contrive*, *deprive*, *revive*, *survive*, etc.

The stressed vowels of the verbs are predictable: *arrive*, *entice*, *deprive*, etc.

Some names have a modernized <-ice>≡/ɪs/ alongside a classical pronunciation /aɪsɪ/ – *Bernice*, *Eunice*. *Maldive* usually has /iː/.

Efficiency: in words 92 per cent; a marginal rule with a fairly heavy workload and with strong bias towards longer words.

Among the <i>-initial strings of more than one letter, the spelling <ie> can only be read effectively along with grammar-based stress rules. You need to know, for instance, that *denied*, *relied*, have final stress and *sullied*, *varied*, do not. Ainsworth has rule (71) '-C(ie) /aɪ/' covering first-syllable <ie> (which would be 38 per cent efficient in words and only 13 per cent in names), and rule (72) 'VC(ie) /iː/', covering other instances. The first-syllable rule really only applies to monosyllabic words and their inflected forms with <-d> and <-s>. Before the <-ing> form, the <ie> converts to <y> (*lie – lying*).

I.4 <ie>≡/aɪ/ | # <C_1> — ({<d>, <s>}) #
Examples: *cries*, *cried*, *die*, *fie*, *fried*, *fries*, *hie*, *lie*, *pie*, *pied*, *skies*, *tried*, *tries*, *vie*, etc.

Efficiency: in words 100 per cent; a marginal rule for some common monosyllables.

I.5 <ie>≡/aɪ/ | <V> <C_0> {<f>,<l>} — {<d>,<s>} #
Conditions:

- the preceding <l> should not be double (*rallied*, *sullied*, etc.).

This odd-looking rule captures inflected forms of the common verb suffix <-ify> and one or two verbs ending in stressed <-ly>. The rule does not include the <-ier> forms (*intensifier*, etc.), which come out as exceptions to I.7, where they compete with <ier>≡/ɪə/ forms such as *clothier*, *merrier*.

Examples: *applied*, *belied*, *certified*, *countrified*, *dignified*, *implied*, *modified*, *qualified*, *relied*, *satisfied*, etc. and similar forms with <-s>.

Exceptions: *allied*, *allies* are exceptions to the condition on <ll>.

Efficiency: in words 99 per cent; a marginal rule, and not surprisingly, since it deals with a disyllabic suffix, it has very strong bias towards longer words.

I.6 <ie>≡/ɪ/ | <V> <C_0> — ({<d>, <s>}) #
This rule captures final unstressed <-ie> and inflected forms of words ending in unstressed <-ie> or <-y>.

Examples:

- inflected forms – *able-bodied*, *candies*, *candied*, *flurried*, *frenzied*, *hurried*, *ivied*, *jellies*, *married*, *palsied*, *panties*, *salaries*, *studied*, *varied*, etc.;
- final <-ie> – *auntie*, *birdie*, *bolshie*, *boogie*, *bookie*, *brassie*, *budgie*, *calorie*, *camaraderie*, *chappie*, *collie*, *commie*, *conshie*, *cookie*, *coolie*, *coterie*, *cowrie*, *curie*, *darkie*, *dearie*, *genie*, *gillie*, *laddie*, *lassie*, *lingerie*, *prairie*, *quickie*, *sweetie*, *talkie*, etc.

Speakers who have /iː/ rather than /ɪ/ in final open unstressed syllables will have a contrast between *candied* /iː/ and *candid* /ɪ/ or /ə/.

Efficiency: in words virtually 100 per cent; a marginal rule.

I.7 <ie>≡/iː/ – the default rule for <ie>
Examples: *achieve, achievement*, *belief*, *believe*, *besiege*, *brief*, *chief*, *diesel*, *fief*, *field*, *fiend*, *grief*, *grieve*, *hygiene*, *lief*, *liege*, *lien*, *mien*, *niece*, *piece*, *priest*, *reprieve*, *retrieve*, *shield*, *shriek*, *siege*, *thief*, *thieves*, *wield*, *yield*; *Brie*, *Fielden*, *Gielgud*, *Kiel*, *Piedmont*, *Rievaulx*, *Siegfried*, *Siemens*, *Wiesbaden*.

This rule also caters for *fierce* and the unstressed <ier> of *carrier*, *happier*, etc. R.1 inserts the [ə] glide and allows for smoothing to /ɪə/.

Exceptions:

- with /e/ – *friend*;
- various forms of hiatus:

with /aɪə/ – *anxiety*, *impiety*, *notoriety*, *proprietor*, *quiet*, *variety*;
with /ɪ-iː/ – *medieval*;
with /iː-e/ – *acquiesce*, *fiesta*, *quiescent*, *serviette*, *sierra*, *siesta*; *Dieppe*, *Kiev*, *Rienzi*, *Sienna*, *Vienna*, *Vietnam*;
with /ɪə/ – *alienate*, *oriel*, *soviet*, *spaniel*, *veriest*, and a large group of words with <-ient>, <-ience>: *audience*, *gradient*, *lenient*, etc.

- as part of an <ieu> or <iew> spelling of /(j)uː/ – *adieu*, *lieu*, *purlieu*, *purview*, *review*, *view,* and in AmE *lieutenant, milieu.* In SBS *lieutenant* is irregular as /lef-/, and *milieu* as /-jɜː/.

Efficiency: in words 61 per cent; in names 87 per cent; a minor rule.

I.8 <ig>≡/aɪ/ | — {<m>, <n>} #
Examples: *align*, *assign*, *benign*, *condign*, *consign*, *design*, *ensign*, *malign*, *paradigm*, *resign*, *sign*.

Efficiency: in words 94 per cent; a marginal rule with some bias towards high TF words.

I.9 <igh>≡/aɪ/
Examples: *blight*, *bright*, *delight*, *fight*, *flight*, *fright*, *high*, *knight*, *light*, *might*, *nigh*, *night*, *plight*, *right*, *sigh*, *sight*, *thigh*, *tight*, *wight*, *wright*, and derived forms; *Albright*, *Arkwright*, *Bligh*, *Blighty*, *Brighton*, *Cartwright*, *Dwight*, *Higham*, *Knighton*, *Wright*, etc.

Exceptions:

- with /ɪg/ and <h>≡∅ at the boundary in *Bigham*, *Brigham*, *Wigham*;
- with final /ɪ/ – *Denbigh*, *Kirkcudbright*;
- with /iːg/ – *Respighi*.

Efficiency: a core rule with strong bias towards high TF words and some bias towards shorter words;

in words – 100 per cent (= 5 percentage points of 55 per cent correct /aɪ/ predictions);
in names – 82 per cent (= 3 percentage points of 46 per cent correct /aɪ/ predictions).

I.10 <ir>≡/ɜː(r)/ | — {<C>, #}
Conditions:

- not before a further non-final <r> (*irrigate*, *mirror*). Inflected forms, such as *stirring*, *whirred*, of course, keep the /ɜː/ of their base forms.

Examples: final monosyllabic *fir*, *sir*, *stir*; and *birch*, *bird*, *birth*, *circle*, *circumvent*, *dirge*, *dirty*, *firm*, *first*, *flirt*, *girder*, *girl*, *girth*, *irksome*, *mirth*, *quirk*, *shirt*, *sirloin*, *skirmish*, *squirt*, *swirl*, *thirst*, *virgin*, *virtue*, *twirl*, *zircon*, etc.; *Birkbeck*, *Birmingham*, *Birnam*, *Dunkirk*, *Firth*, *Girton*, *Hirst*, *Irvine*, *Irwin*, *Kirby*, *Pirbright*, *Shirley*, *Stirling*, *Thirsk*, *Virgil*, *Virginia*, etc.

Exceptions: with /ɪə/ finally in polysyllabic words – *emir*, *nadir*, *souvenir*, *tapir*; *Aboukir*, *Kashmir*, *Pamir*, *Sapir*, *Vladimir*.

Efficiency: a core rule;

in words – 96 per cent (= 14 percentage points of 90 per cent correct /ɜː/ predictions);
in names – 89 per cent (= 12 percentage points of 96 per cent correct /ɜː/ predictions).

The original rule was plain <ir>≡/ɜː/, which would wrongly apply before vowels (*spiral*, *ironic*) and to non-final <irr>≡/ɪr/ (*irrigate*).

I.11 <i>≡/aɪ/ | — <nd> (<e>) #
Examples: *behind*, *bind*, *blind*, *blindness*, *find*, *grind*, *grinder*, *hind*, *kind*, *mind*, *remind*, *rind*, *wind* (v.), *winder*; *Gradgrind*, *Hind*(*e*).

Exceptions: with /ɪ/ – *hinder*, *tinder*, *wind* (n.); *Brind*, *Ind*, *Lind*, *Rind*, *Sind*.

Efficiency: in words 90 per cent; a marginal rule with very strong bias towards high TF words and towards shorter words.

I.12 <i>≡/aɪ/ | <C_1> — <ld> (<e>) #
– a marginal rule with strong bias towards high TF words and strong bias towards shorter words.

Examples: *child*, *mild*, *wild*; *Fairchild*, *Rothschild*, *Wilde*.

Exceptions: with /ɪ/ – *bewilder*, *gild*, *Brunnhilde*.

The <C>$_1$ of the context excludes *build*, *guild*, where the <u> has been taken as part of <bu>≡/b/, <gu>≡/g/.

I.13 <i>≡/ɪ/ | — #

Examples: *bikini*, *broccoli*, *chilli*, *confetti*, *graffiti*, *khaki*, *kiwi*, *macaroni*, *mini*, *mufti*, *salami*, *scampi*, *semi*, *spaghetti*, *taxi*, etc.; *Adelphi*, *Ashanti*, *Capri*, *Chianti*, *Cincinatti*, *Disraeli*, *Ferranti*, *Fiji*, *Gallipoli*, *Gandhi*, *Israeli*, *Malawi*, *Marconi*, *Missouri*, *Tahiti*, etc. Some speakers have /iː/ rather than /ɪ/ in final unstressed syllables. The rule would be more general if it gave /iː/, optionally reducible to /ɪ/ in the absence of stress. That would also include *ski*.

Exceptions:

- with /aɪ/ – *alibi*, *alkali*, *quasi*, *rabbi*;
- /aɪ/ also occurs in anglicized Latin plurals – *alumni*, *cacti*, *gladioli*, etc. – a more purist pronunciation is /ˈkæktiː/. There is a similar variation in classical names – *Delphi* with /aɪ/ or /iː/, /ɪ/.

Efficiency: in words 57 per cent; in names 86 per cent; a marginal rule with strong bias towards low TF words.

I.14 <i>≡/iː/ | —<C> {<a>, <i>, <o>} #

This rule is an attempt to capture exotic words ending in <a>, <i> or <o> and stressed on the penultimate syllable.

Examples: *albino*, *amino*, *ballerina*, *bikini*, *casino*, *concertina*, *diva*, *farina*, *graffiti*, *incognito*, *kilo*, *kiwi*, *libido*, *maraschino*, *marina*, *merino*, *mosquito*, *scarlatina*, *semolina*, *visa*; *Adelina*, *Afridi*, *Alexandrina*, *Angelina*, *Anita*, *Arequipa*, *Argentina*, *Assisi*, *Dominica*, *Farina*, *Fiji*, *Filipino*, *Frederica*, *Georgina*, *Gita*, *Guido*, *Houdini*, *Juanita*, *Lima*, *Lisa*, *Louisa*, *Martini*, *Medina*, *Messina*, *Mussolini*, *Navarino*, *Ouida*, *Paganini*, *Palestrina*, *Puccini*, *Riga*, *Rossini*, *Ryvita*, *Swahili*, *Tahiti*, *Tanganyika*, *Tsarina*, *Wilhelmina*, etc. *Elvira* has /iː/ – /aɪ/ variation.

Exceptions:

- with unstressed /ɪ/ before /k/ – *angelica*, *arnica*, *basilica*, *brassica*, *calico*, *erotica*, *harmonica*, *japonica*, *majolica*, *medico*, *paprika*, *politico*, *portico*, *replica*, *sciatica*, *silica*, *swastika*; *Armorica*, *Erica*, *Eroica*, *Jessica*, *Mexico*, *Monica*, *Pimlico*, *Salonica*, *Thessalonica*, *Veronica*, etc. The rule could be adjusted to exclude this well-defined class, leaving *mica* and *Dominica*, *Frederica*, *Tanganyika*, as exceptions.
- other instances of unstressed /ɪ/ – *alumina*, *domino*, *generalissimo*, *indigo*, *maxima*, *minima*, *patina*, *retina*, *stamina*, *vertigo*; *Candida*, *Eskimo*, *Fatima*, *Florida*, *Hiroshima*, *Inigo*, *Perdita*, *Shillito*, etc.;
- *Manila* has stressed /ɪ/ and an alternative spelling *Manilla* to suit; *mini* also has stressed /ɪ/;

- with /aɪ/ – *angina*, *giro*, *impetigo*, *lino*, *mica*, *proviso*, *rhino*, *saliva*, *silo*, *vagina*, *viva* ('exam'); *Carolina*, *China*, *Eliza*, *Fido*, *Godiva*, *Jemima*, *Sligo*;
- people not familiar with the regular pronunciation of *Dominica* as /dɒmɪˈniːkə/, will pronounce it /dəˈmɪnɪkə/ (LPD), probably by analogy with *Dominican*.

Efficiency: in words 27 per cent; in names 51 per cent; a marginal rule.

I.15 <i>≡/aɪ/ | — <C>* <e>* #
Conditions:

- the <C>* is not <x> (*fixing*);
- the <C>* may be a <Cl> or <Cr> cluster other than <ll>, <rr> (*trifle*, *fibre*), or <th> (*lithe*);
- the <e>* may be elided before the initial vowel of a suffix as in *riding*, *spicy* (p. 269).

Examples: *admiringly*, *advise*, *agile*, *alkaline*, *astride*, *bike*, *blithe*, *briny*, *chives*, *cider*, *coincide*, *combine*, *crises*, *define*, *desire*, *dice*, *diver*, *emphasise*, *empire*, *entirely*, *expiry*, *filings*, *fiver*, *grimy*, *hireling*, *ice*, *idle*, *jiving*, *liken*, *liner*, *lining*, *liven*, *miser*, *mitre*, *perspire*, *ripen*, *satire*, *spiny*, *swinish*, *textile*, *tidings*, *whitish*, *widen*, *writhe*, etc.; *Clementine*, *Clive*, *Devizes*, *Giles*, *Grimes*, *Irish*, *Jacobite*, *Klondike*, *Miles*, *Niger*, *Nile*, *Palestine*, *Pennines*, *Price*, *Tiber*, *Valentine*, *Viking*, etc.

Exceptions:

- some words ending in <-ish> as part of the stem, not a suffix: *diminish*, *finish*;
- with /iː/ in the ending <-ine> – *amphetamine*, *chlorine*, *dentine*, *dextrine*, *figurine*, *gabardine*, *gasoline*, *gelatine*, *guillotine*, *latrine*, *libertine*, *machine*, *margarine*, *marine*, *quinine*, *ravine*, *routine*, *vaccine*, *vaseline*, etc.; *iodine* has a variant with /aɪ/;
- with /ɪ/ in the ending <-ine> – *destine*, *determine*, *discipline*, *doctrine*, *engine*, *ermine*, *examine*, *famine*, *feminine*, *imagine*, *jasmine*, *urine*, etc.;
- other examples of /iː/ – *automobile*, *chemise*, *elite*, *expertise*, *imbecile*, *marguerite*, *prestige*, *regime*;
- other examples of /ɪ/ – *arbiter*, *caliper*, *conifer*, *consider*, *exquisite*, *favourite*, *granite*, *hypocrite*, *juniper*, *mortise*, *opposite*, *promise*, *river*, *shiver*, *sliver*, *vestige*, etc.

Efficiency: a core rule with a heavy workload;

in words – 77 per cent (= 37 percentage points of 55 per cent correct /aɪ/ predictions);

in names – 50 per cent (= 20 percentage points of 46 per cent correct /aɪ/ predictions).

I.16 <i>≡/aɪ/ | # <C_0>— <C>* ENDING
Conditions:

- the <C>* may be a <Cr> cluster (*vibrant*); there are no examples in the data of <th> as the <C>*.

Examples and exceptions:

with <-al> – *bridal*, *final*, *primal*, *rival*, *sisal*, *spinal*, *spiral*, *tribal*, *vital*;
with <-an> – not *divan*;
with <-ar> – not *cigar*, *vicar*;
with <-is> – *ibis*, *iris*;
with <-on> – *bison*, *icon*, *micron*, but not in *citron*, *prison*;
with <-us> – *minus*, *primus*, *sinus*, *virus*, but not in *citrus*;
with <-acy> – *piracy*, *primacy*, but not in *privacy*;
with <-ant, -ance, -ancy> – *finance*, *migrant*, *vibrant*;
with <-ary> – *binary*, *library*, *primary*;
with <-ent, -ence, -ency> – *licence*, *silent*, *strident*, *trident*;
with <-ine> – not *divine*;
with <-ite> – *finite*;
with <-our> – not *rigour*, *vigour*.

Efficiency: in words 41 per cent; a marginal rule. Some longer stems would also fit, as in *arrival*, *detritus*, *decisive*.

The suffixes <-ic(al)>, <-id>, <-it> have a complementary function in that they mark a short vowel (the default) in *civic*, *clinic*, *critic*, *digit*, *elicit*, *exhibit*, *illicit*, *implicit*, *inhibit*, *insipid*, *livid*, *mimic*, *parasitic*, *rigid*, *solicit*, *spirit*, *timid*, *visit*, *vivid*; *Brigid*, *Pacific*, *Semitic*.

There is no basis in the case of <i>, unlike other vowel letters, for predicting a long vowel before <-CVV>. The many §Latinate words ending in <-tion>, <-sion> have a short vowel in the case of preceding <i> (*derision*, *munitions*); these endings only have a preceding long vowel if it is spelt <a>, <e>, <o>, or <u> (*dictation*, *secretion*, *devotion*, *ablution*).

Hiatus with <-i-> as the first letter also has to be handled differently. The normal /aɪ/ value can certainly be expected when it is the first syllable of the word, partly because of §Greek prefixes such as *bio-*, *dia-*. In other instances the <i>≡/iː/ correspondence seems more predictable. Accordingly we give two hiatus rules:

I.17 <i>≡/aɪ/ | # <C_0> — <V>
As the first vowel of a word and followed by another vowel.

Examples: *bias*, *biochemical*, *biographer*, *biology*, *biopsy*, *briar*, *client*, *diabolic*, *diadem*, *diagnose*, *diagram*, *friable*, *friar*, *giant*, *hiatus*, *iambic*, *iodine*, *ionic*, *liable*, *liar*, *lion*, *phial*, *pioneer*, *pliant*, *riot*, *sciatica*, *science*, *striation*, *triad*, *trial*, *triumph*, *viaduct*, *violin*, etc.; *Brian*, *Diana*, *Diocletian*,

Diogenes, *Guiana*, *Hiawatha*, *Iolanthe*, *Iona*, *Iowa*, *Lionel*, *Miami*, *Niagara*, *Pius*, *Priam*, *Siam*, *Zion*, etc.

Exceptions: with /iː/ – *clientele*, *fiance(e)*, *fiasco*, *fiord*, *kiosk*, *liaise*, *liaison*, *liana*, *miasma*, *piano*, *pianist*, *piastre*, *trio*, *viola*; *Biarritz*, *Chianti*, *Diaghilev*, *Dior*, *Fiat*, *Fiona*, *Giovanni*, *Iago*, *Ian*, *Liam*, *Rio*, etc. When stress is on the second vowel, as in *Fiona*, the <i> may represent /ɪ/ rather than /iː/.

The /iː/ pronunciation is more exotic than the regular /aɪ/. This may help to distinguish *Dior* /iː/ – *Diana* /aɪ/, but it is not a reliable guide, since exotic words can become familiar without changing the vowel. There may even be homograph pairs: *viola* (flower) has /aɪ/, *viola* (instrument) has /iː/.

Efficiency: in words 86 per cent; in names 65 per cent; a minor rule with some bias towards longer words.

I.18 <i>≡/iː/ | — <V>
This applies in syllables other than the first. If the following vowel is unstressed, the two vowels may merge as /ɪə/ (*alien, idiot)*.

Examples: *abbreviate, aerial*, *affiliation*, *alias*, *ammoniac*, *apiary*, *bacteria*, *barium*, *bibliography*, *billiards*, *carrion*, *curious*, *dominion*, *dubious*, *editorial*, *expedience*, *glorious*, *medallion*, *milliamp*, *obvious*, *onion*, *polio*, *radio*, *ruffian*, *trivia*, *verbiage*, etc.; *Adrian*, *Arcadia*, *Assyria*, *Bleriot*, *Elliot*, *Gerontius*, *Julia*, *Julius*, *Lilian*, *Ontario*, etc. The names *Maria* and *Sophia* used to have anglicized forms with /aɪ/, as in 'The Black Maria' (a police van). This pronunciation now seems old-fashioned. The form with /iː/ is now usual for *Maria. Sophia* seems to have become a mere alternative spelling for *Sophie*.

Exceptions:

- with /aɪ/ – *alliance*, *certifiable*, *defiant*, *denial*, *elegiac*, *leviathan*, *verifiable*, etc.; *Ananias*, *Goliath*, *Jeremiah*, *Josiah*, *Mathias*, *Messiah*, *Obadiah*, *Ohio*, *Orion*, etc.
- with merger into a palatal /ʃ, ʒ, ʧ, ʤ/ – *fuchsia*, *Asia*, *Asian*, *Belgian*, etc.

The /iː, ɪ/ pronunciations are largely in unstressed syllables and the /aɪ/ pronunciations in stressed syllables. There is a good case for keeping the <y> spelling of verbs such as *defy*, *verify*, in their derived forms as *<defyant>, *<verifyable>.

Efficiency: a core rule with a heavy workload with strong bias towards low TF words and towards longer words;

in words – 87 per cent (= 24 percentage points of 74 per cent correct /iː/ predictions);
in names – 89 per cent (= 34 percentage points of 94 per cent correct /iː/ predictions).

I.19 <i>≡/ɪ/ – the default rule for <i>
Examples: *brick, fiddle, interesting, lid, prism, tinge, vindicate,* etc.

There are a number of exceptions to the default rule (and hence to the <i>-rules as a set):

- /iː/ – *artiste*, *chic*, *cliche*, *debris*, *fatigue*, *intrigue*, *massif*, *modiste*, *motif*, *piquancy*, etc.;
- inert <i> in *business*, *medicine*.

Efficiency: a core rule; very heavy workload and some bias towards longer words.

in words – 93 per cent (= 51 percentage points of 88 per cent correct /ɪ/ predictions);
in names – 93 per cent (= 49 percentage points of 81 per cent correct /ɪ/ predictions).

<j>-rules

J.1 <j>≡/ʤ/ – the default rule for <j>
Examples: *abject*, *banjo*, *cajole*, *conjugal*, *conjurer*, *dejected*, *eject*, *enjoy*, *jab*, *jackal*, *jade*, *jaguar*, *jail*, *jamboree*, *jam*, *janitor*, *jargon*, *jaundice*, *jaunty*, *javelin*, *jazz*, *jealous*, *jeans*, *jeep*, *jelly*, *jet*, *jewel*, *jingle*, *jittery*, *job*, *jockey*, *join*, *journalism*, *juice*, *just*, *majestic*, *major*, *object*, *prejudice*, *rejuvenate*, *subject*, *trajectory*, etc.; *Ajax*, *Benjamin*, *Darjeeling*, *Fiji*, *Jabberwock*, *Jack*, *Jacobean*, *Jacob*, *Jaffa*, *Jagger*, *Jamaica*, *January*, *Japan*, *Jeffreys*, *Jerusalem*, *June*, *July*, *Joan*, *Joseph*, *Punjab*, *Trajan*, etc.

Exceptions: occasional exotic words with <j>≡/j/ – *hallelujah*, *majolica*. They are likely to be adapted either in spelling (*alleluia*) or in pronunciation (/məˈʤɒlɪkə/). Foreign names with <j>≡/j/ include *Ajaccio*, *Betjeman*, *Jaeger*, *Jantzen*, *Jena*, *Jespersen*, *Joachim*, *Johannes*, *Jugoslavia*, *Reykjavik*, *Sarajevo*, etc.

Efficiency: a core rule with a fairly heavy workload;

in words – 99 per cent (= 21 percentage points of 80 per cent correct /ʤ/ predictions);
in names – 92 per cent (= 42 percentage points of 89 per cent correct /ʤ/ predictions).

<k>-rules

K.1 <k>≡∅ | # — <n>
Examples: *knack*, *knapsack*, *knave*, *knead*, *knee*, *kneel*, *knell*, *knew*, *knickers*, *knife*, *knight*, *knit*, *knob*, *knock*, *knoll*, *knot*, *know*, *knowledge*, *knuckle*, etc.; *Knaresborough*, *Knowles*, *Knox*, *Knutsford*, etc.

Exceptions: an occasional foreign name with /kn/ – *Knesset*, *Knossos*.

Efficiency: in words 100 per cent; a marginal rule with strong bias towards high TF words and very strong bias towards shorter words.

K.2 <kh>≡/k/
Examples: *gymkhana*, *khaki*; *Astrakhan*, *Gurkha*, *Khaled*, *Khan*, *Khartoum*, *Khayyam*, *Khyber*, *Ladakh*, *Oistrakh*, *Sikh*, *Tutankhamun*, etc.

Efficiency: in words 100 per cent; in names 100 per cent; a marginal rule.

In reading, this correspondence presents no problem. Any attempt to pronounce /kh/ as a cluster would simply sound like aspiration of the /k/. English names *Kirkham*, *Oakham*, etc. usually have /h/≡∅ in the final unstressed syllable.

K.3 <k(k)>≡/k/ – the default rule for <k>
Examples: *alkali*, *amok*, *ankle*, *ark*, *bank*, *basket*, *bikini*, *break*, *crook*, *flake*, *honkytonk*, *joke*, *karate*, *kimono*, *kiwi*, *monkey*, *plonk*, *rebuke*, *speak*, *tankard*, *tinkle*, *yoke*, etc.; *Alaska*, *Askew*, *Bangkok*, *Birkbeck*, *Cherokee*, *Dunkirk*, *Dvorak*, *Ezekiel*, *Katherine*, *Oakes*, *Skaggerak*, *Tokyo*, etc. Double <kk> is rare and exotic: *Akkadian*, *Habakkuk*, *Rikki-Tikki-Tavi*, *Sikkim*. The normal <C>-doubling of <k> is <ck>, which is dealt with in the <c>-rules.

Exceptions: <k>≡∅ in *Kirkby* /ˈkɜːbɪ/.

Efficiency: a core rule with a heavy workload and strong bias towards shorter words;

in words – 99 per cent (= 12 percentage points of 90 per cent correct /k/ predictions);
in names – 99 per cent (= 25 percentage points of 89 per cent correct /k/ predictions).

<l>-rules

L.1 <le>≡/əl/ | <C> — #
Examples:

- the common endings <-able>, <-ible> – *available*, *credible*, etc.;
- others – *bangle*, *bible*, *brittle*, *carbuncle*, *cripple*, *gentle*, *gurgle*, *jungle*, *meddle*, *noble*, *obstacle*, *oracle*, *pinnacle*, *quadrangle*, *quadruple*, *rabble*, *throttle*, *tinkle*, etc.; *Ambleside*, *Anglesey*, *Appleby*, *Caudle*, *Pringle*, etc.

Exceptions: with redundant <-e> – *Searle*.

Efficiency: a core rule with a heavy workload and some bias towards longer words;

in words – 99 per cent (= 8 percentage points of 90 per cent correct /l/ predictions);
in names – 72 per cent (= 6 percentage points of 89 per cent correct /l/ predictions).

L.2 <l(l)>≡/l/ – the default rule for <l>
Examples: *alcohol, alibi, alloy, atoll, bell, bullock, climb, droll, elephant, globule, kiln, lollipop, play*, etc.; *Albert, Allen, April, Atlas, Balliol, Blake, Cavell, Dallas, Eli, Flynn, Hillman, Kleenex, Llangollen* (anglicized), *Marvell, Neale*, etc.

Exceptions: <l>≡∅ in *baulk, calf, calve, caulk, folk, half, yolk*; *Anouilh, Axholme, Belvoir* /ˈbiːvə/, *Calne* /kɑːn/, *Chalfont* (var. /ˈʧɑːfənt/), *Colne, Colney, Falconer, Folkestone, Foulkes, Hainault, Holborn, Holkham, Holmes, Hulme, Lincoln, Norfolk, Ralph* (var. /reɪf/), *Renault, Rievaulx, Rolfe* (var. /rəʊf/), *Stockholm, Suffolk, Versailles*, etc.

The instances of <al> in *chalk, calm, bald, malt*, etc., before <k>, <m>, <d>, <t>, have been dealt with as strings under the <a>-rules.

Welsh <ll> represents a voiceless alveolar lateral fricative [ɬ] (*Llandilo, Llangollen*) which is usually anglicized to /l/, though some speakers try to capture it with /θl/ or /fl/ (cf. Shakespeare's character *Fluellen*, a spelling of *Llewellyn*, in *Henry V*).

Efficiency: a core rule with a very heavy workload;

in words – 99 per cent (= 82 percentage points of 90 per cent correct /l/ predictions);
in names – 78 per cent (= 83 percentage points of 89 per cent correct /l/ predictions).

<m>-rules

M.1 <m(m)>≡/m/ – the default rule for <m>
Examples: *amen, ammonia, autumn, blame, comfort, crumb, dimmer, embody, gum, gummy, lemma*, etc.; *Assam, Bahamas, Bellamy, Brahms, Cummings, Emma, Fleming, Gamage, Grimm, Jim, Jimmy*, etc.

Exceptions: <m>≡∅ in one or two Greek loans – *mnemonic, Mnemosyne*.

Efficiency: a core rule with a very heavy workload; in words – 99 per cent, names 99 per cent – the only rule for /m/.

<n>-rules

N.1 <n>≡/ŋ/ | — <g> {<a>, <o>, <u>, <C>, # }

- the context is meant to exclude the possibility of <e>,<i> or <y> following the <ng> in minimal free-forms such as *singe, stingy, tangible*, when the correspondence would be <ng>≡/nʤ/.

Examples: *along, amongst, angry, cling, dangle, distinguish, fungus, hangar, languor, quadrangle, swing*, etc.; *Angola, Bangkok, Bengal, Buckingham, Byng, Fingal, Hastings, Hungary, Ingram, Kinglake, Mongol, Rangoon, Shanghai, Tonga*, etc.

There is free variation between /n/ – /ŋ/ in prefixes ending in <n> – {con-}, {en-}, {in-}, {un-}, as in *congratulate*, *engage*, *engulf*, *inglorious*, *ingredient*, *ungainly*, *ungrateful*, etc. There may also be assimilation of /n/ to /ŋ/ at other internal boundaries – *downgrade*, *greengage*, *sunglasses*, *vainglory*, *vanguard*, etc. Place-names with two elements such as *Cairngorm*, *Dungarvan*, *Glengarry*, *Leningrad*, *Stalingrad*, have similar variation.

Efficiency: a core rule with some bias towards high TF words; heavy workload;

in words – 100 per cent (= 63 percentage points of 98 per cent correct /ŋ/ predictions);
in names – 100 per cent (= 71 percentage points of 91 per cent correct /ŋ/ predictions).

This supposes free assimilation of /n/ to /ŋ/ before /g/.

N.2 <n>≡/ŋ/ | i) — {<k>, <q>, <x>}
ii) — <c> {<a>, <o>, <u>, <C>*, # }

Conditions:

• the C* is not <h> (*inch*, *truncheon*).

These are spellings of /k/ which may condition a previous velar nasal (*link*, *vanquish*, *jinx*). The <c> only counts when followed by a vowel letter other than <e>, <i> or <y> (*bronco*, *incur*), or by a consonant letter other than <h> (*defunct*), or when final (*zinc*). Ainsworth did not cater for a velar nasal before /k/, perhaps because there are rather more spellings to give as a context than in the case of /g/. This rule could equally well be merged with N.1.

Examples: *ankle, anxious*, *anxiety*, *avuncular*, *bank*, *banquet*, *blanco*, *blanket*, *brink*, *bunker*, *canker*, *conquer*, *crinkle*, *defunct*, *donkey*, *kinky*, *larynx*, *lynx*, *rankle*, *sphinx*, *uncle*, *vanquish*, *yank*, *zinc*, etc.; *Algonquin*, *Ankara*, *Bankes*, *Banquo*, *Bentinck*, *Bronx*, *Casblanca*, *Frank*, *Gollancz*, *Helsinki*, *Inca*, *Manx*, *Vancouver*, *Yankee*, etc.

As in N.1, there is free variation in prefixes between /n/ and /ŋ/: *concave*, *conclusive*, *concubine*, *encamp*, *enclave*, *encumber*, *enquire*, *incarnate*, *incognito*, *inquest*, *unclean*, *uncover*, etc. and in names with an element boundary – *Bancroft*, *Doncaster*, *Duncan*, *Duncannon*, *Glencoe*, *Hancock*, etc.

Efficiency: a core rule with a fairly heavy workload;

in words – 100 per cent (= 35 percentage points of 98 per cent correct /ŋ/ predictions);
in names – 100 per cent (= 20 percentage points of 91 per cent correct /ŋ/ predictions).

This supposes free assimilation of /n/ to /ŋ/ before /k/.

N.3 <n(n)>≡/n/ – the default rule for <n>
Examples: *again*, *agent*, *annoy*, *anoint*, *banana*, *bunny*, *condense*, *cunning*, *den*, *inane*, *none*, *picnic*, *senna*, *tunnel*, etc.; *Ananias*, *Annie*, *Athens*, *Cannock*, *Dennis*, *Johannes*, *Napier*, *Nile*, *Thynne*, etc.

Exceptions: <n>≡∅ in *autumn*, *column*, *condemn*, *damn*, *hymn*, *limn*, *solemn*, and their inflected forms (*condemning*, *damned*), but not before a vowel in derived forms – *autumnal*, *columnar*, *condemnation*, *damnation*, *hymnal*, *solemnity*, etc.; there is also a rhetorical *damned* /ˈdæmnɪd/.

Efficiency: a core rule with very strong bias towards low TF words; fairly heavy workload; in words – 99 per cent, in names 99 per cent, – the only rule for /n/.

<o>-rules

Correspondences are dealt with in numbered rules as follows:

O.1 <oa>≡/əʊ/	O.2 <oir>≡/wɑː(r)/	O.3 <oi>≡/ɔɪ/
O.4 <oor>≡/ɔː(r)/	O.5, 7, 8, 9 <oo>≡/ʊ/	O.6, 10 <oo>≡/uː/
O.11 <or>≡/ɜː/	O.12 <or>≡/ɔː(r)/	O.13, 26 <ou>≡/uː/
O.14 <ou>≡/ə/	O.15 <ough>≡/ɔː/	O.16 <ough>≡/aʊ/
O.17, 19 <ough>≡/ʌf/	O.18 <ough>≡/ɒf/	O.20 <ough>≡/uː/
O.21 <ough>≡/əʊ/	O.22 <oul>≡/ʊ/	O.23 <our>≡/ə(r)/
O.24 <our>≡/aʊə(r)/	O.25 <our>≡/ʌ(r)/	O.27 <ou>≡/aʊ/
O.28 <ow>≡/aʊ/	O.29 <ow>≡/əʊ/	O.30 <oy>≡/ɔɪ/
O.31–34,36–40 <o>≡/əʊ/	O.35 <o>≡/ʌ/	O.41 <o>≡/ɒ/-the default.

O.1 <oa>≡/əʊ/
Before //r// the vowel is /ɔː/.

Examples: *approach*, *bloated*, *boast*, *boat*, *broach*, *cloak*, *coach*, *coal*, *coast*, *coat*, *coax*, *cockroach*, *cocoa*, *croak*, *encroach*, *gloat*, *goad*, *goal*, *goat*, *groan*, *hoax*, *load*, *loaf*, *loam*, *loathe*, *moan*, *moat*, *oat*, *oath*, *poach*, *reproach*, *roast*, *shoal*, *soak*, *soap*, *stoat*, *throat*, *toad*, *toast*, etc.; *Arbroath*, *Boadicea*, *Coates*, *Joan*, *Noakes*, *Oakeley*, *Sloane*, *Soames*, etc.; with /ɔː/ before //r// – *boar*, *board*, *coarse*, *hoar*, *hoard*, *hoarse*, *oar*, *roar*, *soar*; *Foard*, *Hoare*.

Exceptions:

- with /ɔː/ (not before //r//) – the very common word *broad* and derived forms (*abroad*, *broaden*; *Broadhurst*, *Broadway*, etc);
- the vowel of *board* is reduced to /ə/ in *cupboard*, *larboard*, *starboard*;
- hiatus with prefixes or stems ending in <o> – *coagulate*, *coalesce*, *coalition*, *coaxial*, *hypoactive*, *oxaloacetic*, *protozoa*, etc.;
- hiatus in non-English names – *Alloa*, *Boas*, *Croatia*, *Genoa*, *Goa*, *Joanna*, *Krakatoa*, *Minoan*, *Moab*, *Noah*, *Samoa*, *Shenandoah*, *Soares*, *Zoar*, etc.

Efficiency: a core rule with a strong bias towards shorter words;

in words – 94 per cent (= 7 percentage points of 53 per cent correct /əʊ/ predictions);

in names – 93 per cent (= 5 percentage points of 55 per cent correct /əʊ/ predictions).

O.2 <oir>≡/wɑː(r)/ | — { <e>, #}

Examples: a marginal rule: *boudoir*, *escritoire*, *memoir*, *repertoire*, *reservoir*, *soiree*; *Renoir*, *Lenoir*.

Exceptions: some irregularities – *choir* /'kwaɪə/; *Belvoir* /'biːvə/, but as a street name /'belvwɔː/; *Moir* /'mɔɪə/. *Lenoir* as a US town is /lə'nɔː/.

O.3 <oi>≡/ɔɪ/

Examples: *adenoids*, *adroit*, *alkaloid*, *appoint*, *avoid*, *boil*, *boisterous*, *celluloid*, *cloister*, *coil*, *coin*, *devoid*, *disappointed*, *embroidery*, *exploit*, *foil*, *goitre*, *join*, *moist*, *noise*, *oil*, *point*, *poison*, *sequoia*, *spoil*, *thyroid*, *toil*, and, if anglicized, *turquoise*, etc.; *Detroit*, *Droitwich*, *Gascoigne*, *Hanoi*, *Iroquois*, *Moira*, *Oistrakh*.

Exceptions:

- hiatus at evident boundaries – *autointoxication*, *coincidence*, *egoism*, *heroine*, *jingoism*, *oboist*, *soloist*, *Shintoism*, *Taoism*; other examples of hiatus – *coitus*, *heroin*; *Coimbra*, *Heloise*;
- §French loans with /wɑː/ or a reduced form of it – *bourgeois*, *chamois*, *coiffure*, *patois*, *toilette*, *turquoise* (if not anglicized); *Antoinette*, *Blois*, *Valois*;
- irregular – *Boivie* /'biːvɪ/.

Some consonant letters and strings found after <oi> will alert the reader to hiatus, since they do not occur after <oi>≡/ɔɪ/: <oic#> *Stoic*, <oism#> *egoism*, <oing> *doing*, *going*, etc.

Efficiency: a core rule with some bias towards low TF words;

in words – 85 per cent (= 27 percentage points of 89 per cent correct /ɔɪ/ predictions);

in names – 53 per cent (= 57 percentage points of 78 per cent correct /ɔɪ/ predictions).

O.4 <oor>≡/ɔː(r)/

A marginal rule with strong bias towards high TF words.

Examples: *door*, *floor*; also in *moor*, *poor*, *spoor*, *Dartmoor*, etc. for speakers who have /ɔː/ in these words rather than /ʊə/.

Exceptions:

- with /ʊ/ – *hooray*;
- with /ʊə/ – *boor*.

In the next six rules, Ainsworth tries to sort out the incidence of /uː/ and /ʊ/ in <oo> spellings. They have little generality, but are motivated by the high text frequency of some of the words.

O.5 <oo>≡/ʊ/ | — <k>
Examples: *book*, *brook*, *cook*, *crook*, *forsook*, *hook*, *look*, *nook*, *rook*, *rookie*, *shook*, *took*, *stook*; *Booker*, *Brook*(*e*)(*s*), *Chinook*, *Cooke*, *Crooke*, *Flook*, *Tooke*, *Wookey*, etc. In Northern England there is usually a long vowel /uː/ in all these words.

Exceptions: with /uː/ – *snook*, *snooker*, *spook* – a small subset of 'familiar' words. These exceptions make the difference between SBS /-ʊk/ and northern English /-uːk/ a difference of lexical distribution and not a general phonotactic difference that can be stated by rule.

Efficiency: a core rule with strong bias towards shorter words;

in words – 94 per cent (= 7 percentage points of 28 per cent correct /ʊ/ predictions);

in names – 99 per cent (= 9 percentage points of 35 per cent correct /ʊ/ predictions).

O.6 <oo>≡/uː/ | <f> — <d>
This Ainsworth rule to cover *food* and its derived forms is, in effect, an exception to the next rule. It is presumably justified on the grounds of text frequency.

O.7 <oo>≡/ʊ/ | — <d> #
Examples: *good*, *hood*, *stood*, *wood*, *woodbine*; the suffix <-hood> – *adulthood*, *babyhood*, *boyhood*, *falsehood*, *hardihood*, *knighthood*, *likelihood*, *motherhood*, *widowhood*, etc.; *Atwood*, *Goodwood*, etc.

Adding the # boundary prevents the rule applying wrongly to *boodle*, *doodle*, *hoodlum*, *hoodoo*, *noodle*, *poodle*, and *voodoo*.

Exceptions:

- with /ʌ/ – *blood*, *flood*;
- with /uː/ – *brood*, *mood*, *rood*; *Strood*.

Efficiency: a core rule with a very heavy workload;

in words – 76 per cent (= 10 percentage points of 28 per cent correct /ʊ/ predictions);

in names – 94 per cent (= 20 percentage points of 35 per cent correct /ʊ/ predictions).

O.8 <oo>≡/ʊ/ | { <f>, <s>} — <t>
Examples: a marginal rule for the words *foot*, *soot*; *Foote*.

O.9 <oo>≡/ʊ/ | <w> —
Conditions:

- not after the cluster <sw> (*swoon*, *swoop*).

Examples: a marginal rule for the words *woof* ('barking'), *wool*; *Woollard*, *Woolsey*, *Wootton*.

Exceptions: with /uː/ – *woo*, *woof* (in weaving); *Wooburn*.

O.10 <oo>≡/uː/ – the default rule for <oo>
Examples: *aloof*, *baboon*, *balloon*, *ballyhoo*, *bamboozle*, *bamboo*, *bassoon*, *bloom*, *boo*, *booby*, *boodle*, *boogie*, *boom*, *boomerang*, *boon*, *boost*, *booth*, *boot*, *booty*, *booze*, *cartoon*, *coop*, *croon*, *cuckoo*, *doodle*, *fool*, *googly*, *groove*, *hoodlum*, *hoodoo*, *hooligan*, *hoot*, *kangaroo*, *loot*, *moon*, *noodle*, *noose*, *poodle*, *room*, *smooch*, *smoothe*, *swoon*, *swoop*, *tattoo*, *tooth*, *tycoon*, *voodoo*; *Bakerloo*, *Bloomsbury*, *Boone*, *Boosey*, *Boothby*, *Bootle*, *Broome*, *Cameroon*, *Cooch*, *Coolidge*, *Coombes*, *Googie*, *Hooghly*, *Maynooth*, *Rangoon*, *Sassoon*, *Scrooge*, etc.

The <oo> spelling of /uː/ is not shared by /juː/.

Exceptions:

- with hiatus – *cooperate*, *oolite*, *spermatozoon*, *zoology*; *Laocoon*;
- with /əʊ/ – *brooch* (/uː/ in AmE); *Loos*, *Roosevelt* (alt. /uː/ in SBS).

Efficiency: a core rule with a fairly heavy workload and a very strong bias towards shorter words;

in words – 88 per cent (= 16 percentage points of 76 per cent correct /(j)uː/ predictions);
in names – 93 per cent (= 7 percentage points of 51 per cent correct /(j)uː/ predictions).

O.11 <or>≡/ɜː/ | <w(h)> — <C>
Examples: *whorl*; *word*, *work*, *world*, *worm*, *worse*, *worst*, *worship*, *worth*, *worthy*.

Exceptions: with /ɔː/ – *sword* and the verb forms *sworn*, *worn*; with /ʌr/ – *worry*; with /ʊ/ – *worsted.*

Efficiency: a core rule with a strong bias towards low TF words;

in words – 88 per cent (= 9 percentage points of 90 per cent correct /ɜː/ predictions);
in names – 87 per cent (= 10 percentage points of 96 per cent correct /ɜː/ predictions).

O.12 <or>≡/ɔː(r)/ | — {<C>, #}
Conditions: the <r> is not doubled, which would mark a short vowel (*borrow*, *horrible*, *torrid*).

Examples: *abhor*, *acorn*, *border*, *cantor*, *cord*, *cork*, *corner*, *corps*, *divorce*, *dormitory*, *forfeit*, *formal*, *horse*, *mentor*, *orchid*, *pork*, *shorts*, *storm*, *torso*, etc.; *Bordeaux*, *California*, *Cleethorpes*, *Corfu*, *Cornwall*, *Dorset*, *Forbes*, *Forsyth*, *Norwich* (USA), *Ormskirk*, *Portsmouth*, *York*, etc. There is reduction to /ə/ in unstressed name elements such as {-ford}, {-forth}: *Ashford*, *Beresford*, *Carnforth*, *Clifford*. The suffix <-ory> has a reduced vowel in SBS, but not in AmE.

Exceptions:

- with /ɒ/ – *Borwick*, *Norwich* (UK), where the <w> is an empty letter;
- with /ɜː/ – *attorney*.

Efficiency: a core rule with a heavy workload;

in words – 99 per cent (= 49 percentage points of 82 per cent correct /ɔː/ predictions);
in names – 99 per cent (= 48 percentage points of 84 per cent correct /ɔː/ predictions).

Without allowing reduction to /ə/ in unstressed syllables (*actor*, *camphor*, *doctor*, etc.) the efficiency would be in words 63 per cent, in names 65 per cent; if reduction is allowed, the figures reach 99 per cent.

O.13 <ou>≡/uː/ | <y> —
Examples: a marginal rule for the words *you*, *youth*; *Youmans*.
Exceptions: *young*; *Youghal* /jɔːl/, *Young*(*er*).
Your(*s*) has /ʊə(r)/ smoothing to /ɔː(r)/ for many speakers.

O.14 <ou>≡/ə/ | <V> <C_0> — <s> #
This rule deals with the adjectival suffix {-ous}.

Examples: a large number of adjectives and derived forms – *adventurous*, *ambitious*, *capricious*, *fictitious*, *graciously*, *ludicrous*, *obnoxious*, *piteously*, *righteousness*, *treacherous*, *vigorous*, etc. and a few names such as *Aldous*.

Efficiency: in words 96 per cent; a marginal rule with a fairly heavy workload. Since it deals with a common §Latinate suffix, there is some bias towards low TF words and very strong bias towards longer words.

In the next seven marginal rules, Ainsworth deals with the string <ough> and its variant pronunciations in small clusters of short words. This is worth noting as an attempt to deal with a notoriously intractable group of spellings in a rule format and not by listing, even though some rules refer to a single word. As rules, they are evidently motivated by the high text frequency of just a few words, since their overall lexical frequency is low. In names there is a great deal of free variation. The whole string <ough> is here treated as a unit. There are good reasons for doing so. The correspondences <gh>≡/f/ and <ou>≡/ɔː/ are restricted to <augh> and <ough> strings, so it cannot be said that the <gh> is always empty and the previous vowel letters have normal values.

O.15 <ough>≡/ɔː/ | — <t>
Examples: *bought*, *brought*, *fought*, *nought*, *ought*, *sought*, *thought*, *wrought*.

Exceptions: with /aʊ/ – *doughty*, *drought*. Names such as *Boughton*, *Broughton*, *Houghton*, *Oughton*, *Oughtred*, *Stoughton* have /ɔː/ – /aʊ/

variation and occasionally /uː/ or /əʊ/. Some are only given with one variant by EPD – *Loughton* /aʊ/, *Moughton* /əʊ/, but with the pronunciation of a name one can never be fully certain.

O.16 <ough>≡/aʊ/ | <b> —
Examples: *bough*; *Boughton* (also /ɔː/).
Exceptions: with /əʊ/ – *Boughey*.

O.17 <ough>≡/ʌf/ | <t> —
Examples: only the word *tough*.

O.18 <ough>≡/ɒf/ | <c> —
Examples: only the word *cough*.
Exceptions: *Ayscough* /'æskjuː/ or /'eɪskəf/; *Coughlin* /'kɒglɪn/; *Myerscough* /'maɪəskəʊ/.

O.19 <ough>≡/ʌf/ | # <r> —
Examples: only the word *rough*.
At the level of one rule per word, there might just as well be a rule for the equally common *enough*.

O.20 <ough>≡/uː/ | <r> —
Examples: only the word *through*.
Exceptions:

- with /ə/ – *borough*, *thorough*, *Bamborough*, *Marlborough*, *Scarborough*, etc.;
- with /ɒf/ – *trough*;
- *Brougham* has /uː/, /ʊ/ or /əʊə/.

O.21 <ough>≡/əʊ/ – the default rule for <ough>
Examples: *although*, *dough*, *furlough*, *though*; *Bullough*, *Donough*, *Dougherty*, *Whatmough*.
Exceptions: these are failures for the set of <ough> rules:

- with /ʌf/ – *enough*, *slough* ('cast off');
- with /aʊ/ – *plough*, *slough* ('bog'), *sough*; *Slough*;
- unstressed with /ə/ – *Willoughby*;
- quite peculiar – *hough* /hɒk/.

O.22 <oul>≡/ʊ/ | # <C_1> — <d> #
Examples: a marginal rule for the function words *could*, *should*, *would*.
Exceptions:

- with /əul/ – *mould*;
- with /uːl/ – *Gould*.

The algorithm does not have the information to simply define the class as auxiliary verbs.

O.23 <our>≡/ə(r)/ | <V> <C> — #
– final in a polysyllabic word.

Examples: *ardour*, *armour*, *candour*, *clamour*, *colouration*, *demeanour*, *dishonourable*, *enamoured*, *favourite*, *flavour*, *glamour*, *harbour*, *labour*, *neighbours*, *odour*, *parlour*, *rancour*, *savoury*, *vapour*, *vigour*, etc.; in names such as *Balfour*, *Gilmour*, *Seymour*, there can also be a full /ɔː/, but in names such as *Barbour*, *Turnour*, *Wardour*, *Wintour*, there is only /ə/ – the <-our> in these names is presumably a graphic variant of <-er>.

Exceptions:

- with /aʊə(r)/ – *devour*;
- with /ʊə(r)/ – *amour*, *detour*, *contour*;

Efficiency: in words 78 per cent; in names 94 per cent; with strong bias towards high TF words.

O.24 <our>≡/aʊə(r)/ | — #
– final in a monosyllable (after O.23).

Examples: *flour*, *hour*, *lour*, *our*, *scour*, *sour,* and their derived forms.

Exceptions: with /ɔː(r)/ – *four, pour*; with /ʊə(r)/ – *dour*, *tour*, and when stressed *your.*

The place-name *Stour*, found in half a dozen different areas of England is recorded as having /aʊə/, /ʊə/ and /əʊə/ variants.

Since the [ə] glide to /r/ is predictable, this marginal rule is really part of the default rule for <ou>≡/aʊ/ (O.27).

O.25 <our>≡/ʌ(r)/ | — <V>
– before a vowel.

Examples: a marginal rule for the words *courage*, *flourish*, *nourish.*

Exceptions:

- with /ʊ/ – *courier*, *Fourier*;
- with /ʊə/ – *Douro.*

O.26 <ou>≡/uː/ | — { <V>, # }
Examples: *bivouac*, *caribou*, *denouement*, *marabou*, *pirouette*, *silhouette*, *sou*; *Bedouin*, *Douai*, *Houyhnhnm*, *Louis*, *Louisa*, *Ouida*, *Rouen*, *Zouave*, etc.

This is a §French correspondence; some of these words may be identified as §French by other features, such as the suffix <-ette>. The /uː/ may reduce to /ʊ/ or even /w/ when not stressed: *Bedouin* as /ˈbedʊɪn/ or /ˈbedwɪn/.

Efficiency: in words 75 per cent; in names 66 per cent; a marginal rule.

O.27 <ou>≡/aʊ/ – the default rule for <ou>
Examples: *about*, *account*, *aloud*, *announcement*, *cloud*, *compound*, *couch*, *count*, *doubt*, *espouse*, *flout*, *foundation*, *grouse*, *house*, *lout*, *mountain*, *mouth*, *outfit*, *profound*, *renounce*, *round*, *scout*, *stout*, *thousand*, *voucher*,

wound (partic.); *Avonmouth*, *Backhouse*, *Dalhousie*, *Lounsbury*, *Louth*, *Mounsey*, *Oundle*, *Routledge* (also /ʌ/), *Stroud*, etc.

Exceptions:

- with /uː/ – *accoutrement*, *barouche*, *boudoir*, *boulevard*, *bouquet*, *boutique*, *cantaloupe*, *cartouche*, *cougar*, *coulomb*, *coulter*, *coup*, *coupe*, *coupon*, *couth*, *croupier*, *croup*, *douche*, *ghoul*, *goulash*, *group*, *insouciance*, *louvre*, *oubliette*, *ragout*, *recoup*, *rouble*, *rouge*, *roulette*, *route*, *routine*, *soubrette*, *souffle*, *soup*, *souvenir*, *toupee*, *troubadour*, *troupe*, *wound* (n.); *Bouverie*, *Colquhoun*, *Couper*, *Coupland*; mostly §French – see O.26;
- with /ʌ/ – *country*, *couple*, *couplet*, *cousin*, *double*, *doublet*, *doubloon*, *southern*, *touch*, *trouble*; *Blount*;
- with /əʊ/ – *moult*, *poultice*, *poultry*, *soul*; *Boulger*, *Boult*, *Boulter*, *Boulton*.

Some names have variants with /aʊ/, /əʊ/ and /uː/: *Ffoulkes*, *Joule* (as an English surname). Unstressed place-name elements may have /aʊ/ reduced to /ə/: *Bournemouth*. *Coulsdon* in Greater London has a local pronunciation /əʊ/ and a spelling pronunciation /uː/.

Efficiency: a core rule with some bias towards shorter words; fairly heavy workload;

in words – 81 per cent (= 58 percentage points of 69 per cent correct /aʊ/ predictions);
in names – 38 per cent (= 29 percentage points of 47 per cent correct /aʊ/ predictions).

This shortfall in /aʊ/ predictions is due to the large number of exceptions to O.29, which gives <ow> as /əʊ/ by default.

Some words not dealt with by the <our> rules would wrongly get /aʊə(r)/ by default here;

- with /ɔː/ – *course*, *court*, *Courtald*, *Harcourt*;
- with /ʊə/ – *bourgeois*, *bourn* (also /ɔː/), *gourd*, *gourmand*, *gourmet*, *potpourri*, *tournament*, *tourniquet*, *Courland*, *Gourlay*;
- with /ɜː/ – *adjourn*, *courteous*, *courtesy*, *journal*, *journey*, *scourge*.

There is wide and locally peculiar variation in the <bourne> element of names: *Ashbourne*, *Bourne*, *Pangbourne* vary between /ɜː/, /ɔː/ and /ʊə/; but *Eastbourne*, *Glyndbourne* only seem to have /ɔː/. *Melbourne* has /ə/ in Australia, but occasionally /ɔː/ in British pronunciations.

Ainsworth's treatment of <ow> takes the five consonant letters <c, h, n, r, v> in separate rules as contexts which determine a following <ow>≡/aʊ/, before coming to the default correspondence <ow>≡/əʊ/. In each case only a few words are involved. Here they have been merged into a single rule as follows.

O.28 <ow>≡/aʊ/ | # <C_0> {<c, h, n, r, v>} —
– in the first or only syllable of a word.
Examples:

- after <c-> – *cow, coward, cower, cowl, cowrie, scowl*; *Cowdrey, Cowley, Cowper* (also /uː/);
- after <h-> – *chow, chowder, howitzer, how, howl, shower*; *Howe, Howie, Howson*;
- after <n-> – *now*;
- after <r-> – *brow, brown, browse, crowd, crown, drown, drowsy, frown, frowsty, frowzy, growl, prow, prowl, row* ('quarrel'), *rowdy, rowel, trowel*; *Frowde* (also /uː/);
- after <v-> – *vow, vowel*; *Vowles* has both /əʊ/ and /aʊ/.

Exceptions: with /əʊ/ – *show, shower* ('agent'), *shown, Chowles, Howth*; *know, snow, Knowles, Snow, Snowden, Snowdon*; *crow, grow, grown, growth, throw, thrown, row* ('line'), *Rowland*; with hiatus – *microwave*.

The first-syllable context effectively excludes <ow> as the final syllable of a polysyllabic free-form – *arrow, furrowed, sorrowful*; *Barrow, Arrowsmith, Borrowdale*, etc. The rule shows some bias towards low TF words and very strong bias towards shorter words,

O.29 <ow>≡/əʊ/ – the default rule for <ow>
Examples: *arrow, below, bellows, bestow, billow, blow, bowl, flown, follow, furrowed, hollow, low, lower, meadow, narrow, owe, own, slow, sorrowful, widow*, etc.; *Arrowsmith, Barrow, Barlow, Borrowdale, Bowden, Bowness, Callow, Fellowes, Fowkes, Gillow, Glasgow, Hounslow, Jarrow, Ludlow, Mowbray, Towcester, Wilmslow, Yarrow*, etc.
Exceptions:

- with /aʊ/ – *allow, avow, blowsy, bowels, bower, clown, dowager, dowdy, dowel, dower, down, dowry, flower, fowl, glower, gown, jowl, owl, powder, power, renown, tower, towel, town, yowl*; *Andow, Ashdown, Bowker, Bowra, Dow, Dowland, Downes, Downing, Fowler, Hankow, Kowloon, Lowndes, Lowry, Louth, Lowther, Lucknow, Mowgli, Plowden, Pownell*, etc.;
- with a boundary – *kilowatt, towards*.

Efficiency: in words 53 per cent; in names 46 per cent; with strong bias towards high TF words.

O.30 <oy>≡/ɔɪ/
Examples: *ahoy, alloy, annoy, boy, boycott, buoy, clairvoyant, cloy, convoy, coy, coyote, decoy, deploy, destroy, employ, enjoy, envoy, flamboyant, gargoyle, joy, loyal, oyster, ploy, royal, soya, toy, viceroy, voyage*, etc; *Ackroyd, Boycott, Boyd, Boyle, Burgoyne, Croydon, Doyle, Floyd, Foyle, Hoylake, Joyce, Lloyd, Loyola, Royce, Savoy, Toyota, Troy*, etc.

Efficiency: a core rule with a strong bias towards high TF words;

in words – 100 per cent (= 62 percentage points of 89 per cent correct /ɔɪ/ predictions);
in names – 95 per cent (= 21 percentage points of 78 per cent correct /ɔɪ/ predictions).

We now deal with the long value of <o> without <e>-marking before <l> in the clusters <ld>, <lt>, <ll>, <lst> and before <st> (*bold, bolt, boll, bolster, post*). Phonetically, these contexts are a well-defined natural class. They are found mostly in monosyllabic words and derived forms. Ainsworth's rule only caters for <ld>, which is the most common.

There is no clear-cut choice of correspondence before <-st>. We are balancing *almost*, *host*, *ghost*, *most*, *post*, against *cost*, *frost*, *lost, costume*, *ostensible*, *posterior*, etc. There would be less of a problem if we could keep to /-əʊst/ within monosyllabic free-forms, but this algorithm cannot deal with the different structures of *postage–hostage*, *poster–foster*, *hostess–hostile*. By default we shall get <ost>≡/ɒst/, with /-əʊst/ words as exceptions.

O.31 <o>≡/əʊ/ | — <ld>
Examples: *behold*, *blindfold*, *bold*, *cold*, *cuckold*, *fold*, *gold*, *manifold*, *marigold*, *old*, *scold*, *soldier*, *sold*, *threshold*, *told*, *wold*, etc.; *Barnoldswick*, *Cotswolds*, *Golding*, *Goldschmidt*, *Holden*, *Humboldt*, *Leopold*, *Mold*, *Newbold*, *Oldenburg*, *Oldham*, *Southwold*, etc.;

Exceptions:

- with /ɒ/ – *doldrums*, *solder*; *Isolde*;
- with /ə/ – *scaffold*; *Arnold*, *Clissold*, *Harold*, *Reynolds*.

Efficiency: in words 93 per cent; in names 71 per cent; a minor rule with some bias towards shorter words.

O.32 <o>≡/əʊ/ | — <ll> #
Examples: a marginal rule for the words *boll*, *droll*, *enroll*, *knoll*, *roll*, *scroll*, *stroll*, *toll*.

Poll is a homograph: /əʊ/ = 'head','vote'; /ɒ/ = 'parrot'; *boll* may have /ɒ/. The vowel of the Norse loan-word *troll* has been anglicized to /əʊ/, which is perhaps an indication of the normality of <oll>≡/əʊl/ in monosyllables.

Exceptions:

- with /ɒ/ – *atoll*, *doll*, *loll*.

Dolly follows *doll,* as a derived form with <-y>, and wrongly gets /əʊ/. Words with <-olly> which do not have the simple suffix <-y> escape to the default /ɒ/ – *brolly, folly*, *golly*, *holly*, *jolly*, *lolly*, *mollycoddle*. The spelling <roly-poly> ('pudding'), which is presumably based on *roll*, avoids confusion by having a single <l>.

O.33 <o>≡/əʊ/ | — <l(s)t>
Examples: *bolt*, *colt*, *dolt*, *jolt*, *molten*, *revolt*, *volt*, etc.; *Bolton*, *Holt*, *Newbolt*, etc.; *bolster, holster*.

Exceptions: with /ɒ/ – *voltaic*. Some speakers may have short /ɒ/ in *bolt*, *volt* (LPD).

Efficiency: in words 87 per cent; in names 70 per cent; a marginal rule.

O.34 <o>≡/əʊ/ | — #
Examples: *adagio*, *ago*, *albino*, *also*, *ammo*, *armadillo*, *audio*, *auto*, *banjo*, *bingo*, *calico*, *cargo*, *ditto*, *dynamo*, *flamingo*, *go*, *grotto*, *jumbo*, *kilo*, *limbo*, *momento*, *no*, *photo*, *ratio*, *so*, *solo*, *tempo*, *tobacco*, *video*, *yobbo*, *zero*, etc.

Exceptions: with /uː/ in the function words *do* (and similarly *ado*, *outdo*, etc.), *to* (*unto*, *thereto*, etc.), *who*, the numeral *two*, and in *lasso*, which ought perhaps to be spelt **lassoo* since it breaks the regularity for lexical words.

Ainsworth's four rules for final <-o> (rules 116–119, table 41 p. 265) seem to be entirely dictated by the high TF of a few common words: *go*, *no*, *so*, and, purely in consequence, *calypso*, *domino*, *lumbago*, *torso*, *vertigo*, *volcano*. They inexplicably leave the irregular /uː/ of *do*, *to*, *two*, *who*, as the default, ignoring all the other lexical words with final <-o>.

Efficiency: a core rule with some bias towards low TF words;

in words – 99 per cent (= 9 percentage points of 53 per cent correct /əʊ/ predictions);
in names – 99 per cent (= 16 percentage points of 55 per cent correct /əʊ/ predictions).

O.35 <o>≡/ʌ/ | — <v>
Examples: *above*, *coven*, *covenant*, *cover*, *covet*, *covey*, *discover*, *dove*, *glove*, *govern*, *love*, *oven*, *plover*, *recover*, *shove*, *shovel*, *slovenly*; *Aberdovey*, *Bovey*, *Glover*, *Govan*, *Lovat*, *Lovell*, *Tovey* (also /əʊ/), etc.

Exceptions:

- with /əʊ/ – *alcove*, *bovine*, *clove*, *clover*, *cove*, *drove*, *grove*, *hove*, *mangrove*, *oval*, *ovary*, *over*, *rove*, *stove*, *strove*, *throve*, *wove*; *Bolsover*, *Casanova*, *Clovis*, *Dover*, *Hanover*, *Hovis*, *November*, *Slovak*, *Soviet*, etc.;
- with /ɒ/ – *grovel*, *hovel*, *hover*, (these three are regular with /ʌ/ in AmE); *novel*, *novelty*, *novice*, *poverty*, *provenance*, *provender*, *proverb*, *provocation*, *provost*, *sovereign*, *Covent* (*Garden*), *Coventry*, *Coverack*, etc.;
- with /uː/ – *approve*, *improve*, *move*, *prove*, *remove*.

The rule tries to capture the small group of words, some quite common, where a letter <o> has been adopted in place of <u> to prevent minim confusion before <v>. This spelling is not consistent and it inevitably conflicts with the usual function of <o>, to represent /əʊ/ and /ɒ/. Moreover, except for a few marginal words (see under v-rules), the writing system does not allow a doubled <vv> to mark a previous short vowel, since double <vv> would look too much like <w>. Surprisingly, an <-e> is used instead, so neutralizing the two normal markers of vowel length in pairs such as *clove–glove*, *clover–plover*.

Efficiency: in names 19 per cent; in names 23 per cent; a marginal rule.

O.36 <o>≡/əʊ/ | — <C> { <a>, <i>, <o>} #
The first of the sequence of general rules for long vowels. The vowel is /ɔː/ before <r>.

Examples: *aroma*, *aurora*, *carcinoma*, *coda*, *coma*, *corona*, *diploma*, *flora*, *glaucoma*, *gondola*, *hobo*, *iota*, *kimono*, *mimosa*, *pagoda*, *persona*, *photo*, *pianola*, *polo*, *quota*, *rota*, *soda*, *sofa*, *solo*, *tapioca*, *toga*, *viola*, *virtuoso*, etc.; *Angola*, *Arizona*, *Barcelona*, *Dakota*, *Desdemona*, *Dodo*, *Europa*, *Fiona*, *Formosa*, *Gorgonzola*, *Iona*, *Loyola*, *Manitoba*, *Minnesota*, *Mona*, *Oklahoma*, *Orinoco*, *Rhoda*, *Saratoga*, *Soho*, *Xhosa*, *Zola*, etc.

Exceptions: with /ə/ – *amphora*, *cupola*, *gondola*, *parabola*, *pergola*, *piccolo*, *plethora*, *tremolo*, etc.; *Catriona*, *Agricola*, *Bogota*, *Ladoga*. *Catriona* has a variant /kætrɪˈəʊnə/.

For <o> this rule has the usual long vowel value /əʊ/ (/ɔː/ before <r>), unlike the non-§Basic <a>≡/ɑː/ (*tomato*) and <i>≡/iː/ (*albino*).

Efficiency: in words 90 per cent; in names 86 per cent; a marginal rule with strong bias towards low TF words, certainly more so than in the corresponding rule for other vowel letters.

O.37 <o>≡/əʊ/ | — (<C>*) <e>* #
Conditions:

- the <C>* is not <x> (*boxing*);
- the <C>* may be <th> (*clothe*), a <Cl> or <Cr> cluster other than <ll>, <rr>, (*noble*, *ogre*), or, as the brackets indicate, it may be zero (*woeful*). Before <r> (*boring*, *sore*) the vowel is /ɔː/.
- the <e>* may be elided before the initial vowel of a suffix such as <-y> (*smoky* p. 269).

Examples: *alone*, *anecdote*, *antelope*, *artichoke*, *ashore*, *bloke*, *bone*, *bony*, *boredom*, *broken*, *casserole*, *cathode*, *chore*, *closeness*, *composed*, *condole*, *cosy*, *crony*, *devote*, *diagnose*, *dozy*, *elopement*, *envelope*, *explode*, *frozen*, *gory*, *grocery*, *holy*, *hopeful*, *hormone*, *ignore*, *microbe*, *modish*, *noble*, *noted*, *poser*, *posy*, *proneness*, *restorer*, *rigmarole*, *rosy*, *smoky*, *store*, *story*, *tadpole*, *token*, *total*, *vote*, etc.; *Athlone*, *Basingstoke*, *Bolinger*, *Coleman*, *Cromer*, *Homer*, *Moses*, *Polish*, *Rathbone*, *Rhodes*, *Walpole*, *Woking*, etc.

Examples of <oe> with no intervening consonant are: *aloes*, *doe*, *dominoes*, *floe*, *foe*, *hoe*, *mistletoe*, *oboe*, *roe*, *sloe*, *throes*, *toe*, *woe*, etc.; *Beddoes*, *Clitheroe*, *Coe*, *Cottesloe*, *Crusoe*, *Defoe*, *Faeroes*, *Glencoe*, *Ivanhoe*, *Jellicoe*, *Monroe*, *Roedean*, *Roscoe*, *Sillitoe*, etc.

In names such as *Salome*, *Volpone*, and in exceptions such as *Antigone*, *Penelope*, the <-e> represents /ɪ/ (or /iː/).

Exceptions:

- with /ɒ/ – *begone*, *bother*, *choler*, *gone*, *honest*, *moderate*, *modest*, *proper*, *scone* (also /əʊ/), *shone* (/əʊ/ in AmE), etc.; *Aristotle*, *Roger*; there is also a group of words ending in <-ish> as part of the stem, not a suffix: *admonish*, *demolish*, *polish*;
- with /ʌ/ – *anyone*, *become*, *brother*, *come*, *done*, *does*, *dozen*, *mother*, *none*, *nothing*, *one*, *other*, *smother*, *some*, etc.;
- with /uː/ – *canoe*, *doer*, *lose*, *loser*, *shoe*, *whose*; *Brome*, *Scone*, *Scrope*;
- with /ə/ – *almoner*, *anemone*, *astrologer*, *astronomer*, *customer*, *hyperbole*, *pardoner*, *summoner*; *Alverstone*, *Antigone*, *Europe*, *Gladstone*, *Johnstone*, *Maidstone*, *Penelope*, *Trollope*;
- with /ʊ/ – *Bolingbroke*, *Broke*, *Pembroke*.

The long <o>≡/əʊ/ correspondence does not have <e>-marking with the final letter clusters in *cold, roll*, *bolt*, etc., which have been dealt with by O.31 to 33.

Efficiency: a core rule with a fairly heavy workload and with some bias towards shorter words;

in words – 76 per cent (= 17 percentage points of 53 per cent correct /əʊ/ predictions);
in names – 69 per cent (= 9 percentage points of 55 per cent correct /əʊ/ predictions).

O.38 <o>≡/əʊ/ | #<C_0> — <C> ENDING
Examples and exceptions:

with <-al> – *chloral*, *choral*, *focal*, *floral*, *global*, *local*, *modal*, *oral*, *oval*, *tonal*, *total*, *vocal*, but not in *moral*;
with <-an> – *slogan*, but not in *woman*;
with <-ar> – *molar*, *polar*, *solar*, *sonar*, but not in *scholar*;
with <-on> – *boron*, *colon*, *croton*, *moron*, *proton*, *stolon*;
with <-us> – *bogus*, *bonus*, *chorus*, *crocus*, *focus*, *locus*, *lotus*;
with <-age> – *dosage*, *dotage*, but not in *homage*;
with <-ant, -ance, -ancy> – *romance*;
with <-ary> – *notary*, *rosary*, *rotary*, *votary*;
with <-ent, -ence, -ency> – *cogent*, *moment*, *potent*, *rodent*;
with <-ine> – *bromine*, *chlorine*;
with <-ite> – not *polite*;
with <-ive> – *motive*, *votive*;
with <-our> – not *colour*, *honour*.

Efficiency: in words 41 per cent; in names 33 per cent; a marginal rule.

There are similar instances in longer words: *anecdotal*, *disposal*, *pro-*

posal, etc. and suffixes other than these that might be explored, such as *gonad*, *nomad*; *bromide*, *chloride*; *acidosis*, *diagnosis*, *neurosis*.

The suffixes <-ic(al)>, <-id>, <-it> have a complementary function in that they mark a short vowel (the default) in *atomic*, *boric*, *carbolic*, *chaotic*, *deposit*, *exotic*, *florid*, *frolic*, *harmonic*, *posit*, *solid*, *stolid*, *tonic*, *vomit*, etc.; *Doric*, *Ovid*; but *chromic*, *phobic*, with /əʊ/ are exceptional.

O.39 <o>≡/əʊ/ | — <C>* <i> <V>
Conditions:

- the <C>* is not <x>, but may be <th> or <Cr>.

This captures a large number of §Latinate words; the many words ending in <-tion>, <-sion> regularly have a long preceding vowel if it is spelt <a>, <e>, <o>, or <u>.

Examples: *ammonia*, *armorial*, *begonia*, *ceremonial*, *chromium*, *colonial*, *commotion*, *copious*, *custodian*, *devotion*, *emporium*, *explosion*, *euphoria*, *ferocious*, *foliage*, *magnolia*, *memorial*, *moratorium*, *notion*, *opium*, *pandemonium*, *social*, *sodium*, *symposium*, *tutorial*, etc.; *Caledonia*, *Estonia*, *Lothian*, *Malvolio*, *Mongolia*, *Ohio*, *Orient*, *Polonius*, *Victoria*, etc.

Exceptions:

- with /ʌ/ – *onion*;
- with /ə/ – *proprietor*, *sobriety*, *society*, etc.;
- with /ɒ/ – *Sonia*.

Efficiency: in words 91 per cent; in names 88 per cent; a minor rule with strong bias towards longer words.

Having dealt with <oe> in O.37 as a final <e>-marked vowel with no intervening consonant before the <-e>, we now have to sort out the remaining examples of <oe>. There are two general categories to consider as the basis of a rule: either <oe>≡/iː/ in §Greek words such as *amoeba*, *phoenix*, or the <o>≡/əʊ/ of hiatus in *coerce*, *poetic*. In this algorithm we cannot exploit any markers of '§Greek'-ness, so we opt for the usual hiatus rule.

O.40 <o>≡/əʊ/ | — <V>
Examples: – a marginal rule: *coeducational*, *coerce*, *coexist*, *dioecious*, *hydroelectric*, *loess*, *monoecious*, *poem*, *poesy*, *poetic*; *Citroen*, *Genoese*, *Joel*, *Noel*, etc. *Loewe* is /ˈləʊɪ/.

Exceptions: with <oe>≡/iː/ – *amoeba*, *coelacanth*, *diarrhoea*, *foetus*, *oedipal*, *oesophagus*, *phoenix*, *pyorrhoea*, *subpoena; Croesus*, *Oedipus*, *Phoebus*.

Some foreign names with <oe> representing an original [ø] (a mid front rounded vowel), such as *Froebel*, *Loeb,* may have /əʊ/ as a spelling pronunciation or, as a phonetic attempt, may have /ɜː/. *Bloemfontein* has /uː/.

Examples of hiatus previously mentioned in the <o>-rules as exceptions to the complex spelling of a single vowel include: *coagulate*, *coalesce*, *coaxial*, *protozoa*; *Croatia*, *Genoa*, *Joanna*, *Noah*, *Samoa*, *Soares*; *coincidence*, *egoism*, *going*, *heroin*, *heroine*; *Stoic*.

O.41 <o>≡/ɒ/ – the default rule for <o>
Examples: in stressed syllables – *across*, *belong*, *block*, *bobbin*, *bronze*, *catalogue*, *choreography*, *confident*, *dog*, *donkey*, *glottal*, *jolly*, *obstinate*, *off*, *olive*, *plonk*, *stock*, *tonsils*, etc. Before <-st>, *cost*, *lost*, *frost*, *costume*, *ostensible*, *posterior*, are correct by default. If we assume that the stress pattern becomes apparent by a parallel process, then we would expect vowel reduction to occur in the unstressed syllables of *agony*, *anatomy*, *apron*, *atom*, *carbon*, *carrot*, *consent*, *continual*, *contingency*, *dollop*, *ebony*, *idiot*, *petrol*, *recognition*, etc.; some unstressed syllables in non-§Basic disyllabic words may keep a full vowel – *atoll*, *compost*, *micron*, *plankton*, etc.

Efficiency: a core rule with some bias towards low TF words and a very heavy workload;

in words – 74 per cent (= 72 percentage points of 81 per cent correct /ɒ/ predictions);
in names – 64 per cent (= 69 percentage points of 74 per cent correct /ɒ/ predictions).

There are a number of exceptions to the default rule (and hence to the <o>-rules as a set). In particular, no provision has been made in the rules for the following:

- <o>≡/ʌ/ in contexts other than before /v/ (O.35) – *accomplice*, *accomplish*, *among*, *another*, *borough*, *brother*, *colour*, *comfort*, *company*, *compass*, *conjure*, *fishmonger*, *front*, *frontier*, *ironmonger*, *mongrel*, *monk*, *monkey*, *month*, *mother*, *nothing*, *one*, *once*, *other*, *smother*, *son*, *sponge*, *ton*, *tongue*, *won*, *wonder*; *Monday*, etc. These exclude words such as *constable* which vary in SBS with /ɒ/ – /ʌ/. Other accents may have the default /ɒ/ in some words: *among*, *mongrel*, *nothing*, *one*, *once*, *tongue*. AmE may have /ʌ/ in *donkey*, so that it rhymes with *monkey*. In names, SBS has /ʌ/ in *Blondell*, *Bompas*, *Bromwich*, *Cadogan*, *Colombo*, *Crompton*, *Donne*, *London*, *Pomfret*, *Tonbridge*, *Yonge*;
- <ol>≡/əʊl/ finally in verbs – *control*, *enrol*, *extol*, *patrol*. One would normally expect the <V> of a -<VC># string to represent a short vowel. It would be an advantage to have them spelt with <-ole> like *console*, *parole*, or <-oll> like *unroll*. Nouns ending in <-ol> do have the default /ɒ/ – *alcohol*, *folderol*, *methanol*, *parasol*, *phenol*, *protocol*, etc.; disyllabic nouns usually have reduction to /ə/ – *carol*, *petrol*, as does *vitriol*;
- the <o>≡/əʊ/ ending of §Latinate or §Greek initial elements in compounds: *angiosperm*, *astrophysics*, *autocoder*, *baroreceptor*, *axiomatic*, *biophysics*, *carbohydrate*, *cryptogram*, *electrotherapy*, *hydrocarbon*, *idiomatic*, *microdot*, *monoplane*, *photogenic*, *physiotherapy*, *thermo-*

plastic, *videotape*, etc. This correspondence occurs at word boundaries (O.34) and indeed some of these elements are used as free forms: *auto*, *hydro*, *micro*, *photo*, *video*;

- <o>≡/əʊ/ before some instances of <-st>, as in *almost*, *host*, *ghost*, *most*, *post* (p. 350);
- other instances of <o>≡/əʊ/: *betroth*, *bohemian*, *bosun*, *both*, *brochure*, *cobra*, *cocoa*, *codeine*, *cohort*, *cologne*, *comb*, *depot*, *folk*, *gross*, *grotesque*, *kodak*, *robust*, *rogue*, *rotund*, *topee*, *troth*, *wont*, *yodel*, *yokel*, *yolk*;
- miscellaneous: with /ʊ/ – *bosom*, *wolf*, *woman*, *Boleyn*; with /uː/ *caisson*, *cantonment*, *catacomb*, *whom*, *tomb*; and the maverick spelling *colonel*.

<p>-rules

P.1 <ph>≡/f/

Examples: *alphabet*, *amphibian*, *aphid*, *asphalt*, *atmosphere*, *biography*, *catastrophe*, *cellophane*, *cenotaph*, *chlorophyl*, *diphthong*, *elephant*, *emphasis*, *lymph*, *metaphor*, *orphan*, *pamphlet*, *phantom*, *phase*, *pheasant*, *phial*, *phlegm*, *phlox*, *phrase*, *physics*, *prophecy*, *syphon*, *sphere*, *sphinx*, *sulphur*, *syphilis*, *telephone*, *typhoon*, etc.; *Adelphi*, *Asaph*, *Bardolph*, *Biddulph*, *Christopher*, *Daphne*, *Elphinstone*, *Ephraim*, *Humphrey*, *Joseph*, *MacPherson*, *Mustapha*, *Orpheus*, *Phelps*, *Philbrick*, *Philpot*, *Phyllis*, *Randolph*, *Westphalia*, etc.

Exceptions:

- with /v/ – *Stephen* (hence alternative spelling *Steven*);
- with <p>+<h> straddling a boundary – *haphazard*, *upheaval*, *upholstery*. How apparent such a boundary is varies. The word *shepherd* is an extreme example of an opaque boundary, as are the names *Clapham* and *Felpham*.

Bispham as a surname, though not as a place-name, may have /f/ instead of /p/ (LPD). This shows that <-ham>, even when reduced to /əm/, is still seen in some place-names to be an element. It also shows an appreciation of the difference between §Basic and §Greek names: <ph>≡/f/ is a §Greek correspondence and *Bispham* is clearly a §Basic name. There is no reluctance to have a similar spelling pronunciation with <sh>≡/ʃ/ in *Bosham*, *Masham*.

Efficiency: a core rule with a fairly heavy workload, with a very strong bias towards low TF words and strong bias towards longer words;

in words – 96 per cent (= 11 percentage points of 87 per cent correct /f/ predictions);

in names – 94 per cent (= 13 percentage points of 94 per cent correct /f/ predictions).

P.2 <p>≡∅ | # — { <n>, <s>, <t>}
Examples: *pneumatic*, *pneumonia*, *psalm*, *psalter*, *pseudo*, *psi*, *psittacosis*, *psyche*, *psychology*, *ptarmigan*, *pterodactyl*, *ptomaine*, etc.; *Ptolemy*.

The rule covers a few §Greek words. It has been altered to include not only the common initial cluster <ps->, but also <pn-> and the much rarer <pt->.

Efficiency: in words 100 per cent; a marginal rule with strong bias towards low TF words and towards longer words.

P.3 <p(p)>≡/p/ – the default rule for <p>
Examples: *bump*, *captive*, *copper*, *corpse*, *equip*, *grapple*, *improve*, *map*, *pimple*, *pop*, *poppy*, *pyramid*, *rope*, *shrapnel*, *tipper*, *up*, etc.; *Agrippa*, *Allsopp*, *Chaplin*, *Chappell*, *Crippen*, *Cupid*, *Dunlop*, *Europe*, *Hopkins*, *Packard*, *Palgrave*, *Pegge*, *Trollope*, etc.

There are a number of exceptions to the default rule (and hence to the <p>-rules as a set):

- with <p>≡∅ – *corps*, *coup*, *cupboard*, *raspberry*, *receipt*, *sapphire*; *Beauchamp* (/ˈbiːʧəm/; = *Beecham*), *Campbell*, *Deptford*, *Lympne* (/lɪm/; = *Lymm*), *Sappho*;
- <p>≡∅ often occurs as a natural cluster simplification in *Hampden*, *Hepburn*, *Lampson*, *Sampson*.

Efficiency: a core rule with a very heavy workload; in words – 99 per cent; in names – 99 per cent; the only /p/ rule.

<q>-rules

Q.1 <que>≡/k/ | — #
Examples: *antique*, *arabesque*, *baroque*, *barque*, *bisque*, *boutique*, *brusque*, *burlesque*, *casque*, *catafalque*, *cheque*, *clique*, *critique*, *junoesque*, *opaque*, *peruque*, *picturesque*, *physique*, *pique*, *plaque*, *statuesque*, *technique*, *torque*, *unique*, etc.; *Bisque*, *Braque*, *Cinque* (*Ports*), *Martinique*, *Monegasque*, *Mozambique*, etc.; and derived forms (*brusquely*, *obliquely*, *uniqueness*, etc.).

Exceptions: with /keɪ/ – *communique* (unless written with an acute accent).

Efficiency: in words 91 per cent; in names 100 per cent; a marginal rule with some bias towards low TF words and very strong bias towards shorter words. The length bias, measured in syllables, is rather disguised, since <que> corresponds to just one phoneme and there are few derived forms of these words.

Q.2 <(c)qu>≡/kw/
Examples: *acquire*, *adequate*, *antiquity*, *aquarium*, *conquest*, *consequently*, *enquire*, *equal*, *equipment*, *frequent*, *inadequate*, *inquisitive*, *liquefy*, *liquid*,

quack, *quadrangle*, *quaint*, *qualified*, *quarter*, *queen*, *quench*, *question*, *quick*, *quiet*, *quite*, *require*, *sequence*, *square*, *tranquil*, *ventriloquist*, etc.; *Aquarius*, *Aquitaine*, *Banquo*, *De Quincey*, *Don Pasquale*, *MacQuoid*, *Marquand*, *Squeers*, *Tarquin*, *Don Quixote*.

Exceptions:

- with <qu>≡/k/ – *bouquet*, *chequer*, *conquer*, *croquet*, *croquette*, *exchequer*, *etiquette*, *lacquer*, *liqueur*, *liquor*, *liquorice*, *mannequin*, *marquee*, *marquetry*, *masquerade*, *mosquito*, *parquet*, *piquant*, *piquet*, *quay*, *queue*, *sobriquet*, *tourniquet*, etc.; *Jaques* /ʤeɪks/ (but Shakespeare's character is /ˈʤeɪkwɪz/), *Algonquin* (also /kw/), *Arequipa*, *Bosanquet*, *Chequers*, *Esquimau* (= *Eskimo*), *Henriques*, *Iroquois*, *McCorquodale*, *Roquefort*, *Tanqueray*, *Torquay*, *Torquemada*;
- with <quh>≡/k/ – a small group of Scottish names – *Colquhoun*, *Farquhar*, *Urquhart*.

Efficiency: a core rule with a fairly heavy workload, covering some very high frequency words;

in words – 91 per cent (= 5 percentage points of 90 per cent correct /k/ predictions);
in names – 56 per cent.

Q.3 <q>≡/k/
Examples: a very marginal rule; only in exotic names – *Iraq*, *Iraqi*.

<r>-rules

Postvocalic <r> has been treated as part of a complex spelling in <aer>, <air>, <ar>, <er>, <ir>, <oir>, <our>, <or>, <ur>, with one of the phonemes /ɪə/, /ɛə/, /ʊə/, /ɑː/, /ɔː/, /ɜː/ followed by /r/ before a vowel.

R.1 <r>≡/ə(r)/ | {/aɪ/, /aʊ/, /iː/, /uː/, /ɔɪ/} —
SBS usually has a [ə]-glide after these vowels and before //r//. Cf. *tie* /taɪ/, *tied* /taɪd/ with *tire* /taɪə/, *tired* /taɪəd/.

Examples: *acquire*, *adherent*, *cereal*, *chimera*, *environs*, *esquire*, *fierce*, *fire*, *giro*, *irony*, *neuron*, *pier*, *piracy*, *require*, *steroid*, *virus*, *weir*, *weird*, etc.; *Elvira*, *Gowrie*, *Hiram*, *Moira*, *Nero*, etc.

Exceptions: /eɪ/ in recent French loan-words – *atelier*, *croupier*, *dossier*; these do not have linking /r/.

R.2 <re>≡/ə(r)/ | <C> — #
Examples: *acre*, *calibre*, *centre*, *fibre*, *goitre*, *litre*, *louvre*, *lucre*, *lustre*, *manoeuvre*, *massacre*, *meagre*, *mediocre*, *metre*, *mitre*, *ochre*, *ogre*, *reconnoitre*, *sabre*, *saltpetre*, *sceptre*, *sepulchre*, *sombre*, *spectre*, *theatre*, etc. and inflected forms in <-s> and <-d>; *Dacre*, *Petre*.

Exceptions:

- with /eɪ/ – *padre*, *emigre* (unless written with an acute accent);
- recent French loans and names, such as *genre*, *macabre*; *Le Havre*, *Lefevre*, usually have /rə/.

There may be confusion between an inflected form such as *centred* and words such as *hatred*, *hundred*, *kindred*, *sacred*. This would not be true of names such as *Alfred*, *Mildred*, which as names are not inflected.

Efficiency: in words 77 per cent; in names 40 per cent; a minor rule.

R.3 <rh>≡/r/
Examples: *rhapsody*, *rhea*, *rheostat*, *rhetoric*, *rheumatism*, *rhinoceros*, *rhodium*, *rhododendron*, *rhubarb*, *rhyme*, *rhythm*; *Penrhyn*, *Rhine*, *Rhodes*, *Rhodesia*, *Rhondda*, *Rhone*, *Rhyl*, *Rhys*, etc.

Exceptions: *myrrh* is exceptional. There is an obvious boundary in *Fairhaven*, *Fairholt*.

Efficiency: in words 94 per cent; in names 99 per cent; a marginal rule with some bias towards low TF words.

R.4 <r(r)>≡/r/ – the default rule for <r>; see pp. 55, 177.
Examples: *borrow*, *breed*, *crash*, *draw*, *grow*, *jury*, *purr*, *pray*, *sheriff*, *sherry*, *tray*, *wary*, etc.; *Barry*, *Brahms*, *Farr*, *Christy*, *Kerr*, *Storr*, etc.

Efficiency: a core rule with a very heavy workload; in words 99 per cent; in names 98 per cent.

<s>-rules

Correspondences are dealt with in numbered rules as follows:

S.1 <sch>≡/sk/ S.2 <sc>≡/s/ S.3 <sh>≡/ʃ/
S.4 <st>≡/s/ S.5, 6 <s>≡/s/ S.7–10 <s>≡/z/
S.11 <si>≡/ʒ/ S.12 <s(s)i>≡/ʃ/ S.13 <s>≡/ʒ/
S.14 <s(s)>≡/ʃ/ S.15 <s (s)>≡/s/ – the default rule.

S.1 <sch>≡/sk/
Examples: *schematic*, *scheme*, *schismatic*, *schizoid*, *scholar*, *school*, *schooner*; *Aeschylus*, *Ascham*, *Muschamp* /ˈmʌskəm/, *Scheldt* (also /ʃ/), *Schofield*, *Scholes*. In a poll conducted by Wells for LPD, 71 per cent preferred /sk-/ in *schism* to the older /sɪ-/.

Exceptions:

- with /s-ʧ/ across a boundary – *discharge*, *eschew*, *mischance*, *mischief*; *Rothschild*;
- with /ʃ/ – *maraschino*, *meerschaum*, *schedule* (AmE /sk/), *schnapps*, *schnozzle*, *seneschal*; *Herschel*, *Porsche*, *Scheherezade*, *Schiller*, *Schleswig*, *Scholl*, *Schubert*, *Schumann*, *Schwann*, *Schweppes*, etc.

Efficiency: in words 68 per cent; in names 32 per cent; a marginal rule with some bias towards low TF words.

S.2 <sc>≡/s/ | — {<e>, <i>}
Examples: *abscess*, *acquiesce*, *adolescent*, *ascend*, *ascertain*, *ascetic*, *coalesce*, *convalesce*, *crescent*, *descend*, *discern*, *disciple*, *discipline*, *fascinate*, *lascivious*, *obscene*, *obsolescent*, *omniscient*, *proboscis*, *reminiscent*, *rescind*, *resuscitate*, *scene*, *scent*, *sceptre*, *sciatica*, *science*, *scissors*, *viscera*, etc.; *Lascelles*, *Priscilla*, *Scillies*.

Exceptions: with /ʃ/ – *conscience*, *conscious*, *crescendo*, *fascia*, *fascism*, *luscious*; *Priscian*, *Roscius*. In some of these the <i> is absorbed into the /ʃ/ spelling.

Efficiency: in words 86 per cent; in names 71 per cent; a marginal rule with strong bias towards low TF words and strong bias towards longer words.

S.3 <sh>≡/ʃ/
Examples: *abolish*, *ash*, *brush*, *fashion*, *nourishment*, *perish*, *shady*, *shop*, *sponsorship*, *worship*, etc.; *Ashton*, *Carshalton*, *Cushing*, *Gresham*, *Heysham*, *Horsham*, *Isherwood*, *Kashmir*, *Lewisham*, *Macintosh*, *Pershing*, *Rusholme*, *Shanklin*, *Sheila*, *Walsh*, etc.

Exceptions:

- *Bysshe* has an irregular <ssh>≡/ʃ/;
- with a boundary – *disharmony*, *dishearten*, *dishonest*, *goshawk*, *mishandle*, *mishap*, *mishear*, and an opaque German boundary in *dachshund*. The boundary before the placename element {-ham} may be observed in a local pronunciation (e.g. *Bosham* as /ˈbɒsəm/ or /ˈbɒzəm/; *Masham* as /ˈmæsəm/), but not necessarily in the spelling pronunciation of newcomers (/ˈbɒʃəm/) or as a surname (/ˈmæʃəm/). The boundary is effective in *Cheshunt*, *Chisholm*, *Gadshill*, *Gateshead*, *Penshurst*, *Townshend*, which do not have /ʃ/.

Efficiency: a core rule with some bias towards shorter words and a heavy workload;

in words – 98 per cent (= 31 percentage points of 89 per cent correct /ʃ/ predictions);
in names – 95 per cent (= 66 percentage points of 79 per cent correct /ʃ/ predictions).

S.4 <st>≡/s/ | — {<le>, <en>} #
This rule accounts for an empty or inert <t> after <s>.

Examples:

- with <-stle> – *apostle*, *bristle*, *bustle*, *castle*, *epistle*, *gristle*, *hustle*, *jostle*, *mistletoe* (also /z/), *nestle*, *pestle*, *rustle*, *thistle*, *throstle*, *trestle*, *whistle*, wrestle, etc.; *Astle*, *Birtwistle*, *Whistler*, etc. There may be similar /t/ elision in *costly*, *listless*, *restless*, *wristlet*; *Astley*, etc. This elision is peculiar to the <le> spelling of /əl/ – cf. *bristle–Bristol*;

- with <-sten> – *chasten*, *christen*, *fasten*, *glisten*, *hasten*, *listen*, *moisten*, etc.

Exceptions: *tungsten*; *Austen*.

Efficiency: in words 99 per cent ; in names 99 per cent; a marginal rule with some bias towards high TF words.

We now come to rules to distinguish between /s/ and /z/ in consonant clusters. Ainsworth's only such rule was S.8, giving /z/ after a voiced consonant, with /s/ by default elsewhere. Voicing in clusters is rather more complex, so three extra rules have been added. Rules S.6 and S.8 are ordered to give *first*, *firs* correctly; otherwise, S.6 is really unnecessary, since S.15 gives /s/ by default.

S.5 <s>≡/s/ | # {<ab>, <ob>, <sub>} —
The <b> in these §Latinate prefixes does not make a voiced cluster /bz/ except in a very few cases.

Examples: *abscond*, *absent*, *absolute*, *absorb*, *abstain*, *abstemious*, *abstract*, *abstruse*, *absurd*, etc.; *obscure*, *obsequious*, *obsessed*, *obsolete*, *obstinate*, *obstruct*; *subsequent*, *subserve*, *subside*, *subsist*, *substance*, *subsume*, etc.

Exceptions: *absolve*, *observe* have /z/ and *absorb* may have /z/.

Efficiency: in words 99 per cent; a marginal rule.

S.6 <s>≡/s/ | — {<c>, <f>, <k>, <p>, <q>, <t>}
This covers the three very common clusters /sp/, /st/, /sk/ and the less common /sf/.

Examples: *ask*, *cast*, *clasp*, *scan*, *skin*, *square*, *sphinx*, *sport*, etc.

Exceptions: the rule may not apply in careful speech across free form boundaries: *clothespeg*, *newsprint*, *painstaking*, but is likely to in less formal registers. /s/ is the usual pronunciation in *newspaper*.

In names such as *Beresford*, *Ormskirk*, *Stansfield*, where the cluster is split by an element boundary, there may be /s/ – /z/ variation. The clear boundary in *Charlestown* /ˈʧɑːlztaʊn/ usually gives /z/, but *Charleston* has /s/, since the boundary is obscured.

Efficiency: a core rule with a very heavy workload;

in words – 99 per cent (= 28 percentage points of 78 per cent correct /s/ predictions);
in names – 96 per cent (= 25 percentage points of 76 per cent correct /s/ predictions).

S.7 <s>≡/z/ | <e> — #
Examples: *allies*, *aloes*, *caries*, *dominoes*, *monies*, *rabies*, *series*, *skies*, *tidies*, *undies*, etc.; *Amies*, *Beddoes*, *Indies*, *Jefferies*, *Ramillies*, *Surtees*, etc.

Exceptions: with /s/ – *Davies*, *Dumfries*, *Fries*, *Gillies*, *Harries*, *Herries*, *Margulies*, *Rees*, etc. Some of these have a regular spelling: *Davis*, *Harris*.

Efficiency: in words 99 per cent; in names 61 per cent; this is an inflectional spelling.

S.8 <s>≡/z/ | i) {<b>, <d>, <g>, <m>, <n>, <v>, <w>, <y>} —
ii) {<l>, <r>} — #

This represents Ainsworth's only rule for consonant phoneme clusters with an <s> spelling. He specifies the context as a previous voiced consonant; <s> in other clusters would get the default value /s/. The rule would be true for word-final {-s} inflections for plural, possessive and third person singular present tense (*dogs*, *hoards*, *pulls*, *sums*, *turns*, etc.) and so would have a high level of accuracy in text. It would often fail, however, when applied lexically to word stems. We have specified the context in terms of letters and taken 'voiced consonant' to include underlying //r// (*stars*) and <w>,<y>, as part of a complex vowel spelling (*saws*, *days*). As a simple vowel spelling, <y> is indeterminate (with /z/ in *physics*, /s/ in *chrysalis*). The distinction between speech and writing gets a little blurred here in deciding what to treat as a 'voiced consonant'. Medial <ls> and <rs> seem to give too many counter-examples – *alsatian*, *compulsive*, *cursory*, *dorsal*, *Belsize*, *Elsa*, *Forsyth*, etc., so <ls> and <rs> have been restricted to word-final position.

Examples: *adenoids*, *afterwards*, *arms*, *always*, *arrears*, *balls*, *bellows*, *bonkers*, *cars*, *cleanse*, *crimson*, *drowsy*, *fittings*, *flimsy*, *helmsman*, *jeans*, *plebs*, *summons*, *transact* (also /s/), *whimsical*, etc.; *Adams*, *Atkins*, *Barnsley*, *Brunswick*, *Evans*, *Gadsby*, *Ginsburg*, *Hensley*, *Sainsbury*, etc.

Exceptions: with /s/ – *answer*, *censor*, *compensate*, *dense*, *pensive*, etc.; *Branson*, *Dunsinane*, *Plimsoll*, etc.; there are predictable exceptions across element boundaries: *alongside*, *godson*, *jigsaw*, etc. and many involving §Latinate elements such as <con->, <in->: *consider*, *console*, *consult*, *enslave*, *inside*, *insincere*, *insist*.

Efficiency: in words 31 per cent; in names 69 per cent. This is largely an inflectional spelling.

The next rule tries out a further context for <s>≡/z/ in clusters.

S.9 <s>≡/z/| <V> — {<b>, <d>, <g>, <l>, <m>, <n>, <r>, <w>}
Examples:

- – <sm>≡/zm/ in *archaism*, *baptism*, *bismuth*, *charisma*, *chasm*, *cosmetic*, *cosmic*, *cosmopolitan*, *dismal*, *egoism*, *enthusiasm*, *heroism*, *iconoclasm*, *jasmine*, *jingoism*, *mesmerize*, *miasma*, *microcosm*, *numismatics*, *orgasm*, *osmosis*, *plasma*, *prismatic*, *sarcasm*, *seismic*, *spasmodic*, *talisman*, *truism*;

Bismarck, *Ellesmere*, *Esmond* etc. and, with a boundary, in *salesman*, *tradesman*, etc.;
- in other consonant-letter clusters – *busby*, *husband*, *lesbian*, *presbyter*, *Brisbane*, *Crosby*, *Gisbourne*, *Lesbos*, *Lisbon*, *Nesbitt*, *Wisbech*; *wisdom*, *Bethesda*, *Desdemona*, *Dresden*; *phosgene*, *Cosgrave*, *Musgrave*; *Boswell*, *Cosway*, *Griswold*, *Oswald*; *gosling* (cf. /s/ in *goose*), *grisly*, *muslin*, *quisling*, *Bisley*, *Breslau*, *Haslam*; *Basra*; *Bosnia*, *Chesney*, *Disney*.

Cottesloe is /ˈkɒtsləʊ/, but there is a spelling pronunciation /ˈkɒtɪzləʊ/. When the <th> is not pronounced, *Frithsden* is /ˈfrizdən/, but otherwise /ˈfriθsdən/.

There is free variation between /z/ and /s/ in *asbestos* and the names *Chesney*, *Cresswell*, *Glasgow*, *Glaswegian*, *Jasmine*, *Ruislip*, *Spottiswoode*, *Wesley*.

Exceptions: with /s/ – *Aisgill*, *Asgard*, *Bledisloe*, *Conisbee*, *Conisborough*, *Glasneven*, *Islip*, *Grasmere*, *Sigismund*, etc. In some of these names there is an obvious element boundary before or after the <s>.

Efficiency: in words 30 per cent; in names 69 per cent; a minor rule with very strong bias towards low TF words.

Ainsworth makes no provision for intervocalic <s>, which by default is taken to be /s/. We can test the alternative assumption that <s> between vowel spellings is /z/, but excluding prefixes such as <dis->.

S.10 <s>≡/z/ | <V> — <V>
Conditions:

- not in the prefixes <dis->, <mis->.

Examples: *abuse* (v.), *accusative*, *advise*, *amuse*, *applause*, *arouse*, *artisan*, *bruise*, *causal*, *chisel*, *composer*, *cruiser*, *deserve*, *erase*, *expertise*, *expose*, *improvise*, *museum*, *nasal*, *paralyse*, *phrase*, *presentation*, *represent*, *suppose*, *televise*, *visage*, etc.; *Ambrose*, *Arethusa*, *Boosey*, *Bosanquet*, *Brasenose*, *Caesar*, *Chinese*, *Denise*, *Elisabeth*, *Fraser*, *Griselda*, *Isaac*, *Isobel*, *Isambard*, *Kaiser*, *Louise*, *Medusa*, *Naseby*, *Susan*, etc.

There may be either /s/ or /z/ in *nausea*, *vaseline*, *Besant*, *Cusack*, *Druse*, *Livesey*. *Joseph* has /z/, but *Josephus* has /s/.

Exceptions: with /s/ – *abuse* (n.), *abstruse*, *adipose*, *base*, *carcase*, *case*, *cease*, *cellulose*, *concise*, *decrease*, *dose*, *grouse*, *kerosene*, *lease*, *loose*, *mortise*, *mouse*, *noose*, *palisade*, *paradise*, *practise*, *precise*, *recluse*, *sausage*, etc.; *Casablanca*, *Casey*, *Creasey*, *Esau*, *Feisal*, *Formosa*, *Heseltine*, *Jerusalem*, *Lusaka*, *Mombasa*, *Nagasaki*, *Osaka*, *Pasadena*, *Sisam*, etc.; and where there is a free form boundary before the <s> – *aforesaid*, *antiseptic*, *bisect*.

The rule obviously cannot cater for the functional difference between a verb with /z/ and a noun/adjective with /s/ in forms such as *abuse*, *close*, *excuse*, *house*.

There is smoothing to /zj/ or /ʒ/ after the stressed syllable in *ambrosia*, *amnesia*, *anaesthesia*, *analgesia*, *artesian*, *casual*, *fantasia*, *freesia*, *hosiery*, *usual*.

Efficiency: a core rule with a heavy workload;

in words – 57 per cent (= 33 percentage points of 74 per cent correct /z/ predictions);
in names – 49 per cent (= 15 percentage points of 78 per cent correct /z/ predictions).

The next six rules are an attempt to capture the palatalization of an underlying //s// to /ʃ/ before /j/ or a close front vowel – or, with further complications, to /ʒ/ or /ʧ/. Most instances are found with §Latinate endings such as {-sion}, {-sious}. S.11 and S.12 simply reflect, rather clumsily, two variant pronunciations of the ending <-sion>

S.11 <si>≡/ʒ/ | <V> — <on>
Examples: *abrasion*, *adhesion*, *allusion*, *cohesion*, *collision*, *conclusion*, *confusion*, *corrosion*, *decision*, *delusion*, *division*, *erosion*, *illusion*, *occasion*, *persuasion*, *precision*, *provision*, *seclusion*, *vision*, etc.

Efficiency: in words 100 per cent (= 45 percentage points of 64 per cent correct /ʒ/ predictions); a core rule for the uncommon phoneme /ʒ/ with very strong bias towards high TF words and some bias towards longer words.

S.12 <s(s)i>≡/ʃ/ | — <on>
Examples: *admission*, *commissioner*, *compassionate*, *compulsion*, *convulsion*, *discussion*, *diversionary*, *emulsion*, *expression*, *fission*, *mansion*, *passionately*, *procession*, *professional*, *succession*, *tension*, *version*, etc.

Efficiency: in words 100 per cent; a minor rule with strong bias towards high TF words and towards longer words.

S.13 <s>≡/ʒ/ | <V> — <ur> <V>
Examples: *closure*, *composure*, *displeasure*, *erasure*, *exposure*, *foreclosure*, *leisure*, *measure*, *pleasure*, *treasure*, *usury*, etc.

In formal registers, less common words such as *caesura*, *cynosure*, may have /zj/.

Efficiency: in words 98 per cent (= 19 percentage points of 64 per cent correct /ʒ/ predictions); a core rule for /ʒ/ with strong bias towards high TF words.

S.14 <s(s)>≡/ʃ/ | — <ur> <V>
Examples: *assured*, *censure*, *cocksure*, *commensurate*, *ensure*, *fissure*, *insurance*, *pressure*, *sure*, *tonsure*, etc.

Efficiency: in words 100 per cent; a marginal rule with strong bias towards high TF words and very strong bias towards longer words.

S.15 <s(s)>≡/s/ – the default rule for <s>
There are a number of exceptions to the default rule (and hence to the <s>-rules as a set):

- the function words *as*, *has*, *his*, *is*, have /z/ (cf. similar voiced obstruents in *of*, *with*);
- there is a zero correspondence <s>≡∅ medially in *aisle*, *island*, *isle*, *Basle*, *Carlisle*, *Delisle*, *Grosvenor* and word-finally in the overtly §French words and names *apropos*, *bourgeois*, *chamois*, *corps*, *debris*, *fracas*, *patois*, *Beaujolais*, *Dumas* and in *Arkansas* /ˈɑːkənsɔː/;
- <ss>≡/z/ in *dessert*, *dissolve* (cf. /s/ in *dissolution*), *hussar*, *possess*, *scissors*; *Aussie*, *Bessborough*, *Missouri*.

Efficiency: a core rule with a very heavy workload;

in words – 97 per cent (= 35 percentage points of 78 per cent correct /s/ predictions);
in names – 89 per cent (= 41 percentage points of 76 per cent correct /s/ predictions).

<t>-rules

We can begin with the string <th>, which represents either /θ/ (*thigh*) or /ð/ (*thy*). We have already seen that this fact is bandied about as an argument either for the irregularity of the English writing system or, with more justification, for its relative regularity (p. 13). Ainsworth, working with a synthesizer which could probably not differentiate [θ] and [ð] very well for the listener, simply opts for <th>≡/ð/ apart from the cluster <thr>≡/θr/. This is no doubt because of the high text frequency of deictic ('pointing') function words (*the*, *that*, *those*, *this*, *these*, *there*, *then*, *thus*, *they*, etc), which begin with /ð/.

The optimal strategy would be to assign /ð/ to deictic function words and then treat lexical words in two subsystems: §Basic words would have <th>≡/θ/ as an initial or final spelling (*thin*, *bath*), but <th>≡/ð/ as a medial spelling (*bathe*, *bother*), while §Greek words would have <th>≡/θ/ throughout (*theory*, *pathos*, *polymath*) except in some voiced clusters (*rhythmic*). Since the present algorithm cannot work with subsystems or grammatical classes, we have to rely purely on distribution, so some otherwise well-marked classes are stranded as exceptions. Ainsworth's rule that gives /θ/ in <thr> clusters, as in *anthropology*, *arthritis*, *philanthropy*, *thrash*, *threaten*, *three*, *throne*, *throng*, etc., is not really needed, even though it would be a core rule for /θ/, since it falls in with the new default. The problem now is to provide a satisfactory rule for §Basic medial /ð/.

T.1 <th>≡/ð/ | <V>* — {<e>, <ed>, <en>, <er>, <es>, <est>, <ing>} #
Conditions:

- the <V>* will include complex vowel spellings ending in <w> or <r> (*Crowther*, *farther*).

This rule captures final <-e>-marked /ð/ in §Basic words and their inflected and derived forms (*breather*, *scathing*, *tithes*) and a large group of words, mostly disyllabic, ending in <-er>. The rule covers inflections, as in *breather*, *scathing*, and the same strings ending a base morpheme, as in *farthing*, *rather*. The usual free-form suffixes can be added after the '#'.

Examples: *altogether*, *another*, *bathe*, *blithe*, *bother*, *breathe*, *brother*, *either*, *farther*, *farthest*, *farthing*, *father*, *feather*, *further*, *gather*, *heathen*, *heather*, *hither*, *lathe*, *lather*, *loathe*, *mother*, *other*, *rather*, *scathing*, *scythe*, *seething*, *sheathe*, *slither*, *smoothed*, *smother*, *soothe*, *swathe*, *teething*, *tethered*, *thither*, *tithes*, *together*, *unscathed*, *weather*, *whether*, *wither*, *wreathe*, etc. We can include the <-ern> suffix of *northern*, *southern*, here and a quasi-derivation *smithereens*. *Smooth* itself has no final <-e>.

Some of the above words are derived from §Basic words ending in <th>≡/θ/ – *teeth*, *wreath*, etc. Many of them contain letter strings that do not occur in §Greek words – <sh>, <sw>, <wr>. It is not suggested that readers are consciously aware of these details, but it is suggested that many words covered by this rule have a recognizably §Basic profile. There are similar §Basic names: *Blythe*, *Crowther*, *Hatherton*, *Hythe*, *Netherlands*, *Smithers*, *Smythe*, *Wuthering*, etc.

Exceptions: *ether*, *Luther*; in names there is occasional uncertainty: *Atherton*, for example, usually has /θ/. There are relatively few instances of words with final /-θ/ which persists before <-ed>, <-er> or <-ing> as in *berthed*, *frothed*, *unearthing*. *Bathing* is taken to be from *bathe*; *bathing* from *bath* is an exception. *Earthen* has variation between /ð/ and /θ/. The free-form boundary in *nothing*, *plaything* has to be recognized and the absence of a boundary in *atheist*. No provision is made for /ð/ in *smithy*, *worthy*, because /θ/ is usually unchanged before <-y>, as in *pithy*, *frothy*. These and other instances of /ð/ that are uncatered for end up as exceptions to T.2, the default rule for <th>.

Efficiency: a core rule, indeed the only rule for /ð/ in the absence of a rule for deictic words; in lexical words it is 90 per cent efficient, in names 68 per cent. There is some bias towards shorter words.

T.2 <th>≡/θ/ – the default rule for <th>
Examples:

- with /θr/ – *anthracite*, *anthrax*, *anthropology*, *arthritis*, *philanthropy*, *thrash*, *thread*, *threaten*, *three*, *threw*, *thrice*, *thrift*, *thrill*, *throne*, *throng*, *throttle*, *throw*, *thrush*, *thrust*, etc.; *Guthrie*, *Jethro*, *Mithras*, *Thrace*, *Thring*, *Throgmorton*;

- with a previous voiceless consonant – *aesthetic*, *anaesthetic*, *callisthenic*, *depth*, *diphtheria*, *diphthong*, *eighth*, *fifth*, *naphtha*, *ophthalmia*, *sixth*, *twelfth*; the /θ/ may be elided in *asthma*, *isthmus*;
- with initial /θ/ – *thalidomide*, *thane*, *thank*, *thatch*, *thaw*, *theatre*, *theft*, *theistic*, *thematic*, *theory*, *therapist*, *thermal*, *thesis*, *thick*, *thief*, *thigh*, *thimble*, *thin*, *third*, *thirst*, *thistle*, *thong*, *thorax*, *thorn*, *thorough*, *thought*, *thousand*, *thumb*, *thunder*, *thwack*, *thwart*, *thyroid*, etc.; *Thackeray*, *Thanet*, *Thebes*, *Thelma*, *Theseus*, *Thirsk*, *Thorpe*, etc.;
- with final /θ/ – *bath*, *beneath*, *berth*, *both*, *cloth*, *broth*, *dearth*, *death*, *earth*, *filth*, *fourth*, *froth*, *growth*, *health*, *hearth*, *heath*, *mirth*, *month*, *moth*, *mouth*, *myth*, *path*, *plinth*, *sheath*, *sleuth*, *smith*, *stealth*, *strength*, *warmth*, *worth*, etc.; *Arbroath*, *Asquith*, *Builth*, *Carnforth*, *Corinth*, *Dalkeith*, *Edith*, *Elisabeth*, *Garth*, *Howarth*, *Hesketh*, *Judith*, *Kenneth*, *Lambeth*, *Leith*, *Macbeth*, *Meredith*, *Nazareth*, *Ruth*, etc. These also include free-forms with added suffixes, as in *deathly*, *faithful*, *filthy*, *frothy*, *lengthen*, *monthly*, *truthful*;
- with medial /θ/ – *amethyst*, *anthem*, *anther*, *apathetic*, *arithmetic*, *athlete*, *authentic*, *author*, *authority*, *brothel*, *cathedral*, *cathode*, *catholic*, *enthusiasm*, *epithet*, *ethics*, *ethnic*, *ethylene*, *hypothesis*, *lethal*, *lethargy*, *leviathan*, *marathon*, *mathematics*, *methane*, *method*, *orthodox*, *panther*, *pathetic*, *sympathise*, *synthetic*, etc.; in names – *Atholl*, *Batho*, *Bertha*, *Bethel*, *Bentham*, *Cuthbert*, *Cynthia*, *Dorothy*, *Ethel*, *Hathaway*, *Ithaca*, *Jonathan*, *Katherine*, *Martha*, *Methuen*, *Othello*, *Pythagoras*, etc.

Also covered are derived and compound forms of words with §Basic initial or final <th>≡/θ/ – *bethink*, *birthday*, *forethought*, *mothball*, etc.

Exceptions:

- we have already noted the obvious group of exceptions with initial /ð/ in the deictic words *that*, *the*, *their*, *them*, *then*, *thence*, *there*, *these*, *they*, *this*, *thither*, *those*, *thus*, and their compounds *themselves*, *thereupon*, etc.;
- with final /ð/ – *booth*, *mouth* (v.), *smooth*, and usually *bequeath*, *betroth*, though this latter pair may also have /θ/; usually the /ð/ of verbs is marked by a final <e> and it would be more consistent if these, too, were spelt *<bequeathe>, *<mouthe>, *<smoothe> – cf. *wreath* /θ/, *wreathe* /ð/ (T.1); *with* is /wɪð/ in SBS, except for assimilation to /θ/ before voiceless consonants, but in Northern England it is generally /wɪθ/. As one might expect, names provide a few oddities: the name *Blyth* has both /θ/ and /ð/ (or zero), but there is also a regular alternative spelling *Blythe* with /ð/; *Louth* in Lincolnshire has /θ/, but *Louth* and *Meath* in Ireland have /ð/; *McGrath* is /mə'grɑː/ with <th>≡∅;
- with medial /ð/ – *betrothal*, *fathom*, *smithy*, *swarthy*, *worthy* (see T.1); *Botham*, *Clitheroe*, *Latham*, *Lytham*, *Swithin*. The plural *brethren* is only exceptional because it is truncated from *bretheren*. EPD has a name *Ruthrieston* with /ðr/ – possibly truncated from /-ðər-/. The ending

<thm>≡/ðm/ in some §Greek words (*algorithm*, *rhythm*) is parallel to voiced <sm>=/zm/ in *sarcasm*, etc.;

- with <th>≡/t/ – *thyme* and in some non-§Basic names from various sources – *Anthony*, *Bayreuth*, *Beethoven*, *Berthold*, *Botha*, *Gotha*, *Goethe*, *Hindemith*, *Lesotho*, *Marathi*, *Mathilda*, *Pathan*, *Thailand*, *Thames*, *Theresa*, *Thomas*, *Thompson*, *Walther*, etc. Some more common personal names have spelling pronunciations: *Anthony* as /'ænθənɪ/; some have <t> spellings: *Antony*, *Matilda*. In the ending <-ham> in names, theloss of /h/ gives effectively <th>≡/t/ – *Chatham*, *Cheetham*, *Streatham*, *Trentham*;
- the plural of words ending in /θ/ is usually regular as /θs/: *births*, *deaths*, *faiths*, *heaths*, *lengths*, *months*, *sleuths*, *smiths*. This is so of all non-§Basic words such as *hyacinths*, *labyrinths*, *monoliths*, *osteopaths*, *sabbaths*. In some §Basic words, however, the usual plural is /ðz/: *baths*, *oaths*, *paths*, *sheaths*, *truths*, *wreaths*, *youths*, though some speakers may have /θs/. Wells in a poll for LPD found 'surprisingly' that half his informants preferred /bɑːθs/. Some had /θs/ for 'acts of bathing' and /ðz/ for 'bathtubs', 'bathhouses'. LPD gives preference to /θs/ in *births*, *broths*, *cloths*, *hearths*, *laths*, but notes /ðz/ as a possible variant, sometimes dialectal. *Moths* may have /ðz/ as an American pronunciation;
- where a boundary splits the <th> – *goatherd*, *knighthood*, *lighthouse*, *outhouse*, *penthouse*, *posthaste*, *posthumous*, *sweetheart*; *Fonthill*, *Spithead*, etc.

We should also take into account that the tongue-twisting sequence /sθm/ is almost always reduced to /sm/ in *asthma* and *isthmus*.

Efficiency: a core rule, indeed the only rule for /θ/, with strong bias towards low TF words and towards longer words; in words it is 93 per cent efficient; in names 84 per cent.

T.3 <tch>≡/ʧ/

Examples: *batch*, *bitch*, *blotch*, *butcher*, *catch*, *clutch*, *crotch*, *crutch*, *despatch*, *ditch*, *etch*, *fetch*, *hatch*, *hatchet*, *hitch*, *itch*, *kitchen*, *latch*, *match*, *notch*, *patch*, *pitcher*, *ratchet*, *scratch*, *sketch*, *snatch*, *stitch*, *stretch*, *switch*, *thatch*, *twitch*, *watch*, *witch*, *wretch*, etc.; *Aitchison*, *Batchelor* [*sic*], *Bletchley*, *Cesarewitch*, *Cratchit*, *Dutch*, *Hitchin*, *Hutchinson*, *Kitchener*, *Mitchell*, *Redditch*, *Ritchie*, *Saskatchewan*, *Thatcher*, etc.

Since <tch> does not appear initially in §Basic words, the initial <tch> of *Tchad*, *Tchaikovsky*, marks these names as §Exotic.

Efficiency: a core rule with a very strong bias towards shorter words;

in words – 100 per cent (= 13 percentage points of 91 per cent correct /ʧ/ predictions);
in names – 100 per cent (= 15 percentage points of 85 per cent correct /ʧ/ predictions).

T.4 <tz>≡/ts/
Examples: a marginal rule – *blitz*, *chintz*, *howitzer*, *quartz*, *seltzer*; in *waltz* there is variation between /s/ and /ts/. German names – *Austerlitz*, *Berlitz*, *Horowitz*, *Kreutzer*, *Rosencrantz*, *Switzerland*, and names with the prefix <Fitz-> – *Fitzgerald*, *Fitzpatrick*, *Fitzroy*, etc.

The next few rules deal with palatalization of /t/ to /ʧ/.

T.5 <tur>≡/ʧə(r)/ | <V> <C_0> — <V>
Examples: *adventure*, *adventurer*, *agriculture*, *architecture*, *capture*, *conjecture*, *creature*, *culture*, *departure*, *expenditure*, *feature*, *fixture*, *fracture*, *furniture*, *future*, *gesture*, *horticulture*, *lecturer*, *literature*, *manufacturer*, *miniature*, *mixture*, *moisture*, *nature*, *pasture*, *picture*, *posture*, *puncture*, *rapture*, *sculpture*, *signature*, *temperature*, *texture*, *vulture*, etc. and forms with other vowel-initial endings <-al>, <-ate>, <-ist>, <-ous>, <-y>, etc. – *agricultural*, *adventurous*, *century*, *futuristic*, *natural*, *saturate*, *structural*, etc.

Exceptions: with /tjʊə/ or /ʧʊə/ – *immature*, *mature*, *overture*, *premature*; *Angostura*.

Efficiency: a core rule; in words – 85 per cent (= 13 percentage points of 91 per cent correct /ʧ/ predictions).

T.6 <t>≡/ʧ/ | — <u> <V> (OPT.)
This is an optional rule (*punctual* as /-ʧʊəl/ or /-tjʊəl/).

Examples: *actual*, *conceptual*, *contemptuous*, *estuary*, *eventual*, *factual*, *fatuous*, *fluctuate*, *gargantuan*, *habitual*, *impetuous*, *intellectual*, *mortuary*, *mutual*, *perpetual*, *presumptuous*, *punctuate*, *ritual*, *sanctuary*, *situated*, *spiritual*, *statue*, *virtuous*, etc.; *Cophetua*, *Mantua*, *Septuagint*, *Stuart*, *Tuesday*, etc.

Efficiency: a core rule; in words – 100 per cent. Since it applies in common §Latinate suffixes, it has some bias towards longer words.

T.7 <t>≡/ʧ/ | <s> — <io>
This is a marginal rule with very strong bias towards high TF words and towards longer words, since this is in effect the ending <-ion>.

Examples: *combustion*, *congestion*, *digestion*, *exhaustion*, *question*, etc.

Exceptions: *bastion*.

If the context were generalized as — <i> <V>, the take-up would wrongly include unassimilated /t/ in words such as *bestial*, *celestial*, *fustian*, *nastier*, *Sebastian*, etc.

T.8 <t>≡/ʃ/ | — <iat>
This rule differs from the next since the <i> stays as a vowel. It is a marginal rule with strong bias towards low TF words and very strong bias towards longer words.

Examples: *differentiate*, *ingratiate*, *initiate*, *negotiate*, *propitiate*, *satiate*, *substantiate*, *vitiate*, etc. and derived forms with <-ative>, <-atory>, <-ator>.

T.9 <ti>≡/ʃ/ | — {<a>, <e>, <o>}
Here the <i> can be taken as part of the /ʃ/ spelling in a number of §Latinate suffixes.

Examples:

- the common ending <-tion> – *abbreviation*, *abolition*, *accusation*, *action*, *addition*, *affection*, *convention*, *construction*, *devotion*, *promotion*, etc.;
- other endings – *bumptious*, *cautious*, *confidential*, *conscientious*, *credentials*, *deferential*, *dementia*, *dissentient*, *essential*, *evidential*, *fractious*, *gentian*, *impatience*, *inertia*, *infectious*, *martial*, *militia*, *nuptials*, *palatial*, *partial*, *patient*, *potential*, *prudential*, *quotient*, *spatial*, *vexatious*, etc; *Aleutian*, *Croatian*, *Diocletian*, *Domitian*, *Egyptian*, *Haitian*, *Lilliputian*, *Titian*, *Venetian*, etc. *Scrumptious* may have /ʃ/ or /ʧ/. The rule works in these particular §Latinate endings; with other endings it will fail.

Exceptions:

- the suffixes <-er> (*frontier*), <-eth> (*fortieth*), <-able> (*pitiable*); occasional names such as *Antioch*;
- where the /t/ of a personal name is preserved before the suffix – *Gilbertian*, *Kantian*;
- where the vowel after the <i> is stressed – *Christiana*, *Santiago*, *Tatiana*;
- *cation* (cf. *anion*) has /ˈkætaɪən/.

A similar rule for <te>≡/ʧ/ would be needed for *righteous*.

Efficiency: a core rule with a heavy workload with a very strong bias towards longer words;

in words – 96 per cent (= 47 percentage points of 89 per cent correct /ʃ/ predictions);
in names – 73 per cent (= 8 percentage points of 79 per cent correct /ʃ/ predictions).

T.10 <t(t)>≡/t/ – the default rule for <t>.
There are a number of exceptions to the default rule (and hence to the <t>-rules as a set):

- there is a zero correspondence for final <-t> in §French words and names – *argot*, *ballet*, *beret*, *bouquet*, *buffet*, *cabaret*, *cachet*, *chalet*, *crochet*, *croquet*, *debut*, *depot*, *gourmet*, *mot*, *parquet*, *ragout*, *rapport*, *ricochet*, *sabot*, *sachet*, *tourniquet*, *tricot*; *Bizet*, *Camembert*, *Chevrolet*, *Margot*, *Peugeot*, *Renault*, *Roquefort*, etc., and for medial <t> in *mortgage*;
- cluster simplification also gives <t>≡∅ in *chestnut*, *lastly*, *nestling*, *waltz*, *Christmas*.

Efficiency: a core rule with a very heavy workload; in words – 99 per cent; in names – 99 per cent.

<u>-rules

There is predictable variation in the long vowel values of <u>. After <l>, <r> and after spellings representing a palatal, such as <ch> or <j>, there is no palatal /j/ glide before the /uː/. Compare /uː/, /ʊə/, in *rule*, *lute*, *lurid*, *June*, *anchusa*, with /juː/, /jʊə/, in *mule*, *repute*, *cure*, *tune*. In AmE the /j/ tends also to be dropped after <d>, <t>, <n>, <s>, representing alveolar consonants, as in *dune, tune, nude, assume* (see p. 200). This predictable variation between /juː/ and /uː/ will not be split into separate pairs of rules.

U.1 <ui>≡/uː/
Conditions:

- in initial or final syllables;
- not before <d>,<n> (*fluid*, *ruin*; *Druid*, *Bruin*).

Examples: a marginal rule: *bruise*, *bruit*, *cruise*, *fruit*, *juice*, *recruit*, *sluice*, *suit* and derived forms.

Exceptions: suite /swiːt/.

This rule is worth the attempt, since it tries to account for some quite common words. Lexically, however, <ui> most commonly represents a hiatus /uː-ɪ/ in §Latinate words such as *casuistic*, *continuity*, *fluid*, *ingenuity*, *suicide*. The conditions eliminate a good many of these. The /uː-ɪ/ of *fruition* may trap the reader, since <fruit> does not have its isolate pronunciation. The <u> has been taken out as part of the consonant spelling in *build*, *guild*.

U.2 <ur>≡/ɜː(r)/ | — { <C>*, (<r>) # }
Conditions:

- the <C>* does not include <r> (*hurry*).

The rule applies before a consonant letter (*burn*), unless it is a further <r>. It also applies before a boundary, where there may be <C>-doubling (*recur, purr*). The boundary allows <-rr-> in inflected forms (*recurred, recurring*).

Examples: *burden*, *burglar*, *burn*, *church*, *curl*, *curse*, *curtain*, *disturb*, *excursion*, *fur*, *furniture*, *hurt*, *larkspur*, *murder*, *nursery*, *purple*, *purpose*, *purr*, *recur*, *suburb*, *surgeon*, *survey*, *turbine*, *urgent*, etc.; *Bathurst*, *Burgoyne*, *Burke*, *Burma*, *Churchill*, *Curzon*, *Gurkha*, *Hapsburg*, *Hurd*, *Hurford*, *Kilburn*, *Murdoch*, *Purcell*, *Swinburne*, *Turkey*, *Ursula*, etc.

Exceptions: with /ʌ/ – *Durham*. The place name element <burgh> is troublesome: it represents /ɜː/ in *Burghley*, /ɜːg/ in *Pittsburgh*, /bərə/ in *Edinburgh*, *Fraserburgh*, *Happisburgh* /ˈheɪzbərə/, *Helensburgh*, *Jedburgh*, *Musselburgh*, *Newburgh*, and as *Burgh* it may be /bɜːg/, /ˈbʌrə/, or /brʌf/.

Since /ɜː/ and /ə/ are so similar in vowel quality, it does not seem to matter for the reader whether unstressed syllables (*liturgy*, *penury*, *sulphur*;

Aylesbury) are tentatively read with /ɜː/ rather than /ə/ – *murmur* as */ˈmɜːmɜː/.

Efficiency: a core rule with a fairly heavy workload;

in words – 100 per cent (= 24 percentage points of 90 per cent correct /ɜː/ predictions);
in names – 95 per cent (= 37 percentage points of 96 per cent correct /ɜː/ predictions).

U.3 <u>≡/ʌ/ | # — <n>
This represents the common prefix <un->, which can be freely added to adjectives and verbs. There is naturally very strong bias towards low TF words and some bias towards longer words.

Examples: *unable*, *unaffected*, *undone*, *uneven*, *unforgettable*, *unidentified*, *uninformed*, *uninspired*, *unusual*, etc.

Exceptions: with /juː/ – *unanimous*, *unicorn*, *uniform*, *unify*, *unilateral*, *unique*, *union*, *unison*, *unit*, *unity*, *universe*, *university*, etc. These all have Latin *unus* 'one' in their etymology, but that is too remote to be exploited semantically by the common reader. Nor can we profitably hive off the string <uni-> in a previous rule, since there are too many words beginning with <i> to which <un-> can be prefixed (*unideal*, *unimpaired*, *uninvited*, etc.). There is an outside chance of reading *unideal* as */ˈjuːnɪdiːl/ perhaps, but otherwise this would be prevented by the irregularity of the 'initial' consonant string after the mistaken *<uni-> boundary: *<-mpaired>, *<-nvited>.

We now explore the long vowel value of single <u> as /juː/ or /uː/. The /j/ glide does not occur after /r/ or palatals /ʃ ʒ ʧ ʤ/ in SBS and AmE (*rule, chute, June*). Most speakers also have /uː/ rather than /juː/ after /l/ (*ludicrous*). AmE speakers usually do not have the /j/ glide after /t d n s/ (p. 200). /tj/ and /dj/ frequently palatalize into /ʧ/ and /ʤ/ (*tune*, *dune*).

U.4 <u>≡/(j)uː/ | — (<C>*) <e>* #
Conditions:

- the <C>* is not <x> (*fluxing*);
- the <C>* may be a <Cl> or <Cr> cluster other than <ll>, <rr> (*scruple*, *lucre*), or <th> (*Luther*), or, as the brackets indicate, it may be zero (*glue*);
- the <e>* may be elided before the initial vowel of a suffix as in *plumy*, *tubing* (p. 269).

The vowel glides on to a following //r// to give /(j)ʊə(r)/ (*endure*).

Examples: *accuse*, *alluring*, *amusing*, *brute*, *brutish*, *commune*, *computer*, *consumer*, *cured*, *demure*, *dispute*, *duly*, *duty*, *fury*, *globule*, *gluten*, *introduce*, *minute* (adj.), *module*, *perfume*, *polluted*, *pure*, *puny*, *reputed*, *ruby*, *secluded*, *tuner*, *truly*, etc.; *Bruce*, *Danube*, *Gertrude*, *Jude*, *June*, *Kruger*, *Luke*, *Neptune*, *Shute*, etc.

Examples of <ue> with no intervening consonant are: *accrue, avenue, barbecue, blue, clue, continue, cue, due, ensue, flue, glue, hue, issue, pursue, rescue, revenue, statue, subdue, tissue, true, value, virtue*; *Bellevue, Fortescue. Donohue* has either /-hu:/ or /-hju:/.

Exceptions:

- with /ɪ/ – *busy, lettuce, minute* (n.);
- with /ʌ/ – *butler, punish, study*; *Anstruther, Carruthers, Wuthering*;
- some unstressed syllables may have reduction to /ə/ – *fortune*.

The regular <ue> of *argue* and *Montague* fails because the <u> is pre-empted by G.4 <gu>≡/g/ – cf. *fatigue, plague, rogue*.

Efficiency: a core rule with a fairly heavy workload and with some bias towards high TF words;

in words – 93 per cent (= 20 percentage points of 76 per cent correct /(j)u:/ predictions);
in names – 24 per cent (= 6 percentage points of 51 per cent correct /(j)u:/ predictions).

U.5 <u>≡/(j)u:/ | — <C>* ENDING
Conditions:

- the <C>* may be a <Cr> cluster (*hubris*).

Examples and exceptions:

with <-al> – *brutal, ducal, frugal*;
with <-an> – *human*;
with <-ar> – *lunar*, but not in *sugar*;
with <-is> – *hubris*;
with <-us> – *humus, lupus, mucus*;
with <-acy> – *lunacy*;
with <-ant, -ance, -ancy> – *mutant*;
with <-ary> – not in *sugary*;
with <-ent, -ence, -ency> – *lucent, prudent, student*;
with <-ine> – *supine*;
with <-our> – *humour, rumour, tumour*.

Efficiency: in words 94 per cent; in names 74 per cent; a marginal rule.

Unlike the other vowel letters <a>, <e>, <i>, <o>, the letter <u> does not represent a short vowel before the endings <-Cid> and <-Cit> (*lucid, lurid, putrid, stupid, cubit, unit*). These will be exceptions to the default rule.

U.6 <u>≡/(j)u:/ | — <C>* <i> <V>
Conditions:

- the <C>* is not <x>.

This captures a large number of §Latinate words; the many words ending in <-tion>, <-sion> regularly have a long preceding vowel if it is spelt <a>, <e>, <o>, or <u>.

Examples: *communion*, *conclusion*, *crucial*, *delusion*, *dubious*, *enthusiasm*, *junior*, *minutiae*, *peculiar*, *pollution*, *studio*, etc.; *Andalusia*, *Confucius*, *Julia*, *Julian*, *Julius*, *Mancunian*, *Mercutio*, *Nubia*, etc.

Exceptions:

- with /ʌ/ – *bunion*;
- with /ʊ/ – *Margulies*.

Efficiency: a core rule; since the rule is largely involved with §Latinate suffixes, there is some bias towards high TF words and very strong bias towards longer words;

in words – 95 per cent (= 5 percentage points of 76 per cent correct /(j)uː/ predictions);
in names – 95 per cent (= 3 percentage points of 51 per cent correct /(j)uː/ predictions).

U.7 <u>≡/(j)uː/ — <V>
Examples: *affluent*, *annual*, *casual*, *cruel*, *dual*, *duel*, *fluent*, *fuel*, *genuine*, *influenza*, *sensual*, *sinuosity*, *tenuous*, *truant*, *vacuum*, etc.; *Bruin*, *Emanuel*, *February*, *January*, *Papua*, *Samuel*, etc. Some of these will be smoothed to /ʊə/.

Exceptions: with /w/ – *assuage*, *dissuade*, *persuade*, *suave*, *suede*; *Suetonius*, *Venezuela*, etc.

Efficiency: a core rule;

in words – 82 per cent (= 9 percentage points of 76 per cent correct /(j)uː/ predictions);
in names – 56 per cent (= 2 percentage points of 51 per cent correct /(j)uː/ predictions).

There is a problem with the short-vowel values of <u> for speakers of SBS and regional accents in England south of a line running roughly from the Wash to the Severn. The historical correspondence <u>≡/ʊ/ has been complicated by a phonemic split (Wells 1982:196 'the FOOT-STRUT split'). The SBS default correspondence is <u>≡/ʌ/. The words spelt with <u> which retain a /ʊ/ frequently have some lip articulation or protrusion in adjacent consonants /p, b, ʃ, ʧ/ – *bull*, *push*, *put*, *butcher*, etc. This is not, however, consistent enough to form the basis of a spelling rule. Before the default rule, there are some very common affixes which can be worth taking out.

U.8 <u>≡/ʊ/ | <f> — <l>
A marginal rule capturing *full* and the common suffixes <-ful>, <-fully>, <-fulness>. This actually represents 7 percentage points of 28 per cent correct /ʊ/ predictions.

Examples: *awful*, *awfully*, *awfulness*, etc.; the /ʊ/ often reduces to /ə/ or merges in a syllabic /l/, except in nouns – *armful*, *basketful*, *bellyful*, *cupful*, *glassful*, *pailful*, *spoonful*, etc., where the /ʊ/ remains.

Because of the frequency of this §Basic string, readers may wrongly read /ʊ/ instead of /ʌ/ in §Latinate words – *fulcrum*, *fulminate*, *fulvous*, *Fulvia*. Indeed *fulcrum* does have a variant with /ʊ/. On the other hand, the /ʊ/ in *fulsome*, *Fulham*, is marked as §Basic by the endings. There are no system clues to help the reader with *fulmar*, which is in fact also §Basic (from Norse).

U.9 <u>≡/ə/ | <i> —
Deals with the /ɪə/ of §Latinate endings such as <-ius>, <-ium>.

Examples: *auditorium*, *calcium*, *chromium*, *cranium*, *delirium*, *genius*, *geranium*, *gymnasium*, *medium*, *opium*, *pandemonium*, *radium*, *radius*, *stadium*, *tedium*, *triumph*, *uranium*, etc.; *Aquarius*, *Byzantium*, *Claudius*, *Elysium*, *Julius*, *Marius*, *Sibelius*, etc.

The preceding <i> may be merged with the previous consonant by palatalization – *Belgium* /-ʤəm/, *Mauritius* /-ʃəs/.

Efficiency: in words 92 per cent; in names 95 per cent; a marginal rule with strong bias towards low TF words.

U.10 <u>≡/ʌ/ – the default rule for <u>
Examples: *abrupt, adjust*, *annul*, *begun*, *blunder*, *brush*, *buffalo*, *butter*, *crux*, *cuddle*, *cuff*, *curry*, *dumdum*, *dungeon*, *dumb*, *dung*, *fluff*, *flurry*, *hubbub*, *hundred*, *hurry*, *husband*, *judge*, *luggage*, *mud*, *plump*, *sculpt*, *sulk*, *truncate*, *up*, *viaduct*, etc. There are many common words with <u>≡/ʌ/, but no statistical bias to high TF, since they are offset by a great many §Latinate words: *indulgence*, *presumptuous*, *sublimate*, *subterfuge*, etc.

There are a number of exceptions to the default rule (and hence to the <u>-rules as a set):

- the main class of exceptions are those words which avoided the change of original /ʊ/ to /ʌ/ in the seventeenth century: *ambush*, *bull*, *bullion*, *bulrush*, *bulwark*, *bush*, *bushel*, *butcher*, *cuckoo*, *cushion*, *fulfil*, *fulsome*, *hurrah*, *hurray*, *hussar*, *pudding*, *pull*, *pulpit*, *push*, *puss*, *put*; recent introductions with similar contexts such as *cushy*, *sputnik* also tend to have /ʊ/. If the boundary is recognized in words such as *blurry*, *demurring*, *furring*, *furry*, they will have been given /ɜː/ by U.2, leaving hurry, scurry, for the /ʌ/ default;
- §Latinate words with a long vowel /(j)uː/ before a plosive and liquid cluster – *cuprous*, *duplicate*, *duplicity*, *lubricate*, *lucrative*, *nutrition*, *putrid*, *rubric*, *supra-*;
- others with /(j)uː/– *debut*, *fuchsia*, *impugn*, *truth*.

Efficiency: a core rule with a heavy workload;
in words – 66 per cent (= 19 percentage points of 45 per cent correct /ʌ/ predictions);

in names – 66 per cent (= 14 percentage points of 17 per cent correct /ʌ/ predictions).

<v>-rules

V.1 <v(v)>≡/v/ – the default rule for <v>
Examples: *active*, *advise*, *alive*, *chivy*, *civil*, *covet*, *crave*, *delve*, *dove*, *even*, *ivy*, *lever*, *salvo*, *sever*, *vex*, *virtue*, *volley*, etc. Examples with <vv> are rare and usually abbreviations or slang: *bovver* ('bother'), *civvy* ('civilian'), *revving*, *savvy*, etc.

The <v> of German names is anglicized as /v/ and German <w> as /w/, so *Volkswagen* has the spelling pronunciation /ˈvɒlkswægən/ (LPD) instead of an easy phonetic matching /ˈfɒlksvɑːgən/.

Efficiency: a core rule with virtual 100 per cent efficiency in words and names and with a heavy workload.

<w>-rules

W.1 <wh>≡/h/ | — <o>
Examples: *who*, *whom*, *whose*, *whole*, *whoop*, *whore*.

Exceptions: with /w/ – *whoa*, *whoopee*, *whopper*, *whopping* (cf. *Wapping*), *whorl*, *whortleberry*.

Efficiency: in words 81 per cent, including compound words such as *whoever*, *wholesome* ; a marginal rule.

W.2 <wh>≡/w/
AmE, Irish and Scottish speakers will usually have a voiceless /hw/.

Examples: *overwhelm*, *whack*, *whale*, *wham*, *wharf*, *wheat*, *wheedle*, *wheel*, *wheeze*, *whelk*, *whelp*, *wherry*, *whet*, *whey*, *whiff*, *whig*, *whim*, *whine*, *whip*, *whisker*, *white*, etc.

Efficiency: a core rule with a strong bias towards high TF words and strong bias towards shorter words;

in words – 100 per cent (= 6 percentage points of 63 per cent correct /w/ predictions);
in names – 100 per cent (= 6 percentage points of 89 per cent correct /w/ predictions).

W.3 <w>≡∅ | — <r>
Examples: *awry*, *wrack*, *wraith*, *wrangle*, *wrap*, *wrath*, *wreak*, *wreath*, *wreathe*, *wreck*, *wren*, *wrench*, *wrest*, *wrestle*, *wretch*, *wrist*, *write*, *wrought*, *wry*, etc.

Efficiency: in words 100 per cent; in names 100 per cent; a marginal rule with some bias towards high TF words and very strong bias towards shorter words.

W.4 <w>≡/w/ – the default rule for <w>
Examples: *away*, *beware*, *dwell*, *swear*, *twice*, *wander*, *went*, *will*, *window*, *word*, etc.; *Baldwin*, *Cotswold*, *Kuwait*, *Webb*, *Wembley*, *William*, *Wyld*, etc.

The letter <w> forms part of the complex vowel spellings <aw>, <ew>, <ow> as an auxiliary letter.

There are a number of exceptions to the default rule (and hence to the <w>-rules as a set):

- <w> represents a vowel /u/ in Welsh placenames such as *Bettws*, *Clwyd*, *Ebbw*;
- the <w> of the unstressed place-name elements <-wick>, <-wich>, represents an elided /w/ in *Alnwick*, *Berwick*, *Beswick*, *Borwick*, *Bromwich*, *Chiswick*, *Dulwich*, *Greenwich*, *Keswick*, *Norwich*, *Warwick*, *Woolwich*, etc. – cf. also *Mainwaring* /ˈmænərɪŋ/;
- <w> in German names represents /v/ – *Volkswagen*, *Wagner*, *Weber*, *Weimar*;
- <w>≡∅ in *sword*.

Efficiency: a core rule with some bias towards shorter words and a heavy workload;

in words – 96 per cent (= 57 percentage points of 63 per cent correct /w/ predictions);
in names – 90 per cent (= 83 percentage points of 89 per cent correct /w/ predictions).

<x>-rules

X.1 <x>≡/z/ | # —
Examples: – a marginal rule: *xenon*, *xenophobia*, *xylophone* and a few other §Greek scientific terms; *Xanadu*, *Xanthippe*, *Xavier*, *Xenia*, *Xenophon*, *Xerxes*.

Exceptions: *Xhosa* – the initial lateral click sound is anglicized as /k/. The <X> of the abbreviation *Xmas* represents the cross as an ikon of {Christ}; it sometimes attracts a spelling pronunciation /ˈeksməs/ – cf. *X-ray*.

X.2 <x>≡/gz/ | #<e> — <V>
The prefix <ex-> has a variant with voiced consonants before a vowel, usually in unstressed syllables, but the incidence varies from speaker to speaker.

Examples: with unstressed /egz/ or /ɪgz/ – *exact*, *exaggerate*, *exalt*, *examine*, *example*, *executive*, *exempt*, *exert*, *exhibit*, *exhort*, *exist*, *exonerate*, *exotic*, *exult*, etc. *Exhaust* /ɪgˈzɔːst/ belongs here in the absence of /h/.

Exceptions: with stressed /ˈeks/ – *execrate*, *execute*, *exercise*, *exodus*, *Exeter*, etc.

Efficiency: in words 64 per cent; a marginal rule with strong bias towards high TF words and strong bias towards longer words.

X.3 <x>≡/ks/ – the default rule for <x>.
Examples: *axe*, *boxing*, *extra*, *fox*, *mixture*, *orthodox*, *praxis*, *texture*, *vixen*, *wax*, etc.

Exceptions: before <i> or <u> the <x> may represent /kʃ/ rather than /ks/ because of palatal assimilation: *anxious*, *connexion*, *flexure*, *luxury*, etc.

Efficiency: in words 94 per cent; in names 83 per cent; a core rule with fairly heavy workload.

<y>-rules

Y.1 <y>≡/j/ | {#, <n>} — <V>
The consonantal value of <y>. The <y> of <ay>,<ey>,<oy> has been read as an auxiliary letter in the vowel spelling of *betrayal*, *conveyance*, *joyous*, etc.

Examples:

- word-initial – *yacht*, *yak*, *yam*, *yank*, *yap*, *yard*, *yarn*, *yarrow*, *yashmak*, *yawl*, *yawn*, *yaws*, *yea*, *yeah*, *year*, *yearn*, *yeast*, *yell*, *yellow*, *yelp*, *yen*, *yeoman*, *yes*, *yesterday*, *yet*, *yew*, *yield*, *yobbo*, *yodel*, *yoghourt*, *yoke*, *yolk*, *yonder*, *you*, *young*, *your(s)*, *youth*, *yucca*, etc.; *Yale*, *Yalta*, *Yarmouth*, *Yehudi*, *Yemen*, *Yokohama*, *Yorick*, *York*, *Yoruba*, *Yucatan*, *Yugoslavia*, etc.;
- medial examples after <n> in a single morpheme are rare – *banyan*, *canyon*, *lanyard*.

Efficiency: 100 per cent of the consonantal use of <y>; a core rule with strong bias towards high TF words.

Because of this consonantal use, <y> does not serve as the first letter of complex vowel spellings, as do the other vowel letters in strings such as <ai>, <eu>, <ie>, <oi>, <ue>, apart from <e>-marking (*dye*, *dyke*). Since <y> as a vowel spelling is less common than spellings with the other five vowel letters, the workload of the remaining <y>-rules will be relatively slight.

Y.2 <yr>≡/ɜː(r)/ | — {<C>*, #}
Conditions:

- the <C>* does not include <r> (*Tyrrell*);
- reduction to /ə/ in unstressed syllables.

Examples: a marginal rule: *myrmidon*, *myrtle*; *Byrd*, *Byrne*, *Kyrle* and with reduced /ə/ – *martyr*, *satyr*, *zephyr*; *Merthyr*.

Exceptions: The conditions would have to be adjusted to accommodate *myrrh*. With /ɪ/ – *Tyrwhitt* /ˈtɪrɪt/.

Y.3 <y>≡/aɪ/ | <if> — #

The verb suffix <-ify> has a long /aɪ/. There is naturally strong bias towards longer words. Other examples of final <-y> will have /ɪ/ by default (Y.6).

Examples: a marginal rule: *amplify*, *beautify*, *certify*, *falsify*, *gratify*, *notify*, *pacify*, *terrify*, etc.

Exceptions: /ɪ/ in the noun *salsify*.

Though <y> is a relatively uncommon spelling for stressed vowels, we can explore the long value <y>≡/aɪ/ with the usual contexts beginning with the main <e>-marking rule.

Y.4 <y>≡/aɪ/ | — (<C>*) <e>* #

Conditions:

- the <C>* may not be <x> (though there are no competing forms with short <y> similar to *taxing, vexing, fixing, boxing, fluxing*);
- the <C>* may be <th> (*scythe*) or a <Cl> cluster (*cycle*), or, as the brackets indicate, it may be zero (*lye*);
- the <e>* may be elided before the initial vowel of a suffix as in *analysing* (p. 269).

Examples: a marginal rule with very strong bias towards low TF words: *acolyte*, *analyse*, *cyclist*, *dyne*, *enzyme*, *lyre*, *paralysed*, *rhyme*, *shyly*, *slyly*, *style*, *stylish*, *thyme*, *type*, *tyre*, etc.; *Argyle*, *Blantyre*, *Byron*, *Carlyle*, *Clyde*, *Khyber*, *Kintyre*, *Pyke*, *Sykes*, *Tyler*, *Tyre*, etc.

Examples of <ye> with no intervening consonant are *bye*, *dye*, *goodbye*, *lye*; *Frye*, *Pye*, *Skye*.

Exceptions:

- with /ɪ/ – *polymer*, *tricycle*; *Euphrosyne*, *Hippolyte*, *Lyly*, *Maskelyne*, *Powyke*, *Wykeham*; the <e> of *Battye* is mere padding;
- with /iː/ – *Denyse*, *Ypres*;
- at internal free form boundaries which should be obvious to the reader – *jellyfish*, *ladylike*, *storyline*; *Runnymede*. A preceding double consonant letter <CCy> is a fairly powerful §Basic marker for unstressed <y>≡/ɪ/.

Y.5 <y>≡/aɪ/ | — <C>* ENDING

Examples: a marginal rule:

- with <-on> – *nylon*, *pylon*;
- with <-us> – *thymus*;
- with <-ant, -ance, -ancy> – *hydrant*.

The suffix <-ic(al)> has a complementary function in marking a short vowel (the default) in *analytic*, *catalytic*, *cynic*, *physic*.

Exploring the context before <C> <i> <V> is hardly worthwhile since there are only occasional examples with stressed <y>, such as *forsythia*.

Y.6 <y>≡/ɪ/ – the default rule for <y>
In effect this is final <-y>, less the ending <-ify> (Y.3). In conservative RP and in much of Northern England this correspondence occurs in final unstressed syllables – the most frequent context for <y>. Many SBS speakers, however, have final <y>≡/iː/.

Examples: *accordingly*, *almighty*, *angry*, *aptly*, *assembly*, *beastly*, *coldly*, *cuddly*, *frankly*, *naughty*, *pygmy*, *softly*, *wealthy*, etc.

Exceptions: verbs with stressed /aɪ/ – *apply*, *comply*, *descry*, *imply*, *supply*, etc.

Efficiency: a core rule with a very heavy workload with some bias towards longer words;

in words – 95 per cent (= 18 percentage points of 88 per cent correct /ɪ/ predictions);
in names – 90 per cent (= 20 percentage points of 81 per cent correct /ɪ/ predictions).

If this final <-y> is taken to be /iː/ rather than /ɪ/, it would represent about 50 per cent of successful /iː/ predictions.

As an auxiliary letter, <y> forms part of the complex vowel spellings <ay>, <ey>, <oy>.

<z>-rules

Z.1 <z(z)>≡/z/ – the default rule for <z>
Examples: *amazing*, *blaze*, *boozer*, *brazen*, *breeze*, *buzz*, *crazy*, *dazzle*, *dizzy*, *embezzle*, *enzyme*, *fizz*, *gauze*, *hazel*, *horizon*, *jazz*, *kazoo*, *muzzle*, *plaza*, *sneeze*, *zeal*, *zest*, *zinc*, *zoo*, etc.

Exceptions:

- with <zz>≡/ts/ in *intermezzo*, *mezzanine*, *mezzotint*;
- with <z>≡/ts/ in *bilharzia*, *nazi*, *scherzo*, *schizophrenia*; *Danzig*, *Franz*, *Herzog*, *Mozart*, etc.; however, the advertising slogan 'beans means Heinz' implies an anglicized /haɪnz/ rather than /haɪnts/;
- with /ʒ/ in *azure*, *crosier*, *seizure*; *Brazier*;
- with /s/ in *eczema*.

Efficiency: a core rule with a fairly heavy workload and a very strong bias towards low TF words;

in words – 97 per cent (= 24 percentage points of 74 per cent correct /z/ predictions);
in names – 86 per cent (= 16 percentage points of 78 per cent correct /z/ predictions).

Summary list of text-to-speech spelling rules analysed above in §4.3

The rules are reprinted here with a few keywords to facilitate cross-reference. The text of §4.3 should be consulted for details of their limitations, relative importance and efficiency.

A.1 <age>≡/ɪʤ/ | <V> <C$_0$> — #
– *average, frontage, garbage, haulage, manage, roughage, sewage,* etc.

A.2 (OPT.) <a>≡∅ | <V> <C$_0$> —<lly>
– *critically, dramatically, historically,* etc.

A.3 <ative>≡/ətɪv/ | <V> <C$_0$> — #
– *affirmative, decorative, evocative, laxative, lucrative, sedative,* etc.

A.4 <a>≡/ə/ | <V> <C$_0$> — <bl> {<e>, <y>} #
– *available, capably, enjoyable, habitable, reliably, syllable,* etc.

A.5 <aer>≡/ɛə(r)/ (AmE /ɛr/)
– *aeration, aerial, aerobic, aerodrome, aeronaut, aerosol, anaerobic,* etc.

A.6 <ae>≡/iː/
– *aegis, aeon, anaemia, anaesthetist, archaeology, encyclopaedia, leukaemia,* etc.

A.7 <ai>≡/eɪ/ (before //r// the vowel is /ɛə/)
– *abstain, bait, campaign, faint, rainy, sailor, terrain, waiver,* etc.

A.8 <ay>≡/eɪ/
– *away, bayonet, day, delay, essay, popinjay, play, portray, pray, say,* etc.

A.9 <augh>≡/ɔː/
– *caught, daughter, distraught, fraught, haughty, naughty, slaughter, taught,* etc.

A.10 <au>≡/ɔː/
– *applaud, astronaut, author, auxiliary, bauble, caucus, haunt, laundry, saucer,* etc.

A.11 <aw>≡/ɔː/ | — {<C>, # }
– *awful, crawl, dawdle, gawky, jaw, lawn, prawn, raw, saw, scrawl, yawn,* etc.

A.12 <ah>≡/ɑː/ | — {<C>, #}
– *bah, hurrah; Ahmed, Bahrain, Brahmin, Brahms, Mahler, Mahmud,* etc.

A.13 <al>≡/ɔː/ | — {<k>, <l>} {<C>, # }
before <k> – *balk, chalk, stalk, talk, walk;*
before <l> – *all, ball, call, fall, gall, hall, mall, pall, small, squall, stall, tall, thrall,* etc.

A.14 <al>≡/ɑː/ | — <m>
– *almond, alms, balmy, calm, embalmer, napalm, palm, psalm, qualm,* etc.

A.15 <al>≡/ɔːl/ | — {<d>, <t>}
– *alder, altar, alternate, bald, exalt, falter, halt, malt, paltry, salt, scald,* etc.

A.16 <ar>≡/ɔː(r)/ | {<qu>, <w>, <wh>} — {<C>, #}
– *quart, thwart, sward, swarm, swarthy, war, warble, warden, wharf, warm,* etc.

A.17 <a>≡/ɒ/ | {<qu>, <w>, <wh>} — <C> {<C>, #} (AmE /ɑ/)
– *quantity, quarrel, squabble, squash, swamp, swan, swap, waddle, watch, what,* etc.

A.18 <ar>≡/ɑː(r)/ | — {<C>, #} (AmE /ar/)
– *arm, bar, barn, carbon, cigar, guardian, large, pharmacy, star, yard,* etc.

A.19 <a>≡/ɑː/ | — <sk> (default /æ/ in AmE)
– *ask, bask, basket, cask, casket, flask, mask, task;* etc.

A.20 <a>≡/ɑː/ | <C> — <st> (default /æ/ in AmE)
– *aghast, alabaster, castle, disaster, fast, master, nasty, pastime, plaster, vast,* etc.

A.21 <a>≡/ɑː/ | — <th> (default /æ/ in AmE)
– *bath, lath, path*, and for some speakers *aftermath.*

A.22 <a>≡/ɑː/ | — <ft> (default /æ/ in AmE)
– *abaft, aft, after, craft, graft, haft, raft, rafter, shaft,* etc.

A.23 <a>≡/ɑː/ | # <C_1> — #
– *bra, ma, pa, spa.*

A.24 <a>≡/ə/ | — #
– *algebra, aroma, banana, bonanza, camera, comma, data, drama, opera, soda,* etc.

A.25 <a>≡/ɑː/ | — <C> {<a>, <i>, <o>} #
– *armada, avocado, banana, desperado, drama, pastrami, safari, saga, soprano,* etc.

A.26 <a>≡/eɪ/ | — <ng> <e> #
– *arrange, change, danger, grange, range, strange, stranger,* etc.

A.27 <a>≡/eɪ/ | — (<C>*) <e>* #
– *ache, awaken, bravery, butane, cable, fatal, gravy, paste, rating, space,* etc.

A.28 <a>≡/eɪ/ | # <C_0> — <C>* ENDING
– *basal, pagan, planar, nadir, apron, bathos, status, vagary, cadence, latent,* etc.

A.29 <a>≡/eɪ/ | — <C>* <i> <V>
– *alias, amiable, contagion, cranium, gymnasium, labial, maniac, occasion,* etc.

A.30 <a>≡/eɪ/ | — <V>
– *aorta, chaos, kaolin.*

A.31 <a>≡/æ/ – the default rule for <a>

B.1 <bu>≡/b/ | — <V>
– *build, buoy, buy.*

B.2 <b>≡∅ | <m> — (e) #
– *bomb, catacomb, climb, comb, dumb, lamb, limb, numb, succumb, thumb, tomb,* etc.

B.3 <b(b)>≡/b/ – the default rule for <b>

C.1 <che>≡/ʃ/ | — #
– *barouche, cache, creche, douche, gauche, moustache, niche, panache,* etc.

C.2 <ch>≡/k/ | — {<l>, <r>}
– *chloroform, chromatic, chronicle, chrysalis, cochlea, lachrymose, sepulchre,* etc.

C.3 <ch>≡/ʧ/ — the default rule for <ch>
– *beech, bench, beseech, birch, cheap, cheese, child, church, leech, teach,* etc.

C.4 <ck>≡/k/
– *acknowledge, attack, barracks, black, crackle, hijack, hockey, packet, stickler,* etc.

C.5 <cc>≡/ks/ | <a> — {<e>, <i>}
– *accelerate, accent, accept, access, accident, flaccid, vaccine,* etc.

C.6 <c>≡/s/ | — <ae>
– *caecum, caesura; Alcaeus, Caesar, Nicaeus.*

C.7 <ce>≡/ʃ/ | — {<an>, <ous>} #
– *crustacean, ocean(ic); cretaceous, herbaceous, sebaceous, siliceous.*

C.8 <c>≡/s/ | — <e>
– *absence, ace, adjacent, advice, cancel, centre, divorce, glycerine, police, wince,* etc.

C.9 <c>≡/ʃ/ | — <iat> <V> (OPT.)
– *appreciate, emaciated, glaciation, officiate,* etc.

C.10 <ci>≡/ʃ/ | — <V>
– *ancient, artificial, efficient, gracious, malicious, politician, social, special, vicious,* etc.

C.11 <c>≡/s/ | — <i>
– *acid, anticipate, city, crucible, decide, icing, lucid, precinct, precise, tenacity,* etc.

C.12 <c>≡/s/ | — <y>
– *agency, bouncy, celibacy, cyanide, cyclamen, cycle, cypress, leucocyte, salycylic,* etc.

C.13 <c>≡∅ | — <qu>
– *acquaint, acquiesce, acquire, acquit, lacquer; Jacqueline, Jacques,* etc.

C.14 <c(c)>≡/k/ — the default rule for <c>
– *academic, acclaim, accompany, according, alcohol, balcony, cable,crude, duct,* etc.

D.1 <dg>≡/ʤ/ | — {<e>, <i>, <y>, #}
– *abridge, badger, bludgeon, budgie, dodgy, gadget, judgement, knowledge, stodgy,* etc.

D.2 <dj>≡/ʤ/
– *adjacent, adjective, adjoin, adjourn, adjudge, adjudicate, adjust, adjutant,* etc.

D.3 <d(d)>≡/d/ – the default rule for <d>

E.1 <e>≡/iː/ | # <C_1> — #
– the function words *be, he, me, she, the, we,* and archaic *ye.*

E.2 <e>≡∅ | — #
– *avenue, blameless, careful, comedienne, corpse, dye, indorsement, judgeship,* etc.

E.3 <es>≡/ɪz/ | <V> <C_0> {<c>, <ch>, <sh>, <g>, <s>, <z>} — #
– after sibilants in *races, churches, matches, wishes, ages,* etc.

E.4 <es>≡/s/ | <V> <C_0> {<f>, <k>, <p>, <qu>, <t>} — #
– after other voiceless consonants in *chafes, rakes, ropes, writes,* etc.

E.5 <es>≡/z/ | <V> <C_0> — #
– by default in *archives, besides, clothes, homes, knives, measles, tales,* etc.

E.6 <ed>≡/ɪd/ | <V> <C_0> {<t>, <d>} — #
– after alveolar plosives in *guarded, wooded; addicted, antiquated,* etc.

E.7 <ed>≡/t/ | <V> <C_0> {<c>, <f>, <ch>, <sh>, <k>, <p>, <Cs>, <x>} — #
– after other voiceless consonants in *laced, glanced, chafed, watched, missed, boxed,* etc.

E.8 <ed>≡/d/ | <V> <C_0> — #
– by default in *ashamed, reserved, tattered,* etc.

E.9 <er>≡/ə(r)/ | <C> — # (AmE /ər/)
– *after, barrier, canister, diameter, draper, driller, lesser, outer, poorer, soccer,* etc.

E.10 <er>≡/ɜː/ | — <C> (AmE /ɜr/)
– *adverse, certain, determine, hermit, inertia, person, reserve, revert, vertigo,* etc.

E.11 <ear>≡/ɜː/ | — <C> (AmE /ɜr/)
– *dearth, earl, early, earn, earnest, earth, heard, hearse, learn, pearl, etc.*

E.12 <eau(x)>≡/əʊ/
– *bureau, chateau, plateau, portmanteau, tableau, trousseau,* etc.

E.13 <ea>≡/iː/
– *appeal, beam, cheap, clean, creature, eagle, flea, heathen, squeak, stream, wreath,* etc.

E.14 <ee>≡/iː/
– *agree, asleep, beef, degree, feeble, jubilee, reel, refugee, speech, teeth, tweezers,* etc.

E.15 <eigh>≡/eɪ/)
– *eight, freight, inveigh, neigh, neighbour, sleigh, weigh, weight,* etc.

E.16 <ei>≡/iː/ | <c> —
– *ceiling, conceit, conceive, deceit, deceive, perceive, receipt, receive,* etc.

E.17 <ei>≡/aɪ/ – the default rule for <ei>

E.18 <eur>≡/ɜː(r)/ | — # (AmE /ɜr/)
– *amateur, amateurism, chauffeur, connoisseur, entrepreneur, raconteur, restaurateur,* etc.

E.19 <eu>≡/(j)uː/
– with no /j/ after <l> or <r>: *leukaemia, sleuth, rheumatism*, etc.;
– with /j/ in SBS but not usually in AmE: *deuce, neutral, pneumonia,* etc.;
– with /j/ in both SBS and AmE: *eucalyptus, eucharist, eulogy, feud,* etc.

E.20 <ew>≡/(j)uː/ | i) # <C_0> —
ii) — <C_0> # – the default rule for <ew>
– with no /j/ after <l> or <r>: *blew, lewd, screw, Andrew,* etc.;
– with /j/ in SBS but not usually in AmE: *dew, new, steward,* etc.;
– with /j/ in both SBS and AmE: *askew, few, sinew,* etc.

E.21 <ey>≡/ɪ/ | <V> <C_0> — #
– the vowel is /iː/ rather than /ɪ/ for many speakers.
– *abbey, alley, barley, blimey, chimney, honey, jockey, journey, valley,* etc.

E.22 <ey>≡/eɪ/ – the default rule for <ey>
– *abeyance, conveyance, grey, heyday, prey, purveyor, surveying, they, whey,* etc.

E.23 <e>≡/e/ | — <ver>
– *asseverate, beverage, clever, every, ever, never, reverent, sever, several,* etc.

E.24 <e>≡/iː/ | — <C> {<a>, <i>, <o>} #
– *edema, ego, emphysema, eta, hyena, magneto, torpedo, verbena, veto, zeta,* etc.

E.25 <e>≡/iː/ | — <C>* <e>* #
– *athlete, austere, cashmere, cede, centipede, complete, extreme, here, journalese,* etc.

E.26 <e>≡/iː/ | <C_0> — <C>* ENDING
– *legal, pecan, cedar, thesis, demon, ethos, femur, genus, secant, plenary, decent,* etc.

E.27 <e>≡/iː/ | — <C>* <i> <V>
– *anterior, bacteria, comedian, experience, heliotrope, immediate, mediocre,* etc.

E.28 <e>≡/iː/ | — <V>
– *alveolar, aqueous, creosote, erroneous, geodetic, leonine, meteor, neon,* etc.

E.29 <e>≡/e/ – the default rule for <e>

F.1 <f(f)>≡/f/ – the default rule for <f>

G.1 <gg>≡/g/
– *bragging, buggy, digger, druggist, egg, nugget, straggly, thuggery, wriggle,* etc.

G.2 <gh>≡/g/
– *aghast, burgher, ghastly, gherkin, ghetto, ghost, sorghum, spaghetti, yoghourt,* etc.

G.3 <gu>≡/gw/ | <n> — <V> <C>
– *anguish, distinguish, language, languid, lingual, linguist, penguin, sanguine,* etc.

G.4 <gu>≡/g/ | — <V>
– *beguile, beleaguer, demagogue, disguise, fugue, guard, guess, league,* etc.

G.5 <g>≡∅ | <n>* — { #, <C>* }
– *accordingly, amongst, hangman, kingdom, lengthwise, oblong, provoking, sling,* etc.

G.6 <g>≡∅ | i) — {<m>, <n>} (<e>) #
ii) # — <n>
– *alignment, apothegm, campaign, champagne, diaphragm, feigning, gnarled,* etc.

G.7 <g>≡/g/ | — <et> {<C>, #}
– *altogether, beget, forget, get, target, together; Gethsemane, Getty, Gettysburg.*

G.8 <ge>≡/ʤ/ | — <V>*
– *advantageous, cagey, congeal, courageous, dungeon, gorgeous, pigeon,* etc.

G.9 <g>≡/ʤ/ | — <e>
– *age, algebra, angel, apologetic, challenge, change, cogent, genius, progeny,* etc.

G.10 <g>≡/ʤ/ | — <iat>
– *collegiate, intercollegiate.*

G.11 <gi>≡/ʤ/ | — {<a>, <o>}
– *allegiance, collegian, contagious, legion, nostalgia, regional, religion, vestigial,* etc.

G.12 <g>≡/ʤ/ | — {<i>, <y>}
– *agile, agitated, angina, biology, clergy, digit, fragile, hygiene, magic, origin,* etc.

G.13 <g>≡/g/ – the default rule for <g>

H.1 <h>≡/h/ – the default rule for <h>

I.1 <i>≡/ə/ | <V> <C_0> — <bl> {<e>, <y>}
– *audibly, compatible, crucible, fallible, feasibly, flexible, horribly, possibly,* etc.

I.2 <i>≡/iː/ | — <que> #
– *antique, boutique, clique, oblique, physique, piqued, technique,* etc.

I.3 <i>≡/ɪ/ | <V> <C_1> — {<c>, <v>} <e> #
– <-ice> – *apprentice, liquorice, malice, notice, office, practice, service,* etc.
– <-ive> – *active, adhesive, endive, festive, forgive, fugitive, massive, olive,* etc.

I.4 <ie>≡/aɪ/ | # <C_1> — ({<d>, <s>}) #
– *cries, cried, die, fie, fried, fries, hie, lie, pie, pied, skies, tried, tries, vie,* etc.

I.5 <ie>≡/aɪ/ | <V> <C_0> {<f>, <l>} — {<d>, <s>} #
– applied, belied, certified,dignified,satisfied; implies, modifies, relies, etc.

I.6 <ie>≡/ɪ/ | <V> <C_0> — ({<d>, <s>}) #
– *able–bodied, candies, candied, hurried, jellies, married, varied,* etc.
– *auntie, birdie, boogie, bookie, budgie, calorie, lassie, lingerie, prairie, sweetie,* etc.

I.7 <ie>≡/iː/ – the default rule for <ie>

I.8 <ig>≡/aɪ/ | — {<m>, <n>} #
– *align, assign, benign, consign, design, ensign, malign, paradigm, resign, sign,* etc.

I.9 <igh>≡/aɪ/
– *blight, bright, delight, fight, high, knight, light, might, night, right, sigh, thigh,* etc.

I.10 <ir>≡/ɜː(r)/ | — {<C>, #}
– *birch, bird, birth, circle, dirty, firm, first, flirt, irksome, mirth, skirmish, thirst,* etc.

I.11 <i>≡/aɪ/ | — <nd> (<e>) #
– *behind, bind, blindness, find, grinder, kind, mind, remind, rind, winder,* etc.

I.12 <i>≡/aɪ/ | <C_1> — <ld> (<e>) #
– *child, mild, wild.*

I.13 <i>≡/ɪ/ | — #
– *bikini, graffiti, khaki, kiwi, macaroni, mini, salami, scampi, semi, spaghetti, taxi,* etc.

I.14 <i>≡/iː/ | — <C> {<a>, <i>, <o>} #
– *albino, ballerina, casino, concertina, incognito, kilo, kiwi, mosquito, visa,* etc.

I.15 <i>≡/aɪ/ | — <C>* <e>* #
– *advise, agile, alkaline, bike,chives, cider, coincide, desire, emphasise,* etc.

I.16 <i>≡/aɪ/ | <C_0> — <C>* ENDING
– *final, iris, bison, minus, piracy, finance, migrant, library, licence,* etc.

I.17 <i>≡/aɪ/ | # <C_0> — <V>
– *bias, biology, biopsy, diagnose, giant, liable, liar, lion, riot, triumph, viaduct,* etc.

I.18 <i>≡/iː/ | — <V>
– *alias, alien, glorious, idiot, onion, polio, radio, ruffian, trivia, verbiage,* etc.

I.19 <i>≡/ɪ/ – the default rule for <i>

J.1 <j>≡/ʤ/ – the default rule for <j>

K.1 <k>≡∅ | # — <n>
– *knack, knee, knew, knickers, knife, knit, knob, knock, knot, know, knuckle,* etc.

K.2 <kh>≡/k/
– *gymkhana, khaki*; and names such as *Astrakhan, Gurkha.*

K.3 <k(k)>≡/k/ – the default rule for <k>

L.1 <le>≡/əl/ | <C> — #
– *available, credible, cripple, gentle, jungle, meddle, noble, obstacle, rabble, tinkle,* etc.

L.2 <l(l)>≡/l/ – the default rule for <l>

M.1 <m(m)>≡/m/ – the default rule for <m>

N.1 <n>≡/ŋ/ | — <g> {<a>, <o>, <u>, <C>, # }
– *along, amongst, angry, cling, dangle, distinguish, fungus, hangar, languor, swing,* etc.

N.2 <n>≡/ŋ/ | i) — {<k>, <q>, <x>}
ii) — <c> {<a>, <o>, <u>, <C>*, # }
– *ankle, anxious, banquet, blanket, brink, crinkle, defunct, larynx, lynx, zinc,* etc.

N.3 <n(n)>≡/n/ – the default rule for <n>

O.1 <oa>≡/əʊ/
– *approach, boast, cloak, coax, goat, groan, hoax, load, roast, shoal, soak, soap,* etc.
– before //r// the vowel is /ɔː/: *boar, board, coarse, hoard, hoarse, oar, roar, soar,* etc.

O.2 <oir>≡/wɑː(r)/ | — { <e>, #}
– *boudoir, escritoire, memoir, repertoire, reservoir, soiree,* etc.

O.3 <oi>≡/ɔɪ/
– *adenoids, coil, coin, devoid, disappointed, exploit, noise, oil, point, thyroid, toil,* etc.

O.4 <oor>≡/ɔː(r)/
– *door, floor* and also *moor, poor, spoor,* etc. for speakers who do not have /ʊə/.

O.5 <oo>≡/ʊ/ | — <k>
– *book, brook, cook, crook, forsook, hook, look, nook, rookie, shook, took,* etc.

O.6 <oo>≡/uː/ | <f> — <d>
– *food.*

O.7 <oo>≡/ʊ/ | — <d> #
– *good, hood, stood, wood, woodbine;* the suffix <-hood> as in *boyhood,* etc.

O.8 <oo>≡/ʊ/ | { <f>, <s>} — <t>
– *foot, soot.*

O.9 <oo>≡/ʊ/ | <w> —
– *woof* ('barking'), *wool*; and some names.

O.10 <oo>≡/uː/ – the default rule for <oo>

O.11 <or>≡/ɜː | <w(h)> — <C>
– *whorl; word, work, world, worm, worse, worst, worship, worth, worthy,* etc.

O.12 <or>≡/ɔː(r)/ | — {<C>, #}
– *absorb, acorn, chord, cord, cork, corner, corps, divorce, morning, storm, torso,* etc.

O.13 <ou>≡/uː/ | <y> —
– *you, youth.*

O.14 <ou>≡/ə/ | <V> <C_0> — <s> #
– *ambitious, capricious, fictitious, graciously, ludicrous, vigorous,* etc.

O.15 <ough>≡/ɔː/ | — <t>
– *bought, brought, fought, nought, ought, sought, thought, wrought.*

O.16 <ough>≡/aʊ/ | <b> —
–*bough.*

O.17 <ough>≡/ʌf/ | <t> —
– *tough.*

O.18 <ough>≡/ɒf/ | <c> —
– *cough.*

O.19 <ough>≡/ʌf/ | # <r> —
– *rough.*

O.20 <ough>≡/uː/ | <r> —
– *through.*

O.21 <ough>≡/əʊ/ – the default rule for <ough>

O.22 <oul>≡/ʊ/ | # <C_1> — <d> #
– the function words *could, should, would.*

O.23 <our>≡/ə(r)/ | <V> <C> — #
– *ardour, armour, dishonourable, enamoured, favourite, neighbours, odour,* etc.

O.24 <our>≡/aʊə(r)/ | — #

– *flour, hour, our, scour, sour.*

O.25 <our>≡/ʌ(r)/ | — <V>

– *courage, flourish, nourish.*

O.26 <ou>≡/uː/ | — { <V>, # }

– *bivouac, caribou, denouement, marabou, pirouette, silhouette, sou,* etc.

O.27 <ou>≡/aʊ/ – the default rule for <ou>

O.28 <ow>≡/aʊ/ | # <C_0> {<c, h, n, r, v>} —

– *scowl, shower (as in 'rain'), now, crowd, vowel,* etc.

O.29 <ow>≡/əʊ/ – the default rule for <ow>

O.30 <oy>≡/ɔɪ/

– *annoy, boy, boycott, buoy, clairvoyant, destroy, employ, oyster, royal,* etc.

O.31 <o>≡/əʊ/ | — <ld>

– *cold, fold, gold, manifold, marigold, old, scold, soldier, sold, told,* etc.

O.32 <o>≡/əʊ/ | — <ll> #

– *droll, enroll, knoll, roll, scroll, stroll, toll,* etc.

O.33 <o>≡/əʊ/ | — <l(s)t>

– *bolster, bolt, colt, dolt, holster, jolt, molten, revolt, volt,* etc.

O.34 <o>≡/əʊ/ | — #

– *ago, albino, also, bingo, calico, cargo, flamingo, go, grotto, jumbo, photo, video,* etc.

O.35 <o>≡/ʌ/ | — <v>

– *above, covenant, cover, dove, glove, govern, love, oven, recover, shove, shovel,* etc.

O.36 <o>≡/əʊ/ | — <C> {<a>, <i>, <o>} #

– *aroma, diploma, pagoda, persona, photo, polo, quota, solo, tapioca, virtuoso,* etc.

O.37 <o>≡/əʊ/ | — (<C>*) <e>* #

– *alone, anecdote, bony, boredom, cathode, diagnose, grocery, noble, noted,* etc.

O.38 <o>≡/əʊ/ |#<C_0> — <C> ENDING

– *floral, slogan, solar, proton, bonus, dosage, romance, rotary, moment, bromine,* etc.

O.39 <o>≡/əʊ/ | — <C>* <i> <V>

– *ammonia, chromium, devotion, notion, opium, pandemonium, social, sodium,* etc.

O.40 <o>≡/əʊ/ | — <V>

– *coerce, coexist, dioecious, hydroelectric, loess, monoecious, poem, poesy, poetic,* etc.

O.41 <o>≡/ɒ/ – the default rule for <o>

P.1 <ph>≡/f/
– *alphabet, asphalt, catastrophe, elephant, emphasis, pamphlet, phantom,* etc.

P.2 <p>≡∅ | # — { <n>, <s>, <t>}
– *pneumatic, pneumonia, psalm, pseudo, psychology, pterodactyl, ptomaine,* etc.

P.3 <p(p)>≡/p/ – the default rule for <p>

Q.1 <que>≡/k/ | — #
– *antique, arabesque, baroque, cheque, clique, opaque, physique, technique, unique,* etc.

Q.2 <(c)qu>≡/kw/
– *acquire, adequate, conquest, equal, liquid, quaint, qualified, quite, require, square,* etc.

Q.3 <q>≡/k/
– only in exotic names – *Iraq, Iraqi.*

R.1 <r>≡/ə(r)/ | {/aɪ/, /aʊ/, /iː/, /uː/, /ɔɪ/}
– *acquire, cereal, fierce, fire, giro, irony, neuron, require, steroid, virus, weir, weird,* etc.

R.2 <re>≡/ə(r)/ | <C> — #
– *acre, calibre, centre, fibre, massacre, meagre, mediocre, metre, sombre, theatre,* etc.

R.3 <rh>≡/r/
– *rhapsody, rheumatism, rhinoceros, rhododendron, rhubarb, rhyme, rhythm,* etc.

R.4 <r(r)>≡/r/ – the default rule for <r>

S.1 <sch>≡/sk/
– *schematic, scheme, schismatic, schizoid, scholar, school, schooner,* etc.

S.2 <sc>≡/s/ | — {<e>, <i>}
– *abscess, adolescent, ascend, disciple, fascinate, obscene, scene, scent, science,* etc.

S.3 <sh>≡/ʃ/
– *abolish, ash, brush, fashion, nourishment, perish, shady, sponsorship, worship,* etc.

S.4 <st>≡/s/ | — {<le>, <en>} #
– with <-stle> – *apostle, bristle, gristle, hustle, jostle, thistle, trestle, whistle,* etc.
– with <-sten> – *chasten, christen, fasten, glisten, hasten, listen, moisten,* etc.

S.5 <s>≡/s/ | # {<ab>, <ob>, <sub>} —
– *abscond, absent, abstruse, absurd, obscure, obsequious, subside, substance,* etc.

S.6 <s>≡/s/ | — {<c>, <f>, <k>, <p>, <q>, <t>}
– *ask, cast, clasp, scan, skin, square, sphinx, sport,* etc.

S.7 <s>≡/z/ | <e> — #
– *allies, aloes, caries, dominoes, monies, rabies, series, skies, tidies, undies,* etc.

S.8 <s>≡/z/ | i) {<b>, <d>, <g>, <m>, <n>, <v>, <w>, <y>} —
ii) {<l>, <r>} — #
– *adenoids, balls, bonkers, crimson, drowsy, fittings, flimsy, summons, whimsical,* etc.

S.9 <s>≡/z/ | <V> — {<b>, <d>, <g>, <l>, <m>, <n>, <r>, <w>}
– *baptism, busby, husband, presbyter, sarcasm, truism,* etc.

S.10 <s>≡/z/ | <V> — <V>
– *advise, applause, artisan, bruise, chisel, composer, museum, televise, visage,* etc.

S.11 <si>≡/ʒ/ | <V> — <on>
– *abrasion, collision, conclusion, decision, division, precision, seclusion, vision,* etc.

S.12 <s(s)i>≡/ʃ/ | — <on>
– *admission, discussion, emulsion, expression, passionately, tension, version,* etc.

S.13 <s>≡/ʒ/ | <V> — <ur> <V>
– *closure, composure, displeasure, leisure, measure, pleasure, treasure, usury,* etc.

S.14 <s(s)>≡/ʃ/ | — <ur> <V>
– *assured, censure, cocksure, ensure, fissure, insurance, pressure, sure, tonsure,* etc.

S.15 <s(s)>≡/s/ – the default rule for <s>

T.1 <th>≡/ð/ | <V>* — {<e>, <ed>, <en>, <er>, <es>, <est>, <ing>} #
– *altogether, another, bathe, brother, either, lathe, scythe, seething, sheathe,* etc.

T.2 <th>≡/θ/ – the default rule for <th>

T.3 <tch>≡/ʧ/
– *batch, butcher, catch, sketch, snatch, switch, watch; Kitchener, Thatcher,* etc.

T.4 <tz>≡/ts/
– *blitz, chintz, howitzer, quartz, seltzer; Berlitz, Rosencrantz, Switzerland,* etc,.

T.5 <tur>≡/ʧ/ə(r)/ | <V> <C_0> — <V>
– *moisture, picture, sculpture, signature, temperature, texture, vulture,* etc.

T.6 <t>≡/ʧ/ | — <u> <V> (opt.)
– *actual, estuary, factual, fatuous, punctuate, ritual, statue, virtuous,* etc.

T.7 <t>≡/ʧ/ | <s> — <io>
– *combustion, congestion, digestion, exhaustion, question,* etc.

T.8 <t>≡/ʃ/ | — <iat>
– *differentiate, ingratiate, initiate, negotiate, propitiate, substantiate, vitiate,* etc.

T.9 <ti>≡/ʃ/ | — {<a>, <e>, <o>}
– *affection, convention, cautious, confidential, impatience, inertia,* etc.

T.10 <t(t)>≡/t/ – the default rule for <t>

U.1 <ui>≡/uː/
– *bruise, bruit, cruise, fruit, juice, recruit, sluice, suit,* etc.

U.2 <ur>≡/ɜː(r)/ | — { <C>*, (<r>) # }
– *burden, curse, curtain, disturb, hurt, nursery, purple, purpose, suburb, urgent,* etc.

U.3 <u>≡/ʌ/ | # — <n>
– *unable, unaffected, undone, uneven, unforgettable, uninspired, unusual,* etc.

U.4 <u>≡/(j)uː/ | — (<C>*) <e>* #
– *accuse, brute, computer, dispute, duty, fury, globule, reputed, ruby, secluded* etc.

U.5 <u>≡/(j)uː/ | — <C>* ENDING
– *brutal, human, lunar, hubris, mucus, lunacy, mutant, prudent, supine, rumour,* etc.

U.6 <u>≡/(j)uː/ | — <C>* <i> <V>
– *communion, conclusion, crucial, delusion, dubious, peculiar, pollution, studio,* etc.

U.7 <u>≡/(j)uː/ — <V>
– *affluent, annual, duel, fluent, fuel, influenza, sensual, tenuous, truant, vacuum,* etc.

U.8 <u>≡/ʊ/ | <f> — <l>
– *armful, basketful, bellyful, cupful, glassful, pailful, spoonful,* etc.

U.9 <u>≡/ə/ | <i> —
– *auditorium, calcium, chromium, genius, geranium, radius, stadium, triumph,* etc.

U.10 <u>≡/ʌ/ – the default rule for <u>

V.1 <v(v)>≡/v/ – the default rule for <v>

W.1 <wh>≡/h/ | — <o>
– *who, whom, whose, whole, whoop, whore.*

W.2 <wh>≡/w/
– *overwhelm, whack, whale, wheat, wheedle, wheel, wheeze, white, whisker,* etc.

W.3 <w>≡∅ | — <r>
– *awry, wrangle, wrap, wreck, wren, wrench, wrestle, wretch, write, wrought, wry,* etc.

W.4 <w>≡/w/ – the default rule for <w>

X.1 <x>≡/z/ | # —
– *xenon, xenophobia, xylophone.*

X.2 <x>≡/gz/ | # <e> — <V>
– with unstressed /egz-/ or /ɪgz-/ – *exact, exaggerate, exalt, examine, example*, etc.

X.3 <x>≡/ks/ – the default rule for <x>

Y.1 <y>≡/j/ | {#, <n>} — <V>
– *yawn, yeast, yes, you, young, youth, yucca; banyan, canyon, lanyard,* etc.

Y.2 <yr>≡/ɜː/(r)| — {<C>*, #}
– *myrmidon, myrtle*, and with reduced /ə/ – *martyr, satyr, zephyr, Merthyr.*

Y.3 <y>≡/aɪ/ | <if> — #
– *amplify, beautify, certify, falsify, gratify, notify, pacify, terrify,* etc.

Y.4 <y>≡/aɪ/ | — (<C>*) <e>* #
– *analyse, cyclist, enzyme, lyre, paralysed, rhyme, style, stylish, thyme, type, tyre,* etc.

Y.5 <y>≡/aɪ/ | — <C>* ENDING
– *nylon, thymus, hydrant.*

Y.6 <y>≡/ɪ/ – the default rule for <y>

Z.1 <z(z)>≡/z/ – the default rule for <z>

Chapter 5

Identical forms – homographs and homophones

5.1 HOMOGRAPHS AND HOMOPHONES

Sharing a written or spoken shape or even both

In any writing system that has evolved over a long period of time, it often happens that phonetically quite different words are found with the same spelling and, conversely, phonetically identical words may have quite different spellings. These pairs of forms are called **homographs** and **homophones** respectively. Both groups represent only a fraction of English vocabulary, since different words are normally expected both to sound different and to look different.

Homographs may in theory require some effort of the reader in identifying the lexeme:

The bass was remarkably good

'Fish' (/'bæs/) or 'singer' (/'beɪs/)? Similarly, homophones may cause the writer (or the listener) some difficulty:

/ðə 'beɪs laɪn wəz 'tuː 'ləʊ/

'Singer' (<bass>) or 'position' (<base>)? Only very occasionally will such identities, homographs or homophones, entail misunderstandings in practice. Usually the meaning is apparent from the context. But consider the following:

The Fayed bid was waived [*sic*] through without reference to the Monopolies Commission by the then Trade and Industry Secretary.
(*Guardian* 21/9/90: 15).

This should presumably have been <waved through>, but the Secretary did *waive* his right to interfere with the bid. However, this is probably a simple spelling mistake rather than a nuance of style.

Homographs and homophones can safely exist because both spoken and written language have a high level of redundancy. Nevertheless, the poet laureate Robert Bridges wrote an inaugural tract (Bridges 1919) for the Society for Pure English, claiming that homophones were ultimately detrimental in a language. He points out that a careful writer (or speaker, too, no doubt) avoids placing homophones too close to each other. Tennyson clearly could not use the word *sea*, rather than *deep* in the line:

I see the deep's untrampl'd floor (not 'I see the sea's un .....').

This is evidently part of the same stylistic principle that avoids the repetition of a word in close context, a principle which replaces the word *said* in dialogue with *asserted*, *replied*, *maintained*, and other words denoting speech. To discourage homophones, Bridges hoped that schools would actively promote a more formal style of speech in which, for instance, full vowel quality was used rather than /ə/ in unstressed syllables: 'the *o* of the word *petrol* should be preserved, as it is now universally spoken, not having yet degraded into *petr'l*' (ibid.: 22). He also wanted a phonemic contrast between /ɔː/ and /ɔə/, as in *caught–court*, to be maintained as a last defence against the loss of 'post-vocalic' /r/ in SBS (ibid.: 35). He found evidence of the undesirability of homophones in the work being done in historical studies of language, which showed that new words were often developed to bypass the danger inherent in a pair of homophones.

We shall take homophones to be identical strings of phonemes in the citation form of the words. We cannot take into account pairs of words which in running speech or across accents are liable to be confused:

Son: What's a vulture, Daddy?
Father: It's a big bird, like an eagle.
Son: Why did the driver on the school bus ask me if I had a vulture? (sc. 'voucher').

Nor shall we consider units larger than a single word, as in:

I do expect students to know what /ənæləʤɪ/ is.

Where 'analogy' and 'an allergy' may have exactly the same pronunciation in SBS and other accents in which the //r// is lost before a consonant.

Linguists use the terms 'homograph' and 'homophone' for forms which involve a difference in meaning. With that restriction, variant spellings such as *jail* and *gaol* would not be classified as homophones. This would apply to pairs such as *caraway–carraway*, *connection–connexion*, *flier–flyer*, *gibe–jibe*, *gray–grey*, *hiccough–hiccup*. These pairs are all found as alternative spellings for the same lexeme. Bridges (1919: 4) would even treat *draught* and *draft* as variant spellings of the same word in spite of their semantic specialization. Generally speaking one would expect an individual to keep to one such spelling in any of these pairs fairly consistently. So, between individuals, such variation represents a difference of incidence of spellings in words (/ʤeɪl/ as *gaol* or *jail*) parallel to a difference of incidence of phonemes in words (e.g. whether *scone* is pronounced as /skəʊn/ or /skɒn/). American spelling conventions and British spelling conventions represent the two main written 'accents'.

Similarly, linguists would not consider the noun *conflict* /ˈkɒnflɪkt/ and the verb *conflict* /kənˈflɪkt/ to be homographs in the strict sense, nor the noun *advocate* /ˈædvəkət/ and the verb *advocate* /ˈædvəkeɪt/, since the same lexeme is involved in different syntactic uses. Our main purpose here, however, is simply to explore the writing system, so there is no harm done in taking some of these instances into account as interesting identities of spelling or of sound.

A number of two-syllable or three-syllable homographs (in this wider sense) in the §Latinate vocabulary differ only in stress pattern (usually with consequential vowel reduction). The same lexeme functioning as a verb may have final stress, and as a noun or adjective non-final stress:

You should dis*count* it. They gave me a *dis*count.

Here the vowels are more or less unchanged in quality, though, due to the stress shift, the pitch, duration and intensity patterns will vary. Other pairs may have vowel reduction on the first syllable when unstressed:

They con*struct*ed a bridge. (/kənˈstrʌkt/)
A peculiar *con*struct. (/ˈkɒnstrʌkt/)

The writing system does not attempt to show these differences; it prefers to keep a constant spelling for the lexeme.

Other examples: *absent*, *abstract*, *accent*, *access*, *addict*, *advert*, *affix*, *alloy*, *ally*, *augment*, *combine*, *commune*, *compact*, *compound*, *compress*, *conduct*, *confine*, *conflict*, *conscript*, *consort*, *contest*, *contrast*, *convert*, *convict*, *decoy*, *decrease*, *dictate*, *digest*, *discourse*, *excerpt*, *excise*, *export*, *extract*, *ferment*, *fragment*, *frequent*, *implant*, *import*, *impress*, *imprint*, *incense*, *increase*, *indent*, *insert*, *insult*, *intern*, *inverse*, *perfect*, *perfume*, *permit*, *pervert*, *presage*, *present*, *produce*, *progress*, *project*, *prospect*, *prostrate*, *protest*, *rebel*, *rebound*, *record*, *regress*, *reject*, *relay*, *second*, *segment*, *subject*, *surmise*, *survey*, *suspect*, *torment*, *transfer*, *transplant*, *transport*. Some of these examples may be much more common as a verb than as a noun or adjective (*construct*) or vice versa (*compound*), but with some allowance for personal variation, the potential contrast is there.

There are similar examples where the pairs do not discernibly represent the same lexeme in present-day usage:

collect ('prayer' as noun; 'gather' as verb);
console ('control panel' as noun; 'comfort' as verb);
content ('what is contained' as noun; 'satisfy' as verb);
contract ('agreement' as noun; 'become less' as verb);
converse ('opposite' as noun; 'chat' as verb);

defile ('a narrow gorge' as noun; 'contaminate' as verb);
entrance ('way in' as noun; 'charm' as verb);
object ('thing' as noun; 'protest' as verb);
proceeds ('result' as noun; 'carries on' as verb).

Almost all the above examples of stress variation are §Latinate minimal free-forms, but the same kind of functional phonetic difference may occur, though with some rhythmical variability, in words with stressable prefixes:

A nice piece of *un*dercut. Our price has been under*cut*.
You need a *re*fill. You'll have to re*fill* it.

A similar functional difference occurs in three-syllable lexemes with the endings <-ate> and <-ment>. Here there is no difference in the place of primary stress between noun and verb, but the verb has full vowel quality on the last syllable and the noun or adjective tends to have a reduced vowel (/ɪ/ or /ə/):

verbs: *advocate* /ˈædvəkeɪt/, *implement* /ˈɪmplɪment/;
nouns: *advocate* /ˈædvəkət/, *implement* /ˈɪmplɪmənt/.

Other examples: *aggregate*, *animate*, *appropriate*, *approximate*, *articulate*, *associate*, *certificate*, *co-ordinate*, *correlate*, *degenerate*, *delegate*, *deliberate*, *duplicate*, *elaborate*, *emasculate*, *estimate*, *expatriate*, *graduate*, *importunate*, *incorporate*, *initiate*, *intimate*, *moderate*, *postulate*, *precipitate*, *predicate*, *separate*, *subordinate*, *syndicate*; *complement*, *compliment*, *document*, *implement*, *increment*, *ornament*, *supplement*. In these latter words <-ment> is added to a bound form, not to a free-form that is itself a verb, as in *appeasement*, *inducement*, etc.

Stress differences (with vowel reduction) also occur in other lexemes larger than two syllables.

5.2 TYPES OF HOMOGRAPH

Sharing the same spelling: 'if a year is short, a minute is minute'

We turn now to distinct lexical homographs. Some homographs differ not only in lexical meaning but in structure: *flatter* ('fawn upon') is a single morpheme, *flatter* ('more flat') is a comparative adjective (cf. *madder*); *analyses* may be a third person singular verb form /ˈænəlaɪzɪz/ or a noun plural /əˈnæləsiːz/. There is homography in the identical spelling of the noun suffix {-er} and the comparative suffix {-er}: *cleaner*, *commoner*, *cooler*, *damper*, *dryer*, *fuller*, *furrier*, *slacker*, *slicker*, *stranger*. These homographs are also homophones.

With some verbs the <-ed> form covers two different functions and pronunciations: *blessed* may be past tense /ˈblest/ or adjectival /ˈblesɪd/.

Other examples are: *aged*, *crooked*, *cursed*, *dogged*, *learned*.

The ending <-es> may represent the normal noun plural /-ɪz/ or the §Latinate plural /-iːz/ of singular nouns ending in /-ɪs/: *axes* (may relate to *axe* as /ˈæksɪz/, or to *axis* as /ˈæksiːz/. Other examples are: *bases* (from *base*/*basis*), *ellipses* (from *ellipse*/*ellipsis*). A similar identity occurs with the third person singular present of the verb in *analyses* and *diagnoses*.

The ambiguity of <s> as a spelling of both /s/ and /z/ produces homographs in: *abuse*, *close*, *diffuse*, *excuse*, *house*, *use*. The /z/ form is the verb, the /s/ form is the noun or adjective. *Refuse*, however, (/ˈrefjuːs/ noun, /rɪˈfjuːz/ verb), represents different lexemes. A similar voiceless/voiced contrast is found in *mouth* /maʊθ/ (noun), /maʊð/ (verb). Here the <th> is the normal spelling of both /θ/ and /ð/. One might have expected <*mouthe> for the verb – cf. *loath–loathe*, *bath–bathe*. Analogous pairs with a /f/ – /v/ contrast show it in the spelling: *wife–wives*, *leaf–leaves*, *strife–strive*, *life–live*.

Most of the above examples of spelling identity would not usually be considered as homographs since, in spite of the contrasting phonetic differences, the same lexeme is usually involved. Identities of spelling in pairs of completely different lexemes are not very common. Some of these homographs have different phonetic forms:

bass (/bæs/ – /beɪs/)
bow (/bəʊ/ – /baʊ/)
buffet (/ˈbʊfeɪ/ – /ˈbʌfɪt/)
does (/dʌz/ – /dəʊz/)
gill (/gɪl/ – /ʤɪl/)
lead (/liːd/ – /led/)
live (/lɪv/ – /laɪv/)
minute (/ˈmɪnɪt/ – /maɪˈnjuːt/)
putting (/ˈpʊtɪŋ/ – /ˈpʌtɪŋ/, from *put* and *putt*)
read (/riːd/ – /red/)
resume (/rɪˈzjuːm/ – /ˈrezjuːmeɪ/)
tear (/tɛə/ – /tɪə/)
tinged (/tɪnʤd/ – /tɪŋd/ (LPD)
wind (/wɪnd/ – /waɪnd/)
wound (/wuːnd/ – /waʊnd/)

Ay /eɪ/ ‘forever’ and *aye* /aɪ/ ‘yes’ have alternative forms <aye> and <ay> respectively, which makes them potential homographs.

Other homographs may also be homophones. These identities are sometimes referred to as **homonyms**:

bank (1. ‘mound of earth’; 2. i.e. for money)
bark (1. ‘b. of dog’; 2. ‘b. of tree’)
barrow (1. ‘hill’; 2. ‘wheel-barrow’)
bellows (1. ‘fan’; 2. ‘shouts’)
bound (1. ‘leap’; 2. ‘tied up’)
can (1. ‘tin’; 2. ‘be able’)
champ (1. ‘chew’; 2. ‘champion’)
cricket (1. ‘game’; 2. ‘insect’)
fell (1. ‘cruel’; 2. ‘mountain’; 3. ‘tumbled’)
fare (1. i.e. cost of ticket; 2. ‘food’)

fine	(1. 'good'; 2. 'penalty')
firm	(1. 'solid'; 2. 'company')
fit	(1. 'healthy'; 2. 'seizure')
flat	(1. 'level'; 2. 'apartment')
hail	(1. 'greet'; 2. 'snow')
hamper	(1. 'impede'; 2. 'basket')
last	(1. 'final'; 2. 'cobbler's last')
leaves	(1. from noun *leaf*; 2. from verb *leave*)
mews	(1. from verb *mew*; 2. 'back street')
mine	(1. 'of me'; 2. 'colliery')
mould	(1. 'form'; 2. 'mildew')
pants	(1. 'breaths'; 2. 'trousers')
plane	(1. 'tree'; 2. 'surface')
quarry	(1. 'prey'; 2. 'stone-quarry')
rest	(1. 'repose'; 2. 'remainder')
rose	(1. 'flower'; 2. 'nozzle'; 3. 'got up')
row	(1. i.e. with oars; 2. 'line')
stable	(1. i.e. for horses; 2. 'constant')

These variants clearly represent different lexemes. However, the full extent of the class of homonyms is bound to be indeterminate since it depends on what constitutes a difference of meaning.

Before discussing homophones, we should note that homophones in one accent may not be homophones in another. In AmE *hostel* and *hostile* are homophones with a syllabic /l/ in the unstressed syllable; in SBS *hostile* ends in /-aɪl/. Two accents may differ in their range of contrasts: *fair* and *fur* are homophones with the same vowel phoneme on Merseyside, but not in SBS, where /ɛə/ and /ɜː/ contrast (Wells 1982: 372). In AmE the short open back vowel /ɒ/ has lost its rounding and fallen in with /ɑ(ː)/ so that *balm* and *bomb* are homophones in AmE, but not in SBS. There may be general differences in the distribution of phonemes: *pour* and *paw* are homophones in SBS as /pɔː/ and so are *whacks* and *wax* as /wæks/. They are not homophones in Scottish English or in AmE, where they are differentiated by the presence/absence of final /r/ and of /h/ (Wells 1982: 407f). An individual speaker may sometimes differentiate potential homophones by contrasting full vowel quality in one word with reduced vowel quality in the other. So, SBS can differentiate *chorale* as /kɒˈrɑːl/ and *corral* as /kəˈrɑːl/. In AmE these two may be homophones with /kəˈræl/. Conversely, *barrage* represents /ˈbærɪʤ/ as 'dam' and /bəˈrɑːʒ/ as 'artillery fire' for AmE speakers, but for SBS speakers they are homophones as /ˈbærɑːʒ/. *Primer* represents /ˈpraɪ-/ as 'paint' and /ˈprɪ-/ as 'textbook' for AmE speakers, but for SBS speakers they are homophones with /ˈpraɪ-/. Some speakers have the same pronunciation for *bolero* as 'dance' and 'garment' /bəˈlɛərəʊ/, others differentiate them as /bəˈlɛərəʊ/ and /ˈbɒlərəʊ/.

Spelling reform based on regular phoneme correspondences cannot do away with homographs: it will resolve some, but create others. In *New Spelling* (Ripman and Archer 1948: 83), *abuse* with /s/ and with /z/ gives **abues*, **abuez*; *bow* with /əʊ/ and with /aʊ/ gives **boe*, **bou*; *lead* with /iː/ and with /e/ gives **leed*, **led*; *wind* with /ɪ/ and with /aɪ/ gives **wind*, **wiend*, etc. On the other hand, following the same principles, new homographs are created from pairs such as *aloud*, *allowed*; *coarse*, *course*; *meat*, *meet*; *taught*, *taut*; etc.

5.3 TYPES OF HOMOPHONE

Sharing the same pronunciation: rite, right and write

Homophones can be divided into several types. Inflected forms with final /s/ or /z/ frequently form homophones with single morphemes: *adds*, *adze*; *bays*, *baize*; *boos*, *booze*; *brays*, *braze*, *braise*; *brews*, *bruise*; *brows*, *browse*; *chews*, *choose*; *claws*, *clause*; *cocks*, *cox*; *cops*, *copse*; *crews*, *cruise*, *cruse*; *days*, *daze*; *does*, *doze*; *flecks*, *flex*; *flocks*, *phlox*; *frays*, *phrase*; *frees*, *freeze*, *frieze*; *gores*, *gauze*; *greys*, *graze*; *guys*, *guise*; *hoes*, *hose*; *knows*, *nose*; *lacks*, *lax*; *laps*, *lapse*; *lays*, *laze*; *links*, *lynx*; *loos*, *lose*; *masseurs*, *masseuse*; *minks*, *minx*; *nicks*, *nix*; *packs*, *pax*; *paws*, *pores*, *pours*, *pause*; *pleas*, *please*; *prays*, *preys*, *praise*; *pries*, *prise*, *prize*; *pros*, *prose*; *quarts*, *quartz*; *rays*, *raise*; *roes*, *rows*, *rose*; *rues*, *ruse*; *sacks*, *sacs*, *sax*; *sighs*, *size*; *tacks*, *tax*; *teas*, *tees*, *tease*; *treaties*, *treatise*; *whacks*, *wax*.

Inflected forms with final /t/ or /d/ also frequently form homophones with single morphemes: *allowed*, *aloud*; *balled, bawled*, *bald*; *banned*, *band*; *barred*, *bard*; *billed*, *build*; *bowled*, *bold*; *brayed*, *braid*; *brewed*, *brood*; *chased*, *chaste*; *ducked*, *duct*; *fined*, *find*; *guessed*, *guest*; *holed*, *hold*; *candied*, *candid*; *cowered*, *coward*; *crewed, crude; mined*, *mind*; *missed*, *mist*; *mowed*, *mode*; *mooed*, *mood*; *mustered*, *mustard*; *owed*, *ode*; *paced*, *paste*; *packed*, *pact*; *pried*, *pride*; *rapped*, *wrapped*, *rapt*; *ribboned*, *riband*; *sighed*, *side*; *stayed*, *staid*; *swayed*, *suede*; *tacked*, *tact*; *tied*, *tide*; *towed*, *toad*; *trussed*, *trust*; *warred*, *ward*; *weighed*, *wade*; *welled*, *weld*; *wheeled*, *wield*; *whiled*, *wild*; *whined*, *wind*; *whirred*, *word*.

The pair *passed*, *past*, are, in origin, simply variant spellings. A 'past master' of a guild is one who has 'passed' his term of office. Examples with final /aɪ/ before the /-d/ suffix, such as *tied*, *tide*, will not be homophones for those Scottish speakers who have two different allophones – [ae] in *tied* before the morpheme boundary and [ʌi] medially in *tide* (Wells 1982: 405). The words do not then contrast as a string of phonemes, but through the presence/absence of a morpheme boundary.

Comparative adjectives and agent nouns ending in <-er> also form homophones with single morphemes: *bolder*, *boulder*; *boarder*, *border*; *conker*, *conquer*; *doer*, *dour*; *dyer*, *dire*; *fisher*, *fissure*; *fryer*, *friar*; *grosser*, *grocer*; *hanger*, *hangar*; *higher*, *hire*; *leaver*, *lever*; *meatier*, *meteor*; *rigger*, *rigour*; *roomer*, *rumour*; *saver*, *savour*; *seeder*, *cedar*; *seller*, *cellar*; *sucker*, *succour*; *tenner*, *tenor*; (cf. also *plainer*, *planer*, *planar*). Other examples of two-morpheme and single-morpheme homophones are: *bridal*, *bridle*; *chilly*, *chilli*; *lessen*, *lesson*.

In two-morpheme homophones there is often a difference in the location of the morpheme boundary: *tax* + {plural} and *taxi* + {plural} are both /ˈtæksɪz/ for some SBS speakers (though /ˈtæksɪz/ – /ˈtæksiːz/ for others). Consider the following radio news item: 'Both parties are using /ˈtæksɪz/ to capture the floating voter'. *Taxis* or *taxes*? Other examples are: *banded*, *bandied*; *budges*, *budgies*; *eyelet*, *islet*; *fallacies*, *phalluses*; *lasses*, *lassies*; *leased*, *least*; *mashes*, *mashies*; *misses*, *missies*; *pitted*, *pitied*; *poses*, *posies*; *pusses*, *pussies*; *studded*, *studied*; *tided*, *tidied*; *verdure*, *verger*. Though these are homophones for some SBS speakers, pairs such as *tided*, *tidied* will be different for the growing number of SBS speakers who have /iː/ rather than /ɪ/ in final open unstressed syllables: /ˈtaɪdɪd/ – /ˈtaɪdiːd/. For other speakers these may contrast as /ˈtaɪdəd/ – /ˈtaɪdɪd/.

In polysyllabic words, homophones may result from the reduction of different underlying vowels to /ə/: *confirmation*, *conformation*; *complement*, *compliment*; *interpellation*, *interpolation*; *literal*, *littoral*; *vacation*, *vocation*; *veracious*, *voracious*. Particularly where one of the words has an <o> spelling, careful speakers aware of the possible confusion may have an unreduced vowel (/veɪˈkeɪʃn/ ≠ /vəʊˈkeɪʃn/, /veˈreɪʃəs/ ≠ /vɒˈreɪʃəs/) to maintain the difference. Some BBC announcers pronounce *guerrilla* with /e/, rather than the normal /ə/, in reporting events in Africa, where 'attacked by gorillas' is a remote possibility.

Phonetic identity between function words and lexical words is of no more importance than mere curiosity: *aren't*, *aunt*; *be*, *bee*; *been*, *bean*; *but*, *butt*; *by*, *buy*; *for*, *fore*, *four*; *I*, *eye*; *I'll*, *aisle*, *isle*; *in*, *inn*; *might*, *mite*; *our*, *hour*; *we*, *wee*; *we're*, *weir*; *were*, *whirr*; *we've*, *weave*; *won't*, *wont*; *would*, *wood*; *you*, *ewe*, *yew*; *you're*, *your*, *yore*.

Phonetic reductions in the weak forms of function words that might cause confusion are avoided. The preposition *on* does not usually reduce to /ən/ because of possible confusion with *and* in a phrase such as /ən ðə ˈteɪbl/. However, it does not matter that both the auxiliaries *is* and *has* are homophones when reduced to /s/, since the verb form that follows is distinctive: 'he's gone', 'he's going'. Context should also distinguish *there*, *their*, and *they're*, but in practice these three are frequently misspelt.

Homophones in SBS due to the loss of //r// before a consonant or finally will not be homophones in 'rhotic' accents such as AmE or Scottish and Irish English or where /ɔː/ (paw) and /ɔə/ (*pour*) are distinct phonemes: *alms*, *arms*; *area*, *airier*; *awe*, *or(e)*; *bawd*, *board*; *beta*, *beater*; *calve*, *carve*; *canna*, *canner*; *caught*, *court*; *caulk*, *cork*; *cause*, *cores*; *cawed*, *chord*; *cheetah*, *cheater*; *cilia*, *sillier*; *coma*, *comber*; *cornea*, *cornier*; *curricula*, *curricular*; *eta*, *eater*; *father*, *farther*; *flaw*, *floor*; *formally*, *formerly*; *fought*, *fort*; *gnaw*, *nor*; *lava*, *larva*; *laud*, *lord*; *law*, *lore*; *lawn*, *lorn*; *ma*, *mar*; *manna*, *manner*, *manor*; *maw*, *more*; *nebula*, *nebular*; *pa*, *par*; *panda*, *pander*; *paw*, *poor*; *peninsula*, *peninsular*; *raw*, *roar*; *rhea*, *rear*; *rota*, *rotor*; *sauce*, *source*; *saw*, *soar*; *schema*, *schemer*; *sought*, *sort*; *spa*, *spar*; *stalk*, *stork*; *talk*, *torque*; *taught*, *taut*, *tort*; *taw*, *tor*; *tuba*, *tuber*; *uvula*, *uvular*.

Not many homophones involve differences in consonant spellings. Some of them reflect the difference between §Basic and §Romance conventions: *ark*, *arc*; *bark*, *barque*; *block*, *bloc*; *cash*, *cache*; *check*, *cheque*; *frank*, *franc*; *mannikin*, *mannequin*; *mark*, *marque*; *mask*, *masque*; *peak*, *pique*; *shoot*, *chute*. Other homophones with consonant spellings from different subsystems are: *chord*, *cord*; *scull*, *skull*; *tocsin*, *toxin*.

The endocentric spellings <kn>≡/n/, <wh>≡/h/, <wh>≡/w/, <wr>≡/r/, <gu>≡/g/, <mb>≡/m/ and <ch>≡/k/ provide quite a few homophones: *knave*, *nave*; *knead*, *need*; *knew*, *new*; *knight*, *night*; *knot*, *not*; *know*, *no*; *whole*, *hole*; *whoop*, *hoop*; *whale*, *wail*; *what*, *watt*; *wheel*, *weal*; *whet*, *wet*; *whether*, *weather*; *which*, *witch*; *whig*, *wig*; *while*, *wile*; *whine*, *wine*; *whit*, *wit*; *whither*, *wither*; *wrack*, *rack*; *wrap*, *rap*; *wreak*, *reek*; *wreck*, *reck*; *wrest*, *rest*; *wretch*, *retch*; *wright*, *write*, *right*, *rite*; *wring*, *ring*; *wrote*, *rote*; *wrung*, *rung*; *gauge*, *gage*; *guild*, *gild*; *guilt*, *gilt*; *climb*, *clime*; *jamb*, *jam*; *plumb*, *plum*; *lichen*, *liken*; *loch*, *lock*. The pairs with <wh>≡/w/ are not homophones for Irish and Scottish speakers and the many AmE speakers who have <wh>≡/hw/ in *what*, *wheel*, etc. If <bu> is taken to be a consonant spelling analogous to <gu>, then *boy*, *buoy* belong here too, at least for SBS speakers. AmE speakers may, however, pronounce *buoy* as /buːi/ rather than /bɔɪ/.

The <n> in *dam*, *damn* and the <g> in *sine*, *sign* are inert letters (cf. *damnation*, *signature*).

The different spellings of /s/ produce quite a few homophones. Since <c> and <s> both occur as spellings of /s/ in §Latinate vocabulary, the homophones may both be in the same subsystem (*cereal*, *serial*), rather than in different subsystems (§Basic: *seed*, §Latinate: *cede*). Other examples with different spellings of /s/ are: *ascent*, *assent*; *descent*, *dissent*; *psalter*, *salter*; *cession*, *session*; *cell*, *sell*; *cent*, *scent*; *ceiling*, *sealing*; *scene*, *seen*; *supercede*, *supersede*; *council*, *counsel*.

Some homophones differ in <C>-doubling (and in some cases vowel spelling as well): *banns*, *bans*; *barren*, *baron*; *bass*, *base*; *batten*, *baton*; *berry*, *bury*; *cannon*, *canon*; *carrot*, *carat*; *dessert*, *desert* (v.); *matt*, *mat*; *meddle*, *medal*; *palate*, *palette*, *pallet*; *speck*, *spec* (*specification*); *specks*, *specs* (*spectacles*); *steppe*, *step*.

Variation in vowel spelling is, as one might expect, the most fruitful source of homophones. Some of the following SBS examples may not be homophones in other accents of English. In North Lancashire *wait* /eː/ and *weight* /ɛɪ/ differ (Wells 1982: 357). In rhotic accents such as Scottish

English, the <er>, <ir>, <ur> spellings of /ɜː/ may represent different vowels plus /r/ (Wells 1982: 407). Conversely, some accents may have homophones that differ in SBS. Merseyside speakers who do not distinguish /ɜː/ and /ɛə/ will have as homophones *fur – fair/fare*, *stir – stair/stare*, *were – where/wear*, etc. (Wells 1982: 372). Examples of SBS homophones with long vowels are:

/iː/ – *beach, beech*; *beat, beet*; *beetle, betel*; *breach, breech*; *cede, seed*; *ceiling, sealing*; *cheap, cheep*; *feat, feet*; *flea, flee*; *heal, heel*; *eaves, eves*; *creak, creek*; *quean, queen*; *leach, leech*; *leaf, lief*; *leak, leek*; *leas, lees*; *mean, mien*; *meat, meet*; *pea, pee*; *peak, peek, pique*; *peal, peel*; *peace, piece*; *read, reed*; *sea, see*; *seam, seem*; *scene, seen*; *steal, steel*; *suite, sweet*; *tea, tee*; *team, teem*; *weak, week*; *discreet, discrete*;

/eɪ/ – *ail, ale*; *bail, bale*; *brake, break*; *faint, feint*; *fate, fete*; *gait, gate*; *grate, great*; *lain, lane*; *made, maid*; *male, mail*; *mane, main*; *pail, pale*; *pain, pane*; *plain, plane*; *place, plaice*; *pray, prey*; *sail, sale*; *slay, sleigh*; *stake, steak*; *straight, strait*; *tail, tale*; *vale, veil*; *vain, vane, vein*; *way, weigh*; *wain, wane*; *waist, waste*; *wait, weight*; *waive, wave*;

/aɪ/ – *die, dye*; *dine, dyne*; *giro, gyro*; *liar, lyre*; *pi, pie*; *sign, sine*; *cite, sight, site*; *sleight, slight*; *stile, style*; *tike, tyke*; *tire, tyre*. Due to a transitional [ə] glide between /aɪ/ and a following 'dark' /l/, some speakers do not distinguish *file, phial* or *vile, vial.* This was the basis for a slogan protesting against a new airport runway at Styal, Cheshire: 'a new runway is not our Styal';

/əʊ/ – *bole, boll*; *beau, bow*; *broach, brooch*; *doe, dough*; *floe, flow*; *groan, grown*; *load, lode*; *loan, lone*; *mot, mow*; *moat, mote*; *pole, poll*; *rondeau, rondo*; *roe, row*; *road, rode*; *role, roll*; *sloe, slow*; *sew, so, sow*; *sold, soled*; *sole, soul*; *toe, tow*; *told, tolled*; *yoke, yolk*; *throes, throws*; *throne, thrown*;

/aʊ/ – *bow, bough*; *foul, fowl*; *flour, flower*;

/ɑː/ – *hart, heart*;

/ɔː/ (+ //r//) – *boar, bore*; *born, borne*; *fore, four*; *forth, fourth*; *hoard, horde*; *hoarse, horse*; *coarse, course*; *morn, mourn*; *aural, oral*; *war, wore*; *warn, worn*;

/ɔː/ – *aureole, oriole*; *balk, baulk*; *ball, bawl*; *faun, fawn*; *hall, haul*; *mall, maul*; *naught, nought*; *aught, ought*; *all, awl*;

/uː/ – *pleural, plural*; *rood, rude*; *root, route*; *troop, troupe*; *threw, through*;

/juː/ – *dew, due*; *hew, hue*; *review, revue*;

/ɪə/ – *beer, bier*; *dear, deer*; *hear, here*; *peer, pier*; *sear, sere*; *tear, tier*;

/ɛə/ – *bare, bear*; *fair, fare*; *flair, flare*; *hair, hare*; *pair, pare, pear*; *stair, stare*; *tare, tear*; *wares, wears*; *their, there*;

/ɜː/ – *berth, birth*; *fir, fur*; *heard, herd*; *per, purr*; *pearl, purl*; *serf, surf*; *tern, turn*; *whirl, whorl*; *earn, urn.*

Homophones involving spelling variation in short vowels are, again as one might expect, much less common than with long vowels. The reason is that the short vowels have been subject to less phonetic change over the centuries and the spelling has remained fairly stable. Examples:

/e/ – *bread*, *bred*; *lead*, *led*; *leant*, *lent*; *read*, *red*;
/ʌ/ – *none*, *nun*; *one*, *won*; *rough*, *ruff*; *ton*, *tun*;
/ɒ/ – *swat*, *swot*.

Variant spelling of an unstressed syllable differentiates several groups of homophones. The endings <-ous> and <-us> are homophones: *callous*, *callus*; *citrous*, *citrus*; *fungous*, *fungus*; *humorous*, *humerus*; *mucous*, *mucus*; *phosphorous*, *phosphorus*. Similarly there is *populace*, *populous*. It requires quite a high degree of literacy to distinguish the <-ous> and <-us> words in, say, 'citrus fruits' and 'mucous membrane'. Other homophonous affixes are found in: *elicit*, *illicit*; *eruption*, *irruption*; *caster*, *castor*; *censer*, *censor*; *miner*, *minor*; *storey*, *story*; *caddie*, *caddy*; *pinkie*, *pinky*; *stationary*, *stationery*; *pendant*, *pendent*; *currant*, *current*. Homophonous affixes are discussed in detail in §5.5 (pp. 417–42).

Since the difference between opposite meanings 'out' and 'in' is not reflected in the pronunciation of *eruption* and *irruption*, we have all the ingredients for a spelling mistake. Compare 'the action is at its funniest with the eruption [*sic*] of the fanatical innocent into [*sic*] this world of bent cynicism' (*Guardian* 13/8/87: 10). Many people would be at a loss to find any error here. They may well use *eruption* for both 'in' and 'out', neutralizing the contrast. *OED* has quite a few earlier examples of this prefix confusion: 'emerge it into a cistern of cold water', 'I have been emerged in calculation ever since', 'emersed under the waters of the ocean', 'on no occasion (unless very immergent ones)' – this from a letter of George Washington. There are other possible confusions between *eradicate* 'to uproot' and the less common *irradicate* 'to enroot' (as correctly used in: 'to tear up what has become irradicated in his intellectual and moral being' *OED*). The prefix pairs *ante-*, *anti-*, and *hyper-*, *hypo-*, are also a source of confused spelling.

Different spellings of /əl/ give a number of homophones: *cubical*, *cubicle*; *principal*, *principle*; *radical*, *radicle*; *gamble*, *gambol*; *idle*, *idol*; *mantel*, *mantle*; *muscle*, *mussel*; *pedal*, *peddle*; *petrel*, *petrol*; *dual*, *duel*; *naval*, *navel*; *vial*, *viol*.

Other homophones with differently-spelt unstressed syllables are: *altar*, *alter*; *auger*, *augur*; *lumbar*, *lumber*; *marten*, *martin*; *meter*, *metre*; *taper*, *tapir*.

Unusual use of final <-e>, in particular after two consonant letters, gives the following homophones: *aid*, *aide*; *bell*, *belle*; *born*, *borne*; *cast*, *caste*; *grill*, *grille*; *heroin*, *heroine*.

French masculine and feminine endings <-é> and <-ée> are homophonous; they are frequently spelt without an accent mark in English: *fiance*, *fiancee*; *protege*, *protegee*.

Though, as we have seen, most homophone pairs only differ in a vowel spelling or a consonant spelling, there are more complex differences: *choir*, *quire*; *choler*, *collar*; *colonel*, *kernel*; *cue*, *queue*; *genes*, *jeans*; *geezer*, *geyser*; *gneiss*, *nice*; *key*, *quay*; *mare*, *mayor*; *profit*, *prophet*; *raiser*, *razor*; *cymbal*, *symbol*; *caeca*, *seeker*; *gorilla*, *guerrilla*; *chorale*, *corral*.

Homophones in figurative language for which there is no clear derivation, often generate a great deal of speculation. A *holy-stone* is a form of soft sandstone used for scrubbing decks. Is it a porous stone with holes in it, or is it a stone that has *holy* (= 'sacred') properties as an amulet? Imagination costs nothing. Smyth's *Sailor's Word-book* of 1867 (quoted by *OED*) suggests the sacred interpretation 'from being originally used for Sunday cleaning, or obtained by plundering church-yards of their tombstones, or because the seamen have to go on their knees to use it'. Is this speculation *hair-brained* or *hare-brained*? Similarly, do we leave *fairway* or *fareway*? In spite of associations with *fare* in the sense of 'travel' and compounds such as *wayfarer*, *thoroughfare*, *OED* considers *fareway* an erroneous spelling.

Identity or near-identity of sound or spelling has long been exploited for stylistic purposes. Word-play does not require absolute identity of sound or spelling: the available homophones and homographs would be too few and in the long run too hackneyed to serve. Puns have to run the risk of not being noticed, so near-identity often serves very well:

Antony: 'These Arabs are intense lovers.'
Caesar: 'Of course. They do everything in tents.'

(Film: *Carry on Cleo*)

Here there is only a strict homophone for those who do not contrast /nts/ and /ns/ as in 'a pound of mints/mince', but have /nts/ for both. For speakers who do make the contrast, near-identity may suffice.

Punning and word-play became a revered art-form with Elizabethan authors. Several quite different layers of meaning could be provocatingly sandwiched together in the same passage. Some favourite Elizabethan puns are still quite accessible (e.g. *dear–deer*, *hart–heart*, *choler–collar*). Others have to be excavated by philologists with a good eye for the bawdy and an ear trained in Shakespeare's pronunciation. Later on, the strict classicism of the later seventeenth century and eighteenth century frowned on such exuberance and it did not appeal to the Romantics either, since it was a matter for the head rather than the heart. Robert Bridges (1919) castigates John Donne for:

'pretending or thinking that genuine feeling can be worthily carried in a pun. So that in his impassioned 'Hymn to God the Father', deploring his own sinfulness, his climax is

But swear by thyself that at my death Thy Sonne
Shall shine as he shines now,

the only poetic force of which seems to lie in a covert plea of pitiable imbecility'

(Bridges 1919: 19n)

Perhaps Robert Bridges would take the Greek New Testament to task for calling Simon Bar-Jonah by the nickname 'Rocky' (in Greek 'Petros'): 'Thou art Peter and upon this rock I will build my church' (St. Matthew XVI.17).

Nowadays word-play is back in favour. At one end of the scale it adds to the impact of advertisements and newspaper headlines: 'Lancaster canvasses support for right to keep paintings' (*Guardian*, 14/3/90) and at the other it reached its literary apotheosis in the work of James Joyce.

5.4 NEW WORDS FROM VARIANT SPELLINGS

Many pairs of homophones developed out of variant spellings of the same word: <flower> and <flour>

Variant spellings of a word have frequently become associated with discrete ranges of meaning in the course of time. The meaning of the two forms may still show some similarity, but often there is no remaining semantic link and the two spellings have become quite independent words – a new pair of homophones.

One can catch a glimpse of this process of semantic differentiation at work in the case of *gray/grey*. In 1893 as part of the editorial work for the *New English Dictionary*, which later became *OED*, Murray asked various printing houses and other correspondents whether they used the spelling <grey> or <gray>. Dr Johnson had preferred <gray>, but it turned out that the majority of people consulted by Murray preferred <grey>. Interestingly some correspondents used both forms but with a difference of meaning: 'the distinction most generally recognized being that *grey* denotes a more delicate or a lighter tint than *gray*. Others considered the difference to be that '*gray* is a "warmer" colour or that it has a mixture of red or brown' (*OED* under *grey*). This might possibly be explained as a transfer of sound association to letters. The vowel of both words is, of course, the same phoneme /eɪ/, but the letter <a> is associated with vowels more open and further back than those represented by the letter <e>. This letter association tallies with the darker-and-warmer versus lighter-and-cooler association of vowel sounds with which the letters are otherwise associated (see Jakobson *et al.* 1951: 32).

Scientists often establish a manipulated spelling or an existing spelling variant as a technical term. In botany, the creation of new terms by varying the spelling becomes almost an art form. A favourite device is metathesis. For instance, the two species of cacti *Mila* and *Lobivia* are anagrams of the place-names *Lima* and *Bolivia*. Similarly in 1883, in physics, Lord Kelvin proposed the term *mho*, which was *ohm* spelt backwards, as the unit of conductivity. This had the virtue of shortness, though it introduced an alien correspondence <mh>≡/m/; even so, <h> was familiar enough as the second letter of a complex consonant spelling. <Mho> also had the advantage of being iconic, since this backward-spelt unit is the reciprocal of the ohm. The advantage is now lost, since the *mho* has since been renamed honorifically as the *siemens*. In geology in the mid-nineteenth century the spelling *terrane*, rather than *terrain*, was introduced for a fault-bounded body of rock. Indeed *OED* gives this as 'the usual spelling' for this technical sense. Recently *terrane* has been given a more specific meaning in plate-tectonic theory as a fragment of a crustal plate. Again in botany, our common *sycamore*, a kind of maple, is not a native tree in Britain, but was introduced from the continent (French *sycomore*). The <a> and <o> spellings which were at first mere variants for the maple, have now been exploited in English for two trees of entirely different genera, a maple and a fig: *sycamore* is Acer Pseudoplatanus (French *Érable sycomore*); *sycomore* is Ficus Sycomorus (French *Figuier sycomore*). This is putting quite a strain on the <a>/<o> variation in the spelling of an unstressed syllable, but it might work for specialist botanists. In this case the spelling variation might be reinforced by a pronunciation difference: <syca>≡/ˈsɪkə/ and <syco>≡/ˈsɪkəʊ/.

A good example of an innovative use of existing variant spellings to make a technical distinction can be found in various technical differences placed on the two spellings <disc> and <disk>. These normally differ only in that they are the British (<c>) and American (<k>) spellings of the same word. However, attempts have been made to harness this difference. A careful distinction between the two spellings is made in the publisher's manual for the machine-readable version of the *OED* (1989). The glossary of terms has:

Disc Describes a compact dis**c**, as opposed to magnetic dis**k** or dis**k**ette.
Disk Describes a floppy or hard dis**k**, as opposed to a compact dis**c**.

In industry there are various other conventions. The Hewlett-Packard computer company gives the <c> and <k> spellings different technical uses: a *disc* is a place in a file system where a hard *disk* is located; a *disk* is accessed through a *disc* directory.

There seems to be a general tendency to use *disc* in scientific senses and for more advanced technology. It seems, however, very doubtful, in such a critical technical context, whether such fine distinctions will prove workable and survive.

It is quite common for a word to split semantically in the course of time, and for different spellings to attach themselves to the different meanings.

This process should be distinguished from instances where a loan-word is readopted a second time with a different spelling and a different meaning. A good example of the latter is the pair *complement–compliment*. The basic meaning is 'fulfilment', but the former was developed from the Latin with this basic meaning, while the second came as a loan from Italian, where it had specialized as 'fulfilment of the requirements of courtesy'. Similarly, the pair *antique–antic* both derive from Latin *antiquus* or *anticus*, but the special meaning 'grotesque' always seems to have been attached to <antic> and not to have developed from *antique* within English. On the other hand, although *common* and *commune* look as if they might be an early French loan and a later second borrowing, both senses developed within English from an early loan. The record of early forms and evidence of meanings is not always easy to interpret, however. *Cask* 'wooden barrel' and *casque* 'helmet' are presumably both related to French *casque*, but the first meaning only occurs in English. In most of the examples given below, the differentiation took place as a process within English.

A further problem is to decide when there is a significant difference of meaning between two forms. In marginal cases the difference may simply be that one form came to be used exclusively by a particular group of people. One might draw the line at including instances such as *camomile – chamomile*, where the 'learned' <ch> spelling was used by pharmacists for the plant processed for medical use, or *centring–centering*, where *OED* notes that the latter, though not the regular British spelling, tends to be used in technical senses. One or two similar examples are included below, nevertheless, if only to show that there are fuzzy instances.

Some archaic specialized spellings

We can look first at just a few examples of specialized or technical differentiation of spellings which never became current. Even the more archaic of these are interesting because they show how such a differentiation could begin. In citing the pair of forms, I have put the common form first and the archaic specialized form second.

bat–batt : the <tt> spelling was commonly used for the layers of felt used in hat-making, which were presumably 'batted' flat.

bead–bede : 'beads' are so called from the prayers of the rosary; the spelling <bede> is found as a deliberate archaism in literature in the sense of 'prayer', as in *bedesman*, *bedesong*.

beadle–bedel, *bedell* : the latter are ceremonial officials at Oxford (one <l>) and Cambridge (two <l>'s). This resembles the totemism of proper names (§6.3).

carcase–carcass : the latter was the regular spelling of an early kind of mortar shell.

child–childe : the latter, as in Byron's *Childe Harold*, is an archaic literary form meaning 'a youth of gentle birth'.

coin–coign, *quoin* : the basic meaning of *coin* was a wedge, corner or stamping-die; the spelling *coign* came to be used for a wedge in gunnery and *quoin* for a corner-stone in building.

domain–demesne : both came from French, originally meaning the property of a lord (Latin *dominus*); *domain* (modern French *domaine*) is used in a general sense of 'territory' and *demesne* is an archaic technical term in law.

housewife–huswife, *hussive* : this is very sad – the latter is a small cloth pouch in which troops keep needle and cotton.

picket–picquet, *piquet* : the latter spelling was formerly standard use in the British army – 'in the Army Regulations spelt piquet' (*OED*).

Variants which retain a semantic link

Of the differentiated spellings which have become current, we can look first at those which retain some semantic link. The strength of the link varies:

adapter–adaptor: the <-or> spelling tends to be used for specialized gadgets which adapt, as in *an adaptor socket*. The <-er> spelling is used for human agents: 'In adapting his novel for the screen he proved to be a very skilful adapter'. Cf. *sailer–sailor* (below).

artist–artiste : the French spelling was introduced in the mid-nineteenth century for actors, singers and dancers (the performing arts), because *artist* had become restricted to graphic art. The <-e> spelling marks a final stress.

balk–baulk : these are still alternative spellings, but in billiards the spelling *baulk* (part of the billiard table) has become standardized.

bans–banns : there is still a notion of potential 'banning' in the specialized form 'marriage banns'.

block–bloc : in the sense of a combination of political parties, *bloc* was introduced as a loan-word from French just after 1900 and retained its French spelling. In early instances of its use it was italicized, perhaps to show that it was a tentative loan-word and not just a misprint for *block*. This spelling difference is unlikely to survive partly because a final <c>≡/k/ in a monosyllable is so unusual and partly because the meaning of *bloc* is well within the semantic range of *block*.

borne–born : *born* is only used in the passive and only without 'by': 'He was born in a stable', 'a lady born and bred', but 'of the three children borne by her'. *Borne* as the past participle of *bear* has the general sense of 'carried'.

blond–blonde : the <e> refers specifically to a blonde woman, a §French gender marker.

brier–briar : these refer, with little consistency, to two different types of plants: rose species and a Mediterranean heath. The spelling <briar> is generally used for tobacco pipes made from the root of the heath. Roses can be either *brier* or *briar*.

calibre–caliper(*s*), *calliper*(*s*) : 'calliper compasses' were used to measure the calibre of a bullet.

courtesy–curtsey, curtsy : the <cur-> spellings are used for the specialized meaning as an act of courtesy or greeting.

critic–critique : the spelling *critic* was originally used both for the person and the critical article; the §French spelling *critique*, along with a stress shift, came in as an eighteenth century differentiation of the two.

curb–kerb : this is one of the neatest examples of differentiation: *kerb* in British English has the specialized sense of a stone edging to a pavement. The <curb> spelling is still used for both in AmE. Mencken (1948: 278) mentions a New York street sign misunderstood by British visitors: 'Curb your dog!', where *curb* means 'take to the kerb', not 'restrain'.

draught–draft : both represent the noun /drɑːft/, connected with the verb *to draw*, but they have become assigned to different applications: *a banker's draft*, *a written draft*, *a military draft*, as against *a draught of ale*, *a draught of air*, *the draught of a ship*. The American spelling is uniformly *draft*.

enquiry–inquiry: see p. 442).

faint–feint : the *feint* spelling is used in the printing trade for faint lines used to guide handwriting. It has nothing to do with *feign*.

fantasy–phantasy : the shortened form, *fancy*, had already been hived off with a range of separate meanings; *OED* suggests that a further difference was developing between the <f> and <ph> forms: 'the predominant sense of *fantasy* being "caprice, whim, fanciful invention", while that of the latter is "imagination, visionary notion"'; the §Greek <ph> spelling would then go with the more serious range of meanings. The same applied with nineteenth century writers to *frenzy–phrenzy* : 'some writers show a tendency to prefer *phrenzy* when the reference is to prophetic ecstasy or demoniacal possession' – clearly a case for the §Greek spelling.

human–humane : the <-e> spelling was usual down to the eighteenth century, when the spelling <human> took over; this left the <-e> spelling for the specialized meaning 'what befits a human being'.

jewellery–jewelry : *OED* draws a nice distinction – 'in commercial use commonly spelt jewellery; the form jewelry is more rhetorical and poetic, and unassociated with the jeweller'. This is odd. *Jewellery* would seem more formal and so 'rhetorical', since it reflects the fuller pronunciation. The usual American spelling is *jewelry*.

knob–nob: the slang use of *nob* to mean 'head' loses the archaic <kn-> spelling.

license–licence : a number of §Latinate words ending in /s/ have an <s>

spelling for the verb and a <c> spelling for the noun in British English (cf. *practise–practice*, *prophesy–prophecy*). This seems to have come about by analogy with pairs such as *advise* with /z/, *advice* with /s/. The <c> spelling is reinforced in the noun *practice* by the frequency of <ice> as a noun ending in *justice*, *notice*, *service*, etc. This tendency helped to select the variants *defence*, *offence* as the current British spelling rather than *defense, offense*, which is standard in the USA. The adjective always has <s>: *defensive, offensive.*

lightening–lightning : this pair is rather like *jewellery* and *jewelry*: the specialized meaning in 'thunder and lightning' has a phonetic spelling reflecting the elision of /ə/. This divorces it from the verb *lighten*. This elision of a medial /ə/ is treated very variably in spelling – cf. *remembrance*, *severance*, *wondrous*, *ponderous*.

local–locale : the <-e> spelling, with a final stress, came into use towards the end of the nineteenth century, at first in italic print, to mean 'the place of a particular event'. This meaning had previously had the ordinary spelling 'local'. The first edition of *OED* considered *locale* 'erroneous'. Fowler (1926: 331), however, shows the thinking that must underlie the process of differentiation: 'The word's right to exist depends on the question whether the two indispensable words *locality* & *scene* give all the shades of meaning required, or whether something intermediate is useful'. He then proceeds to show that it does fill such a gap.

pendent–pendant : the latter is the usual noun spelling, as in a piece of jewellery.

plain–plane : the latter was hived off in the seventeenth century for geometrical uses; there is still a semantic link between *plain* 'flat terrain' and *plane* 'a flat surface' in geometry. The navigational phrase *plane sailing* was originally a geometrical use; as a figurative expression meaning 'straightforward' it has the other spelling *plain sailing*.

reflection–reflexion : these have been free variants for the noun corresponding to *reflect*, but since the verb *reflex* needs a companion form *reflexion* we have a potential distinction 'the *reflection* of light', 'the *reflexion* of a muscle'.

set–sett : (cf. *bat–batt* above) the <tt> spelling is standard in some technical uses, such as the setting of a loom, or a square paving-stone. Fowler does not like it:

> the extra *t* is an arbitrary addition in various technical senses... Each class of persons has doubtless added it to distinguish the special sense that means most to it from all others; but so many are the special senses that the distinction is now no more distinctive than an Esq. after a man's name, & all would do well to discard it.
>
> (Fowler 1926: 525)

This is far too strict. The unexpected letter doubling might well be thought a useful flagging of a particular technical use. Any two different technical uses will not be likely to occur in the same text.

review–revue : the spelling *revue,* in the sense of a satirical review on stage of fashions and events, only dates from 1913 (*OED*).

troop(*er*)*–troupe*(*r*) : the French spelling was introduced in the mid-nineteenth century to refer specifically to actors and dancers (cf. *artiste* and *revue* above). This use of French <-e> spellings is presumably responsible for a spelling mistake I have seen on circus posters: 'Large *caste of artistes'. The pair *cast* 'distributed roles in a play' and *caste* 'hereditary social class' were never simply variant spellings.

urban–urbane : the specialized <-e> form here is the older. Classical Latin *urbanus* already had connotations of 'refined', 'polished'. The *urban* form came into use largely in the nineteenth century as the neutral adjective 'pertaining to cities'.

whisky–whiskey : the first spelling is Scottish, the second Irish and American.

Variants where the semantic link has been eroded

Finally, there are instances where the semantic link is no longer really apparent. For instance, *chord* was separated from *cord* for its academic uses in music and mathematics in the sixteenth century. The <ch> spelling reflected the Latin <ch> and Greek <χ> spellings and so was more appropriate for academic use (see §7.2 on etymology as a force in English spelling). *OED* quotes Dr Johnson: 'when it signifies a rope or string in general, it is written *cord*: when its primitive signification is preserved, the <h> is retained'. This use of 'it' is interesting. In actual usage we are now dealing with two different words which happen to be homophones: there is no clear semantic link between a piece of string and a combination of musical notes. They can only be 'it' from the viewpoint of distant and irrelevant etymology.

Other examples where the semantic link seems to have been lost are:

bail–bale : one meaning of *bail* was 'bucket' and the verb meaning 'to throw water out of a boat with buckets' attracted the differentiated (*OED* 'erroneous') spelling *bale.*

broach–brooch : they both derive from French *broche* 'pin, spike'; 'to broach a subject' originates as a metaphor from broaching or piercing a barrel with a pointed spigot.

canvas–canvass : the latter is the verb form meaning 'to solicit votes'; this figurative meaning comes from *canvas* 'cloth' by way of 'to be tossed in a sheet' – a fairly accurate description of the electoral process.

caster–castor : both are agent nouns from the verb *cast*, an early loan from Old Norse; in present usage *caster* usually attaches to the basic sense 'throw', so *pepper caster*, *sugar caster*, *caster sugar*. The spelling *castor* attaches to the less common use of *cast* to mean 'turn, veer' (as in 'to cast about for something') and is used for the little wheels on furniture. How *castor oil* relates to all this is a mystery, but, being medical, the §Latinate <-or> suffix fits in. There may be a connection with the Greek word for a beaver κα'στωρ. Beaver gland extract was used as a purgative and the name was later transferred to a vegetable equivalent *Ricinus communis* (*OED* does not make the connection). See also *sailer* and *adapter* above.

cattle–chattel (as in 'goods and chattels') : the two forms are historically the same word; the spelling *cattle* is largely found after 1700 for livestock; the Anglo–French legal term for property *chattel* survives 'as a distinct modern form and sense'(*OED*).

check–cheque (not in US) : the financial use of *cheque* dates from the eighteenth century; it relates to the verb *check* 'verify' by way of counterfoil.

course–coarse : both could be spelt *course* down to the eighteenth century; the adjective seems to have come about by way of 'ordinary' cloth, which was *coarse* in the same pejorative way that 'ordinary-looking' has come to mean 'plain'.

differ–defer : both these stem from medieval Latin *differo* (**dis-fero*) 'move', 'carry apart'. The prefixes {de-} and {dis-} were frequently confused in Medieval Latin and hence in Middle English.

discreet–discrete : the former is 'the popular sense, leaving *discrete* for the scholastic and technical sense in which the kinship to L. *discretus* is more obvious' (*OED*).

flower–flour : the latter is metaphorically the 'flower' of the ground meal.

groin–groyne : the latter means 'part of a sea-wall' and it may have come from the basic *groin* for part of the body. The spelling in both cases is <groin> in AmE.

mantle–mantel : the original meaning was 'a cloak, or covering'; the <-el> spelling is used for the specialized meaning *mantel*(*shelf*), *mantel*(*piece*).

metal–mettle : the latter is a figurative use – an *iron lady* can be *on her mettle*.

of–off : these are historically the same word; the spelling *off* attached to the emphatic form. They are now distinguished by the /v/ – /f/ pronunciation.

patron–pattern : both come from French *patron*, which still has both meanings; the stress shifted to the first syllable when referring to things as a 'pattern' and the spelling was anglicized; the stress shifted later in *patron* too, but the French spelling was kept.

person–parson : both are from Latin *persona* by way of French. The specialized ecclesiastical use with the <a> spelling gradually established itself in early modern English. In Middle English the two had been variant spellings with either meaning.

plait–pleat : the differentiation seems to have come about from different dialectal pronunciations of the word *plait*.

premise–premiss : this pair has not quite settled down; it would be convenient to have *premiss*, *premisses*, for uses in logic and *premise*, *premises*, to mean buildings and property.

price–prize : these began to be differentiated as early as 1600.

queue–cue (as in billiards). Both are late eighteenth century borrowings of French *queue*. The spelling differentiation has evolved in English.

rout–route : the semantic relationship between these variants is completely lost; they both come from Latin *ruptus* 'broken'. A *rout* is a broken-off body of people, a *route* is a broken-through road. Both are pronounced /raʊt/ in the US and, formerly but seemingly no longer, in the British army.

shagreen–chagrin : the first, an anglicized spelling of French *chagrin*, is a rough kind of skin used for polishing; this was the original meaning – the emotion *chagrin* is a figurative use; no spelling distinction has been made in French.

stanch (v.)–*staunch* (adj.) : here, too, the semantic relationship is quite tortuous; they both come ultimately from Latin *stagnum* 'a pool' (cf. *stagnant*) by way of French. The verb *stanch* means 'to stop the flow of blood', the adjective *staunch* means 'determined' (by way of 'water-tight').

temper–tamper : 'to temper clay' was to mix it thoroughly for the potter; a dialect version of this was *tamper*, which is now used figuratively for 'to meddle, interfere' (cf. modern slang 'to mix it' = 'to brawl'). Curiously, the original sense of *meddle* was 'to mix'.

tire–tyre : both were formerly used for 'attire, clothing'; the alternative spelling *tyre* fell into disuse quite early but was revived in British English (not US) in the nineteenth century for the *tyre* (i.e. 'clothing') of a wheel.

ton–tun : both variants meant originally a cask; the Old English spelling was *tunne*, the Old French spelling was *tonne*; since the eighteenth century *tun* has been used for 'cask' and liquid measure and *ton* for 'weight'.

Dialect variants are responsible for some differentiation. *Hale* (as in *hale and hearty*) is a Northern form of *whole*. *Glamour*, according to *OED* may be a Scottish corruption of *grammar*. It first appeared in Sir Walter Scott's novels in the sense of 'magic, enchantment' and in recent times has become a stock term of advertising and the film industry. Alternatively, it may be a variant of *glimmer*, with the basic meaning of 'brightness'.

There are occasional examples of two differently-spelt and quite distinct words being distanced still further by spelling manipulation. *OED* mentions the deliberate use of *cokernut* in the Port of London instead of *coconut* to avoid confusion with *cocoa*. The two pronunciations of *invalid* /ɪn'vælid/ 'not valid' and /'ɪnvəliːd/ 'infirm' could be usefully differentiated, with the latter having the §French spelling **invalide*.

The French loan-word *design* covers two meanings which have become differentiated in spelling in the original French: *dessein* ‘purpose, plan’ and *dessin* ‘design in art’.

There are many instances of the reverse process to differentiation, where two distinct words become confused into one, but these are of less direct interest for English spelling. One curious literary example is Sir Thomas More’s *Utopia* ‘no-place’. This has been widely reinterpreted with the meaning of *Eutopia* ‘good-place’, a fictitious name also used in the sixteenth century. In the sixteenth century the word *concent* was used to mean ‘musical harmony’; the <cent> related to Latin *cantus* ‘song’. However, it soon became confused with its homophone *consent* (from Latin *con* + *sentire*) ‘to agree together’ – a natural enough interpretation of harmony.

The existence of variant spellings clearly invites semantic differentiation. On the other hand there are variant spellings which have persisted as variants, presumably because the semantic range of the word is fairly restricted: *caldron*, *cauldron*; *despatch*, *dispatch*. In the case of *lour*, *lower* ‘to look threatening’, it would be sensible to drop the spelling *lower* because of confusion with *lower* ‘more low’ in, for instance, *lowering clouds*. Some spelling variants, as one might expect, simply reflect variant pronunciations: cf. *scallop* with /æ/, *scollop* with /ɒ/. But even here there is some fuzziness: *scallop* may have /ɒ/; *scollop* is largely found in a figurative use as a kind of pleating or lacework (*OED*). The suffix pair <-able>, with a free stem, and <-ible>, with a bound stem, allow competing forms which may develop a different meaning. Fowler (1926: 2) cites *uncorrectable* and *incorrigible*, *destroyable* and *destructible* (see §5.5 p. 424ff).

Prescriptive writers on English usage like to encourage specific uses for varying spellings. Fowler (1926: 371), the most prestigious, lends his weight to the general tendency to use <nought> for the number ‘zero’ and <naught> for figurative uses (‘to set at naught’). Similarly, he wants to assign <spirt> to the ‘spirting’ of blood (cf. squirt??) and <spurt> as ‘final effort’. On the other hand, he refuses to accept the growing tendency to have <premiss>, <premisses> for use in logic and <premises> ‘building’. Vallins (1965: 157) suggests that <cypher> should be assigned to ‘zero’ and <cipher> to ‘secret writing’, and also <syren> to ‘nymph’ and <siren> to ‘loud warning device’. This is consistent, since he gives the §Basic <i> spelling to the derived figurative use. However, pundits are less influential than the example set by printers.

While variant spellings, such as *metal–mettle*, *block–bloc* and even *gray–grey*, may come to differentiate two distinct meanings, it is not so easy to find examples of free variant pronunciations of the same spelling gradually acquiring a difference of meaning. This may be so with the two pronunciations of *greasy*: ‘Some people use the forms /ˈgriːsɪ/ and /ˈgriːzɪ/ with a difference of meaning, /ˈgriːsɪ/ having reference merely to the presence of grease and /ˈgriːzɪ/ having reference to slipperiness caused by grease' (EPD). The following examples are taken from LPD. Some people distinguish two meanings of *baths*: with /θs/ as 'acts of bathing', with /ðz/ as 'bathtubs, bathhouses'. Some British speakers distinguish between a wall *plaque* as /plæk/ and dental *plaque* as /plɑːk/ or /pleɪk/. In the case of *fascia*, 'In BrE generally ˈfeɪʃ-, but as a medical term, ˈfæʃ-; as a term in classical architecture, also ˈfeɪs i .ə. In AmE, generally ˈfæʃ i ə, but ˈfeɪʃ ə in the sense of 'board above shopfront' (LPD p. 268). These have to be interpreted as spoken variants of {fascia} conditioned by different technical jargons. LPD notes that British speakers will have /-ɑːd/ in *promenade* as 'sea-front', but /-eɪd/ for a movement in square dancing. This is using an American pronunciation in an American cultural context.

5.5 HOMOPHONOUS AFFIXES

Identifying affixes

Spelling is often discussed as if it were simply a matter of phoneme and letter correspondences with no regard to the structure of words. But for words consisting of more than one morpheme, the internal structure of the word strongly conditions the written form. Spellers can only perform efficiently by taking this structure into account. The text-to-speech algorithms discussed in §4.1, with the exception of Ainsworth's deliberately simplified model, all exploit word structure by affix stripping. The pioneering speech-to-text algorithm of Hanna did not (§2.8.5). Yet the identification of an affix by its meaning or grammatical function is particularly important to the writer, since many recurrent affixes are homophonous with other strings. The words *hydrometer* and *arbiter* both end in /-ɪtə(r)/; the words *physician* and *repetition* both end in /-ɪʃn/. Anyone who can associate *hydrometer* with 'measuring' and {meter} is not likely to write **hydromiter*. Anyone who associates <-ician> with 'human, professional' is not likely to write **physition* (cf. *position*). Similarly, the endings <-ence>, <-ance>, both pronounced /-əns/ in *sequence*, *substance*, can be differentiated in spelling if we are aware of the stressed vowels in *sequential*, *substantial*. There can be no doubt that an awareness of word-structure in a particular word and in semantically related words may play an important role in selecting the correct spelling when pronunciation alone is not decisive. This is particularly so in unstressed syllables where the vowel may have been reduced or adjacent consonants merged.

The identification of a particular affix may be worthwhile in two different respects:

1 The affix itself may have a spelling which is in some way peculiar – in terms of the spelling correspondences which otherwise apply in root morphemes. The correspondence <ti>≡/ʃ/ is only found in association

with suffixes, as in <-tion>, where it is a consequence of palatalization. Selecting <ti>≡/ʃ/ as the correct correspondence involves knowing that you are dealing with a §Latinate suffix.

2 The affix may mark the word as belonging to a particular subsystem and so condition the correct spelling of the stem to which it is attached. The <ex-> and <-ive> of *exclusive* together mark it as a §Romance or §Latinate word and so the §Basic correspondence <oo>≡/uː/ (*<excloosive>) is ruled out.

The recognition of a particular affix may depend on any of three factors:

1 phonetic: recognizing the phonetic structure of the word, its stress pattern, or the number of syllables;
2 semantic/syntactic: recognizing meaning or grammatical function;
3 morphological: recognizing word formation potential and morpheme boundaries.

What is involved in spelling *pallid* correctly? Leaving aside the problem of the double <-ll->, why not spell it *pallied* (like *rallied*)? In terms of meaning and function *pallid* clearly has an adjective-forming <-id>: it can have a comparative 'more pallid'. In terms of morphology we may recognize that the boundary is /ˈpæl+ɪd/ not /ˈpælɪ+d/ and that it associates with *pallor*, not with a verb **pally*. There are analogous pairs: *squalid–squalor*, *torpid–torpor*. In terms of phonology we may be aware that some speakers have long /iː/ in final open unstressed syllables rather than /ɪ/ (/ˈræliː/ rather than /ˈrælɪ/). So we have potential variation /-iːd/ ~ /-ɪd/ in *rallied*, which we do not have in *pallid*. This is not to say that, when someone writes the word *pallid*, any single one of these considerations will come to the level of awareness. But they are factors which may influence people when they originally learn the spelling or try to bolster their memory when they come to write it down.

Wrongly spelt affixes form a large proportion of all spelling errors. Yet, simply because most accounts of English spelling conventions are written in the direction spelling-to-sound, the problems posed for the writer by affixes have not received much attention. It is no trouble at all, in one direction, to state that both *sequence* and *substance* are pronounced with the same ending /-əns/. It is rather more difficult, working in the other direction, to identify possible clues for a successful spelling of /-əns/. We can, however, examine some of the more troublesome affixes to see what phonetic, semantic, grammatical and morphological cues might be available to the speller. The problems are mostly found with suffixes rather than prefixes. We need not, however, be too particular about what constitutes a 'prefix' or a 'suffix'. Indeed, in a prior sifting of the material it is better to think in terms of 'beginnings' and 'endings' and then, if necessary, sort out the morphology at a later stage. The letter string need not represent a discrete functional part of the word. There is no point in excluding the <-ant> of *elephant* from a discussion of <-ant> in *elegant, important*.

Starting with the phonetic string itself we shall try to find means of associating it with all the variant spellings. The endings discussed below are known to cause problems:

1 /-ʒn/, /-ʧn/, /-ʃn/ as in <-sion>, <-tion>, <-cion> p. 420
2 /-ʃəs/, /-ʧəs/ as in <-cious>, <-tious> p. 421
3 /-ənt/, /-əns/ as in <-a/ent>, <-a/ence>, <-a/ency> p. 422
4 /-əbəl/ as <-able>, <-ible> in adjectives p. 424
5 /-ə(r)/ as <-er>, <-or> in agentive nouns p. 426
6 /-ə(r)/ as <-or>, <-our>, <-ure> in mass nouns p. 428
7 /-ə(r)/ as <-ar> in adjectives p. 429
8 /-ɪə(r)/ in <-eer>, <-ier> in agentive nouns p. 429
9 stressed /-et/ as <-ette>, <-et> p. 429
10 /-eɪ/ in French loans as <-e>, <-ee>, <-er>, <-et> p. 430
11 /-ɪd/ as <-ied>, <-id> p. 430
12 /-ɪs/ as <-ice>, <-is> in nouns p. 430
13 /-ɪ/ (AmE /i(:)/) in nouns as <-y>, <-ey>, <-ie> p. 431
14 /-ərɪ/ as <-ary>, <-ery>, <-ory>, <-ury> in nouns p. 431
15 /-iːn/ in nouns as <-ene>, <-ine> p. 432
16 /-iːz/ in nouns as <-ese>, <-ise> p. 433
17 /-aɪz/ in verbs as <-ise>, <-ize> p. 433
18 /-əl/ as <-le>, <-al>, <-el>, <-il>, <-ol> p. 433
19 /-əm/ as <-am>, <-em>, <-om>, <-um> in nouns p. 438
20 variation in <e>/<i> at suffix boundaries p. 438
21 miscellaneous suffix problems p. 440
21 miscellaneous prefix problems p. 441

To some extent the material presented here will recur in §3 and §4 under the spelling of individual phonemes and letters, but it is worth bringing together in this 'identical forms' section some of the main problems posed by homophonous affixes as they present themselves to a writer. The numbers of instances quoted for any particular affix refer to the words in the database used to provide material for §3 and §4. They will serve as a rough indication of the number of words in current use with that particular affix. The database is described in §3.1.1: it is simply a comprehensive word list culled from very large bodies of text. The figures quoted are only rough proportional indicators, since there are hundreds of obscure or archaic technical terms that might be found in historical or specialist dictionaries that are not represented in the database, or in any practicable corpus of text. On the other hand, the relative figures quoted probably correspond to the day-to-day experience of the average speller.

1 /-ʒn/, /-ʧn/, /-ʃn/ as in <-sion>, <-tion>, <-cion>

This group of noun endings is generally thought to be a considerable spelling problem, though investigation shows more regularity than one would suppose. We also need to refer to adjectives and derived nouns in <-ian> such as *alsatian* ‘an Alsatian dog’. That this is an adjective meaning ‘from Alsace’ is opaque to most people, so there is every temptation to write *<alsation>. The connection between *Mars* and *Martian* is more obvious.

The spelling of /-ʒn/ (29 examples) is almost always <-sion> (*confusion*, *invasion*, *decision*). The only exceptions are, very curiously, the word *equation*, where many speakers have /ʒ/ rather than /ʃ/ and one or two words with <-ian> formed from proper names: *artesian* (from *Artois*), *Friesian*.

The spelling of /-ʧn/ (8 examples) is also consistent in the database as <-tion> after <s> (*suggestion*, *exhaustion*, *combustion*). Some individual speakers may have /-ʧn/ rather than /-ʃn/ after /n/ in words like *abstention*, *tension*, but we have assumed such words to have /-nʃn/ and these are dealt with below.

The spelling of /-ʃn/ is the main problem. Some groups of words can be identified by meaning. The <-ician> (23 examples) spelling of /-ɪʃn/ is quite consistent; the referent is always ‘human, professional’: *politician*, *mathematician*. Similarly there is no problem with the §Basic words *ashen*, *freshen*, *harshen* since there is a clear boundary after the free forms *ash*, *fresh*, *harsh*.

The words *fashion*, *cushion*, with <sh> and *luncheon*, *stanchion*, with <ch> represent single morphemes, not a stem and suffix.

We can consider the remaining words in the context of the phoneme immediately preceding the /-ʃn/; in practice this also means in the context of the preceding letters. One ending in particular outnumbers all the others – <-ation>≡/eɪʃn/ (825 examples). The other less common endings are shown in table 45 below.

Table 45 Consonants preceding <-ion> suffix

Phonemes	/p/	/k/	/l/	/n/	/ɪ/	/e/	/æ/	/ʌ/	/iː/	/ɜː/	/əʊ/	/ɔː/
Letters	< p	c	l	n	i	e	a	u	e	Vr	o	Vr/au>
<-sion>	–	–	8	20	–	–	–	–	–	14	–	1
<-tion>	39	128	–	15	72	2	1	–	7	4	9	8
<-cion>	–	–	–	–	1	–	–	–	–	1	–	–
<-ssion>	–	–	–		12	29	2	4	–	–	–	–

Examples:

- <-sion> : *compulsion*, *pension*, *immersion*, *incursion*, *torsion*;
- <-tion> : *adoption*, *selection*, *invention*, *inhibition*, *discretion*, *ration*,

deletion, *assertion*, *lotion*, *contortion*;
- <-cion> : *suspicion*, *coercion*;
- <-ssion>: *mission*, *recession*, *passion*, *discussion*.

It is clear from the above table that in many cases the stem-final phoneme does condition the choice of spelling. It is also clear that there are a sprinkling of isolated spellings which will inevitably need individual treatment: *suspicion*, *coercion*, (*com*)*passion*, *ration*, (*in*)*discretion*, and *torsion* (cf. *contortion*). The main indecisive phonetic contexts are after /n/, /ɪ/ and /ɜː/ affecting the choice of <-(s)sion> or <-tion>, as in *tension–detention*; *mission–inhibition*; *immersion–exertion*.

Word-formation potential supports the phonetic context in most cases and is clearly an easy criterion to exploit in practical teaching (*opt* gives <t> for *option*, *compulsive* gives <s> for *compulsion*, *ignite* gives <t> for *ignition*, *digress* gives <ss> for *digression*, *elated* gives <t> for *elation*, etc.). There is a conflict in words containing {vert}, such as *convert–conversion*.

2 /-ʃəs/, /-ʧəs/ as in <-cious>, <-tious>

This is a further palatalization problem. Of the two main spellings, <-cious> and <-tious>, the former is more common. For the words in the database, the previous phoneme(s) predict the spelling to some extent.

After /teɪ/ and /kseɪ/ only <-tious> occurs: *flirtatious*, *ostentatious*, *vexatious*; otherwise there is <-acious>: *audacious*, *capacious*, *contumacious*, *curvacious*, *efficacious*, *fallacious*, *gracious*, *loquacious*, *mendacious*, *pertinacious*, *pugnacious*, *rapacious*, *sagacious*, *salacious*, *spacious*, *veracious*, *vivacious*, *voracious*. They are distinguishable, too, by different derivation patterns: <-atious> – <-ation> *flirtation*, *ostentation*, *vexation*; <-acious> – <-acity>, with <c>≡/s/, *audacity*, *mendacity*, *pertinacity*, *rapacity*, *sagacity*, *veracity*; /s/ also figures in *fallacy*, *grace*, *space*.

After /ɪ/, it is not so easy to distinguish <-icious> (15 examples) and <-itious> (13 examples). Expect <-itious> after /t, b, d, ʤ/: *adventitious*, *ambitious*, *seditious*, *flagitious*. Otherwise expect <-icious>: *auspicious*, *avaricious*, *capricious*, *delicious*, *malicious*, *meretricious*, *officious*, *pernicious*, *suspicious*, *vicious*. Exceptions: *judicious*, *nutritious*, *propitious*.

Apart from *conscious*, we find <-ntious> with <t>: *conscientious*, *contentious*, *licentious*, *pretentious*, *sententious*.

Otherwise, there are just odds and ends. After /p/, /ɔː/ there is <-tious> with <t>: *bumptious*, *captious*, *cautious*. With /k/ there is either a <ct> spelling: *factious*, *fractious*, *infectious*, or an <x> spelling: *anxious*, *noxious*, *obnoxious*. After /əʊ/ there is <-cious> with <c>: *atrocious*, *ferocious*, *precocious*. On its own is *luscious*, and we have *specious* set against *facetious*.

3 /-ənt/, /-əns/ as in <-a/ent>, <-a/ence>, <-a/ency>

The difference in <a> and <e> spellings in these suffixes largely derives from different Latin verb conjugations. This is a notorious source of misspellings in present-day English because the vowel in both pairs of suffixes is reduced to /ə/. There is some guidance on the choice of <a> or <e> spellings from related forms with a stressed vowel (*consequent–consequential*; *substance–substantial*), but many of these related words are rather remote from daily use. Words with these suffixes were usually borrowed by way of French, where the Latin <a> and <e> had been merged into a regular <-ant> <-ance>. Spellings with <e> in words such as *dependence* (Latin *dependere*) are due to later qualms by English scholars. But etymological respectability did not always weigh heavily with the public and so the dictionary makers have had to allow both spellings in some common words, notably *dependent*, *dependant*, *dependence*, *dependance*. To allow free variation like this in some particular words only serves to confuse spellers still further. These relaxations are not, however, very consistent: **independant*, unlike *dependant*, is not permitted. The speller may feel entitled to ask: if I am allowed a free choice in *dependent/dependant*, why is this choice not allowed in *independent*, *resplendent* and *abundant*? An out and out free thinker might even wonder: if a Romance language such as French, regulated as it is by a fearsomely conservative Academy of scholars, can fix the spelling in French as <dépendant>, <dépendance>, <indépendant>, <indépendance>, very conveniently but quite unetymologically, why cannot it be done for English? If this were done across the lexicon, some homophones would then have the same spelling (*current*, *currant*), but very few. If spelling standardization of awkward suffixes were ever undertaken, these two would be a prime target.

Table 46 < -ent/-ant> and <-ence/-ance> spelling variability (Webster)

'almost always' spelt	'usually' spelt	'about equally' spelt
ascendant *attendance* *descendant* *intendant* *pendant (n.)*	*expellant* *propellant*	*ascendancy/ascendency* *dependant/dependent (n.)* *pendant/pendent (adj.)*
dependency *dependent (adj.)* *tendency* *transcendent* *superintendent*	*impellent* *repellent*	

W3NID (p. 25a) estimates various degrees of variability for some of the variable words, presumably with reference to American practice. Examples are shown in table 46.

Since spellers tend to use the <-ant>, <-ance>, <-ancy> spellings by default, we can usefully list the more important stems which are followed by <e> spellings. These represent a 55 per cent majority over <a> spellings. Rare or archaic words such as *attingence*, *comburence*, *frugiferent*, *lutulence*, *regredience*, have not been included. All three endings <-ent>, <-ence>, <-ency> are potential, but sometimes there are gaps: we have *different*, *difference*, but rarely *differency*; we have *delinquent*, *delinquency*, but rarely *delinquence*. Forms with <-esc->≡/es/ *crescent*, *effervescent*, predictably have <e> and are not included. A range of prefixes found with each root have been included, to indicate that roots such as {curr} (*recurrent*, etc.) and {fer} (*different*, etc.) are more widely distributed than roots such as {dulg}, or {nasc}.

Table 47 Consonants preceding <-ant/-ent> <-ance/-ence> suffixes

Phonemes	/p/	/b/	/t/	/d/	/k/	/g/	/ʧ/	/ʤ/	/m/	/n/	/l/	/r/
Letters	<*p*	*b*	*t*	*d*	*c*	*g*	*ch*	*g*(*e*)	*m*	*n*	*l*	*r* >
<-ant/ce>	4	1	62	26	13	9	2	4	6	40	24	62
<-ent/ce>	8	5	33	62	–	–	–	42	1	24	48	27
Phonemes	/f/	/v/	/s/	/z/	/ʃ/	/w/	/eɪ/	/aɪ/	/ɔɪ/	/aʊ/	/ɪ/	/ʊ/
Letters	< *f*	*v*	*s*/*c*	*s*	*ti*	(*q*)*u*	*a*	*i*	*oy*	*ow*	*i*	*u* >
<-ant/ce>	4	14	10	13	–	–	2	11	6	1	16	6
<-ent/ce>	–	4	66	4	15	17	–	–	–	–	49	13

abhorr-, abs-, abstin-, accid-, adher-, afflu-, ag-, anci-, ambi-, ambival-, anteced-, appar-, ard-, astring-, audi-, belliger-, benevol-, benefic-, cad-, circumfer-, clem-, cli-, coher-, coincid-, compet-, complac-, compon-, concurr-, condol-, confer-, confid-, congru-, consci-, consequ-, consist-, constitu-, contin-, conveni-, converg-, corpul-, correspond-, cred-, credul-, curr-, decad-, dec-, decumb-, defer-, defici-, delinqu-, depend-, despond-, deterg-, deterr-, differ-, diffid-, dilig-, dissid-, diverg-, divulg-, ebulli-, effici-, efflu-, effulg-, eloqu-, emerg-, emin-, emolli-, ess-, evid-, excell-, exist-, expedi-, experi-, expon-, exud-, ferv-, flatul-, floccul-, flu-, fraudul-, frequ-, gradi-, imman-, immin-, impati-, impot-, impud-, inadvert-, incid-, incipi-, incongru-, incumb-, independ-, indiffer-, indig-, indol-, indulg-, infrequ-, inher-, innoc-, insist-, insol-, insolv-, instrum-, insurg-, intellig-, interfer-, intermitt-, intransig-, lat-, leni-, magnific-, malevol-, munific-, nasc-, neglig-, obedi-, occurr-, omnipot-, omnisci-, oppon-, opul-, pat-, pati-, penit-, perman-, persist-, pestil-, pot-, preced-, prefer-, presci-, pres-, preval-, profici-, promin-, provid-, prud-, pruri-, pung-, rec-, recipi-, recumb-, recurr-, redol-, refer-, refulg-, reg-, reminisc-, repell-, resid-, resili-, resplend-, respond-, resurg-, retic-, rever-, sali-, *sent-*, *senti-*, *sequ-*, *sil-*, *solv-*, *somnol-*, *string-*, *strid-*, *subsequ-*, *subservi-*, *subsid-*, *succul-*, *suffici-*, *tang-*, *tend-*, *transcend-*, *transi-*, *transpar-*, *transluc-*, *trucul-*, *turbul-*, *urg-*, *val-*, *vehem-*, *viol-*, *virul-*.

If we try to find regularities in the present system, we can see that to some extent the spelling of the suffix is determined by the previous (stem-final) phoneme. In practice this also means by the stem-final spelling. In 754 words found in the database (including monomorphemic words such as *merchant*, *elephant*), the preceding phoneme contexts were as shown in table 47.

In table 47 the common ending <-ment> is not included; the endings <-escence>, <-escent> are included; /ʃ/≡<sci> also has <-ence> in *conscience*.

Positive cues for <a> spellings are accordingly a stem-final /k, g, ʧ, f/ or any of the diphthongs /eɪ, aɪ, ɔɪ, aʊ/. The only positive cue for <e> spellings is a previous /kw/. Stems ending in <-ul-> tend to have <-ent>: *corpulent*, *flatulent*, *flocculent*, *fraudulent*, *opulent*, *succulent*, *truculent*, *turbulent*, *virulent*. Exceptions are: *ambulance*, *petulant*, *stimulant*.

The spelling is therefore predictable in words such as: *significance*, *elegance*, *trenchant*, *infant*, *abeyance*, *reliance*, *annoyance*, *allowance*, *eloquent*, *consequence*. If the complex suffix <-escence>/<-escent> can be identified by its meaning: 'growing x, becoming x', then the suffix spelling in these words is also determined.

4 /-əbl/ as <-able>, <-ible> in adjectives

These are rather a mess. The productive suffix is <-able>. It can be added to any vaguely transitive verb: *actable*, *awakenable*, *bemoanable*, *chattable*, *crammable*, *dethronable*, *garbleable*, *kissable*, *trafficable*, etc., – all from *OED*. Very occasionally it is added to a noun: *marriageable* (= *marriable*), *peaceable*; but this is quite exceptional for <-ible>: *contemptible*, *digestible*. Though the suffix <-able> and the free form *able* have different Latin origins, they have a similarity of meaning in modern English, since both involve, in most instances, the ability or desirability of someone doing something. Words with the structure *X-able*, where *X* is a free-form, can usually be glossed as 'able to be X-ed'. This association does not easily carry over into <-ible>, where the bound form needs paraphrase: *visible* is glossed as 'able to be seen'.

There are conflicting criteria, and hence a spelling problem, in the choice of <-able> or <-ible>. Etymological spellers prefer <-ible> in all words that would have <-ibilis> in Latin. But some words, such as *tenable*, have come into English by way of French, where they have been standardized on <-able>. In other cases the English <-ible> follows the Latin etymology: English *responsible*, French *responsable*. If the stem is (phonetically) an English free-form verb, it is fairly safe to use <-able>: *admittable*, *comprehendable*, *defendable*, *dividable*, *permittable*, *reprehendable*, *transmittable*. A bound stem may require <-ible>: *admissible*, *comprehensible*, *defensible*, *divisible*, *permissible*, *reprehensible*, *transmissible*. These examples show a free-form ending in /d/ or /t/ with <-able> and a bound form with /s/ which has <-ible>. But usage is not always consistent: *OED* has *extendible* and *W3NID* has *comprehendible*. There is, surprisingly, a potential difference of meaning between *contractable* 'capable of being contracted' as in 'a c. disease', and *contractible* 'capable of contracting, contractile'. There are a few near synonyms such as *believable–credible, eatable–edible.*

Words which go against the trend of having <-able> after a free-form, and instead have <-ible>, include: *accessible*, *controvertible*, *convertible*, *corruptible*, *deducible*, *deductible*, *destructible*, *digestible*, *discernible*, *exhaustible*, *expressible*, *flexible*, *forcible*, *reproducible*, *reversible*, *suggestible*. They tend to have in common a final /d/, /t/, or /s/, and occasionally /n/, before the suffix. *W3NID* has either <-able> or <-ible> in the following words: *collapsible*, *collectible*, *discernible*, *expressible*, *extendible*, *gullible*, *perfectible*.

One group of words with <-able> after a bound form are *abominable, appreciable, calculable, demonstrable, educable, equable, palpable*, where the free-form of the verb ends in <-ate>, or where there is a noun in <-ation> as *durable–duration*. Other instances of <-able> after a bound form are *amiable, capable, despicable*.

Words which have <-ible> after a bound form include: *audible*, *combustible*, *comestible*, *corrigible*, *credible*, *dirigible*, *edible*, *eligible*, *fallible*, *feasible*, *horrible*, *intelligible*, *invincible*, *irascible*, *legible*, *negligible*, *ostensible*, *plausible*, *possible*, *refrangible*, *susceptible*, *tangible*, *terrible*, *visible*.

The spelling problems are compounded by variability in adaptation rules before <-able>. A consonant that normally doubles does so after a stressed vowel: *barrable*, *beggable*, *biddable*, *clubbable*, *crammable*, *diggable*, *stoppable*, etc., but not after an unstressed vowel: *covetable*, *focusable*. An <e> is naturally kept when it marks a consonant, as in <ge>≡/ʤ/, <ce>≡/s/: *changeable*, *gaugeable*, *serviceable*. The spelling <dge>≡/ʤ/ is sufficiently explicit to allow either *bridgeable* or *bridgable*. There is some variability with <-ve> spellings and with the <e> that marks a long vowel: *bribeable*, *bribable*; *blameable*, *blamable*; *chaseable*, *chasable*; *moveable*, *movable*; *solveable*, *solvable*; *unmistakeable*, *unmistakable*, etc. *OED* comments: 'As much reason can be given and as much authority cited for one spelling as the other, and until a reform of English spelling is made, the double form of these words must continue'. The snag is that, if you allow variability before <-able>, it becomes difficult to insist on <e>-deletion before other vowel-initial suffixes. Stem-final <-y> becomes <i> before <-able> as in: *dutiable*, *enviable*, *reliable*, but not when the <y> is an auxiliary letter in a vowel spelling: *assayable*, *enjoyable*. Exceptions are *flyable*, *fryable* (from *fry*; cf. *friable* 'crumbly').

An interesting insight into the incidence of bound forms with <-ible> and free forms with <-able> can be seen with *confer*, *prefer*, *refer*, *transfer*. *Collins Concise English Dictionary* (1978) has *conferrable*, but *referrable* or *referrible*, *transferable* or *transferrable*, all with stress on the <-fer-> With initial stress it has *preferable*, *referable*. These spellings may well be a statement of what is acceptable, but it is hardly subject to rule.

5 /-ə(r)/ as <-er>, <-or> in agentive nouns

We can begin with some advice which clearly will not work as it stands: 'usually use *-er* as a suffix for one-syllable [*sic*] words meaning a person who "does", e.g. *diner*, *jumper*, *runner*; use *-or* for words of two or more syllables, meaning a person or thing that "does", e.g. *actor* [*sic*], *editor*, *incinerator*' (Longley 1975: 49). The only reason why this advice, when disentangled, might have some apparent success is simply that §Romance stems are frequently polysyllabic.

At first sight the difference between <-er> and <-or> in agentive nouns formed from verbs is one between native §Basic words and §Latinate words, but the distribution of the two forms proves to be more complicated and by no means fully regular.

The agentive ending <-er> only attaches to free forms, either §Basic or §Latinate: *commuter*, *drinker*, *killer*, *lover*, *liquefier*, *remembrancer*, *subscriber*. There are similar occupational terms: *hatter*, *jailer*. The spelling *sailor* replaced earlier **sailer* in the professional sense in the nineteenth century. Occupational §Greek words have <-er> after a bound stem: *astrologer*, *astronomer*, *biographer*, *geographer*, *philosopher*, where the <-er> replaces <-y>. *Chorister* is ultimately also §Greek. *Beggar*, *liar* and *pedlar* are irregular.

The ending <-or>, which only occurs in §Romance and §Latinate words, attaches to both free-forms (*alternator*, *confessor*, *elevator*, *grantor*, *reactor*, *rotator*) and bound forms (*predecessor*, *sponsor*, *tutor*). In some cases dictionaries allow either spelling, with no semantic difference: *adviser–advisor*, *vender–vendor*. Purists do not like <-or> to be used in non-§Latinate words, even if they are §Romance. Manchester University had 'advisors and tutors' up to 1954, but thereafter we have had 'advisers and tutors'.

The productive ending <-er> is found after a free form in a number of senses which are not agentive and where the spelling <-or> would not usually occur; moreover, <-or> cannot be added to a compound:

(a) 'native of X': *Londoner*, *New Yorker*;
(b) 'one that has X': *double-decker*, *six-shooter*.

There are many simple nouns in both systems ending in <-er> where it does not represent a suffix (§Basic: *water*, *ladder*, *thunder*; §Latinate: *slander*, *tuber*, *cancer*). Word-formation potential marks the latter group as §Latinate words (*slanderous*, *tubercule*, *cancerous*), though mixed forms can occur: *thunderous*. Among words which can be classified by their meaning as agentive nouns, it is only really the <-or> words which can be largely identified by rule.

The ending <-or> is normally unstressed and the vowel is reduced to /ə/. A small group of various nouns ending in <-or> have a pronunciation /-ɔː(r)/: *matador*, *humidor*, *cuspidor*, *corridor* and so present no spelling problem. Pronunciation as /-ɔː(r)/ for agentive nouns is functional when the usual pronunciation with /-ə(r)/ would cause confusion with the comparative or with some other form. This would account for *humidor* and for words such as *lessor* (where **humider* and *lesser* are potential comparatives). In fact, *lessor* can have the pronunciations /'lesɔː/ or /le'sɔː/, with the second syllable stressed, to further pinpoint the contrast with *lessee;* (cf. *settler*, *settlor*). Otherwise in agentive nouns the /-ɔː(r)/ pronunciation is only found in very formal registers (*actor* as /'æktɔː/).

In the database there are some 300 agentive nouns ending in <-or> and there are no doubt as many again in the remote fringes of §Latinate vocabulary. There are several distinct sub-groups clearly marked as §Latinate <-or> words. The largest of these is of words ending in <-ator> (105 examples) formed as agent nouns from verbal stems ending in <-ate>: *creator*, *insulator*, *agitator*. In some cases the equivalent verb is not usually found (*aviator*, *curator*, *spectator*), though it may be produced by back-formation as with *commentate* (from *commentator*). In words of four or more syllables the nuclear stress is two syllables before the <-at-> (*administrator*) and in three-syllable words on the <-at-> itself (*dictator*). The words *orator* and *conspirator* with /ətə/ are exceptions. A spelling algorithm could exploit this by identifying <-ator> in words of three or more syllables and not in *crater*, *freighter*, *waiter* etc. nor in *traitor*. The <-er> suffix is only occasionally used after <-ate>: *collater*, *relater*. The next largest group is words ending in <-ctor> (52 examples), since several common roots happen to end in <ct>, (*detector*, *conductor*, *constrictor*). These are clearly marked as §Latinate words by their word-formation potential; the only exceptions in the database are the §Greek non-agentive *character* and *aerobacter*.

A group of nouns ending in <-itor> (20 examples) are another well-defined sub-group (*inhibitor*, *capacitor*, *depositor*). There are no *<-mitor> endings to cause confusion with <-meter>≡/-mɪtə(r)/ (*pedometer*, *galvanometer*); in any case the unstressed {meter} is readily identifiable from the meaning. The word *arbiter* is clearly a §Latinate word; it is exceptional in that the /ə(r)/ is part of the base form (cf. *arbitration*).

Morphological markers of §Latinate origin, and hence <-or> rather than <-er>, are rather scattered in the remainder of the words. There are a few word-formation links for agentive <-or> words. There are related words ending in:

- <-al> (n.) for *survivor*;
- <-al> (adj.) for *pastor*;
- <-ance> for *conveyor*, *capacitor*;

- <-ate>, <-ation> for *donor*;
- <-ial> for *tutor*, *dictator*;
- <-ion>, <ive> for *incisor*, *inventor*, *successor*, *distributor*.

A dozen or so more-or-less agentive nouns, some of them fairly common, have at best a non-§Basic appearance rather than positive markers: *abettor*, *conqueror*, *councillor*, *counsellor*, *emperor*, *suitor*, *traitor*, *tormentor*.

The /ə(r)/≡<yr> of the §Greek words *martyr*, *satyr*, *zephyr* is clearly not agentive.

6 /-ə(r)/ as <-or>, <-our>, <-ure> in mass nouns

These endings present a minor, but fairly intractable problem, partly in distinguishing <-or> from <-our> (*stupor–vapour*), partly in distinguishing these endings from the <-er> of some §Basic mass nouns (*liquor–wicker*). The pronunciation of all three spellings is usually a common /-ə(r)/. The Americans have simplified matters by standardizing on <-or>: *armor*, *clamor*, *color*, *honor*, *vapor*. This is all the more reasonable since the <u> does not occur in British spelling in derived forms: *coloration*, *glamorous*, *honorific*, *vaporize*, etc. More particularly, there is the §Latinate <or>≡/ɔː/ correspondence in stressed syllables, as in *armorial*, *laborious*. Curiously, in *W3NID ardor* is given with the variant *ardour*; *savior* has the variant *saviour*; *glamour* is given first place, with *glamor* as a variant.

There are a dozen or so mass nouns ending in <-or> in British spelling, including some of Greek origin: *camphor*, *error*, *horror*, *languor*, *liquor*, *metaphor*, *pallor*, *phosphor*, *squalor*, *stupor*, *terror*, *torpor*; many of these were earlier written with <-our> **errour*, **terrour*. Some of this group can be countable (*errors*, *metaphors*). There are twice as many mass nouns with <-our>, but this is still rather a small group: *armour*, *behaviour*, *candour*, *clamour*, *clangour*, *colour*, *endeavour*, *fervour*, *flavour*, *glamour*, *honour*, *labour*, *rancour*, *rigour*, *rumour*, *splendour*, *succour*, *valour*, *vapour*, *vigour*. Some of these can also be countable (*honours*, *rumours*). There are a few nouns ending in <-our> which are only countables and which have no particular marking: *harbour*, *parlour*, *tumour* and the agentive *saviour*.

Mass nouns ending in <-ure> can be identified by a preceding /ʧ/ as a palatalization of //tj//: *architecture, literature, moisture*. Some occur also as count-nouns: *adventure, conjecture, curvature, structure, temperature*. There are also /ʃ/ in *pressure* and /ʒ/ in *leisure, measure, pleasure, treasure.*

Apart from this, numbers are too small to warrant any rules based on the preceding stem-final phoneme. Both <-our> and <-or> pattern with adjectives in <-id>: *fervour–fervid*, *candour–candid*, *horror–horrid*, *torpor–torpid*, which at least prevents confusion with <-er>.

7 /-ə(r)/ as <-ar> in adjectives

This is a §Latinate ending, forming a potential word-formation cluster with <-arity> or occasionally <-ous>: *popular–popularity–populous*. The majority of these adjectives have a preceding /l/: *globular*, *particular*, *jugular*, *popular*, *scalar*. Others are: *lumbar*, *vulgar*, *familiar*, *peculiar*, *planar*, *lunar*.

Apart from the comparative, which is readily identified by meaning, very few adjectives end in <-er>. Examples: *bitter*, *chipper*, *eager*, *neuter*, *proper*, *slender*, *sober*, *yonder*.

8 /-ɪə(r)/ in <-eer>, <-ier> in agentive nouns

These suffixes also occur in nouns denoting human agents. The <-eer> spelling is a productive suffix that freely attaches to minimal free-forms: *engineer*, *mountaineer*, *mutineer*, *auctioneer*, *profiteer*. It often has contemptuous overtones: *pamphleteer*, *sonneteer*. It always carries primary stress. The <-ier> spelling corresponds either to a stressed suffix (*cashier*, *bombardier*, *grenadier*, *brigadier*, *gondolier*) or unstressed suffix (*farrier*, *clothier*, *furrier*). Stressed <-ier> is usually attached to §Romance words: *brigade–brigadier*. When unstressed, it is homophonous with agentive <-er> added to stems ending in /ɪ/: *carrier*, *fancier*, *harrier*. There is no similar overlap with agentive <-or> except in the word *warrior*, which must be regarded as exceptional.

For the words in the database, the stressed endings can be largely differentiated by the preceding consonant: <-ier> after /d/ and /ʃ/; <-eer> after /t/ and /n/. This, however, seems to be a purely fortuitous consequence of the small number of words involved.

9 stressed /-et/ as <-ette>, <-et>

The ending <-ette> usually has primary stress in SBS: *brunette*, *cassette*, *chiffonette*, *cigarette*, *coquette*, *corvette*, *croquette*, *etiquette*, *flanelette*, *gazette*, *georgette*, *kitchenette*, *launderette*, *layette*, *lorgnette*, *marionette*, *mignonette*, *novelette*, *pipette*, *pirouette*, *rosette*, *roulette*, *serviette*, *silhouette*, *soubrette*, *statuette*, *suffragette*, *usherette*, *vignette*. The stress may shift to the antepenultimate syllable in one or two of the more frequent of these words, such as *cigarette*. The word *omelette* is quite exceptional in that the stress is never on the last syllable and the vowel of that syllable is reduced to /ə/ or /ɪ/.

There is a spelling problem here since a final stressed /-et/ may also be spelt simply as <-et> as in: *bassinet*, *cadet*, *clarinet*, *curvet*, *duet*, *epaulet*, *flageolet*, *martinet*, *minuet*, *spinet*, *stockinet*; *quartet*, *quintet*, *sextet*, *septet*, *octet*, *nonet*. In the latter group alternative spellings *quartette* and *quintette* sometimes occur.

Semantic indicators such as ‘female’ for <-ette> and ‘male’ for <-et> (*martinet*, *usherette*), or ‘diminutive’ for <-ette> (*kitchenette*) are not very reliable. One would get better results from the quite arbitrary notion that military and musical words had <-et>. The only firm rule seems to be that, if the ending follows a free-form, then you have the ending <-ette>. The <-ette> ending is so clearly §French that purists object to its unrestricted use after any minimal free-form: ‘most of these, as leaderette, sermonette, essayette, can scarcely be said to be in good use’ (*OED*). This, however, was before the public had been softened up to accept *kitchenette*, *launderette*, and similar neologisms.

10 /-eɪ/ in French loans as <-e>, <-ee>, <-er>, <-et>

The problem is to distinguish words such as *cafe*, *fiancee*, *foyer*, *ballet*. For detailed lists, see under /eɪ/ in §3.3.2.3, p. 167. Words such as *cafe* need not necessarily occur with a French acute accent mark as <é(e)>. In spite of their French origin, these words do not usually have final stress; they are mostly nouns, with a few adjectives.

11 /-ɪd/ as <-ied>, <-id>

For some SBS speakers *candied–candid*, *jellied–gelid* are homophones ending in /ɪd/. In spite of phonetic identity this should not be a spelling problem. Speakers should be aware that in *candied* the suffix {-ed} has been added to a free form, *candy*. No-one should be tempted to write **frenzid* for *frenzied*.

A growing number of English speakers (certainly within SBS) tend to have /iː/ rather than /ɪ/ in final open unstressed syllables. This difference in distribution (or perhaps in realization – Wells 1982: 4.1.7) makes *candied* and *candid* phonetically distinct: /ˈkændiː+d/ – /ˈkændɪd/.

12 /-ɪs/ as <-ice>, <-is> in nouns

The ending <-ice> comes through French from a number of Latin origins. Apart from being a marker of nouns, it has no particular consistent meaning: *accomplice*, *apprentice*, *armistice*, *artifice*, *auspice*, *avarice*, *benefice*, *bodice*, *chalice*, *cornice*, *cowardice*, *crevice*, *dentifrice*, *edifice*, *hospice*, *interstice*, *jaundice*, *justice*, *lattice*, *liquorice*, *malice*, *notice*, *novice*, *office*, *orifice*, *poultice*, *practice*, *precipice*, *prejudice*, *pumice*, *service*, *solstice*, *surplice*, etc.

The ending <-is> is found in §Greek nouns, if these can be identified as such: *acropolis*, *aegis*, *amaryllis*, *analysis*, *aphis*, *axis*, *chrysalis*, *dermis*, *dialysis*, *electrolysis*, *epidermis*, *genesis*, *hubris*, *hydrolysis*, *hypothesis*, *ibis*, *iris*, *metropolis*, *necropolis*, *nemesis*, *oxalis*, *parenthesis*, *penis*, *syphilis*, etc.

There are, however, a few words of Romance origin: *tennis*, *trellis*, *portcullis*.

There is little guidance for the speller from word-formation here. Only <-ice> is added to free forms: *cowardice*, *service*. Only <-ice> allows further affixation that modifies the stem phonetically: *auspicious*, *avaricious*, *beneficial*, *justiciary*, *malicious*, *novitiate*, *official*, *practical*, *precipitous*, *prejudicial*.

13 /-ɪ/ (AmE /iː/) in nouns as <-y>, <-ey>, <-ie>

Adjectives will normally select the ending <-y>. When <-y> is added to a noun or verb to form the adjective, a final <e> may or may not be deleted: *gamey, gamy, horsey, horsy, jokey, joky, shakey, shaky*. An <-e-> is inserted after a stem-final <y>: *clayey*, since *<yy> is not a permitted string.

After free-forms the diminutive or familiar noun suffix is usually <-ie>: *bookie, cookie, darkie, movies, quickie, rookie, talkie, undies*. *Junky–junkie*, *hanky–hankie* (*handkerchief*), and *loony–looney–loonie* (*lunatic*) are variants. When the final /ɪ/ is not a suffix, the spelling is usually <-ey> after a /k/: *donkey*, *flunkey*, *hockey*, *jockey*, *lackey*, *monkey*, *whiskey* (Irish w.; or the usual American spelling). After /n/ there is some variation: *blarney*, *chimney*, *chutney*, *cockney*, *hackney*, *honey*, *journey*, *kidney*, *money*, *tourney*; *crony* (not apparently connected with *crone*), *pony*, *tunny*. *Acne* is §Greek.

There is free variation between <-y> and <-ie> in 'pet' (hypocoristic) names: *Johnny–Johnnie*, *Willy–Willie*. The <-ie> ending is more endearing and tends to be used for a female when the name can be either male or female: *Billie*, *Bobbie*. An exception would be *Billy Jean King*, the tennis player, but her other name, *Jean*, already indicates that she is a woman. *Georgy* is from *George, Georgie* is usually from *Georgina*. However, the <-ie> forms are commonly used for males in Scotland. Final <-i> shows a name to be foreign: *Willi*.

14 /-ərɪ/ as <-ary>, <-ery>, <-ory>, <-ury> in nouns

Of these <-ory> and <-ary> have unreduced vowel quality in AmE as /-eri/ and /-ɔri/. There are various types of structure:

- <-ary>: *anniversary*, *antiquary*, *apothecary*, *capillary*, *centenary*, *commissary*, *constabulary*, *dignitary*, *dromedary*, *granary*, *itinerary*, *library*, *luminary*, *ovary*, *pituitary*, *quandary*, *salary*, *secretary*, *seminary*. There are some instances of an apparent free-form before <-ary>: *adversary*, *boundary*, *burglary*, *commentary*, *dispensary*;
- <-ery>: a free form + <-ery> in *bravery*, *cajolery*, *fernery*, *forgery*, *prudery*, *refinery*. In some cases it is difficult to decide whether we have

<-ery> as a simple suffix or <-er->+<-y>: is *gunnery* like *fern+ery* or *master+y*? There is a stem ending in <-er> + <-y> in *mastery*, *misery*, *recovery*, *upholstery*. The stem is not a free-form in *artery*, *celery*, *chancery*, *emery*, *livery*, *monastery*, *surgery*;

- <-ory> (excluding stressed <-atory> as in *ambulatory*): *allegory*, *category*, *chicory*, *factory*, *hickory*, *history*, *ivory*, *memory*, *oratory*, *pillory*, *promontory*, *purgatory*, *rectory*, *refectory*, *repertory*, *signatory*, *suppository*, *territory*, *trajectory*. In *oratory*, *rectory*, *victory*, there is <-or->+<-y>, and in *consistory*, *depository*, *directory*, the <-ory> is added to a free-form;
- <-ury>: *injury*, *luxury*, *perjury*, *treasury*, – all with a previous palato-alveolar consonant /ʤ, ʃ, ʒ/.

There are two possibilities outside these four endings:

- with §French <-ie>: *calorie*, *camaraderie*, *gaucherie*, *lingerie*, *menagerie*, *reverie*;
- the noun *armoury*.

Association with parallel §Latinate forms may indicate the spelling of the /ə/ in some instances: relating to <-ory> are *categorial*, *factorial*, *memorial*; but in that case, *armorial* would prompt the American spelling *armor*; relating to <-ary> are *antiquarian*, *commissariat*, *illumination*, *ovarian*.

15 /-iːn/ in nouns as <-ene>, <-ine>

Chemical and medical substances may have the ending <-ene> (*phosgene*) or <-ine> (*iodine*). The difference is of systematic importance in chemistry, though over the years different conventions have been adopted. The present position is that hydrocarbons with double bonds have <-ene> and amines have <-ine>. Given the formula, the spelling is clear. Also, <-ine> is more generally used for medical substances. The <-ine> suffix for some substances has had a variant <-in> (*gelatin*, *gelatine*). The words in the database are clearly not a complete list of such terms because of the highly-specialized nature of the terminology:

<-ene> : *acetylene*, *anthracene*, *benzene*, *ethylene*, *methylene*, *naphthalene*, *phosgene*, *polystyrene*, *polythene*, *styrene*, *terylene*, *toluene*, *tolylene*;
<-ine> : *amphetamine*, *aniline*, *benzedrine*, *bromine*, *chlorine*, *dentine*, *dexedrine*, *dextrine*, *fluorine*, *gelatine*, *iodine*, *isodine*, *melamine*, *morphine*, *nicotine*, *promazine*, *quinine*, *saccharine*, *strychnine*, *tricotine*, *tyrosine*.

A peculiar example of a clear contrast between the two spellings, but where <-ene> is not in one case a suffix, is: *phosphene* – 'an appearance of rings of light due to irritation of the retina', where the {phene} element relates to 'appear'; *phosphine* – 'phosphorous ammonia'.

Some trade-names with the <-ene>/<-ine> suffix are *gasolene/gasoline*, *glycerine* (properly *glycerol*), *kerosene*, *margarine*, *vaseline*.

Codeine is exceptional with <ei>≡/iː/. The medical term *gangrene* is peculiar in having <-ene> (cf. *vaccine*). In adjectives, where the ending <-ine> is pronounced /aɪn/, there is no spelling problem (*adamantine*, *alkaline*, *bovine*, *calcimine*, *crystalline*, *elephantine*, *labyrinthine*, *philistine*, *serpentine*). In AmE these adjectives are usually /-iːn/.

16 /-iːz/ in nouns as <-ese>, <-ise>

The problem here is to distinguish the <-ise> of *expertise* from the <-ese> of *journalese*. The <-ese> ending seems to have come about by comparison with names of languages: *Chinese*, *Portuguese*, etc. It is similarly used with the names of authors: *Byronese*, where it tends to be pejorative. It does not seem to be used with monosyllabic names to give **Popese*, **Shawese*. The <-ise> of *expertise* is added to a free form, unlike the French loans ending in <-ise>: *cerise*, *chemise*, *valise*.

17 /-aɪz/ in verbs as <-ise>, <-ize>

The <-ize> spelling reflects a Greek verbal ending in English words, such as *baptize*, *organize*, which represent actual Greek verbs. There are also words that have been made up to imitate Greek, in later Latin or in French (*humanise*), or within English itself (*bowdlerise*). Some printers adopt a purist approach and spell the first group with <-ize> and the second group with <-ise>, others have <-ize> for both.

Since this difference is opaque to the ordinary speller, there is pressure to standardize on the <s> spelling, as French has done. To standardize with a <z> spelling as American spelling has done has disadvantages, because there are §Latinate verbs ending in <-ise> which have historically nothing to do with this suffix: *advertise*, *apprise*, *circumcise*, *comprise*, *compromise*, *despise*, *devise*, *excise*, *exercise*, *improvise*, *incise*, *supervise*, *surmise*, *surprise*. If you opt for a scholarly <organize>, you are likely to get an unscholarly *<supervize>. The *OED* argues that the pronunciation is /z/ and that this justifies the <z> spelling. But this ignores the fact that <s>≡/z/ happens to be the commonest spelling of /z/. To introduce more <z> spellings would probably complicate matters for the speller.

18 /-əl/ as <-le>, <-al>, <-el>, <-il>, <-ol>

Syllabic [l̩] and [əl] are different realizations of /əl/. Allegro forms contain more instances of [l̩] than do lento forms, but some contexts tend to favour [əl]. Before a stressed vowel, for instance, where the /l/ is naturally syllable initial we are unlikely to find [l̩] (*malinger*, *political*).

The [ə] is also usual (at least in SBS) after /r/ in *squirrel*, *laurel*, etc.

The relative frequency of the spellings of final /əl/ is shown in table 48.

Table 48 Relative frequency of the spellings of final /əl/

<-le>	TF 57.6 %	LF 55.7 %
<-al>	TF 32.5 %	LF 36.9 %
<-el>	TF 6.6 %	LF 5.8 %
<-il>	TF 2.1 %	LF 1.0 %
<-ol>	TF 1.2 %	LF 0.7 %

Spellings with <-ul>, such as *consul, mogul*, and especially in the common suffix <-ful>, vary in pronunciation between /ʊl/ and /əl/ and are not included. There is very little discrepancy between the text and lexical frequencies, but <-al> does show a tendency to occur in lower-frequency words.

The <-le> spelling typically occurs in disyllabic minimal free-forms which are nouns or verbs. Many of them are Romance in origin (e.g. *battle*, *bottle*, *sample*, *supple*) but without §Latinate word-formation potential. *Uncle* has an exceptional <c> spelling rather than <k> because of its Romance origin. If the first vowel is short, there is <C>-doubling (with the usual conditions, such as no doubling if the previous vowel is spelt with a digraph). The preceding consonants form a fairly homogeneous set: the plosives /p, b, t, d, k, g/ and the fricatives /f, s, z/. For the six plosives we find most of the examples with either a single plosive preceding (with <C>-doubling) or a homorganic [nasal]+[plosive] cluster. There are also some <rC> clusters of underlying //r//+consonant, where the /r/ survives in AmE and other rhotic accents, but where it merges into a vowel /ɜː/, /ɑː/ or /ɔː/ in SBS. Long vowels are relatively uncommon. Fairly full lists are given below to illustrate these contexts for the six plosives:

- /p/ – (<C>-doubling) – *apple*, *cripple*, *dapple*, *grapple*, *nipple*, *ripple*, *stipple*, *supple*, *tipple*, *topple*; (*couple*);

(nasal + plosive) – *ample*, *crumple*, *dimple*, *example*, *rumple*, *sample*, *simple*, *temple*, *trample*, *wimple*;

(<rC>) – *purple*;

(long vowel) – *maple*, *people*, *scruple*, *staple*, *steeple*.

- /b/ – (<C>-doubling) – *babble*, *bubble*, *cobble*, *dabble*, *dibble*, *dribble*, *gabble*, *gobble*, *hobble*, *nibble*, *nobble*, *pebble*, *quibble*, *rabble*, *rubble*, *scrabble*, *scribble*, *squabble*, *stubble*, *wobble*; (*double*, *trouble*);

(nasal + plosive) – *amble*, *assemble*, *bramble*, *bumble*, *crumble*, *dissemble*, *ensemble*, *fumble*, *gamble*, *grumble*, *humble*, *jumble*, *mumble*, *nimble*, *ramble*, *resemble*, *rumble*, *scramble*, *shamble*(*s*), *stumble*, *thimble*, *tremble*, *tumble*;

(<rC>) – *burble*, *garble*, *marble*, *warble*;

(long vowel) – *bauble*, *bible*, *fable*, *foible*, *noble*, *rouble*, *table*.

- /t/ – (<C>-doubling) – *battle, bottle, brittle, cattle, cuttle, fettle, kettle, little, mettle, mottle, nettle, pottle, prattle, rattle, scuttle, settle, shuttle, skittle, spittle, tattle, throttle, tittle, wattle, whittle*; (*subtle* is exceptional);

(nasal + plosive) – *cantle, gentle, mantle*;
(<rC>) – *chortle, hurtle, kirtle, myrtle, startle, turtle*;
(long vowel) – *beetle, title*.

- /d/ – (<C>-doubling) – *addle, coddle, cuddle, diddle, fiddle, fuddle, griddle, huddle, meddle, middle, muddle, paddle, peddle, puddle, riddle, saddle, straddle, swaddle, toddle, twaddle, twiddle, waddle*;

(nasal + plosive) – *brindle(d), bundle, candle, dandle, dwindle, fondle, handle, kindle, spindle, swindle, trundle*;
(<rC>) – *curdle, girdle, hurdle*;
(long vowel) – *beadle, boodle, bridle, cradle, dawdle, idle, ladle, needle, noodle, poodle, sidle, treacle, wheedle*.

- /k/ – (<C>-doubling) – *buckle, cackle, chuckle, cockle, crackle, fickle, freckle, grackle, hackle, heckle, knuckle, pickle, prickle, shackle, sickle, stickle, suckle, tackle, tickle, trickle, truckle*;

(nasal + plosive) – *ankle, crinkle, rankle, sprinkle, tinkle, twinkle, winkle, wrinkle*; *uncle*;
(<rC>) – *snorkle, sparkle*; *circle*;
(long vowel) – *cycle*.

- /g/ – (<C>-doubling) – *boggle, draggle(d), gaggle, giggle, goggle, haggle, jiggle, joggle, juggle, smuggle, snuggle, straggle, struggle, toggle, waggle, wiggle, wriggle*;

(nasal + plosive) – *angle, bangle, bungle, dangle, dingle, jangle, jingle, jungle, mangle, mingle, shingle, single, spangle, strangle, tangle, tingle, wangle, wrangle*;
(<rC>) – *gargle, gurgle*;
(long vowel) – *beagle, bugle, eagle, ogle*.

The fricatives /f, s, z/ have a more limited range of contexts. The commonest pattern for /s/ is with <-st-> rather than <-ss->; /z/ has <-zz->.

- /f/ – (<C>-doubling) – *baffle, muffle, piffle, raffle, riffle, ruffle, scuffle, shuffle, snaffle, sniffle, snuffle, truffle, waffle*;

(long vowel) – *rifle, stifle, trifle*.

- /s/- (<C>-doubling) – *tussle*;

(quasi-doubling) – *bristle, bustle, castle, epistle, gristle, hustle, jostle, justle, nestle, pestle, rustle, thistle, throstle, trestle, whistle, wrestle*; *muscle*.

- /z/ – (<C>-doubling) – *dazzle, drizzle, fizzle, frazzle, frizzle, guzzle, muzzle, nozzle, nuzzle, puzzle, schnozzle, sizzle*;

(long vowel) – *tousle(d)*.

In many of the <-le> words there is a frequentative meaning (*fumble, guzzle, squabble, tipple, tremble, wobble*, etc.) especially in those which are onomatopoeic (*jingle*, *sizzle*, *shuffle*, etc.). This reinforces the overall group identity of the graphic-phonetic pattern. Where the first vowel is a long /iː/, this is always a digraph <ea> or <ee>, never a single <e> (**egle*, **betle*). Other single vowel letters do occur: *table*, *bible*, *ogle*, *bugle*.

There are, however, quite a few words in which /p, b, t, d, k, g/, or /f, s, z/, are followed by /əl/ and which do not have the <-le> spelling. Most of these have a clear suffix attached either to a free or to a bound morph and many of them have three or more syllables:

- <-al> forming nouns from verbs – *appraisal*, *arousal*, *causal*, *dispersal*, *disposal*, *espousal*, *perusal*, *proposal*, *recital*, *refusal*, *reversal*;
- <-al> forming adjectives from nouns – *basal*, *bridal*, *brutal*, *colloidal*, *digital*, *fatal*, *fugal*, *homicidal*, *modal*, *orbital*, *oriental*, *tidal*, *triumphal*, *universal*;
- <-al> as an adjective suffix with bound forms – *conjugal*, *dental*, *frugal*, *fungal*, *glottal*, *legal*, *marital*, *mental*, *municipal*, *natal*, *papal*, *principal*, *rectal*, *regal*, *skeletal*, *vital*.

There are also three longer endings to consider: <-acle>, <-icle>, <-ical>. The noun endings <-acle> and <-icle> are distinguished by some speakers with /ə/ and /ɪ/, but this is tenuous; other speakers may have /ɪ/ for both.

- <-acle> – *barnacle*, *binnacle*, *coracle*, *manacle*, *miracle*, *obstacle*, *oracle*, *pinnacle*, *receptacle*, *spectacle*, *spiracle*, *tabernacle*, *tentacle*;
- <-icle> – *article*, *auricle*, *canticle*, *chronicle*, *conventicle*, *cubicle*, *curricle*, *cuticle*, *fascicle*, *follicle*, *icicle*, *particle*, *radicle*, *testicle*, *ventricle*, *vehicle*, *vesicle*;
- <-ical> – *historical*, *radical*, etc. (some 224 examples in the database).

Homophones are a good test of whether these categories can be made obvious to the speller. Unfortunately, mistakes such as *a *radicle design*, *the *principle reason* are quite common.

There are no <-le> spellings after the palato-alveolars /ʃ, ʧ, ʤ/, but we have:

- /ʃ/ – *marshal*, *bushel*, and with palatalization: *initial*, *martial*, *nuptial*, *partial*, *spatial*, *substantial*;
- /ʧ/ – *satchel*;
- /ʤ/ – *angel*, *cudgel*, *evangel*.

There are no <-le> spellings after the nasals /m, n/ or the liquid /r/ but we have:

- /m/ – *dismal*, *formal*, *primal*, *thermal* and other adjectives in <-al>; *mammal*; *calomel*, *camel*, *caramel*, *enamel*, *pommel*, *pummel*, *trammel*;
- /n/ – *final*, *nominal*, *ordinal*, *renal*, *spinal*, *tonal* and other adjectives in <-al>; *channel*, *charnel*, *colonel*, *fennel*, *flannel*, *funnel*, *grapnel*, *kennel*,

kernel, *panel*, *runnel*, *sentinel*, *shrapnel*, *signal*, *tunnel*;

- /r/ – *central*, *mural*, *sacral*, *several*, *ventral* and other adjectives in <-al>; *apparel*, *barrel*, *cockerel*, *doggerel*, *laurel*, *mackerel*, *minstrel*, *mongrel*, *quarrel*, *scoundrel*, *sorrel*, *spandrel*, *squirrel*, *timbrel*, *wastrel*; *carol*, *petrol*.

There are no <-le> spellings after /v/, but there are quite a number of <-el> spellings in disyllabic minimal free forms with a short vowel before the /v/ (*gravel*, *hovel*, etc.). This is a context in which we would normally expect <C>-doubling, but /v/ is a consonant which rarely has it (§3.2.2 #D3, p. 120).

Examples of /əl/ after /v/: *festival*, *interval*, *larval*, *medieval*, *naval*, *oval*, *removal*, *rival*; *bevel*, *drivel*, *gavel*, *gravel*, *grovel*, *hovel*, *level*, *marvel*, *navel*, *novel*, *ravel*, *revel*, *shovel*, *shrivel*, *snivel*, *swivel*, *travel*.

After /θ/ we have *lethal* and *brothel*.

We are left with a very mixed group of words which cause problems for the speller. Some seem to fit the pattern of words which have <-le> but they have final <-Vl> instead. If they have §Latinate word-formation (*opal* – *opaline*), then this rules out an <-le> spelling. If in addition the unstressed vowel is stressed when suffixes are added, this will also indicate the right vowel spelling (*metal–metallic*). Examples:

- <-al> – *opal*, *sepal*; *cymbal*, *gimbal*; *petal*; *medal*, *pedal*, *sandal*, *scandal*, *vandal*; *offal*; *missal*, *vassal*; *sisal*;
- <-el> – *carpel*, *chapel*, *gospel*, *scalpel*; *babel*, *label*, *libel*, *rebel* (n.); *betel*, *chattel*, *hostel*, *lintel*, *mantel* (var. *mantle*), *pastel*; *nickel*, *shekel*, *yokel*; *cancel*, *chancel*, *counsel*, *morsel*, *mussel*, *tassel*, *vessel*; *bezel*, *chisel*, *damsel*, *diesel*, *easel*, *hazel*, *tinsel*, *weasel*;
- <-il> – (these words may have /ə/ or /ɪ/) *council*, *pencil*, *stencil*; *basil*;
- <-ol> – *gambol*, *symbol*; *idol*; *mongol*.

A further feature of some of these words is consonant clustering not found in the <-le> words: *central*, *dismal*, *hostel*, *pencil*, *pistol*, *tinsel*, *petrol*, *signal*. This makes *axle* an exception. The fact that the usual clusters found before <-le> are [nasal]+[plosive] or <rC> can hardly be a crutch for the poor speller, but it may subconsciously add to the profile of words which do not have and words which do have an <-le> spelling.

Finally there are some words which have an <-le> spelling outside the main group which might be expected to have <C>-doubling: *treble*, *triple*, and some words of three syllables which have <-le>: *disciple*, *multiple*, *principle*; *carbuncle*, *tubercle*; *inveigle*; *apostle*; *bamboozle*, *embezzle*.

The various spellings of /-əl/ illustrate an important and little-understood aspect of the English writing system. They do not lend themselves to explicit, recallable rules, but they are not without a profile of phonetic and morphological regularities that may underpin the competence of a literate adult.

19 /-əm/ as <-am>, <-em>, <-om>, <-um> in nouns

The <-um> spelling is usual in §Latinate words (e.g. *medium*). The <-om> spelling occurs, much less frequently, in §Greek words (e.g. *axiom*). There are also a few native words, such as *besom*, *bosom*, with <-om> spellings. A normal adult speller is probably not attuned to these particular differences of system, so it would be useful to identify any learnable contexts and markers. The <-um> spelling is clearly the default.

We find <-ium>≡/ɪəm/ in *bacterium*, *calcium*, *compendium*, *chromium*, *delphinium*, *geranium*, *gymnasium*, *helium*, *medium*, *podium*, *premium*, *radium*, *sodium*, *stadium*, *tedium* and many more. The <-eum> ending of *linoleum*, *mausoleum*, *museum*, *petroleum*, may easily be confused with <-ium>. *Axiom* and *idiom* are the only exceptions with <-iom>; their Greek origin shows in word-formation potential: *axiomatic*, *idiomatic*. There are a few <-uum> words (*continuum*, *residuum*, *vacuum*).

After a consonant, however, there is clearly some possibility of confusion. However, we can note in passing that the native suffix <-dom> (*kingdom*, etc.) can easily be identified since it is added to free forms (*kingdom*, *freedom*, etc.; with vowel shortening in the case of *wisdom*). The range of other /əm/ spellings is as follows; those which are not nouns are bracketed:

- <-am> – *amalgam*, *balsam*, *bantam*, *bedlam*, *buckram*, *flotsam*, *gingham*, *jetsam*, *macadam*, *madam*, *marjoram*;
- <-em> – *anthem*, *emblem*, *item*, *problem*, *stratagem*, *system*, *tandem*, *theorem*, *totem*;
- <-om> – *atom*, *besom*, *blossom*, *bosom*, *bottom*, (*buxom*), *custom*, *fathom*, *hansom*, *maelstrom*, *phantom*, *pogrom*, (*random*), *ransom*, *symptom*, *transom*, *venom*;
- <-um> – *album*, *alum*, *asylum*, *capsicum*, *carborundum*, *chrysanthemum*, *decorum*, *forum*, *interregnum*, *laburnum*, *maximum*, *modicum*, *optimum*, *pendulum*, *platinum*, *quorum*, *referendum*, *sedum*, *sorghum*, *talcum*, *vellum*, *velum*; non-§Latinate *hokum*, *hoodlum*. In *autumn* and *column* there is a further spelling problem in the inert letter <n>.

How our normal adult speller finds a way through these variant spellings is difficult to account for. A potential stress shift to show the quality of the underlying vowel, and so select the spelling, is only possible in one or two words: *atom–atomic*, *system–systemic*. Stress shifts such as *emblem–emblematic*, where the /ə/ remains, do not help. As a rule of thumb, words of three or more syllables usually have <-um>.

20 variation in <e>/<i> at suffix boundaries

As a stem-final vowel before a suffix, /iː/ or /ɪ/ may be spelt either as <e> or as <i>. The <e> spelling is the minority spelling. Sometimes dictionaries allow either spelling in *liquefy–liquify*. The minority endings with <-e-> are as follows; the relative frequency of <-e->/<-i-> is given for each ending as a proportion of the <-i-> and <-e-> forms in the database.

We can take the <-eous> adjectives first and group them by the preceding consonant:

- where underlying //sɪ// has become /ʃ/: 4 <e>/ 49 <i> – *cretaceous*, *herbaceous*, *sebaceous*, *siliceous*; cf. *audacious*, *capacious*, *delicious*, etc.;
- after /d/: 1 <e>/ 11 <i> – *hideous*; cf. *compendious*, *fastidious*, etc.;
- after /ʤ/: 4 <e>/ 9 <i> – *advantageous*, *gorgeous*, *outrageous*, *umbrageous*; cf. *contagious*, *litigious*, *prodigious*, *religious*, *sacrilegious*, etc.;
- after /n/: 13 <e>/ 24 <i> – *contemporaneous*, *cutaneous*, *erroneous*, *extraneous*, *heterogeneous*, *homogeneous*, *igneous*, *instantaneous*, *miscellaneous*, *sanguineous*, *simultaneous*, *spontaneous*, *subterraneous*; cf. *acrimonious*, *arsenious*, *calumnious*, *ceremonious*, *euphonious*, *felonious*, *harmonious*, *ignominious*, *ingenious*, *parsimonious*, *sanctimonious*, etc.;
- after /r/: 4 <e>/ 37 <i> – *calcareous*, *nectareous*, *sulphureous*, *vitreous*; cf. *laborious*, *penurious*, *precarious*;
- after /s/: *gaseous*, *osseous*, *nauseous*;
- after /kw/: *aqueous*;
- after /t/: 7 <e>/ 36 <i> – *beauteous*, *bounteous*, *courteous*, *duteous*, *piteous*, *plenteous*, *righteous*; cf. *propitious*, *sententious*, etc.

Some tendencies can be seen in these examples. The suffix <-age> naturally gives <-ageous>, using the <-e-> to mark the /ʤ/ pronunciation of the <g>. A free-form stem ending in <-y> usually gives <-ious>, but there are exceptions (*bounteous*, *piteous*, *plenteous*). The spelling <-aneous> is consistent.

Other endings with <-e-> rather than <-i-> are:

- <-eate> : 5 <e>/ 53 <i> – *create*, *delineate*, *nauseate*, *nucleate*, *procreate*; cf. *calumniate*, *luxuriate*, etc.;
- <-eo> : 5 <e>/ 21 <i> – *cameo*, *rodeo*, *romeo*, *stereo*, *video*; cf. *audio*, *patio*, *radio*, *studio*, etc.;
- <-eage> : *lineage*; cf. *foliage*, *verbiage*;
- <-ear> : *linear*; cf. *foliar*;
- <-eon> : *chameleon, melodeon, Napoleon, pantheon.* The <-e-> of *bludgeon, gudgeon; dungeon, pigeon, sturgeon, surgeon*, is simply a marker of the palatal consonant.
- <-ety> : the suffix <-ity> (*amenity, infirmity*) has a variant <-ety> after a stem-final <i>: *anxiety, gaiety, notoriety, piety, propriety, society, variety,* etc.

21 miscellaneous suffix problems

The phonetic identity of endings does not necessarily make for spelling errors. Much depends on the lexical awareness of the speller (see §2.9.3). An essential requirement for successful spelling in English is the recognition of boundaries. The suffix <-less>, as in *hopeless*, *penniless*, *shameless*, is added to free-forms, but it is homophonous with <-ous> added to a bound stem ending in /l/, as in *callous*, *credulous*, *jealous*, *meticulous*, *parlous*, *tremulous*, *scurrilous*, and occasionally to a free stem, as in *marvellous*, *perilous*, or to a slightly modified free stem as in *ridiculous*, *zealous*. A normally intelligent human speller would recognize the difference in structure and indeed the different meaning: *perilous* means 'full of', not 'lacking in' peril.

There are occasional homophonous endings, in addition to the ones considered above, that may result in spelling errors when lexical awareness or system awareness is lacking. For instance, <-us> would seem at first sight to be quite predictable in §Latinate nouns such as *apparatus*, *fungus*, *typhus*. But if the only clue to its identification is the phonetic form /-əs/, there is scope for spelling errors. Other nouns ending in /-əs/ include:

- with <-as> – *atlas*, *bias*, *canvas*, *pampas*, *pancreas*;
- with <-ass> – *compass*, *cutlass*, *windlass*;
- with <-ace> – *necklace*, *palace*, *preface*, *populace*, *solace*;
- with <-ase> – *carcase*, *purchase*;
- with <-oise> – *porpoise*, *tortoise*;
- with <-os> – *rhinoceros*, *thermos*;
- with <-uce> – *lettuce*.

These are a possible source of spelling errors – *<tortus> for *tortoise*. For speakers who have /ɪs/ rather than /əs/ in some of these, such as *lettuce*, *necklace*, there will be other homophony problems (e.g. *lettuce* – *lattice*). There are only a few parallel forms which might associate the /ə/ with a stressed vowel, except perhaps *palatial*, *pancreatic*, *thermo-nuclear*. It is misleading that *rhinoceros* should have a §Greek <-os> and *hippopotamus* should have a §Latinate <-us>; both are formed from Greek elements.

Other §Latinate endings that cannot safely be identified by sound alone include the following:

- /-ʃə/≡<-tia> would seem regular enough in view of the frequency of <-tial>, <-tially>, but there are only three examples in the database: *dementia*, *inertia*, *militia*, along with *acacia*, *fascia*, *fuchsia*, *magnesia*.
- /-əlɪst/≡<-alist> occurs in §Latinate nouns such as *finalist*, *idealist*, *instrumentalist*. There are, however, other words in which the /əl/ part does not represent the adjective suffix <-al>: *duellist*, *evangelist*, *monopolist*, *novelist*, *symbolist*; but not *cymbalist*, *dualist*. In two §Greek exceptions: *analyst*, *catalyst*, the /ɪst/ is not a suffix.

- /-ətɪv/≡<-ative> occurs in §Latinate adjectives such as *combative*, *demonstrative*, *laxative*. There is possible confusion with *additive*, *definitive*, *competitive*, *inquisitive*, *insensitive*, *positive*, *repetitive*, *secretive*, *transitive*. Most of these, however, have parallel forms with stressed /ɪ/: *addition*, *definition*, *position*, etc.
- /-əlɪ/≡<-ally> occurs in §Latinate adverbs such as *centrally*, *finally*, *ideally*. As part of <-ically>, it is predictable. For SBS and other non-rhotic speakers, /-əlɪ/ also occurs in different structures: with <-er>+<-ly> *bitterly*, *cleverly*, *soberly*, *tenderly*, etc.; with <-ar>+<-ly> *particularly*, *peculiarly*, *regularly*, *similarly*, etc.; with <-ary>+<-ly> *contrarily*, *extraordinarily*, *fragmentarily*, *necessarily*, etc.; and the irregular *thoroughly*. In SBS *formally* – *formerly* are homophones. This would not be so for speakers with a rhotic accent, who still retain a pre-consonantal /r/ in the word *formerly*. One would expect journalists on the *Irish Times* to be rhotic speakers with //r// retained in all contexts, yet, under a heading 'Corrections and Clarifications', there appeared: 'the new development officer of the Irish Farmhouse Cheese-Makers Association, Cairin O'Connor, is formerly of the Traditional Cheese Co. not "formally" as was stated' (*Irish Times*, 8 August 1992).
- /-əltɪ/≡<-alty> occurs in §Latinate nouns such as *casualty*, *penalty*, *royalty*. /-əltɪ/ also occurs in different structures: with stem+<-ty> *cruelty*, *novelty*, *subtlety*; with stem+<-y> *difficulty*; and, as a minimal free form, *faculty*.
- /-əsɪ/≡<-acy> in nouns such as *adequacy*, *conspiracy*, *fallacy*, *legacy*, and §Greek <-cracy> as in *aristocracy*, *democracy*. There are other competing endings: with <-asy> *apostasy*, *ecstasy*, *fantasy*; with <-assy> *embassy*; with <-esy> *courtesy*, *heresy*; with <-ecy> *prophecy*; with <-icy> *policy*; with <-osy> *argosy*; with <-ocy> *idiocy*; with <-ousy> *jealousy*.
- /-aɪt/≡<-ite> in §Latinate nouns such as *anthracite*, *appetite*, *gelignite*. There may be confusion with <-yte> in §Greek words (for which <y> is the only spelling of /aɪ/) *acolyte*, *electrolyte*, *leucocyte*, *lymphocyte*, *neophyte*, *phagocyte*, *proselyte*, *saprophyte*. *Delight* would still be spelt *delite* if it were not for past tinkering.
- /-ətɪ/≡<-ity> in §Latinate nouns such as *equality*, *hilarity*, *rapacity*. There is possible confusion: with <-ety> *entirety*, *gaiety*, *moiety*, *naivety*, *surety*; with <-erty> *liberty*, *poverty*, *property*, *puberty*.

Affixes account for a large number of spelling errors. One answer to the problem would be to develop more system awareness and lexical awareness in literacy teaching.

22 miscellaneous prefix problems

Prefixes prevent fewer problems than suffixes. The most frequent spelling problem is the doubled consonant letter of §Latinate prefixes. Two identical consonant letters may occur in §Romance words with a Latin prefix (ad-, com-, e(x)-, in-, ob-, per-, sub-) as in *adduce*, *command*, *innate*. The prefix often assimilates to the initial consonant of the stem, as in *approve*, *affect*, *announce*, *connect*, *immerse*, *illegal*, *occlude*, *offend*. These are discussed as a group in §3.2.2 and under the different phonemes elsewhere in §3.

<ante-> 'before' and <anti-> 'against' are both /æntɪ/ in SBS. In AmE *anti-* may have /-aɪ/. The meanings are fairly obvious in compounds with free forms as in: *ante-chamber, antedate, ante-room, ante-natal; anti-body, anti-climax, anti-cyclone, anti-freeze, anti-hero, antiseptic, anti-social, anti-toxin* (hyphen use varies). The meanings are less obvious to the speller in *antecedent, antediluvian, antidote, antipathy*.

The prefixes <en->≡/ɪn/ and <in-> (meaning 'in') are often mere variants. The <en-> spelling is supposedly to be used for words which have come from Latin through French and the <in-> for words direct from Latin. In practice, this is not much use to anyone. There is a choice of *enquire* or *inquire*. *The Times* newspaper, for instance, seems to prefer the <en->. Some people make a tentative difference between *enquiry office* 'asking about something' and *government inquiry* 'investigation' and similarly 'He enquired after your health' and 'They inquired into the price fixing'. The following words may have either <en-> or <in-> with no difference in use: *enclose, encrust, endorse, enfold, engrain, engraft, entrench, entrust, entwine*.

The following is a sample of purely <en-> words: *enable, enact, encamp, encash, enchain, enchant, encipher, encircle, encounter, encourage, endanger, endear, enfeeble, enfranchise, engrossed, enjoy, enkindle, enlarge, enlist, enliven, ennoble, enrage, entangle, enthrone, entomb,* etc. With bound stems there are: *encroach, endeavour, endorse, endow, enhance, entice,* etc. Most people store a spelling pronunciation /en-/ for these words and tend to use it in more literary words such as *engender*.

Chapter 6

Conventions used in the spelling of names

6.1 THE SPELLING OF NAMES

Names have a wider range of spelling correspondences

The spelling of names – personal names and place-names – brings the reader and the speller special problems. One can sympathise with an American senator, hesitating in the middle of a prepared speech, who said: 'the meeting of our two leaders in R....., er, in ....., in Iceland', evidently backing off from deciding on a suitable pronunciation of *Reykjavik*. How, too, might we pronounce *Purkinjean capsules*, a term for anatomical structures in the grinding teeth of elephants? Do we take this to be a discrete name *Purkinjean* /ˈpɜːkɪnʤiːn/ (without an adjectival suffix as in the *Doppler effect*)? Or do we assume it to be an adjective formed with a name *Purkinje* plus <-an> and so /pɜːˈkɪnʤɪən/? A name ending in <-inje> would be distinctly exotic; <-inge> is the norm. So, it does look as if the name of this person might well be *Purkinjean*. But that is not in fact the case. *Purkinje* was a Bohemian physiologist (*OED*).

Names do not have to be foreign to be difficult. It is not by any means obvious to strangers that *Hawick* is pronounced /hɔɪk/ by those who know the place, or that a place referred to as /hɔɪk/ is *Hawick* on the signposts. No stranger reading the place-name *Keighley* could guess the /-θl-/, or hearing the place-name /ˈheɪzbərə/ could possibly imagine that the spelling was *Happisburgh*. Correspondences turn up in names which are simply not found in non-names: <sh>≡/ʒ/ in *Bosher*, or <gh>≡/ʤ/ in *Bargh*, or <al>≡/eɪ/ in *Ralph*. It would be wrong, however, to regard the spelling and pronunciation of the names we meet to be quite unsystematic. Many names, both personal names and place-names, are spelt with the same conventions as non-names and show no peculiarities of correspondence. However, there are many conventions which are peculiar to names and which link up with a more complex set of subsystems than are found in non-names. This is only to be expected since most foreign names come with a spelling provided by their local writing system. So, to a much greater extent than in the spelling of ordinary words, in the spelling of names there are degrees of literacy, degrees to which a person may be sensitive to patterns of correspondence. Accounts of English spelling usually have little to say on the spelling of names, taking the view of Cummings that 'each proper name can be pretty much a rule unto itself' (1988: xxiv). But if we set out to examine the problems encountered by users of the writing system, some exploration of the conventions used in the spelling of names is clearly required.

It will be assumed that the phonetic or written forms of foreign names have been interpreted in some conventional way as a string of English phonemes, however crudely. How a native English speaker goes about this translation of foreign sounds or foreign spellings into English phonemes is a matter of some interest, but lies outside our scope. We shall ignore deliberate phonetic approximations to the phonemes of other languages, such as contrastive vowel nasalization (*Caen* as [kɑ̃]).

What in practice constitutes a 'name' will also be left unexplored: a recent definitive study is Allerton (1987). For present purposes there is adequate material in the large sample of names given in LPD, backed up by the more conservative EPD. This is a useful enough sample for examining recurrent correspondences and patterns of variation. Needless to say, I do not pretend to have commented on every recorded idiosyncracy and variant. A source of this size can give us a good indication of the lexical frequency of correspondences found in names, but text frequency in any general sense could only come from an impossibly large database. That is partly because the names found in any given sample are bound to be more peculiar to that sample than ordinary words. So, although *John* is likely to occur much more frequently than *Jeremiah*, there is no obvious way to provide reliable quantitative data for the whole range of names.

A further reason why it is difficult to make any statistical comments on the spelling of names, as compared with ordinary vocabulary, is that names often have a range of variant pronunciations and spellings. Even though the pronouncing dictionaries record a wide range of variation in pronunciation and spelling, one cannot be certain that variants which are not given do not actually occur. The name that is spelt *Froud*, *Froude* is only recorded by LPD as *Froud* with /aʊ/ and *Froude* with /uː/. One suspects that /fraʊd/≡<Froude> may well exist somewhere, since in names a final <-e> is often mere padding, but how are dictionary compilers and their informants able to be certain? There is a similar problem with the frequency ranking between variants from one name to another. Both *Holbrook* and *Holburn* vary in EPD with /əʊ/ and /ɒ/, but *Holbrook* has /əʊ/ as the principal variant and *Holburn* has /ɒ/. This may well be the case, but such rankings are inevitably based on informed personal judgements by the authors, rather than actual pronunciation counts. Indeed it is difficult to see how pronouncing dictionaries could be compiled otherwise. But, even though the relative frequency of these spelling and pronunciation variants is to some extent uncertain, the patterns of variation recorded do represent an important aspect of the competence of adult English spellers.

Linguistically, this type of variation in the spelling and pronunciation of names is slightly odd. In ordinary words any free variant pronunciations (/skəʊn/ or /skɒn/ for {scone}) and free variant spellings (<gray> or <grey> for the colour) have the same referent. One cannot say: '/skəʊnz/ are not the same type of cake as /skɒnz/' or '*grey* is not the same colour as *gray*' (but see §5.4 p. 407). With names this need not apply. The variants can be made distinctive. To distinguish two known different people, and not merely to correct a spelling, one can write: 'I am referring not to my friend Calcott, but to my friend Calcot', or one can say, not merely to correct a pronunciation: 'I am referring not to my friend /ˈkɔːlkɒt/, but to my friend /ˈkɒlkət/'. The variant spellings *Jonson* and *Johnson* suffice in English literary criticism to distinguish the playwright *Ben* from the lexicographer *Samuel*. Yet generally speaking one can regard such pairs as 'the same' name not only because there is a high degree of phonetic and graphic similarity, but also because the graphic and phonetic differences are a known paradigm of difference which recurs in other names. Variation between <alt>≡/ɔːlt/ and <alt>≡/ɒlt/, as in *Alton*, also occurs in non-names: some people will say /sɔːlt/, some people /sɒlt/ for {salt}. There is a difference, however, in that a given speaker in a given register will usually have one of these correspondences consistently. This same speaker, however, may refer to a particular person or place by the variant which seems locally appropriate. *Calton* near Edinburgh has /ɔː/ and *Calton* near Glasgow has /ɑː/. Changed circumstances may associate with a different pronunciation: *Kenya* before independence was usually pronounced with /iː/, but now it usually has /e/. I pronounce *Austin*, *Austria* and *Australia* with /ɒ/, but *Jane Austen* with /ɔː/, simply because she was introduced to me in that form by a particular teacher. Anthony Powell, the novelist, and Baden-Powell of the Scout movement pronounced their name with /əʊ/ instead of the more common /aʊ/, making it equivalent to *Pole*. No doubt their personal circle respected this, but as they recede into history it can hardly matter.

Getting the variant spelling right is a problem which also carries over to derived adjectives. We have <Thomsonian> blank verse, after James Thomson the poet, and <Thomsonian> medicine after Samuel Thomson a nineteenth century physician. But most of the *OED* examples have the latter as <Thompsonian>. This is presumably because the poet's name is always printed with the poems, but the doctor's medical theories were mediated through others, who got the wrong spelling.

Variant spellings of the 'same' name may come about when the structure of the name as a string of elements ceases to be obvious. Spellings with <x> may obscure such a boundary in *Dixon*, *Nixon*, and *Hauxwell*, which are opaque compared with *Dickson*, 'son of Dick', *Nickson* and *Hawkswell*. *Dixon* has the spelling of a single morpheme, as does *tax* compared with *tacks*. The common place-name element <-ham> usually reduces to /əm/ and the <h> may be taken to be part of the previous consonant spelling. So we have a reinterpretation of *Bispham* /ˈbɪspəm/ as /ˈbisfəm/. The reinterpretation is likely when the name is used as a personal name and is no longer bound by local tradition. Compare *Walsham* as /ˈwɒlsəm/ and /ˈwɒlʃəm/, *Lydgate* as /ˈlɪdgeɪt/ and /ˈlɪʤɪt/. A reader must always be aware that a name, in spite of appearances, may be a single unit. A good example is the names ending in <-er>: *Banger* and *Comber* are /ˈbeɪnʤə/, /ˈkɒmbə/, not /ˈbæŋə/, /ˈkəʊmə/. There is, furthermore, some reluctance to alter the appearance of a name by morphological processes: 'the two Germanys' (not *<Germanies>) is the preferred spelling. This does not apply, however, when the morphology is §Latinate: *Bodley–Bodleian*, *Shaw–Shavian*.

Different standards of stringency in what constitutes the 'same' name may apply for purely pragmatic reasons. My bank manager will readily accept cheques on my behalf made out to **Carnay* or even **Kearney*, presumably relying on phonetic identity. When it comes to paying money out, he insists on *Carney* and all the allographic detail of my handwritten signature. When names are used in commerce and industry, stringent phonetic and graphic identity is clearly necessary. Otherwise, English law is fairly flexible on what constitutes the 'same' name. Courts will not set aside proceedings on account of the misspelling of names (such as *Lawrance* for *Lawrence*), provided that the variance is so slight as not to mislead, or the different spellings 'sound alike' *idem sonans*.

6.2 MANIPULATED SPELLINGS IN TRADE-NAMES

'Klean Shyne' for 'clean shine', 'Tracc-Tac' for 'track tack'

A name is a valuable property and can be registered as such. Indeed, names suitable for perfumes or sports cars are frequently staked out and registered by industrial companies long before work on the product that will eventually receive the name is ever begun. Recently, computers have been brought in to generate arbitrary names as random strings of syllables; *Teflon* and *Mylar* seem to come from this source. The property in trade-names is well-protected by law. The United States Trade-Mark Act (1946) requires, among other things, that a registered trade-mark should not resemble a mark which has been previously registered or used, to an extent that may cause confusion or deception. Nor is a mark allowed to be merely descriptive or simply an existing surname. Since this Act, there has been a predictable increase in the use of trade-marks with manipulated and irregular spellings (Jacobson 1966; Praninskas 1968).

The use of spelling manipulation in advertising became commonplace in the early years of the century. Writing in the first volume of *American Speech* (1925), Louise Pound, in an article 'The Kraze for "K"', commented on how manipulated <k>-spellings had been increasing in the 1920s. Alliterative use of <k> was common in the text of posters and advertisements ('Katie the Komical Kow') and was rife in newspaper headlines. It even became a fetish in the house-style of the Ku Klux Klan, who apparently have terms such as *klansmen*, *kloncilium*, *kludd*, *kleagle*, *klaliff*. Her comparison with alliterative headlines is a fruitful one, since in many of her examples a medial <c> is left unchanged (e.g. *Kompact*, *klonvocation*) and only the initial letters alliterate. In advertising she found names such as *Kwik-Pak*, *Kwality Kut Klothes*, *Klay Kompact for Komplexions*, etc. She thought, however, that there were signs of this craze beginning to pall, but it is by no means dead. One can still find, for example, *Likker Pikker* as the name of a self-service liquor shop. There may well be lasting damage: the American vice-presidential (Dan Quayle) Christmas card for 1990 is said to have read: 'May our nation continue to be the *beakon of hope for the world' (*Observer* 3/2/91).

Re-spelling may also be used to identify a whole advertising slogan and the product: *Drinka Pinta Milka Day*, with the consequent creation of <pinta> as a product name for a pint of milk, no doubt by analogy with the word *cuppa* 'cup of tea'. Spelling manipulation is more stridently assertive than the simple assonance of that classic slogan *My goodness! My Guinness!* Present-day newspapers still use alliteration in headlines for comic effect and still exploit <k> spellings. The *Daily Mail* of 8/6/1989, hardly the gutter press, had articles headed 'Katie's kolourful kanines' and 'Tale of tips, tans 'n' titfers'.

The material collected by Jacobson and Praninskas shows similar spelling manipulation. Here, too, alternative spellings are used in irregular contexts. So <k>≡/k/ is used before <a, o, u> and in consonant clusters instead of <c>: 'Kote' *coat*, 'Krush' *crush*, 'Kleen' *clean*, 'Kontakt' *contact*, etc. There are very few examples in reverse, where <c> is preferred to <k>: 'Tracc-Tac' *track tack*. The correspondence <x>≡/ks/ is allowed across a morpheme boundary: 'Protex' *protects*, with a cluster simplification of /-kts/ to /-ks/ (cf. *tax–tacks)*. Simple vowel letters are untypically used to represent long vowels in final position: 'Tru-Blu' *true blue*, 'Fre-Flo' *free flow*, 'Mildu' *mildew*. Final <C>-doubling is frequently simplified: 'Hot-Stuf' *hot-stuff*, 'Chil-Gard' *chill guard*, 'Fly-Kil' *fly kill*, 'Pul-Jak' *pull jack*, etc. Conversely, <C>-doubling occurs in unusual contexts: 'Hott Patch' *hot patch*, 'Strypp' *strip*, 'Kuvver' *cover*, etc. A normally word-final <ay>≡/eɪ/ is used medially: 'Rayn' *rain*. Independently of context, <y..e> is commonly substituted for <i..e>: 'Tyme' *time*, 'Bykes' *bikes*, 'Slyde' *slide*. It is often used as an archaic marker: 'Olde Tyme Dancing'.

Letters are also used in advertising as in a 'rebus' puzzle (*non verbis sed rebus* 'not by words but by things'): 'an enigmatical representation of a name, word or phrase, by figures, pictures, arrangement of letters, etc., which suggest the syllables of which it is made up' (*OED*). For instance, the letter <u> may be used to stand for the word *you*, since /juː/ is the name of the letter and the sound of the word, as in an 'IOU' 'I owe you'. This is quite different as an exploitation of the letter names from mere abbreviation such as 'IOW.' for 'Isle of Wight'. There appears to be no current technical term for this device. Trade examples are 'Spud-U-Like' (a baked potato shop) or 'Serve-U-Rite' (a delivery service). Names of current pop bands include 'U2' ('you too') and 'INXS' ('in excess'). This last example is difficult because there is no marker, such as a hyphen, to show where the letter names 'XS' start. There are similar uses in 'customized' car number plates, such as 'O2BINLA' ('Oh to be in Los Angeles').

A trade-name may apparently wish to be identified as an institutionalized spelling mistake. Theakston's traditionally brewed ale is sold as 'Old Peculier'. The desired association may be: this is drunk by robust workers, who have never worried about spelling. The name has iconic peculiarity.

There seems to be no compulsion to be consistently radical in making these changes. There are many examples in Jacobson's data where changes are made only to parts of the name: 'Light Wryter' *light writer*, 'Klean Shyne' *clean shine*, 'Bild-a-Clock' *build a clock*. Readers must feel very uncertain about pronunciation and morpheme recognition in the more bizarre manipulations: 'Driv-Gyds *drive guides*, 'Myhrmade' *mermaid*, 'Taprite' *tape right*, 'Kul Ryde' *cool ride*.

In some ways the liberty taken with trade-names mirrors the variability found in place-names and personal names, but it goes far beyond this. The free manipulation of spelling in trade-names could soften up public opinion for planned spelling reform by familiarizing people with workable alternative spellings. Trade-names have become institutionalized spelling mistakes. Some trade-names even leave one with a sneaking suspicion that the inventor may not know the real spelling: is the <on> in 'Pollon-Eze' (a hay-fever remedy) deliberate? Since trade-name coinage relies so heavily on the breaking of whatever rules exist, it is undoubtedly a nuisance for those learning to read. But what will happen to trade-names if a regular reformed spelling is introduced? The public's attitude to variant spellings would then be difficult to assess.

6.3 VARIANTS AND TOTEMS

Allsopp, Alsopp, Allsop, or Alsop?

Both readers and writers nowadays expect there to be a standard spelling of ordinary words, but are prepared to accept a considerable degree of variability in the spelling and pronunciation of names. We are all aware of the range of conventional spellings of family names and within quite wide limits variant spellings are tolerated. A person answering to /ˈgɪlmɔː/ may spell it *Gilmore* or *Gilmour*; /liː/ may be spelt *Lea*, *Lee*, or *Leigh*; /ˈgreɪnʤə/ may be spelt *Grainger* or *Granger*, and so on. The variation cuts both ways: not only are *Allsopp*, *Alsopp*, *Allsop* and *Alsop* spelling variants of what people take to be 'the same' name, but that name may be pronounced /ˈɔːlsɒp/, /ˈɔːlsəp/, /ˈɒlsɒp/ or /ˈɒlsəp/ with any of the four spellings. 'How do you spell your name?' – is a question which reflects this freedom. It also implies that nowadays people are expected to keep to their particular spelling all the time. In earlier centuries people could and did vary the spelling of their own name from occasion to occasion, but the needs of bureaucracy soon stifled that freedom. Rapid changes in technology may well bring about a further standardization of names. If speech-to-print on microcomputers ever becomes a normal administrative tool in office-work, there will be pressure to standardize the written shape of personal names. Families named *Lea*, *Lee* and *Leigh*, for instance, may all eventually have to agree to a common spelling.

Why the variability of personal name spellings should still thrive becomes clear if we compare first names and surnames. First names are common property and so one would expect a standard spelling. Even so, rather more variability is allowed than in non-names: *Anthony–Antony*, *Brian–Bryan*, *Caroline–Carolyn*, *Catherine–Katherine–Kathryn*, *Jeffrey–Geoffrey*, *Lewis–Louis*, *Marjorie–Margery*, etc. Surnames, however, are the totem-poles of language. The pressure of distinctive function puts a value on different and even bizarre spellings.

The prestige value of archaic spelling

Archaism, too, has a value. A spelling which looks old and is out of step with present-day spelling conventions shows that the family is 'old', in the sense of having a long recorded history. Only occasionally does the difference from the spelling of non-names show greater regularity, as in *Flite–flight*. Particularly prestigious are names that preserve Norman-French spellings which diverge considerably from the present pronunciation, such as *Beaulieu* /ˈbjuːlɪ/, since these are both old and aristocratic. There seems to be no association of archaism in similarly divergent Celtic names such as *Meagher* /mɑː/ or *Siobhan* /ʃɪˈvɔːn/. They are probably just regarded as inadequate anglicizations, but they do have a strong totemic value. The Marquis of Cholmondeley, whose name, when spoken, is /ˈʧʌmlɪ/, probably has the ultimate Norman totem, while the ultimate in native Anglo-Saxon is probably *Featherstonehaugh*, pronounced /ˈfænʃɔː/, or *Woolfardsworthy*, pronounced /ˈwʊlzərɪ/. Noble families choose their own particular variant of the pair *marquis–marquess*, so that this effectively becomes part of the name-totem.

On a smaller time scale we can see the development of archaism in the spelling of names in languages where there have been recent spelling reforms. Spelling reforms are applied to non-names and usually to place-names, but personal names are generally not interfered with. It is worth looking in some detail at the treatment of names in one such writing system which, unlike English, is 'managed' by authority. The spelling of Swedish is regulated by recommendations of the Swedish Academy in a 'word-list' published at regular intervals and by occasional parliamentary statutes. The last of these was the spelling reform of 1906. This did away with the <q> spellings of /k/ and the <w> spellings of /v/, so that <q> and <w> are no longer used outside loan-words in official Swedish spelling. This allows these letters to be exploited unofficially for their antiquarian value. Hotels often carry the sign *Wärdshus* instead of the normal *Värdshus* and the names of historic towns often appear unofficially, for example in the tourist trade, in their unreformed spelling (e.g. *Waxholm*). Antiquarianism, however, is not the only influence at work. In December 1970 the town of *Hälsingborg* was granted special dispensation by the Swedish government to spell its name officially with the archaic spelling *Helsingborg*; <e> and <ä> are both possible spellings of /e/. The reason here was presumably that the usual Swedish spelling with the modified Roman <ä> was awkward in business correspondence and information processing. Swedish industrialists have done likewise: *Skånska Cement* (<å>≡/oː/) now call themselves *Skanska*, which results in a quite alien correspondence <a>≡/oː/ and perhaps ultimately in an irrelevant pronunciation /ˈskanska/. Nor does <Skanska> relate any longer to the province of *Skåne*. The spelling of family names may similarly be altered to make them orthographically distinct. *Moberg* may have a deliberate respelling <Mobärg>, which loses the identity of the second element *berg* 'mountain'.

Family names do not have to correspond to standard spelling conventions and are allowed to vary between archaic and new. So alongside a 'normal' *Lindkvist* we find just as often *Lindquist*. The majority of family names with initial /v/ are still spelt with <w> (e.g. *Wallin*). In the family name *Wahlquist* there are usually three archaisms: <w>≡/v/, <ah>≡/ɑː/ and <qu>≡/kv/. One hardly ever sees a normally spelt *Valkvist*. Family names in Swedish thus retain and frequently use types of correspondence which have been stringently engineered out of ordinary spelling. Vowel length can be represented in names by vowel-letter doubling: *Höök*, *Wiik*, *Roos*, *Leek* (which are *hök*, *vik*, *ros*, *lek* as non-names), or by using <h> as a length marker: *Ahl*, *Rehn*, *Pihl* (which are *al*, *ren*, *pil* as non-names). This means, of course, that names have some fairly recognizable markers in addition to their capital letters. There is also the slight advantage that texts in the pre-reform spelling can be read with little hesitation by anyone, because the conventions of the older spelling system are still familiar from names. However, since archaism in the spelling of Swedish family names is so common, one can hardly consider it a marker of prestige. The obverse is probably true: people who spell their name as *Valkvist* would seem to have an overtly modern, even 'leftish' outlook.

'New Spelling' as a scheme for English spelling reform realizes that names present problems (Ripman and Archer 1948: 88), but comes out in favour of re-spelling all names, including anglicized foreign names. These include: **Inggland*, **Jurmany*, **Ooroogwie*, **Uerop*, **Aesha*, **Juulyus Seezar*, **Vurjil*, **Hoemer*, **Konfueshyus*.

Even though English tolerates a good deal of irregular archaism, most of the variation in the English spelling of personal names follows the conventions of ordinary spelling and only varies within a restricted range of patterns. Overall there is greater plurality of symbolization (several spellings to one phoneme) and greater plurality of correspondence (several phonemes to one spelling) than in the spelling of non-names, but we expect the usual range of spelling correspondences to apply for most of the time. If you have never come across the surname *Mearns* but are asked to pronounce it, there is only one possibility for the <M-ns> part: /ˈm-nz/. The <m> and <n> only allow /m/ and /n/; the final <s> cannot be /s/ in this context, only /z/. The <ear> restricts the SBS vowel choice to /ɜː/, /ɪə/, /ɛə/ or /ɑː/ and you would no doubt put the probability of pronunciation in that order. In non-names there are /ɜː/≡<ear> correspondences in *learns*, *yearns* and *earns*. The potential pronunciations /mɪənz/, /mɛənz/ and /mɑːnz/ seem much less likely, but with names one can never know. All the above pronunciations of the name *Mearns* (except /mɑːnz/) are in fact found in EPD. Since the totem value of any correspondence is in inverse proportion to one's expectations, anyone with the surname *Mearns* wishing to stand out from the crowd should certainly adopt /mɑːnz/ and then have the pleasure of correcting people.

Plurality of potential correspondence is a problem for readers rather than writers. Writers, on the other hand, have problems with plurality of symbolism. For a name you might hear pronounced /mɜːnz/, the spellings *<Murns>, *<Merns>, and *<Mirns> seem possible in addition to <Mearns>. But *<Mourns> (cf. *scourge*) hardly suggests itself. That, however, would be the spelling to go for if you wished to achieve maximum totemicity. One can imagine someone saying: 'No, no! Not /mɔːnz/, but /mɜːnz/, as in *scourge*! There aren't many of us.'

The sensitivity factor

There are sometimes good social reasons for avoiding the usual pronunciation of a name. Some names have unpleasant or embarrassing associations, but the inconvenience can be eased by choosing an unusual pronunciation. The spelling may also be adjusted to match. Though one can never be certain that this embarrassment factor lies behind a particular pronunciation or spelling, the following examples are likely cases: *Astle* /ˈæsl/ (where /ˈɑsl/

as in *castle* might suggest *arsehole*); *Belcher* with /ʃ/ not /ʧ/; *Bottome* /bə'təʊm/; *Buggs* /bju:gz/; *Death* /deɪθ/, /di:θ/, /di:'æθ/; *Fudge* /fju:ʤ/. Consider names with final <-gge>, where both the <C>-doubling and the <e>-marking are irregular – *Bigge*, *Fagge*, *Legge*, *Pegge*, *Snagge*. They do look like a deliberate avoidance of association with the ordinary meanings. *Poe* is sometimes pronounced as two syllables like *Chloe*. To keep the Latin stress on the penultimate syllable of *Uranus* is clearly asking for trouble, so /'jʊərənəs/ is a common alternative form.

Personal first names also vary in their associations with gender roles. In a survey of the influence of names on personality by Carol Johnson and Helen Petrie (University of Sussex), reported in *The Independent* (18 December 1991: 4), the ten most 'masculine' names (in the names of the sample of 286 people tested) were perceived to be *John, David, Richard, Peter, Mark, James, Paul, Michael, Matthew, Edward*, and the ten most 'feminine' names were perceived to be *Sophie, Elizabeth, Emily, Lucy, Rose, Emma, Katherine, Mary, Diana, Victoria*. The research showed that the personalities of women were affected by the relative femininity of their name. Women with an overtly 'feminine' name, such as *Sophie*, seemed to conform more to female stereotypes. Some women reacted to this in choosing to be known by a diminutive which could refer to either sex, such as *Nick, Jo*, or *Chris*.

If we now look at the structure of the two quoted lists of 'marked' names, we can see interesting differences in sound and also in spelling. In the women's names there are five stop consonants and the mean length in syllables is 2.5. In the men's names there are thirteen stops and the mean length in syllables is 1.6. The three names which do not have initial stress are women's. Of the ten women's names seven ended in a vowel, but only one man's name (if we exclude *Peter*). The spelling makes this difference even more salient. All the men's names ended in a consonant letter, but only one of the women's names (*Elizabeth*). All these phonetic and graphic features conspire to produce an effect of 'softness' or 'less abruptness' in women's names and 'hardness' or 'more abruptness' in men's names. This is further evidence that a personal name, written or spoken, is often more than just an arbitrary sign.

The phonetic erosion of place-names. Spelling pronunciations

English place-names, many of which also figure as personal names, also show considerable variety in pronunciation. Over the centuries, common place-name elements have suffered phonetic reduction in local use until the pronunciation is often very much out of step with ordinary spelling patterns. Local pronunciations of places such as *Leominster* /'lemstə/, *Congresbury* /'ku:mzbrɪ/, *Bicester* /'bɪstə/, *Cirencester* /'sɪsɪtə/, *Puncknowle*

/ˈpʌnl/, are not deducible by rule. This wearing down of a place-name by frequent local use is similar to the reduced forms of words found in jargons. The terms *foresail*, *forecastle*, *foremast* are /ˈfɔːsl/, /ˈfəʊksl/ and /ˈfɔːməst/ in nautical jargon; *sail*, *castle* and *mast* have reduced forms. A stranger will naturally attempt a spelling pronunciation of a reduced place-name, and this alternative may gain currency alongside the original local form. Cirencester locals may nowadays have a guilty feeling that they ought really to be calling the place /ˈsaɪərənsestə/. So, for *Hawarden*, /ˈheɪwɔːdn/ is found alongside /ˈhɑːdn/; for *Uttoxeter*, /juːˈtɒksɪtə/ is found alongside /ˈʌksɪtə/, and so on. When a place-name is transferred from its traditional locality to serve as the name of a road or company or product, or a new locality elsewhere, it will usually get a regularized spelling pronunciation in its new home. EPD records *Blawith* as /ˈblɑːɪθ/ (in Cumbria), but as /ˈbleɪwɪθ/ (road at Harrow). This may even happen to personal names: EPD cites *Beethoven Street* in London with the spelling pronunciation /iː/. Foreign place-names borrowed in the U.S.A. for new settlements are regularized: *Cairo* as /ˈkɛərəʊ/ (AmE /ˈkɛroʊ/) not /ˈkaɪərəʊ/, *Norwich* as /ˈnɔːwɪtʃ/ (AmE /ˈnɔrwɪtʃ/) not /ˈnɒrɪtʃ/, *Lima* in Ohio with /aɪ/ not /iː/. Warwick as an American personal name is /ˈwɔːwɪk/ (AmE /ˈwɔrwɪk/). These spelling pronunciations serve to indicate what is regarded as the more regular correspondence. *Coulsdon* in Greater London has a local pronunciation with /əʊ/; the regularized pronunciation is /ˈkuːlzdən/. This may indicate that the correspondence <oul>≡/uːl/ in *boulevard*, *coulter*, *ghoul*, *roulette*, is regarded as more 'normal' than <oul>≡/əʊl/ in *moult*, *poultice*, *poultry*, *soul*.

It is not surprising then that a considerable sense of insecurity attaches to the pronunciation of an English place-name. EPD lovingly records the following variation for the place-name *Stour*:

(in Suffolk, Essex) /stʊə/
(in Kent) /stʊə/, rarely /ˈstaʊə/
(in Hampshire) /ˈstaʊə/, /stʊə/
(in Warwickshire) /ˈstaʊə/, /ˈstəʊə/
(in Dorset) /ˈstaʊə/.

Analogy is never quite safe. Despite the above, *Stourmouth* in Kent has /ˈstaʊə/, rarely /stʊə/. *Stourton* in Wiltshire and as a surname has /ɜː/. All the places containing initial <Hey-> are pronounced /heɪ-/: *Heycock*, *Heyno*, *Heytesbury*, *Heywood*; but *Heysham* has /hiː-/. The element {holy} has an unshortened vowel /ˈhəʊlɪ-/ in *Holycross*, *Holyoake* but a shortened vowel /ˈhɒlɪ-/ in *Holyhead*, *Holyrood*, *Holywell*.

Variability also flourishes in the pronunciation of foreign place-names and personal names. Important foreign names have long been fixed in an institutionalized English pronunciation: *Paris*, *Rome*, *Moscow*; the most bizarre correspondence is probably *Leghorn* for *Livorno* in Italy, which in earlier times was *Legorno*. *Leghorn* also shows how a foreign name can sometimes be restructured into native English elements, a kind of 'popular etymology'. For those names which have not been institutionalized, there are common patterns of acceptable variation in pronunciation. Latin names are a well-known and highly contentious instance. An anglicized pronunciation of *Getae* is /ˈʤiːtiː/, with the Latin //g// palatalized to /ʤ/ and the vowels raised to /iː/ in line with native English vowels which underwent the Vowel Shift. An attempt to stay more close to the original Latin would give a very different /ˈgeɪtaɪ/. Similarly we have *Longinus* as /lɒnˈʤaɪnəs/ or /lɒŋˈgiːnəs/ or *Mundi* as /ˈmʌndaɪ/ or /ˈmʊndiː/.

6.4 PADDING

Empty letters in names. Unusual final <-CC> and <-e>

Personal names gain advantage by having a certain written bulk since a totem impresses partly by its size. Consequently, names which are phonetically quite short are often padded out with empty letters. The name /leg/ never seems to appear as **Leg* – the usual spelling is *Legge*. Here we see the two most common types of padding: <C>-doubling and a superfluous <-e> in a context where neither is warranted by modern spelling conventions. Such spellings were common in both names and non-names before conventions settled down in the eighteenth century, but archaism is not the only reason for their continued use in names. Since such spellings are most frequently found in monosyllables and since the unpadded spellings are much less common, their written bulk is obviously seen as an advantage. They also reinforce the initial capital letter as a marker of names and help them to stand out from the non-names in written text. In some cases the padding may help to distance the name from an unfortunate homophone, as in *Thynne*.

Less frequently do we find proper names which are iconic with smallness. 'There are specks of towns with short jabs of names: *Dot*, *Fred*, *Frog*, *Grit*, *Gus*, *Joy*, *Jud*, *Nix*, *Pep*, *Uz*' (Trevor Fishlock, *Daily Telegraph* 24 June 1989 in an article on Texas).

Padding takes various forms. A superfluous <-e> is found after a short vowel and a consonant-letter cluster in: *Aske*, *Bigge*, *Cocke*, *Crabbe*, *Cuffe*, *Donne* (but *Dunn*/*Dunne*), *Focke*, *Fulke*, *Gomme*, *Inge* (/ɪŋ/), *Legge*, *Passe*, *Pegge*, *Powicke*, *Prynne*, *Snagge*, *Soffe*, *Thynne*. Names such as *Goodliffe*, *Hinchliffe*, *Iliffe*, *Jolliffe*, *Olliffe*, *Radcliffe*, *Redcliffe*, *Wickliffe* usually have an <-e>, but *Ratcliff*(*e*) and *Cliff*(*e*) often dispense with it. The <-e> is also variable in: *Ann*(*e*), *Ask*(*e*), *Beck*(*e*), *Bewick*(*e*), *Cross*(*e*), *Dunn*(*e*), *Esmond*(*e*), *Fagg*(*e*), *Fisk*(*e*), *Glynn*(*e*), *Goff*(*e*), *Gwynn*(*e*), *Harding*(*e*), *Hardwick*(*e*), *Keating*(*e*), *Lock*(*e*), *Plumb*(*e*), *Webb*(*e*), *Wolf*(*e*), *Wynn*(*e*). Similarly <-e> can occur after <oo>≡/ʊ/ and a consonant, usually /k/:

Foot(e), *Brook(e)*, *Cook(e)*, *Crook(e)*, *Good(e)*, *Hook(e)*, *Holbrook(e)*.

The other main context where <-e> is superfluous is after a long vowel spelt with more than one letter (cf. *loan – lone*) as in: *Berowne*, *Blencowe*, *Brawne*, *Cawse*, *Cheeke*, *Choate*, *Coote*, *Crewe*, *Croome*, *Crowe*, *Crowte*, *Doane*, *Dowle*, *Doyle*, *Elaine*, *Esdaile*, *Foyle*, *Freake*, *Frowde*, *Hewke*, *Holyoake*, *Keyne*, *Keyte*, *Leake*, *Maine*, *Newe*, *O'Keefe*, *Perowne*, *Rowe*, *Soane*, *Scroope*, *Steyne*, *Tamburlaine* (but *Tamerlane* is regular), *Toole*, *Towne*, *Toye*. In these names the <-e> spelling seems fairly standard. Names which have a variable <-e> spelling include: *Alleyn(e)*, *Bagshaw(e)*, *Barlow(e)*, *Beal(e)*, *Boon(e)*, *Broom(e)*, *Froud(e)*, *Claud(e)*, *Daw(e)*, *Dean(e)*, *Down(e)*, *Henslow(e)*, *Freen(e)*, *Kean(e)*, *Keen(e)*, *How(e)*, *Lansdown(e)*, *Low(e)*, *Maud(e)*, *Neal(e)*, *Pain(e)*, *Read(e)*, *Sloan(e)*, *Steel(e)*, *Vail(e)*. The <-e> is also superfluous in *Hind(e)*, *Wild(e)*, *Wyld(e)*.

We can also include here vowel spellings with <r>: *Aherne*, *Beare*, *Bourke*, *Bourne*, *Burke*, *Burne*, *Calthorpe*, *Camborne*, *Corfe*, *Erle*, *Eyre*, *Geare*, *Herne*, *Poore*, *Searle*, *Shearme*, *Smirke*, *Thorne*, *Warne*, *Warre* – which all have <-e>, and, with or without <-e>: *Ayr(e)*, *Blackburn(e)*, *Clark(e)*, *Clerk(e)*, *Earl(e)*, *Fearn(e)*, *Ford(e)*, *Hart(e)*, *Hearn(e)*, *Hoar(e)*, *Horn(e)*, *Kirk(e)*, *Moor(e)*, *Nairn(e)*, *Ord(e)*, *Park(e)*, *Sharp(e)*, *Stearn(e)*, *York(e)*.

This use of <-e> is evidently rather capricious. Moreover, dictionaries can only aim to provide for a reasonable coverage of spellings. An entry only with <-e> cannot be taken to mean that a form without <-e> does not exist. If only *Leake* is given, it does not mean that *Leak* does not figure as a surname. Spellings with an <-e> may well be more common in cases such as *Crowe*, *Leake*, *Thorne* (rather than *Crow*, *Leak*, *Thorn*) where the <-e> has a marking function and distinguishes the name from an ordinary word. On the other hand, there are very many names homophonous with non-names where such a marker is probably never used: we do not seem to find **Blacke*, **Duffe*, **Flinte*.

The superfluous <-e> has archaic associations. These are commonly and sickeningly exploited in advertising: **fayre*, **olde*, **shoppe*. In family names this archaic/quaint effect must be considered minimal since the <-e> spellings are so common. It is difficult to pin down any possible phonetic functions of the <-e>. The spelling *Beare* (/bɪə/) may use the <-e> to indicate that this is not pronounced like the common noun *bear* and so suggest the alternative vowel /ɪə/. *Boase* may exploit the <-e> to indicate a single long vowel /əʊ/ rather than /əʊ/+/æ/, as in *Boas*. On the other hand *Boag* is /bəʊg/. One can only suggest any functional use of <-e> very tentatively since there is so much free variation in its use. Apart from such isolated examples, there is quite a problem for the reader with some non-§Basic names ending in <-e> in knowing whether the <e> is empty or a long vowel marker or whether it represents a separate vowel <e>≡/ə/ (*Isolde*) or <e>≡/ɪ/ (*Iolanthe*). *Metropole* can conceivably be misread as */meˈtrɒpəlɪ/

on the lines of *metropolis* /me'trɒpəlɪs/. Some names have two pronunciations: *Eunice* as /'ju:nɪs/ or /ju:'naɪsɪ/, *Irene* as /'aɪri:n/ or /aɪ'ri:nɪ/, *Rhode* as /rəʊd/ or /'rəʊdɪ/. Readers have to be aware of a final <-e> corresponding to /ɪ/ (or /i:/) in: *Amphitrite*, *Andromache*, *Antigone*, *Apache*, *Aphrodite*, *Arachne*, *Chichele*, *Chile*, *Chloe*, *Circe*, *Cloete*, *Cyrene*, *Gethsemane*, *Giuseppe*, *Hermione*, *Iolanthe*, *Matabele*, *Mohave*, *Montefiore*, *Niobe*, *Penelope*, *Persephone*, *Phoebe*, *Veronese*, *Volpone*, *Yosemite*. The final vowel may be /eɪ/ in *Dante*, *Kobe*. After consonant clusters which would not occur finally the <e> obviously has to represent a vowel: *Ariadne*, *Daphne*, *Kresge*, *Zimbabwe*. Sequences such as <-ite>, <-ene>, <-ate>, <-phone> clearly set a trap for the unwary and are a temptation to anglicize. Wordsworth rhymes *Amphitrite* with /-aɪt/.

An ill-advised use of <-e> is in the spellings *Hardinge*, *Inge*, *Keatinge*, which have /ɪŋ/ as an alternative pronunciation to the regular /ɪn(d)ʒ/. A similar misleading use of <e> is found in *Davies*, *Gillies*, *Harries*, *Herries*, *Margulies* – all of which usually end in /ɪs/, not /ɪz/ (except as a spelling pronunciation).

Final <-e> also occurs in the ending <-ie> as an alternative to <-y>. The <-ie> is a 'pet-name' (hypocoritic) suffix in some cases (*Archie*) competing with the <-y> form of the suffix (*Billy*). There is a tendency, too, to use <-ie> for a female version of an otherwise male name – *Bobbie* is much more likely to be a woman than *Bobby*. The <-ie> form also avoids similarity with adjectival <-y>. Presumably it is more endearing to be referred to as *Smellie* than as *Smelly*.

<C>-doubling may be found unexpectedly, sometimes with <-e> as well, in final position or before final /s/ with the consonants /p b t d g m n/ and //r//. These normally have a single-letter spelling in this context in non-names (*rip*, *rib*, *lit*, *lid*, *leg*, *ram*, *ran*, *far*). Examples are:

- with <pp> – *Alsopp*, *Chipp*, *Copp*, *Krupp*, *Lapp*;
- with <bb> – *Chubb*, *Cobb*, *Dibb*, *Dobb*(*s*), *Gibb*(*s*), *Hobbs*, *Jebb*, *Robb*, *Stubbs*, *Tibbs*, *Webb*(*e*);
- with <-tt> in a large number of disyllabic and occasional trisyllabic names – *Abbot*(*t*), *Alcott*, *Allbutt*, *Arnot*(*t*), *Barnet*(*t*), *Barrat*(*t*), *Bartlett*, *Basset*(*t*), *Becket*(*t*), *Bennet*(*t*), *Birkett*, *Blackett*, *Blewett*, *Blissett*, *Bockett*, *Bonnett*, *Boycott*, *Bunnett*, *Burdett*, *Burnett*, *Calcot*(*t*), *Calcutt*, *Caldecott*, *Catcott*, *Cobbett*, *Cockshott*, *Corbett*, *Cubitt*, *Daggett*, *Dannatt*, *Debrett*, *Doggett*, *Domett*, *Elliot*(*t*), *Endicott*, *Everitt*, *Evett*(*s*), *Fawcett*, *Follett*, *Folliott*, *Ganett*, *Garbutt*, *Garnet*(*t*), *Garratt*, *Garret*(*t*), *Giblett*, *Gillott*, *Gimblett*, *Grocott*, *Gwinnett*, *Hackett*, *Halkett*, *Haslett*, *Hewitt*, *Hewlett*, *Howitt*, *Hudnott*, *Ivatt*, *Jarratt*, *Jowett*, *Knyvett*, *Leavitt*, *Leggatt*, *Leverett*, *Levett*, *Lintott*, *Lippincott*, *Lycett*, *Melchet*, *Mockett*, *Murcott*, *Muskett*, *Mynott*, *Nesbit*(*t*), *Olcott*, *Ossett*, *Owlett*, *Parratt*, *Powitt*, *Peckitt*, *Perrett*, *Pig*(*g*)*ott*, *Plunket*(*t*), *Poulett*, *Prescot*(*t*), *Secrett*, *Sinnett*, *Smollett*, *Tippett*,

Truefitt, *Truscott*, *Tyrwhitt*, *Upcott*, *Uthwatt*, *Walcott*, *Westcott*, *Wilmot*(*t*), *Wolcott*, *Wyat*(*t*);

- with <-tt> in monosyllabic names – *Brett*, *Butt*, *Coutts*, *Kitts*, *Lett*(*s*), *Mott*, *Pett*, *Pitt*(*s*), *Platt*, *Pott*(*s*), *Pratt*, *Putt*, *Scot*(*t*), *Spratt*, *Strutt*, *Trott*, *Watt*(*s*), *Whytt*;
- with <dd> – *Bodd*, *Budd*, *Dodd*(*s*), *Fludd*, *Judd*, *Kidd*, *Lydd*, *Rudd*, *Todd*;
- with <gg> – *Askrigg*, *Beggs*, *Bigge*, *Biggs*, *Bragg*, *Brigg*(*s*), *Brownrigg*, *Buggs*, *Clegg*, *Cragg*, *Fagg*(*e*), *Figg*, *Flagg*, *Fogg*, *Glegg*, *Grigg*(*s*), *Hogg*, *Kellogg*, *Legge*, *Pegge*, *Skeggs*, *Snagge*, *Sprigg*, *Twigg*;
- with <mm> – *Gomme*, *Grimm*, *Mumm*, *Wimms*;
- with <nn> – *Binn*(*s*), *Blunn*, *Donne*, *Dunn*(*e*), *Fenn*, *Finn*(*s*), *Flynn*, *Ginn*, *Glynn*(*e*), *Gwynn*(*e*), *Lynn*, *McCann*, *Mann*(*s*), *Nunn*, *Penn*, *Prynne*, *Thinn*, *Thynne*, *Venn*, *Wann*, *Wrenn*;
- with <rr> – *Barr*, *Burr*, *Carr*, *Dorr*, *Farr*, *Kerr*, *Parr*, *Spurr*, *Starr*, *Storr*. *Orr* is regular in having at least three letters (§3.2.5 p. 131).

There is little comment one can make on these departures from the <C>-doubling conventions that apply in non-names. The doubling of final <t> in the second, unstressed syllable of disyllabic words may be designed to avoid a §French pronunciation as <-et>≡/eɪ/ or <-ot>≡/əʊ/. Monosyllables are bulked up by <C>-doubling and final <-e> almost as if a minimum four-letter rule applied to names. A particularly bizarre example is the surname *Icke* /aɪk/ (cf. *Ike*), which has the double letter <ck> plus <e>-marking of the long vowel. There are, however, a number of exceptions with less than four letters, such as *Cam*, *Esk*, *Ham*, *Kyd*, *Lot*, which are not bulked up to four letters.

Abbreviated names do not usually have unconventional <C>-doubling, since this extra padding would be at odds with their abbreviation: *Bet* (*Elizabeth*), *Bob* (*Robert*), *Brit* (*-ish*), *Dan* (*-iel*), *Don* (*-ald*), *Fan* (*-ny*), *Fred* (*-erick*), *Jap* (*-anese*), *Jim* (*James*), *Ken* (*-neth*), *Meg* (*Margaret*), *Pam* (*-ela*), *Pip* (*Phillip*), *Rob* (*-ert*), *Rod* (*-ney*), *Sam* (*-uel*), *Strad* (*-ivarius*), *Ted* (*Edward*), *Tim* (*-othy*), *Tom* (*Thomas*), *Wat* (*Walter*), *Whit* (*-suntide*). Nor do abbreviated names have conventional <C>-doubling: *Vic* (*-toria*) not *<Vick>, *Gus* (*Augustus*) not *<Guss>, *Reg* (*-inald*) not *<Redge>, *Sol* (*-omon*) not *<Soll>. Consequently, forms such as *Robb*, *Watt* are marked by the <C>-doubling as surnames rather than first names. If the form is not simply a truncation, but has some other alteration as well, there may be conventional doubling: compare the simple abbreviations *Gus*, *Vic*, with *Bess* (*Elizabeth*), *Dick* (*Richard*), *Mick* (*Michael*), *Nick* (*Nicholas*). *<Nich> would represent /ˈnɪʧ/.

6.5 VARIABILITY IN VOWEL CORRESPONDENCES

'How do you pronounce your name, Miss er Batho'?

A recurrent problem in attempting to pronounce an unfamiliar name is whether a sequence of vowel letters should be treated as one unit or as two. The uncertainty is reduced if there is some evidence to show whether the name is native or foreign. The vowel sequence alternative is likely to be in a foreign name. For instance, *Ife* as an English surname is /aɪf/; as a Nigerian town it is /ˈiːfeɪ/ with two vowels. There is always a tendency for two contiguous vowels to merge into one syllable peak because of the lack of an intervening consonant, so Laos /ˈlɑːɒs/ has been adapted to /laʊs/. *Kaunda* /kɑːˈʊndə/ is tending to become */ˈkaʊndə/. There are similar problems with apparent <e>-marking: the <e> represents a vowel in *Bethphage*, *Lalage*, *Beves*, *Purves*. *Forbes* allows both /ˈfɔːbz/ and /ˈfɔːbɪs/. There are sometimes markers to alert the reader. *Hakodate* is marked as exotic by the single <k> rather than <ck> after a presumably short /æ/. So the <-ate> is not going to be the familiar /-eɪt/ but /-ɑːtɪ/. *Alcinous*, if it is a man's name, is unlikely to have the <-ous> adjectival suffix, so one might suspect that it is /ælˈsɪnəʊəs/.

The most striking difference between the vowel correspondences of non-names and those of names is not so much in the actual correspondences found in names, as in the patterns of free variation allowed. The simple letter <a> may correspond to /æ/, /ɑː/, or /eɪ/ as usual, but names such as *Glasgow* may have /æ/ or /ɑː/, names such as *Bader* may have /eɪ/ or /ɑː/, names such as *Batho* may have /æ/ or /eɪ/. Some variants may be qualified as 'old-fashioned' (e.g. *Gloucester* with /ɔː/, *Lombard* with /ʌ/, or *Salonica* with /aɪ/). Some variants represent spelling pronunciations of a place-name used as a personal name or street name away from the practice of the locality (e.g. *Bury* not as /ˈberɪ/, but as /ˈbjʊərɪ/). Some variants are regional. Some variants are strangely at odds with the original pronunciation. EPD, which includes a greater proportion of eccentric pronunciations than LPD, allows /əʊ/, a long vowel, in *Agamemnon*. Some variants are learned. *Viking* looks §Basic and normally has /aɪ/, but there is an academic variant with /iː/ based on the Scandinavian pronunciation. Readers will have their own idea of what the 'usual' pronunciation is, but may be aware of the other possibilities as part of their competence and general background.

Variants of place-names in the rest of this chapter are not assigned to the 'context' of particular localities. For instance, Houston is given as an example of /uː/ – /juː/ – /aʊ/ variation, but it is not noted that /ˈhuːstən/ is a Scottish name, /ˈhjuːstən/ is the Texas city, /ˈhaʊstən/ is a street in New York City and a place in Georgia, USA (LPD).

<a> spellings

<a> spellings show the most variation. The pair /æ/ – /eɪ/ are short and long variants in allomorphic variation (*flammable–flame*, *manic–mania*, etc.). In some cases a context which usually dictates a short vowel rather than a long one may or may not be active: three-syllable names such as *Atchison*, *Blakiston*, *Cananite*, *Jamieson*, *Lavery*, have /æ/ variants presumably because of third-syllable shortening, but they may well have an unshortened /eɪ/. The difference could be associated with the recognition or not of an element boundary (*Jamie+son* giving /eɪ/, *Jamieson* taken to be one unit, giving /æ/). Personal names, however, are not usually seen to contain elements and internal boundaries. Names are institutionalized. You usually take them as you find them. If I knew one family called /ˈʤeɪmɪsn/ and another called /ˈʤæmɪsn/, I would try to respect their particular totems. Even if I invariably pronounce *salt*, *alter*, *fault*, *false*, etc. with /ɒ/, I would be perfectly willing to accommodate the *Alsopp* family with their /ɔː/ (and their single <s> and double <pp>). Other names with /æ/ – /eɪ/ variation are: *Agate*, *Athos*, *Avon*, *Basford*, *Blackie*, *Capel*, *Haslett*, *Jacques*, *Sabin*, *Shadrach*, *Zilliacus*. Some of these variants, however, are distinctly uncommon. Before //r// the parallel of this variation is between /æ/ and /ɛə/: *Aries*, *Baring*, *Darien*.

The /æ/ – /ɑː/ variation is rather different. An original short open vowel was lengthened to /ɑː/ in Southern England in the early seventeenth century before the fricatives /f, θ, s/ (*after*, *bath*, *pass*) and before a nasal plus consonant (*dance*). North of a line stretching roughly from the Wash to the Bristol Channel this change did not take place. So present-day variation in British English between a short and a long open vowel in a particular word exists across different accents, and it is an accent difference of which most people would be aware (Wells 1982: 3.1.9). This same difference may occur in names as free variation.

Names which may have /æ/ – /ɑː/ variation across SBS speakers in the lengthening contexts of the sound change are: *Alexander*, *Bantu*, *Basque*, *Damascus*, *Dante*, *Ghandi*, *Glastonbury*, *Granton*, *Jasper*, *Las (Vegas)*, *Lhasa*, *Madras*, *Mander*, *Maskell*, *Mombasa*, *Pasteur*, *Pavlova*, *Penzance*, *Prendergast*, *Sandra*, *Taft*. Variation between /æ/ – /ɑː/ also occurs in elements of names where the equivalent non-names would have only /ɑː/ in SBS: *Dance*, *Passfield*, *Passmore*. There is usually /ə/ in the name element <-caster> (*Lancaster*), but LPD also gives variants with /ɑː/.

Variation between /æ/ – /ɑː/ is found before a range of other consonants (ignoring syllable boundaries) in names which are distinctly exotic:

- /p/ : *Capri*, *Capua*, *Papua*;
- /b/ : *Abishai*, *Aboukir*, *Lochaber*, *Calabria* (+ /eɪ/);
- /d/ : *Adler*, *Adolf*, *Allahabad* (and other *-bad* names), *Kaliningrad* (and other *-grad* names);

- /k/ : *Balakirev*, *Braque*, *Dvorak*, *Nagasaki*, *Yakutsk*;
- /g/ : *Zagreb*;
- /ʧ/ : *Pagliacci*;
- /z/ : *Plaza*;
- /ʃ/ : *Pasha*;
- /l/ : *Guatemala*, *Salzburg*, *Stalin*;
- /m/ : *Famagusta*, *Islam*, *Nizam*, *Seringapatam*, *Vietnam*;
- /n/ : *Fezzan*, *Montana*, *Pakistan* (and other *-stan* names), *Sudan*, *Taiwan*, *Urbana*;
- /ŋ/ + /k/ : *Franck*;
- /w/ : *Gawain*.

The following consonant, irrespective of any perceived syllable boundary, is only of interest in the above examples in that it is not usually one of the contexts in which, in the absence of underlying //r//, we would expect /ɑː/. These names are consequently marked as exotic by an /ɑː/ pronunciation. Since there is no normal lengthening context in this group of names, the speller has to be aware that an /ɑː/ pronunciation is not here associated with //r// (**Garwain*). But if the speller knows that an /æ/ pronunciation is possible as an alternative to /ɑː/ (/ˈgæweɪn/ – /ˈgɑːweɪn/), this will rule out any <r> spelling. The reason is that /r/ cannot remain after a short /æ/ and before a consonant in SBS and similar accents. This reason may seem tortuous but there is no reason why a speller should not become aware from experience that a short vowel before a consonant does not involve <r> spellings.

Stress variation can also can link /æ/ and /ɑː/. *Anakim* is pronounced /ˈænəkɪm/ with antepenultimate stress and /əˈnɑːkɪm/ with penultimate stress. /æ/ – /ɑː/ variation also occurs with a following /r/: *Barham* (/ˈbɑːrəm/ or /ˈbærəm/), *Cesario*, *Karen*, *Marham*, *Polaris*, *Zarathustra*. *Fahrenheit* also has /æ/ – /ɑː/ variation in spite of the spelling <ah>; normally this spelling would only represent a long vowel, but the short vowel in this word may be seen as third-syllable shortening.

Variation between the two long vowels /eɪ/ and /ɑː/ also occurs. The difference here is usually between old-established and recent names, between familiar and distinctly exotic. This group does not include <ar> spellings, of course. Borrowed names with a long [ɑː] will keep it as long as the name has foreign associations, hence the term ‘continental *a*’. General acceptance will change the vowel to /eɪ/. So, the woman’s name *Ada* is usually /ˈeɪdə/; a known foreigner, however, might be marked as foreign with /ˈɑːdə/. This distinction is one of the differences between the old anglicized and new purist pronunciations of Latin. Examples of /eɪ/ – /ɑː/ variation from a wide range of origins: *Africanus*, *Anastasia*, *Apis*, *Asa*, *Ate*, *Ava*, *Bader*, *Bilbao*, *Cahill*, *Lestrade*, *Manes*. Before /r/ this type of variation is between /ɛə/ and /ɑː/, as in: *Apollinaris*, *Aral*, *Aryan*, *Baruch*, *Harewood*, *Sharon* (also /æ/), *Stradivarius*, *Tocharian*.

The most common variation involving <a> is the /ɔːl/ – /ɒl/ pronunciation of <al>. This free variation is also found in non-names in the SBS pronunciation of words such as *salt*, *altar*, *false*. A large number of place-names containing the Old English element *ald-* or *all-* ('old') show this variation: *Albury*, *Alcott*, *Aldenham*, *Aldgate*, *Alford*, *Allchin*, *Allcorn*, *Allcroft*, etc. Other examples are: *Balchin*, *Balkan*, *Baltic*, *Baltimore*, *Calcott*, *Caldecott*, *Calder*, *Caldwell*, *Dalton*, *Falconbridge*, *Falkirk*, *Falstaff*, *Galt*, *Gibraltar*, *Haldane*, *Maldon*, *Maldive*, *Malta*, *Malvern*, *Palfrey*, *Salford*, *Salisbury*, *Spalding*, *Talbot*, *Wallrook*, *Walcheren*, *Walden*, *Waldorf*, *Wallwork*, *Walpole*, *Walsall*, *Walsh*, *Walter*, etc. The further possibility of /æl/ in addition to /ɔːl/, /ɒl/ is found in: *Albany*, *Alcock*, *Aldous*, *Calderon*, *Calthorpe*. But /æl/ also varies with /ɔːl/ in: *Albania*, *Breadalbane*, *Calvert*, *Dalby*, *Galsworthy*, *Gilgal*, *Halsey*, *Palgrave*, *Palsgrave*, *Yalding*. Within these groups the relative frequency of one or other variant will differ from name to name: with *Dalby* /ɔː/ is more frequent than /æ/, but the reverse is the case with *Calvert*.

Long/short variation is similarly found, as in non-names, in <au> spellings as /ɔː/ – /ɒ/: *Austen*, *Austell*, *Austin*, *Australia*, *Austria*, *Fauntleroy*, *Hainault*, *Mauretania*, *Sauchiehall*. The non-§Basic correspondence for <au> is /aʊ/, so we have /aʊ/ – /ɔː/ in: *Audi*, *Braun*, *Munchausen*, *Nassau*, *Saudi*. More marginal are the variations /ɔː/ – /əʊ/ in *Faulds*, *Kefauver*, and /ɔː/ – /ɑː/ before <-nd>, <-nt> in *Saunders*, *Saunderson*, *Staunton*, *Taunton*.

There is similar variation between <ai> (or <ay>) as /aɪ/ – /eɪ/, where /aɪ/ is the more §Exotic: *Bulawayo*, *Cetewayo*, *Cyrenaica*, *Haydn*, *McKay*, *McKie*, *Paraguay*, *(Port) Said*, *Stainer*, *Tokay*, *Uruguay*.

There are a few minority variations involving <a>:

- <a>≡ /ɪ/ – /eɪ/ : *Alsager*;
- <a>≡ /æ/ – /ʌ/ : *Basra*, *Hassah*, *Jamia*, *Pahang*; this is due to English listeners identifying a short fully open vowel [a] as /ʌ/ rather than a fronted /æ/;
- <a>≡ /eɪ/ – /ɔː/ : *O'Brady*, *Whalley* (+ /ɒ/);
- <a>≡ /ɑː/ – /ɔː/ – /æ/ – /ɒ/ : *Wrath*;
- <al>≡ /æl/ – /ɑː/ : *Chalfont*;
- <al>≡ /ɑːl/ – /ɔːl/ : *Calton*, *Nepal*;
- <aa>≡ /ɑː/ – /ɔː/ : *Haakon*;
- <ae>≡ /æ/ – /eɪ/ : *Gaelic*;
- <ah>≡ /ɑː/ – /ɔː/ : *Strahan*, *Utah*;
- <ai>≡ /æ/ – /eɪ/ : *Laing*.

<e> spellings

For <e>, the usual long/short alternation /iː/ – /e/ (*serene – serenity*) occurs in free variation across SBS speakers in *Bevis*, *Cedric*, *Cheviot*, *Devers*, *Evelyn*, *Eveline*, *Greta*, *Hebron*, *Kedron*, *Kenya*, *Leven*, *Levy*, *Nepos*,

Nevis, *Teviot*, *Thetis*. There is similar variation in *Carnegie*, *Pedro*, but these also have variants in /eɪ/. The two alternative long pronunciations /iː/ and /eɪ/ occur in *Lena*, *Cheney*, *Chenies*, *Eugene*, *Galileo*, *Manresa*, *Rehan*, *San Remo*, *Veda* and, in spite of the <-ic> ending, which usually has a preceding short vowel, in *Vedic*.

In final open syllables, where /e/ cannot occur, there is /ɪ/ – /eɪ/ variation in *Bronte*, *Zimbabwe*.

Variations in other spellings where <e> is the first letter are:

- <ea>≡/iː/ – /e/ : *Greatham*, *Polzeath*;
- <ea>≡/iː/ – /eɪ/ : *Eames*, *Greaves*, *Hargreaves*, *Yeatman*;
- <ee>≡/ɪ/ – /e/ : *Greenwich*;
- <ei>≡/iː/ – /ɪ/ : *Leishman*;
- <ei>≡/iː/ – /aɪ/ : *Bernstein*, *Keightley*, *Stein*; *Keighley* /ˈkiːθlɪ/ (place-name), /ˈkaɪlɪ/ or /ˈkiːlɪ/ (personal name);
- <eigh>≡/eɪ/ – /aɪ/ : *Deighton*, *Heigho*, *Zuleika*;
- <ey>≡/e/ – /eɪ/ : *Meynall*, *Meyrick*, *Reynard*;
- <ey..e>≡/iː/ – /eɪ/ : *Alleyne*;
- <ey>≡/iː/ – /aɪ/ : *Keyser*;
- <eu>≡/ɔɪ/ – /ɜː/ – /uː/ : *Breughel*;
- <eu>≡/ɔɪ/ – /juː/ : *Euler*;
- <eu>≡/juː/ – /uː/ : *Leuchars*;
- <er>≡/er/ – /ɪər/ : *Cherith*, *Eros*, *Hyperion*, *Tera*, *Very*;
- <er>≡/ɑː/ – /ɜː/ : *Berkeley*, *Berkshire*, *Bertie*, *Herford*, *Herts*., *Hervey*, *Jervaulx*, *Jervis*, *Ker(r)*, the /ɑː/ pronunciation has also developed a more realistic alternative spelling in some of these names: *Barclay*, *Harford*, *Harvey*, *Jarvis*, *Carr*;
- <er>≡/ɛə/ – /ɜː/ : *Berlioz*, *Berne*, *Brer*, *Clermont*, *Pergolese*, *Puerto Rico*, *Sauterne*, *Vermeer*, *Verne*, *Verner*, *Versailles*, *Wittenberg* and other <-berg> names; the /ɛə/ pronunciation is probably thought to be less anglicized and a better approximation to the pre-consonantal <er>≡/er/ which these foreign names would have by rights;
- <ear>≡/ɪə/ – /ɜː/ : *Kearsley*, *Kearton*, *Sheard*, *Shearn*;
- <ear> /ɜː/ – /ɑː/ : *Kearney*.

<i> and <y> spellings

There are a few instances of long/short variation /aɪ/ – /ɪ/ (as in *vice – vicious*) in names such as *Delphi*, *Hindley*, *Icarus*, *Idris*, *Ind*, *Phidias*, *Philemon*, *Pisces*, *Simond*, and with <y>: *Dionysius*, *Symonds*, *Smyth*(*e*), *Tyzack*, *Wyck* etc.; before //r// /aɪər/ – /ɪr/ in *Sirius*, *Syracuse*.

The two alternative long pronunciations /aɪ/ and /iː/ occur in names such as *Adeline*, *Aldine*, *Dion*, *Geraldine*, *Ivor*, *Levantine*, *Lima*, *Lisa*, *Lisle*, *McKie*, *Medina*, *Milo*, *Riga*, *Salonica*, *Vigo*, *Viking*. Before //r// the equivalent is /aɪə(r)/ – /ɪə(r)/: *Elvira*, *Spiers*. There is also /ɪə(r)/ – /ɜː(r)/ in *Nirvana*, *Virgo*.

Cliveden unexpectedly has /iː/ – /ɪ/ variation.

<o> spellings

There is long/short alternation /əʊ/ – /ɒ/ (as in *tone – tonic*) in *Aumonier*, *Bogota*, *Bolinger* (but *Bollinger just has* /ɒ/), *Cocke*, *Cocksedge*, *Cockcroft*, *Colgate*, *Conan*, *Gotham*, *Holtham*, *Jolyon*, *Lothbury*, *Mocha*, *Mosley*, *Ophelia*, *Osiris*, *Otago*, *Pinocchio*, *Pomeroy*, *Robins*, *Roche*, *Romany*, *Scholl*, *Sofia*, *Soviet*. *Ovid* has a variant with /əʊ/ as an American surname. Dickens' pen-name *Boz* originally had /əʊ/, now /ɒ/.

The use of <o> instead of <u> alongside <m>, <n>, <v> or <w> to avoid too many vertical pen strokes in sequence (see p. 148) results in /ɒ/ – /ʌ/ variation, as in *Abercrombie*, *Blondel*, *Bromley*, *Bromwich*, *Brompton*, *Colombia*, *Colombo*, *Conduit*, *Conisborough*, *Constable*, *Conybeare*, *Covent*, *Coventry*, *Crompton*, *Cromwell*, *Donegal*, *Donne*, *Honiton*, *Molyneux*, *Monmouth*, *Pomfret*, *Romford*, *Romney*, *Sonning*, *Sotheby*, *Thorold*. Less common is /ɒ/ – /ʊ/ variation in *Blomfield*, *Moslem*, *Wombwell*.

Other variation involving simple <o> includes: /əʊ/ – /uː/ in *Lesotho*, *Mahon*, *Pole*, *Scrope*, *Roding*; /əʊ/ – /juː/ in *Home*; /əʊ/ – /ʊ/ in *Coke*; /əʊ/ – /ʌ/ in *Tovey*; /ɔː/ – /ɒ/ in *Andorra*, *Boreas*, *Chloris*, *Cross*, *Crossley*, *Doris*, *Florinda*, *Lorelei*, *Korea*, *Koran*, *Moran*, *Oran*.

Minority variations with <o> in complex spellings include:

- <oo>≡/uː/ – /ʊ/ : *Goodge*, *Woomera*;
- <oo>≡/əʊ/ – /uː/ : *Loos*, *Woburn*;
- <ou>≡/əʊ/ – /uː/ : *Goulburn*, *Joule* (+ /aʊ/), *Moule*, *Outhwaite*, *Poulson*;
- <ou>≡/uː/ – /aʊ/ : *Froud*, *Frowde*, *Houston* (+ /juː/), *Tout*;
- <ou>≡/əʊ/ – /aʊ/ : *Blougram*;
- <oul>≡/əʊ/ – /aʊ/ : *Foulkes*;
- <ow>≡/əʊ/ – /aʊ/ : *Bowden*, *Cowen*, *Cracow*, *Fowke*, *Jowett*, *Lowson*, *Mowatt*, *Powis*, *Rowan*, *Sowerby*, *Rowell*, *Rowney*, *Trowell*, *Vowles*;
- <ou>≡/aʊ/ – /ʌ/ : *Routledge*, *Southey*;
- <ow>≡/ɔː/ – /aʊ/ : *Rowton*;
- <our>≡/ɜː/ – /ɔː/ : *Ashbourne*, *De Courcy*, *D'Eyncourt*;

The spelling <ough> becomes even more inscrutable in names. As a non-name, *hough* is /hɒk/, but in place-name elements it can be /hɒf/ in *Houghall*, /hʌf/ in *Hougham*, /həʊ/, /haʊ/ or /hɔː/ in *Houghton*.

<u> spellings

There is free variation between /juː/ and /uː/ in *Arethusa*, *Corfu*, *Cuvier*, *Dudeney*, *Sue*, *Suez*, *Sumatra*, *Sumerian*, *Udolpho*, but the /j/ is no longer found with <lu> spellings: *Lucerne*, *Lucie*, *Lucifer*, *Lucrece*, *Luke*, *Lusiad*, *Lusitania*, *Mameluke*, etc.

There is also variation between long/short vowels in:

- /uː/ – /ʊ/ : *Brunel*, *Drusilla*, *Guggenheim*, *Gujarat*, *Istanbul*, *Jupiter*, *Kaunda*;
- /juː/ – /ʌ/ : *Uttoxeter*. In *Buggs*, *Fudge*, *Muggins*, the /juː/ variant given in EPD seems to be an avoidance of an unpleasant association. The long vowel before the doubled <gg> is distinctly odd.

In non-names, earlier /ʊ/ has become /ʌ/ in SBS, except in a small group of words which usually have an adjacent labial consonant (e.g. *bush*, *put*, *pudding*). Foreign names, especially German, generally have /ʊ/: *Bruckner*, *Buddha*, *Gluck*, *Innsbruck*. Some free variation can be found in *Gustavus*, *Humboldt*, *Hunyadi*, *Krupp*, *Mogul*, *Muslim*, *Uppsala*. The /ʌ/ pronunciation is the more anglicized, as in *Bunsen*.

6.6 STRESS PLACEMENT AND VOWEL REDUCTION

'Is Dominica stressed on the <min> or on the <nic>'?

The placement of primary stress may vary in names without affecting the quality of the vowels, that is, without reducing the vowel of the unstressed syllable. There are many two-syllable names which have final stress in isolation and unchanging full vowels; in many of these names the stress may shift forward onto the first syllable if a stress follows closely in the context. Names which fit this pattern, at least for some speakers, include *Aline*, *Annagh*, *Annam*, *Anthea*, *Argyll*, *Assam*, *Bagdad*, *Belfast*, *Bombay*, *Bolshoi*, *Burgoyne*, *Cargill*, *Clonmel*, *Cornell*, *Culross*, *Dior*, *Dundas*, *Dunbar*, *Eugene*, *Fermoy*, *Fitzroy*, *Gerard*, *Gillard*, *Gillett*, *Hindu*, *Manchu*, *Marlene*, *Maureen*, *Munro*, *Oolong*, *Osage*, *Pauline* (girl's name), *Tangier*, *Tucson*.

Most of these are not native and come from a range of foreign sources: Celtic, French, Arabic and other languages. The variation in stress placement that occurs is largely conditioned by context. A speaker who has variable stress in the name *Pauline*, will say '*Pau*line *Smith*' but 'S*end* Pau*line*' (rather than '*Send Pau*line). Similar variation is found in longer names: *Ataturk*, *Cameroon*, *Finisterre*, *Ibrahim*, *Malabar*, *Paraguay*, *Spitzbergen*, *Trinidad*. Stress variation between the penultimate and antepenultimate syllables of names usually involves a difference between long and short vowels, an effect of third-syllable shortening:

Andronicus (/-əˈnaɪ-/, /-ˈɒnɪ-/), *Damara(land)* (/ˈdæmə-/, /dəˈmɑː-/), *Dominica* (/-ˈmɪnɪk-/, /-mɪˈniːk-/).

Similar stress variation is found in some native place-names consisting of two elements, each with an unreduced vowel, such as *Caithness*, *Cheapside*, *Eastleigh*, *Edgehill*, *Minehead*, *Mountjoy*, *Scawfell*, *Spithead*, *Woodside*.

Stress variation seems to be more frequent with some final elements than with others. This can be seen in the different compound names made up with initial *Black-*. Stress varies rhythmically in *Blackfriars* and *Blackheath* but does not appear to do in *Blackpool*, which has initial stress only. We would certainly not expect to find *'We *went* to Black*pool*' from native English speakers.

Most second elements, even those with underlying long vowels, tend to have a reduced form if the name has first-element stress. This is so, for instance, with the elements *-borough* as /-brə/, *-bourne* as /-bən/, *-burgh* as /-brə/, *-bury* as /-brɪ/, *-cester* as /-stə/, *-combe* as /-kəm/, *-dale* as /-dl/, *-ford* as /-fəd/, *-gate* as /-gət/, *-holm* as /-əm/, *-house* as /-əs/, *-land* as /-lənd/, *-man* as /-mən/, *-mouth* as /-məθ/, *-shire* as /-ʃə/, *-son* as /-sn/, *-stead* as /-stɪd/, *-tree* as /-trɪ/, *-well* as /-wəl/, *-wick* as /-ɪk/, *-worth* as /-wəθ/, *-yard* as /-jəd/ as in *Marlborough*, *Brabourne*, *Edinburgh*, *Salisbury*, *Alcester*, *Addiscombe*, *Bedale*, *Brentford*, *Lidgate*, *Axholm*, *Lofthouse*, *Lapland*, *Newman*, *Plymouth*, *Yorkshire*, *Tennyson*, *Plumstead*, *Daintree*, *Blackwell*, *Barwick*, *Ainsworth*, *Ledyard*. There is, however, a tendency to avoid reduction if the first element occurs as a free form: *Exmouth* at the mouth of the Exe has either /-maʊθ/ or /-məθ/. If the first element has more than one syllable, a rhythmical stress on the last will help to keep the unreduced vowel as in *Avonmouth*. Names which have had no long period of familiar use, such as *Tynemouth*, are less likely to be reduced.

6.7 Variability in consonant correspondences

'Is it with an /s/ or a /z/, Miss er Besant'?

Consonant variation is not so common. There is only one very frequent instance: uncertainty about whether <s> (or occasionally <ss>) corresponds to /s/ or /z/. Examples with either /s/ or /z/ in their English pronunciation are: *Asa*, *Alfonso*, *Alsace*, *Ambrose*, *Aussie*, *Basra*, *Basuto*, *Besant*, *Bismarck*, *Breslau*, *Casanova*, *Cluse*, *Crees*, *Crusoe*, *Cusack*, *Disraeli*, *Druse*, *Dysart*, *Eloisa*, *Elsa*, *Elstree*, *Formosa*, *Glasgow*, *Glaswegian*, *Grase*, *Hals*, *Halses*, *Halsey*, *Hanseatic*, *Hausa*, *Iseult*, *Islip*, *Jasmine*, *Johannesburg*, *Josiah*, *Hosias*, *Maas*, *Manresa*, *Marquesas*, *Masaryk*, *Missouri*, *Muslim*, *Nasmyth*, *Oronsay*, *Osler*, *Oslo*, *Osman*, *Pilsener*, *Salzburg*, *Sion*, *Thurso*, *Visigoth*,

Wiesbaden, *Wrase*. There is also /s/ – /z/ variation in native English names at the boundary between elements. This is due to presence or absence of voicing assimilation with an adjacent consonant: *Beresford*, *Bosham* (/ˈbɒsəm/ – /ˈbɒzəm/), *Carisbrooke*, *Chesney*, *Cresswell*, *Crosby*, *Daylesford*, *Horsley*, *Kelsey*, *Macclesfield*, *Masefield*, *Spottiswoode*, *Stansfield*, *Swansea*, *Walsingham*, *Wesley*.

There are a few oddities in this type of variation. *Bessborough* only has /z/ in spite of the <ss> spelling; *Chastney* only has /-sn-/, the lost /t/ still exerting an influence; the alternation in *Dickensian* depends on whether analogy follows the stem /ˈdɪkɪnz/ (/dɪˈkenzɪən/) or the more usual pronunciation of <-sian> as /-sjən/ (/dɪˈkensjən/, cf. *Albigensian*).

The other consonant variations are very minor. <ch> shows variation across /ʧ/, /ʃ/ and /k/:

- <ch>≡ /ʧ/ – /ʃ/ : *Belcher*, *Lechmere*, *Chandos*, *Channon*, *Daiches*, *Pondicherry*;
- <ch>≡ /ʧ/ – /k/ : *Michelson*, *Murchie*, *Murchison*;
- <ch>≡ /ʃ/ – /k/ : *Leuchars*.

There is unusual variation with <g> between /g/ – /ʤ/ before front vowel <e>, <i>, <y> spellings, where one would normally expect only /ʤ/. This is partly between the old (/ʤ/) and new (/g/) pronunciations of Latin, partly §Basic /g/ and §Romance /ʤ/ and partly inexplicable: *Albigenses*, *Areopagite*, *Benger*, *Burgin*, *Geeson*, *Gell*, *Genseric*, *Gerry*, *Gibben*, *Gifford*, *Gill*, *Gillingham*, *Gillott*, *Gilson*, *Gimson*, *Gye*, *Gyp*, *Magi*, *Sagittarius*. A difficult pair are the names *Gilliam* /g/ and *Gillian* /ʤ/. A previous nasal also varies giving /ŋ/ and /nʤ/ in names such as *Bellingham*, *Kissinger*.

We have already noted /s/-/z/ variation due to voicing assimilations at element boundaries. Optional assimilations may also affect the place of articulation of /n/≡<n>. The alveolar nasal will tend to anticipate a following labial consonant giving /m/≡<n> in *Banbury*, *Banff*, *Canberra*, *Downpatrick*, etc. In some cases the labial assimilation has been recorded in a variant spelling: *Barnby/Barmby*.

Consonant digraphs can be ambiguous at element boundaries in native names. An initial <h> in suffixes such as *-hall*, *-ham*, *-home*, after a stem ending in <p>, <s>, or <t> can produce alternative spelling pronunciations with <ph>≡/f/, <sh>≡/ʃ/, and <th>≡/θ/. *Bispham* as a surname may be either /ˈbɪspəm/ or /ˈbɪsfəm/, though the place-name stays as /ˈbɪspəm/. *Coggeshall* in Essex is pronounced /ˈkɒgɪʃl/, but the surname is usually pronounced /ˈkɒgzɔːl/; here the place-name is the spelling pronunciation. A /ʃ/ pronunciation is possible in *Masham*, *Pattershall* and *Walsham*.

Chapter 7

Standardization and spelling reform

7.1 SIXTEENTH AND SEVENTEENTH CENTURY STANDARDIZATIONS

The first concerted movement for the reform of English spelling gathered pace in the second half of the sixteenth century and continued into the seventeenth as part of a great debate about how to cope with the flood of technical and scholarly terms coming into the language as loans from Latin, Greek and French. It was a succession of educationalists and early phoneticians, including William Mulcaster, John Hart, William Bullokar and Alexander Gil, that helped to bring about the consensus that took the form of our traditional orthography. They are generally known as 'orthoepists'; their work has been reviewed and interpreted by Dobson (1968). Standardization was only indirectly the work of printers. It was too well-designed to be a simple settling down of printing-house practices.

> Above all it is significant that the English spelling system that emerged from the seventeenth century is not a collection of random choices from the ungoverned mass of alternatives that were available at the beginning of the century but rather a highly ordered system taking into account phonology, morphology and etymology and providing rules for spelling the new words that were flooding the English lexicon. Printed texts from the period demonstrate clearly that, during the middle half of the seventeenth century, English spelling evolved from near anarchy to almost complete predictability.
>
> (Brengelman 1980: 334)

Brengelman singles out five particularly important improvements brought about at the suggestion of seventeenth century scholars:

1 The rationalization of the use of final *e*.
2 The rationalization of the use of consonant doubling, including the use of *tch* and *ch*, *dg* and *g*, *ck* and *k*.
3 The rationalization of the use of *i* and *j*, *v* and *u*.
4 Resolution of the worst problems relating to the use of *i*, *y*, and *ie*.

5 The almost total regularization of morphemes borrowed from Latin, including those borrowed by way of French. (ibid.: 347)

These measures left English spelling largely in the form we have today. That there should have been so few changes since then is in itself a testimony to the work of the sixteenth and seventeenth century orthoepists. But that does not mean that there is no scope for further reform.

Standardization came about by gradual consensus, drawing on the work of individual scholars and stimulated by general public interest. English spelling has never been officially managed. There is no recognized academy or educational agency in Britain appointed to monitor the use and development of the language, as there often is for the languages of other countries. However, since the middle of the last century, both in Britain and the United States, there has been a long succession of individual scholars, writers and even politicians with strong views on spelling reform and offering a wide spectrum of proposals for change. Why should spelling not be open to reform in the same way as currency, weights and measures and other institutions of society? The main argument for reform is self-evidently valid: that the removal of irregularities in our present writing system would make for greater and easier literacy.

7.2 ETYMOLOGY – FAMILIARITY AND RESPECTABILITY

'The desire to avoid certain vulgar associations' (OED on 'coney')

Since the Renaissance, etymology has been the main criterion in deciding on the spelling of a word. Before you could provide a word with a suitable spelling, you had to make a decision about its origins. There is plenty of evidence for etymological guesswork in the variant spellings recorded in *OED*. Suppose you are writing about life at sea and find that a favourite dish of working seamen was called /bɜːˈguː/. If you think that this word is just nautical slang, you will spell it <burgoo>. But if you think, perhaps because of the final stress, that it may have something to do with French cooking, you will look for possible French elements and spell it <burgout>, presumably by analogy with *ragout*. An old variety of blood-red apple was called a *biffin*, at least that is its §Basic spelling. It came from *beef* + *-ing*, with vowel shortening. The spelling <beaufin> also exists, a clear attempt to give the apple some culinary status. A *buffet* 'sidetable' was frequently but inaccurately spelt **beaufet* in the eighteenth century; this would distance it from *buffet* 'blow'. An early type of perambulator was called a *bassinet*; this related ultimately to *basin*. However, in the 1880s, some tradesmen decided to upmarket their product by calling it a **berceaunette*, linking it to French *berceau* 'cradle'. This kind of manipulation is very common in trade-names. The French appearance of *barouche*, a four-wheeled carriage, belies the fact that there is no such French word; it may have come from Italian or even German, but elegance seems to have required a French spelling. *Biscuits* were happily spelled **biskets* until the eighteenth century, which saw 'the senseless adoption of the mod. French spelling, without the French pronunciation' (*OED*). Even the common word *blue* owes its ending to the same process: before 1700 the usual spelling was *blew*.

There are occasional instances of the contrary, where a word has been given a §Basic spelling because of its down-to-earth meaning. The origin of the word *blight* is uncertain. Since it 'entered literature from the speech of farmers or gardeners in the 17th century' (*OED*), it was spelt as §Basic *blight* rather than **blite*.

As with names (§6.3, p. 451f.), there is a tendency to avoid embarrassing pronunciations and their associated spellings. When rabbits were introduced into Britain, they were called *cunnies* or *cunneys*, with a short vowel. The spelling <coney>, with a long vowel pronunciation, probably came in because:

> the desire to avoid certain vulgar associations with the word in the cunny form, may have contributed to the preference for a different pronunciation in reading the scriptures. . . . Smart (1836) says 'it is familiarly pronounced cunny', but cony is 'proper for solemn reading'.
>
> (*OED*).

A similar case is that of an important dignitary of the King's court called 'the Groom of the Stole' (as /stəul/). This sounded quite prestigious, because it seemed to imply that he was in charge of the royal wardrobe, since a *stole* is a garment. The origin was more humble. This <stole> was a spelling variant of *stool* and the office was originally that of lavatory attendant.

Tinkering with spelling and pronunciation also took effect in the opposite direction, by making learned words more homely. This is 'popular etymology'. Two well-known examples are **cowcumber* for *cucumber* and **sparrow-grass* for *asparagus*. Food items seem a natural area for imaginative tinkering. In 1836 Smart wrote: 'no well-taught person, except of the old school, now says cow-cumber . . . although any other pronunciation . . . would have been pedantic some thirty years ago' (*OED*). Similarly, Walker wrote in 1791: 'sparrow-grass is so general that asparagus has an air of stiffness and pedantry'(*OED*).

Final unstressed syllables are obvious targets for reinterpretation. The French loan *ambergris* literally means 'grey amber', but in popular etymology it was thought to be **amber-grease*. *Curtail* was originally formed from an adjective *curtal*. The verb apparently took on final stress and the last syllable became associated with *tail*. Similarly, *tafferel*, a loan-word from Dutch for part of a ship's stern, was reinterpreted in the nineteenth century as *taffrail*. That strange word *frontispiece* came from medieval Latin *fronti-spicium*, literally 'looking at the forehead'. The notion of 'front' remains, but the <(s)picium> part was taken quite arbitrarily to be *piece*. Similarly, *templet*, 'a supporting rafter' in building, has a more common variant *template*. *OED* has a nicely contrastive quotation: 'the purpose of templates is similar to that of wall-plates', from a technical manual of 1879. Still more natural is the association of *hair* with *mohair* (French *mouaire*, now *moire*, from Arabic).

Before the eighteenth century *cupboard* was frequently spelt **cubberd* or **cubbard*, but the analytical spelling <cup>+<board> has since prevailed, even though the object has now little to do with cups and nothing at all with boards. A happier notion was a seventeenth century spelling of *jolly* as **joyly*, associating it with *joy*.

Exceptionally, spelling may be changed so as to distance a word from its etymology. Our present day words *woman* and *women* come from Old English *wif-man* and *wif-men*. The <wo> part is the remains of *wif*, the Germanic word for woman, which now only survives on its own in the specialised sense of *wife*. Many people would support a respelling of *women* as *<wimmin>, a perfectly regular and reasonable spelling. It avoids any assumption that women are merely a derivative or appendage of men. Had this not been a strictly neutral study of English spelling conventions, I might have been tempted to say that both <woman> and <women> are really quite ridiculous spellings and that *<wummun> and *<wimmin>, with their flowing minim strokes are both phonetically apt and graphically pleasing.

Why people should prefer a dubious compound such as *cupboard* to a regular phonetic spelling is puzzling. A good story helps and there is none better than the knighting of the loin of beef. *Sirloin* is a French loan-word, originally spelt **surloin* (cf. *surname*), from French *sur* 'over'. The story has it that Henry VIII (or James I, or Charles II, or any king with a little flair) was so impressed by his dinner that he knighted it. Hence the <sir>. Jonathan Swift puts this story into his *Polite Conversation* of 1738, a treasure-house of clichés.

> *Miss*. But, pray, why is it call'd a sir-loin?
>
> *Ld. Smart*. Why, you must know, that our King James the First, who loved good eating, being invited to dinner by one of his nobles, and seeing a large loin of beef at his table, he drew out his sword, and in a frolic knighted it. Few people know the secret of this.
>
> (Dialogue II).

The prefix <sur-> in *surname* was similarly thought to be *sire* (**sirename*).

In the sixteenth and seventeenth centuries, the academic respectability of Latin and Greek prompted the respelling of a number of words which had come into English via French and with a French spelling. The best known of these are *debt* and *doubt*, which came in from French as *dette* and *doute* and which got their superfluous <b> from a re-association with Latin *debitum* and *dubitare*. Shakespeare makes fun of this in *Love's Labours Lost*, where the curate Sir Nathaniel is condemned by the schoolmaster Holofernes:

> I abhor such fanatical phantasms, such insociable and point-device companions; such rackers of orthography, as to speak dout, fine, when he should say doubt; det, when he should pronounce debt, – d, e, b, t, not d, e, t: he clepeth a calf, cauf; half, hauf; neighbour *vocatur* nebour; neigh abbreviated ne. This is abhominable, – which he would call abbominable: it insinuateth me of insanie . . .
>
> (*Love's Labours Lost* Act V(i))

The spelling of *abominable* is even more contentious than the <b> of *debt* and *doubt*. From medieval Latin the <om> was thought to refer to *ab homine* ('away from man') and so 'beastly'; hence the <h> in early spellings and indeed in all the Shakespeare first folio spellings. Actually, the <om> is related to Latin *omen*; neither **abhominable* nor **abbominable* are justified. In cases like this, where the semantic relations are so obscure, the spelling reformers may well point out that there is little to lose.

There were other mistaken etymologies. *Abound* was supposed to be related to Latin *habere* 'to have' and was spelt with an initial <h> by Caxton. Reality is stranger: it is ultimately derived from Latin *unda* 'wave' and so 'overflowing'.

Some etymologically unjustified spelling changes proved relatively harmless, since they did not introduce peculiar spelling correspondences. The word *scent* came from French *sentir* (Latin *sentire*); the <sc> appeared for no good reason after 1600. It does have the virtue of differentiating the homophones *sent* and *scent*. On the other hand, the perfectly respectable §Greek spelling *skeptic* used in Johnson's Dictionary and standard in the US, never really caught on in Britain. That is a pity, since <sce-> usually corresponds to /se/ rather than /ske/; this causes problems in differentiating *sceptic* and *septic*. The <th> spelling of *author* and its spelling pronunciation, wherever it may have come from, helped to differentiate **auctor* and *actor*. The <ch> of *anchor*, *lachrymal*, *sepulchre*, comes from the medieval Latin practice of writing <chr> rather than <cr>, so if the notion of 'correctness' only takes in classical Latin, these would not be 'theoretically correct'. *Anchor* had originally been borrowed into Old English as *ancor* from Latin *ancora*. A Greek /h/, the so-called 'rough breathing', is ignored in the variant spelling *odometer* (*hodometer*), but this may be due to borrowing via French. Archimedes, on discovering specific gravity in his bath, is said to have cried **eureka* 'I have found (it)'; a proper spelling would be *heureka* (as in *heuristic*). Spellers sometimes proved to have, as Ben Jonson rather pompously said of Shakespeare, 'little Latin and less Greek'.

Some tinkerings may cause irregularity of correspondence as in the case of *debt* and *doubt*. The <ch> of *ache* was standardized by Johnson; he evidently thought it had a Greek origin. In fact it derives from Old English, as do the verbs *bake*, *make*, *wake* and their corresponding nouns *batch*, *match*, *watch*. If the two had not become confused in course of time, we should now have a verb **to ake* /eɪk/ and a noun **an atch*. Whether the word is §Basic or §Greek matters little, but we now have a correspondence <ch>≡/k/ in an unusual context: word-finally after a long <a..e> vowel. The spelling **ake* would be regular.

Not only did Shakespeare's schoolmaster Holofernes want the <b> to be seen in the spelling of *debt* and *doubt*, he also wanted it pronounced. In this instance, he was asking too much, because obstruent clusters in English are all fortis (≅ 'voiceless') as in /pt/, /kt/, /ts/, or all lenis (≅ 'voiced') as in /bd/, /gd/, /dz/. Mixed clusters such as */bt/ are not found and would not survive. Other new etymological spellings were more successful in attracting a new pronunciation.

Unfamiliar letter strings in loan-words may attract a spelling pronunciation. *Dais* was borrowed from French as a monosyllable, but EPD and LPD give /deɪɪs/ as the commoner pronunciation now. Though <ai>≡/eɪ/ and <s>≡/s/ are familiar correspondences, the more normal spelling of final /eɪs/ would be <ace> (*lace*) or occasionally <ase> (*base*); so, *dais* was ripe for reanalysis.

Normal phonetic processes of reduction and smoothing are, however, always working in the other direction to produce anomalous spellings. *Diamond* has /aɪə/ in EPD and LPD, but the common pronunciation without /ə/ (also given in LPD) is evidenced by early instances of **dimond* and by the surname *Dimond*. The simple /aɪ/ pronunciation gives us either anomalous <ia>≡/aɪ/, or an empty <a>. There seems to be no similar phonetic reduction in *diadem*, *dialogue*, *diaper*.

Words may have their internal structure obscured or revamped and so attract a different spelling. A *bodice* was originally *a pair of bodies* (cf. *a pair of stays*); the plural notion became lost and the /z/ became an /s/ with a spelling to match. *Pox* is an altered spelling of the plural *pocks*, now used as a singular noun. A similar instance in names is the <x> spelling of *Dixon*, *Nixon*, for *Dickson*, (< 'Dick's son'), *Nickson*.

Etymology has always been constantly tempered by analogy in deciding or adjusting the spelling of a word. Analogy can be seen as the regularities of the system asserting themselves. Thus in British English spelling there has been a strong generalizing tendency for nouns such as *licence*, *practice*, *prophecy*, to be spelt with <c> and verbs such as *license*, *practise*, *prophesy*, to be spelt with <s>. The word *accurse* is spelt as if it had a §Latinate <ad-> prefix by analogy with *account*, *acclaim*, even though *curse* is an Old English root and the /ə/ prefix is that found in §Basic *arise*, *awake*, *awhile*. *Ammunition* looks at first sight as if it began with an assimilated Latin prefix <ad-> + <m-> giving <amm>. But this assimilation is not found in either French or English. *Munition* is indeed related to Latin *munire* 'to fortify' and came via French, but the <am-> has nothing to do with Latin <ad->. *OED* quotes French sources to show that a pronunciation **amonition* was used by common soldiers, *monition* by officers; the soldiers had mistaken *la monition* for *l'amonition*. There was also confusion with *admonition* 'warning'. *Delight* as a Romance borrowing should have kept the form **delite*, but it was refashioned by analogy with §Basic *light*, *flight*. There were similar forms **despight*, **spight*, in use right up to the eighteenth century, but for these words the spelling *despite*, *spite*, is now standard. After the Latinizing <b> was inserted in *doubt*, some writers even spelt §Basic *doughty* as **doubty*. The Latinizing <p> inserted in *receipt* did not, however, copy itself analogically in *conceit* and *deceit*. The earlier consistent spelling *flexion* (cf. *to flex*), has been respelt as *flection* by analogy with *reflection*, *direction*, etc. *Flotation* is a hybrid of §Basic *float* plus §Latinate *-ation*; the <o> spelling disguises the subsystem mismatch.

7.3 SPELLING REFORM IN BRITAIN AND THE USA

The standardizations of the sixteenth and seventeenth centuries gave English a writing system which preserved the cultural history of English words in a complex of subsystems (§2.9). For literature and scholarship, that is a perfectly reasonable arrangement. Since then, however, those who have wanted to reform the writing system have worked to other criteria: the educational needs of initial literacy teaching, or the economic cost of irregularity and diversity. Reform proposals have usually aimed to introduce a single, more or less uniform system of spelling conventions.

In Britain the reform debate has largely been channelled through the Simplified Spelling Society, which was founded in 1908 as a successor to a number of Victorian enterprises. The Society has published various kinds of detailed reform proposals and has a regular journal. Similar societies exist in other English-speaking countries (see p. xix).

The Simplified Spelling Society's aims, as stated in a current promotional leaflet, are:

> working towards the modernization of English spelling for more effective education, higher standards of literacy, easier mastery of the language, a more efficient writing system, better communication worldwide.

Former members of the Simplified Spelling Society have included scholars such as Gilbert Murray, Daniel Jones, Walter Skeat and public figures such as Bernard Shaw, H.G. Wells, Archbishop William Temple, Mont Follick and Sir James Pitman. The Society's early history is briefly described in Ripman and Archer's *New Spelling* (1948: 5ff.).

The United States had its own organization devoted to spelling reform, The Simplified Spelling Board. Before his death in 1919, its patron, Andrew Carnegie, poured a great deal of money into its activities. Since then, like the spelling reform movement as a whole, it has become less active. In its heyday its members included a justice of the Supreme Court, several publishers, Samuel L. Clemens (Mark Twain) and Melvil Dewey, the author of the decimal system of cataloging books in libraries. Mencken (1948: 287ff) provides a useful critical survey of the American spelling reform movement.

A wide range of spelling reform schemes have competed, with little tangible success, for public approval. The most extreme proposal was undoubtedly **the Shaw alphabet**, subsidized by the estate of George Bernard Shaw (Shaw 1962, discussed in §7.3.5). This was based on the strict alphabetic principle of one consistent symbol per phoneme. The new alphabet could have been contrived by augmenting the 26 letters of the Roman alphabet with extra letters or accents, but Shaw took the extreme option of commissioning a completely new set of 40 letter shapes in which, to a limited extent, phonetically similar sounds had a similar form. Other proposals have sought a system based on the phonemic principle, but have eked out the set of single Roman letters with digraphs such as <th> and <dh>. The Simplified Spelling Society's '**New Spelling**' is in this category (Ripman and Archer 1948, discussed in §7.3.2). The criterion of economic cost, which was Shaw's main argument for his experimental alphabet, underpins the system of '**Cut Spelling**' proposed by Upward (1992, discussed in §7.3.3), which dispenses with any letters considered to be redundant. The least radical proposal, and one that would least offend conservative opinion, was the general tidying-up of English spelling conventions worked out in detail by the Swedish scholar Axel Wijk as '**Regularized Inglish**' (1959, discussed in §7.3.4). For our purposes, it seems best to examine each of these very different schemes in some detail, rather than attempt a rollcall of all the would-be reformers and the ebb and flow of controversy. But before that, we must mention the work of a reformer who did succeed in introducing changes, Noah Webster.

7.3.1 AMERICAN SPELLING: THE INFLUENCE OF WEBSTER

When the United States won their independence from Britain, it was only natural that they should take a critical look at the institutions they had inherited. In 1786, Noah Webster wrote to Benjamin Franklin: 'the minds of the people are in a ferment, and consequently disposed to receive improvements' (quoted in Krapp 1925: 331). The differences between present-day American spelling and British spelling are the result of reform proposals by various American scholars, of whom Noah Webster was the most important. Webster published a *Spelling Book* in 1783 which sold hundreds of millions of copies over the next century and a half. In 1828 he published the first of the dictionaries that still bear his name.

During his lifelong interest in spelling reform, Webster proposed a whole range of changes, most of which did not find approval after his death and which attracted criticism and controversy in his lifetime. Webster, like many others before and since, proposed cutting out superfluous letters, especially final <-e>, as in: **gazell, *carmin, *definit, *disciplin, *doctrin, *granit, *imagin, *maiz, *nightmar, *vultur*. Superfluous consonant letters were also to be dropped, which would leave the following still recognizable: **chesnut*, **crum*, **diaphram*, **grotesk*, **ile*, **ieland*, **istmus*, **mosk*, **thum*. Vowel digraphs were simplified where possible: **bredth*, **fether*, **lepard*, **stelth*, **thred*; **cloke*, **soe* (for *sew* and *sow*); **juce*, **nusance*.

In his *Dictionary* and *Spelling Book*, however, he kept to changes which he felt would not be too controversial and which the public would take to. Some of his changes, such as <-ic> instead of <-ick> in *heroic, public*, etc., have also been adopted independently in British spelling. He also gave English versions of Indian place-names instead of the French versions then commonly found in books of travel: *Wisconsin* for **Ouisconsin*, *Wabash* for **Ouabasche*.

Webster's dictionaries did ensure the acceptance of several important changes. The mass nouns *armour, behaviour, colour, favour, honour, labour, odour, vapour, vigour,* have the ending <-or> in American spelling. See §5.5.6 (p. 428). It might be said in favour of the British spelling that it usefully distinguishes these mass nouns from agent nouns ending in <-or>, such as *author, collector*. The case is complicated by various factors, however. Some mass nouns in medical use have <-or> in British spelling: *pallor, rigor, stupor*, and some count nouns have <-our>: *harbour, parlour, tumour*. In derived forms the <or> spelling is actually used in British English: *coloration, laborious, vaporize*. But there are also: *behavioural, colourful, flavoursome*.

The ending <-re> in *centre, fibre, litre, theatre*, became American <-er> (*center*, *fiber*, etc.). The older <-re> spelling does however have a useful marking function: it marks such nouns as different from agent nouns in <-er>. There is a contrast in British spelling between *metre* 'unit of length' and *meter* 'instrument'. If you do have spellings such as *center*, then for consistency *battle, candle*, etc. ought to be spelt **battel, *candel*. This has often been proposed, but never adopted.

In the suffix <-ise>/<-ize> as in *capitalize, dramatize, naturalize*, where British practice varies, American spelling has adopted a standard <-ize>. The <z> spelling is also used in *analyze* and *paralyze*. See §5.5.17, p. 433 The unstressed prefix <en->≡/ɪn/ in the British spelling of some words has a corresponding American spelling <in->: *encase, enclose, endorse, enquire, ensure*, giving *incase, inclose*, etc. This does not apply to all <en-> words: *encamp, enchant, endow*, etc.

The British <c> spelling of the nouns *defence, licence, offence, pretence*, and *practice* has an <s> counterpart in American spelling: *defense, license*, etc. The British distinction between the noun spelling (*licence, practice*) and verb spelling (*license, practise*) is lost. Rather confusingly, the form *practice* can also be found as an American spelling of both noun and verb. The British use of the <c> – <s> difference to mark nouns and verbs is also found to some small extent in *advice–advise, device–devise, prophecy–prophesy* .

The digraph spellings <ae> and <oe> for /iː/ in Greek and Latin loanwords have been reduced to simple <e> in American spelling: *anaemia, anaesthetic, diarrhoea, encyclopaedia, foetus mediaeval, oestrogen, paedriatrics, subpoena,* giving *anemia, fetus,* etc. This is also the case with <ae>≡/e/ in *haemhorrhage*. A similar reduction has been made with the ending <-ogue> in *analogue, catalogue, dialogue, epilogue, monologue, travelogue*, giving *catalog*, etc., and with omission of the stem-final <e> in *abridgement, acknowledgement, judgement,* etc., giving *abridgment*, etc.

There are differences in <C>-doubling. The single <l> at the end of *appal, enthral* (but cf. *thrall*), *instil, fulfil*, is doubled in American spelling to give *appall*, etc., but on the other hand the double <CC> in the unstressed syllables of British *counsellor, kidnapper, traveller, worshipping*, is usually single in American spelling: *counselor, kidnaper, traveler, worshiping.*

In addition to these groups of words, there are a number of individual British/American spelling differences, including: *artefact–artifact, carcase–carcass, gaol–jail, mould–mold, moult–molt, moustache–mustache, plough–plow, pyjamas–pajamas, smoulder–smolder, sulphur–sulfur, toffee–taffy, tyre–tire, waggon–wagon, whisky–whiskey, woollen–woolen.* The American reduction of the pairs *cheque–check, draught–draft, kerb–curb, storey–story*, to the second of these spellings is not necessarily an advantage (§5.4, pp. 407ff.).

The Webster dictionaries have standardized American practice in these respects. It is evidence of the reforming spirit of the times that Webster even thought it possible to put such changes in a reference book. He himself would have liked to go much further, but he was constrained by what the American paying public were willing to accept. Krapp (1925: 347) concludes his survey of Webster's work by suggesting that 'Webster's project of a distinctive American spelling for the American people was doomed to failure because the people did not want such a spelling'. Nevertheless, the changes that did come about through Webster show that piecemeal and cumulative reform is possible. Curiously though, the very authority of the Webster dictionaries set up a new American orthodoxy and seemed to halt further spelling reform.

There is still a willingness to experiment with spelling in informal genres. In American popular newspaper headlines and in advertising, there is widespread creative respelling similar to that used in invented trade-names

(§6.2, pp. 446ff.). Common words often respelt include *buy* as *<bi>, *Christmas* as *<Xmas>, *cool* as *<kool>, *crossing* as *<Xing>, *doughnut* as *<donut>, *high* as *<hi>, *low* as *<lo>, *night* as *<nite>, *please* as *<pleez>, *quick* as *<kwik>, *right* as *<rite>, *socks* as *<sox>, *thanks* as *<thanx>, *though* as *<tho>, *through* as *<thru>, *you* as *<U>. Such spellings are sometimes seen as an indication that the American public would be receptive to further reform. That may be a false conclusion. Such creative spellings need to contrast with an existing formal spelling to have the desired effect of casualness.

7.3.2 'New Spelling' Ripman and Archer (1948)

Reform proposals which try to remodel the whole writing system by design are even more difficult to sell to a conservative public. 'New Spelling' represents the Simplified Spelling Society's long-term scheme for reformed spelling on a more or less phonemic basis:

> a rational phonetic spelling will do much to steady our language in the perilous seas upon which it has embarked.
>
> (Ripman and Archer 1948: 6)

The 'peril' they feared was that English, as an international language, would break up into mutually unintelligible dialects, as Latin did into the different Romance languages, unless the spelling became a reliable indication of the pronunciation.

A great deal of work and debate has gone into 'New Spelling' (see also MacCarthy 1969b) and it can be regarded as a definitive radical scheme for a spelling system founded on the premiss that English spelling should simply reflect surface phonetic contrasts. The basic principle is that anyone who knows the pronunciation of a word should be able to spell it. There are no morphemic spellings: the {ed} of *hoped*, *rushed*, *begged*, *skimmed*, *played*, *emptied*, has a phonemic spelling as **hoept*, **rusht*, **begd*, **skimd*, **plaed*, **emptid*, so *tacked* and *tact*, *allowed* and *aloud*, are not distinguished: they are spelt **takt*, **aloud* (ibid.: 80). The <-ate> of nouns and verbs is similarly distinguished: **deliberet*, **deliberaet*; **estimet*, **estimaet*. Different vowel spellings for stressed and unstressed syllables attempt to show the difference between *permit* (noun and verb): **purmit*, **permit*; *protest* (noun and verb): **proetest*, **protest* (ibid.: 85). The prefix <ex-> becomes *<eks-> in *exodus* and *<egz-> in *exotic*. On the other hand, there is no attempt to represent vowel reduction to /ə/ in unstressed affixes with a common single letter. Endings such as <-ant> and <-ent> are kept intact because of the stressed variants, as in *pedant–pedantic*, *president–presidential*, *increment–incremental*.

Consonants (ibid.: 19ff) required little alteration: <g> is reserved for /g/, so /ʤ/ is spelt with <j> – *rage* as **raej*. Originally, /k/ was represented by

<c>, but later versions switched to <k>, largely because of its more distinctive shape. This means that <c>, <ck>, <q> and <x> were no longer needed. The digraph <ch>, however, is required for /ʧ/, since *church* (unchanged) is clearly preferable to **tshurtsh*. The <h> of <ch> is in fact redundant and there were tentative plans to drop it at a later stage, leaving **curc* for *church*. With single <c> gone, <s> and <z> were consistently used for /s/ and /z/. Consistency also meant that if <ng> were kept for /ŋ/, then /ŋg/ would have to be represented as *<ngg>, giving *longer* as **longger*. Other consonant digraphs are used: *<zh> for /ʒ/, giving *leisure* as **lezher*, and *<dh> for /ð/, giving *leather* as **ledher*. Double consonants were not used to mark short vowels since vowel digraphs with <e> are used to show vowel length consistently: *doll*, *dole* became **dol*, **doel*. Geminated consonants at word boundaries are naturally kept (*meanness* as **meennes*) and <orr> retains its double <rr> in **forren*, **majorrity*, to avoid confusion with <or>≡/ɔ:(r)/.

Vowel spellings presented a range of problems and solutions too wide to deal with here. The measures taken can best be seen in a sample of text in 'New Spelling':

> Agaen, let us not forget huu form dhe graet majorrity ov dhoez dhat lurn to reed and riet. Dhae ar dhe children dhat atend priemary skuulz; dhaer tiem iz limited. We hav noe riet to impoez on dhem a kaotik speling for dhe saek ov posibly teeching dhem a litl historrikal gramar.
>
> (Ripman and Archer 1948: 93f)

First impressions on reading a 'New Spelling' text are the sheer obtrusiveness of the <dh> spelling. This was admitted. For many reformers it seemed that:

> the proposed use of <dh> for the voiced sound will not only be too great a shock to conservative sentiment, but will also scarcely effect any substantial simplification. . . . Those who favour the use of *th* and *dh* consider that failure to show the distinction would be an arbitrary breach of consistency in the interests of the adult generation.
>
> (ibid.: 99)

More recently, the <dh> has been dropped in favour of retaining <th>. By comparison, the moving forward of the <e> marker for long vowels (**biet*, not *bite*) is much less startling, since the digraph is familiar anyway from open syllables such as *lie*, *toe*, *due*.

A compromise has to be reached between a consistency obligation towards those who would learn the system as children, and the need not to stray too far from traditional spelling to preserve links with the past. In political terms that might mean not alarming the voters. Indeed, proposals for spelling reform were brought before Parliament in a private member's bill in 1949 by Mont Follick (MP for Loughborough) and again in 1953, when the Bill reached the Committee Stage (Pitman 1969). Sufficient interest and support was aroused to make the Government agree, as a compromise, to consider the possibility of spelling reform if the Bill were withdrawn. On this understanding, Mont Follick withdrew, the wave of public interest died down and nothing further was done. An account of the campaign is given in Follick (1965).

7.3.3 'Cut Spelling' Upward (1992)

In recent years, the Simplified Spelling Society has explored a gradualist approach to reform. The word 'reform' itself, so very Victorian, is now glossed alternatively as 'modernization' in the Society's literature. One main proposal under active consideration is a scheme to introduce 'Cut Spelling' (Upward 1992). This, in principle, simply involves getting rid of redundant letters, an idea central to most spelling reform proposals. Apart from general economy of writing effort and the cost of printing, there are clear advantages in getting rid of some redundant letters. If *organ* is spelt *<orgn>, *stationary* and *stationery* as *<stationry>, *principal* and *principle* as *<principl>, there is no longer any spelling problem for the writer in how to represent the vowel of the unstressed syllable. There is no need to refer to the stressed vowel of *organic*, or *principality*. So, letters representing /ə/ before <l, m, n, r> are cut out along with empty letters such as the <b> of *debt.* Most doubled <C>-letters become single. So, *add* becomes *<ad> and *added* becomes *<add>.

The alterations are made solely by cutting. With a loss of <a> and <i>, *peace* and *piece* both become *<pece>. On the other hand, the spelling of *vane, vain, vein,* remains unchanged. The scheme does not seek to alter correspondences where there are no redundant letters. It does, however, replace <igh> with <y> as a spelling of /aɪ/ (*<fytng> *fighting*), and has <j> as a consistent spelling of /ʤ/ (*<brij> *bridge*). The {-ed} suffix is replaced by <d>, cutting the <e> to give *<ripd>, *<relentd>, *<flekd>, etc. This preserves the identity of the suffix morpheme in most cases, since there are no final phoneme clusters such as */pd/, */td/, */kd/ to cater for in writing (cf. *<rapt>, *<rapd> for *rapt*, *rapped*). The 'short word rule' (p. 131) is not maintained. The lexical words *pea, sea, tea,* become *<pe>, *<se>, *<te>.

Occasional homographs such as *<latrly> for *latterly* and *laterally* are not thought to be serious. On the other hand, groups of spellings which would become ambiguous by cutting are preserved: *chilled, milled, willed, binned, finned, grinned*, retain their letter doubling to avoid confusion with *grind, mild*, etc. *Thumb, bomb, lamb, plumb,* have their <b> cut to give *<thum>, etc., but *climb, comb, tomb, womb*, keep their <b>, somewhat oddly, as a marker of the long vowel. Here is a small sample of text in 'Cut Spelling':

> Th tourists swirl past in a cloud of dust in ther safari vehicls without stopng, wile th elefnts move in and out of th parks causing widespred damaj to tres, soil and crops. Tres ar regulrly pushd over so they can graze on th leavs. Maze crops ar even mor atractiv. Th truth of this unromantic pictur is undenybl: but th solution wich som hav now sujestd – th reopenng of th ivory trade – must be oposed.
>
> (Upward 1992: 229)

Most of the cutting, as can be seen, applies to the vowel letters of unstressed syllables. The cut spelling is easiest to read when there can be a parallel phonetic elision, as in *<oprate>, *<mislaneus>, or when a consonant can be syllabic, as in *<simpl> or *<systm> (cf. normal *prism*). It is more difficult for the reader to cope with longer compressed strings of consonant letters, such as the *<-rwrdl-> of *<forwrdly>, or *<regmntd> for *regimented*.

Yet, as with all schemes for a reformed spelling, readers need to take some trouble to judge the proposals only after they have become familiar with them. Instant judgements are biased towards conservatism. One consequence of adopting such changes might be a long transitional period of permissive spelling, until practice settled down.

The extent of the economy in print and writing effort can be gauged from the difference in the number of letters in Upward's four text samples (1992: 227–230). These have a total of 4243 letters in traditional orthography and 3865 letters in 'Cut Spelling', which represents a reduction of 9 per cent. This is, naturally enough, seen to be advantageous. It may well prove to be so. However, this basic 'economy' assumption needs to be tested and explored.

One of the striking features of human language is its high redundancy. It is meant to be used in adverse conditions of communication. Not every part of a written or spoken message needs to be consciously monitored by the listener or reader. But if cut spelling takes out some of the slack in the system, then more attention and conscious effort may be required as a result. How is that to be costed? It is tempting to cut out the <o> in the adjectival ending <-ous> to give *<piteus>, *< hideus>, *< famus>, *< rigrus>, but that gets rid of a marker which separates adjectives from nouns (*radius, citrus*). It is tempting to reduce *tea, fee, key,* to *<te>, *<fe>, *<ke>, but then we have lost a marker of the difference between lexical words and function words such as *be, me, we*. That difference, embodied in the 'short word rule' (§3.2.5 p. 131), was thought to be necessary in the evolution of the present writing system. Skilled readers can piece together the sequence of function words by skimming over them only if they can be seen to be different in size from the lexical words. Whether the 'Cut Spelling' changes are an advantage to the learner-reader is yet another open question. The redundant letters, naturally enough, have been identified as redundant by people who are already highly literate. They ask themselves in effect: 'Are these cuts possible for a skilled reader like me'? But a learner who is dependent on reference back to speech is not necessarily going to find *<regmntd> easier to tackle, either in reading or writing, than <regimented>, which clearly has its four syllables marked. The 'Cut Spelling' system presented by Upward is a practicable suggestion for spelling reform, but, as with the Shaw alphabet (§7.3.5 p. 483), the underlying notion of economy may be too simplistic and needs to be explored.

7.3.4 'Regularized Inglish' Wijk (1959)

Any changed spelling is bound to look on first impact like a spelling mistake that you are being asked to overlook. That is why the best hope of reform lies in the gradual ironing out of irregularities: it should be possible to lead the public through a series of gradual permissive changes. British institutions tend to change gradually through inspired tinkering, not as a stringent redesign dictated by theory. A gradualist approach to spelling reform was suggested by Fowler:

> English had better be treated in the English way, & its spelling not be revolutionized but amended in detail, here a little & there a little as absurdities become intolerable, till a result is obtained that shall neither overburden schoolboys nor stultify intelligence nor outrage the scholar.
>
> (Fowler 1926: 553)

The more radical attempts at spelling reform have always attracted more opposition that they could cope with. Andrew Carnegie poured money generously into The Simplified Spelling Board in the United States at the turn of the century. But by 1915 he was in despair at the lack of practical progress.

> 'A more useless body of men never came into association, judging from the effects they produced. Instead of taking twelve words and urging their adoption, they undertook radical changes from the start and these they can never make... I have much better use for twenty-five thousand dollars a year.'
>
> (quoted in Venezky 1980: 28)

Wijk's (1959) proposals for the reform of English spelling are based on minimal changes to the existing system. Strictly speaking, they are not a new system for spelling English, but the result of putting the regular English spelling in place of irregular spellings. He simply set out to 'regularize' English by keeping the most regular correspondences unchanged and bringing unpredictable spellings into line. He did not subscribe to the principle adopted in 'New Spelling' that writers ought to be able to spell any word they could pronounce. His primary aim was to make things easier for the native reader. For instance, he did not try to provide consistent marking for the usual long and short values of the simple vowel letters <a e i o u>.

> The important thing to note in this connection is that the choice between the short and long pronunciation of the simple vowels is a difficulty which as a rule only exists for the foreign learner of the language. The native speaker who is confronted with words like *famous*, *famine*, *evil*, *devil*, *tiger*, *vigour*, *sober*, *proper*, *super*, *suburb*, etc., usually knows at once whether the vowel has its long or short pronunciation. And since the foreign learner of the language will always have to learn the meaning of the words anyway, he might as well learn their pronunciation at the same time.
>
> (ibid.: 106).

This point of view clearly limits any reform to a tidying-up of irregularities and does not require the pronunciation to be shown unambiguously in the spelling. So Wijk did not suggest that <C>-doubling should be extended to give spellings such as *<devvil>, *<propper>. If, however, a word was to be respelt for some other reason, then <C>-doubling could be added if there was a short vowel to be marked. In regularizing the <ea> of *ready* to <e>, the <o> of *women* to <i>, or the <eo> of *leopard* to <e>, we might just as well add <C>-doubling to give *<reddy>, *<wimmin>, *<leppard>.

Here is a short specimen of 'Regularized Inglish':

> The sport woz at its hight, the sliding woz at the quickest, the laafter woz at the loudest, when a sharp smart crack woz herd. Thare woz a quick rush tordz the bank, a wilde scream from the ladies, and a shout from Mr. Tupman. A large mass ov ice disappeard; the wauter bubbled up over it; Mr. Pickwick's hat, gluvs and hankerchif wer floating on the surface and this woz aul ov Mr. Pickwick that enybody cood see.
>
> (Wijk 1959: 335)

Overall, about 70 per cent of the words in running text would be regularized and about 10 per cent of the total vocabulary.

Notice in the small specimen above that the <ea> remains in *scream* along with the <ee> in *see*. One wonders whether there is any point in the <aa>≡/ɑː/ of *<laafter>, when Northerners and others will retain a short vowel and when it is suggested that the long and short vowels of *evil* and *devil* can easily be sorted out by a native reader. The morpheme spelling for {-ed} remains in <bubbled>, as elsewhere in <hurried>, <emerged>, *<disclozed>, <affected>, <declined>, but is shortened in <*disappeard>, as elsewhere in *<bawld>, *<occurd>, *<relievd>, *<performd>, *<offerd>, *<wrapt>, *<fixt>. Notice, too, that <igh> is used in respelling *height* as *<hight>. This certainly marks off Wijk from other, more radical reformers:

> Actually the spelling *igh* is one of the very few really reliable spellings in English, since this combination is always pronounced like long *i*, practically without exception. Why then should it be changed. especially as it is one of the characteristic peculiarities of English?
>
> (ibid.: 83)

Wijk also points out that the retention of *igh* serves to distinguish homophones such as *might–mite*, *sight–site–cite*. This defence of <igh> shows that his scheme is meant to serve the needs of reading rather than spelling.

7.3.5 The Shaw alphabet and the Initial Teaching Alphabet

The most radical proposal for the reform of English orthography in this century was potentially the best funded and, ironically, the least regarded. George Bernard Shaw died in 1950. His estate was immensely rich from the royalties of plays, films and the musical *My Fair Lady,* which was based on his play *Pygmalion.* He had intended that the income from his estate, for a period of twenty one years, should be poured into a scheme to provide English with a radically new alternative alphabet of at least 40 different letters. After that, the estate would go to the British Museum and other institutions. The provision in the Will for the launch of the new alphabet was successfully challenged by these other legatees, but an agreement to make some provision for promoting the alphabet was finally reached. Small-scale funding was made available for an international competition to design the new letter shapes and for printing books in the new alphabet (Shaw 1962). Shaw's intention was that the first books to be printed in his alphabet would have the usual Roman spelling on each facing page for comparison with the Shaw alphabet. He supposed that, purely by demonstration, the reading public would be immediately convinced of the advantages of phonemic spelling in the new alphabet. He believed that the new alphabet would find a place for itself alongside the existing Roman alphabet, just as the decimal system of Arabic numerals 0, 1, 2, 3, 4, 5, 6, 7, 8, 9, has replaced the cumbersome Roman numerals I, II, III, IV, V, VI, VII, VIII, IX, and reduced them to decorative curiosities. Even though the Shaw alphabet failed to catch the public imagination and is now consigned to history, there are worthwhile lessons to be learnt from its design concepts.

For the latter part of his long life, Shaw had repeatedly trumpeted the advantages of a phonemic spelling system using at least 40 completely new letter shapes. His central argument was not educational but an economic one, based on the cost in time and effort caused by the irregularities in traditional spelling:

> To any others the inadequacies of our 26 letter alphabet seem trifling, and the cost of a change quite prohibitive. My view is that a change, far

> from being an economic impossibility, is an economic necessity. The figures in its favor, hitherto uncalculated and unconsidered, are astronomical. . . . To spell "Shaw" with four letters instead of two, and "though" with six, means to them only a fraction of a second in wasted time. But multiply that fraction by the number of "thoughs" that are printed every day . . . and the fractions of a second suddenly swell into integers of years, of decades, of centuries, costing thousands, tens of thousands and millions. . . . Shakespear [*sic*] might have written two or three more plays in the time it took him to spell his name with eleven letters instead of seven.
>
> (From a letter published in *The Author*, Summer 1944)

This is essentially the economic argument that is put forward in favour of 'Cut Spelling' (p. 479), but here it is tied in with the economy of a one-symbol-per-phoneme spelling. The advantages claimed for the new alphabet are largely advantages for the writer. The symbols of the Shaw alphabet are shown in table 49 below.

'Short' letters do not project above or below the line of print, as represented by the pairs of hyphens in the table. 'Tall' letters project above, and 'Deep' letters below the line of print. In addition to these symbols, abbreviations are used for common function words: *the, of, to,* are represented by the single consonant letter; *and* by the symbol for /n/. There are no different shapes for capital and lower-case letters: capitals are simply written larger. Nor is there any difference between the printed shape of the letters and their handwritten shape.

What, more than anything else, made the scheme uncomfortable for the reading public was the radical design of the characters. They are not an augmented Roman alphabet with 14 extra letter shapes but a completely new set of letters. Phonetically, the design of the letters is quite ingenious and to some extent inspired by Henry Sweet's 'Current Shorthand'. The pairs of fortis – lenis consonants ('voiceless' – 'voiced') share the same symbol, but reversed, as do the two nasals /m/ and /n/, the two liquids /l/ and /r/, the two semivowels /j/ and /w/ and some related pairs of vowels such as /ʊ/ and /uː/. To benefit fully from that design principle, the user would have to learn a little basic phonetics for the similarities of shape to have a mnemonic value. A few of the symbols show some slight or twisted resemblance to an equivalent Roman letter, particularly the symbols covering /f/, /s/, /t/ and /əʊ/.

The letters have bending, flowing shapes for ease of writing. Indeed, the whole scheme was formulated with the writer, not the reader in mind. No psychological tests were made to check the visual efficiency and contrastiveness of the letter shapes for the reader. Even so, Sir James Pitman asserts in the introduction to the Shaw alphabet edition of *Androcles and the Lion* (Shaw 1962: 107): 'Shaw's alphabet is both more

Table 49 The symbols of the Shaw alphabet.

Sound	(Tall)	(Deep)	Sound	Sound	(Short)	(Short)	Sound
/p/ peep	𐑐	𐑚	/b/ bib	/ɪ/ if	𐑦	𐑰	/iː/ eat
/t/ tot	𐑑	𐑛	/d/ dead	/e/ egg	𐑧	𐑱	/eɪ/ age
/k/ kick	𐑒	𐑜	/g/ gag	/æ/ ash	𐑨	𐑲	/aɪ/ ice
/f/ fee	𐑓	𐑝	/v/ vow	/ə/ ado	𐑩	𐑳	/ʌ/ up
/θ/ thigh	𐑔	𐑞	/ð/ they	/ɒ/ on	𐑪	𐑴	/əʊ/ oak
/s/ so	𐑕	𐑟	/z/ zoo	/ʊ/ wool	𐑫	𐑵	/uː/ ooze
/ʃ/ sure	𐑖	𐑠	/ʒ/ measure	/aʊ/ out	𐑬	𐑶	/ɔɪ/ oil
/ʧ/ church	𐑗	𐑡	/ʤ/ judge	/ɑː/ ah	𐑭	𐑷	/ɔː/ awe
/j/ yea	𐑘	𐑢	/w/ woe	/ɑː(r)/ are	𐑸	𐑹	/ɔː(r)/ or
/ŋ/ hung	𐑙	𐑣	/h/ ha-ha	/ɛə(r)/ air	𐑺	𐑻	/ɜː(r)/ err
	(Short)	(Short)		/ə(r)/ array	𐑼	𐑽	/ɪə(r)/ ear
/l/ loll	𐑤	𐑮	/r/ roar			(Tall)	
/m/ mime	𐑥	𐑯	/n/ nun	/ɪə/ Ian	𐑾	𐑿	/juː/ yew

legible and one-third more economical in space than traditional printing and this should lead to a great increase in reading speed. The characters themselves are very distinct'. There is no denying that interested literate readers can learn to use it very quickly. How it would fare without the help of enthusiastic curiosity has never been tested. In spite of Sir James Pitman's confidence in the legibility of the symbols, their designer, Kingsley Read, did show some awareness (ibid.: 148) that the shapes were not well differentiated: 'Be sure to distinguish properly between these Short letters', citing the following letter groups:

This is an admission of the problems of the reader and focusses on the whole untested notion of economy. If one has to be careful in distinguishing between the letters, then more processing time inevitably has to be used in reading them. The same reservation applies to the writer. If letters can easily be confused unless they are written with great care, there will be no real saving in time and effort. One can only write fast in a system of well-differentiated letter shapes. Some redundancy is not necessarily wasteful. The Shaw letter shapes seem to show an over-reliance on minimal distinctive features.

Readers may form their own opinion from the following short passage copied from the *Androcles* text (ibid.: 107).

FERROVIUS. Man there is no terror like the terror
of that sound to me. When I hear a trumpet or
a drum or the clash of steel or the hum of the
catapult as the great stone flies, fire runs through
my veins: I feel my blood surge up hot behind
my eyes: I must charge: I must strike: I must
conquer: ·Caesar himself will not be safe in his
imperial seat if once that spirit gets loose in me.

A very different modification of the alphabet was widely canvassed and used in primary education in the 1960s and 1970s in Britain. This was the 'Initial Teaching Alphabet' invented and funded by the publisher Sir James Pitman. It provides support for the first steps in learning to read by using slightly modified Roman letters to relate more effectively and consistently to the child's speech. There were 21 of these modified characters. For instance, the <th> digraph for the /θ/ of *thin* and the /ð/ of *then* were modified by turning the tail of the <t> to the left for /ð/ and by extending it under the <h> for /θ/. To show the /z/ value of an <s> spelling as in *has*, the

<z> symbol was flipped over. The digraphs used in 'New Spelling' <ae>, <ee>, <ie>, <oe> and <ue> for the long vowels of *take, she, prize, ago, beauty,* were woven into single letter shapes. The child would learn a single letter for a phoneme which in overall shape would show some resemblance to a traditional spelling. In addition to these special characters, there was a large measure of regularization. For instance, /ʤ/ was consistently spelt with <j> in words such as *page, large, anthology*. These and other 'i.t.a.' conventions can be seen in the following passage.

> **ie hav just cum from a scɷl whær ŧhe nue reediŋ iz taut. ie met ŧhær a littl girl ov siks. ʃhee is ŧhe œldest ov a larj family liviŋ on an œldham housiŋ estæt. tɷ yeers agœ ʃhee wos a ʃhie nervus ɕhield, tɷ frietend tɷ tauk. ʃhee has wun priezd personal posseʃhon—a dog-eerd anŧholojy ov vers, given tɷ her bie an œlder ɕhield. ŧhat littl girl ov siks has just red tɷ mee very buetifɷlly wurdswurŧh's daffodils. ie askt her whie ʃhee ɕhœs ŧhat pœem. ʃhee replied ŧhat ʃhee luvd daffodils.**

M. Harrison (Wijk 1969: 87)

As a means of teaching reading in the primary school, 'i.t.a.' is no longer advocated by teacher training programmes and is only used by a declining band of enthusiasts. The main problem in the use of 'i.t.a.' was not the association of sound and symbol by the child, but the transition which the child had to make from reading 'i.t.a.' texts to reading normal orthography. Dedicated teachers seemed able to manage this quite well. Those who were less enthusiastic about the scheme found problems.

The sample passage above shows what changes a child would need to make to arrive at the traditional spelling. Some change-overs were easy: the two <th> symbols simply merged. Many transitions involved learning an irregularity: <tauk> ⇒ <talk>, <hav> ⇒ <have>, <cum> ⇒ <come>, <ov> ⇒ <of>, <scool> ⇒ <school>, <frieten> ⇒ <frighten>. Other transitions applied to groups of words. The child had to recognize when <sh> persisted, as in *shop*, or changed to <si> as in *possession*, or <ti> as in *nation*; and to recognize when <ie> changed as in *child, shy*.

From the point of view of spelling reform, the special 'i.t.a.' symbols are irrelevant. They would probably have had a conservative influence by simplifying the learning of traditional spelling. Some of the spelling regularizations borrowed from 'New Spelling' may have gained a foothold through 'i.t.a.', if the transition to traditional spelling had been eased by allowing spellings such as <agoe> for *ago* or <larje> for *large* to continue in use. See also Wijk (1969: 87), who makes a detailed comparison of the relative advantages for initial readers of 'i.t.a.' and his own 'Regularized Inglish'.

With the death of Shaw in 1950 and of Dr Mont Follick, the crusading

Labour MP for Loughborough, in 1958, English public life lost two influential and persistent advocates of spelling reform. Since then, no public figure has taken up the cause. In comparison, Mont Follick's other crusades, for the adoption of the metrical system and for a decimal currency, did eventually see a successful outcome. The desire for radical changes in the traditional English spelling system is presently at a very low ebb. However, there are still good reasons for making some changes and no lack of suggestions. There is a wide spectrum of opinions about what spellings should be altered and what should replace them, and what should be the pace of reform. The best hope for change seems to be that the growing concern over standards of literacy will lead to a permissive tidying-up of irregularities for purely educational reasons.

References

Aderman, D. and Smith, E. E. (1971) 'Expectancy as a determinant of functional units in perceptual recognition', *Cognitive Psychology* 2: 117–129.

Ainsworth, W. A. (1973) 'A System for Converting English Text into Speech', *IEEE Transactions on Audio and Electroacoustics* AU–21 (3): 288–290.

Albrow, K. H. (1972) *The English writing system: notes toward a description*, London: Longman.

Allen, J., Hunnicutt, M. S. and Klatt, D. (1987) *From text to speech. The MITalk system*, Cambridge: Cambridge University Press.

Allen, W.S. (1978) *Vox Latina – a guide to the pronunciation of Classical Latin,* Cambridge: Cambridge University Press.

Allerton, D. J. (1982) 'Orthography and dialect', in W. Haas (ed.) *Standard Languages: Spoken and Written*, Manchester: Manchester University Press.

—— (1987) 'The linguistic and sociolinguistic status of proper names', *Journal of Pragmatics* 11: 61–92.

Bojarsky, C. (1969) 'Consistency of spelling and pronunciation deviation of Appalachian students', *Modern Language Journal* 53: 347–50.

Brengelman, F. H. (1980) 'Orthoepists, printers and the rationalization of English spelling', *Journal of English and Germanic Philology* 79: 332–54.

Bridges, R. (1919) 'On homophones', *Society for Pure English*, Tract II, Oxford: Oxford University Press.

Brown, A. (1988) 'A Singaporean corpus of misspellings: analysis and implications', *Journal of the Simplified Spelling Society* 3: 4–10.

Brown, H. D. (1970) 'Categories of spelling difficulty in speakers of English as a first and second language', *Journal of Verbal Learning and Verbal Behaviour* 9: 232–6.

Carroll, J. B., Davies P. and Richman B. (1971) *The American Heritage Word Frequency Book*, New York: American Heritage.

Cheshire, J., Edwards, V., Munstermann, H. and Weltens, B. (1989) *Dialect and Education*, Clevedon, Philadelphia: Multilingual Matters Ltd.

Chomsky, C. (1970) 'Reading, writing and phonology', *Harvard Educational Review* 40: 287–309.

Chomsky, N. and Halle, M. (1968) *The Sound Pattern of English*, New York: Harper & Row.

Clymer, T. (1963) 'The utility of phonic generalisations in the primary grades', *The Reading Teacher* 16: 252–8.

Cordts, A. D. (1965) *Phonics for the Reading Teacher*, New York: Holt, Rinehart.

Cox, B. (1989) *English for Ages 5 to 16*, London: Department of Education & Science.

Cruttenden, A. (1994) Gimson's *Pronunciation of English*, London: Edward Arnold.

Crystal, D. (1987) *The Cambridge Encyclopedia of Language*, Cambridge: Cambridge University Press.

Cummings, D.W. (1988) *American English Spelling – An Informal Description*, Baltimore: John Hopkins.

Desberg, P., Elliott, D. E. and Marsh, D. (1980) 'American Black English and spelling', in Frith, U. (ed.) *Cognitive Processes in Spelling*, London and New York: Academic Press.

Dobson, E. J. (1968) *English Pronunciation 1500 – 1700*, 2 vols Oxford: Oxford University Press.

Ellis, N. and Cataldo, S. (1990) 'The role of spelling in learning to read', *Language and Education*: 1–28.

EPD – see Jones, D. (1980).

Follick, M. (1965) *The Case for Spelling Reform*, London: Pitman.

Fowler, H.W. (1926) *A Dictionary of Modern English Usage*, Oxford: Oxford University Press.

—— (1965) *Fowler's Modern English Usage*. 2nd edn revised by Sir Ernest Gowers, Oxford: Oxford University Press.

Gibson, E.J., Pick, A. D., Osser, H. and Hammond, M. (1962) 'The role of grapheme–phoneme correspondence in the perception of words', *American Journal of Psychology* 75: 554–70.

Gibson, E. J., Shurcliff, A. and Jonas, A. (1970) 'Utilization of spelling patterns by deaf and hearing subjects', in Levin, H. and Williams, J. P. (eds.) *Basic Studies on Reading*, New York: Basic Books Inc.

Haas, W. (1970) *Phonographic Translation*, Manchester: Manchester University Press.

—— (1976) 'Writing: the basic options', in W. Haas (ed) *Writing without Letters*, Manchester: Manchester University Press.

Hall, R. A. (1961) *Sound and Spelling In English*, New York: Chilton.

Hanna, P. R., Hanna, J. S., Hodges, R. E. and Rudorf, E. H. (1966) *Phoneme–Grapheme Correspondences as Cues to Spelling Improvement*, Washington: US Department of Health, Education and Welfare.

Henderson, L. and Chard, J. 'The reader's implicit knowledge of orthographic structure', in Frith, U. (ed.), *Cognitive Processes in Spelling*, London and New York: Academic Press.

Higginbottom, E. M. (1962) 'A study of the representation of vowel phonemes in the orthography', *Language and Speech* 5: 67–117.

Hill, L. A. and Ure, J. M. (1962) *English Sounds and Spellings*, London: Oxford University Press.

Hook, J. N. (1976) *Spelling 1500: A Program* (2nd edn), New York: Harcourt, Brace, Jovanovich.

Hornby A. S. (1974) *Oxford Advanced Learner's Dictionary of Current English* (3rd edn), Oxford: Oxford University Press. (The 1st edn (1948) had the title: *A Learner's Dictionary of Current English*.)

Jacobson, S. (1966) *Unorthodox spelling in American trademarks,* Stockholm: Almqvist & Wiksell.

Jakobson, R., Fant, C. G. M. and Halle, M. (1951) *Preliminaries to Speech Analysis*, Cambridge, Mass.: MIT Press.

Jespersen, O. (1909) *A Modern English Grammar. Part I: Sounds and Spellings*, Copenhagen: Munksgaard.

Johansson, S. and Hofland, K. (1989) *Frequency Analysis of English Vocabulary and Grammar*, Oxford: Clarendon Press.

Jones, D. (1956) *An Outline of English Phonetics* (8th edn), Cambridge: Heffer.
— (1980) *English Pronouncing Dictionary* (14th edn), London: Dent Dutton.
Krapp, G. P. (1925) *The English Language in America*, New York: Century Co.
Kucera, H. and Francis, W. N. (1967) *Computational Analysis of Present-day American English*, Providence, RI: Brown University Press.
Lester, A. (1964) 'Graphemic-phonemic correspondences as the basis for teaching spelling', *Elementary English* 41: 748–52.
Longley, C. (1975) *BBC Adult Literacy Handbook*, London: BBC
LPD – see Wells, J. C. (1990).
MacCarthy, P.A.D. (1969a) 'New spellings with old letters', in W. Haas (ed.) *Alphabets for English*, Manchester: Manchester University Press.
— (1969b) 'The Bernard Shaw Alphabet', in W. Haas (ed.) *Alphabets for English*, Manchester: Manchester University Press.
McIlroy, M.D. (1974) *Synthetic English Speech by Rule*, Computing Science Technical Report 14, New Jersey: Bell Telephone Laboratories, Inc.
McLeod, M. E. (1961) 'Rules in the teaching of spelling', in H. J. L. Robbie *Studies in Spelling*, Publications of the Scottish Council for Research in Education XL, London: ULP.
Mencken, H.L. (1948) *Supplement II: The American Language*, New York: Alfred A. Knopf.
Morris, J. M. (1984) 'Focus on phonics: Phonics 44 for initial literacy in English', *Reading* 81. 1: 13–24.
Nauclér, K. (1980) *Perspectives on Misspellings*, Travaux de l'Institut de Linguistique de Lund XV, Malmö : CWK Gleerup.
OED = The Oxford English Dictionary (1933). Murray, J. A. H., Bradley, H., Craigie, W. A. and Onions, C. T. (eds), Oxford: Clarendon Press.
O'Neal, V. and Trabasso, T. (1976) 'Is there a correspondence between sound and spelling? Some implications for Black English speakers', in Harrison, D. S. and Trabasso, T. (eds) *Black English: A Seminar*, Hillsdale, NJ: Erlbaum.
Perera, K. (1980) 'Review of Smith' (1978) in *Journal of Linguistics* 16.1: 127–31.
Perera, S. (1983) *A Guide to some Alphabet Books*, Knowsley, Merseyside: Knowlsey Education Authority.
Peters, M. L. (1985) *Spelling: Caught or Taught?* (2nd edn), London: Routledge.
Pitman, Sir James (1969) 'The late Dr Mont Follick – an appraisal. The assault on the conventional alphabets and spelling', in W. Haas (ed.) *Alphabets for English*, Manchester: Manchester University Press.
Pomfret, J. (ed.) (1969) *Lancashire Evergreens*, Nelson, Lancs.: Gerrard.
Pound, L. (1925) 'The Kraze for "K"', *American Speech*: 43–4.
Praninskas, J. (1968) *Trade Name Creation: Processes and Patterns*, The Hague: Mouton.
Ripman, W. and Archer, W. (1948) *New Spelling. Being Proposals for Simplifying the Spelling of English Without the Introduction of New Letters* (6th edn revised by D. Jones and H. Orton), London: Pitman. (Previous editions had had the alternative title *Simplified Spelling.*)
Rusk, R.R. (1961) 'The Scottish pupil's Spelling Book', in H. J. L. Robbie *Studies in Spelling*, Publications of the Scottish Council for Research in Education XL, London: ULP.
Sampson, G. (1985) *Writing Systems*, London: Hutchinson.
Scragg, D.G. (1974) *A History of English Spelling*, Manchester: Manchester University Press.
Shaw, G.B. (1962) *Androcles and the Lion* (Shaw Alphabet Edition), Harmondsworth.

Sheridan, T. (1780) *A General Dictionary of the English Language*, London: Dodsley, Dilly & Wilkie.
Simon, D. P. and Simon, H. A. (1973) 'Alternative uses of phonemic information in spelling', *Review of Educational Research* 43: 115–37.
Smith, F. (1971) *Understanding Reading – A Psycholinguistic Analysis of Reading and Learning to Read*, New York: Holt, Rinehart.
— (1973) 'Alphabetic writing – a linguistic compromise?' in F. Smith *Psycholinguistics and reading*, New York: Holt, Rinehart.
— (1978) *Reading*, Cambridge: Cambridge University Press.
Sterling, C. M. (1983) 'Spelling errors in context', *British Journal of Psychology* 74: 353–64.
Stubbs, M. (1980) *Language and Literacy: the Sociolinguistics of Reading and Writing*, London: Routledge Kegan Paul.
— (1986) 'The Synchronic Organisation of English Spelling', *CLIE Working Papers*, 10: The Linguistics Association of Great Britain.
Thorndike, E. L. and Lorge, I. (1944) *The Teacher's Word Book of 30,000 Words*, New York: Teacher's College, Columbia University.
Underwood, B. J. and Schultz, R. W. (1960) *Meaningful and Verbal Learning*, Philadelphia: Lippincott.
Upward, C. (1988) 'English Spelling and Educational Progress', *CLIE Working Papers* 11: The Linguistics Association of Great Britain.
Upward, C. (1992) *Cut Spelling. A Handbook to the Simplification of Written English by Omission of Redundant Letters*, Birmingham: The Simplified Spelling Society.
Vallins, G. H. (1965) *Spelling*, London: Andre Deutsch.
Venezky, R. L. (1967) 'English orthography: its graphical structure and its relation to sound', *Reading Research Quarterly* 2: 75–105.
— (1970a) 'Linguistics and spelling', in A. H. Marckwardt *Linguistics in School Programs. Yearbook of the National Society for the Study of Education* 69.2. Chicago: The University of Chicago Press.
— (1970b) 'The structure of English orthography', in *Janua Linguarum, series minor* 82, The Hague: Mouton.
— (1980) 'From Webster to Rice to Roosevelt', in U. Frith (ed.) *Cognitive Processes in Spelling*, London and New York: Academic Press.
W2NID – *Merriam-Webster's New International Dictionary of the English Language* (1957), Nelson, W. A. (ed.) 2nd edn, Springfield, Mass.: Merriam.
W3NID – *Webster's Third New International Dictionary of the English Language* (1961), Gove, P. B. (ed.) 3rd edn, Springfield, Mass.: Merriam.
Wardhaugh, R. (1971) 'Linguistics and Phonics', in Braun, C. (ed.) *Language, reading and the communication process*, Newmark, Delaware: International Reading Association.
Wells, J. C. (1982) *Accents of English*, Cambridge: Cambridge University Press.
— (1990) *Longman Pronunciation Dictionary*, Harlow: Longman.
Whiteman, M. F. (1981) 'Dialect influence in writing', in Whiteman, M. F. *Writing: The Nature, Development and Teaching of Written Communication*, vol. 1, Hillsdale, N.J.: Lawrence Erlbaum.
Wijk, A. (1959) *Regularized English: An Investigation into the English Spelling Reform Problem*, Stockholm: Almqvist & Wiksell.
— (1966) *Rules of Pronunciation for the English Language*, Oxford: Oxford University Press.
— (1969) 'Regularized English. The only practicable solution of the English Spelling Reform Problem', in W. Haas (ed.) *Alphabets for English*, Manchester: Manchester University Press.

—— (1977) *Regularized English . . . A Proposal for an Effective Solution of the Reading Problem in the English-speaking Countries*, Stockholm: Almqvist & Wiksell.

Willis, G. (1919) *The Philosophy of Language*, London: Geoge Allen & Unwin.

Yannakoudakis, E. J. and Fawthrop, D. (1983) 'The rules of spelling errors', *Information Processing and Management* 19: 87–9.

General Index

Selective Word Index

This is a selective index of word forms that are commented on in the text . Those marked with an asterisk '*' are hypothetical forms. Spelling errors, dialect spellings, creative and reformed spellings are listed in the **Spelling Error Index**

Index of spelling correspondences

This is a selective list of spelling-phoneme correspondences discussed in the text. They are listed here in the text-to-speech direction for alphabetic convenience and easy reference. Those marked with an asterisk are unusual or in some way unrewarding as mappings of letters onto phonemes.

Index of initial and final letter strings in words

This is a selective list of initial and final letter strings in words. The list includes arbitrary strings as well as affixes proper.

1 Initial letter strings in words

2 Final letter strings in words

Index of spelling errors and re-spellings

This is a selective list of abnormal and unusual spellings. It brings together instances of
1 spelling errors (including false etymologies, confusions between word forms and deliberate use of mis-spellings for effect), which are classified or discussed in the text; these are marked with an asterisk '*'.
2 re-spellings used in literary texts to indicate dialect pronunciations or even lack of education - marked with a '≈';
3 a few historical spellings of interest, some of which are in use as deliberate archaisms - marked with a '♠';
4 a small selection of alternative spellings used creatively or suggested as possible spelling reforms - marked with a '®'.